Online Learning Communities and Teacher Professional Development:
Methods for Improved Education Delivery

J. Ola Lindberg
Mid Sweden University, Sweden

Anders D. Olofsson
Umea University, Sweden

INFORMATION SCIENCE REFERENCE

Hershey · New York

Director of Editorial Content:	Kristin Klinger
Senior Managing Editor:	Jamie Snavely
Managing Editor:	Jeff Ash
Assistant Managing Editor:	Michael Brehm
Publishing Assistant:	Sean Woznicki
Typesetter:	Jeff Ash
Cover Design:	Lisa Tosheff
Printed at:	Yurchak Printing Inc.

Published in the United States of America by
Information Science Reference (an imprint of IGI Global)
701 E. Chocolate Avenue
Hershey PA 17033
Tel: 717-533-8845
Fax: 717-533-8661
E-mail: cust@igi-global.com
Web site: http://www.igi-global.com/reference

Library of Congress Cataloging-in-Publication Data

Online learning communities and teacher professional development: methods for improved education delivery / J. Ola Lindberg and Anders D. Olofsson, editors.
     p. cm.

Includes bibliographical references and index.
Summary: "This book features innovative applications for the integration of technology into everyday teaching practices"--Provided by publisher.

ISBN 978-1-60566-780-5 (hardcover) -- ISBN 978-1-60566-781-2 (ebook) 1. Professional learning communities. 2. Teachers--In-service training. 3. Educational technology. I. Lindberg, J. Ola, 1966- II. Olofsson, Anders D., 1973-

  LB1731.O54 2010
  370.71'55--dc22
                    2009017417

British Cataloguing in Publication Data
A Cataloguing in Publication record for this book is available from the British Library.

All work contributed to this book is new, previously-unpublished material. The views expressed in this book are those of the authors, but not necessarily of the publisher.

Trond Eiliv Hauge, *University of Oslo, Norway*
Svein Olav Norenes, *University of Oslo, Norway*
Diana Laurillard, *London Knowledge Lab, Institute of Education, UK*
Elizabeth Masterman, *University of Oxford, UK*
Pamela Whitehouse, *West Virginia University, USA*
Erin McCloskey, *Harvard Graduate School of Education, USA*
Diane Jass Ketelhut, *Temple University, USA*
Raija Hämäläinen, *University of Jyväskylä, Finland*
Maarit Arvaja, *University of Jyväskylä, Finland*
Helena Rasku-Puttonen, *University of Jyväskylä, Finland*

Table of Contents

Section 1
Theoretical and Technological Foundations

Chapter 1

Ingrid Helleve, University of Bergen, Norway

Chapter 2

Shelleyann Scott, University of Calgary, Canada

Section 2
Methods and Models of Online Communities in TPD

Chapter 3

Rebecca Scheckler, Radford University, USA

Chapter 4

Margaret Lloyd, Queensland University of Technology, Australia
Jennifer Duncan-Howell, Queensland University of Technology, Australia

Section 3
Innovations in the Use of technology and TPD

Detailed Table of Contents

Section 1
Theoretical and Technological Foundations

Chapter 1
Ingrid Helleve, University of Bergen, Norway

Throughout this chapter the author argues for a close connection between teachers and teacher educators as a prerequisite for ongoing professional development in education. Possibilities to communicate through online learning communities have made reflective activities through action research between distant educational environments easier to organize and facilitate.

Chapter 2
Shelleyann Scott, University of Calgary, Canada

This chapter explores the divide between theories of effective TPD and the realities of practice within educational contexts. Two case studies, one from Australia and the other from Canada are presented to illustrate the positives and negatives inherent within professional development approaches in these contexts. A number of key dimensions are identified, which when coalesced inform the establishment and sustainability of effective programmes. Online technologies present innovative ways to overcome the impediments to effective professional development. Online communities of practice utilising social networking technologies provide new opportunities for initiating "webs of enhanced practice' (Scott, 2009), where individuals around the globe can engage in collegial collaborations that enhance the passion of teaching.

Section 2
Methods and Models of Online Communities in TPD

Chapter 3

Two intense case studies were done of teachers using the Inquiry Learning Forum (ILF), an online space for professional development in inquiry pedagogies. Major findings included: The ILF initially conceived as an online professional development tool in the form of a Community of Practice (COP) was reconceived as an electronic tool within a larger space that included the online tool but also many co-present spaces pertinent to a teacher's practice of inquiry pedagogy. These case studies also demonstrated the transformative nature of teachers engaging in a COP. Not only is the teacher changed but also the COP is changed by the practice. The cases demonstrated the need for teachers to feel disequilibrium in their practice before they are willing to engage in change of those practices. Lastly immersion in practice described as The Pedagogy of Poverty hampered one teacher's progress in the ILF. These findings are based upon my empirical observations with the backdrop of John Dewey's Theory of Inquiry and of Etienne Wenger's concept of communities of Practice. Future trends in using online COPs for professional development need to look at practice in these terms where allowance for transaction, support outside the electronic space, and disequilibrium are considered.

Chapter 4

This chapter will map data from a doctoral study to a recently-developed model of professional development to offer a new perspective of how online communities can add to a teacher's personal and professional growth and, in so doing, add to the small number of studies in this field. This chapter will conclude with a call for a revision of the way we approach professional development in the 21st century and suggest that old models and metaphors are hindering the adoption of more effective means of professional development for teachers.

Chapter 5

The authors present the current contexts affecting professional development in England and discuss the significance of the shift towards collaborative and community approaches to teachers' learning. The authors argue that transformation is a key, though troublesome, concept in considering the aims of professional development for teachers' use of technologies in their everyday practice. They explore these ideas by presenting the case of the Transformation Teachers Programme (TTP), a wide-scale teachers' development project carried out in a London borough by Haringey City Learning Centre (CLC), and they examine how this project has implemented new approaches to Information and Communications Technology (ICT) and teachers' professional development, based on collaborative experimentation, enquiry and risk-taking within online and other community-based arrangements.

Chapter 6

The chapter uses current research literature on teacher professionalism and professional learning in Scotland to establish the context in which Scottish teachers are currently working. It then draws on three vignettes drawn from research within AERS to argue that the development of virtual environments to support professional learning in Scotland requires further, significant collaborative working between the practitioner, policy and research communities.

Chapter 7

This chapter presents examples of success and challenges associated with a large-scale U.S. statewide online teacher professional development community. It also makes the case for implementing a systematic approach to investigating the effectiveness of online teacher professional development communities through ongoing assessment and responsive evaluation.

This chapter analyses the relationships between professional development, organisational development and the creation and management of collective knowledge. These three concepts can be interrelated and contribute to change when we place ourselves within the framework of autonomous organisations with collective projects focused on lifelong learning. It also outlines the Accelera experience of knowledge creation and management in communities, describing the model and process used. This article examines some of the findings and future prospects of the methodology presented.

Chapter 9

One of the most powerful ways of changing our thinking about how we teach and learn is to experience for ourselves the power of collaborative project-based experiential learning. Few teachers have had the opportunity to learn in this way, and this creates barriers for those who want to change their pedagogy. The Oracle Education Foundation's Project Learning Institute provides teachers with the experience of collaborative project-based learning, using ThinkQuest® to create their own curriculum project. By collaborating with their peers, tutors and mentors, teachers are able to model the projects, environment and experiences they want for their classes through a blended learning experience. This chapter describes the model of continuing professional development and its impact on schools, pedagogies and professional philosophies.

Section 3
Innovations in the Use of technology and TPD

Chapter 10

This chapter explores the innovative uses of technology for teachers' professional development as well as its impact in the classroom on learning and teaching. Two international case studies are included. The first outlines technological innovations in graduate programme delivery within the university context in Canada. The second case presents a multi-dimensional professional development initiative in Australia which has influenced teachers' and students' learning. Two models are described: the macro-oriented "Webs of Enhanced Practice" that addresses the professional development of educators and experts; and the micro-oriented "Webs of Enhanced Learning" focusing on the learning occurring at the classroom level. These two models represent innovations in the use of technology as they conceptualise the eclectic use of multi-modal, varied technologies to advance the professional development of communities of learners.

Chapter 11

Here, the authors describe our approach to the development of virtual patient resources and in particular how this iterative dialogue arising from the allied processes of practice, reflection and pedagogy required to create new learning tools and resources has contributed to professional development of those engaged in teaching medical students and in building online learning communities at the University of Edinburgh.

Chapter 12

Trond Eiliv Hauge, University of Oslo, Norway
Svein Olav Norenes, University of Oslo, Norway

This study demonstrates the possibilities of new media and affordable technological tools that support teacher professional development in a workplace setting. A team of 5 mathematics teachers in a secondary school is followed over a period of six months as they work jointly to improve their teaching and team practice using a multimedia Web developer system (VideoPaper). VideoPaper is an easy-to-use tool for developing and sharing of Web documents that integrates video resources, images, and texts reflecting local practices. The framework of Developmental Work Research methods aligned to historical-cultural activity theory (Engeström, 2001, 2008) was adapted to the local needs and workplace conditions. The findings point to changes in teachers' conceptual approaches to learning and teaching, and to the significance of technology-enhanced support for professional development. The study contributes to an understanding of the complexities in bridging practices between social and technological design for teacher development and the development of learning communities.

Section 4
Pedagogies Afforded by Technology in TPD

Chapter 13

Diana Laurillard, Institute of Education, UK
Elizabeth Masterman, University of Oxford, UK

This chapter focuses on supporting university teachers in the UK in the more innovative use of digital technologies. Although the use of these technologies is now widespread and increasing, it is not always optimised for effective learning. It is important that teachers' use of technology should be directed towards innovation and improvement in teaching and learning, and should not merely replicate their current practice in a digital medium. The authors therefore make the case for an online collaborative environment to scaffold teachers' engagement with technology-enhanced learning. the chapter outlines the findings of our recent research into a blended approach to TPD, and use these to identify the requirements for an online collaborative environment: tools for learning design, guidance, and access to relevant resources to support teachers in their discovery of new forms of technology-enhanced teaching and learning. Such an environment, they argue, would provide a framework for a "community of innovation" in which teachers participate both as learners and researchers.

The purpose of this chapter is to examine the shifting priorities of online teacher professional development design, particularly through the lens of online pedagogies. Whether one's purpose is to design an online teacher learning community or formal professional development program, decisions about technology use will mediate how the learning communities or training programs function. Designers, when choosing communication tools or digital media for inclusion in their program, ideally draw from their technological pedagogical content knowledge, or TCPK – that is, their understanding of which technologies will support pedagogy appropriate for the content and learners being targeted. The model we offer for online teacher professional development program design makes visible the interaction between the technology, the content, the pedagogy and the learner.

This chapter discusses challenges related to teachers' pedagogical activities in facilitating productive discussions among students in Computer-Supported Collaborative Learning (CSCL) contexts. In the light of two different cases from secondary-level and higher education contexts, the authors examine how teachers' pedagogical choices influenced the quality of students' activity, namely Web-based discussion. The results of our studies indicated that rich moments of collaboration were rare and distributed unequally among the students. The obvious weakness from the perspective of teachers' pedagogical activities was that in neither of the studies was the students' interaction in the discussion forum supported in any way. A future challenge is, therefore, to develop both pedagogical and technological tools to support the monitoring and enhancement of students' learning process during online learning. Furthermore, we discuss how teachers' professional development (TPD) is challenged by new technological tools in formal learning environments.

Foreword

Dear Reader. May I have your attention for a moment? Why did you buy this book? Was it intellectual hunger? Pure curiosity? Or even irritation on the continuing bombardment of education with new metaphors? I think for many of us, it is a mix. If you share with me the passion to check if and how education in the western world is going to evolve from an institutionalized- back into a more existential- and, if you like, into a more pedagogical process, then I think buying this book is an excellent choice.

What is happening to education? And will the notion of the networked society be a vital one for education in the years the come?

Going back in my own years as an arriving pupil in the first grade elementary school it is a mild fragrant of memory that pops up: the large crowds of students, the immense number of pages in a book, and the decisiveness of the teachers to make us climb this tower of conventions. Most importantly: they only way to escape from this place was to succeed the tests.

Now, if we quickly scan the innovative paradigms since my first school day in august 1957 you might agree that there are typically four phases: Making schools more

1. democratic (60-70ties),
2. systematic/Instructional (80ties),
3. constructivist/individualized (90ties) and
4. attempts to broaden the concept of what learning actually is. (this decade)

In fact the pure consequence of accepting that learning is endemic to life anyway is that we question the overall contract: Can society afford institutional schooling that *consolidates* rather than *developing* new understanding mainly?

And here we arrive at the point: what actually means "learning in a networked society?" As long as solid hierarchies in reputation and strict disciplines rule the authority, there only a small reason to innovate education; it is just to provide learners with the suggestion that they have the right to take a preferably-small detour in the from ignorance to the arrival at common understanding. As soon as we face the gap between knowing and thinking, or between thinking and problem solving, we admit that education only touches the "tip of the iceberg".

Most important is the scope of this book: Its underlying question is: 1. Is education going to adopt the full impact of the network society in culture and etiquette? Or: 2. Will education just accept the cosmetic features of the networked society?

Of course given the scope and the mission of this book we hope to acknowledge the first option. However, clearly the correct answer is the second one; Education has the job to precede societal impact of ICT; Its stakeholders are *architects* rather than its *inhabitants*. In having that ambition this book took the challenge to make a panoramic tour along the major roads in teacher education, learning communities and in life-long learning. Its goal is to make you courageous for joining and anticipate to the evolution to come in 3 or 4 years from now.

The first notion is that learners need to become owners if their learning ambitions and process. This leads to revisited teacher training programs where learning "consciousness" is at stake. As a consequence we see the trend to improve team learning like now vital when parts of face-to-face teaching is supplanted by e-learning and blended learning. The underlying fundamental question is whether e-learning is becoming a goal rather than a provocative method; It can well be that e-learning works out as a trigger for restructuring the essence of learning in higher education. Traditionally "learning" was apprehended as incorporating what "others already mastered before".

This book comes down to the fact that effective learning implies that the learner chases new; (not yet uncovered) perspectives. In this case we face the job to educate teachers and learners nowadays to have the courage to jump to rather unexplored areas and excavate authentic approaches via inquiry learning, communities of practice and finally knowledge societies. Identity is an important aspect that highlights the learner to start from existential rather than from career incentives. Higher education indeed has (over-)articulated the relevance of employment perspectives. By "Identity" we reschedule the notion that students need to build their attitude and mental predisposition as well.

This book offers new framework for the new professionalism in teacher training and in teacher team building like the networks and web-based communities. The book exemplifies that the new media landscape offers a rich repertoire of cooperation modalities: Best practices by video, animations, simulations and eventually collaborative student projects across institutions even. The awareness of quality assurance and summative quality output is inherent to professionalism. So far the labeling of a student as "customer in the future" (alumni) has propagated quite wide. We see now an ever more competitive struggle between universities to attract the "best" students. International students have become part of this game as well. We may expect that universities make consortia like under the Erasmus Mundi formula that even exceeds the European countries quite soon.

As Epitomes of the new ICT-supported teacher-/learner communities we meet the aspects of mobile, virtual and the gaming presence. It implies the more essential questions like: Can teacher practices be "shared"? Or do we face a high level of idiosyncrasy as it comes to improving the personal touch in pedagogy? Yes games and virtual presence have potential as it comes to flexibility and the copying with a lack of time all over. As main dimensions are listed: Pedagogy, community, domain knowledge, reflective-, clinic- and ethical issues. The challenge for this book is to sketch a roadmap to be expected in few years time.

Finally: Education is not a world in itself any more. In terms of culture and communication it gets more and more compliances to societal trends and processes. Internet plays a crucial liason here; we may expect youngsters to link to many more sources of expertise and social cohesion. Education now faces the challenge to catch up in the conceptual and in the ideological sense. There is the risk that we narrow our goal to "How can education incorporate the "Network Society"? This book shows the ambition to rephrase and ask ourselves: "How can education co-design the society of tomorrow". ICT in this respect has an obligatory, however not a satisfactory role. Most important is that both teachers and students are aware that they are both the architects and the inhabitants; there is no reason to accept a less crucial role, even if ICT seems to play an autonomous and transformative role in cultural and societal evolutions today.

Piet Kommers
University of Twente, The Netherlands
February 24, 2009

Piet Kommers *is associate professor at the University of Twente. His prime field of expertise is media for education. He specialized in the various roles and modalities of conceptual representations. In the early nineties he pioneered in the new-coming domain of cognitive learning tools. As instructional approaches got more and more sophisticated in terms of student modeling and adaptive strategies, his attempt was to introduce and evaluate metacognitive awareness at the learner. Piet Kommers initiated the NATO Advanced Research Workshop on the learning support environments like concept mapping, micro worlds, modeling and simulations in 1989. In 1991 his PhD thesis "Hypertext and the Acquisition of Knowledge" found slight indications that non serialistic students benefitted more from conceptual schemes, while in fact the students with a holistic cognitive style were more inclined to make schematic representations. This led to the hypothesis that the non-serial learning style rested upon a weaker short term memory. His research together with Dr. Heling Huai revealed that indeed the serialistic students rely more on literal rehearsal while the holistic students "survived" by elaborating their long term semantic repertoire. As also it proved that students with a holistic style were superior in meaningful retrieval in the range of years, and much more flexible problem solvers, the theory started to fit together. Piet Kommers was involved in projects on educational technology around the world. His UNESCO chair position in the Kiev International Research and Training Centre and his honorary professorship by the Capital Normal University in Beijing allowed him to dedicate more to explore the ICT effects on cultural and societal processes. His recent work is on the growing potential of web-based communities for learning and social awareness. He initiated the International Journal for Web-based Communities (IJWBC) and the yearly conference Web-based Communities by IADIS. His web page: http://users.edte.utwente.nl/kommers/*

Preface

This book is about online learning communities (OLC) and teacher professional development (TPD). Borko (2004), put forth that "We are only beginning to learn, however, about exactly what and how teachers learn from professional development, or about the impact of teacher change on student outcomes" (p. 3). In this book, the ambition is to contribute to such knowledge by focusing what OLCs in various forms have to offer to practising teachers and teacher trainees when it comes to professional development. As such, what is the character of teachers' professional development? Is it workshops and seminars, could it be a life-long continuous learning and development process towards some unidentified goal? Should it be formally orchestrated on state, local or school level, or informally chosen by the teacher as a self-directed learner, searching for a continuously informed and better understanding of the conditions of teaching and learning? Further, what is this phenomenon called OLC? When does accessing a website or reading and communicating in an online forum become a membership in an OLC, and what keeps this assumed community together? Does it differ to be a member of an OLC from being a member in communities in real life? In this book, questions like these are addressed, some answered, yet others are raised. We will start by giving a brief orientation relating to OLCs before readers head into the chapters. Thereafter, we provide some initial concerns about teacher's professional development that can be equally valuable for the potential reader.

Before presenting some possible cornerstones of OLC we would like to start with directing the readers' interest towards some central notions of the concept of community. That is before community goes online. According to Selznick (1996), community is a dynamic concept. It should according to him not to be associated with a predetermined and objective definition with a clear and central meaning open to only one specific understanding. It is rather the opposite. The concept is open to different kinds of meanings and understandings, depending on social, cultural and societal frameworks. This understanding is also present in Bauman (2001). He argues that community is related to a tension between safety and freedom, which gives a two-folded understanding. Almost like Janus, the Roman god of doorways and passages: one face showing the concept of community associated with a feeling of being part of and sharing something positive with others, another showing the community as threatening our autonomy, demanding us to give up our sense of individuality. Another distinction can be addressed with help from Tönnies (1963). He describes the concept as either being a coherent community in which culture and social practices are infused with moral unity and intimacy or a place in which each member's autonomy and mobility is favoured. Regardless of which understanding, community seems to be an illusive concept, letting itself be defined and used in multiple ways (Delanty, 2003), and in addition we argue that the social and moral dimensions of being together as humans are equally important as always present (Lindberg & Olofsson, 2008; Olofsson & Lindberg, 2006).

Through the writings of for example Lave & Wenger (1991) and Wenger (1998), the concept of community became intertwined with the L in the acronym of OLC. The learning community was in addition given a central role of their concept of Community of Practice (CoP). A concept that seems possible to relate to all three notions about community presented above. Relating to an educational context, Grant and Agosto (2008) sum up ideas such as:

"...a community of practice is a site of learning and action where participants engage in a joint enterprise to develop a whole repertoire of activities, common stories, and ways of speaking and acting for social justice. This endeavor diminishes the borders between community and school, as well as between virtual paces and physical spaces [...] enabling other social arenas to incite new ways of relating and inciting solidarity that is characterized by conviviality and criticality" (p. 189).

So then, what does the concept of community imply when it goes online? In the past decade, the emergence of information and communication technology (ICT) and the development of the Internet also allow people to socialise with others using blogs, wikis, social software, tagging and sharing information, personalising the web, reaching out to and becoming part of the world in ways unprecedented. This makes technology a means for creating new forms of being together in what we know as OLCs. Trying to understand what constitutes an OLC is not an easy task (Preece & Maloney-Krichmar, 2003). In this book, five basic constituents of OLC seem, in different ways and within different practices, are present. Those are, *people, purposes* and *policies* (De Souza & Preece, 2004) and *activities* and *tools* (Carlén & Jobring, 2005). From the positions sketched out, there are apparent possibilities for an OLC to foster its members, and for a membership in an OLC to harbour processes of learning and development. For teachers of today, the OLC is the place to be when it comes to professional growth and development.

In fact, when turning the focus for a moment to TPD, what different views could be elucidated? Fraser, Kennedy, Reid and McKinney (2007) suggested a joint framework of three different models wherein several dimensions of TPD are included when discussing a possible framework to examine TPD. First, the three interrelated aspects of professional learning suggested by Bell and Gilbert (1996): personal, social and occupational. Second, the analytical framework of Kennedy (2005), in which the purpose of the TPD could be located along a continuum of being transmissive, transitional or transformative. Third, Reid's quadrant of teacher learning (McKinney et al, 2005), which is comprised of two dimensions: formal-informal and planned-incidental. Through this joint framework, the complex nature of TPD is recognized. Villegas-Reimers (2003) also gives broad background descriptions of different views on TPD. Starting in professional development, referred to as the development of a person in his or her professional role, Villegas-Reimers continues to include in TPD the professional growth of a teacher as a result of gaining increased experience after examining his or her teaching systematically. This process which includes formal and informal experiences in which the content of these experiences, the processes by which they occur and the contexts in which they take place must be included. Only recently, according to Villegas-Reimers, has TPD come to be considered a long term process, which would include regular opportunities and experiences that are planned systematically to promote professional growth. This is a new perspective for teaching, Villegas-Reimers continues, since the TPD available to teachers has for years been in-service training or staff development usually consisting of workshops or short courses. She summarizes this new perspective in seven characteristics. First, it is based on constructivism rather on a transmission-model. Second, it is conceived of as a long-term process. Third, it is conceived of as a process that takes place in a particular context. Forth, it is intimately linked to school reform. Fifth, a teacher is conceived of as a reflective practitioner. Sixth, professional development is seen as a collaborative process. Seventh, professional development may look and be very different in diverse settings. All of these characteristics appear in different and innovative ways in the chapters of this book, and as such they mirror the complexity of TPD.

Starting in the foundation of this book; the teachers participating in and communicating with others in an OLC are in one way or another active in a process of professional growth and development. According to Vrasidas and Glass (2004, p.3), "Innovative professional development for teachers will involve opportunities for teachers to share their expertise, learn from peers, and collaborate on real-world projects". In the cases and models, methods and pedagogies included in this book, opportunities in Vrasida's and Glass' sense are provided and discussed. OLC and TPD could therefore be seen as endeavours for both understanding TPD, framed within OLCs, and understanding the design of virtual arenas in which teachers have possibilities to develop into what Triggs & John (2004) call an "enabled professional"; i.e. "one who has the capacity to respond to changing conditions, anticipate future technologies and re-define their practice so that they are enabled rather than constrained by external policy agendas" (p. 427). The collaborative work described in this book might well be a way to expand the scope of OLCs, bridging teacher-training practices to teacher practices, and thus including already practising teachers, teacher trainers, and teacher trainees, school-leaders, policy-makers, educational researchers and other stakeholders in joint educational communities (Olofsson & Lindberg, 2007).

This book is divided into four different but interrelated themes. Chapters 1 and 2 represent the first, "Theoretical and Technological Foundations". Chapters 3-9 represent the second theme "Methods and Models of Online Learning Communities in TPD". Chapters 10-12 represent the third theme "Innovations in the Use of Technology and TPD". Chapters 13-15 represent the fourth and final theme "Pedagogies afforded by technology in TPD". The positioning of chapters within different themes has been a difficult task. It is most likely that each chapter respectively could be suitable for more than one theme, which highlights the interrelated nature of them. Nevertheless, the themes are only there to give the reader an orientation within the context of the book, and the position is not to be considered a mutually exclusive categorisation. However, making these distinctions is the power invested in us as editors and we have executed this power for the good of the reader and for the good of the book.

In Chapter 1, "Theoretical Foundations of Teachers' Professional Development", Ingrid Helleve from Norway, shows a possible understanding of how the theoretical foundation of the concept of TPD has changed over time. In the chapter she states that being a professional teacher or teacher educator also means to participate in an ongoing learning process and that the main concern of teachers is to guide and help students to learn. According to Helleve, this means that teaching is in its nature closely connected to personal attitudes and values. This gives that policy-makers and ongoing learning cannot dictate teaching and TPD and that reflection has to be built on teachers' own participation in defining their own profession. The chapter suggests a close connection between teachers and teacher educators as a prerequisite for ongoing professional development in education. Further, the possibility to communicate through OLCs has made reflective activities through action research between distant educational environment easier to organize and facilitate. Finally, the chapter claims that future school development depends on personal engagement from teachers and teacher educators in an ecological learning process supporting students, student teachers, novice teachers and experienced practitioners.

Shelleyann Scott from Canada, in Chapter 2, "The Theory and Practice Divide in Relation to Teacher Professional Development", explores the divide between theories of effective TPD, particularly the potential inherent in OLCs, and the realities of practice within educational contexts. Two case studies, one from Australia and the other from Canada, illustrate the positives and negatives inherent within professional development approaches in these contexts. A number of key dimensions are identified, which when coalesced inform the establishment and sustainability of effective programmes. She argues that online technologies present innovative ways to overcome the impediments to effective professional development. The chapter suggests that online communities of practice utilising social networking technologies provide new opportunities for initiating so-called 'webs of enhanced practice' (Scott, 2009) (see also Chapter 10), where individuals around the globe can engage in collegial collaborations that enhance the passion of teaching.

Chapter 3 is written by Rebecca Scheckler from the USA, and is titled "Case Studies from the Inquiry Learning Forum: Stories Reaching Beyond the Edges". Two intense case studies of teachers using the Inquiry Learning Forum (ILF), an online space for professional development in inquiry pedagogies, are presented. The chapter shows that the ILF initially conceived as an online professional development tool in the form of a Community of Practice (COP) was reconceived as an electronic tool within a larger space that included the online tool but also many co-present spaces pertinent to a teacher's practice of inquiry pedagogy. Further, the case studies also demonstrate the transformative nature of teachers engaging in a COP. Not only does the teacher change, but also the COP changes by the practice. The author addresses the need for teachers to feel disequilibrium in their practice before they are willing to engage in change of those practices. In the end of the chapter it is argued that future trends in using online COPs for professional development need to look at practices in these terms where allowance for transaction, support outside the electronic space, and disequilibrium are considered.

In Chapter 4, "Changing the Metaphor: The Potential of Online Communities in Teacher Professional Development", Margaret Lloyd and Jennifer Duncan-Howell from Australia address that belonging to an online community offers teachers the opportunity to exchange ideas, make connections with a wider peer group and form collaborative networks. The authors suggest that the increasing popularity of teacher professional communities calls for a deepened understanding of how they work and to determine the role they may play in TPD. The chapter maps data from a doctoral study to a recently developed model of professional development to offer a new perspective of how online communities can add to a teacher's personal and professional growth and, in so doing, add to the small number of studies in this field. This chapter is concluded with a call for a revision of the way professional development in the 21st Century is approached. The authors suggest that old models and metaphors hinder the adoption of more effective means of professional development for teachers and that a new metaphor is needed to show how new tools require a rethinking of professional development strategies particularly in how individual teachers take ownership of their own learning.

Chapter 5 is written by Norbert Pachler, Caroline Daly and Anne Turvey, all from the UK, and is titled "Teacher Professional Development Practices: The Case of the Haringey Transformation Teachers Programme". This chapter discusses the need for new models of TPD in the context of established and emerging technologies and socio-constructivist theories of teacher learning within online and other communities. The authors present the current contexts affecting professional development in England and discuss the significance of the shift towards collaborative and community approaches to teachers' learning. The chapter argues that transformation is a key concept, however troublesome, in considering the aims of professional development for teachers' use of technologies in their everyday practice. The authors explore these ideas by presenting the case of the Transformation Teachers Programme (TTP), a wide-scale teachers' development project carried out in a London borough by Haringey City Learning Centre (CLC), and they examine how this project has implemented new approaches to Information and Communications Technology (ICT) and teachers' professional development, based on collaborative experimentation, enquiry and risk-taking within online and other community-based arrangements.

Alastair Wilson and Donald Christie from Scotland, in Chapter 6, titled "Realising the Potential of Virtual Environments: A Challenge for Scottish Teachers" describe how one national school's intranet with universal access is currently being developed in Scotland (anticipated completion in late 2009). In the chapter, they claim that this new technology will provide teachers with access to a variety of tools with which to develop their teaching and learning. Drawing on the experience of the Applied Educational Research Scheme (AERS), a five-year research programme funded to build research capacity in Scottish

Education, the chapter seeks to explore the potential for teachers in Scotland to realise effective use of this new technology in their professional learning. The chapter uses current research literature on teacher professionalism and professional learning in Scotland to establish the context in which Scottish teachers are currently working. The chapter then utilises three vignettes drawn from research within AERS to argue that the development of virtual environments to support professional learning in Scotland requires further, significant collaborative working between practitioner, policy and research communities.

In Chapter 7, "Challenges of Online Teacher Professional Development Communities: A Statewide Case Study in the United States", Vassiliki I. Zygouris-Coe and Bonnie Swan from USA, state that with so many educators needing either initial preparation or ongoing professional development to build and sustain expertise in their discipline, online professional development arises as a viable, effective, and timely vehicle for teacher training. They argue that online learning technologies have the potential to transform professional development of teachers; penetrate cultural, discipline, and other barriers; bring educators together to learn, share successes and challenges; and co-construct and transfer learning. The chapter presents examples of success and challenges associated with a large-scale U.S. state-wide online teacher professional development community. Further, the authors also make the case for implementing a systematic approach to investigating the effectiveness of online teacher professional development communities through ongoing assessment and responsive evaluation.

Chapter 8, written by Joaquin Gairin-Sallán and David Rodriguez-Gómez from Spain, and titled "Teacher Professional Development through Knowledge Management in Educational Organisations". They address that professional development has mainly centred on training processes that involve updating knowledge, yet it has made little headway as a construction that includes both professional and personal characteristics and working conditions. It has in addition focused more on developing training programmes than on analysing the tools for continuous training. The chapter analyses the relationships between professional development, organisational development and the creation and management of collective knowledge. The authors claim that these three concepts can be interrelated and contribute to change when we place ourselves within the framework of autonomous organisations with collective projects focused on lifelong learning. The chapter outlines the 'Accelera experience' of knowledge creation and management in communities, describing the model and process used. It is put forth that the 'Accelera experience' combines the creation of OLCs and the philosophy and technology of what is known as social software.

Chapter 9, "Thinking Things Through - Collaborative Online Professional Development" is written by John P. Cuthell from the UK. In the chapter, he proposes that one of the most powerful ways of changing the thinking about how we teach and learn is to experience for ourselves the power of collaborative project-based experiential learning. According to the author, few teachers have had the opportunity to learn this way, and this creates barriers for those who want to change their pedagogy. The Oracle Education Foundation's Project Learning Institute is said to provide teachers with the experience of collaborative project-based learning, using ThinkQuest® to create their own curriculum project. The author argues that by collaborating with their peers, tutors and mentors, teachers are able to model the projects, environment and experiences they want for their classes through a blended learning experience. The chapter describes a model of continuous professional development and its impact on schools, pedagogies and professional philosophies.

Chapter 10, titled "Innovations in the use of Technology and Teacher Professional Development", is written by Donald E. Scott and Shelleyann Scott from Canada. The chapter explores the innovative uses of technology for TPD as well as its impact in the classroom on learning and teaching. The chapter includes two international case studies. The first outlines technological innovations in graduate programme delivery within the university context in Canada. The second case presents a multi-dimensional professional development initiative in Australia that has influenced teachers' and students' learning. Scott and Scott describe two models: the macro-oriented "Webs of Enhanced Practice" that addresses the professional development of educators and experts; and the micro-oriented "Webs of Enhanced Learning" focusing on the learning occurring at the classroom level. In the chapter, they argue that these two models represent innovations in the use of technology as they conceptualise the eclectic use of multi-modal, varied technologies to advance the professional development of communities of learners.

In Chapter 11, titled "Game Informed Virtual Patients: Catalysts for Online Learning Communities and Professional Development of Medical Teachers", Michael Begg, David Dewhurst and Michael Ross from Scotland emphasize that modern medical education necessitates a complex interleaving of issues relating to practice, professional and personal development, teaching and learning. In the chapter, the authors argue that this complexity has led, in part, to medical education being persistently located in the vanguard of eLearning development. The formation of online communities of practice in medical education is explored and ways in which the technologies at their disposal in an online environment can support multi-specialty and multi-professional development are described. The authors state that it is clear that eLearning and ICT more generally can provide a vehicle for enhancing professional engagement with the education of students and for self-development in numerous ways. Further, they describe their approach to the development of virtual patient resources and in particular, how this iterative dialogue arising from the allied processes of practice, reflection and pedagogy required to create new learning tools and resources has contributed to professional development of those engaged in teaching medical students and in building OLCs at the University of Edinburgh.

Chapter 12, titled "Videopaper as a Bridging Tool in Teacher Professional Development", is written by Trond Eiliv Hauge and Svein Olav Norenes from Norway. The chapter demonstrates the possibilities of new media and affordable technological tools supporting TPD in a workplace setting. In the chapter, the authors describe how they over a period of six months followed a team of five mathematics teachers in a secondary school working jointly to improve their teaching and team practice by the support of a multimedia web developer system (VideoPaper). According to the authors, VideoPaper is an easy-to-use tool for development and sharing of web-documents integrating video resources, images and texts reflecting local practices. The authors describe the study as taking the form of developmental work research aligned to historical-cultural activity theory in line with the work of the Finnish professor Yrjö Engeström and was adapted to local needs and conditions of work. Hauge and Norenes put forth that their findings point to changes in teachers' conceptual approaches to learning and teaching and consequences for technology enhanced support for professional development. They argue that the study contributes to the understanding of the complexities in bridging practices between social and technological design for teacher development and the development of learning communities. In addition, that design of online learning systems fostering TPD must seek to explore and find innovative ways to support transformative actions, where participants are able to create, discuss and connect representations of collective objects of activity to their workplace setting.

Diana Laurillard and Elizabeth Masterman, both from the UK, focus in Chapter 13, "TPD as Online Collaborative Learning for Innovation in Teaching", on supporting university teachers in the UK in more innovative uses of digital technologies. The authors claim that although the use of these technologies is widespread and increasing, it is not always optimised for effective learning. Further, according to the authors it is important that teachers' use of technology should be directed towards innovation and improvement in teaching and learning, and should not merely replicate their current practice in a digital medium. The authors therefore make the case for an online collaborative environment to scaffold teachers' engagement with technology-enhanced learning. The authors' findings from their recent research are outlined into a blended approach to TPD, and they use these to identify the requirements for an online collaborative environment: tools for learning design, guidance, and access to relevant resources to support teachers in their discovery of new forms of technology-enhanced teaching and learning. In the chapter, they argue that such an environment would provide a framework for a "community of innovation" in which teachers participate both as learners and as researchers.

Pamela Whitehouse, Erin McCloskey and Diane Jass Ketelhult from USA, in Chapter 14, titled "Online Pedagogy Design and Development: New Models for 21st Century Online Teacher Professional Development" examine the shifting priorities of online teacher professional development design, particularly through the lens of online pedagogies. They argue that the teaching profession is changing as a response to multiple outside pressures and the rising importance of digital media and digital literacies in teaching and learning. Further, that whether one's purpose is to design an online teacher learning community or formal professional development program, decisions about technology use will mediate how the learning communities or training programs function. Whitehouse, McCloskey and Ketelhut put forth that designers, when choosing communication tools or digital media for inclusion in their program, ideally draw from their technological pedagogical content knowledge, or TPCK – i.e., their understanding of which technologies will support pedagogy appropriate for the content and learners targeted. In the chapter, the authors offer a model for online teacher professional development program design that makes visible the interaction between the technology, the content, the pedagogy and the learner.

The final Chapter 15, "Challenges for the Teacher's Role in Promoting Productive Knowledge Construction in Computer-Supported Collaborative Learning Contexts", Maarit Arvaja, Raija Hämäläinen and Helena Rasku-Puttonen from Finland put forth that contexts resting upon a theoretical base of Computer-Supported Collaborative Learning (CSCL) are productive for TPD and teachers' pedagogical activities. In the light of two different cases from secondary-level and higher education contexts, the authors examine how teachers' pedagogical choices influence the quality of students' activity, namely web-based discussion. They state that a future challenge is to develop both pedagogical and technological tools to support the monitoring and enhancement of students' learning process during online learning. The chapter further argues that TPD is challenged by new technological tools in formal learning environments. They conclude that teachers need possibilities to share their thoughts, reflections and good ideas for making progress and that teacher collaboration within work communities is a powerful element in teachers' workplace learning.

Our idea with this publication was already from the beginning to find ways of moving away from TPD-barriers such as top-down decision making and little or no support in transferring professional development ideas to the classroom. This could, as touched upon above, be achieved by adopting the concept of community (Lave & Wenger, 1991; Wenger, 1998), linking it to TPD, and situating it online. We were convinced that TPD in that way could be practiced within the contexts of OLCs, and be enhanced and sustained over time by the informed use of technology (Henderson, 2007). In addition, TPD in OLCs could thereby be framed by social processes such as mutual engagement, shared repertoire of interest and joint enterprise, always in relation to the teacher's practices and with a point of departure in each teacher's needs (see also Marks, 2005). All 15 chapters address, in various ways, important aspects and dimensions related to our idea. They provide theoretical foundations for developing research on this topic together with cases, models, methods and pedagogies for improved education delivery with great potential to improve practice. The chapters give the readers a solid ground when working towards enhancing TPD using OLC.

In line with the overall idea with this publication, from the onset we also had a clear picture of the potential audience. We had envisioned a publication with potential to attract various, but equally important, stakeholders. A book suited for professionals who, on a daily basis, work with issues concerning OLC, TPD and ICT, i.e. teachers, principals, educational researchers, technologists and designers, curriculum developers, teacher professional associations, teacher training staff, teacher trainees, universities and colleges. Hopefully, the contents of this book at its completion, has enabled this vision to come true.

We in addition hope and believe that this book will be important and cause debate, discussion and development within this specific area. Further that its informed use in policies, learning and teacher developing activities enhance the insight of what impact learning designs and learning arenas can have in order to enrich the practices of both staff and students and how they engage in it on a daily basis. The issue of OLC and TPD combined with methods for improved education for sure deserves such attention.

REFERENCES

Bell, B., & Gilbert, J. (1996). *Teacher development: a model from science education.* London: Falmer Press.

Bauman, Z. (2001). *Community. Seeking safety in an insecure world.* Cambridge: Polity Press.

Borko, H. (2004). Professional development and teacher learning: mapping the terrain. *Educational Researcher, 33*(8), 3-15.

Carlén, U., & Jobring, O. (2005). The rationale of online learning communities. *International Journal of Web Based Communities, 1*(3), 272 – 295

Delanty, G. (2003). *Community.* Routledge: London.

De Souzaa, C., & Preece, J. (2004). A framework for analyzing and understanding online communities. *Interacting with Computers, 16*, 579–610

Grant, C.A., & Agosto, V. (2008). Teacher capacity and social justice in teacher education. In M. Cochran-Smith, S. Feiman-Nemser, & D.J. McIntyre (Eds.), *Handbook of research on teacher education. Enduring questions in changing contexts* (pp. 175-200). New York: Routledge.

Henderson, M. (2007). Sustaining online teacher professional development through community design. *Campus-Wide Information Systems, 24*(3), 162-173.

Kennedy, A. (2005). Models of continuing professional development (CPD): a framework for analysis. *Journal of In-Service Education, 31*(2), 235-250.

Lave, J., & Wenger, E. (1991). *Situated learning: legitimate peripheral participation.* Cambridge: Cambridge University Press.

Lindberg, J. O., & Olofsson, A.D. (2008). OLC in the context of the Other – face, trace and cyberspace. *International Journal of Web Based Communities, 4*(2), 188-198.

Marks, A. (2005). A post-Gesellschaft-Gemeinschaft?. A sociological account of the `Pips` project. In S. Rodrigues (Ed.). *International perspectives on teacher professional development* (pp. 149-164). New York: Nova Science Publishers, Inc.

McKinney, S., Carroll, M., Christie, D., Fraser, C., Kennedy, A., Reid, L., & Wilson, A. (2005). *AERS: Learners, Learning and Teaching Network Project 2 – progress report.* Paper delivered at the Scottish Educational Research Association Annual Conference, Perth, Scotland, 24-26 November.

Olofsson, A.D., & Lindberg, J.O. (2006). "Whatever happened to the social dimension? Aspects of learning in a distance-based teacher education programme. *Education and Information Technologies, 11*(1), 7-20.

Olofsson, A.D., & Lindberg, A.D. (2007). Enhancing phronesis. Bridging communities through technology. In L. Tomei (Ed.). *Online and distance learning. concepts, methodologies, tools, and applications (6-volume set)* (pp. 3157-3175). Hershey, PA: Information Science Reference.

Preece, J., & Maloney-Krichmar, D. (2003). Online communities: design, theory, and practice. *Journal of Computer-Mediated Communication, 10*(4), article 1.

Selznik, P. (1996). In search of community. In W. Vitek & W. Jackson (Eds.), *Rooted in the land: essays on community and place* (pp. 195-203). New Haven: Yale University Press.

Triggs, P., & John, P. (2004). From transaction to transformation: information and communication technology, professional development and the formation of communities of practices. *Journal of Computer Assisted Learning, 20*, 426-439.

Tönnies, F. (1963). *Community and Society* (Charles P. Loomis, Trans.). New York: Harper.

Vrasidas, C., & Glass, G.V. (2004). Teacher professional development. In C. Vrasidas & G.V. Glass (Eds.), *Online professional development for teachers* (pp. 1-11). Greenwich, CT: IAP.

Wenger, E. (1998). *Communities of practice. Learning, meaning and identity.* Cambridge: Cambridge University Press.

Acknowledgment

This book is the hard work of many people that in various ways has supported the process from start to finish. In particularly we will genuinely thank all the authors of the individual chapters for their excellent contributions. We will also thank our colleagues around the globe who, with their deep knowledge in this research area, have participated in the review process. Without your support this book project could not have been satisfactorily completed. In this respect special gratitude shall be given to Ken Fernstrom, Brian Hudson, Theo Wubbels, Shirley Simon, Stefan Hrastinski, Monica Liljeström, Anneli Hansson, Jimmy Jaldemark, and of course the contributing authors in this book that have, in a most productive way, peer-reviewed the chapters.

A special note of thanks is due to the staff at IGI Global whose support throughout the process has been most valuable. In addition we will thank the Faculty of Social Sciences, Department of Education, Mid Sweden University and Faculty of Social Sciences, Department of Education, Umeå University for providing both of us generous opportunities for working with this book. We will also thank our research groups, Digital Competence in Teacher Education and LICT, (Learning & ICT) for encourage and academic support.

Finally, we would like to thank our families for their love, understanding and patience throughout this book project. In Ola´s case his spouse Anne and their children Joakim, Sanna and Martin. In Anders case his fiancée Tina and their children Neo and Wille.

J. Ola Lindberg, Mid Sweden University, Sweden
Anders D. Olofsson, Umeå University, Sweden
March 2009

Section 1
Theoretical and Technological Foundations

Chapter 1
Theoretical Foundations of Teachers' Professional Development

Ingrid Helleve
University of Bergen, Norway

ABSTRACT

To be a professional teacher or teacher educator means to participate in an ongoing learning process. The main concern of teachers is to guide and help students to learn. This means that teaching is by its nature closely connected to personal attitudes and values. Accordingly teaching and teachers' professional development cannot merely be dictated by policy-makers. Ongoing learning and reflection concerning education has to be built on teachers' own participation. Recent research shows that teacher educators undergo the same kind of development as teachers do. Throughout this chapter the author argues for a close connection between teachers and teacher educators as a prerequisite for ongoing professional development in education. Possibilities to communicate through online learning communities have made reflective activities through action research between distant educational environments easier to organize and facilitate.

INTRODUCTION

As a young teacher I yearned for the day when I would know my craft so well, be so competent, so experienced, and so powerful, that I would walk into any classroom without feeling afraid. (P. J. Palmer, 1998, p. 57).

DOI: 10.4018/978-1-60566-780-5.ch001

According to Hargreaves (2000) we are at a crossroad for teachers' professionalism and professional learning at the beginning of this century. One possible future road is that of teachers' diminished professionalism through regulations, another is to maintain and pursue professionalism based on teachers' own participation. Teaching is closely connected to the affective aspect of human minds, and being a teacher means to be emotionally involved. Education is deeply rooted in personal attitudes and values. The fact that teachers' lives are closely

Figure 1. Continuous reflection through action research in learning communities

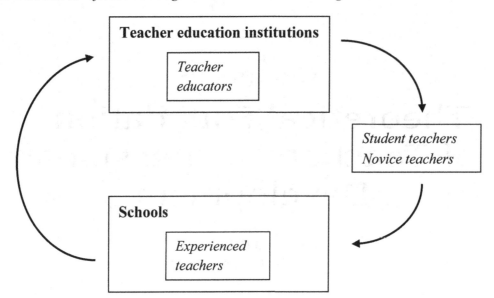

linked to emotions, means that teaching by its' nature is impossible to dictate. Consequently the idea of teachers' professional development should be built on the acknowledgement that teachers' concern is their pupils. Through the chapter I also want to draw attention to teacher educators' professional development, and the necessity of a close connection between teachers and teacher educators in an ongoing learning process. A significant amount of research claims that teachers' professional learning is closely connected to reflection. Research documents that reflection, through action research is a support for teachers' professional development. I intend to argue that teachers' professional development through action research is the bridge between teacher education and teaching in schools, and reflection seems to be the material to build the bridge. Isolated schools as well as teacher education institutions are unable to become learning communities. Professional development for student teachers' and novice teachers' is a common concern for teacher education and schools. The type of support they need is different from experienced teachers' and teacher educators' professional development. I

want to argue that if schools and teacher education institutions are to become learning communities experienced teachers and teacher educators, as well as student teachers and novice teachers need to participate in professional development by continuing reflection through action research, see figure 1.

BACKGROUND

Teachers' professional development is an elusive term. To some it may conjure images of short term courses and workshops. Others may associate it with ongoing learning and reflective practice. So, what does the term teachers' professional development actually mean? According to Darling-Hammond (1994) teachers' professional development is a process of enhancing teachers' status through increased awareness and an expanding knowledge base. Interpretation of teachers' professional development as an investigation of their practice is shared by other researchers. Linda Evans claims that in spite of the fact that many people write and talk about teachers' professional development there are few definitions of what it actually means. She defines teachers' professional development as follows:

an ideologically-, attitudinally-, intellectually- and epistemologically-based stance on the part of an individual, in relation to the practice of the profession to which s/he belongs, and which influences her/his professional practice. (Evans, 2002, p.130).

Like Darling Hammond she is concerned with the fact that teachers' professional development is an ongoing process. Her definition implies that professionalism should be enhanced through a developmental process. Kelly (2006) argues that so far teachers' professional development has been defined through a cognitive perspective on learning. If knowledge and teachers' expertise is perceived as residing inside the head of the individual and knowledge is transferable then courses outside schools are the correct way of enhancing *teachers' professional development*. In a cognitive perspective, knowledge learned in de-contextualized situations can be transferred to the teacher's own schools and class-rooms. To date, courses and learning programs outside school have been a common way of supporting teachers' professional development. A situated perspective accounts for teachers' learning based on their own experiences, tacit knowledge and knowledge-in-practice (Schön, 1983, 1987). Teachers' movement from novice to expert is rooted in engagement in reflective, discursive, collaborative and inclusive practices in order to improve their work (Kelly, 2006). Bell & Gilbert (1994) also argue for the term teachers' *learning* as an alternative to development. *Development* reflects a passive attitude from the teacher as if somebody else has to take responsibility for the process. As different aspects of human nature like personal, professional and social development contribute to the continual process, learning is a better suited concept. According to the authors, an

important way of enhancing teachers' professional development is through action research. Teachers should have the possibility of initiating new learning activities combined with a collaborative process of theoretical input and evaluation. Support as well as critical feedback from colleagues is necessary in order to develop personally, as well as socially and professionally. Accordingly teachers' professional development is part of a systematic ongoing learning process for the individual teacher as well as the community in order to articulate tacit knowledge. In this chapter teachers' professional development is defined as an ongoing reflective learning process in which teachers and teacher educators engage to learn how to adjust their teaching to the learning needs of their students. The process is rooted in critical self-analysis.

In spite of geographical and cultural differences, some common features concerning the changing nature teachers' professionalism and professional learning are identified. Hargreaves (2000) has divided the last century into four different periods called the *pre-professional age*, the age of the *autonomous professional*, the age of the *collegial professional* and finally what he calls the *post-professional* or *post-modern age*. The pre-professional age is the first half of the twentieth century which is described as a demanding, but not always technically difficult period for teachers. They often had few resources and were struggling alone. Still, the frames of what he calls "grammar of schooling" were obvious (ibid. p. 153). The basic methods were recitation, or lecturing, note-taking, questions and answers, and assessment through final tests. Teachers were supposed to maintain attention from the pupils and to cover the curriculum content. How to become a teacher was learnt through apprenticeship, trial and error. The ideal teacher was a person who knew the subject, knew how to "get it across" to the students and who was able to keep control and order in their classes. The term pre-professional period might be exchanged with restricted professionalism (Hoyle, 1974). The next period from the 1960's onwards is described as the *age of the autonomous professional*. Characteristic for this period is a growing focus on child-centred education and on an extended interest in different teaching and learning activities. Teachers were autonomous in the sense that they had the right to choose their own methods. Still there was little further professionalism in terms of quality of the work. The 1970 and 80's were characterized by isolation. Collaboration was occasional and not a part of an explicit national educational policy. There was little or no integration between teacher education and in-service teaching. Consequently ideas prescribed from teacher educators became lost ideals for many novice teachers. The third period is called *the age of the collegial professional*. By the end of the 1980's policy-makers started to mandate teachers to teach in particular ways. Due to societal changes such as inclusion of all pupils, requirements from policy-makers of *what* and *how* teachers should perform their profession changed dramatically. Changes were brought about through organizational structures and a more distinct school leadership. A growing awareness of collaboration as a means for professional development for individual teachers and schools has resulted in increased collaborative structures. Some of these structures are imposed from policy-makers, others are emerging from teachers themselves out of a growing awareness of increased professionalism as a result of collaborative activities among colleagues; a *moving mosaic*. The fourth period is called *the post-professional period* from the beginning of the twenty-first century. This period is characterized by globalization of economies, and a rapid development of educational technology causing uncertainty among teachers as well as policy-makers of what knowledge actually is, and what kind of knowledge is worthwhile to pass on from one generation to the other. So far politicians in many countries have answered these questions by centralizing curricula and imposing test-regimes.

Teachers are rewarded and can earn more than their colleagues for pupils' high score on individual tests. Teaching as a profession is subject to blaming, shaming and intrusive inspection. According to Hargreaves (1994, 2000) the turn of the century is a cross-road for teachers' professionalism and the way professional development for teachers should be perceived and interpreted. One possibility is that policy-makers diminish teachers' autonomy through further regulations. Another possibility is to build on teachers' own contribution and participation. This can only happen through extending and enriching the idea and practice of collegial professionalism, the moving mosaic (Hargreaves, 1994).

THE INDIVIDUAL TEACHER AND THE COMMUNITY

Mentors and apprentices are partners in an ancient human dance…It is the dance of the spiralling generations, in which the old empower the young with experience and the young empower the old with new life, reweaving the fabric of the human community as they touch and turn. (P. J. Palmer, 1998, p. 25)

Student Teachers and Novice Teachers

Novice teachers need for professional development is different from experienced teachers'. Generally there seems to be little connection between teacher education and the teaching profession as it is experienced in the classroom. Since many teachers will retire in the next few years it is necessary to educate more student teachers. The fact that many novice teachers leave the profession after a short while makes it urgent to investigate what kind of professional development student teachers and novice teachers need if they are going to stay in the profession.

The expression *practice shock* (Achinstein, 2006, p.123) can be defined as the conflict between an ideal and the reality novice teachers' experience when starting their first job (Flores & Day, 2006). Newly qualified teachers who are given the full responsibility for their profession find it difficult to maintain the ideal view of what teaching should be. One reason for the shock might be that student teachers are not prepared adequately from their teachers' education to be confronted with the challenges a teacher has to cope with in a classroom Darling-Hammond et al. 2002 found that certified teachers feel better prepared than non-certified. Still, teacher education seems to lack relevance. Recent research shows that teacher education does not seem to influence student teachers' beliefs and practice when they begin teaching (Lunenberg et al. 2007; Wilson, 2006). An extensive review of international research on the impact of teacher education on teachers' practice shows that it is fairly limited (Wideen et al. 1998). This corresponds to the conclusion made by the AERA (American Educational Research Association) (Cochran-Smith & Zeichner, 2005). Teacher education cannot possibly prepare teachers for every situation they encounter in the profession. Biesta (2007) claims that teachers constantly face unexpected situations and that it is impossible to provide recipes of response for each and every one. Initially, teachers deal more with survival than with learning from experiences. Accordingly, there seems to be a growing acknowledgement for student teachers and newly educated teachers' need for support upon entering their career.

The next 5-10 years a large number of teachers in many countries will retire (Teachers Matter, OECD, 2005). This makes it urgent to focus on how to select good teachers and keep them in the profession. Recent research shows that 30-50% of teachers leave the profession during their first 3-5 years (Achinstein, 2006). One explanation is that novice teachers have been found to experience heavy workloads and poor working conditions. They lack sufficient and suitable support to keep them in the profession. Often the most talented teachers leave first (Firestone, 1996). Rots et al. (2007) found that experiences from the novice teachers' first teaching period create the factor with the strongest impact on retention. This fact stresses the importance of providing new teachers with a positive entrance into the profession. Positive experiences the first year will make new teachers more committed to teaching. Teaching and a good relationship with students are some of the factors newly qualified teachers find most satisfying (Flores & Day, 2006).

Mentoring as part of TPD is often used to support student teachers and novice teachers. The idea of mentoring is grounded in the belief that if newly qualified teachers are offered support, they will experience a greater sense of security and self-confidence, and consequently they will be able to improve their teaching. Newly qualified teachers should have someone to turn to for help when they have need of counsel. Research shows that experienced teachers are of great importance for newcomers (Skovholt, 2001). A mentor should be a model and a support, but also be able to challenge the newcomer (Nielsen & Kvale, 1999). However, schools are complex organizations and the question is if one mentor is sufficient for the novice teachers' professional development. Existence of a mentor program is no guarantee in itself of success. A support-program based on relations between individuals is vulnerable. Individual differences might be the reason for success as well as failure. Some mentor teachers are well qualified while others have nothing else than the title to support them in their efforts (Little, 1990; Meyer, 2002). The success of mentoring often rests on mentors' good will, intuition, and commitment. Mentoring arrangements can be examples of contrived collegiality; a relationship that works better on paper than in reality (Hargreaves, 1992). Collaboration between mentors in schools and teacher educators might be a support for professional development for novice teachers, mentors as well as teacher educators. A newly qualified teacher needs different kinds of support. Disciplinary problems, different subject-matters, dealing with parents and the problem of assessment are some examples of some of the many challenges that novice teachers experience. Some of these questions might easily be answered by one person, others need more time for reflection. Newly qualified teachers should have the opportunity to collaborate with teacher educators and other novices as well as experienced teachers. To summarize, a newly qualified teacher has many different needs, and requires different kinds of settings and people to solve the problems. Therefore one mentor is probably not enough to give all the answers. Furthermore, a mentor program consisting of a novice and an experienced teacher signalizes that the new teacher is helpless and needs care and support, while the experienced teacher is an expert who is self-sufficient and has no more to learn. On the contrary, experienced teachers often express that they learn from novice teachers. This leads to the question of how experienced teachers learn. Is it possible to become a finished expert as a teacher, or is teaching by its nature an ever-learning process?

Experienced Teachers' Learning Processes

Current research shows a strong correlation between teachers' teaching and students' school success (Darling Hammond, 1998; Teachers Matter OECD, 2005). Professional development has become increasingly important as a way to ensure that teachers succeed in matching their teaching goals with their students' needs. According to Beijaard et al. 2007, it is remarkable that with so much attention paid to student learning in schools, the issues of teacher learning has until recently drawn relatively little attention from researchers. Having finished teacher education these teachers see no more of their colleagues in their classrooms. They receive no feedback on their practice and make changes mainly through trial and error

(Hargreaves, 2000; Hoyle, 1974). According to Kelly (2006) the most important influence factor in the process of teacher learning or knowing-in-practice are the ways in which the working practice of the school engages them in thinking. The way the community values what an expert teacher is like, will influence the newcomers' way of learning. If the school community is dominated by an instrumental perspective on learning, it is more likely that the novice will adopt the same way of understanding students', as well as teachers' learning. Arfwedson (1984) describes the difference between schools through what he calls the *code* of the school. This code is so different that one school might be perceived as belonging to another universe than the neighboring school. According to Arfwedson groups of teachers have a strong impact on what counts and what does not within a given school culture. Strong groups of teachers have great influence on school culture and school development. The code is decisive for how new teachers and even principals learn and develop within the given community. The strong group of teachers may enhance or counteract against collaborative learning. Learning within a counteracting context can lead to *restricted professional development* which can hardly be called professional (Hoyle, 1974; Hargreaves, 2000). The fact that the impact of the culture is so strong and difficult to change supports the idea that teachers' professional development as well as development of schools as learning communities, is depending on continual influence from communities outside the school context. Schools are not self-sufficient as learning communities.

The teacher who engages fully in reflective discursive collaborative and inclusive practices is an expert (Kelly, 2006). During the movement from novice to expert, a teacher's identity is ever changing. Identities are in a state of constant evolution through a process "which consists of negotiating the meanings of our experiences of membership in social communities" (Wenger, 1998, p. 145). Teachers' identities are neither located within the individual nor entirely a product of others and the social setting. Education is a complex process. Teachers constantly face unexpected situations and it is impossible to provide guidelines of how to respond to each and every one. A teacher has to make decisions every minute, according to Firestone (1996). This means that knowing-in practice is a distributed and dynamic process resulting from the collaborative actions of students, novice and experienced teachers together. In conclusion, promoting teachers learning from novice to expert will depend on the possibility for approaching critically to reflective practices. An important question though, is how reflective practices are initiated and guided. The connection between schools and teacher education has so far mainly been limited to student teachers' practicum. In the next paragraph I will argue for an extended connection between the two institutions for the benefit of novice teachers, experienced teachers and teacher educators as well as student teachers.

Teacher Educators' Professional Development

Working as a teacher educator is a complex profession, and a profession that has not gained too much attention to date. Initial or pre-service teacher education is, almost everywhere, one of the most obsolete pieces of education systems (Moreno, 2007).

Actually, little empirical research focusing on teacher educators has been done and not until recently has there been any focus at all on professional development of teacher educators (Korthagen 2001; Murray & Male 2005). Loughran (2006) advocates the urgency of developing a new pedagogy for teacher education. Recent research documents that it is often a frustrating process for teacher educators to leave their position as expert teachers in schools and become novice teacher educators. Novice teacher educators undergo the same process as un-experienced teachers. (Murray & Male, 2005; Ritter, 2007; Zeichner, 2005).

Teacher education is different from the school environment in many aspects. The academic context surrounding teacher education has demands concerning research as well as education. Teacher educators with backgrounds in schools usually have no research experience. Teaching adult student teachers in a period of insecurity of what teacher education should be is different from teaching pupils in community schools. Altogether this means that teacher educators' professional development is parallel to teachers' professional development. Consequently institutions of teacher education should be compared to communities of learners as well as schools. Novice teacher educators should have the possibility to collaborate and learn from experienced teacher educators, while experienced teacher educators just like teachers in schools are in a continuing learning process of how to design and participate in a community. Teachers' professional development is closely connected to teacher education and teacher educators' professional development. Viewed from an individual and cognitive perspective on learning, the newly qualified teacher should be prepared for the profession after graduation from teacher education. Gradually there has been a growing dissatisfaction with the traditional model of teacher education where pre-service teachers are told what works well in the classroom before they have experienced what it is like to be a teacher (Korthagen, 2001; Niemi, 2002). A new model of teacher education is rapidly emerging based on a situated and socio-cultural approach to learning. In order to promote learning processes inside schools as well as teacher education, there should be a continual connection between teacher education and the school environment based on action research (Gitlin et al. 1999; Levin & Rock, 2003; Schön, 1983, 1987; Spilkova; 2001; Valli, 2000). Learning to teach is an ongoing process of lifelong professional learning for teacher educators as well as teachers (Cochran Smith & Lytle, 1999). Research is part of teacher educators' responsibility. As consumers of research they are able to inform practicum. Through reflective activities based on action research teacher education should also be involved in producing new knowledge in collaborative activities with student teachers, newly qualified teachers, teachers and other teacher educators.

Development through Stages

Teaching career for teachers and teacher educators requires constant upgrading and improvement. However the needs are different from one stage to the other in a lifelong continuum. Different metaphors are used to illustrate how teachers and teacher educators go through a development process from their starting point as novice teachers until they retire. Research within this field of teachers' professional development shows the same change from an individual to a collective perspective. Fuller and Bown (1975) presented a model where *survival* was described as the first phase. They argue that not until later are newly qualified teachers able to move their attention from their own person to the well-being of their pupils.

Watzke (2007) criticizes the theory of phases, claiming that beginning teachers go beyond the survival phase when they start teaching. They are often deeply concerned with students as learners and are capable of complex and student-oriented thinking. Still there is no doubt that teachers undergo some sort of learning processes that might be compared to stages. Like Fuller and Bown, the traditional stage theory conceptualizes teachers' professional learning and development through a number of linear skill-developmental stages. The movement from novice to advanced beginner, competent proficient and expert is described by Dreyfus & Dreyfus (1986). Kolb (1984) made a model to illustrate how the practitioner learns through reflection from a meta-cognitive perspective. An abstract understanding of experience is the starting-point for changed practice in the future. What characterizes these first models of stage

development and reflection is that the individual teacher is focused. What is going on within the rest of the school context is not described. The traditional stage models are underpinned by the belief that "experience is the way of learning and it is the adult learners' text-book" (Day & Gu, 2007, p.425).

Later research has not left the stage theory. What is changed is the growing awareness of the influence and impact from the surroundings on teachers' professional development. The longitudial VITAE-project (Variations in teachers' work, lives and effectiveness) involved 300 teachers. The aim of the project was to investigate different aspects contributing to variations in teachers' effectiveness in different phases of their professional lives. The result shows that the success of professional development is dependent on teachers' opportunities for professional learning mediated by two factors. First, the sense of professional identity is decided by a range of personal conditions. Professional and situated factors are embedded in teachers' work and social lives. Secondly, professional identity is mediated by the teachers' professional life phases. Teacher identity comprises the interaction between professional, situated and personal dimensions. The professional dimension reflects the expectation a teacher has of what it means to be a good teacher. The situated dimension is decided by the local conditions at the school, while family life and social positions outside school influence what is called the personal dimension (Day & Gu, 2007). The results from the VITAE project show that teachers' work and life spanned what they called six professional life phases. It is notable that a distinctive group of the oldest teachers demonstrated a high level of motivation and engagement for their pupils throughout the different periods. Their main concern was students' learning and what was happening in their class-rooms. The research project shows that teachers, independent of life-phases, were confronted by professional and personal pressure, tensions and challenges concerning values, belief as well as practices. Still many of them had the capacity to learn to build upon influences and opportunities to maintain the commitment that had initially attracted them to teaching. The two aspects that were most important for teacher retention and resilience were the support from principals and colleagues, and secondly the ability to create and maintain a learning climate within the school society. Doubtless teachers appreciate the possibilities of common reflection by colleagues, but what does it mean to be reflective? In the following section I want to focus on how research has changed focus from an individual to a collective perspective on reflection as a way of supporting teachers' and teacher educators professional development.

REFLECTION

As important as methods may be, the most practical thing we can achieve in any kind of work is insight into what is happening inside us as we do it. The more familiar we are with our inner terrain, the more surefooted our (work) –and living- becomes. (P.J.Palmer, 1998, p. 5).

Like other professions where the aim of the activity is to help other people, an important quality for a teacher or teacher educator is the ability to be empathic and to appreciate the perspective of others. Contribution to students' learning and development requires active engagement from the teacher. Research shows that caring and understanding are the qualities students value most highly (Skovholt, 2001). Looking at learning from the teacher's perspective, the greatest reward for him or her is to see their pupils grow and develop. The fact that teachers judge their success from their pupils' progression means that by its nature teaching is a vulnerable profession. The importance of personal investment and engagement means that when something goes wrong the

teacher is to blame. Actually there are many possibilities for undesired or unexpected outcomes. To be an educator means to work in an area of constant stress and emotions. Not all students are motivated for learning. On the contrary they sometimes project their negative feelings about schools onto their teachers. There are no limits for the workload. A teacher may spend day and night preparing for a lesson that still does not work because of loss of control in the classroom. Distended demands from students and parents on one hand and policy-makers and school leaders on the other means that the teacher often is in a cross-fire, and confidentiality makes it difficult to talk about problems concerning students and parents. Another aspect is that it is difficult to judge or measure the success of your own work. The personal investment in a profession where the main aim is to help others means the boundaries between the needs of others and the needs of self are difficult to distinguish. In a profession where care is judged to be the most important attribute by the people you are serving it is of extreme importance to be aware of the limits between taking care of others and taking care of oneself. Indifference, ignorance, burnout, or leaving the profession are strategies teachers use to meet a multitude of challenges. Consequently a core question concerning professional development for teachers is how to develop professional self-understanding. Education and experience is not enough to ensure professional development. A reflective attitude is necessary for ongoing professional self development. Professional development cannot be forced. The teacher has to be open to engage in reflective dialogues, to take personal responsibility and not leave it to others. There seems to be an agreement in the educational research field that the ability to reflect is of essential importance for teachers if they are to learn from their experiences (Calderhead, 1989; Korthagen & Vasalos, 2005; LaBosky, 1994; Schön, 1987). What has been questioned lately is what it actually means to reflect and to be reflective. Almost all research seems to agree on the fact that reflection is a special form of thought (Korthagen & Kessels, 1999). The main characteristics of effective teachers seems to be their ability and need to think about their experiences and to examine their own beliefs and practices (Ginns et al. 2001). Dewey (1910) says about reflection that it involves not simply a sequence of ideas, but a con-sequence- a consecutive ordering in such a way that each idea determines the next as its proper outcome, while each in turn leans back on, or refers to, its predecessors (p. 2-3). He gives the following definition of the term reflection:

Active, persistent, and careful consideration of any belief or supposed form of knowledge in the light of the grounds that support it and the further conclusions to which it tends, constitutes reflective thought. (Dewey, 1910, p. 6).

Reflection requires that the teachers become aware of their conceptions of practice, and that they be guided to restructure these conceptions if another way of perceiving is more fruitful. The so-called ALACT-model aims at structured reflection. Korthagen & Wubbels (2001) advocate the ALACT-model as five cyclical phases of reflection; action, looking back on the action, awareness of essential aspects, creating alternative methods for action, and trial. The authors argue that reflection is necessary to promote sound professional behaviour and development of growth competence for teachers and student teachers. The model is based on reflection on the four levels of environment, behaviour, competences, and beliefs. Beliefs are often deep-rooted and persistent (Calderhead & Robson, 1991; Korthagen & Vasalos, 2005), and therefore difficult to change. Reflection can help teachers to become conscious of moral, ethical and political aspects embedded in everyday practice by stepping back and analyzing actions (Handal & Lauvås, 1987). Korthagen & Kessels (1999) portray reflection as a way to gain "insights into the development of the nature of the relationship between teacher cognition

and teacher behaviour" (ibid. p.4). What Korthagen later calls "the onion-model" represents an alternative to, or an extension of, the ALACT model (Korthagen & Vasalos, 2005). In addition to the four competences mentioned above, the concepts of professional identity and mission are added. Reflection on the level of mission triggers such issues as to why the person has decided to become a teacher, or even what he sees as his calling in the world. It is concerned with what inspires us, and what gives meaning and significance to our lives (Korthagen & Vasalos, 2005). Reflection is a way of bringing tacit knowledge to a level of awareness enabling teachers to develop their practical theory of teaching (Handal & Lauvås, 1987). Another major influence for the importance of reflection in teaching is Donald Schön (1983, 1987). Schön's notion of reflection is rooted in practice-based common knowledge and to a certain extent rejects scientific and intellectual knowledge: According to Schön, practitioner's reflection can serve as a corrective to over-learning. Through reflection one can surface and criticize the tacit understandings that have evolved around the repetitive experiences of a specialized practice. One can then make new sense of the situations of uncertainty and uniqueness which he may allow himself to experience (Schön, 1983, p. 61). Schön makes a distinction between reflection-in-action and reflection-on-action that has had an important impact on education. Teaching is by its nature known for frequent decision making. Reflection-in-action is defined as:

When someone reflects-in-action, he becomes a researcher in the practice context. He is not dependent on the categories of established theory and technique, but constructs a new theory of the unique case. His inquiry is not limited to a deliberation about means which depends on a prior agreement about ends. He does not keep means and ends separate, but defines them interactively as he frames a problematic situation". (Schön, 1983, p. 68).

Reflection-in-action implies inquiry into personal theories in the zone of time in which action can still make a difference to the situation. Based on a socio-cultural perspective on learning Wegerif (2007) argues for a focus of attention away from abstract, individual cognitive structures and towards the way people respond to each other in dialogues. A *reflective dialogue* is creative, caring and critical. In this perspective reflection not only enhances the individual teachers' but the community's professional development or learning. In the next paragraph I will give an outline of some possibilities I see for collaborative reflective dialogues across schools and teacher education.

Professional Development Activities

Action research is a way of building a bridge between schools and teacher education with possibilities for collaborative as well as individual professional learning (Smith & Sela, 2005). Action research can be defined as "the study of a social situation with a view to improving the quality of action within it" (Elliot, 1991, p. 69). It is not explicitly connected to teaching as a profession, but in the last decade it has been most often used within this field (Cochran-Smith & Lytle, 1999). Educational action research is a systematic inquiry by teachers with the goal of improving their teaching practices (Levin & Rock 2003). Schön's (1983, 1987) concept reflection-on-action might be understood as an inherent part of action research since action research is a particular way of researching your own learning. The activity is also described as self-reflective practice, or as learning in and through action (McNiff, 2002, p.15). McNiff defines the term *action research* as a process of improving one's own understanding of how to improve social situations. Knowledge is understood as something people *do*. There are no fixed answers. Rather answers are transformed into new questions. A classic definition of action research is:

Action research is simply a form of self-reflective enquiry undertaken by participants in social situations in order to improve the rationality and justice of their own practices, their understanding of these practices, and the situations in which these practices are carried out. (Carr & Kemmis, 1986, p.162).

According to Stenhouse (1975) teaching and research are closely related. As a form of curriculum theorizing, teachers in collaboration with higher education should reflect critically and systematically on their own practice. McNiff is critical to the earliest action research models for different reasons. Firstly she argues that the definitions are performed like recipes or prescriptions of how the research process should be conducted. Second, because they are linear and sequential and thirdly because they might be interpreted as if the initiative has to come from a researcher, and that the researcher should come from higher education. In her view there is a considerable dividing line between this group and the other group who aim to develop new metaphors which show life and living as fluid processes. The first category of action research, called *interpretive and critical theoretic*, works at the level of abstraction and uses metaphors of static reality. The purpose of this kind of research is to observe, describe behaviour and to understand what is going on. The second category called *living theory approach* moves beyond the first one. McNiff underlines that in addition to making observations and descriptions the researcher should show his own process of learning and development. Education is predicated on values. How we act as action researchers will depend on what we believe we are acting for. Action research in an educational setting is a way of researching one's own learning process; a process in which everyone involved is prepared to grow, rather than one person telling others how it should be done. Educational inquiries lead to knowledge of self within a world which the researcher co-creates with others who are similarly occupied. Action research only has meaning when practice is seen in relation to others in a process of dialogue and encounters (McNiff, 2002). Action research should be regarded as a tool for reflection which contributes to teachers' collective and individual learning. When working on action research projects, teachers have to articulate personally constructed knowledge. Knowledge acquired in action research is common knowledge for the members of the professional community. Teachers who engage in action research projects do not only become more professional, they also become actively involved in improving the profession (Smith & Sela, 2005). Accordingly action research can function as a bridge between teachers in schools and teacher educators. Portfolios can be used to encourage reflective dialogues (Helleve, 2007; Klenowski, 2002). The main aim of using portfolios is to encourage student teachers and teachers to think more deeply about their teaching process, to become more conscious of the theories and assumptions that guide their practices, and to engage in collaborative dialogues about teaching in order to support and document professional development. For portfolio implementation to be a success it must contribute to constructing personal knowledge and insights into performance, and possibly support competence development (Anderson & DeMeulle, 1998; Darling Hammond & Snyder 2000; Elminn & Elminn, 2005; Klenowski, 2002; Smith & Tillema, 1998, 2001; Zeichner & Liston, 1998). However, it is necessary to look at the particular conditions under which the portfolios are constructed, and the purpose towards which they are directed. We need to learn more about the nature and quality of reflection that emerges under different conditions of portfolio use (Zeichner & Liston, 1998). Some countries have developed a progressive career route for teachers as a way of enhancing professional development. An example of this is Scotland, with a Chartered Teachers Certificate (Scottish Executive, 2002). Teachers within schools are invited to work on a portfolio where they document formal and informal devel-

opment processes in a professional portfolio. Peer feedback among teachers and teacher educators is another tool for reflective dialogues that has proved to be an important contribution to teachers' professional development (Dochy et al. 1999; Handal & Lauvås, 1987). Teacher educators should profit from the same reflective collaborative activities as in-service teachers such as use of peer feedback and portfolio as earlier suggested for schools and teachers. The ability to communicate and reflect upon one's own teaching seems to be just as important for teacher educators as for teachers (Koster et al. 2005). Recent research shows that teacher educators serve as models for learning and professional development for pre-service student teachers (Lunenberg et al. 2007). Even though teaching pre-service teachers is looked upon as a difficult activity by teacher educators' research is perhaps judged to be even more stressful (Murray & Male, 2005). Still it should be claimed that it is just as important. Research is essential in improving practice in schools as well as teacher education. Teacher and teacher educators' professional development within schools and teacher education is totally dependent upon collaboration between the two institutions. Both depend on each other in an open and ongoing learning process. Action research is a way of building the bridge between the two.

Professional Development through Learning Communities

The model of community we seek is one that can embrace, guide and refine the core mission of education- the mission of knowing, teaching, and learning (J. P. Palmer, 1998, p. 94)

The terms community of practice and community of learners are often used to describe educational contexts. Online collaboration has significantly increased the use of these expressions. In this section I will give an account for why the two concepts are useful in understanding professional development for teachers and teacher educators as part of an ongoing learning process for schools and teacher education institutions. *Communities of practice* are characterized as groups who share a common engagement, tasks and a shared repertoire. There is a close connection between participation, identity and learning because learning is changing who we are as individuals. Learning, meaning and negotiating identity are deeply rooted in the cultural context. According to a situated perspective on learning, psychological phenomena such as thinking, memory and reflection cannot be separated from the activity. We are always reflecting or thinking about something. Reflection is therefore deeply grounded in people's background and community. Schools and teacher education institutions are examples of communities where certain goals are defining what should be validated as important. New teachers learn to understand what counts as valuable for becoming a professional teacher within the community they enter (Lave & Wenger, 1991; Wenger, 1998). Looking at educational contexts as communities is fruitful given the tangled nature of dilemmas, challenges and problems in teaching. Looking at the educational context as a *community of practice*, the movement from novice to expert teacher or teacher educator can be understood as legitimate peripheral participation. Through engagement in practice the novice learns what it means to become a professional teacher, or an expert in this specific community of practice (Lave & Wenger, 1991). What it means to be an expert differs according to the profession of the community you enter, either you are to develop an identity as a carpenter, a nurse or a teacher you learn what counts as professional practice. I have earlier argued for the importance of continual learning for all the participants in an educational context. *Practice* in an educational community is intentional, ongoing learning for students, teachers, and teacher educators. To become a professional teacher or teacher educator means to participate in ongoing, collaborative

reflection including theoretical perspectives and experiences from practice. The roots of the term *community of learners* are different from the *community of practice* metaphor. The term is used to emphasize the importance of interaction between peers, and the necessity of an instructor that can design and guide the learning process (Brown, 1994; Brown & Campione,1994; Rogoff, 1994; Rogoff et al. 1996). The members of a community work together, although not necessarily working in agreement, yet they strive toward a shared and common understanding. That is, they ask questions about their teaching in order to learn from and improve it (Cassidy et al. 2008). Access to a learning community could provide novice teachers, experienced teachers, and teacher educators an opportunity for professional development and a possibility to "offer each other moral support, intellectual/ academic help, and solid friendship" (Noddings, 1992, p. 179). This means that in the *community of practice* metaphor learning is primarily invoked by communication between the participants while the term *community of learners* acknowledges guidance from outside the community. Educational institutions are not self sufficient as learning communities. Facilitators from outside can ask questions and add theory that is necessary in order to promote reflection in an ongoing learning process. External input from other communities, formal theories, and literature is needed to support teachers' professional development. Ongoing professional learning is dependent on external input. Initiative to create and maintain the learning community has to be taken by facilitators outside the community. Teaching is traditionally an isolated profession. Schools and teachers tend to be occupied with their own activities and one might question the possibility for school contexts to create learning communities. Systematic and organized collaboration between teacher education institutions and collaborating schools might ensure that learning communities are designed and guided. Combining the understanding of the concepts *community of practice*, teaching and *community of learners* accounts for the continual reflection that is necessary for school development and teachers' professional development.

FUTURE TRENDS

The ecologic connection between teacher education and teaching in order to stimulate professional development for teachers, student teachers and teacher educators should play an important part in future policy and research. Focus should be on action research creating a bridge between teaching and teacher education As argued earlier, action research within education is a way of understanding one's own learning process; a process in which all are prepared to grow, not one dictating to others how to learn. Educational change has little chance of success unless it actively involves teachers and teacher educators in the change process (Lederman & Niess, 1997; Stenhouse, 1975; Valli, 2000). Teacher educators, student teachers and teachers engaged in systematic enquiries in the local context contribute to reflection and continuing professional learning for teachers as well as teacher educators. There should be a close link between research and practice of teacher education. Positive professional development opportunities related to research are necessary in order to become a resilient practitioner (Cochran-Smith & Zeichner, 2005; Zeichner, 2007). In educational contexts, online or face-to-face continual learning is practice. If these *communities of practice* are going to be *learning communities* then new theoretical perspectives should continuously be brought into the community for discussion and reflection. Formal theories based on empirical data and external research should be used to support and challenge the collaborative reflection process and self-study taking place inside the communities. This continual learning process does not work by itself. It must be guided by a facilitator who can act as a teacher in a classroom. The facilitator should be responsible for designing the activi-

ties and for stimulating theoretical thinking by asking reflective questions (Wubbels, 2007). The facilitator might be a teacher, a teacher educator, schools themselves, or teacher education institutions. Possibilities for online communication make systematic collaboration between different educational communities easier. Reflective activities through action research might as well be organized through online learning communities. An essential requirement is that a learning community, either online or face-to-face has to be designed and supported. Teaching in schools should be closely linked to teaching in teacher education through reflective learning processes, in order to stimulate and support teachers' and teacher educators' continual professional development. Recent research shows that members of online learning communities; teachers, student teachers and teacher educators are not self-sufficient. In an embodied context like an online learning community someone has to be responsible for including theoretical perspectives and maintaining rules for the work with the portfolio (Helleve, 2007; Wubbels, 2007). Further research within this area is needed.

CONCLUSION

What makes a person a teacher is his or her deliberate attempt to involve another person (Matusov, 1998, p. 3).

The OECD-report, Teachers Matter, states that there is substantial research indicating that the quality of teachers and their teaching are the most important factors in student outcomes that are open to policy influence. Teachers are highly motivated by the intrinsic benefits of teaching – working with children and young people helping them to develop and making contributions to society. System structures and schools as workplaces need to ensure that teachers are able to focus on these tasks (Teachers Matter OECD, 2005). Hargreaves (2000) argues that the beginning of this century is a cross-road for teachers' diminished or increased professionalism depending on increased regulations on one hand and teachers' own participation on the other. What is claimed throughout this chapter is that teaching is closely connected to feelings, personal values and attitudes. Caring for others as the core in teaching makes teachers vulnerable, and I have argued for reflective dialogues within confident communities of learners for teachers and teacher educators in a lifelong learning process. Still there is another fact connected to a profession where the feelings of care and commitment play the most central part. It cannot be predicted by policy-makers. This means that teaching is by nature a profession where the practitioners have to participate in defining their own profession. Future school development depends on personal engagement from teachers and teacher educators in an ecological learning process supporting students, student teachers, novice teachers and experienced practitioners.

REFERENCES

Achinstein, B. (2006). New teacher and mentor political literacy: reading, navigating and transforming induction contexts. *Teachers and Teaching: theory and practice, 12*(2), 123-138.

AERA. American Educational Research Panel. Retrieved 27th of December from: http://www.aera.net/newsmedia/?id=763

Anderson, R., & Demeulle, L. (1998). Portfolio use in twenty-four teacher education programs. *Teacher Education Quarterly, 25*(1), 23–32.

Arfwedson, G. (1984). Why schools are different (In Norwegian). Oslo: Tanum.

Beijaard, D., Korthagen, F., & Verloop, N. (2007). Understanding how teachers learn as a pre-requisite for promoting teacher learning. *Teachers and Teaching, 13*(2), 105–108. doi:10.1080/13540600601152298

Bell, B., & Gilbert, J. (1994). Teacher development as professional, personal, and social development. *Teaching and Teacher Education, 10*(5), 483–497. doi:10.1016/0742-051X(94)90002-7

Biesta, G. (2007). Why "what works" won't work: Evidence-based practice and the democratic deficit in educational research. *Educational Theory, 57*(1), 1–22. doi:10.1111/j.1741-5446.2006.00241.x

Brown, A. (1994). The Advancement of Learning. *Educational Researcher, 23*(8), 4–12.

Brown, A., & Campione, J. (1994). Guided discovery in a community of learners. In K. McGilly (Ed.), *Classroom lessons: integrating cognitive theory and classroom practice* (pp. 229-270). Cambridge, MA: Bradford Books.

Calderhead, J. (1989). Reflective teaching and teacher education. *Teaching and Teacher Education, 5*(1), 43–51. doi:10.1016/0742-051X(89)90018-8

Calderhead, J., & Robson, M. (1991). Images of teaching: Student teachers' early conceptions of classroom practice. *Teaching and Teacher Education, 7*(1), 1–8. doi:10.1016/0742-051X(91)90053-R

Carr, W., & Kemmis, S. (1986). *Becoming Critical: Education, Knowledge and Action Research*. Basingstoke: Falmer Press.

Cassidy, C., Chrisite, D., Coutts, D., Dunn, J., Sinclair, C., Skinner, D., & Wilson, A. (2008). Building communities of educational inquiry. *Oxford Review of Education, 34*(2), 217–235. doi:10.1080/03054980701614945

Cochran-Smith, M., & Lytle, S. (1999). The teacher research movement: a decade later. *Educational Researcher, 28*(7), 15–25.

Cochran-Smith, M., & Zeichner, K. M. (Eds.). (2005). *Studying teacher education: the report of the AERA panel on research and teacher education.* Mahwah, NJ: Lawrence Erlbaum.

Darling-Hammond, L. (1994). *Professional Development Schools: schools for developing a profession.* New York: Teachers' College Press.

Darling-Hammond, L. (1998). Teacher learning that supports student learning. *Educational Leadership, 55*(5), 6–11.

Darling-Hammond, L., Chung, R., & Frelow, F. (2002). Variation in teacher preparation. How well do different pathways prepare teachers to teach? *Journal of Teacher Education, 53*(4), 286–302. doi:10.1177/0022487102053004002

Darling-Hammond, L., & Snyder, J. (2000). Authentic assessment of teaching| in context. *Teaching and Teacher Education, 16*(5-6), 523–545. doi:10.1016/S0742-051X(00)00015-9

Day, C., & Gu, Q. (2007). Variations in the conditions for teachers' professional learning and Development: sustaining commitment and effectiveness over a career. *Oxford Review of Education, 33*(4), 423–443. doi:10.1080/03054980701450746

Dewey, J. (1910). *How we think.* Boston: DC Heath & Co.

Dochy, F., Segers, M., & Sluijsmans, D. (1999). The use of self, and peer, and co-assessment in higher education: A review. *Studies in Higher Education, 24*(3), 331–350. doi:10.1080/03075079912331379935

Dreyfus, H. L., & Dreyfus, S. E. (1986). *Mind over machine: the power of human intuition and expertise in the era of the computer.* New York: The Free Press.

Elliot, J. (1991). *Action research for educational change.* Milton: Open University Press.

Ellminn, R., & Elminn, B. (2005). Working with portfolio. (In Norwegian). Oslo: Interface Media A/S.

Evans, L. (2002). What constitutes teacher development? *Oxford Review of Education, 28*(1), 123–137. doi:10.1080/03054980120113670

Firestone, A. W. (1996). Images of Teaching and Proposals for Reform: A Comparison of Ideas from Cognitive and Organizational research. *Educational Administration Quarterly, 32*(2), 209–235. doi:10.1177/0013161X96032002003

Flores, M. A., & Day, C. (2006). Contexts which shape and reshape new teachers' identities: A multy-perspective study. *Teaching and Teacher Education, 22,* 219–232. doi:10.1016/j.tate.2005.09.002

Fuller, F. F., & Bown, O. H. (1975). Becoming a teacher. In K. Ryan (Ed.), *Teacher Education The 74th Yearbook of the National Society for the Study of Education, Part 11.* Chicago: University of Chicago Press.

Ginns, I., Heirdsfield, A., Atweh, B., & Watters, J. (2001). Beginning teachers becoming professionals through action research. *Educational Action Research, 9*(1), 111–133. doi:10.1080/09650790100200140

Gitlin, A., Barlow, L., Burbank, M. D., Kauchak, D., & Stevens, T. (1999). Pre-service teachers thinking on research: implications for inquiry oriented teacher education. *Teaching and Teacher Education, 15*(7), 753–769. doi:10.1016/S0742-051X(99)00015-3

Handal, G., & Lauvås, P. (1987). *Promoting reflective teaching: supervision in practice.* Milton Keynes, UK: SRHE/Open University Enterprises.

Hargreaves, A. (1992). Cultures of teaching: A focus on change. In A. Hargreaves & M. Fullan (Eds.), *Understanding teacher development* (pp. 216-240). London: Teachers' College Press.

Hargreaves, A. (1994). *Changing teachers, changing time*. London. Cassell.

Hargreaves, A. (2000). Four ages of Professionalism and Professional Learning. *Teachers and Teaching: History and Practice*, *6*(2), 151–182.

Helleve, I. (2007). In an ICT-based teacher- education context: Why was our group "The magic group"? *European Journal of Teacher Education*, *30*(3), 267–284. doi:10.1080/02619760701486118

Hoyle, E. (1974). Professionality, professionalism, and control in teaching. *London Educational Review*, *3*, 13–19.

Kelly, P. (2006). What is teacher learning? A socio-cultural perspective. *Oxford Review of Education*, *32*(4), 505–519. doi:10.1080/03054980600884227

Klenowski, V. (2002). *Developing Portfolios for Learning and Assessment*. London: Routledge Falmer.

Kolb, D. A. (1984). *Experiential Learning: Experience as the Source of Learning and Development*. Englewood Cliffs, New Jersey: Prentice Hall.

Korthagen, F. (2001). Teacher education a problematic enterprise. In F.A.J. Korthagen, J.P. Kessels, B. Koster; B. Lagerwerf, & T. Wubbels (Eds.), *Linking practice and theory. The pedagogy of realistic teacher education* (pp. 1- 19). Mahwah, N.J.: Lawrence Erlbaum Associates.

Korthagen, F., Keesels, J., Koster, B., Lagerwerf, B., & Wubbels, T. (Eds.). (2001). *Linking practice and theory. The pedagogy of realistic teacher education*. Mahwah, NJ: Lawrence Erlbaum Associates.

Korthagen, F., & Kessels, J. P. (1999). Linking theory and practice: Changing the pedagogy of teacher education. *Educational Researcher*, *28*(4), 4–17.

Korthagen, F., Klaassen, C., & Russel, T. Simons, R. J., van der Linden, J., & Duffy, T. (Eds.). (2000). *New learning in teaching training. New learning*. Dordrecht, The Netherlands: Kluwer Academic.

Korthagen, F., & Vasalos, A. (2005). Levels in reflection: core reflection as a means to enhance professional growth. *Teachers and Teaching*, *11*(1), 47–71. doi:10.1080/1354060042000337093

Korthagen, F., & Wubbels, T. (2001). Learning from practice. In F.A.J. Korthagen, J.P. Kessels, B. Koster; B. Lagerwerf, & T. Wubbels (Eds.), *Linking practice and theory. The pedagogy of realistic teacher education* (pp. pp. 32-50). Mahwah, N.J.: Lawrence Erlbaum Associates.

Koster, B., Brekemans, M., Korthagen, F., & Wubbels, T. (2005). Quality requirements for teacher educators. *Teaching and Teacher Education*, *21*, 157–176. doi:10.1016/j.tate.2004.12.004

LaBosky, V. K. (1994). *Development of reflective practice: A study of preservice teachers*. New York: Teachers College Press.

Lave, J., & Wenger, E. (1991). *Situated learning. Legitimate peripheral participation*. Cambridge: Cambridge University Press.

Lederman, N. G., & Niess, M. L. (1997). Action research: our actions may speak louder than our words. *School Science and Mathematics*, *97*(8), 397–399.

Levin, B. B., & Rock, T. C. (2003). The effects of collaborative action research on preservice and experienced teacher partners in professional development schools. *Journal of Teacher Education*, *54*(2), 135–149. doi:10.1177/0022487102250287

Little, J. W. (1990). The mentor phenomenon and the social organization of teaching. *Review of Research in Education, 16,* 297–351.

Loughran, J. (2006). *Developing a Pedagogy for Teacher Education.* London: Routledge.

Lunenberg, M., Korthagen, F., & Swennen, A. (2007). The teacher educator as a role model. *Teaching and Teacher Education, 23*(5), 586–601. doi:10.1016/j.tate.2006.11.001

Matusov, E. (1998). When Solo Activity Is Not Privileged: Participation and Internalization Models of Development. *Human Development, 41,* 326–249. doi:10.1159/000022595

McNiff, J. (2002). *Action Research. Principles and Practice.* London: Routledge Falmer.

Meyer, T. (2002). Novice teacher learning communities: An alternative to one-on-one mentoring. *American Secondary Education, 31*(1), 1–27.

Moreno, J. M. (2007). Do the initial and continous teachers' professional development sufficiently prepare teachers to understand and cope with the complexities of today and tomorrow's education? *Journal of Educational Change, 8*(2), 169–172. doi:10.1007/s10833-007-9027-9

Murray, J., & Male, T. (2005). Becoming a teacher educator: evidence from the field. *Teaching and Teacher Education, 21,* 125–142. doi:10.1016/j.tate.2004.12.006

Nielsen, K., & Kvale, S. (1999). Apprenticeship. (In Norweigian). Oslo: AdNotam.

Niemi, H. (2002). Active learning- a cultural change needed in teacher education and schools . *Teaching and Teacher Education, 18*(7), 763–780. doi:10.1016/S0742-051X(02)00042-2

Noddings, N. (1992). *The challenge to care in schools.* New York: Teachers' College Press.

Palmer, P. J. (1998). *The Courage to Teach. Exploring the Inner Landscape of a Teacher's Life.* San Fransisco: Jossey-Bass.

Ritter, J. K. (2007). Forging a pedagogy of teacher education: The challenges of moving from classroom teacher to teacher educator. *Studying Teacher Education, 3*(1), 5–22. doi:10.1080/17425960701279776

Rogoff, B. (1994). Developing Understanding of the Idea of Communities of Learners. *Mind, Culture, and Activity, 1*(4), 209–299.

Rogoff, B., Matusov, E., & White, C. (1996). Models of teaching and learning: Participation in a community of learners. In D. R. Olsen & N. Torrance (Eds.). *Handbook of education and human development* (pp. 388-415). Cambridge: Blackwell Publishers.

Rots, I., Aelterman, A., Vlerick, P., & Vermeulen, K. (2007). Teacher education graduates. Teaching commitment and entrance into the teaching profession. *Teaching and Teacher Education, 23,* 543–556. doi:10.1016/j.tate.2007.01.012

Schön, D. (1983). *The reflective practitioner: How professionals think in action.* New York: Basic.

Schön, D. (1987) *Educating the reflective practitioner.* San Francisco. Jossey-Bass.

Scottish Executive (2002). *Standard for Charted Teachers, Continuing Professional Development.* GTC Scotland: Scottish Executive.

Skovholt, T. (2001). *The Recilient Practitioner.* Boston: Allyn & Bacon.

Smith, K., & Sela, O. (2005). Action research as a bridge between pre-service teacher education and in-service professional development for students and teacher educators. *European Journal of Teacher Education, 28*(3), 293–310. doi:10.1080/02619760500269418

Smith, K., & Tillema, H. (1998). Evaluating portfolio use as a learning tool for professionals. *Scandinavian Journal of Educational Research*, *42*(2), 193–205. doi:10.1080/0031383980420206

Smith, K., & Tillema, H. (2001). Long-term Influences of Portfolios on Professional development. *Scandinavian Journal of Educational Research*, *45*(2), 183–203. doi:10.1080/00313830120052750

Spilkova, V. (2001). Professional development of teachers and student teachers through reflection on practice. *European Journal of Teacher Education*, *18*(7), 815–830.

Stenhouse, L. (1975). *An introduction to curriculum research and development*. London: Heinemann.

Teachers Matter. (2005). *Attracting, developing and retaining effective teachers, OECD rapport*. Retrieved Oct.ober 9, 2007, from: http://www.oecd.org/document/52/0,3343,en_2649_201185 _34991988_1_1_1_1,00.html

Valli, L. (2000). Connecting teacher development and school improvement: ironic consequences of a preservice action research course. *Teaching and Teacher Education*, *16*(7), 715–730. doi:10.1016/S0742-051X(00)00021-4

Watzke, J. L. (2007). Longitudinal research on beginning teacher development: Complexity as a challenge to concerns-based stage theory. *Teaching and Teacher Education*, *23*, 106–122. doi:10.1016/j.tate.2006.04.001

Wegerif, R. (2007). *Dialogic Education and Technology*. New York: Springer.

Wenger, E. (1998). *Communities of practice: learning, meaning and identity*. Cambridge: Cambridge University Press.

Wideen, M., Mayer-Smith, J., & Moon, B. (1998). A critical analysis of research on learning to teach: Making the case for an ecological perspective on inquiry. *Review of Educational Research*, *68*(2), 130–178.

Wilson, E. K. (2006). The impact of an alternative model of student teacher supervision: Views of the participants. *Teaching and Teacher Education*, *22*, 22–31. doi:10.1016/j.tate.2005.07.007

Wubbels, T. (2007). Do we know a community of practice when we see one? *Technology, Pedagogy and Education*, *16*(2), 225–233. doi:10.1080/14759390701406851

Wubbels, T., & Korthagen, F. (1990). The effects of a pre-service teacher training program for the preparation of reflective teachers. *Journal of Education for Teaching*, *16*(1), 29–43. doi:10.1080/0260747900160102

Zeichner, K. (2005). Becoming a teacher educator: A personal perspective. *Teaching and Teacher Education*, *22*, 32–41.

Zeichner, K. (2007). Accumulation knowledge across self-studies in teacher education. *Journal of Teacher Education*, *58*(1), 36–46. doi:10.1177/0022487106296219

Zeichner, K., & Liston, D. (1998). *Reflective teaching*. NJ: Lawrence Erlbaum.

Chapter 2
The Theory and Practice Divide in Relation to Teacher Professional Development

Shelleyann Scott
University of Calgary, Canada

ABSTRACT

The 21st century is a time of rapid change and increasing accountability within education contexts and teacher professional development (TPD) is frequently perceived to be crucial in instituting reforms. This chapter explores the divide between theories of effective TPD and the realities of practice within educational contexts. Two case studies, one from Australia and the other from Canada are presented to illustrate the positives and negatives inherent within professional development approaches in these contexts. A number of key dimensions are identified, which when coalesced inform the establishment and sustainability of effective programmes. Online technologies present innovative ways to overcome the impediments to effective professional development. Online communities of practice utilising social networking technologies provide new opportunities for initiating "webs of enhanced practice' (Scott, 2009), where individuals around the globe can engage in collegial collaborations that enhance the passion of teaching.

INTRODUCTION

The 21st century has yielded a time of rapid-paced change – socio-political and technological - and this has resulted in even greater need for more effective teacher professional development (TPD) to ensure that our children, teachers and their leaders have access to the most productive learning environments.

Since the 1970s onwards, there has been considerable research undertaken about TPD, establishing a solid knowledge base about what TPD processes work in effecting change in teaching behaviours in the classroom with the view to positively influencing student outcomes (Darling-Hammond & McLaughlin, 1995; Goodlad, 1994; Guskey, 1986; Guskey & Sparks, 1991; Joyce & Showers, 1980; 1995; Lieberman & Miller, 2000; Lieberman & Pointer Mace, 2008). Even so there are still poor

DOI: 10.4018/978-1-60566-780-5.ch002

and fragmented TPD proliferated within school systems. It is clear, therefore, that there is still a divide between the theory of effective TPD and the 'reality' of practice within educational systems. This chapter explores these theories and uses two international examples, one from Western Australia and the other from Alberta, Canada to illustrate that this divide still exists. With the world shrinking due to globalisation and innovations in technology, challenges within education show striking similarities regardless of geographical location. The professional responsibilities for the range of roles, such as, teachers, leaders, policy-makers and government are also discussed. A number of dimensions are presented which, acting in concert, can facilitate the establishment and sustainability of effective TPD initiatives, thereby bridging the gap between theory and practice. The final dimension discussed is that of innovations in TPD, particularly the potential inherent in online learning communities. Technology presents real advantages to supporting the development of communities of teachers, not only within their own school districts, but also across the globe. Scott's (2009) "webs of enhanced practice" offer teachers greater opportunities to reduce their isolation and expand their knowledge about good practice, share resources and gain global insights.

BACKGROUND

Theoretical Framework Underpinning Teacher Professional Development

School teachers, leaders, and support staff are all adults who have ongoing learning needs in order to keep abreast of the changes required by society, the profession, and their disciplines. These adults have different learning needs and motivations to those of their students (Knowles, Holton III, & Swanson, 2005). Merriam (2001) indicates adults must be self-determining in their choice of professional learning opportunities. They

have a wealth of life experience which influences their learning. Adults' motivations frequently relate to managing their changing life and professional roles, which makes them more receptive to problem-solving and relevant learning experiences. For example, teachers are most concerned with teaching- and student-related issues, while leaders are predominantly interested in administrative and people management-oriented learning opportunities (Scott, 2003; Scott & Webber, 2008). Even though not limited to adult learners, their motivation tends to be intrinsic rather than extrinsic, in that, they seek to find answers to their real-life questions and curiosity (Knowles, et al., 2005; Wlodkowski, 2004). Adults know what they want and generally how to get it. They are intolerant of professional development perceived to be a waste of time, irrelevant to their own or their students' needs, or which is delivered poorly by non-credible, 'expert' presenters (Long, 2004). Hence, adult learners frequently are perceived by teachers to be demanding, opinionated, and difficult, however, Newton presents a less negative perspective stating "[t]he adult as a learner is pictured as an autonomous, experience-laden, goal-seeking, 'now' oriented, problem-centered individual" (1977, cited in Clardy, 2005, p. 7). Therefore the principles of adult learning indicate that adults gravitate towards professional development which is contextually relevant, pragmatic, delivered by credible facilitators, career oriented, interesting and engaging, and is inclusive of their prior experiences (Knowles, et al., 2005).

Professional development is not a new concept as illustrated by Joyce and his associates early definition that it was "formal and informal provisions for the improvement of educators as people, educated persons, and professionals, as well as in terms of the competence to carry out their assigned roles" (1976, cited in Gall, Renchler, Haisley, Baker, & Perez, 1985, p. 6). Later Gall and his associates proffered a more specific definition being "efforts to improve teachers' capacity to function as effective professionals by having them learn new knowledge, attitudes, or skills" (1985, p. 6). Over the past 30 years, many descriptions of professional development tended to be founded upon the notion that teachers were "deficient", "needed fixing" or were falling short in their professional capacities and this needed to be rectified (Brandt, 1994, p. 4; Clarke & Hollingsworth, 1994; Goodlad, 1994). Therefore, most professional development focused on addressing a lack in teaching skills, perceiving teachers as empty vessels that needed "to be filled" (Garmston, 1991, p. 64). As time passed this view of the 'deficit' rectifying nature of professional development has altered to a more enlightened one, whereby teachers as professionals need to maintain the currency of their knowledge and to continue to expand and enhance their professional practice. It is also now recognised that teachers have significant impact and influence on their students' learning outcomes, therefore investing in effective professional development is highly worthwhile. As Wolfe stated …

what teachers know and can do is the most important influence on what students can learn. We believe that the quality of teachers is a major factor in determining the quality of schools. Paying direct attention to ongoing teacher development is the key to maintaining quality in our profession (Steffy, Wolfe, Pasch, & Enz, 2000, p. i).

With increasing demands for more skilled teachers in the 70s and 80s, Joyce and Showers ran professional development introducing teachers to innovations in complex teaching strategies, namely, "models of teaching" (Joyce & Weil, 1986; Joyce, Weil, & Showers, 1992; Joyce, Weil, & Calhoun, 2004). These models were actually models of learning for students. Each model is a strategy that teachers can implement for specific pedagogical purposes, for example, many of the models promote critical and creative thinking, others structure for debating topics, some for investigation and research, and others to explore

conceptual development. These models are complex strategies and require teachers to understand the rationale for the model, how to select appropriate content for use with the model, as well as, its skilled implementation.

As the models of teaching represent complex learning, Joyce and Showers undertook research into teachers' capacity to transfer these strategies into their regular classroom repertoire. Traditionally, professional development consisted of short-term, isolated events, such as, one-shot workshops, or conferences, lectures with guest speakers, and staff meetings focused on policy implementation or pragmatic matters of school procedure. Joyce and Showers, later reinforced by other researchers, found these traditional formats were largely ineffective in bringing about change in teacher behaviours in the classroom (Darling-Hammond, 1998; Lieberman & Pointer Mace, 2008; Sparks & Hirsh, 2000). Initially, some researchers felt that this may have been due to teachers' lack of motivation to engage in professional development. Fullan observed, however, that teachers' motivation was high, wanting to become better teachers and perceived professional development to be the best approach to this end (Fullan, 1982 cited in Guskey, 1986). Similarly, Guskey (1986) found that professional development was perceived as a way to overcome the isolation in the job, maintain interest, and to increase competence and professional satisfaction. Contrasting against the negative perceptions of teachers' motivation and engagement, Joyce and Showers professional development programmes established that teachers were excellent learners capable of changing their less innovative practices, provided that the training processes were optimal to support higher levels of transfer (Joyce & Weil, 1986). Their research led to the dismissal of old models of professional development which had the predominant philosophical underpinning that teachers were deficit and needed 'fixing' (Brandt, 1994). They instituted the *Peer Coaching Study Teams* (PCST) model which informed scholarly understandings about the importance of sustained, in-context, student-focused, and collegial support (Showers & Joyce, 1996).

In these PCST, teachers were able to visit peer's classrooms to observe their implementation of complex teaching strategies, planned and discussed together, shared lessons and resources, and reflected on their own and their team's use of the models of teaching. Joyce and Showers altered the 'coaching dialogue' so that critiques were removed, rather the 'coach' was the teacher taking the lesson and the one coached was the observer. The observer gleaned hints and suggestions from watching their peer's implementation and interaction with students. The collegial-support embedded in this model reduced teacher isolation, promoted different ways of thinking about practice, ensured peer accountability to implement the newly learned models, and reduced teacher-workload through the joint planning and resource development. Joyce and Showers promoted the inclusion of these activities within the workday rather than requiring teachers to find the time out of school hours.

There has been an identifiable shift in understanding about professional development from that of the one-shot workshop or single event to a more systematic and sustained processes (Goldenberg, & Gallimore, 1991; Sparks & Hirsh, 2000). Linking to the adult learning literature, professional development should be contextually-relevant to the participants; hence school-based or classroom-orientated programs are perceived to be the most valuable to teachers (Knowles, et al, 2005; Sparks & Hirsh, 2000).

The collegial, social and constructivist dimensions advocated for professional development in the literature have resulted in various "community" orientations. One such community-oriented model was DuFour's Professional Learning Communities (PLC), "characterized by an environment fostering mutual cooperation, emotional support, personal growth, and a synergy of efforts" (DuFour & Eaker, 2004, p. abstract). Professional learn-

ing communities are whole-school approaches wherein teacher-teams work on improving student outcomes by analysing teaching practices, assessments, and student achievement data with the view to bringing about improvement in student outcomes. Similar to Joyce and Showers (1995), DuFour (2004) advocated for time to be allocated within the school workday, ongoing throughout the year, to ensure teams were able to meet and collaborate. All teachers must belong to a team and total participation was expected. DuFour indicated PLCs were "a grand design - a powerful new way of working together that profoundly affects the practices of schooling" but he was also realistic in terms of the amount of hard work required to establish and sustain these in most schools (DuFour, 2004, p. 7). He identified this was professional development focused on learning rather than on teaching which enabled teachers to work collaboratively on issues related to supporting student learning outcomes. His PLC model overtly incorporated the philosophy of evaluating progress to ensure the school community held itself accountable for continual improvement in an ongoing reflective cycle.

Wenger and Synder explored adult learning from the social learning perspective through their "communities of practice" model (2000, p. 139). Wenger stated …

Since the beginning of history, human beings have formed communities that share cultural practices reflecting on their collective learning … Participating in these 'communities of practice' is essential to our learning. It is at the very core of what makes us human beings capable of meaningful knowing (2003, p. 79-80).

Wenger and Snyder labelled their communities of practice as cooperative wherein individuals informally teamed up due to their "shared expertise and passion for a joint enterprise" (2000, p. 139). The power of these communities was leveraged through the galvanising of knowledge sharing, learning and facilitating change. They perceived this to be the "new frontier" within the context of business as it drove strategy, solved problems, developed professional skills and promoted the spread of best practice. Similar to DuFour's views, these communities of practice did not simply evolve and remain self-sustaining, rather, they required time, funding, and ongoing support from leaders, information communication technology (ICT) systems and personnel, and active involvement from participants. Wenger and Snyder (2000) reflected on the importance of ensuring reward structures, including promotion and recognition, were focused on collaboration and the outcomes of these communities.

Acknowledged in educational literature is that teachers frequently work in isolation within the classroom, within the school district, and potentially geographically in remote areas (Guskey, 1986; Scott, 2003). Isolation can be deleterious to teachers' professional growth and efficacy. Therefore, if we know that collaborative models of professional development, such as the peer coaching study teams, PLCs, and communities of practice are highly desirable and effective in producing change in teacher knowledge, beliefs, and behaviours, how can the isolation factor be overcome for all teachers? Technology offers answers in the form of 'online' communities of practice.

With the increase in bandwidth, reduction in the cost of computers and associated peripherals, and increased familiarity with ICT, educators have increasing pathways to collaboration with their peers regardless of their context or geographic locale. For the past decade, teachers have been using email to share with colleagues and friends their thoughts, ideas and resource materials (Scott, 2002). Blogs, forums and wikis emerged as further supporting these isolation-reducing and collaborative endeavours. Even so these technologies, while useful, were still asynchronous, potentially limiting their value in establishing lively conversations and the syner-

gies that result from synchronous interactions. As technologies have been refined, synchronous interaction has become readily accessible and affordable. Now educators have the opportunity to interact with a colleague online through programmes such as Skype®. Newer software such as Elluminate Live!® and Horizon Wimba® even allow for a virtual classroom environment where multiple synchronous conversations, document review, PowerPoint presentations, and linking to the Internet, are possible. These new technologies represent a leap forward in the potential to establish online communities of practice – bringing teachers together with their colleagues and accessing experts from within and external to the school system to expand knowledge, expertise and available resources.

From the 1980s to current, research indicates the importance of constructivist-oriented professional development (Brandt, 1994; Darling-Hammond & McLaughlin, 1995; Lieberman & Miller, 2000; Lieberman & Pointer Mace, 2008; Scott, 2003; Sparks & Hirsh, 1997). This research indicates that for professional development to be effective it must:

- encompass a problem-solving orientation;
- incorporate opportunities for teachers to work together and with experts;
- facilitate exposure to innovations in knowledge, teaching practice, and technologies that can support this;
- enable teachers to try out and hone new teaching skills and strategies;
- promote the creation and sharing of resources with the view to improving student learning outcomes; and
- enable ongoing, purposeful reflection and discussion. (Bandura, 2001; Knowles, et al, 2005; Lieberman & Pointer Mace, 2008; Scott, 2009; Wenger, 2003; Wenger & Snyder, 2000; Zeichner & Bekisizwe, 2008).

One aspect frequently overlooked or ignored is that of evaluating the outcomes of professional development. Professional development is usually undertaken to improve teaching and positively influence students' learning. There is real value in maintaining ongoing school improvement efforts if the outcomes of the professional development are measured, documented, and used to identify future directions (Hirsh, 2004). Guskey's (1991; 2002; 2005) research in this area emphasised the importance of measuring the impact of professional development and using these data to inform further programs and activities. In this world of increasing public accountability for funding, it is also important to know how effective various professional development activities are in order to make informed decisions about ongoing efforts, and to explore issues of sustainability. Firm evidence also can provide positive reinforcement for teachers to continue potentially uncomfortable shifts in knowledge, skills and behaviours.

The following two case studies explore the state of professional development within two international educational contexts from the perspectives of the teachers and other stakeholders. They identify there is still a divide between what we know to be effective professional development and what is the reality of actual practice. They present issues related to teacher motivation to engage, constraints related to time, professional development processes, funding, isolation, and political agenda. In both cases, technology is described as predominantly focused on teaching and learning within classrooms but not as a key factor in the delivery of sustained and flexible professional development.

TWO INTERNATIONAL CASE STUDIES

Having explored the theoretical underpinnings of effective professional development and the fact that there are established technologies that can support these processes; the realities of TPD in two educational contexts are explored in the following case studies. The first case is drawn from the Western Australian government education system, while the second focuses on the public school system in Alberta, Canada. Although these two cases are at opposite ends of the globe, they demonstrate considerable similarities. For example, both sites are vast and resource rich states/provinces; have similar geographic distances (Western Australia - 2,527,621 km^2 and Alberta - 661,848 km^2) with many rural and remote schools and communities; similar teacher qualification expectations; and have Western, democratic governments. They do, however, have significant differences. For example, in Alberta, teachers are employed by the boards of education for each district, rather than having only one centralised employer as is the situation in Western Australia. The Alberta Teachers' Association (ATA) in addition to their traditional union responsibilities, also administers funding for, promotes, and provides TPD, whereas the State School Teachers' Union of Western Australia (SSTWA) is predominantly focused on teachers' work conditions and salary negotiations with limited input into professional development. Additionally, in Alberta regional professional development consortia also provide TPD for teachers. The Provincial education department initially established the regional professional development consortia with funding with the view that eventually they would become self-sustaining. Most professional development in Western Australia is provided on an ad hoc basis by private consultants, Ministry of Education District Office personnel, and subject-based professional associations.

The first case study from Western Australia illustrates there is still a divide between theory and practice in effective professional development. This case identifies the importance of decision makers using the extensive knowledge base on effective professional development to structure, facilitate, promote and appropriately fund teacher these programmes. It reports on teachers' professional development activities and their perceptions of these. It also presents information about their rationales for engagement, and perceptions of the prevailing organisational culture. It highlights the importance of good relationships between the ministry of education and teachers and how these influence teachers' perceptions of their employer, the profession, and their willingness to engage in professional development. Contrastingly, the second case study presents an account of a government ministry for education that uses the knowledge base on effective professional development to design and fund initiatives aimed at supporting teachers' ongoing systematic professional growth. Although this initiative has been well formed the implementation across the province has been problematic and evaluative data has been variable in informing future directions. Both cases emphasise that even with knowledge about what constitutes sound TPD, implementation, decision-making, adult learning motivation, and organisational cultures can influence the success of TPD initiatives. They both highlight the importance of appropriate evaluation of professional development initiatives in order to determine impact, ongoing viability, and value for money.

Teacher Professional Development in the Western Australian Public Education System

Research was undertaken to explore TPD in the Western Australian public education system (Scott, 2002, 2003). Respondents were invited to discuss their professional development activities, perceptions of TPD, and levels of motivation to engage. Exploring a snapshot of an 18 month period prior to the study, the findings revealed that teachers were engaging in approximately seven hours of professional development/working week/person. All teachers had participated in TPD and generally had a positive attitude and strong motivation to engage in these activities, perceiving it as irrevocably linked with maintaining their professional-

ism and high quality teaching and learning. Only two teachers in the entire sample were relatively disengaged from TPD activities. Teachers in rural and remote situations experienced specific issues with professional development. Many teachers were newly graduated and felt that the isolation of living and working in small rural towns was detrimental to their development of expertise. There were insufficient opportunities to collaborate with experienced colleagues and were in schools with limited resources. These teachers generally had to travel to the city centre or to their regional district offices to access most professional development. Travel was usually prohibitive in terms of cost and in obtaining time release from school. In some cases, this isolation was an advantage in that it forced them to demonstrate their leadership qualities and bridge the distances to interact with other teachers across their districts.

Teachers' Choices and Motivations

Teachers in this study viewed 'teaching-related' professional development as their highest priority - associated mainly with extension and/or refinement of discipline knowledge and expertise; curriculum changes; assessment practices and processes; networking with similar-discipline colleagues for resources and ideas; classroom management; and occasionally, specific teaching strategies. Some teachers chose to explore further education through postgraduate programs, while others were involved in their subject specialisation professional associations. Technology-related TPD also emerged as an important topic for teachers. A Ministry of Education policy (Education Department of Western Australia, 2000a, 2000b) recognised the importance of ICT and required all teachers, regardless of their learning area to integrate ICT into their teaching. To facilitate this a 'notebook for teachers' programme was established, however, no systematic TPD was provided to support teachers' development of necessary ICT skills or understandings in the educational uses of technology in the classroom. There were mixed reactions from teachers about the technology emphasis. Some were enthusiastic to be involved while others ranged from hesitant to technophobic. Some were accessing TPD with private consultancies in order to get the best use from their computers, and others were experimenting in order to teach themselves. Curiously, there was no relationship between teachers' age or levels of teaching experience with interest and engagement with technology. In fact, many older, more experienced teachers were fully engaged in exploring technology perceiving this as a pathway to renewal in their interest in teaching, development of resources, and in streamlining their managerial responsibilities.

The technology focus in Western Australia was generally about how it could be used in learning and teaching environments. There were no systematic efforts to coordinate technology-facilitated professional development, although some teachers were attempting to keep in contact with each other. Newly graduated teachers indicated they were encouraged by their university professors to keep in contact with each other either through phone or email and these collegial networks had assisted in reducing the isolation and resource deprivation issues they experienced when in rural schools.

The Shift to Effective Professional Development Approaches

Contrasting with teachers' priorities, the majority of TPD scheduled within the school calendar was mandated, centralised, and generally focussed on policy dissemination and implementation-oriented sessions. Teachers had to engage in teaching-related professional development sessions outside-of-school hours. The vast majority of the TPD described by respondents consisted of whole-staff meeting lectures, one-shot workshops, lectures by guest speakers, and/or conference events. All of these were described to be ineffective in changing

teachers' pedagogical behaviours in the classroom although some were 'interesting'. A feature from this research which indicated that there were some positive shifts in the provision of sound TPD were a small number of action research projects designed to better inform practice through collaboration with colleagues in other schools and districts. The collegial support mechanisms in these activities were perceived as the component that raised the effectiveness of the professional development. Pragmatically, collegiality and sustainability were adversely affected in some projects when teachers had to travel considerable distances to regularly meet with colleagues. The other example of sound TPD was 'moderation' meetings provided and supported by district offices. Two days in the school year were allocated for teachers of upper school grades (years 11 and 12) to collaborate with subject-area colleagues to explore moderation and parity exercises in student assessment. These mandated meetings ensured teachers engaged with TPD to:

1. develop deeper understandings of sound assessment practice;
2. share assessment tasks;
3. compare marking schedules and standards; and
4. team up teachers with small cohorts with teachers with larger ones, across schools and districts to ensure statistical comparability, parity in marking, and to provide much needed mentorship for inexperienced teachers.

To ensure the success of this moderation system, leaders were required to release teachers to attend these fully-funded meetings. These described activities indicate that even though there is some movement towards effective and systematic TPD, the majority still represents a gap between what is known to be effective approaches and what is happening in schools.

Quality Teacher Programme

The most extensive TPD initiative was the federally-funded *Quality Teacher Programme* (QTP) which aimed to "update and improve teachers' skills and help lift the status of the teaching profession" (Department of Education Science and Training [DEST], 2004, p. 4). This programme spanned 1999 to 2009 with funding for professional development made available to each Australian state and territory. For the period of 2006-2009 the Western Australian Department of Education allocated approximately $6 million to TPD activities in the public school system. The focus for this programme in Western Australia was to develop and promote action learning projects within schools with the view to improving teachers' practice. Teachers were generally positive about this initiative as it was the first time that significant funding had been made available to schools for teacher professional development. It was also novel that the determination and control of project activities was within the domain of school decision-makers. Many school districts established ongoing action learning projects supported and facilitated by district office professional developers. Evaluation of these projects generally related to teachers' perceptions and feelings related to the success of the projects as reported by their principals. Unfortunately, as identified in the Government report "[a] direct causal link between improved teacher skills and understanding arising from participation in professional learning and improved student outcomes cannot be demonstrated ... [t]he Programme relies on teacher predictions that their professional learning will impact on students" (Department of Education Science and Training [DEST], 2005, p. iii). This is not to say that there was no impact, simply the evaluation process was too limited and anecdotal to provide firm evidence to identify this.

Professional Development and Organisational Culture

Teacher professional development was perceived by policy-makers to be expedient in ensuring teacher-compliance with policy implementation. Frequently, teachers were required to participate in TPD into which they had no input or choice and that lacked direct relevance to the classroom and/or student outcomes. This lack of self-determination in professional development was both frustrating and disheartening to respondents in the study. To compound this heavy handed approach, policy was established which stipulated a prescribed number of hours of TPD to be undertaken outside-school-hours, sending the implicit message that teachers were not responsible or professional enough to regulate themselves. Teachers' prevailing view was that the employer (the Ministry of Education) lacked trust in teachers.

In light of the findings of this study that teachers actively engaged in TPD, many of the government policies which regulated teacher behaviours and TPD appeared to be unnecessary and overtly damaging to the overall organisational culture. Since this study was concluded, it is evident that this has had a devastating impact on teachers' morale, their level of trust in the employer and the leaders in the schools, and ultimately has led to disenfranchisement with the profession. The increasing levels of teacher-accountability and an apparent lack of acknowledgement of the value of teachers' choices in TPD have led to the systematic disempowerment of the profession. As a result over the past decade there has been a haemorrhaging of educators both novice and highly experienced, resulting in chronic teacher shortages. Clearly, there is a need for policy and decision makers to increase their understandings of the theory about effective TPD and how this should be implemented. They should also understand how this 'theory-practice' disparity influences teachers' behaviours and motivations, and organisational reforms and culture.

Even though there were limited reports of technologically-mediated TPD in this study, there remains considerable potential in these to ameliorate many of the issues related to accessing financially viable TPD, particularly for teachers in rural contexts. With so much technology being readily available, increasingly stable, and affordable many teachers now are able to be more self-determining in their TPD by establishing and controlling technology-facilitated collegial networks. These networks would enable them to discuss their teaching, problem-solve, share resources, and socialise with colleagues regardless of their geographical locale. It would overcome the issue of travelling to large city centres to access TPD and the associated issues of the loss of time and difficulties in obtaining teacher relief. For technology-facilitated collegial networks to be successful however, teachers would need to have sufficient technology efficacy to be able to engage and be comfortable with the new media. Therefore, familiarity with a range of technology would be crucial in establishing these technology networks.

Teacher Professional Development in the Alberta Public Education System

The Alberta case is drawn from provincial-wide research, the Alberta Student Assessment Study (ASAS), initiated in 2008 focusing on exploring assessment theory and practice (Webber, Aitken, Runté, Lupart, & Scott, 2008). It is premised on three main themes. In the first phase of this project, the research team's goals were to establish the current state of assessment knowledge and practice at various levels of the organisation informed by key stakeholder focus group interviews. The first stage findings encompassed stakeholder perspectives, including teachers, principals, superintendants, Ministry of Education personnel, the Alberta Teachers' Association (ATA), parents, board of trustee members, and associated professional development consortia members. The second main theme was to examine the leadership implications; and the third was to explore the current statues of professional development and determine what was required to bring about progress in this area. One of the main findings from this case study was the need for 'more effective' professional development to support the extension and enhancement of both teachers' and leaders' knowledge about, and expertise with, assessment.

Initial Findings about Professional Development

The findings from the first phase of the ASAS indicated that even though there were pockets of good practice, the need for effective TPD was "acute" across the province (Webber, et al., 2008). Teachers, principals and administrators all reported concerns about the prevalence of ineffective TPD epitomised by one-shot workshops, and single conference and lecture events. Participants called for greater access to school-based TPD rejecting these ineffective forms, and "desiring more opportunities for collegial 'rich conversations', all on an ongoing basis" (Webber et al., 2008, p. 17). One potential danger identified from the data was the risk of a 'pooling of ignorance', as a recurrent theme was that all the expertise required already resided within the school and no outside experts were needed (Scott, 2002). This perception contradicted many others' claims that there was a dire need to expand teachers' knowledge and expertise, and that many were floundering in navigating sound assessment with no access to knowledgeable assistance. This situation was further exacerbated, particularly in rural and remote schools, with the high levels of staff and leader turnover.

There were polarised comments regarding the predominant TPD providers such as the ATA and the various professional development consortia. An identified positive was that they are generally run by teachers for teachers, therefore deemed to have increased relevance in topic to classroom issues teachers' face on a day-to-day basis, endorsing the adult learning literature (Merriam, 2001). There was very little, if any, TPD for leaders and this was perceived to be a significant deficit in the system considering their importance as instructional leaders (Leithwood, Seashore Louis, Anderson, & Wahlstrom, 2004; Mulford, 2008; Scott & Webber, 2008). Additionally, teacher-leaders needed further professional development as they were the 'leaders of tomorrow'. There was a need to increase the teachers and leaders "'statistical literacy,' sound assessment strategies, and deep understandings of quality assessment ... as some participants indicated that principals needed only to support skilled teacher leaders while others were convinced that principals themselves must possess in-depth understanding of assessment" (Webber et al., 2008, p. 17 & 20).

The Alberta Initiative for School Improvement (AISI) Project

A project that has a strong TPD element incorporated, called the Alberta Initiative for School Improvement (AISI), was established in 2000 aimed at improving student learning outcomes through school-based initiatives identified as valuable by each school authority (McEwan, 2006). This was a partnership between Alberta Education, school boards, parents, universities, trustees, and business officials designed to be a catalyst for change in teaching and learning (Alberta Education, 2008). It provided a relatively unique combination of partnerships with the majority of stakeholders; significant and sustained funding; supportive infrastructure; and was founded on and promoted positive school cultures aimed at achieving greater yield in student learning outcomes. Since 2000 there has been three, three-year cycles with the last cycle initiated in 2006 and due for completion in 2009. Alberta Education allocated $625 million to support AISI over the nine years. To ensure equity between large and small schools, funding

was apportioned according to student numbers. This initiative was founded on the concepts of inquiry, collaboration, continuous improvement, with professional learning communities perceived to be instrumental in providing the mechanism to support these concepts (McEwan, 2006). Evaluation of district outcomes was required, which set the stage for continuing reflection on outcomes and ongoing improvement. Teachers were generally encouraged to have input and to engage with their school's initiative, as the locus of control and ultimate success resided within the school district. However, there was not necessarily whole-school staff 'buy in' or commitment to these projects, with some schools only having a small group of teachers involved. Professional development was an essential component in this initiative and accounted for many of the successes recorded in the first two cycles.

Perceptions of Effectiveness of AISI Projects

There appeared to be a dichotomy in the perceptions of effectiveness of the AISI projects. From a positive perspective, teachers and leaders indicated these projects facilitated collaboration between teachers; development of resources; increased teachers' understanding of and experimentation with sound assessment and more innovative teaching approaches; and had had a major impact on improving school cultures. Some of the elements distilled as key to the success was 1) genuine input from teachers into the selection of foci for their school's AISI project; 2) support for the involvement and professional development of teacher-leaders; 3) informed and involved leadership; and 4) supportive timetabling to facilitate the collaborations. In some districts TPD that supported AISI projects was systematic. For example, in one rural district teachers participated in seven full-day workshops over the course of the school year. These workshops encompassed the theoretical and practical applications in differentiated instruction. They also allowed time for teacher collaboration and development of practical materials for immediate use in their classroom. The aim was that by the conclusion of the year each teacher would have a complete portfolio of lesson plans, teaching strategies, and assessments. Schools were encouraged to send teams of teachers, ideally from the same grades, so they could more easily support each other in implementing their learning when back at school. Additionally, participants had access to support between sessions from the workshop facilitators. When teams participated the outcomes for the school were more pronounced than for solo participants.

Negative perspectives indicated some school boards controlled the focus of school projects with no consultation with teachers. In some schools, teacher collaboration was engineered and "forced", similar to Hargreaves and Fullan's descriptions of "contrived collegiality" (1992, p. 168). In these situations the result was tension, disengagement, and at worst, open dissension between team members. Leaders in these schools were frequently absent and uninvolved in AISI professional development and school meetings. Leaders' absences sent the message that this was only for teachers and administrators were not interested in the educational improvement of the school. Frequently leaders failed to incorporate time within the school day for peer observation or other AISI-related activities. Teachers tended to be critical of the out-of-school time required. A lack of clear vision, direction, and organisation impeded progress in some districts. This was the case even for teacher-leaders who were frustrated at the ambiguity in expectations of their role and the lack of clarity about how to initiate and support projects. There was little guidance or structure on how teachers should implement their learning from the TPD sessions once back in their classrooms. This may have affected their motivation to transfer their learning into regular repertoire.

Evaluation of AISI projects was problematic in that reports were generally based on the district's progress rather than individual schools. This frequently involved evaluation from participants in workshops, gauging teachers' 'happiness quotient', rather than directly measuring the impact on student achievement using a range of sources. As Guskey stated there appeared to be a certain "innocence" on the part of the professional developers and AISI organisers, similar to most professional developers, that this initiative would have "priceless benefits to students, teachers, parents, board members, and the community at large" and yet the evaluation processes have not encompassed a systematic and comprehensive approach (2005, p. 10-11). Guskey advised school communities that they needed to "get serious about evaluation", because we live in an age of accountability and without this high quality data "programs may get axed" which in the case of AISI would be a significant loss to the teachers in Alberta (2005, p. 10).

Lessons Learned from the Case Studies

It is clear from these two case studies that even though there is extensive knowledge about establishing effective professional development there is still a divide between theory and practice within educational systems. This is surprising considering that both cases are situated within wealthy, educated, resource-rich states/provinces, and yet still there are difficulties encountered in establishing sound, systematic, and sustainable professional development.

It is an indictment on governments and senior administrators when there remains a deficit perception of the knowledge of teachers and doubt in their ability to facilitate positive learning environments for students. This negative view of teachers is particularly evident in Western Australia where the Quality Teacher Programme (QTP), was explicitly designed to improve teachers' knowledge and skills, and their status within the community. The subtext of these aims is that teachers are not competent, therefore, not respected within the community. A further indictment is that contrary to most scholarly literature, the QTP does not have improving student outcomes as its primary stated objective. In both case study countries, teachers must be fully qualified with a minimum of a four-year university-level qualification in order to be accredited. In Alberta, teachers' salary scales and promotional opportunities are linked to their qualification levels, thus establishing their extensive knowledge. It also institutionalises the recognition attributed to further studies. Unfortunately, teachers in Western Australia can access a once-only 'qualification allowance' for any further qualification received, thereby institutionally discouraging teachers from further postgraduate studies.

The Alberta Education-funded AISI projects were founded on the principles of professional learning communities and involved inquiry, collaboration and continuous improvement. Even so implementation has been constrained by a lack of organisation and planning, whole-school staff commitment and involvement, and patchy or poor leadership. There appeared to be a failure in leadership in both case studies. Some leaders failed to explicate and obtain buy-in to their vision for professional development. They appeared to lack understanding about the importance of their role in motivating teachers' engagement. In some cases they were too autocratic in establishing goals, processes, and team work. Although we know effective TPD should be contextually relevant, systematic, supported in situ, and evaluated, there is still a proliferation in both Western Australia and Alberta of one-shot workshops and information dissemination meetings (Knowles, Holton III, & Swanson, 2005).

In response to calls from industry and business during the 1990s, Western Australia decision-makers instituted policy which dictated the integration of technology into the curriculum. However, this integration of ICT appeared to be associated with the expectation that teachers will automatically be able to use these technologies without training and ongoing technical support to improve student outcomes. Drawing upon lesson learned from Australia, USA and other provinces in Canada, Alberta has only recently initiated pilot projects into the use of ICT for educational purposes (Learning Cultures Consulting Inc, 2006). There are a number of laptop pilot projects within Alberta, however, as yet there is limited evidence to indicate success or otherwise. Most TPD related to ICT use in education were conference events, and again there was little indication of systematic, timely TPD in this area. Innovations in technology within these educational systems appear to be restricted to teaching and learning, rather than investigating how TPD can be supported and facilitated utilising technology.

In both case studies there is a divide between theory and practice – in Western Australia there is little knowledge shaping decisions about professional development even though technology access has been well established. Conversely, in Alberta there is considerable understandings about effective professional development, however, within the school system there appears to be little exploration of technology to support ongoing professional development. In both countries technology appears to hold significant potential for supporting teachers' professional development and yet it is not evident in systematic approaches.

FUTURE TRENDS

From the two case studies presented it is clear that teachers concerns related to professional development revolved around self-determination, effective processes, choices and availability, supportive leadership, access, time and travel, and funding. Professional development is a complex topic with many dimensions. This future trends section explores a range of dimensions distilled by this author, which when implemented can contribute to bridging the existing divide between theory and practice in teacher professional development. These dimensions are interwoven where if one fails, is not present, understood, or is ignored, the overall tapestry of effectiveness of the initiative is seriously compromised. These dimensions include:

- understanding effective professional development processes;
- political factors;
- empowerment of teachers;
- sound leadership;
- time;
- personal professionalism;
- supporting sustainability through measuring impact and celebrating successes; and
- technological innovations in teacher professional development.

Understanding effective professional development – There are still teachers, leaders and administrators within educational systems around the world who do not understand what processes are required to support optimal teacher learning. Lacking these theoretical insights results in the institutionalisation of poor TPD practices and contributes to the continuation of fragmented approaches to school improvement. *With knowledge comes power* – knowledge about effective TPD generates the power to avoid unproductive processes and institute best practice, thereby catalysing positive educational change. Therefore, the more that all stakeholders are aware of sound practices in TPD, the more likely it is to be able to establish reasonable policies and expectations for implementation, timelines, processes, infrastructure, and change dynamics all resulting in positive educational cultures.

Political factors – Governments and decision-makers frequently perceive TPD as the 'magic bullet' that will bring about reform and policy implementation. Descriptions of TPD figure strongly in the language of public accountability. Unfortunately, it is the quick fix, short-term and deficit-oriented TPD which is usually politically expedient. Professional development must focus on supporting student learning outcomes not just on fixing the teachers or increasing teacher-efficacy, even though there is a relationship between the two. Although there is considerable knowledge about what constitutes effective professional development these processes are deemed to be too slow in yielding the politically desirable results. The conundrum exists that when one-shot workshops or information dissemination processes fail to bring about the mandated changes, the assumption is made that the fault lies with teachers' abilities and motivations to institute the reforms. When the reforms falter it leads to further policy changes, another round of implementation-focused professional development, and the cycle of blame begins again. This reinforces the decision-makers' negative perceptions of teachers and schools. It also embeds teachers' suspicion of policy and government administrators and enhances the partisan attitudes which are so destructive to progress within educational systems.

Government and their decision-makers have significant power to influence the public's perception of education. The overt marketing of positive educational outcomes, rather than highlighting school shortfalls, increases the status of teachers and education, stems the haemorrhaging of teachers leaving the profession, and encourages student retention. When teachers are respected and valued, educational cultures are positive and all stakeholders benefit. When teachers feel valued it increases their desire to be professional and their willingness to demonstrate this professionalism through ongoing learning.

It is imperative to convene regular forums where all stakeholders meet to discuss the establishment of informed student-focused policies and practices, along with effective TPD that builds commitment and participation to ensure the success of all students. 'Commitment' means all stakeholders put aside their partisan perspectives and willingly engage in transparent and constructive dialogue and action for the betterment of all students' learning and development.

Empowerment of teachers – Teachers associate self-determination in their work context and therefore empowerment, with concepts of professionalism. They are individuals with varied beliefs about good teaching, motivational levels to engage in TPD, and experiences within schools. These varied elements influence teachers' willingness to engage in professional development. Teachers' predominant interest in TPD is for topics directly related to the classroom, their teaching and their students. Some veterans may have a wealth of experience with unsuccessful initiatives over the years which have soured their passion for ongoing learning and growth. Additionally, mandated, top-down professional development initiatives designed to ensure implementation of policy may appear to have little relevance to teachers or students, therefore they disengage or simply pay 'lip service' to the reform efforts. Leaders have the responsibility to meet organisational objectives and to engender teachers' support for these. Teachers' support is negotiated through genuine consultation in establishing the goals, processes, and evaluation measures of the professional development. A balance must be found between the needs of the organisation (accountability) with the needs of the individual (responsibility) in relation to choice of professional development. However, teachers must demonstrate personal responsibility to select TPD that supports their endeavours in the classroom, as well as supporting organisational goals to ensure alignment between the personal and organisational.

Sound leadership– Leaders impact student learning by creating positive school cultures and supporting teachers in their work with students (Fullan, 2007; Hargreaves, 1992; Sergiovanni, 1993). In their vision for improving student learning, school leaders must consider effective TPD processes that include a problem-solving orientation; collegial discussions and reflection; shared planning and resource development; peer observation and feedback; and skill and strategy exploration and adoption. Therefore, for those who want or expect rapid change and immediate results, instituting these previously described elements of TPD will not be desirable as these take time to deliver positive educational outcomes – but they are worth the wait! Leaders are confronted with numerous competing demands on their time and policies requiring implementation, therefore they must resist the temptation to 'jump on the bandwagon' and follow the latest fad and fashion being peddled by professional development consultants. They must remain focused on their long-term vision for school improvement, and cognisant of staff capacities to deal with continual changes from new initiatives.

Instituting more systematic professional development requires significant commitment, thoughtful planning, and sound organisational skills of school leaders. The best results are achieved when teachers have bought into this as a shared vision. There are leadership implications in reconnecting disenfranchised or disengaged teachers with their colleagues, in sound professional development processes (Fullan, 1998; Fullan & Hargreaves, 1991; Hargreaves, 1994). If this reconnection does not occur, disgruntled teachers may potentially disrupt or derail whole-school approaches to improvement and enhancement in learning. Leaders, through positive interactions, can create a close knit educational community which serve to increase commitment to the school vision and goals.

Time – Time is always an issue in educational contexts – the lack of it, who controls it, how it is used, and the wasting of it. Time is very important in relation to TPD in a number of ways. It takes time for teachers to engage in TPD, which has financial implications in requiring the funding of substitute teachers to take their classes. Even though quick fixes are politically desirable, long-term systematic TPD is more effective but does require the commitment of time for the processes to become embedded. Teachers need time to experiment with new strategies and time to become comfortable with unfamiliar pedagogies. Students, like their teachers, need time to adjust to the new approaches to learning. Allowing teachers time to reflect on their teaching and assessment processes and how they can improve these, is a powerful aid to enhancing practice. Additionally, time must be made available during the school day for collegial meetings, as well as visits to peers' classrooms for observation, debriefing and action planning. These activities require creative timetabling, funding allocation, and processes and infrastructure changes to support and promote these collegial professional development activities. Leaders must recognise that it will take time for their staff to engage with their vision, to help shape it, to buy into it, to translate it into action and evaluation. Time must be bought out in order to reflect on the whole-school results and to wholeheartedly celebrate the successes with the students, their teachers, parents and the other educational stakeholders. Time should be considered for dissemination of positive outcomes and the lessons learned, so that others within their district and wider afield can benefit from their efforts. With the ever present shortages of time within schools, leaders must be discerning about which TPD topics and processes to adopt and resist the latest fad and fashions in topics that always seem to emerge to captivate the easily impressed but which have little research-based proof of value to, or impact on student learning. Not all 'time matters' outlined here requires real time to be found. Many of these aspects relate to altering expectations of various individuals – leaders, teachers themselves, and even students and parents.

Personal professionalism – Teachers and leaders have a professional responsibility to maintain their discipline and pedagogical knowledge and skills in order to teach and lead effectively, which is the primary goal of all professional development. All teachers and leaders must be conversant in quantitative and qualitative literacies so that appropriate, evidence-based decisions can be made

to guide future directions. Included in quantitative and qualitative literacies is the capacity to formulate and/or select appropriate evaluation measures for gauging student achievement, as well as, the effectiveness of professional development. These literacies are essential to inform problem-solving and decision-making at the classroom, school, district, and provincial/state levels.

Additional professional skills, such as, the ability to work effectively with colleagues, communication, personal leadership, and inter- and intra-personal skills are essential for teachers, teacher-leaders and principals. For example, some disgruntled and disengaged teachers have not seized opportunities to develop these skills and as a result have actively impeded collegial processes due to their lack of personal development. Collegial processes within TPD should facilitate personal reflection time focused on nurturing these vital professional skills. These skills, which can be honed through effective TPD processes, contribute to the efficient and effective functioning of the school and 'grease the wheels' of collaboration.

Measuring the effectiveness and celebrating successes – It is crucial for school leaders to be aware of the importance of collecting and analysing a range of data to monitor the success or otherwise of school improvement programmes. These data inform future directions, but also enable the school community to celebrate the positive outcomes. All too often professional development initiatives are instituted without any thought to measuring the outcomes in terms of school improvement, developments of teacher knowledge and expertise, student learning, and for gauging the impact on school culture. When there are no measures or evidence of impact it is tempting to assume that the professional development is not effecting change and to discard it for the next option. Therefore, an essential dimension in the planning of effective TPD is to establish alignment between the objectives, processes involved, and the evaluation of the initiative. The objectives must have student learning at the core, even though there may be other associated goals. The processes must be founded on sound adult learning and professional development theory and incorporate reasonable timeframes. Evaluation should encompass a range of sources. These may include samples of students' work, student and staff reflections on learning, student retention data, managing student behaviour referral data, standardised assessment, and other sources deemed relevant by collective staff perspectives. The range of data will provide multi-faceted insights into the success of the TPD initiative and will enable staff, leaders and senior administrators to make informed decisions at the classroom, whole-school and district levels.

Celebrations not only serve to disseminate information about TPD initiatives and its impact, but also to highlight the good work being done in schools. This has a powerful effect on the attitudes of the community towards teachers and schools. Celebrations, like evaluations, can be at the classroom, whole-school, district, and even provincial/state levels. At the class level, student and teachers can celebrate the successes of individuals, teams, or the whole group. This reinforces positive student behaviours and teaching strategies which have worked. Celebrating school success recognises the collective effort, empowers teachers, raises morale, and increases the profile of the school within the community - all highly desirable outcomes. District level successes set up a win-win cycle where leaders, teachers, students and the community have information about effective work in schools and facilitates the dissemination and proliferation of best practice. Teaching has experienced reputation issues for many years and it is timely that the efforts of the professionals are recognised and valued.

Technological innovations in teacher professional development – Having established that sound TPD is essential for maintaining the professionalism of teachers, decision-makers and professional development providers must explore the range of innovations available to

them with new technologies. Over the past decade emerging technologies have presented increasing opportunities for learning, that of both teachers and students, and yet there is a prevailing lack of vision for how it can be conducted. Professional development needs to be reconceptualised from traditional face-to-face approaches to virtual ones, or better still, blended learning approaches. The literature advocates for collegial collaboration, shared planning and resource development and idea generation, and yet distance and time are serious impediments to these valued activities. Using online technologies presents innovative ways to overcome these constraints. Indeed they also provide opportunities for initiating communities of practice to engage in the 'shared expertise and passion' that is teaching. Online communities of practice can reduce the isolation of the classroom by placing teachers in collaboration with peers in their school, across the district and even across the globe. These broader interactions widen teachers' perceptions of teaching and learning in different contexts. Using a spider's web as an analogy, multiple groups can create multidimensional linkages and interactions, thus forming "webs of enhanced practice" spanning international boundaries (Scott, 2009). Webs of enhanced practice can generate a "learning-to-learn effect" whereby collegial collaboration reinforces good practice through enthusiastic responses (Joyce & Showers, 1995, p. 113). Webs of enhanced practice may be formally introduced or informal processes.

Even though ICT has advanced and can support continuous and flexible TPD, the opportunities they present is dependent on teachers' and leaders' willingness to try out these new technologies and to change their 'ways of thinking and doing' from the traditional to the entrepreneurial. They need to become familiar and *au fait* with technologies that facilitate social networking. Initial technology-focused TPD would need to be provided to teachers who lack experience with new technologies so that they can become comfortable interacting online and are able to see the potential for both their own learning and that of their students. As technologically-assisted TPD represents not only good practice but also cost savings in the provision of traditional TPD, education ministries must be responsible in establishing appropriate infrastructure and technical support in order for these webs of enhanced practice to thrive.

CONCLUSION

This chapter explores the divide between theories of effective teacher professional development (TPD) and the realities of practice within educational contexts. There is a significant body of knowledge gathered from scholarly research conducted over four decades detailing optimal conditions, processes, and cultures related to teacher professional development. We know that constructivist learning environments are as valuable in supporting the learning of teachers, as they are for students. Even with this empowering knowledge, transmissive and one-shot approaches still prevail as the predominant forms of delivery. Two case studies from differing systems, namely, Western Australia and Alberta, Canada illustrate the similarities and the variability of approaches to TPD which exist. Although advances have been made in bridging the divide between theory and practice in TPD, there are still concerns about the effectiveness and sustainability of initiatives; impact on student learning; eliciting whole-staff engagement; and the dissemination of lessons learned and celebration of successes. The review of the literature reflected against the realities existing in different systems resulted in the distillation of a number of key dimensions. These dimensions, when coalesced, inform stakeholders on 'the why, how and what' - to institute effective TPD that will positively influence student and teacher learning, school results, and educational cultures. These dimensions encompass the theory and practice through:

- 'understanding effective professional development';
- the 'political factors' which always influence education;
- the crucial 'empowerment of teachers' providing ownership and engagement;
- 'sound leadership' - another essential as good leaders produce healthy schools;
- the provision and recognition of the importance of 'time' required for effective TPD and school improvement;
- aiming TPD increasing 'professional knowledge and skills';
- the value of 'measuring the effectiveness and celebrating successes' to individuals, schools, and the entire educational community; and finally but my no means of lesser importance
- the wealth of opportunities presented by entrepreneurial adoption of ICT-facilitated TPD producing 'webs of enhanced practice'.

Educators at every level of the organisation are faced with increasingly fast-paced change to meet society's expectations. Considering that we are in the 21st century with increasingly sophisticated social networking technologies, combined with students' mind-shift towards, expertise in, and comfort with technologies, teachers are well advised to meet these changes head on by exploring their professional growth through the medium of information communication technology. Not only will teachers experience more collegial collaboration and the other associated advantages, but their technological expertise will also increase. Technology-facilitated professional development generates two positive outcomes – professional learning and ameliorating the differences between the teachers' generation and that of their technologically-sophisticated students.

REFERENCES

Alberta Education. (2008). *Facts about the Alberta Initiative for School Improvement (AISI)*, from http://education.alberta.ca/admin/aisi/about/whatisaisi.aspx

Bandura, A. (2001). Social Cognitive Theory: An agentic perspective. *Annual Review of Psychology, 52*(1), 1–26. doi:10.1146/annurev.psych.52.1.1

Brandt, R. (1994). Reflections on 25 years of staff development. *Journal of Staff Development, 15*(4), 2–25.

Clardy, A. (2005). *Andragogy: Adult learning and education at its best?* Towson, Maryland.

Clarke, D., & Hollingsworth, H. (1994). *Reconceptualising teacher change.* Paper presented at the 17th Annual Conference of the Mathematical Education Research Group of Australasia, Southern Cross University, Lismore, Australia.

Darling-Hammond, L. (1998, February). Teacher learning that supports student learning. *Educational Leadership,* 6–11.

Darling-Hammond, L., & McLaughlin, M. (1995). Policies that support professional development in an era of change. *Phi Delta Kappan, 76*(8), 597–604.

Department of Education Science and Training [DEST]. (2004). *Australian Government Quality Teacher Programme Updated Client Guidelines, 2004 - 05.* Canberra.

Department of Education Science and Training [DEST]. (2005). *An Evaluation of the Australian Government Quality Teacher Programme 1999 to 2004.* Canberra: Atelier Learning Solutions Pty Ltd.

DuFour, R. (2004). What is a "Professional Learning Community"? *Educational Leadership, 1*(8), 6–11.

DuFour, R., & Eaker, R. (2004). *Professional Learning Communities at work: Best practices for enhancing student achievement.* Bloomington, IN: National Educational Service.

Education Department of Western Australia. (2000a). *Learning Technologies Project: 1999 School Computer and Connectivity Census Report.* Perth, AU: Education Department of Western Australia.

Education Department of Western Australia (2000b). *Technology 2000 Expanding Learning Horizons: Draft Strategic Plan Overview 1999-2001*: Education Department of Western Australia. Retrieved 29th Dec. 2000

Fullan, M. (1998). Leadership for the 21st Century breaking the bonds of dependency. *Educational Leadership, 55*(7).

Fullan, M. (2007). *The new meaning of educational change* (3rd ed.). New York, NY: Routledge.

Fullan, M. G., & Hargreaves, A. (1991). Interactive professionalism and guidelines for action. In *Working Together for Your School* (pp. 63-111). Hawthorn, Vic: ACEA.

Gall, M. D., Renchler, R. S., Haisley, F. B., Baker, R. G., & Perez, M. (1985). *Effective staff development for teachers: A research-based model*: College of Education, University of Oregon.

Garmston, R. (1991). Staff developers as social architects. *Educational Leadership, 49*(3), 64–65.

Goldenberg, C., & Gallimore, R. (1991). Changing teaching takes more than a one-shot workshop. *Educational Leadership, 49*(3), 69–72.

Goodlad, J. (1994, April). The national network for educational renewal. *Phi Delta Kappan,* 632–638.

Guskey, T. R. (1986, May). Staff development and the process of teacher change. *Educational Researcher,* 5–12.

Guskey, T. R. (2005). Taking a second look at accountability. *Journal of Staff Development, 26*(1), 10–18.

Guskey, T. R., & Sparks, D. (1991). What to consider when evaluating staff development. *Educational Leadership, 49*(3), 73–74.

Guskey, T. R., & Sparks, D. (2002). Linking professional development to improvements in student learning. In *American Educational Research Association*. New Orleans, LA.

Hargreaves, A. (1992). Cultures of teaching: A focus for change. In A. Hargreaves & F. Michael (Eds.), *Understanding teacher development* (pp. 216 - 241). New York: Teachers College Press, Columbia University.

Hargreaves, A. (1994). *Changing teachers, changing times: Teachers' work and culture in the postmodern age.* Great Britain: Redwood Books.

Hargreaves, A., & Fullan, M. G. (1992). Introduction. In A. Hargreaves & F. Michael (Eds.), *Understanding teacher development* (pp. 1-8). New York: Teachers College Press, Columbia University.

Hirsh, S. (2004). Putting comprehensive staff development on target. *Journal of Staff Development, 25*(1), 12–15.

Joyce, B., & Showers, B. (1980). Improving inservice training: The messages of research. *Educational Leadership, 37*(5), 379–385.

Joyce, B., & Showers, B. (1995). *Student achievement through staff development.* New York: Longman.

Joyce, B., & Weil, M. (1986). *Models of teaching* (3rd ed.). New York: Prentice Hall.

Joyce, B., Weil, M., & Calhoun, E. (2004). *Models of teaching* (7th ed.). New York: Allyn & Bacon.

Joyce, B., Weil, M., & Showers, B. (1992). *Models of teaching* (4th ed.). New York: Allyn & Bacon.

Knowles, M. S., Holton, E. F., III, & Swanson, R. A. (2005). *The adult learner: The definitive classic in adult education and human resource development* (6th ed.). Amsterdam: Elsevier.

Learning Cultures Consulting Inc. (2006). *One-to-one mobile computing – Literature review.* Report for Alberta Education.

Leithwood, K., Seashore, L. K., Anderson, S., & Wahlstrom, K. (2004). *How leadership influences student learning.* New York: Wallace Foundation.

Lieberman, A., & Miller, L. (2000). Teaching and teacher development: A new synthesis for a new century. In R. S. Brandt (Ed.), *Education in a new era* (pp. 47-66). Virginia: Association for Supervision and Curriculum Development.

Lieberman, A., & Pointer Mace, D. H. (2008). Teacher learning: The key to educational reform. *Journal of Teacher Education, 59*(3), 226–234. doi:10.1177/0022487108317020

Long, H. B. (2004). Understanding adult learners. In M. W. Galbraith (Ed.), *Adult Learning Methods: A Guide for Effective Instruction* (3rd ed.). Florida, USA: Krieger Publishing.

McEwan, N. (2006). *Improving Schools Investing in Our Future.* Edmonton: Alberta Education.

Merriam, S. B. (2001). Andragogy and self-directed learning: Pillars of adult learning theory. In S. B. Merriam (Ed.), *The new update on adult learning theory* (Vol. 89, pp. 3-13). San Francisco: Jossey-Bass.

Mulford, B. (2008). *The leadership challenge: Improving learning in schools.* Camberwell, Victoria: Australian Council for Educational Research.

Scott, D. E. (2009). *Effective Voice-over-Internet-Protocol (VoIP) learning experiences: The relationship between adult learning motivation, multiple intelligences, and learning styles.* Doctoral Thesis. Curtin University of Technology.

Scott, S. (2002). *Professional development: A study of secondary teachers' experiences and perspectives.* Doctoral Thesis. Curtin University of Technology. http://adt.curtin.edu.au/theses/available/adt-WCU20030312.145827/.

Scott, S. (2003). Professional development: A study of secondary teachers' experiences and perspectives. *The International Journal of Learning, 10.*

Scott, S., & Webber, C. F. (2008). Evidence-based leadership development: The 4L framework. *Journal of Educational Administration, 46*(6), 762–776. doi:10.1108/09578230810908343

Sergiovanni, T. J. (1993, April 13). *Organisations or communities? Changing the metaphor changes the theory.* Paper presented at the annual meeting of the American Educational Research Association, Atlanta, Georgia.

Showers, B., & Joyce, B. (1996). The evolution of peer coaching. *Educational Leadership, 53*(6), 12–16.

Sparks, D., & Hirsh, S. (1997). *A new vision for staff development*: Association for Supervision and Curriculum Development.

Sparks, D., & Hirsh, S. (2000). *A National Plan for Improving Professional Development.* Oxford, OH: National Staff Development Council.

Steffy, B. E., Wolfe, M. P., Pasch, S. H., & Enz, B. J. (Eds.). (2000). *Life cycle of the career teacher.* Thousand Oaks: Kappa Delta Pi and Corwin Press, Inc.

Webber, C. F., Aitken, N., Runté, R., Lupart, J., & Scott, S. (2008, 30th May-4th June). *Alberta student assessment study: Stage one findings.* Paper presented at the Annual Meeting of the Canadian Society for the Study of Education, Vancouver.

Wenger, E. (2003). Communities of practice and social learning systems. In R. Gardner, D. Nicolini, S. Gherardi, & D. Yanow (Eds.), *Knowing in organizations: A practice-based approach.* Armonk, NY: M.E. Sharpe.

Wenger, E. C., & Snyder, W. M. (2000). Communities of practice: The organizational frontier. *Harvard Business Review, 78*(1), 139–146.

Wlodkowski, R. J. (2004). Strategies to enhance adult motivation to learn. In M. W. Galbraith (Ed.), *Adult Learning Methods: A Guide for Effective Instruction* (3rd ed., pp. 91-112). Florida. USA: Krieger Publishing.

Zeichner, K., & Bekisizwe, N. (2008). Contradictions and tensions in the place of teachers in educational reform: Reflections on teacher preparation in the USA and Namibia. *Teachers and Teaching: Theory and Practice, 14*(4), 331–343.

Section 2
Methods and Models of Online Communities in TPD

Chapter 3
Case Studies from the Inquiry Learning Forum
Stories Reaching Beyond the Edges[1]

Rebecca Scheckler
Radford University, USA

ABSTRACT

Two intense case studies were done of teachers using the Inquiry Learning Forum (ILF), an online space for professional development in inquiry pedagogies. Major findings included: The ILF initially conceived as an online professional development tool in the form of a Community of Practice (COP) was reconceived as an electronic tool within a larger space that included the online tool but also many co-present spaces pertinent to a teacher's practice of inquiry pedagogy. These case studies also demonstrated the transformative nature of teachers engaging in a COP. Not only is the teacher changed but also the COP is changed by the practice. The cases demonstrated the need for teachers to feel disequilibrium in their practice before they are willing to engage in change of those practices. Lastly immersion in practice described as The Pedagogy of Poverty hampered one teacher's progress in the ILF. These findings are based upon my empirical observations with the backdrop of John Dewey's Theory of Inquiry and of Etienne Wenger's concept of communities of Practice. Future trends in using online COPs for professional development need to look at practice in these terms where allowance for transaction, support outside the electronic space, and disequilibrium are considered.

INTRODUCTION

The concept of Community of Practice (COP) as a source for professional development, although originating from examples within industrial practice (Lave, 1991; Wenger, 1998; Wenger, 2002), has gained wide interest within educational contexts in the United States (Preece, Maloney-Krichmar, 2005). The continual development and improvement of digital technology has allowed the deployment of experiments in COP to be preformed online. One such project that originated at Indiana University in Bloomington, Indiana and was funded by the National Science Foundation was the Inquiry Learn-

DOI: 10.4018/978-1-60566-780-5.ch003

ing Forum (ILF), a large-scale project meant to promote the use of inquiry pedagogies among math and science teachers in the state of Indiana via an online Community of Practice[2]. This chapter reports on extensive case studies of two teachers who were involved with the ILF in order to provide information on a topic that is often scarce in studies of online professional development. The question was "How did the ILF affect the teaching practice of participants?"

It is a truism that you do not know what case studies will yield until you collect your data and analyze them. That truism is supported by these studies. I started with the goal of discovering through case studies how the ILF affected the teaching practice of some of the actively participating in-service teachers. I soon had to revise my research question to "How do teachers transact with the ILF with particular reference to their teaching practice?". This change resulted from watching two teachers modify the ILF as much as the ILF modified them. It also resulted in a re-conceptualization of the ILF into an e-ILF or the actual electronic space and the greater ILF or the larger space of teacher engagement including their classrooms, meetings with other teachers, parents, the professional organizations of their field, state standards of learning, and their supervisors.

In this chapter I begin by giving an overview of the motivation for the ILF, my studies of the ILF, and some concepts involved in these studies such as Communities of Practice, differentiating the electronic ILF from the entire ILF, A Deweyan Theory of Inquiry, and Pedagogies of Poverty. I then present the methodology for the case studies, and an in depth view of the case studies. I continue by discussing the case studies in relationship to the theoretical concepts and conclude with future trends for online professional development using online COPs and I finish the chapter with a summary of my conclusions.

MOTIVATION FOR THE ILF

The ILF was designed with the need for providing teacher professional development that promoted inquiry pedagogies against a background of a steadily improving Internet access for teachers and against a background of U.S students losing ground in math and science on an international basis (American Association for the Advancement of Science, 1991; U.S. Department of Education, 1999). A needs analysis of a small sample of science and math teachers in Indiana, U.S.A. showed that these teachers wanted to visit the classrooms of teachers who already had proficiency with inquiry pedagogies but their busy schedules prevented them from doing this (Barab, MaKinster, Moore, Cunningham & The ILF Design Team, 2001). This needs analysis resulted in the design of the ILF where teachers could virtually visit classrooms of other teachers and then interact with the demonstrating teachers about their teaching within non-synchronous threaded discussion forums.

STUDIES OF THE ILF

In creating and supporting an online site for teacher professional development there were many difficulties including motivating teachers to feel ownership and thus participate, instilling trust in teachers that their online words would not be used against them, and being able to determine the effectiveness of the online tool (Barab, MaKinster, & Scheckler, 2004). The case studies described in this paper were an attempt to determine the effectiveness of the ILF albeit a deep and narrow determination since it is difficult to find the resources to do very many of these in depth case studies. However the extreme benefit of them was to discover issues of teachers' practice that researchers had not foreseen.

In the United States there has been some great success in using online professional development tools but not the universal adoption that administrators and researchers would have hoped for. There are numerous cultural, bureaucratic, and financial reasons why online professional development is not the norm in the United States. At the least they include lack of appropriate tools, lack of technological support, and lack of motivation for teachers to work on adopting new practices with the aid of an online tool.

In the particular case of the ILF there was a great deal of interest by the research and design teams in providing appropriate and motivating tools for individual teachers as well as supporting these teachers in both their use of the online tools and most importantly their ability to apply these new teaching skills in their classrooms. Towards these ends the ILF provided workshops both in central sites and school based sites, reimbursed teachers for travel, reimbursed school systems for substitutes to cover the absences at our workshops, and even provided class science tools in some cases for accomplishing inquiry lessons.

However even with all this support there is not a wonderful tale of adoption that I report. Several issues affected the use of the ILF and the pedagogy that it promoted and I will mention some of the important ones here: the pedagogy of poverty, lack of local support for change, local communities of teachers that competed with our online COP, lack of trust in demonstrating ignorance online, and more immediate needs for curricular support in science. First you need to know more about the ILF and what it looked like.

The Setting of the Case Studies: The Inquiry Learning Forum

The Inquiry Learning Forum (ILF), an online community of practice for professional development, was actively supported from 1999 until 2006 by Indiana University in Bloomington, Indiana (http://ILF.crlt.indiana.edu) (Barab, et al. 2004, Scheckler & Barab, 2008). Funded by a grant from the National Science Foundation (NSF) I was extremely lucky to be supported

for two years as a post–doctoral fellow for the sole job of researching and supporting the ILF. While I joined the ILF after the needs analysis, initial design, and rollout were accomplished, I was there to witness and participate in a major redesign and metamorphosis of this large and vibrant project. Part of the metamorphosis was realizing and supporting both the electronic-ILF (e-ILF) or the actual online environment and the ILF or the larger environment around the e-ILF involving all the ways the participants interacted and used the ILF both online and offline.

The e-ILF was designed to meet the needs of pre-service and in-service teachers who were interested in using Inquiry pedagogies for their math or science classes. The needs analysis indicated that teachers wanted to visit the classrooms of other teachers particularly those using unfamiliar teaching methods. Time constraints make such visits nearly impossible for the active teacher. Therefore the ILF was designed around the metaphor of professional development as visiting the classrooms of teachers already using inquiry pedagogies. See figure 1 for the entrance page of the ILF where members can choose to visit classrooms, a library of inquiry resources, lounges in which to discuss teaching problems and solutions, rooms to learn about and practice inquiry skills, and storage space to share and work on joint lesson plans.

Every classroom (see figure 2) includes a short video of teaching practice divided into segments, the teacher's reflections on the lesson, the lesson plan, examples of student work, the relevant standards or learning[3] that were being covered, resources that would be helpful in teaching the lesson, and most importantly discussion forums for asking the teacher about the lesson displayed, for critiquing the lesson, or for making suggestions about the lesson. Classrooms display teachers using inquiry with various levels of students and in many different areas. Early on in the ILF all the classes were math or science classes but later instruction was added in everything from history

Figure 1. The e-ILF entry screen. © Indiana University 2009

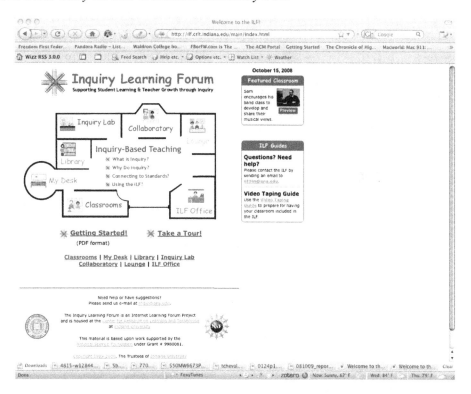

to art to English. The ILF site (http://ilf.crlt.indiana.edu) is password protected in order to protect the children in the videos and in order to obtain consent for research from everyone receiving a password. Passwords were given without charge to teachers, pre-service teachers, administrators, and educational researchers.

Co-present meetings and activities supported the e-ILF. There were meetings for teachers, some at regional math and science organizations in Indiana, some at Indiana University where periodical inquiry workshops, teacher advisory meetings committee meetings, and ILF participant reunions were held. I and other ILF staff members also visited schools in order to present workshops on Inquiry and to demonstrate the e-ILF or to instruct in the use of the ILF. We tried very hard to create an intuitive interface that did not require too much instruction and I think we largely succeeded in doing this.

At its height the ILF had thousands of teachers

registered but of course all were not active participants. Some of the most active teachers created videos of their classrooms to be included in the e-ILF, were members of the participant advisory board (PAB), and posted frequently and passionately in the discussions forums reflecting on their practice as well as the practice of other teachers in the videos. We began to refer to the ILF as having a dual inquiry role. These were encouraging inquiry as pedagogy as well as encouraging inquiry into one's own practice as a teacher.

Two intensive case studies were done in the time period 2001-2002 representing two modes of usage. Ben, an experienced high school science teacher was experimenting with inquiry-based science long before the ILF came along. He used the ILF to gain support for his practices, to gain legitimacy from his administrators and peers, and to find activities outside of the ILF to further his interests in hands on science and on inquiry pedagogy. Helen, a very experienced middle school

Figure 2. An e-ILF classroom. © Indiana University 2009

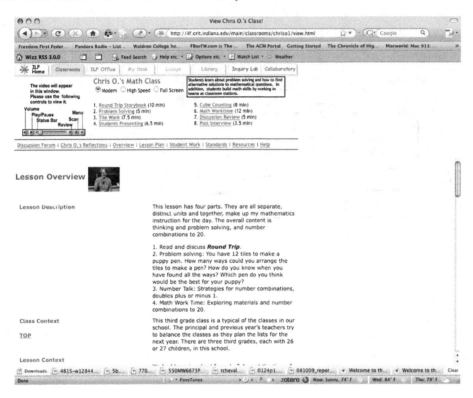

math and science teacher used the ILF when her school decided that its science and math teachers would receive professional development through the ILF. She never did become interested in the ILF beyond the required postings that her site based sessions required. Her teaching practice revolved around preparing her charges for standardized testing, keeping them clothed and fed and parented despite sometimes minimal support from home, and supporting her fellow teachers following constructive as well as destructive practices

Issues in the ILF

In this section I describe some of the theory that is relevant to the case studies. This is somewhat putting the cart before the horse but I will come back to all of these issues after I present the case studies.

E-ILF within the ILF or Where Does Community Occur?

You may be wondering why I take such pains to differentiate the e-ILF from the ILF at large in the section above. Almost as soon as I joined the ILF project the researchers began to debate where the ILF existed which is in a sense an expansion of a discussion about where community exists and particularly where does a COP exist. We saw our participants using relationships that originated online expand out of the virtual space and into other parts of their lived space. We also found teachers selecting to communicate online mostly with people that they knew previously or that seemed similar to them particularly in regard to gender (Herring, Martinson & Scheckler, 2002). We found it necessary to support our participating teachers with offline activities and meetings. We also found their offline or co-present activities affecting how they used the e-ILF. Therefore we began to think of the

Figure 3. The e-ILF within the ILF

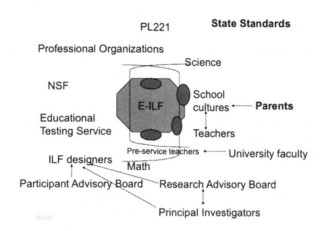

ILF in a broader context but we did not want to ignore the online space as an entity that needed a name and due recognition at various times. Thus we made the differentiation between the ILF (which includes the e-ILF) and the e-ILF.

Figure 3 shows how I saw the ILF composed of the e-ILF in addition to offline activities but also as influenced by the cultures of math and science, by the standards of learning, by Public Law 221 of the State of Indiana that established accountability for K-12 education, by the Educational Testing Service (ETS) creators of college entrance exams in the United States, by parents of current students, by the National Science Foundation (NSF) that funded the project, and by the cultures of individual school systems. Not only did the ILF need to meet the expectations and needs of all these entities but also it needed to motivate teachers to participate despite all these sometimes-conflicting activities and influences. I ultimately concluded that both the practices we were trying to effect and the community we were trying to foster occurred both on and off line, usually simultaneously. Discussing COP and Dewey's Theory of Inquiry will help explain this conceptualization.

Communities of Practice

Etienne Wenger defines a Communities of Practice (COP) as "… groups of people who share a concern or a passion for something they do and learn how to do it better as they interact regularly. (Wenger, no date)". As Wenger further explains a COP requires a domain, a shared practice, and a community where participants are willing to help one another and share knowledge (Wenger, no date). The e-ILF provided a rich and stable electronic domain with tools for discussing and co-creating a common practice of teaching with inquiry pedagogies. However the e-ILF was necessary but not sufficient to supply either a domain or a location for practice. The videos in the ILF were very illustrative of inquiry pedagogy but they did not necessarily represent the reality for an individual teacher. Cultures of schools differ to the degree to which they encourage inquiry. Teachers of math had much different concerns than teachers of science. Teachers had to take what they could from the e-ILF and find a wider domain in which to operate. We helped this process by providing semi-private spaces in the e-ILF where teachers could explore particular interests such as inquiry with special needs children or groups that met each other at our workshops. We frequently took co-present groups and put them into the e-ILF

The most difficult part of establishing COPs in the e-ILF was establishing communities of participants who trusted one another enough to risk making mistakes or being critical of one another's practice (Barab, MaKinster, & Scheckler, 2004). Trust is particularly difficult to establish online where participants do not know who is reading their postings. Members of the ILF worried at times that their supervisors would see their mistakes and judge them as incompetent. In addition teachers are reluctant of being critical of other teachers in what seems to them like a public forum. Here again mixing co-present associations with online spaces encouraged our goal of encouraging teachers to assist one another.

A Deweyan Theory of Inquiry

A Deweyan theory of inquiry is another theoretical tool with which to view design for collaborative professional development spaces. It is another socially and culturally situated theory, similar to the theory of Communities of Practice, with which to examine the inquiry of teachers in the Inquiry Learning Forum. For Dewey, "*Inquiry is the controlled or directed transformation of an indeterminate situation into one that is so determinate in its constituent distinctions and relations as to convert the elements of the original situation into a unified whole.*" (Dewey, 1938/1986, p. 108) Thus for Dewey, inquiry is the transformation of an indeterminate and uncertain situation into one that allows both continuity as a holistic manifestation of life and some stable sense of equilibrium.

It is important to notice from the start, that the end point of inquiry is not an indication of certainty and finality but merely a stable resting spot for further inquiry that will occur in the future. In fact Dewey had no concept of final infallible truths but stressed fallibility and the ongoing quest for increasingly better answers (Dewey, 1929/1982). For Dewey, the only purpose of education was

more education and by extension the only purpose of inquiry is more inquiry. Inquiry is a way to seek consequences that relate to experience and existence. Inquiry has a beginning and an end although this does not mean that every beginning and every end can be identified and separated from all other instances of inquiry. For Dewey inquiry begins when a person's equilibrium is disturbed. This disturbance could be physical such as hunger, thirst, or fatigue or emotional such as fear, confusions or curiosity. The ending point of inquiry is the re-establishment of equilibrium as when one is no longer hungry or thirsty, no longer confused, or satisfied that we are loved or safe from harm. The sense of discomfort that initiates inquiry is the precognitive state.

Following this sense of discomfort or disequilibrium, the inquirer must formulate a question. The precognitive state is usually transformed into a question that can be formulated and understood to have a solution that may be sought (Dewey, 1938/1986, p. 112). Without the transformation of the pre-cognitive to the cognitive, there are just instinctual actions like a hungry animal taking food wherever it lies. Also, without the precognitive discomfort leading to a cognitive positing of a question, there is only the busy work of assigned tasks as are found in many factories and schools.

As one inquires, there is some kind of change in the environment (Dewey, 1938/1986, p. 41). This can be as simple as moving ones head to look to see whether the sun is out. There is usually an empirical part of inquiry that leads to a change in the surrounding environment or ones relations to it. As the one in doubt progresses from doubt to re-establishment of equilibrium, there is a means-ends continuum (Waks, 1999, p. 596)

"Habits are the basis of organic learning" (Dewey, 1938/1986. p. 38). Habits are customary activity. For Dewey, repetitions of activities do not lead to a habit but are the result of a habit (Dewey, 1938/1986, p. 39). In fact, each time an act is repeated, it will be slightly different from other performances of this action since the context is always a little bit different. For a teacher doing professional development, the change in habit might be looking for new sources of lesson plans, thinking about the interactions of students and teachers in new ways, viewing collaboration with other teachers as welcome, looking for new ways to engage students. In short, change in habit might be major or slight, physical and cognitive to varying degrees, and slight or pronounced to observers.

Pedagogies of Poverty

Pedagogy of poverty is a descriptor of problems in sub-standard education as described initially by Martin Haberman (1991). This practice involves teaching children with authoritarian techniques whereby meaning is made by teachers and conveyed to students who are supposed to absorb it without question. As Songer (2002) observed, this type of pedagogy is contrary to inquiry pedagogies where students are given ownership of their learning in varying degrees. This will be important in one case study where it blocked the teacher's use of inquiry pedagogies. Although pedagogies of poverty are attributed to urban settings they are just as prevalent in rural or sub-urban settings. I see them as a class based issue rather than an urban issue. When middle class teachers teach working class or poor children they often teach with a sense of needing to keep control over minimally prepared children who come from inferior settings. Rather than enhancing the skills of these children, these techniques inhibit these student's desires to participate in the educational process. Since these students have much lived experience and the ability to engage in inquiry as described by Dewey, pedagogies of poverty are a demeaning and numbing experience rather than an enlightening one. Haberman (1991) sees these pedagogies as requiring wide scale reforms involving entire schools and even school systems in order to eradicate them.

METHODOLOGY

This chapter presents two intensive cases of teachers involved with the ILF. I investigated via qualitative and ethnographic observations the teachers "in" the ILF, and in their classrooms. I interviewed the teachers and their students, and observed the teachers interacting in the life of their schools. The cases were not selected in any way but are rather the opportunistic cases of two teachers who were willing to have me study them. However they showed me two very different ways that teachers could transact with an online professional development environment and thus represent an interesting story of varying needs, reactions, and utilization of the ILF.

Case Studies

These two case studies are based on an extended period of participant observation, interviews with the teachers, and interviews with the students. Through these observations and interviews I traced networks of how the teachers functioned within and without the ILF, where they interacted with the ILF, and how the ILF seemed to affect their classroom practice. These networks extended far beyond the ILF since the practice of schoolteachers does not stop at the classroom door (Nespor, 1997). I interviewed students of these teachers to find out what they thought they were learning and how they viewed inquiry pedagogy. I sat in many classes and taught or assisted with some classes and field trips. I did not try to be a fly on the wall but instead stayed in the site long enough that both students and teachers looked upon me as part of the class. I ate many lunches with groups of teachers where they seemed to talk very freely about their feelings, successes, and failures. I liberally took field notes and recorded interviews, which were then transcribed verbatim. I also had all online writings of these teachers in searchable text files.

I started out in each case study trying to understand the teacher and their relationship to the ILF (Stake, 2000). This was a daunting job since I could not limit my observations to the classroom or even to the school. I did not follow the teacher home but did listen to many stories about how their home life was entwined with their school life. In one case a spouse was very central to the story of the case. It was not until I finished both case studies that I realized that they were as important in their differences as in their similarities. Neither one represents a typical teacher in the ILF since I would not know how to define such a teacher. Together they give a wide range of practice and involvement that present some important lessons for others who are packaging professional development in an online space. I collected artifacts of student work and teacher's lessons plans.

Ethnography

These cases involve ethnographic methodology as well as case study methodology (Hammersley & Atkinson, 1883). I attempted via participant observation to get an insider's view of the teacher's practice and particularly how it related to the ILF. Case studies may involve ethnography but they do not always involve ethnography. The difference between the two is on the focus. An ethnographic case study focuses on a case and follows the case, whether it is a teachers or a school or a school system with ethnographic methodology.

Qualitative Analysis

It was both a curse and a blessing to be able to collect all this data. The qualitative analysis of such reams of interviews, field notes, and online discourse is daunting. I used both grounded analysis (Strauss & Corbin, 1990) and top down analysis initially. This involved looking for both pre-determined themes such as community, inquiry, computer use, trust, time issues, and also allowing themes to develop from the "ground"

up. Examples of themes that bubbled up were resistance need to maintain authority, care of students, backlash from students preparing for college exams, students enjoyment of inquiry. There was not much overlap in themes between the two cases but there were some such as family stresses, desire to support students, peers lack of understanding of inquiry.

TWO CASES: TWO WAYS OF DOING PROFESSIONAL PRACTICE

This next section introduces you to the two teachers that drove this study. When at all possible I let them speak in their own voices. A brief summary of the cases appears in table 1 and each case is also illustrated with a diagram indicating the far-reaching way the teacher's professional development activities transacted with many other aspects of their lives.

Introducing Ben[4]

Ben was a member of our participant advisory board (PAB) from the very beginning. I don't know how he initially hooked up with the ILF but I do know that he hoped to attend Indiana University as a PhD student in science education in the future. He was using inquiry in his classrooms before I met him and felt isolated from his colleagues who viewed inquiry as easy and not necessarily better than their more traditional lecturing methods of teaching science. Ben said "I feel very isolated in my school and I need feedback about my lessons." 7/20/00. Ben viewed the ILF as a means of gaining support for inquiry and also as a means of providing himself with more nuanced ways of teaching with inquiry. He stated after launching one of his two online classrooms and eliciting comments from other ILF members:

Thanks to everyone who posted comments. I really have gained more (in terms of professional

Table 1. Comparison of cases

	Helen	Ben
Years teaching	35	8
Education	Masters – elementary ed.	Master of Science - hydrogeology
Age	58	mid-30's
Family	Married to an 8th grade science teacher, One grandchild, one son at home, frequently talking about grandchild or complaining about son	Married to an elementary teacher, Two young children, rarely talks about kids
Comfort with technology	"not a computer person"	Likes computers. Always trying to defy school's fire wall to get more services
Involvement with the ILF	Participant in extensive school based workshop, 2 posts to ILF during this workshop-outsider	Member of PAB, made two videos, 51 posts, posted to pre-service class on request insider
# posts	2 – required by workshop	51 – many but not all relating to videos
Type of school	Inner city, lots of poverty, predominantly white, some African-American, lots of turn-over in school year. Several kids leave every year because family moves and some kicked our for behavior problems	Rural -Mixed SEC, some kids children of college faculty others rural poor, entirely white Very stable – most kids have lived in this rural county all their lives
Subjects taught	6th grade math and science	HS chem., physics, environmental science
Leadership in school	Head of 6th grade team Most experienced 6th grade teacher, administers title 1 affairs for 6th grade	Head of science department
Relationship with other teachers	Very close to other teachers in 6th grade team. Does science labs for other 6th grade science/math class Dresses as wizard when she does science labs. Gets most of these science lab ideas form her husband	Doesn't have very high opinion of fellow teachers
Attitude toward science	Science is magic	Science is rational
Attitude toward math	Math is to be discovered	Math is tool for science
Identity as teacher	Very secure as a math teacher but very insecure as a science teacher (discomfort enhanced by recent 6th grade curricular change from life science to physical science and life science), relies heavily on husband	Very secure as a science teacher, somewhat disdainful of other teachers who are not "scientists"
Comfort in school	Lots of peer support and good relationship with principal	Little support in doing inquiry, doesn't think anyone else in his school is like him.
Teaching style	Mainly didactic and directed at entire class, interspersed with attention getting food activities and some small group projects with manipuables Lots of math manipuables Science labs confusing and confused	Very dedicated to inquiry – sometimes does entire unit on inquiry Lots of fields trips, lab activities, many class activities require students to be self directed, lots of small group work
Teaching constraints	ISTEP (Indiana school exams) – constantly mentioned by teacher as motivation for learning new skills	Kids desire to be prepared for college, SATs
Relationship with kids	Motherly – gives them candy for good performance, Very close control of class Teaches after school math class	Interested but detached, down to business, models being a scientist, kids come to him for help in other science classes

continued on following page

Table 1. continued

	Helen	Ben
Views on religion	Active participant in church – many out of school companions from church	Feels need to work with religious issues in school district since teaching a lot about evolution which is controversial in parts of Indiana
Aspirations as teacher	Will retire if teaching stops being fun	Hopes to get PhD at some point
Desires for kids	Get them though middle and high school – prepare them for 7th grade	Wants then to become scientists or at least informed consumers Prepare them for college
Attitude of students	Many think she is the first good math teacher they have ever had and most enjoy the hands on science activities	Highly respected, has inspired some students to study science in college
My effect on teacher	Kids say it is more fun when I am there – I suspect she plans her most student centered lessons for the days I visit	I seem to have no effect on his class or teaching since much of the time kids are working on their own anyway.
My effect (as researcher) on kids	Kids seek me out and want to work with me in small groups or just engage me in conversation. They are very interested in the axolotls I brought to class	Some kids are shy about my eaves dropping on their small group discussions. I respect their reluctance to be observed. It is hard for me to engage them in conversation. They are polite but not forthcoming when I talk to them
Interest in collaborative writing	none	avid
Science competency	Very poor – she seems to have no understanding of what she is teaching in any deep sense	Excellent

development) *by reading your comments than all the administrative evaluations I have had over the past five years. No offense to my administrators:) 7/20/00*

Ben has a sophisticated understanding of inquiry garnered from his own extensive experience and tells me:

All levels benefit. I have taught inquiry in college classes, for adults, high schoolers, and in day care. Younger kids seem to be more comfortable with inquiry learning. They are not scared to ask questions. I would suggest that inquiry learning must be combined with lecture and teacher directed activities. I have had the greatest success when I use inquiry techniques at the end of a unit (maybe one day out of eight will be pure students directed inquiry). The students need to know some basic lab techniques, equations, etc. before they can

investigate on their own. I think this addresses your very legitimate concern about background knowledge. 9/27/01

However Ben also feels pushed by issues outside of the classroom to moderate his use of inquiry:

I can't tell you how many students in my advanced chemistry class who tell me: 'Hey, it's neat that you're letting us solve problems on our own and create them, but you know what? My brother's telling me about Purdue's pharmacy school and if we don't know about [...] we're going to be at a huge disadvantage. 2/01

Issues within his classroom also impede his use of inquiry:

I still encounter a large group of students who say, "You're not teaching us. You never tell us when we are doing something wrong. 7/20/00

However he clearly gets encouragement from his students:

Before that, it was just sort of not applied to real world. So it didn't really mean as much to me, but when you, when I got a chance to apply it to things I could actually see, it sort of had greater weight, guess, seemed more important. Art 8/31/01

Another student who is taking Ben's environmental science class, which is a science elective talks about enjoying options in this class:

It was a breeze. It really was because I got to choose the class I'm taking, and so I cared about it a bit at least, and he didn't just throw stuff at us, like "This is what you have to learn! This is what is required!" You know, we learned what we wanted to learn basically, and so, you know, I wanted to do the work, and I did the work, and

I did it happily, and I wanted to learn it, and so I made sure I learned it. Karen 8/31/01

Ben was a frequent poster to the discussion forums within the ILF and took on a mentoring roll with pre-service teachers who frequently post questions to his classroom forums. I would say that he was as about involved with the ILF as any teacher could be but certainly not the only teacher that was involved with ILF activities. Ben claimed that the most valuable part of his participation was making videos of his classroom inquiry activities. In doing so he was required to write reflections on the segments of the videos and to think hard about what he was teaching and why he was teaching as he did. This is an example of what we called inquiry into one's practice.

Can I say that participation in the ILF changed Ben's teaching practice? This is hard to answer. I can certainly say that the ILF helped Ben feel more comfortable and rewarded for doing inquiry in his science classes. He became friends with other teachers struggling with many of the same issues as he did and then felt much less isolated in

Figure 4. Ben transacting with the ILF

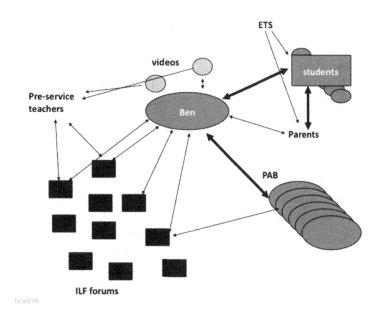

his rural school. He certainly enjoyed the ILF and seemed to be pushing his knowledge of inquiry in the science classroom and trying some new ways of teaching. However he viewed himself as a scientist and would probably have found other ways of "doing science" through inquiry with his students whether supported or not supported by the ILF (cf. Figure 4).

Introducing Helen

Helen is an older teacher who is starting to think about retirement. She got involved with the ILF because her school, an urban, largely white, middle school, requested an extensive multi-session workshop from the ILF in which she was required to participate. The school was targeted by the state for its poor scores in standardized tests and thus was given more resources for professional development. Helen participated in the e-ILF graciously even though she found computer technology taxing. She even volunteered to let me come into her classroom for extensive observations.

Helen is motherly and concerned for her students who are mainly below the poverty level and often living in unstable homes disrupted by absentee parents for reasons of parental criminal activity and/or drug abuse. Helen watches over the health and well being of her students as well as their academic progress. She freely offers sweatshirts to cold students and food to hungry ones. She teaches both math and science to two cohorts of sixth graders and teaches pre-algebra to a third group.

I played a fairly active role in her classroom, bringing in axolotls, aquatic salamanders, for her science classes and modeling guided inquiry for her and her students. Helen never truly accepted that her students, mainly lower socio-economic class could do inquiry:

I think Inquiry, the way I saw it being used with the presentations we had was probably a more in-depth project type based lesson. More like the Annenberg

Foundation does where it will consume a whole class period or several class periods. Because our children have a short attention span and a recall that's not going to necessarily carry them day-to-day. I try to keep the lessons a one day, isolated inquiry and then eventually we'll gain some length and some depth on a project but so far I find that my kids do better on a day-by-day lesson rather than a long term lesson. Their memory is short. Their interest is short and because of that I have adjusted for them not really for what I would like to be doing. 11/13/01

Her participation in the e-ILF never went beyond what was required of her in her school based professional development workshops. She did not enjoy computers and had a rich social and professional life with her school based peers that made the online forums seem superfluous and time consuming to her.

Despite her dislike of the e-ILF, the ILF based workshops did seem to affect her:

Inquiry -based learning has made me think more about using less lecture style teaching and at times less modeling in my classroom. Although both are appropriate teaching tools we need to be open to new methods of doing the same job. I like the process-yet I will have to try it and become accustomed to using it. 1/25/01

Helen's scant knowledge of science made it difficult for her to devise her own inquiry lessons. Instead she relied heavily on me and on her husband for activities that while often hands-on and participatory were never quite inquiry since she had a hard time giving up authority to her students. In general she felt her students were incapable of inquiry despite demonstrations by me to the contrary.

Helen enjoyed teaching math more than science and was able to understand how to apply inquiry for her student's math needs:

Figure 5. Helen transacting with the ILF

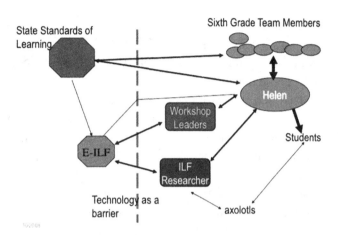

I think I use inquiry learning in possibly a little different format then they taught us, although what I am trying to do with my children, hopefully is that I am trying to get them to think more about what they're doing rather than just necessarily finding an isolated fact in a book. And to draw from what I present to them some conclusions of their own, in other words like in math I'll present them some information but I don't always present them with the algorithm I am hoping that they'll develop the algorithm. 11/13/01.

Helen's students thought that it was fun when I came to class and easily recognized what they disliked about their more usual science lessons:

Interviewer: What don't you like about science?

Interviewee: Nothing. Well when we have chapters of things like they go off on a couple of different things and it has a long chapter and then you take a test and you've got to remember a whole bunch and that's always confusing.

Helen's knowledge of science was not secure. She gave students misinformation such as confus-

ing meiosis and mitosis and easily got rattled by student's questions when class was unstructured. She relied on gee whiz demonstrations and very controlled lab projects, which did entertain her students. Despite her discomfort with science she was the go to person in her team for hands on science. She occasionally traded classes with a colleague so that she could don her wizard hat and coat and do amazing things with pickle based batteries and rubberized eggs. As Ben used the metaphor of "being a scientist", Helen used the metaphor of "doing magic". Figure 5 show my interpretation of Helen' transactions with ILF which were rather limited. I observed that she had plenty of in school support for her teaching practice and had little time or energy for ILF online or offline support.

APPLYING COMMUNITIES OF PRACTICE TO THESE CASES

Ben felt that the ILF and the e-ILF filled a need in his teaching. He was already engaged in the practice of inquiry pedagogy before we came along. That did not mean that his practice was stress free and encouraged. To the contrary he felt that his peers regarded inquiry as the easy way out in teaching science. Her also felt that his principal and other supervisors did not know enough about inquiry to aid his practice. His struggle was not with "if" to use inquiry but "how" to use it. He also tried out different ways of using inquiry in regard to how unstructured he could make it and still cover the basics of chemistry and physics for his college bound students. He was very willing to use inquiry with his environmental studies course since this was not a prerequisite to college courses nor did it cover material on standardized exams. Ben was already engaged with the practice of inquiry but was searching for a community to support it. Ben seemed aloof with the teachers in his school despite being the science coordinator. Since he was a part of the teacher advisory board for the ILF he had many opportunities to meet the other members of this board. Soon he was going fishing with another member, trading lesson plans and doing many of the tasks that we set out to encourage with the ILF. I think that he would have eventually found a COP for inquiry, the ILF made it a little easier for him to do so.

Helen found that technology was a roadblock to her using the ILF. She had computers in her classroom that were adequate for this purpose but she rarely if ever used them except to run drill type software for her students to catch up on math skills. She also had a computer at home but rarely used that since by her admission her home life was very full of church and family activities. Her husband, a science teacher in another urban middle school in a much wealthier area of town was the designated user of the home computer.

Helen's school was organized in teams of teachers and the two sixth grade teams met together daily for a 45-minute planning period. These teachers socialized outside of school, going to the same churches and even taking vacations together. I believe that this very close school community competed with the ILF for Helen's attention and she was clearly more attracted to the local one. Part of this attraction was a long history of contact, proximity, and lack of the need to use a computer for communication.

APPLYING DEWYAN THEORY OF INQUIRY TO THESE CASES

In Deweyan terms both Ben and Helen are placed in states of disequilibrium over and over as they seek new ways of teaching their students or when their satisfaction with their teaching is disrupted by criticisms from parents, students, or scores on standardized tests. Helen's disequilibrium and questions about her teaching practice in science seem to be dealt with in her 6th grade team and from conversations with her husband. In the case of teaching math Helen is much more open to new methods and indeed uses many manipulative math tools that help her students comprehend math, some for the first time in their school careers. Yet the computer is out of her comfort zone and so the ILF is not likely to get her attention since it is based around the e-ILF

Ben finds his reestablishment of equilibrium away from his school. He seems to avoid his school based peers for fear they will mock his teaching methods. The ILF provides solutions, affirmation, and support that he cannot get at school. Surprising to me I never hear Ben talk about his family despite having two small children and a wife who also teaches in the local school system. However issues such as students and parents who are worried about their high achieving students scores on standardized test such as the SAT's that are administered by the College Board do interfere with Ben's desire to use inquiry pedagogies more frequently in his classes. He is afraid that his good intentions will hurt the performance of his students. There is no indication that this is the case, something that Ben probably knows, but he still has conflicts when his students and their parents voice their complaints about his teaching.

APPLYING PEDAGOGY OF POVERTY TO THESE CASES

Helen seems to be a proponent of the Pedaogy of Poverty. She does indeed teach poor students and views her job to control them and get them ready for standardized testing. She does this in a gentle manner and is very motherly to her children who are in turn quite fond of her. However she has not intention of giving any control to her students and views them as needy and not ready for the more advanced science her husband does with his students. It is hard for me to write this, as it is a negative indictment of Helen. However this kind of teaching is said to prepare students to be passive workers in dead end jobs to which they may be forever chained by lack of higher education. In fact when I questioned her students about what they hoped to do when they grew up there was absolutely no mention of anything requiring education beyond high school with the exception of one child who wanted to be a doctor. Nearly all the girls in Helen's class aspired to be dancers or singers and most of the boys aspired to be professional athletes.

FUTURE TRENDS

Dislike of computers will come to a natural end as children who have used computers all their lives grow to become teachers. This has not yet happened although pre-service teachers are certainly more adept at computing than many in-service teachers. In the mean time there are many in-service teachers who could benefit from online professional development. As digital devices evolve I expect there to be more and more telephone sized devices that will be able to deliver professional development. I also expect that the current fascination of U.S. college students with social networking tools such as "Facebook", Myspace", and "Twitter" will give rise to teachers who have no problem with online trust issues, or COPs for professional development. In fact I expect female teachers will demand them in order to more easily combine school and family responsibilities.

If the ILF were still being actively supported it would be interesting to see if a forum on conflicts between inquiry pedagogies and the pedagogies of poverty would help teachers be more positive about fostering ownership of education for the children of poverty. Such an endeavor might be more successful if it engaged an entire school or multi-school system.

CONCLUSION

Observing teachers engaged in professional development with the aid of an online teaching space such as the ILF cannot stop at the ends of the electronic spaces if one wants to get a view of their possibly changing practice. The ILF transacts with its overlapping internal and external cultures and the teachers transact with the ILF, both electronic and co-present, as they also transact with many other aspects of their teaching practice. Thus the ILF comes out very changed from its designer's initial goal and plans. Small private groups replaced large open groups in discussion of teaching practice. Practice emerges that is much more directed than the designers originally planned for.

In terms of the ILF as a community of Practice, there is evidence that it fosters initiation into a practice of inquiry pedagogy and also reflection into one's practice for some of its members. At the same time there is resistance to the sanctioned practice that is fostered by other communities of practice such as Helen's reliance upon her school based peers, one that unfortunately fosters pedagogies of poverty. There is also resistance from Ben's students who want high SAT scores so they can attend highly regarded colleges. Acknowledging these conflicts is important in any type of professional development

In summary I give a detailed view of the Inquiry Learning Forum within the practice of two unique teachers and their students. The focus is not on the teachers or on the ILF but rather on the complex transactions that are created when a teacher engages with an online community of practice. While we can never know if these teachers are "typical" we do learn lessons that merit exploration in other online communities of practice built for teacher professional development.

REFERENCES

American Association for the Advancement of Science. (1993*). Benchmarks for Science Literacy*. New York: Oxford University Press.

Barab, S., MaKinster, J. G., Moore, J., Cunningham, D., & the ILF Design Team. (2001). Designing and building an online community: The struggle to support sociability in the Inquiry Learning Forum. *Educational Technology Research and Development*, *49*(4), 71–96. doi:10.1007/BF02504948

Barab, S. MaKinster, J., & Scheckler, R. (2004). Designing System Dualities: Building Online Community. In S. Barab, R. Kling & J. Gray (Eds.), *Designing virtual communities in the service of learning*. Cambridge, UK: Cambridge University Press.

Dewey, J. (1938). *Experience and education*. New York: Collier Books.

Dewey, J. (1938/1986). *Logic: The theory of inquiry. John Dewey: The later works 1925-1953, 12*, 1-506 J. A. Boydston. Carbondale, Southern Illinois University Press.

Haberman, M. (1991). The pedagogy of poverty versus good teaching. *Phi Delta Kappan, 73*(4), 290–294.

Hammersley, M., & Atkinson, P. (1983). Ethnography: Principles in practice (second ed.). London: Routledge.

Herring, S., Martinson, A., & Scheckler, R. (2002). Designing for community: The effects of gender representation in videos on a web site. *Proceedings of the Thirty-Fifth Hawaii International Conference on System Sciences*. Los Alamitos: IEEE Computer Society Press.

Latour, B. (1987). *Science in action*. Cambridge, MA: Harvard University Press.

Lave, J., & Wenger, E. (1991). *Situated learning: Legitimate peripheral participation*. Cambridge: Cambridge University Press.

Nespor, J. (1997). *Tangled up in school: Politics, space, bodies, and signs in the educational process*. Mahwah, NJ: Lawrence Erlbaum Associates.

Preece, J., & Maloney-Krichmar, D. (2005). Online communities: Design, theory, and practice. *Journal of Computer-Mediated Communication, 10*(4).

Scheckler, R. K., & Barab, S. (2009). Designing for inquiry as a social practice. In J. K. Falk & B. Drayton (Eds.), *Creating and Sustaining Online Professional Learning Communities*. New York: Teachers College Press.

Songer, N. B., Lee, H.-S., & Kam, R. (2002). Technology-rich inquiry science in urban classrooms: What are the barriers to inquiry pedagogy? *Journal of Research in Science Teaching, 39*(2), 128–150. doi:10.1002/tea.10013

Stake, R. E. (2000) Case studies. In N. K. Denzin (Ed.), *Handbook of qualitative research* (2nd ed.). London: Sage Publications.

Strauss, A., & Corbin, J. (1990). *Basics of qualitative research: Grounded theory procedures and techniques*. London: Sage Publications.

U.S. Department of Education. (1999). *TIMSS 1999 Results.* Retrieved 2/14/2009, from http://nces.ed.gov/timss/

Waks, L. J. (1999). The Means-Ends Continuum and the Reconciliation of Science and Art in the Later Works of John Dewey. *Transactions of the Charles S. Peirce Society, XXXV*(3), 595–611.

Wenger, E. (1998). *Communities of practice: Leaning, meaning, and identity.* Cambridge, UK: Cambridge University Press.

Wenger, E. (n.d). *Communities of practice.* Retrieved 2/14/2009, from http://www.ewenger.com/theory/

Wenger, E., McDermott, R., & Snyder, W. M. (2002). *Cultivating communities of practice: a guide to managing knowledge.* Boston: Harvard Business School Press.

ENDNOTES

[1] This paper is based upon work supported by the National Science Foundation under Grant # 9980081.

[2] Although the ILF began as a project to serve Indiana teachers, it was later expanded include teachers to include teachers in all parts of the United States.

[3] Standards of learning refer to state and federal standards for teaching in the United States. These include detailed lists of what will be taught in different subjects at the various grades and thus what will be tested for on standardized state level exams. These have gotten greater attention since "The No Child Left Behind" legislation was passed during the George W. Bush presidency.

[4] Names of teachers are fictitious

Chapter 4
Changing the Metaphor
The Potential of Online Communities in Teacher Professional Development

Margaret Lloyd
Queensland University of Technology, Australia

Jennifer Duncan-Howell
Queensland University of Technology, Australia

ABSTRACT

Belonging to an online community offers teachers the opportunity to exchange ideas, make connections with a wider peer group and form collaborative networks. The increasing popularity of teacher professional communities means that we need to understand how they work and determine the role they may play in teacher professional development. This chapter will map data from a doctoral study to a recently-developed model of professional development to offer a new perspective of how online communities can add to a teacher's personal and professional growth and, in so doing, add to the small number of studies in this field. This chapter will conclude with a call for a revision of the way we approach professional development in the 21st Century and suggest that old models and metaphors are hindering the adoption of more effective means of professional development for teachers.

INTRODUCTION

Online communities provide continuous and self-generating professional development for teachers through flexible, authentic and personalised opportunities for learning. Teachers in many countries are looking to online communities for professional support, guidance and inspiration (Bond, 2004; Chen & Chen, 2002; Cornu, 2004; Matei, 2005) to supplement or replace more traditional forms of professional engagement. These communities – usually grouped around subject area disciplines – differ in their formality but display common characteristics of sharing and collaboration. The current popularity of online communities means that it has now become important to examine how they work and determine their role in facilitating teacher professional development. This chapter will offer a model of how online communities can add to a teacher's personal and professional growth and, in so doing, add to the small number of studies in this field (see, for example, Hawkes, 1999; Hunter,

DOI: 10.4018/978-1-60566-780-5.ch004

2002). This chapter will conclude by arguing for revising the way we approach professional development in the 21st Century and suggest that old models and metaphors are hindering the adoption of more effective means of professional development for teachers.

In order to achieve its aims, this chapter will draw its understandings from two previous studies. The first (Lloyd, Cochrane & Beames, 2005), commissioned by an Australian teacher professional association, suggested an original model of effective teacher professional development that mapped potential reflexive paths between practice and theory. The second is a doctoral study (Duncan-Howell, 2007) investigating the role of online communities in teacher professional development that studied three distinct communities for teachers. Selected data from the latter study will be applied to the model suggested in the former. The outcome will be to validate the model in the context of online communities and to provide new insights into how online communities can support teacher professional development. It will also support the concluding argument of the chapter that a new metaphor is needed to show how new tools require a rethinking of professional development strategies particularly in how individual teachers take ownership of their own learning.

The chapter will develop its argument through four sections. It will begin by presenting the background to the discussion, that is, (a) a definition of online communities, and (b) an explanation of the professional development model (Lloyd & Cochrane, 2006; Lloyd et al., 2005) to be used as the framework for analysis. The second section of the chapter will deconstruct the model and use selected data from teacher focus groups, community transcripts (Duncan-Howell, 2007) and extant literature to substantiate the claim that participation in online communities can provide effective professional development opportunities for teachers. The third section will outline future trends in online collaborations for teachers while the fourth (and final) section will conclude the

chapter by suggesting a new metaphor for teacher professional development.

BACKGROUND

This section is intended to provide background to the discrete areas under review in this chapter. These, as previously noted, are (a) online communities, and (b) the professional development model to be used to interpret selected data.

Online Communities

Communities, or groups of people, are bound together through shared connections that transform individuals from a solitary status to membership of an identifiable group. A community is a phenomenon that is driven rather than something that just happens (Lechner, 1998). While some understandings of an online community can be taken from physical or traditional communities, it is critical to note that they are significantly different in structure and composition and frequently evidence greater diversity in membership than those bounded by location. The obvious and most critical difference is the absence of physical presence in online communities.

In this chapter, online communities for teachers are understood to be open and voluntary gatherings of individuals concerned with the general practice of teaching or specialist disciplines or areas of interest. A community of teachers is, by definition, a community of practice (after Lave & Wenger, 1991). While online communities make use of differing means of synchronous and asynchronous online communication, those considered in this chapter made exclusive use of email which is an asynchronous medium.

What online teacher communities have in common, irrespective of subject affiliation or interest and communication medium, is that individuals communicate in a shared social virtual space and share common goals. The instance of physical meeting or other contact between community members is rare. The community follows a set of unwritten collective rules, rituals and behaviours (Haythornthwaite, 2002). It acts as a sounding board for ideas and provides the space to share dilemmas or success. It is, critically, a space to clarify understandings about issues relating to teaching and learning. The conversations which take place in these communities are wide ranging – they can be as routine as locating a resource or as complex as discussing educational reforms or freedom. Over time, a community develops a shared history and individuals develop a sense of belonging through their membership. This sense of belonging is created by the communicative acts the community engages in and has been referred to as a "narrative of collaboration" (Strehle, Whatley, Kurz, & Hausfather, 2001), derived from shared perspectives or history of the group. Differing hierarchies of novice and expert are forged and, in most cases, a genuine feeling of warmth and scaffolding is generated. Individuals can "drop" in and out of specific conversations or even community membership without explanation. They can be active or passive – "lurking" until a topic of interest or expertise is raised.

Online communities of practice also offer teachers a forum to discuss change and gather evidence, mainly anecdotal, of how successful a change was in a classroom. Participants may then decide, based on discussions in chat rooms (Galland, 2002) and through other online media, whether to try the suggested strategies or approaches for themselves. This is in direct contrast to the noted unwillingness of teachers to use research or implement suggestions by outside experts (Guskey, 1985; 1986; 2002; Richardson, 1992; Richardson & Placier, 2001). Such reported resistance to outsiders supports the suggestion that change is an internal process for teachers (Richardson, 1990) and that the most influential catalyst for change is personal motivation or perceived need (Borko & Putnam, 1995; Richardson, 1990). The

resistance to outside experts – and also to advice from employing authorities - is removed in online communities of practice as change is initiated and supported by trusted peers.

The key process in online communities is collaboration. Collaboration has been widely identified as an important activity in encouraging teacher learning (Richardson, 1990; Richardson, 1992; Richardson & Placier, 2001). Boyle, While and Boyle (2004) proposed that collaborative networks are particularly effective when they are sustained over a long period of time allowing teachers to learn and reflect on their teaching practices. Networking – in all forms - offers teachers the critical opportunity to be exposed to new ideas and practices (Huberman, 2001; Strehle et al., 2001). The greater the number of ideas being offered (after Scardamalia's (2002) description of the role of idea diversity in knowledge building), then the potentially richer the outcome becomes.

The following section brings the discussion in this chapter to teacher professional development. It will introduce the model suggested in a study by Lloyd et al. (2005) which will be used as the basis for analysis in this chapter.

Professional Development Model

Professional development for teachers has generally been offered as face-to-face short courses or workshops conducted after school or during school holidays. Perhaps because these instances "do not reflect the characteristics and approaches of effective professional development suggested by research" (Schlager, Fusco, & Schank, 2002, p. 129), they have often failed to produce positive or ongoing results. They have been "widely criticised as being ineffective in providing teachers with sufficient time, activities, and content necessary for increasing teachers' knowledge and fostering meaningful changes" (Garet, Porter, Desimone, Birman, & Yoon, 2001, p. 920). Further to this, it has been shown that "teachers are discerning about the quality of [professional development] offerings

Figure 1. Iterative connection between practice and theory

and … are impatient with those that are of poor quality and waste valuable time" (Department of Education, Science and Technology (DEST), 2004, p. 164). It is clearly time for a re-evaluation of teacher professional development.

At its simplest, teacher professional development is concerned with practice and theory. Rather than being exclusive entities, these are interconnected and intertwined. One affects the other in persistent, iterative and subliminal ways (see the simple practice-theory model in Figure 1) as they meld into the personal praxis described as a "dialectical union of reflection and action" (Hoffman-Kipp, Artiles, & Lopez-Torres, 2003, p. 248).

While Guskey (1986) inconclusively wrestled with the fundamental question of whether practice followed belief or belief followed practice, it seems more likely that they are simultaneously developed in subtler and more empathetic ways. An understanding of the importance of the connection between practice and theory can be drawn from the literature on self-efficacy and the role of beliefs in influencing teaching practice (see, for example, Albion & Ertmer, 2002; Bandura, 1997; Dwyer, Ringstaff, & Sandholtz, 1990).

Practice provides a lens for examining theory in context while theory provides an explanation and consolidation of what is observed in practice. The connection between practice and theory suggested in Figure 1 underlies Nespor's (1987) view that a change in teachers' practice is coupled with a gradual "replacement" of beliefs. This is an

ongoing and mostly subconscious activity and, as noted, the product of simultaneous rather than sequential processes.

The discussion in this chapter is premised on the belief that online communities can support individual development of both the practice and theory of teaching and thus encourage positive and self-generating professional development for teachers. Participation in online communities sits well with Windschitl's (2002) description of transformative professional development being built by:

(a) interrogating one's own practice and the practices of others;
(b) making assumptions explicit; and,
(c) making classrooms sites for inquiry.

As previously noted, the model to be adopted in this chapter emerged from an investigation by a teacher professional association into the characteristics of effective professional development for teachers (Lloyd et al., 2005). The specific context was professional development in the use of information and communication technologies in the classroom.

The model presented as Figure 2 appears to be complex but, in reality, is an extension of the simpler practice-theory model shown in Figure 1. It positions four elements (time, context, personal growth and community) in the space between practice and theory. These discrete elements will be discussed in greater detail in the following sections of this chapter (see also Lloyd & Cochrane, 2006). Figure 2 can be read from left to right, that is, from practice to theory, or from right to left, that is, from theory to practice. Either directional path moves through *community* – an element that emerged as the central component in literature reviews of teacher professional development and in the research associated with the initial development of the model.

The model can be conceptually divided into two halves or hemispheres. The practice hemisphere

Figure 2. Elements of effective teacher professional development (Lloyd et al., 2005)

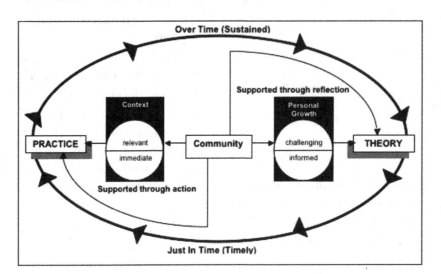

contains the context element that teachers in the Lloyd et al. (2005) study described in terms of immediacy and relevance. Teacher learning is here supported through action. The theory hemisphere contains the element of personal growth which teachers identified through their demand for professional development to be both informed and challenging. Teacher learning is here supported through reflection. In each instance, the consolidation of learning comes through and from within a community of peers. Ideas are challenged and defended or processes are mentored by others. Learning rarely happens in isolation or without feedback from peers.

The element of time is similarly split into two forms. The first is the idea of professional development being sustained or "over time." This is of particular importance in an individual's shift from practice to theory and in developing professional practice informed by theory. The second is the concept of timeliness or "just in time" which has clear ramifications of the path between theory and practice. For example, teachers who encounter a particular situation, perhaps a new student with a specific learning disability, need authoritative advice to inform their daily practice without delay. A common criticism of professional development

for teachers is that it is "just in case" rather than "just in time."

The model is intended to be dynamic rather than static and places the teacher in the role of a lifelong learner. Its complexity comes from the repetition and interweaving of simple elements and in this, it can be likened to the formation of a Celtic knot design (Lloyd & Cochrane, 2006). The centrality of community remains constant although the beliefs and values of the community itself may change and contexts may differ between individual instances.

This model differs radically in form and intention from existing developmental schemas which describe teachers' adoption and curricular integration of ICT (see, for example, ACOT 1996/2006; Trinidad, Newhouse & Clarkson, 2004). Each extant schema is based on progression from an embryonic stage (which Mevarech (1997) referred to as "survival" and others called "awareness" (Hall & Hord, 1987; Russell, 1995)) to a final stage always typified by innovation, reinvention or creative application. These schemas show an increasing transparency and a shift towards using technology in ways to support broader pedagogical goals. It also differs from the metaphor of a journey which is frequently adopted to describe this development and, in likening ICT adoption to a "journey of transformation," King (2001) described the first step as one characterised by fear, uncertainty, disorientation and self-examination. Another metaphor adopted is that of human growth, with Crystal (2001) describing teachers at the introductory level as "neonatal." Through its analogy to infancy, this descriptor carries an implicit determinism for growth and perhaps the slur of immature or ill-formed development. The differences inherent in the model adopted in this discussion will be extended in the conclusion to this chapter.

In the following section, selected data drawn from a study into three online communities for teachers (Duncan-Howell, 2007) will be analysed using the model. The selected communities are all related to teaching with the largest being an international community based in the UK, the next being a national community based in Australia, and the last (and smallest) based in an Australian state. The intention of this analysis is twofold. The first being to validate the model in the context of online communities while the second is to add to understandings of the role of online communities in providing professional development for teachers.

ONLINE COMMUNITIES AS EFFECTIVE PROFESSIONAL DEVELOPMENT

As noted, the model has four key elements: context, personal growth, time and community. Also, as noted, this chapter will use these elements as the means to interpret, or rather re-interpret, the data from a doctoral study that focussed on the role of online communities in teacher professional development (Duncan-Howell, 2007). The specific data sources to be used are an open survey, transcripts of three community archives for one calendar month (comprising of 2827 messages), and discussion board contributions made by an invited focus group.

This section will begin by considering the overall experience of participation in online communities, that is, in terms of the entities of theory and practice which define and delimit the adopted model, before moving into specific detail of the elements. The subjects in the Duncan-Howell (2007) study were members of online communities for teachers who had voluntarily completed the online survey and/or had been specifically invited to join the focus group discussions. This is not seen as a limitation of the conclusions drawn in this chapter. Rather, it is seen as an indication of the genuine potential for professional development of participation in online communities.

Participation in Online Communities

The overall impact of online communities on teaching and learning can be seen in the following statements from the teacher focus groups (Duncan-Howell, 2007). The positivity of the selected representative statements (numbered for later reference in this chapter) is clear as is the conscious understanding of the value of the communities to an individual's professional development.

- *Without a doubt, my classroom practice is informed by participation in online communities.* (Statement 1)
- *Some of my best ideas for the classroom have been spawned from ideas that I never would have come across in the "real world."* (Statement 2)
- *Boy, have I EVER learned a lot and has it changed my teaching! I can't imagine standing in front of a class of students being the font of all knowledge. I started teaching 45 years ago, when that is what you were taught to do.* (Statement 3)
- *Yes ... [I have learnt many new things] – and not only in the areas where I've asked for help. Just following threads makes you stop and think about things you hadn't*

thought of before – and some of these have seen me do a complete turnaround in what I thought was "right." (Statement 4)

While all four statements show evidence of personal praxis (Hoffman-Kipp et al., 2003), Statements 1 and 2 can be seen to belong more specifically to the practice hemisphere while the latter Statements (3, 4) relate to the hemisphere of theory (see Figures 1 and 2). Statement 1 is a straightforward declarative fact that provides a clear indication of the educative and contextual value of membership of an online community of teachers. Statement 2 can be seen as an enactment of the theoretical contentions raised earlier in this chapter relating to collaborative networks (Boyle et al., 2004) and idea diversity (Scardamalia, 2002). Statements 3 and 4 share the common theme of self-initiated change prompted by reflection and peer discussion that demonstrates Freire's (1972) notion of praxis as action and reflection where practice informs theory and theory "illuminates" practice. These statements (3 and 4) also enact the iterative shifting from theory to practice (as shown in Figure 1) and Nespor's (1987) notion of belief replacement. The change articulated in Statement 3 is one which is fundamental to teacher identity (see Albion & Ertmer, 2002) and the change in Statement 4 – "a complete turnaround" - is noteworthy because of its extent. These four statements collectively show the overall impact of online communities and their role in the professional development of teachers.

Further to this, the themes evident in the focus groups in the Duncan-Howell (2007) study showed a resonance with the key messages from the literature relating to the advantages of participation in or membership of online communities. These may be summarised as follows:

1. capacity for networking (Huberman, 2001) and professional conversation (Sorge & Russell, 2000)

2. relevance and immediacy (Richardson, 1992)

3. convenience in terms of time (Garet et al., 2001)

4. pooling of expertise (Sorge & Russell, 2000)

5. building collective knowledge (Boyle et al., 2004)

6. encouragement of active learning (Guskey, 2002

The message from the Duncan-Howell (2007) study was unequivocal. Not only were the entities of practice and theory being addressed through participation in online communities – the iterative transition between them was facilitated through identified means. That these means could be also noted in other studies acted as validation for the metacognitive processes being adopted by community members and informants to the study. The following subsections, which address the elements of context, personal growth, time and community in turn, will evidence similar levels of reflection and metacognition.

Context

One of the defining characteristics of any community is its shared context. Lave and Wegner (1991) first described communities of practice in terms of case studies of such clearly identifiable groups as Yucatan midwives, meat-cutters and Vai and Gola tailors. It is therefore not surprising that teachers similarly seek membership of a group that shares the same environment, challenges and joys of their unique workplace.

In the model being adopted in this chapter, context refers to the practice of teaching and learning which, as noted, is described in terms of *relevance* and *immediacy*. The criteria – determined through a comprehensive literature review and substantiated by data (Lloyd et al., 2005; Lloyd & Cochrane, 2006) - to satisfy the element of *context* are that professional development must:

- be relevant (authentic, local and real)
- be meaningful
- be practical
- meet immediate needs (direct impact)
- meet ongoing needs (sustained impact)

Focus group responses in the Duncan-Howell (2007) study indicated that participation in online communities clearly meets these criteria. This is evident in the following selected representative statements.

- *The whole point of the discussions you get here, compared with professional journals, is that it is practical and to the point.* (Statement 5)
- *It [being a member of an online community] is a worthwhile professional development activity because you are able to initiate topics which are of interest/concern to you when you most need help.* (Statement 6)

Statement 5 emphasises the practicality and conciseness of the advice received through an online community and implicitly accredits credibility to the source of the advice from the community. The sleight on professional journals – as being the diametric opposite of being "practical and to the point" – is of interest and highlights teachers' dislike of "experts" as previously noted in this discussion (see Guskey, 2002; Richardson & Placier, 2001). Rather than being the outcome of empirical educational research, "theory" for many teachers is more commonly a set of innate beliefs and understandings.

Statement 6 emphasises the need for authenticity and timeliness in professional development experiences. There is an indeterminate power in being able to direct one's own learning, an affordance enabled by online communities. The opposite of this, that is, a lack of control and self-direction, emerged as a major criticism of existing professional development experiences

in Lloyd et al.'s (2005) study.

The survey data in the Duncan-Howell (2007) study reinforced the importance of the element of context. An open question was asked as to what teachers were looking for in an online community and the responses were categorised under the general headings of professional requirements and emotional support.

Professional requirements dominated the bulk of the messages (n=1992, 70.46%). Within this category, the majority of messages were concerned with personal professional development needs (n=1173, 41.49%) which specifically related to: (i) learning from other teachers/peers (n=391, 13.83%); (ii) sharing professional knowledge (n=391, 13.83%); (iii) opportunities to develop professional practices (n=270, 9.55%); and (iv) professional discussions (n=121, 4.28%). The other professional requirement noted in the messages related to meeting classroom or student needs (n=819, 28.9%). This comprised of (i) access to expertise to solve classroom problems (n=391, 13.83%); (ii) access to subject-specific resources (n=228, 8.07%); (iii) new relevant content (n=151, 5.34%); and (iv) sharing lesson ideas (n=49, 1.73%).

Emotional support was an unexpected outcome in the survey findings but had previously been noted in the ACOT (Apple Classrooms of Tomorrow) longitudinal research (ACOT, 1996/2006) where it had been given parity with technical support in gaining competence and confidence in the use of information and communication technologies in the classroom. In the Duncan-Howell (2007) study, messages which displayed emotional support *(n*=835) comprised 29.54% of all messages classified. These comprised of (i) the ability to ask for help (n=101, 3.57%); (ii) a sense of belonging (n=121, 4.28%); (iii) collegial support and camaraderie (n=121, 4.28%); and (iv) the provision of "safety-net" if needed (n=492, 17.4%).

The following (Statement 7) is a comment from the focus group which evidences the need for emotional support and the way that one individual chose to test the willingness of others to provide this support.

- *Without doubt – online communities for me are valuable resources that put me in touch with people who know more about stuff than I do – I happily say I do not know how to do something and throw myself on the mercy of the list... – nothing ventured, nothing gained is my online motto.* (Statement 7)

The element of context is clearly important for teachers participating in online communities. It is self-evident that, while individuals may join many communities reflecting their own interests and pastimes, when they join a "teacher" list, they understand that the conversations will be about classrooms and the daily life of a teacher. Lloyd et al.'s (2005) model has identified the element of context and positioned it in relationship to other elements while the data from the Duncan-Howell (2007) study has allowed greater specificity into how online communities can provide the contextualised discussion teachers are seeking.

Personal Growth

Professional development is frequently seen as "training." In the context of information and communication technology, McKenzie (1998) argued that what was needed was "less training and more learning" (p. 2) suggesting that professional development needs to offer more than the expository teaching of skills. The *personal growth* element in the adopted model refers to the cognitive challenges as well as the maintenance of "corporate" knowledge that the teacher needs, for example, in regard to new or altered curriculum and administrative processes. To satisfy the element of personal growth (Lloyd et al., 2005), professional development should:

- add to personal knowledge
- increase personal skills
- enhance status (within learning community)
- take account of teachers' prior knowledge, different levels and learning styles
- enable reflection
- allow personal selection

Active participation in online communities meets the listed criteria for personal growth. This is evident in the following statements from the focus group discussions.

- *Being part of a virtual professional community often fills a void in my professional learning as often there may not be someone with like interests available for the discussions needed and the lists can help to fill this gap and stimulate further thinking.* (Statement 8)
- *I take what interests me, pick at some of the stuff I am not too sure about, and don't bother too much with the stuff that doesn't really grab me. I can engage with, or ignore the stream of ideas in whatever way I choose. The important thing is that I have a steady stream of ideas coming past me every day.* (Statement 9)
- *Can you imagine being a teacher and not understanding things like pedagogy or constructivism? That was me. What else didn't I understand? What else do I still not understand? Man, I *need* to belong to online communities or I'd just be a really ignorant jackass of a teacher.* (Statement 10)

Statement 8 is – as with Statement 1 – a declarative statement which, in this instance, articulates a clear understanding that participation in an online community satisfies a need for personal growth through increasing personal skills and adding to prior knowledge. The statement adds the piquant notion that participation is not simply a question and answer scenario and that an answer or response may be a catalyst to further thinking. The statement also reinforces previously stated notions of networking and collaboration with unknown others- an idea extended in the later subsection on the element of *community*. The people in the online community supplement this individual's network as evident in the caveat that "there may not be someone with like interests available for the discussions needed." If "real" peers are not available or able to help, someone in the broader network will be available. It is of interest that while these people are regarded as expert, they are trusted in a way which "outside" experts or those writing for professional journals are not. There is a seemingly arbitrary division of trusted and not-trusted sources (see also Statement 5). Members of an online community gain credibility by being presumed to be the same or similar to the individual posting the request.

Statement 9 enacts the "personal selection" criterion. It has parity with Statement 6 in its enabling individuals to direct their own learning. This person has articulated the capacity for selection through analogy to a stream. The notion of a "steady stream" has resonance with the element of time (to be discussed in the next sub-section) but can also be seen here as a reliable and ongoing source of support which can be "dipped" into and out of as needed. The implicit notion of trust is arguably a partial explanation for the emotional support offered by online communities.

Statement 10 is a self-deprecating and candid statement of an individual's need to be part of an online community for the sake of his/her own professionalism. To be an "ignorant jackass" meant, for this person, to not understand the theoretical concepts of pedagogy and constructivism. This person may not be opposed to "experts" but would prefer to learn about theoretical concepts through the practical conversations of the community rather than theoretical texts. The rhetorical "What else didn't I understand? What else do I still not

understand" marks this person as a lifelong learner and one for whom an online community provides – and will continue to provide - ongoing generative professional development. Participation in an online community is, for this person, more about sustaining personal growth than short-term answers or quick-fix solutions.

Online communities have the capacity to encourage personal growth because there is no compulsion to participate. Individuals voluntarily select the community/ies they wish to join and then regulate, on a daily basis, their own level of interaction with topics of discussion or with peers. The ultimate selection lies in an individual's decision to remain within a community, to initiate or engage in discussion, to remain silent, or to unsubscribe.

Time

The element of time proved to be the most complex of the four elements to map (Lloyd et al., 2005). It is positioned in the model (Figure 2) as its outer diameter. The arc from practice to theory is labelled as the "over time" (sustained) continuum indicating that the development of a theory or personal philosophy is only achieved through conscious reflection. The arc from theory to practice is labelled as "just in time" (timely) implying that theory can inform practice or assist in finding quick solutions to immediate problems. This often takes the form of direct answers to simple queries about, for example, software issues, purchase of specific equipment, or location of resources.

Time has multiple senses, but generally has a dual definition:

1. *time* as a measure, that is, duration and frequency, expressed as needing to be prolonged, ongoing, sustained, as well as the partition of time within professional development events, extension beyond event, and the issues related to time release;

2.   *time* as a variable of sequence or need, that is its timeliness or being "just-in-time."

To satisfy the dual understandings of *time* (Lloyd et al., 2005), professional development should:

- be timely (just-in-time)
- be sustained (over time)
- provide adequate time for participation, reflection and implementation
- allow teachers to take responsibility for their own learning

The messages which indicated sustained or "over-time" professional development are:

- *Maybe they are not as specific and directed as face-to-face professional development activities, but I find them [online communities] more diverse in scope, more consistent in delivery, and more effective over time. (Statement 11)*
- *The on-going continuous nature of online communities is a big advantage as you know that, at any time or place, you can log on ask a question, make a statement, post a resource and someone else will reply with a positive or negative response that will help clarify your thinking. Love the collective wisdom of the group! (Statement 12)*
- *I think a professional - a true professional - continues to learn/share/collaborate. (Statement 13)*

The messages which indicated timely or "just in time" professional development are:

- *It [participation in an online community] is a worthwhile professional development activity because you are able to initiate topics which are of interest/concern to you when you most need help. (Statement 14)*

- *Just in time models are very powerful. (Statement 15)*
- *It's also often a just-in-time model of professional development, rather than what is so often the case for "real" professional development courses, a just-in-case model. (Statement 16)*
- *When I have a problem I need answers quickly and the discussion groups are as quick as it gets. With such a diverse group, you get a wider range of alternatives/solutions from around the globe. (Statement 17)*

The difference between "over" and "in" time demands is clear in the statements. Neither is more important than the other as they meet differing needs. There is a subtle difference in the outcomes, however, as "in time" demands belong to the practice hemisphere while "over time" demands are the mainstay of the theory hemisphere. The latter is the product of reflection. Time is the critical element which allows the replacement of beliefs and the development of praxis, as action is guided by reflection, and reflection is corroborated by action.

Community

Online communities were briefly defined earlier in this chapter. In the adopted model, *community* refers more generally to collaborations during and following the professional development event and to ongoing connections and professional collaborations within local and extended communities. To satisfy the *community* element (Lloyd et al., 2005), professional development should:

- encourage sharing with others, hearing other stories from the field
- provide ongoing support and heightened collaboration
- expand professional and personal networks

In the model, community is the central element and all action and reflection occurs within or through collaborations with the community. Teachers need reassurance from their peers to validate any potential or planned changes to practice or theory. This is made explicit in discussions in online communities where this process is made visible through posted messages.

The discussion forum comments from the Duncan-Howell (2007) study relating to the sense of community engendered by online communities included the following:

- *[I] think the collective wisdom of groups helps you develop as a teacher.* (Statement 18)
- *The group has the combined knowledge to greatly increase the ability to solve problems compared to an individual. Different members of the group will approach a problem in different ways and will bring different points of view and skills to the problem.* (Statement 19)
- *The problem is that a workplace – school – will only have a small pool, if any, of colleagues with similar needs. Online communities permit contact with colleagues of similar roles, curriculum areas, [and] experience.* (Statement 20)
- *In my workplace, I'm an island. There is no one else there like me, so it's only through the virtual community discussions that I can have relevant professional discussions.* (Statement 21)

Statement 18 includes the evocative phrase, "collective wisdom," which encapsulates what theorists have suggested is the prime value of both on- and off-line communities. The person who posted this message has recognised the abstract value of this group knowledge to an individual's development as a teacher. This statement centralises the role of community in the process of professional development.

Statement 19 acknowledges the power of diversity within a community and enacts the current popular notion of "the wisdom of crowds" (Surowiecki, 2005). A participant in an online community needs, perhaps above all, to be open to such diversity and expect multiple solutions to a posted enquiry or differing responses to a statement of opinion. Participants also need to expect that their voice may not be as dominant as it may be in their classroom where they are the source of knowledge and the arbiter of all decisions and differences of opinion.

Statements 20 and 21, as with the previously cited Statement 8, clearly show the need that individuals have for peer support and interaction. The "isolation" of teachers – even in large schools – has been acknowledged for some time (see, for example, Riel, 1987, 1990). In a study of rural teachers, Gal (1993) noted one teacher's experience that "each day when I go online, it is like being in a room full of very talented teachers who are sharing all these wonderful ideas. The isolation that is common in a rural school is suddenly gone" (p. 39). The statements also resonate with the previously noted value of diversity in communities in providing multiple perspectives and a broad range of experience.

When the twenty-one selected representative statements from the Duncan-Howell (2007) study are mapped to the model from the Lloyd et al.'s (2005) study, the importance of online communities in ongoing and effective professional development for teachers becomes apparent. The conclusion of the Lloyd et al.'s (2005) study was that effective professional development has to immerse individuals in their community, address directly the context of teaching and learning, add to personal growth, and be both "over" time and "in" time. This chapter has demonstrated that participation in online communities meets this definition.

It has, further to this, also shown that the processes of transformative professional development (after Windschitl, 2002) are in place.

There is evidence in the representative statements of individuals who have interrogated their own practice and have made their own classrooms and workplaces sites for research. They have, above all else, made the metacognitive connection between their online interactions and their own professional growth. They generously share their understandings with their communities and, in so doing, make the outcome of their impromptu research explicit to others. Beliefs are confirmed or replaced through dialectical processes. Opinions are defended or modified.

The previously cited theorised and observed benefits of participating in an online community can be noted in the representative statements presented in this section. Perhaps the clearest of these is the notion of collective knowledge building (after Boyle et al., 2004) and the pooling of expertise (Sorge & Russell, 2000). The repeated references – including the explicit acknowledgement of "collective wisdom" (Statements 12 and 18) – are testament to this understanding.

FUTURE TRENDS

As noted, the data for this chapter was drawn from the three online teacher communities investigated through a doctoral study (Duncan-Howell, 2007). Two of these – the large UK community and the small Australian state-based community - were established by professional associations. The third was hosted by a self-funding non-profit group based within a Faculty of Education in an Australian university.

Contrary to this external organisation, an emerging trend is for individuals to form their own communities through free access to online, particularly synchronous, media. An example of this is a community of Australian and New Zealand educators titled Oz/NZ Educators [http://oznzeducators.ning.com] formed in June 2008. The group holds regular meetings through a Web 2.0 application called a Ning. This community

was set up by a teacher who was keen to make meaningful use of new technologies and people, mostly from the Southern Hemisphere, who find the community by word of mouth or invitation attend meetings and engage in open discussion. The group's "flash" meetings are kept in an archive and resources are similarly stored. These can be accessed without password or subscription. Just as the Internet has allowed blogging and social networking to threaten mainstream media as a source of information and entertainment, it has also encouraged the free interchange of ideas and the formation of ad hoc communities of practice.

An immediate benefit of these communities is that they can, through the use of video connections, begin to replicate the physicality of traditional face-to-face communities. The synchronous communication also brings immediacy to the interaction. It remains to be seen, however, if they have the convenience in terms of time afforded by asynchronous media or allow the same time for reflection. The interest in these communities is that they are "grass-roots" allowing small groups of early adopters of new technologies to meet and discuss issues of professional interest.

In the future, online communities of teachers may become more fluid and less formal as groups form and re-form in the free space of the Internet. The same fundamental value of more traditional or asynchronous online communities will be experienced and the role of communities in engendering ongoing professional development – as established in this chapter – will be as effective. Like-minded people will find the means to bond together as communities and will find the most appropriate technology to achieve this goal.

CONCLUSION

This chapter has shown, using an original cyclic model of professional development, that online communities can provide ongoing and effective professional development for teachers. It has also started to question the commonly-applied metaphor that professional development is a sequential or linear process of growth or a journey. For example, growth can be viewed as a sequential process of moving from infancy to maturity (see Crystal, 2001) while many journeys follow a predetermined path from Point A to Point B (see King, 2002). The model in this chapter is, instead, circular in nature and tracks a path through which the individual changes in subtle, iterative and self-determined ways.

The growth metaphor, however, can imply a beginning state which is deficient in some way. A newborn child is dependent on others for its survival. The teacher first joining an online community may depend on others but only in terms of familiarisation and the hesitance that accompanies being in any new environment. Lave and Wenger's (1991) writing of individuals moving from "legitimate peripheral participation" to full membership of a community is not comparable to the notion of growth. You cannot choose not to grow but you might choose not to participate in a community.

The metaphor of the journey is more persuasive as it usually suggests that a person starts out to go somewhere they have never been before, that is, to intentionally reach a place they have not previously visited. Implicit in the notion of travelling is a growth in experience, knowledge and understanding which seems to sit well with the idea of professional development. But a journey can also be quite a plebeian process of reaching a designated destination and tracking along a straight line with towns or landmarks along the way reached in a sequential and unchanging way.

In L. Frank Baum's classic children's story, *The Wizard of Oz,* first published in 1900, the target destination was The Emerald City. The travellers, Dorothy, the Tin Man, the Cowardly Lion and the Scarecrow, were travelling to see the Wizard who they believed would solve all their problems and redress their shortcomings. Many teachers think of professional development in this

way. They believe that there is a magical destination where someone – perhaps a specific trainer or program – will provide an instant solution for them. It is about what will be done to them – they will be magically given the brain or heart or whatever it is they need if only they can reach the destination. This is, as has been shown in this chapter, at odds with the reality of professional development by "experts" as being generally mistrusted (Statement 5). The real power, as the protagonists in the story discovered, lies within you and your travelling companions (Statement 7) rather than external sources. A similar power evident in online communities has been shown in this chapter in the statements relating to diversity and the collective "wisdom" of the group (see Statements 18-20).

Point B – the Emerald City – is fixed and is reached via the Yellow Brick Road, a predetermined linear path. In the ongoing and self-generating professional development offered by online communities, there is no fixed path. Power lies in the capacity to "pick" up topics of interest (Statement 9) or initiate discussion on topics of concern (Statement 6) as needed. Participants in online community set their own path and choose their own detours and speed of progress.

If professional development is a journey, then it is more akin to the Buddhist tradition where value lies in how one travels rather than in reaching the destination. The reality of being a teacher in the 21st Century is that it is unlikely that there *is* a destination, a fixed Point B or Emerald City, to attain. The same issues of social and technological change are reflected in contemporary schooling and being a teacher today is as much about coping with change as it is about having mastery of subject matter.

The participants in the Duncan-Howell (2007) and Lloyd et al. (2005) studies have shown that, like the travellers in the *Wizard of Oz*, they can learn from each other rather than from an external expert. They have also shown that, even when new to a community, they are not helpless infants and that there are multiple paths to the one destination. Growth and journey metaphors are potentially dangerous in limiting teachers' belief in their own ability to control and direct their own learning. The model validated in this chapter has shown that the newer metaphor of the iterative circle, particularly when used to describe participation in online communities, is a powerful way of describing the real ways that teachers use these communities for ongoing generative professional development.

Online communities have the potential to provide effective professional development and to meet the emergent professional needs of teachers in the 21st Century. While participating in an online community requires a sense of confidence in yourself and others, the rewards – as noted in the statements presented in this chapter – are great. Changing the metaphor hands power back to teachers to become independent and effective lifelong learners.

REFERENCES

ACOT. (1996/2006). *Changing the conversation about teaching, learning and technology: A report on 10 years of ACOT research*. Retrieved September 7, 2008, from http://www.images.apple.com/education/k12/leadership/acot/pdf/10yr.pdf

Albion, P., & Ertmer, P. A. (2002). Beyond the foundations: The role of vision and belief in teachers' preparation for integration of technology. *TechTrends*, *46*(5), 34–38. doi:10.1007/BF02818306

Bandura, A. (1997). *Self-efficacy: The exercise of control*. New York: Freeman.

Bond, P. (2004). Communities of practice and complexity: Conversation and culture. *Organisations and People*, *11*(4), 1–7.

Borko, H., & Putnam, R. T. (1995). Expanding a teacher's knowledge base: A cognitive psychological perspective on professional development. In T. R. Guskey & M. Huberman (Eds.), *Professional development in education: New paradigms and practices* (pp. 35-65). New York: Teachers College Press.

Boyle, B., While, D., & Boyle, T. (2004). A longitudinal study of teacher change: What makes professional development effective? *Curriculum Journal*, *15*(1), 45–68. doi:10.1080/1026716032000189471

Chen, T.-L., & Chen, T.-J. (2002). *A strategic analysis of the online learning community for continuing professional development of university faculty in Taiwan: A SWOT analysis*. Paper presented at the International Conference on Computers in Education (ICCE'02).

Cornu, B. (2004). Networking and collecting intelligence for teachers and learners. In A. Brown & N. Davis (Eds.), *Digital Technology, communities and education* (pp. 40-45). London: Routledge Falmer.

Crystal, J. (2001). Building from within: Two professional development models that work. *Technology & Learning*, *22*(2), 62–66.

Department of Education. Science and Technology (DEST) (2004). *PD 2000 Australia - National mapping of school teacher professional development*. Retrieved September 5, 2004, from http://www.qualityteaching.dest.gov.au/Content/SubSection_PD2000.htm

Duncan-Howell, J. (2007). *Online Communities of Practice and their role in the professional development of teachers*. Unpublished doctoral thesis, Queensland University of Technology, Brisbane, Australia.

Dwyer, D. C., Ringstaff, C., & Sandholtz, J. H. (1990). *Teacher beliefs and practices (Part 1): Patterns of change. The evolution of teachers' instructional beliefs and practices in high-access-to technology classrooms* (ACOT Report #8). Cupertino, CA: Apple Computer.

Freire, P. (1972). *Pedagogy of the oppressed.* Harmondsworth: Penguin.

Gal, S. (1993). Teachers and teaching. *Journal of Research in Rural Education, 9*(1), 38–42.

Galland, P. (2002). Techie teachers — Web-based staff development at your leisure. *TechTrends, 46*(3), 11–16. doi:10.1007/BF02784836

Garet, M. S., Porter, A. C., Desimone, L., Birman, B. F., & Yoon, K. S. (2001). What makes professional development effective? Results from a national sample of teachers. *American Educational Research Journal, 38*(4), 915–945. doi:10.3102/00028312038004915

Guskey, T. R. (1985). Staff development and teacher change. *Educational Leadership, 42*(7), 56–60.

Guskey, T. R. (1986). Staff development and the process of teacher change. *Educational Researcher, 15*(5), 5–20.

Guskey, T. R. (2002). Professional development and teacher change. *Teachers and Teaching, 8*(3), 381–391. doi:10.1080/135406002100000512

Hall, G., & Hord, S. (1987) *Change in schools: Facilitating the process.* New York: State University of New York Press.

Hawkes, M. (1999). Exploring network-based communication in teacher professional development. *Educational Technology, 39*(4), 45–52.

Haythornthwaite, C. (2002). Building social networks via computer networks: Creating and sustaining distributed learning communities. In K. A. Renninger & W. Shumar (Eds.), *Building virtual communities: Learning and change in cyberspace* (pp. 159-190). Cambridge: Cambridge University Press.

Hoffman-Kipp, P., Artiles, A., & Lopez-Torres, L. (2003). Beyond reflection: Teacher learning as praxis. *Theory into Practice, 42*(3), 248–254.

Huberman, M. (2001). Networks that alter teaching: Conceptualisations, exchanges and experiments. In J. Soler, A. Craft & H. Burgess (Eds.), *Teacher development: Exploring our own practice.* (pp. 141-159). London: Paul Chapman.

Hunter, B. (2002). Learning in the virtual community depends upon changes in local communities. In K. A. Renninger & W. Shumar (Eds.), *Building virtual communities* (pp. 96-126). Cambridge: Cambridge University Press.

King, K. (2002). *A journey of transformation: A model of educators' learning experiences in educational technology.* Paper presented at the Adult Education Research Conference, Raleigh NC, May. ED 472069.

Lave, J., & Wenger, E. (1991). *Situated learning: Legitimate peripheral participation.* Cambridge: Cambridge University Press.

Lechner, S. (1998). Teachers of the N-Gen need reflective online communities. *Journal of Online Learning, 9*(3), 20–24.

Lloyd, M., & Cochrane, J. (2006). Celtic knots: Interweaving the elements of effective teacher professional development in ICT. *Australian Educational Computing, 21*(2), 16–19.

Lloyd, M., Cochrane, J., & Beames, S. (2005). *Towards a model of effective professional development in ICT for teachers.* Commissioned report for Queensland Society for Information Technology in Education (QSITE). Retrieved September 13, 2008, from http://www.qsite.edu.au/publications/position/PD

Matei, S. A. (2005). *From counterculture to cyberculture: Virtual community discourse and the dilemma of modernity.* Retrieved August 10, 2008, from http://jcmc.indiana.edu/vol10/issue3/matei.html

McKenzie, J. (1998). Creating learning cultures with just-in-time support. *Adult Technology Learning.* Retrieved July 27, 2000, from http://www.staffdevelop.org/adult.html

Mevarech, Z. (1997). The U-Curve process that trainee teachers experience in integrating computers into the curriculum. In D. Passey & B. Samways (Eds.), *Information technology: Supporting change through teacher education.* London: Chapman & Hall.

Nespor, J. (1987). The role of beliefs in the practice of teaching. *Journal of Curriculum Studies, 19*(4), 317–328. doi:10.1080/0022027870190403

Richardson, V. (1990). Significant and worthwhile change in teaching practice. *Educational Researcher, 19*(7), 10–18.

Richardson, V. (1992). The agenda-setting dilemma in a constructivist staff development process. *Journal of Teaching and Teacher Education, 8*(3), 287–300. doi:10.1016/0742-051X(92)90027-Z

Richardson, V., & Placier, P. (2001). Teacher change. In V. Richardson (Ed.), *Handbook of research on teaching.* (4th ed., pp. 905-947). Washington, DC: American Educational Research Association.

Riel, M. (1987). The intercultural learning network. *The Computing Teacher, 14,* 27–30.

Riel, M. (1990). Cooperative learning across rooms. *Instructional Science, 19,* 445–466. doi:10.1007/BF00119390

Russell, A. (1995). Stages in learning new technology: Naïve adult email users . *Computers & Education, 25*(4), 173–178. doi:10.1016/0360-1315(95)00073-9

Scardamalia, M. (2002). Collective cognitive responsibility for the advancement of knowledge. In B. Smith (Ed.), *Liberal education in a knowledge society* (pp. 67-98). Chicago, IL: Open Court.

Schlager, M., Fusco, J., & Schank, P. (2002). Evolution of an on-line education community of practice. In K.A. Renninger, & W. Shumar, (Eds.), *Building virtual communities: Learning and change in cyberspace* (pp. 129-158). New York: Cambridge University Press.

Sorge, D. H., & Russell, J. D. (2000). A strategy for effective change in instructional behavior: Staff development that works. *Educational Technology, 40*(6), 46–49.

Strehle, E. L., Whatley, A., Kurz, K. A., & Hausfather, S. J. (2001). Narratives of collaboration: Inquiring into technology integration in teacher education. *Journal of Technology and Teacher Education, 10*(1), 27–47.

Surowiecki, J. (2005). *The wisdom of crowds.* New York: Random House.

Trinidad, S., Newhouse, C. P., & Clarkson, B. (2004). A framework for implementation of ICT in schools. Paper presented at the Australian Computers in Education Conference. July 2004, Adelaide, Australia.

Windschitl, M. (2002). Framing constructivism in practice as the negotiation of dilemmas: An analysis of the conceptual, pedagogical, cultural, and political challenges facing teachers. *Review of Educational Research, 72,* 131–175. doi:10.3102/00346543072002131

Chapter 5

Teacher Professional Development Practices
The Case of the Haringey Transformation Teachers Programme

Norbert Pachler
Institute of Education, University of London, UK

Caroline Daly
Institute of Education, University of London, UK

Anne Turvey
Institute of Education, University of London, UK

ABSTRACT

This chapter discusses the need for new models of teachers' professional development in the context of established and emerging technologies and socio-constructivist theories of teacher learning within online and other communities. The authors present the current contexts affecting professional development in England and discuss the significance of the shift towards collaborative and community approaches to teachers' learning. The authors argue that transformation is a key, though troublesome, concept in considering the aims of professional development for teachers' use of technologies in their everyday practice. They explore these ideas by presenting the case of the Transformation Teachers Programme (TTP), a wide-scale teachers' development project carried out in a London borough by Haringey City Learning Centre (CLC), and they examine how this project has implemented new approaches to Information and Communications Technology (ICT) and teachers' professional development, based on collaborative experimentation, enquiry and risk-taking within online and other community-based arrangements.

INTRODUCTION

In this chapter we discuss the need for new models of teachers' professional development in the con-text of established and emerging technologies and socio-constructivist theories of teacher learning within online and other communities. We present the current contexts affecting professional development in England and discuss the significance of the shift towards collaborative and community approaches to

DOI: 10.4018/978-1-60566-780-5.ch005

teachers' learning. We argue that transformation is a key, though troublesome, concept in considering the aims of professional development for teachers' use of technologies in their everyday practice. We explore these ideas by presenting the case of the Transformation Teachers Programme (TTP), a wide-scale teachers' development project carried out in a London borough by Haringey City Learning Centre (CLC), and we examine how this project has implemented new approaches to Information and Communications Technology (ICT) and teachers' professional development, based on collaborative experimentation, enquiry and risk-taking within online and other community-based arrangements. The initiative deals with both local and national priorities contained within a government initiative for England, Building Schools for the Future (BSF), which aims to transform teaching and learning so that the learning needs of local populations are better met. The current national focus on equipping schools with 'state of the art' buildings and technology needs to be matched, however, with providing professional development for teachers, which enables them to harness the potential of the initiative from a pedagogical perspective. Having explored the principles and pedagogy of the programme, we present vignettes of two teachers who have been affected by the programme in different, related ways. The chapter concludes with a discussion of what can be learnt from the case regarding the future development of teachers' professional learning and makes recommendations for features of effective Continuing Professional Development (CPD) in ICT for teachers. The term CPD is adopted here as this is the current terminology used by the majority of stakeholders to describe in-service professional development for teachers in the United Kingdom.

THE NEED FOR EFFECTIVE ICT CPD

It is widely recognised that teachers require an ever greater, and ever changing range of skills and understanding, in particular with regard to the increasing proliferation of technological tools for all aspects of work, be it pedagogical or administrative. For example, recent years have seen a considerable growth in the popularity of interactive whiteboards and the use of virtual learning environments including e-portfolios in- and outside schools in the UK for teaching, learning and assessment. Increasingly schools are also considering how to harness the proliferation of sophisticated portable devices owned by the learners themselves, in particular smartphones, for teaching and learning, a phenomenon known as 'mobile learning'.

Yet, we diagnose a disappointing history in the adoption of technologies by teachers for improving their own learning and that of their students (see e.g. Preston & Cuthell, 2007). A historical focus on techno-centric aims for CPD, generic skills training, top-down frameworks for CPD and outcomes-driven CPD programmes has meant that the potential of technology to enhance the learning experiences of students remains largely unfulfilled (see for example reports on Interactive Whiteboard use in the UK by Moss et al., 2007 or Preston, 2004). Similarly, there has been relatively little focus on *how* school teachers learn with technologies within online collaborative contexts (see e.g. Fisher et al., 2006; Dede, 2006). The importance of secure subject knowledge and subject-based pedagogical understanding has been highlighted for the effective use of technologies in education (see Cox et al. 2003), but there is relatively little that examines how teachers' professional development with technologies might be enhanced, and how collaborative arrangements can be enhanced by technologies.

We argue that, with some exceptions (e.g. Pachler & Daly, 2006), teachers' professional development involving technologies has been largely un(der)theorised. A theoretically sound and conceptually coherent approach to CPD and 'new' technologies needs to be based on an explicit definitional base.

For the purposes of this chapter, ICT CPD is understood as professional development activities and experiences, including skills training, which enhance pedagogy across the curriculum and beyond, and which help to deepen teachers' knowledge and understanding of how to use technologies effectively in teaching and learning, including for professional administrative activities. It includes a spectrum of both formal and informal arrangements, which help teachers use technology, and may involve both in-house and a range of external or networked bodies, which contribute to those arrangements. The focus, therefore, is very firmly on developing practice. Our discussion also focuses on practice and learning across the curriculum that is enhanced by new technologies; it is not only concerned with ICT as a school subject.

CPD of Teachers and 'New' Technologies

Teachers in England are entitled to five days of continuing professional development a year, which focuses on enabling them to meet wider school development priorities as well as their individual needs. ICT CPD has been an important element in contributing to both types of needs. The current standards for Qualified Teacher Status (QTS) integrate ICT into the professional knowledge, skills and understanding expected of all qualified teachers. Although teachers qualifying to teach in recent years have had to meet standards by demonstrating ICT skills and the use of technologies in their lessons, in-service CPD is the main vehicle by which the majority of teachers acquire new skills and learn about the integration of technologies into classroom practice. There is growing evidence that the greatest influence on teachers' ongoing professional development is in fact their school

environment, and the extent to which it provides the conditions for a productive learning community by which practice is developed among groups and networks of individuals (see e.g. Bolam et al, 2005; Fielding et al, 2005; Schifter, 2008). It may well be that, even for recently trained teachers, sustainable pedagogical capacity around the use of new technologies will be greatly determined by the school environments and CPD experiences to which they are exposed in their early careers, and how these are connected to external training bodies and networks, both online and face to face. It is important that any study of contemporary approaches to ICT CPD acknowledges the *centrality of teachers' experiences of CPD in practice* when it comes to developing professional capacity. The case of the Haringey TTP addresses this need to focus on identifying models which enable teachers to develop new collaborative practices and bring about change in order to identify effective models for ICT CPD.

Recent years have seen the growing diversification in the provision of ICT CPD. There is an increased involvement of the commercial sector in offering ICT support and training to schools, mainly linked to the use of their own resources and products, together with a wide range of specialist technology providers and freelance trainers. Whilst we know that provision is growing ever more varied, we know much less about what types of provision make a difference, and enable teachers in England to become 'e-mature' (Becta, 2008) and contribute to the e-maturity of their schools. By e-maturity, technologies become embedded in everyday work and pedagogical practices to enhance "the capacity of a learning institution to make strategic and effective use of technology to support educational outcomes" (ibid. p. 20).

The key challenge for us is to understand how certain types of engagement with ICT CPD can change professional behaviours. This question is connected to the ability for a pedagogic model or professional development programme to impact on teachers' beliefs and attitudes. Changes in motivation, confidence, attitudes and belief emerged as key drivers in making CPD effective in Cordingley et al's (2005, 2007) reviews of the literature on CPD. These core features were found to result from collaborative approaches to CPD, and may be crucial to overcoming barriers to change such as frustrations brought about by lack of technical support and access to technology.

The Shift to Collaborative CPD

There has been a move away from a transmission model of CPD which relies chiefly upon 'expert' trainers and attendance at externally provided courses, to models which build on 'knowledge construction' by participants which takes place within learning communities. Evaluation of The New Opportunity Funding (NOF) ICT national training programme 1999-2003 (see Preston, 2004) revealed problems for teachers in incorporating new practices into their everyday practice, with lack of motivation and the need for ongoing access to technology and support being key factors. Since then, the move has been away from national programmes of ICT training in the UK, to one where school leaders have far greater control over CPD priorities and over funding of professional development. The focus on meeting local, identified needs is to be welcomed, but with this comes the need for models which have been shown to foster teacher learning and innovate new pedagogical practices.

There is growing interest in the concept of online learning communities for professional development based on their capacity to support bottom-up interactive practices of inquiry. Cordingley et al (2005, 2007) have conducted systematic reviews of the CPD literature concerning both collaborative CPD and the intervention of specialists in CPD programmes. Overall findings are that collaborative CPD, in which teachers work together and with specialist input to undertake a variety of tasks such as planning, observation, shared reflection and classroom enquiry, provides

benefits which lead to the adoption of new practices. Benefits, according to Cordingley (2005, pp. 65-66) result from:

- the use of peer support
- explicit use of specialist expertise
- applying and refining new knowledge and skills and experimenting with ways of integrating them in day-to-day practice
- teachers observing one another
- consultation with teachers either about their own starting points, focus of CPD, or the pace and scope of CPD
- involving specialists in observation and reflection.

Particularly significant are Cordingley's findings about the organisation of collaborative work, "that shorter, smaller and more frequent collaborative work is more effective than larger, infrequent meetings" (Devereux, 2009).

A further finding from Cordingley (2007) is that when specialists contribute to CPD programmes, teachers learn more about their subject, more about learning and new ways of teaching. Sometimes CPD can result in all three of these types of learning. The challenge is how to develop models where collaborative learning can be achieved which is 'shorter, smaller and more frequent' and in which judicious use is made of a range of specialists, so that learning about technologies for teaching is embedded in both local school networks and in external expertise. There is a key role here for the use of a variety of online social networking tools to support collaborative processes between the various parties, in conjunction with other face to face approaches. Crucially, in the Haringey case, the technologies of collaboration and communication (Web 2.0 software such as blogging, podcasting, flickr, Animoto, Slideshare, Openmind) are also pedagogical tools with which the teachers become familiar and use as part of their classroom practice and to share action research with their peers and programme leaders. As far as we are aware, the Haringey case is unusual in its attempt to establish a model for collaborative ICT CPD, and to date there has been little work to develop collaboration using the utilities of Web 2.0 social software for teacher learning within an action research approach. This represents a key 'transformational' approach to teachers' professional development. It has set out to harness Web 2.0 to bring about fundamentally altered ways for teachers to experience CPD, and it conceptualizes how CPD can be constructed by the teachers' themselves in collaboration with ICT 'experts'. Such a transformational approach integrates the use of technologies with community perspectives on professional learning.

The work of Fielding et al. (2005) on 'joint practice development' and Bolam et al. (2005) on effective professional learning communities, has focused on the potential impacts on teacher learning of collaborative, learner-engaged practices. The unifying theoretical assumption is that communities (whether online or face to face) help constitute professional learning, which forms a shift away from a focus on individual teacher learning as a purely cognitive matter which happens through increased isolated understanding. Such teachers' professional learning communities are based on moral concerns and shared ideas about educational purpose and 'socially responsible goals' (Sachs, 2003, p.135). Pickering et al (2007) established three core design principles for effective teachers' professional learning, based on a series of research studies into professional development in a variety of contexts. Professional development should not come from a top-down model of best practice, but should focus on:

- the co-construction of shared teacher knowledge through shared practice;
- collaboration through learning networks or communities; and
- scholarly reflection on practice.

A similar focus on collaborative practices as key to effective teacher development in the use of technologies for learning has been identified by Schifter (2008) in her assertion that working in groups is the prime factor underpinning effective CPD in this area.

The Contemporary Technological Context and Collaborative Teacher Development

We very briefly want to consider the contemporary technological contexts here which, we argue, demand a reconceptualisation of teachers' professional learning. What, for example, are the implications for teachers of the ubiquitous nature of Web 2.0 technologies, with their capacities for altering social communication, and for altering how learners access, change and exchange ideas and information (see e.g. Pachler & Daly, 2008)? What are the implications of the agency afforded by increasingly powerful handheld devices owned and used by learners outside of formal education? They confront educators with a need to re-align educational endeavours and to engage with the fundamental socio-cultural changes manifesting themselves in the life-worlds of young people where practices and experiences of everyday use can be, and are being brought into the school and should be enhanced and augmented inside the school to in turn be fed back into everyday life practices. The prime need for altered relationships between teachers, students and networks for learning with technologies was highlighted by DEMOS (2007), based on the gulf between young people's use of technologies to access information and share personal responses, and the learning practices they encounter in schools. We consider new technologies to have transformative effects on student learning as well as the professional practice of teachers (see e.g. Chapter 12 in Pachler, Barnes & Field, 2008). We view these new technologies as cultural resources that promote the bridging of the gap between formal and informal learning

Figure 1. The Networked Teacher. (2006, Couros. Used with permission under Creative Commons licensing).

(see the work of the London Mobile Learning Group at http://www.londonmobilelearning.net). For a discussion of the new habitus of learning see Kress & Pachler, 2007. Couros (2006) has captured the notion of 'the networked teacher' as existing in potential connection with a range of contemporary technologies and resources for their own learning and in relation to the learning of others (Figure 1).

The image may be a long way from the way many teachers practise in schools, but contemporary approaches to CPD need to be aligned with such a 'worldview'. It signifies the possibilities of finding support, collaboration and creative inspiration in the various connections. Teachers need to develop deep knowledge about how learning is situated in different ways, is shaped by new collaborative practices, and how learners are capable of embracing informal as well as formal learning opportunities. These factors need to be reflected in transformed learning practices of the teachers themselves. Conventional approaches to ICT CPD are no longer appropriate for the transformation

of pedagogy and practice. The case provides one example of how a collaborative CPD model can help to embed learning with technologies in how teachers live their professional lives.

THE CASE

We consider these issues by presenting a 'case' of teachers' professional development in the Transformation Teachers Programme (TTP), which is an ongoing CPD initiative in the London Local Authority of Haringey which started in 2007. The case formed part of a year-long funded research project, 'Teachers and Technology', at the Centre for Excellence for Work-based Learning at the Institute of Education, University of London (http://www.wlecentre.ac.uk). The research was a qualitative investigation into differing models of ICT CPD, which involved: recorded interviews with teachers who had attended the programme, their school colleagues and a headteacher during the year following the CPD; recorded interviews with the programme leader and CLC leader; site visits on programme days at the Centre to collect field notes about the programme activities and talk informally with teachers currently enrolled; views of the programme area on Haringey CLC Virtual Learning Environment (Fronter Open Learning Platform ©) and its evidence base of teacher engagement with social software and other technologies, and the teachers' collection of electronic teaching and learning artefacts; and detailed discussions with the teachers on the programme about the topics for their 'teacher enquiries' into a pedagogical innovation using technologies.

The Case Context

The TTP is an initiative which seeks to build a collaborative learning community among teachers from every secondary school and secondary special school in the Borough of Haringey in order to enable them to work with technologies to improve students' learning. The borough is one of the most socially and economically disadvantaged in London, and the imperative to improve students' motivation and achievement at school is strong. Technologies are viewed as having a vital role to play, but this cannot happen without a 'transformed' workforce, capable of harnessing the potential of technologies in new and creative ways. The project brings together teachers from a range of curriculum areas who have been identified by their headteachers as excellent practitioners, but not with any particular expertise in using technologies. The aim is to facilitate a programme by which the teachers become part of a learning community which fosters and supports their own development and is part of a wider pattern of networks which bring about change in their schools. Their pedagogical knowledge is an important foundation – technologies are not seen as the antidote to poor teaching – they are seen as enhancing tools in the hands of excellent teachers, who are willing to take risks and explore further how young people

learn. The community is facilitated in several interrelated ways with a range of technological and face to face infrastructure. Two teachers from every secondary and special school in the borough are recommended by their headteachers as having particular potential to benefit from the programme in terms of making an impact on their practice, and on the practice of their colleagues. Thus, senior management is expected to have a particularly active and focused investment in the CPD from the start, and a Senior Leader is assigned to the two teachers within each school to form a learning 'triad' which will provide mutual support for developing practice and carrying out teacher enquiry as part of the CPD.

Overview of the Programme

The programme takes place with between 24-28 teachers over one year, from April – April. It is run by a project developer in conjunction with the CLC manager, and a team of CLC staff. There is also involvement on training days from the Local Authority advisor for ICT and a university tutor who specialises in teacher education. It has three core components:

- skills training in a range of Web 2.0 and more established technologies
- collaborative work, both face to face and via Web 2.0
- teacher enquiry and critical reflection on developing practice.

For the first six months, teachers receive basic training in five short sessions (usually after school or as part of whole day meetings) at the City Learning Centre in a range of technology applications. Participants are given a range of hardware (e.g. MacBooks©, digital cameras, microphones) and software (e.g. video and audio editing packages plus the usual Microsoft Office© packages. The emphasis is on providing a range of tools and software, some freeware, that can enhance teaching and learning). They are expected to work in their own time familiarising themselves with the software and hardware, before framing a research question to address the effect of one or two aspects on a specific group of students. They are expected to carry out small-scale innovations with the students within their schools, supported by the Centre staff who can carry out planned site visits on a needs basis to install software, provide further skills training and advise on pedagogy. Ongoing support is thus provided by programme staff, but participants are encouraged to collaborate and support each other electronically through a shared 'room' on Fronter Open Learning Platform©, and through their blogs. The senior staff member is also required to hold regular meetings in school to monitor and support the teachers' developing practice and enquiry.

Communication within the community is maintained in a variety of ways during the year. The teachers blog their experiences on Edublogs© throughout the programme, and share online their teaching artefacts and experiences of using the technologies. They meet face to face at the CLC with the whole group of teachers, with other TTP teachers in their local school 'clusters' and in their learning 'triads' within their schools. Their enquiries are planned and published within the online community, and are aimed at focusing wider development work in their schools. At the end of the programme, the teachers can choose to submit their multimodal presentation of their enquiries (which is a compulsory requirement) for accreditation with local universities who have developed awards for higher level professional development which can lead to a masters qualification. There is an expectation that, along with their fellow TTP teacher and support from the school 'transformation manager', each participant will become a leader of 'transformation' in her school, providing INSET, support and training to groups of teachers in implementing and embedding new technologies across the curriculum. The Haringey teachers, working in some of the most challenging schools in the country, were subject to high expectations. In return they were transparently valued. The face to face events were well-organised and generously catered, and they attended a programme dinner with relevant speakers in a prestigious location as part of the social networking aspect of the course.

The Technologies

It was viewed as essential that teachers become familiar with technologies by "owning" equipment (the equipment is actually owned by the school but teachers are allowed to keep it full time until they leave) and being able to experiment with it at home in their own time. By doing this, they could take advantage of their private networks, drawing on personal support from friends and family as well as colleagues as part of their immersion in the new technologies. Embedding technologies in teachers' lives outside as well as inside school is seen as an essential aspect of 'transformation', enabling informal experimentation and online networking to take a central place in professional development. This is a significant departure from conventional ICT CPD previously experienced by most teachers. Each teacher is provided with the following equipment, which must be included in their schools' insurance arrangements, and which becomes available for them to keep for use in school when they complete the course. If they do not carry out innovations and teacher enquiry, the equipment must be returned:

MacBook© – with both Windows© and Mac© software using VM Fusion© to allow teachers to use both PC and Mac platforms simultaneously
Button mouse
Monitor cable
Flashdrive to enable staff to move resources around

Table 1. Programme equipment. (Transformation Teachers Programme, 2008).

Software – PC	Software - Mac
Microsoft Office for Windows XP©	
OpenMind©	Smart Board Software©
	iWorks '08©
PhotoShop Elements©	iLife '08©
Smart Board Software©	iMovie©
2 Kar2ouche titles©	Skype©
Audacity©	ScreenFlow©
Skype©	Quick Time Pro©
Quick Time Pro©	PulpMotion©
Microsoft Photo Story©	Banner Zest©
MemoryMiner©	
Dida Support pack© – includes media players	Dida Support pack© – includes media players

Digital still camera with video capability
Rucksack/laptop bag
Microphone.

Programme equipment and software was ambitious in its scope. It was not intended that teachers would use all the available packages and equipment, but that they would all be able to develop practice with particular ones according to a variety of factors: confidence levels, personal enthusiasms, school development priorities, subject preferences and knowledge of the particular needs of their learners and what might motivate and enhance their learning. Giving teachers genuine choices about what to focus on and at what pace to progress according to their individual needs and a level playing field in terms of everyone having the same tools and quality of hardware was an important element of the flexible approach of the programme. The range and variety of programme software was a vital aspect of CPD and actively promoted Web 2.0 technologies (see Table 1).

In addition, kits were provided for specific project loan during the course:
ActivStudio Voting Kit© x 3

Video cameras
Visualisers x 4
Senteo Voting Kit©
Genee Census Voting Kit©
Digital SLRs with Live view capacity

The programme was sponsored in part by commercial providers who assisted with discounts on various licences and kit items, and this was a further crucial element in enabling a wide range of software to be introduced:

Immersive Education (Kar2ouche) ©
Matchware (OpenMind) ©
Techknowledgey (Crazy Talk) ©
Toucan Computing (Apple kit) ©

The Training Days

Field notes taken on the face to face programme days contain observation evidence of the co-constructivist model which underpins the teachers' learning on the CPD programme:

The afternoon is devoted to two sessions focused on introducing software, one on using StopMotion© animation, and the other is 'MemoryMiner'©.

Teachers have a choice of attending one, both or none. They have the option to network with each other, to attend the training workshops, or to work alone on their skills development in any area with support from the CLC team. Choice is important – most teachers attended the animation session, but they could choose to consolidate previous knowledge or knowledge from the morning workshops (Smart Board© and Garageband©). Twenty-two teachers attended the animation session (two are 'graduates' from last year, assisting). Having had a twenty minute demo, they are invited to get into groups, one camera and tripod per group, and make an animation, one group to a computer. The trainer emphasizes that making an animation is a powerful collaborative tool. They are encouraged to work with models (lego, playmobil people, cut outs). They are sitting on the floor in groups around large pieces of card with cut-out figures, camera poised, fervently discussing the next shot. Another cry goes up… There's a palpable sense of learning…

The whole building is a hub of activity, of animated and highly engaged talk. In the corridor, a woman sits and works away at her laptop; in another room, teachers are working at different speeds, on different activities, in groups, alone, with other teachers helping, with last year's teachers helping, with CLC technical support…a whole constellation of ways of working according to teachers' readiness, aptitudes, needs.

The CPD arrangements reflect the features of school classrooms which are built on co-constructivist approaches – the teachers are engaged in flexible, multiple activities; group talk is central to the learning; collaborative group work is the vehicle for learning, and premised on the belief that the teachers will achieve more together than they could alone within a context of challenging 'instruction'. There are spaces to work alone to consolidate and practise, drawing on further individual help if needed, which might come from other teachers or CLC staff. It is CPD based on a pedagogical model which fosters the co-construction of knowledge and practice, driven by a strong sense of purpose, with teachers motivated by creativity, exploration and, essentially, risk-taking. This is a context where they can take a leap into the unknown with colleagues in support and with no fear of recrimination if things do not go as expected. Technologies are not just for production of resources or creative task-making, but for networking and sharing the learning – which of course can be embedded within 'task-making'. An audio-recording becomes a podcast. Digital photographs are to be shared on flickr. Outcomes and artefacts are to be embedded in blogs and commented upon. Text-based powerpoint 'delivery' is banned.

The School-Based Learning

Within the space allowed here, we present examples from the case in the form of two 'vignettes' of teachers whose practice has been affected in different ways. One is of a teacher, Tessa, who has completed the programme, and the other is of Sasha, one of the school colleagues to whom Tessa is charged with 'passing on' the new practices she has developed. The vignettes help to distil the essential features of the kinds of impact such a programme can have – where it matters most, back with the school's wider network of teachers. The vignettes can help to provide an in-depth look at the micro-level processes which enable practice to change for both the TTP teacher and her colleague, as a result of collaborative CPD.

Two Vignettes

The experiences of two teachers working in one of the schools involved in the Haringey project illuminate the ways in which the 'core design principles' for effective professional learning (Pickering et al, 2007) are played out in practice. The vignettes illustrate how they engage with the various learning communities they belong to or are brought into contact with – the community of Haringey TTP teachers; the subject department at school; the wider school community. Significance lies in the inter-relationship between their individual experiences and the social contexts and community dimensions which help shape them. Teachers' learning experiences are distributed across technologies, communities and people. What ties them together is a community perspective which informs both practice with pupils in classroom and teachers in CPD contexts. The community element of the TTP is one key component which affects a range of other contexts where teachers use both online and classroom-based technology like an IWB. The two teachers were interviewed once in the autumn term of 2007 and then in April, 2008. Our first interview question – 'Tell us about a time in your teaching when you think learning has gone well' – led to a series of questions that focus on the ways in which the teachers use technology and have developed their confidence and competence in this area.

Sasha

Sasha is an English teacher with considerable experience of teaching media studies at her previous school. Her response to the opening question of the interview comes from a confident and informed understanding of what studying a 'literary text' could mean for a class of fifteen year olds. She speaks of 'the learning from a class novel' that she wants to encourage, using terms such as 'empathy with the characters', the 'relevance of the themes to students today' and 'the power of Steinbeck's writing'. She is clear too about helping the pupils themselves to 'write about literature and become more aware of the skills they are using and those they need to work on'. When she speaks of developing her use of IWB technology, it is in the context of this literary subject knowledge and her own developing classroom practice. Here she is speaking about teaching another literary

text, in response to the question: Tell me about some good things that have happened as a result of using the IWB.

Well, just this morning, use of images, it sounds silly, but just the size of the images on the whiteboard. The way you can use them. I was telling students about the social, historical context of 'A View from the Bridge'. Showing pictures, getting them to talk about emotions and so on. I used a resource Tessa put together for 'Of Mice and Men', and we were debating issues around power between the characters, and we were able to move characters around and got students to think about where they would position them… Also, kids do presentations for me on 'Of Mice and Men' characters, and all of those have been saved in shared resources, so for revision they can go back to that.

It is in many ways a very 'simple' view of the affordances of the technology – moving things around on an IWB – but this teacher's understanding of learning and progress in English that underpins the practice, as well as her view of a classroom pedagogy, are complex. She says elsewhere in the interview that she wants her classroom to be a place where pupils 'interact with each other' and where they can express their own opinions about literature and 'develop independence as readers and Smart Boards© can do that'. She speaks confidently about the technology because it is embedded in her own rationale for the co-construction of knowledge by teachers and pupils alike:

So the use of Smart Board©, becoming more the way we are teaching, and trying to use it more interactively, to use it to differentiate, to support students in the class, alongside me as a professional. And we have had a lot of talking in the school this year, about the future of schools and where teaching is going. Some people talk about a time when you won't need teachers or you will have a virtual teacher who will talk to millions of people across the world and so on. But I feel the value of a teacher as an individual, it is something I would never want to see disappear. But as somebody who isn't great with technology I can still see the value of it. I think the Smart Board© is a fantastic resource.

A major factor in Sasha's professional learning is the sharing of practice with colleagues she trusts and in situations where she feels free to experiment and 'play around on her own'. She says at one point that she needs to 'believe in the learning' before she feels 'pushed to find out more about the technology' and it is clear that her belief in Smart Board© begins with a view of learning before the practice becomes an integral part of her professional life as an English teacher. The colleague, Tessa the TTP 'graduate' whose work she refers to here, had offered a session to newly qualified and student teachers on using Smart Board© and Sasha decided to go along.

It was funny, actually, because I thought I was going to be the only teacher going along, and I walked along and there were about six other people who had heard about it. Someone from languages, a [student teacher] from languages, another member from the English department, Louise, came in as well, to kind of see what was happening, and since then my confidence has gone right up because Tessa did it in a very considered way and she took us through how to produce ... And I have been sitting down and adapting things and producing my own stuff ... Now I have got to the stage where I think – how would I teach without a Smart Board©? Which is the point you want to get to, in a sense, isn't it? And not feeling – oh gosh, I have got to use that today!

Sasha thinks she is at the point with the software where she needs more training, but only because, as she puts it, 'I know what I can do with it for my teaching'. She points to the kind of 'playing

around time' that she needs if the technology is to really shape her practice:

After the session finished last week, Louise and Tessa were playing around with it. And I stayed for a while, and then I thought I had to leave, because my brain can't cope with all of this yet. I just need to go and fix everything they have told me. So I know there is so much capability and I am not up to speed on that yet. So I need more training on that.

For Sasha, crucial to her professional learning in this area is her collaboration with others in the department and with one particular teacher, Tessa, who is one of the participating teachers in the Haringey project.

Tessa

At the time of the first interview Tessa had responsibility for 'i-learning in the English department'. In this school, 'i-learning' indicates a specific view of ICT as supporting 'independent learning that is interactive and inclusive'. At the session on the use of IWBs that Sasha found so effective, Tessa describes in detail the kind of collaborative, 'figuring it out together' atmosphere she wanted to create.

So when I led that session on Thursday it was quite nice because Louise came in at some point and initially I thought – oh Louise, don't watch me. It is bad enough teaching your colleagues, without someone else ... But every so often Louise would go – ooh, I didn't know how to do that. I have learnt something today. And similarly there was one point where Louise, I can't remember what it was now, but she showed me and said – you know you can do this. And by the end of that session, because a couple of questions I couldn't answer, and I had said – oh, I will try and figure that out. And we got to the end and I started playing around and by the end of the session I had figured out how to do three or four more things .... I quite like being able to model to students the not knowing as well as the knowing!

This is someone with a strong belief in the co-constructed nature of knowledge, who sees the learning of both teachers and pupils as very much a collaborative venture. She says she doesn't feel 'qualified to be an expert' which perhaps calls into question the discourse around 'expert' in relation to many aspects of education, including technology. From a community perspective, the concept of 'expert' needs to be revised, and investment in the collaborative responsibility for growing professional knowledge among teachers is more appropriate. Tessa understands the learning needs of her department and how to capitalise on her colleagues' strengths as well as to develop their expertise. Sasha, she says:

… is not 'instinctively' good with technology, therefore just to say to her – these are blogs, they are technology, they are great, look – she is not going to go for that. But if you say – these are great because – she will go for it. And the kind of picture of her as being someone who is a bit technophobe, was proved totally wrong… She was the only one after the first session who had gone away and done anything.

Tessa is explicit about her own view of the value of collaboration and it underpins her work on a new project with her A level students – the development of personal blogs to support their reading and writing about literature. This idea came from one of the Haringey TTP training sessions:

I picked blogs because it was the only thing I could straightaway see, easily see a learning use for… I had used them, I had realised how collaborative they could be. On one level I think I just thought – won't it be nice, (the students) will like it more. But I think I had also seen the pedagogical benefits and the collaborative benefits.

For Tessa, using the blogs with her students comes out of her own experiences of using them as part of the Haringey TTP programme. 'I think it does help,' she says 'if you have used it to support your learning, you can immediately see how it supports other people's'. She is able to engage in 'scholarly reflection on practice' (Pickering et al, 2007 p. 6) and her comments about the students' learning come from her own strong subject and pedagogical base. Scholarly reflection is core to her teacher enquiry about introducing blogging to students, entitled 'How can blogs be used to increase motivation, independence and collaboration in students making the transition from AS to A2 English?' Increasing motivation, independence and collaboration are precisely the drivers behind the TTP approach she has experienced.

One example of her critical awareness about her practice is what she says about the way the literature blogs support a particular aspect of teaching and learning: using questions to consolidate understanding and to move students forward.

And by making the students ask a question (about the reading), the second homework was – you must go on to your blog and answer all the questions that have been asked you. And that then functioned as a kind of higher order questioning that I do in class when they [?] much more developed answers that were in lots of cases more articulate somehow, than their initial posts… I think the same level of improvement happens when you say to a student – tell me more about what you mean. Because they do kind of elaborate more. To see that in writing is powerful… I suppose, yeah, again, it was a basic pedagogical technique that a good teacher uses all the time, just being done in a different way. So I think for me, that kind of technological thing is saying – what can I do already that is good? Because I want to keep doing that. How can I use technology to make it better?

Community Perspectives in the Teachers' Experiences

When Tessa presents her work to a small group of 'interested teachers' from several departments in an after-school session, Sasha 'went along and learned how to create a blog'. It is clear that Sasha's belief in the value of the blogs was very much the result of her respect for both Tessa's sensitivity as a teacher working with peers and her values as an English teacher. The values and pedagogy of the Haringey TTP have filtered through to her own practice, although she herself never participated directly. The learning community is widely distributed and takes on different forms of membership where individuals form their own relationship with it according to their practice contexts. In the April 2008 interview, Sasha describes her own work on developing the reading blogs with the Year 7 (twelve and thirteen-year-olds) as 'the main thing I've done'. Everything she says about the 'online reading community' that she is trying to build is consistent with her ideas about the ways young people learn to read critically and to talk about their reading in a variety of ways, within and beyond the classroom or school. It is also consistent with the pedagogical approach to online collaborative learning which was a feature of the TTP. She is asked about the value of the blogs for the students and she says:

I think it's...collaborative learning. I also think it is an online reading community. And I think it is important to model how to read. And I think that part of reading, not just sitting in your room and reading, is actually discussing your reading... I want them to develop the independence, first of all, the collaborative learning, the ability to discuss and articulate interpretations. A desire to discuss their reading, to discuss anything really. Motivation to learn independently.

Much of this is embedded in Sasha's view of herself as a 'teacher of reading': the technology simply would not work without this underpinning view of reading as a social practice. Introducing blogs and encouraging the students to engage in the kind of 'talk about reading' that research suggests is important in developing independence and enthusiasm for reading has helped Sasha to develop and refine her own views in ways that might not have been possible without what she calls 'taking a chance with the technology'. Setting up 'collaborative reading activities' and 'getting (the students) to listen to each others' views and to disagree about books' is of course possible in the classroom; but it seems the technology has helped to embed literacy practices in the pupils' wider social and cultural lives, where social networking is becoming ubiquitous, as well as shaping the teachers' own learning.

For Tessa and Sasha, the technology supports a clear, powerfully articulated view of learning and the role of the teacher. The formal and informal networks that exist in the school or are being put into place by committed teachers are valuable in so far as these draw on perceived interests and ongoing need.

DISCUSSION

The case provides a complex picture of the range of interactions which support the learning process and allow teachers to be self-directing within flexible and supportive environments which constitute professional learning communities, as described by Bolam et al, 2005 and Pickering et al, 2007. This has been crucial to enable each participant to learn as a 'networked teacher' (Couros, 2006). Being 'networked' in terms of professional learning requires careful facilitation, so that the teachers benefit from a spectrum of collaborative arrangements, social and technological, which enable them to function as a community. Essential to Couros' model is the teacher's two-way engagement with all the learning resources available – the teacher is both a 'maker' as well as a 'user' of these, an active participant in their own learning but also affecting the learning of others. The online element of the case is critical to this. Fronter© is not used as a repository, but as a space for critical sharing. The requirement to blog within the VLE is core to the teachers' commitment to their own development and to the fact that it is a shared experience within a community. Using the VLE to share progress in terms of planning, resources and reflection on experiences is vital for maintaining the group cohesion and impetus for learning between face to face meetings. It can be recognized as a component of Fielding et al's (2005) 'joint practice development' which takes place within teachers' learning communities. This is because it supports a wide diversity of development to take place among teachers who are different subject specialists but who are encouraged to develop shared pedagogical principles based on collaboration, embracing diversity, active engagement and creativity. This principled pedagogical core is supported by the ways the teachers are expected to engage with the VLE. The CPD experience is not without firm leadership and accountability – the parameters are very strict, and the teachers must carry out an innovation, or they lose the equipment. They must also carry out teacher enquiry, and must make their work shareable on the VLE so that it becomes a facet of the community. They must blog and make their professional activities accessible to others by using Web 2.0 utilities. The demands are clear, and act as a supportive framework in which teachers take charge of their development, take the degrees of risk for which they are ready, they to a large extent, determine how they will be accountable – how they can show what they have learnt. These examples from the case study of the TTP suggest that it reflects the three core principles identified by Pickering et al (2007), which – it is argued here – underpin effective teachers' professional development: the co-construction of shared teacher knowledge; collaboration through learning networks; and scholarly reflection on practice. The

case reflects many of Cordingley's (2005, 2007) findings about effective CPD recorded earlier (i.e. the use of peer support; applying and refining new knowledge and skills and experimenting with ways of integrating them in day-to-day practice; consultation with teachers about their own starting points, focus or pace and scope of development). It further suggests that combined online and face to face provision can help teachers to actively engage with peers to allow them to benefit from expert input (Cordingley, 2007) and grow their own practice by experimentation, sharing practice and consultation.

FUTURE TRENDS

In the light of these perspectives, it is not helpful to describe what has happened to the teachers as 'going on a course' and the case indicates that a new and different kind of ICT CPD provision is required for teachers to meet the needs of contemporary learners. Transformational learning here has required immersion in a complex learning experience, which is made up of many parts. This of course, raises troubling questions about how possible it may be to replicate such a model. The implication is that, in the future, a transformational model is not located in one place. It will be distributed. It will involve fluctuating cohorts of participants who come into contact with each other in varying ways at different times for differing purposes, in different groupings, in different patterns of partnerships based on expert-learner, learner-leaner, learner-'new' expert, etc. It will have multiple locations – online learning environments (which can be accessed, increasingly, by mobile devices); government-sponsored centres such as the CLC; cluster schools; the classrooms of the teachers; teachers' homes. It will move between different constellations of teachers – whole cohorts, the groups they join for workshops etc, cluster groupings, school pairings, triads and so forth. All the collaborations have had roles to play in this case of developing pedagogy, but this gives a glimpse of a possible future CPD scenario which is highly complex. There is no attempt to 'simplify' the kinds of interactions which are needed, and the fact that they are multilayered and 'multi-played' means that there are significant challenges in re-producing such a programme in its widest sense. In the case, there are inconsistent patterns in the amount of time and support available from the senior transformation managers within the triads. Some schools already had the infrastructure to support the dissemination of new expertise, but for others there was no clear way for the teacher to assume a catalytic role and support colleagues' individual needs. Much of this depends on highly skilful teacher qualities in terms of professional relationships and leadership approaches. The se-lection of the teachers by headteachers is crucial, but so is school leaders' perceptions of what the model means for their school and its wider ethos of CPD. Central to the programme is the 'vision' of the CLC staff, and their considerable skills in being able to lead and co-ordinate such a ven-ture and inspire 'non-expert' teachers to take up catalytic roles. Even within the borough, shifting funding priorities mean that the continuation of the programme in this form is by no means certain, despite the extremely positive feedback received from schools and teacher evaluations. One way into the future is in sight here, and yet to bring it into being would require a fundamental shift in the ways CPD is currently organized.

At the core of what is difficult, is that informal, genuinely enquiry-based and collaborative prac-tices for teachers and students require changes in the ways that learning (for students and teachers) is currently organised in many schools. The roles of 'catalysts' within effective learning commu-nities for technology-related CPD are vital and complex. The community fostered both online and face to face by the TTP is centred on both skills training and critical enquiry, within a col-laborative approach. The demand that Tessa has to blog her CPD experiences has been crucial to bringing about critical awareness of changes in the teachers' practices, and to Tessa's self-perception as a non-specialist teacher regarding ICT, who can assume a hands-on role in the development of pedagogies within her school.

A further issue which emerges is the issue of how teachers can be enabled to appropriate new technologies in their personal, social and profes-sional lives in order for a transformed relationship with technologies to become embedded. This is, in our estimation, an important pre-requisite for use in their pedagogical practices. The programme was in part reliant on funding being available via the BSF initiative to support such an ambitious vision, including the personal provision of equip-ment for teachers and access to the latest software, frequently discounted by commercial providers. The role of a variety of stakeholders in new models for ICT CPD needs to be understood if teachers as learners are indeed to be 'networked' in appropriate ways. As government policy initiatives continue to change at increasing rates in attempts to 'keep up with technology', the issues of sustainability, funding priorities and sources of funding for CPD need serious consideration.

CONCLUSION

In considering collaborative approaches to CPD, the case suggests that teachers' participation in online communities exists in complex interrela-tionship with other learning practices, only some of which use technology. Collaborative professional development involves the use of technologies for the sharing of experiences and artefacts within and across schools as a basis for critical reflection on pedagogy; it helps teachers to take account of the context-specific nature of professional practice, whilst remaining outward-looking in their pro-fessional discussions; it is based on the premise that peers act as critical friends in evaluating professional practices around new technologies. In particular, we consider collaborative professional development mediated by technology, and the relationship between this learning experience and how teachers re-assess their students' learning practices in their classrooms, as important.

In this way, we see new technologies afford certain opportunities and present certain challenges to teachers' continuous professional development. Lee and Judy Shulman (2004) have recently updated the original, cognitive, individually and subject specialism orientated notion of pedagogical content knowledge (PCK) to add the notion of what they call teacher learning communities and posit that "an accomplished teacher is a member of a professional community who is ready, willing, and able to teach and to learn from his or her teaching experiences" (Schulman & Schulman, 2004, p. 259). By ready, they mean 'possessing vision', by willing 'having motivation', by able 'both knowing and being able 'to do'", reflective 'learning from experience' and communal 'acting as a member of a professional community'; these are the key elements of their theory. They also note that each of these elements and dimension has implications for personal and professional development. What is the potential and what are the challenges of using new technologies to operationalise such a vision of professional teacher learning? Engström (2005), for example, offers a very interesting analysis of what factors make social networking services useful, which seems to be of relevance for our purposes here and poses a key challenge. Engström argues that there exists a profound confusion about the term 'social network' as a 'map of relationships between individuals' and argues instead for a view of it as 'object-centred sociality'. In other words, effective networks are predicated on a shared object (understood here in the tradition of Activity Theory) by which people are connected. This notion, if accepted, has clear implications for the use of social networking tools and online networks for continuing professional development and suggests the central importance of a shared object. The 'shared object' in our case can be seen as the ongoing body of pedagogical

knowledge and practice which is at the core of the various networks. It is knowledge which both helps constitute the networks, and which is developed by them.

Finally, we summarise here the key points concerning ICT CPD, focusing on the future development of collaborative networks between and within schools, based on the case. Teachers should have a tangible sense of being valued as part of the CPD process. It seems clear that an inspirational 'vision' of what is possible needs to inform ambitious CPD design, based on sound understanding of how teachers learn, how technologies are integral to students' and teachers' learning, and how schools can work as learning organisations. Collaboration is a key feature of all this, and we need to consider how, in the future, to include a wide range of participants, locations and formats for collaborative work to underpin CPD activities. Teacher enquiry is a further important element of CPD, involving critical and reflective processes. Higher Education has a role to play in ensuring that teacher enquiry is embedded as an achievable programme activity, and that the quality of outcomes can lead to professional accreditation, where appropriate. On an operational level it is vital that headteachers and senior school leaders are fully engaged with CPD processes from the start, with time available for senior staff to support the activities and that they are sympathetic to flexibility as a key feature of CPD designs. This allows teachers to make meaningful choices about the focus of their ICT development based on personal enthusiasms, knowledge of students' needs and subject differences. Time to allow for full participation of teachers in distributed CPD activities should be built into CPD design at school level. As for technology skills training, there needs to be a mixture of core training to enable Web 2.0 communication to underpin shared learning processes, and specialised options according to individual needs and preferences. Equipment and up-to-date software needs to be made available to teachers for their long-term use, in order to integrate their personal, social and professional use of technologies. This is an essential informal aspect of skills development. Investment from a range of stakeholders, e.g. commercial providers, should be considered to develop the best means by which they can help to ensure access to the latest technologies and secure sustainability for collaborative CPD in uncertain economic and political climates.

ACKNOWLEDGMENT

The 'Teachers and Technology' research study was funded by the Centre for Excellence for Work-based Learning for Education Professionals, Institute of Education, University of London.

Thanks are due to Judith Jakes (TTP project developer) and Lincoln Fisher (Haringey City Learning Centre manager) for their considerable help and in contributing to the case and allowing access to the programme. Thanks also to the teachers involved in the programme who gave freely of their time to talk about their experiences.

REFERENCES

Becta (2007). *Harnessing Technology Review 2007: progress and impact of technology in education*. Coventry: Becta.

Bolam, R., McMahon, A., Stoll, L., Thomas, S., & Wallace, M. (2005). *Creating and Sustaining Effective Professional Learning Communities*. London: Department for Education and Skills.

Cordingley, P., Bell, M., Evans, D., & Firth, A. (2005). The impact of collaborative continuing professional development (CPD) on classroom teaching and learning. Review: How do collaborative and sustained CPD and sustained but not collaborative CPD affect teaching and learning? In *Research Evidence in Education Library*. London: EPPI-Centre, Social Science Research Unit, Institute of Education, University of London.

Cordingley, P., Bell, M., Isham, C., Evans, D., & Firth, A. (2007). What do specialists do in CPD programmes for which there is evidence of positive outcomes for pupils and teachers? In *Research Evidence in Education Library*. London, EPPI-Centre, Social.

Couros, A. (2006). *Examining the open movement: possibilities and implications for education*. Unpublished doctoral dissertation, University of Regina, Saskatchewan.

Cox, M., Webb, M., Abbott, C., Blakeley, B., Beauchamp, T., & Rhodes, V. (2003). *ICT and pedagogy. A review of the research literature*. London: Becta for the Department for Education and Skills.

Dede, C. (2006). *Online Professional Development for Teachers*. Cambridge, MA: Harvard Education Press.

Department for Children. Schools and Families (2008). *Harnessing Technology: Next Generation Learning 2008-14*. Coventry: Becta.

Devereux, C. (2009). *Beyond the curriculum: The positive effects of Continual Professional Development for a group of post-16 science teachers*. Occasional Paper, London: WLE Centre, Institute of Education.

Engeström, J. (2005). *Why some social network services work and others don't – Or: the case for object-centred sociality*. Retrieved June 10th, 2007, from: http://www.typepad.com/t/trackback/242863/2243067

Fielding, M., Bragg, S., Craig, J., Cunningham, I., Eraut, M., Gillinson, S., et al. (2005). *Factors Influencing the Transfer of Good Practice*. London: Department for Education and Skills.

Fisher, T., Higgins, C., & Loveless, A. (2006). *Teachers Learning with Digital Technologies: a review of research and projects*. Futurelab series, No 14. Retrieved December 20th 2006, from: http://www.futurelab.org.uk/research/lit_reviews.htm#lr14 20.12.06).

Green, H., & Hannon, C. (2007). *Their Space. Education for a digital generation.* London: Demos (available at www.demos.co.uk).

Kress, G., & Pachler, N. (2007). Thinking about the 'm' in m-learning. In N. Pachler (Ed.), *Mobile learning: towards a research agenda* (pp. 7-32). London: WLE Centre, Institute of Education. Available at: http://www.wlecentre. ac.uk/cms/files/occasionalpapers/mobilelearning_pachler_2007.pdf

Moss, G., Jewitt, C., Levacic, R., Armstrong, V., Cardini, A., & Castle, F. (2007). *The interactive whiteboards, pedagogy and pupil performance evaluation: an evaluation of the Schools Whiteboard Expansion (SWE) project: London Challenge.* Nottingham: DfES.

Pachler, N., Barnes, A., & Field, K. (2008). *Learning to teach modern foreign languages in the secondary school.* (3rd ed.). London: Routledge.

Pachler, N., & Daly, C. (2008). Narrative and social networking technologies. In Y. Gächter, H. Ortner, C. Schwarz, & A. Wiesinger, (Eds.), *Storytelling – Reflexionen im Zeitalter der Digitalisierung / Storytelling – Reflections in the Age of Digitalization* (pp. 196-201). Innsbruck: iup.

Pachler, N., & Daly, N. (2006). Online communities and professional teacher learning: affordances and challenges. In E. Sorensen & D. Murchú, (Eds,), *Enhancing learning through technology* (pp. 1-28). Hershey, PA: Idea Group.

Pickering, J., Pachler, N., & Daly, C. (Eds.). (2007). *New designs for teachers' professional learning.* Bedford Way Papers. London: Institute of Education, UoL

Preston, C. (2004). *Learning to use ICT in classrooms: teachers' and trainees' perspectives. An evaluation of the English NOF ICT teacher training programme 1999 – 2003* London: Mirandanet and the Teacher Training Agency

Preston, C., & Cuthell, J. (2007). *Perspectives on ICT CPD: The experiential learning of advisers responsible for school teachers' ICT CPD programmes.* London: WLE Centre Occasional Papers in Work-based Learning 3.

Sachs, J. (2003). *The Activist Teaching Profession.* Buckingham: Open University Press.

Schifter, C. (2008). *Infusing Technology into the Classroom: Continuous Practice Improvement.* IGI Global.

Shulman, L., & Shulman, J. (2004). How and what teachers learn: a shifting perspective. *Journal of Curriculum Studies, 36*(2), 257–271. doi:10.1080/0022027032000148298

Chapter 6
Realising the Potential of Virtual Environments
A Challenge for Scottish teachers

Alastair Wilson
University of Strathclyde, UK

Donald Christie
University of Strathclyde, UK

ABSTRACT

A national schools intranet is currently being developed in Scotland with universal access anticipated in late 2009. This new technology will provide teachers with access to a variety of tools with which to develop their teaching and learning. Drawing on the experience of the Applied Educational Research Scheme (AERS), a five year research programme funded to build research capacity in Scottish Education, this chapter seeks to explore the potential for teachers in Scotland to realise effective use of this new technology in their professional learning. The chapter uses current research literature on teacher professionalism and professional learning in Scotland to establish the context in which Scottish teachers are currently working. It then draws on three vignettes drawn from research within AERS to argue that the development of virtual environments to support professional learning in Scotland requires further, significant collaborative working between the practitioner, policy and research communities.

INTRODUCTION

Glow, the national schools intranet, is currently being made available to Scottish schools with universal access expected in 2009. In essence GLOW will offer schools, teachers and pupils: secure and personalised access to the intranet and internet; virtual learning opportunities; and a range of tools to enable users to collaborate, cooperate and communicate across the network (GLOW, 2008). Almost in parallel with the development of GLOW the Applied Educational Research Scheme[1] (AERS) has been striving to build educational research capacity, support and sustain the research infrastructure and, crucially, to develop more effective collaboration among researchers, policy-makers and practitioners. In the early developmental stages of AERS the potential of virtual environments was recognised as a possible means of supporting these aims. Working in collaboration with the Centre for Applied Research

DOI: 10.4018/978-1-60566-780-5.ch006

in Educational Technology (CARET) at the University of Cambridge, AERS adopted the Sakai virtual environment in late 2004 primarily as a platform for a diverse range of research and other collaborative activity. Within AERS the Learners, Learning and Teaching Network (LLTN) consisted of three substantive research projects examining teachers as learners in the context of professional development; the impact of neighbourhood on pupil engagement in learning and the concept of 'community of enquiry' as a collaborative model of engagement in educational research. The LLTN recognized the potential of virtual environments to impact on each of these areas and took a lead in developing the Sakai virtual environment as a means of supporting collaborative research and enquiry. Initial interest in using virtual environments in this way was extensive with a broad spectrum of different types of groups seeking support from the LLTN in their use of the environment. These included special interest groupings involving practitioners, policymakers and researchers engaging in joint discussion and collaborative enquiry and small, often dispersed Higher Education (HE) educational research teams.

As the work of the LLTN further developed it afforded researchers the opportunity to work more closely with schools and teachers, and in particular, to explore the use of virtual environments as a means of supporting teaching and learning. At the time of print participating schools were developing virtual environments in a range of different ways:

- As a means of engaging pupils by collating subject-based resources and access to discussion with other pupils and teachers outside school hours;
- As a supportive environment for specific classes and a means to increasing engagement of parents/carers;
- As a resource supporting professional learning by facilitating virtual collaboration within and between schools.

This varied application of the Sakai virtual environment within the AERS community provided researchers within the LLTN the opportunity to explore the potential impact of virtual environments on a range of different areas of Scottish education. In the sections which follow, this chapter seeks to outline the ways in which the LLTN progressed this work (which was effectively an action research project). The chapter discusses some of the theoretical ideas which informed the work as well as briefly describing the context in terms of teacher professional learning in which it developed. An illustration of the empirical work of the project is presented in the form of three vignettes which form the basis of discussion and reflection. In this way the chapter seeks to offer insight into how teachers may realise the potential of virtual environments and the GLOW digital network to impact positively on both their own and subsequently, pupil learning. Three key questions provide the framework for this analysis:

- What is the current landscape of teacher professionalism in Scotland?
- How fertile is this environment in terms of nurturing teacher learning and innovation?
- In what ways can virtual environments support teacher engagement in collaborative enquiry and research?

Engaging Teachers in Virtual Collaboration

There is now a strong body of literature supporting the need for teachers to be engaged in collaborative working '...to build strong professional cultures of collaboration to develop common purpose, to cope with uncertainty and complexity' (Hargreaves 2000; p.165). In addition it has been widely recognised that there is a need for more effective collaboration in research between policy makers, practitioners and educational researchers (Furlong and Oancea 2005; Smedley 2001; McLaughlin and Black-Hawkins, 2004) both UK wide and specifically within Scotland (Baron, 2004). Within AERS the LLTN has explored the concept of 'community of enquiry' as a potential means of facilitating these ambitions (AERS 2008; Cassidy, Christie, Coutts, Dunn, Sinclair, Skinner & Wilson, 2008; Christie, Cassidy, Skinner, Coutts, Sinclair, Rimpilainen & Wilson, 2007). Such interest and enthusiasm for collaborative working has been paralleled with increased possibilities for using new internet technologies to facilitate collaborative activities (*see*Carusi, 2006 and Laterza *et al.*, 2007). Furthermore a range of recent research indicates that the use of these new technologies and virtual environments in particular, can play a vital role in supporting '… communities of professionals to better understand the learning practices they are engaged in' (Pachler & Daly, 2006).

The Concept of 'Community of Enquiry'

As indicated above LLTN developed dual purposes, firstly by identifying and nurturing collaborative research groups and secondly, by investigating their ongoing development. In the initial phase of the work the research team undertook a review of a wide range of related literature (see Cassidy *et al*, 2008). The theoretical perspective adopted centred on the concept of community of enquiry. This concept is associated with 'community of philosophical inquiry' (Lipman, 1988, 1991; Pardales and Girod, 2006) which Lipman adapted from C.S. Pierce's collaborative approach to scientific research, community of inquiry. Communities of enquiry also have a tradition in adult education (Bray *et al.,* 2000) using a reflective enquiry process but again with little emphasis on empirical enquiry. For LLTN community of enquiry was an appropriate choice of concept given the emphasis on building collaboration and a sense of community between groups enquiring into issues of mutual concern in the field of learning and teaching. These groups were composed

of individuals from varying backgrounds and perspectives, committed to creating deeper, more rounded understanding, knowledge and practical solutions to the issues being considered (Cassidy *et al.,* 2008).

The related concept community of practice developed by Lave and Wenger (1991), widely employed in educational circles, is a somewhat elusive one, generally referring to informal groups which develop around an established work activity. The community of practice engenders a communal spirit, norms and mutual support to sustain the practice and initiate novices. Another more recent idea, increasingly discussed in relation to electronic networks, is that of 'innovative knowledge communities' (Hakkarainen *et al.*, 2004). Innovative knowledge communities are closely related to the developing LLT conceptualization of community of enquiry. In contrast to communities of practice, innovative knowledge communities are focused on knowledge creation rather than knowledge transfer, and are concerned with more than the socialisation and maintenance of existing social practices (Hakkarainen, *et al*, 2004). In addition, a community of enquiry is seen as a potentially powerful organising concept for developing collaboration between the policy, practice and research communities in an educational context (Christie, *et al.,* 2007; Wilson, *et al.*, 2007). The challenge to the LLT has been to find ways in which to realize some of this potential. The availability of virtual environments to researchers within LLTN provided a platform for the network to engage with and support collaborative working. This effectively demanded an action research approach.

Realising Communities of Enquiry?

From a process of progressive filtering and interpretation of the literature seven factors were identified by the research team (Cassidy *et al.,* 2008) as important considerations in the establishment and investigation of collaborative communities of enquiry in the context of educational research:

- dialogue and participation – a community depends on its members' opportunities to engage in dialogue and other modes of participation;
- relationships – participation in a community is sustained through the quality of its relationships;
- perspectives and assumptions – valuing different perspectives and assumptions underpins the relationships of a community and may offer insights into its dynamics and operation;
- structure and context – how a community operates is governed by its structure and context, including the extent to which its structure is imposed or constrained either internally or externally;
- climate – as a community develops, a climate for its operation also emerges – involving aspects such as tone, environment and potential conflict;
- purpose – the purpose of an enquiry will influence this climate and there may be a need to accommodate or harmonise a multiplicity of purposes arising from the complex interrelationships, perspectives and assumptions involved;
- control – a key issue for all communities is control, in relation to who has access to the community, to resources, constraints and power within it

Potential communities of enquiry within LLTN (including that illustrated in Vignette 1) were encouraged to consider these issues in the formation and nurturing of their groups. In addition they provided a useful lens for LLTN to explore and analyse data generated by emerging communities.

A Fertile Environment for Virtual Working?

As indicated above introducing virtual environments to schools and teachers requires their engagement in learning and appropriate resourcing. For teachers, in particular those wanting to develop innovative pedagogical approaches, realising effective use of virtual environments places considerable demands on their capacity to engage in appropriate professional development and learning. The developing LLTN research on teachers as learners (Kennedy *et al*, 2008; Fraser *et al* 2007) provided researchers with an insight both into the existing structure of teacher professional learning in Scotland and the cultural context in which this was established. In the following sections we explore the extent to which this specific cultural and political context provided a fertile environment for nurturing such innovation.

In a broad survey of professionals and professionalism in the UK Friedman and Philips (2004) highlight the ambiguity and tensions inherent in Continuing Professional Development (CPD), arguing that while professional associations are committed to establishing CPD as a crucial dimension of their members' lives, they have not 'developed a clear vision of what CPD is for' (p.361). They emphasize the ways in which CPD can be established as a means of ensuring lifelong learning, professional and personal development but also, crucially, as a means of ensuring competence. The extent to which these aims can co-exist, however, is contested. This is illustrated in Scotland by the General Teaching Council (GTC) referring to CPD as '...the ongoing learning and development of teachers throughout their careers' a statement that is immediately followed by 'all teachers have a contractual commitment to undertake 35 hours of CPD per year' (GTC Scotland 2008). A number of writers have explored the impact of this contested vision of CPD within teaching. In a study of 240 teachers in England Day *et al* (2007) describe teachers as holding positive views of their professionalism including the importance of continuing learning and collaborative cultures. However, this analysis also underlines teachers feelings of '...ambivalence and conflict, associated with increased bureaucracy, cultures of loneliness and the lack of understanding and ownership of the process of change' (Day *et al.*, 2007, p.264). Day and Sachs (2005) elaborate on this with the description of two current forms or versions of professionalism. The first, 'managerial professionalism' it is argued is advocated by employers and asserts itself in the '..promulgation of policies and the allocation of funds associated with these policies' (Day & Sachs, 2005; p.6). In this way 'managerial professionalism' becomes a tool for shaping teacher professionalism in order to ensure accountability and compliance. Perhaps a more cutting analysis of this conceptualization of teacher professionalism is provided by Ball (2003) through his analysis of the policy technologies of educational reform. Ball argues that policy technologies are not simply mechanisms for initiating organizational change but are also a means of 'reforming' teachers. This is what Ball refers to as the 'struggle for the teacher's soul' and, he argues, constitutes a direct threat to 'the act of teaching and the subjectivity of the teacher (Ball, 2007, p. 147). It is a process which changes the 'social identity' (Ball reference to Bernstein, 1971 p. 6) of teachers.

Co-existent with these formulations of professionalism are those which emphasize teacher autonomy, lifelong learning and crucially, the value of informal learning. In an interesting analogy Coffield (2000) argues that if learning was represented by an iceberg then the third of the mass above water would represent formal learning and the submerged two thirds '...would be needed to convey the importance of informal learning' (2000: p.1). Coffield expands on this to argue that despite is importance informal learning is largely ignored by government, employers and indeed researchers. In a discussion of implicit learning and tacit knowledge, Eraut (2000) argues

that policy makers and educators must understand 'the role played by tacit knowledge in all parts of our lives and avoid the delusion of hyper-rational interpretations of professional action' (2000: p.29). Turner (2006) provides an interesting analysis of the ways in which informal learning can be conceptualised as a model including three distinctive elements: reactive, deliberative and implicit. In his model Turner describes the ways in which cognitive, emotional and behaviourally based developmental processes influence the actions of inexperienced teachers (2006: p.315). The second form of professionalism described by Day & Sachs (2005) offers 'democratic professionalism' which attempts to avoid an entrenched response to managerialism by seeking to locate teacher professionalism within a wider context. In this form of teacher professionalism collaborative and collegial forms of working are nurtured to realize a version of professionalism which addresses reform but maintains professional autonomy (Day & Sachs, 2005; p.7).

However in an analysis of the experience of a group of teachers of professional development across a cluster of six schools in south-east Queensland, Australia, Hardy & Lingard (2008) illustrate the ways in which professional development constituted a local response to broader policy initiatives. In particular, teachers resisted *both* 'performative' and 'social democratic policy pressures associated with the reform agenda' (Hardy & Lingard, 2008, p. 77). For these teachers it was clear that the complex nature of the reform agenda coupled with further demands for measurable pupil gains made professional development, even when framed as collaborative, across school learning, something to be resisted. Teachers, under pressure from various dimensions of educational reform and accountability may then resist all forms of professional learning including collaborative and collegial opportunities for learning.

It is against these tensions in teacher professionalism that the LLTN has researched the use of the Sakai virtual environment as a means of engaging teachers in collaborative, professional development. Initially this work conceptualised virtual environments essentially as tools to support extant communities of enquiry. However further research has recognised virtual environments as potentially creating new environments in which participants engage and generate new forms of knowledge (Wilson *et al*, 2007). Hence, practitioner use of virtual environments needs to be recognised as a distinct and legitimate approach to collaborative working. However, this may create a tension between existing collaborative practice and that encouraged and supported by virtual environments. Drawing from a study of a pilot online environment Carr and Chambers (2006) argue that the teaching profession is not yet at the point were theory and practice about online professional learning are aligned (Carr & Chambers, 2006, p.155). They identify three key conditions that inhibited the use of the online community studied: a lack of perceived commonality of purpose which influenced time and effort; a lack of culture of shared critical reflection and a lack of familiarity and experience of using computer mediated communication tools (p.155). Schlager & Fusco (2003) recognise this and argue the need to understand existing communities within education before making use of new internet based technology to '..strengthen, grow, sustain…[extant communities] structures and processes' (p.207). Clearly then virtual environments, despite their innovative potential are dependent on and cannot be separated from the specific contexts in which they are to be realized.

Barriers to Teachers Developing Virtual Working

The development of virtual environments to support learning is not unproblematic and teachers will be expected to bridge pupils' personal experience of virtual environments from a variety of contexts (primarily from social networking sites) with educational activities and learning.

While an extensive literature informs on solely virtual learning environments (e.g. university provided distance learning course) much less is written about the ways in which ICT and virtual environments can support classroom teaching in a form of hybrid environment, supportive of classroom teaching but not intended to replace it. In a very clear analysis Richards (2006) highlights the need for various kinds of ICT infrastructure '..to be reconciled, approached and understood in terms of constructivist learning principles' (p.252). Richards also argues the need to move away from a transmission approach in which ICT is harnessed as a mere add on to existing practice to one in which technology and pedagogy are more carefully integrated. These are clearly issues which teachers will need to supported to address. Liu & Huang (2005) identified a number of administrative interventions such as providing teachers with positive examples of technology integration; incentives for teachers in terms of release time and summer courses; workshops and demonstrations of technology integration across the curriculum (p.46).

Research also indicates that teachers in particular face a number of barriers to engaging with internet technologies such as competence in using IT, access to networked computers and time to engage with such activity (Ottesen, 2006; Wilson, *et al* 2007). Similarly Dawson (2008) in a study of science teachers identified the factors that most inhibited ICT use as workload, behaviour management issues access to computers and the Internet (p.203). Allied to this is concern that were teachers develop their use of ICT and virtual environments problems experienced when the technology doesn't work properly can have a negative impact on their confidence (Somekh, 2008 p.28). Resolution of such difficulties may come from a more careful alliance and collaboration between teachers and technologists in the software development process. Laterza *et al* (2007) argue that this requires increased understanding of different educational contexts and mediation between technologists, researchers and practitioners (p.265).

In summary it is clear that the literature indicates effective use of virtual environments can make a potentially valuable contribution to both teacher professional development and pupil learning. However, it is also clear that realising such effective use requires teacher engagement which, in the current context in Scotland, may be problematic to realise. In the remainder of this chapter we first present an example of the virtual environment used in the research process before using data in the form of three vignettes, to illustrate and explore teacher engagement with virtual environments.

The AERS Virtual Environment

This is an example of a virtual worksite (this site was used to engage pupils working towards their Higher (upper secondary school certificate) examinations. However it is identical to the environment offered to teachers engaging in collaborative enquiry). 'Worksite' is the key unit within the Sakai virtual environment and it comprises a distinct virtual environment equipped with a set of tools selected to support the activities of individual groups. The tools are arranged on the left hand side tool panel and include various synchronous and asynchronous communication tools, (e.g. Discussion forum, Chat Room, Announcements, Email Archive, Mail Tool, or a Blog), or tools geared to support collaborative working, including a Resources area for sharing and storing digital files (texts, audio, video etc.) and a Wiki tool for collaborative writing. There is also an integral Schedule for organising dates and deadlines and an individual Drop Box accessible only to individual pupils and their teacher and especially useful for individual teacher-pupil exchange such as the handing in of homework and receiving of comments online. The Web content tool enables the collation of relevant external websites which can be accessed without leaving the Sakai envi-

ronment. The flexible, modular structure of the environment means that the number and type of tools can be selected according to the specific needs of the users of a particular worksite.

Access to the environment is password controlled, which makes it a secure collaboration space. The worksites can be either private, available only to those registered on the site, or publicly joinable by anyone registered in the environment. There are two main types of users within the environment, maintainers or accessors, whose permissions can vary between being equal to highly differentiated depending, again, on the purpose of the worksite. For example in school based worksites teachers can moderate the use and availability of resources for their pupils (Rimpilainen & Carmichael, 2006).

THREE VIGNETTES

In this section we present three vignettes of experience within LLTN illustrating specific examples of teacher engagement in virtual environments. The first vignette explores the development of a single virtual environment for teachers with responsibility for developing a collaborative, curriculum development initiative, within their own schools. The second vignette captures the experience of teachers from a large secondary school exploring the use of virtual environments primarily as a potential means to increase pupil engagement in learning but also, crucially, as a means of sharing and developing their professional learning with regard to new technologies. The third vignette draws from an action research project in adult literacies to illustrate the ways in which a virtual research environment facilitated collaborative enquiry between researchers, practitioners and policymakers. The data from which these vignettes are drawn was collated from a number of sources, effectively constructing an ethnography of each group:

- The virtual environments themselves generated data in terms of participants' contributions (use of communication tools such as email and chat facilities as well as more formal contributions to discussion areas). This data was constantly monitored and analysed by the research team. In the project described in Vignette 3 the virtual environment permitted this initial analysis to be discussed and further developed with participants.
- The research teams conducted observation of the virtual environments, in particular their patterns of use. In addition any actual meetings of participants were attended, observed and recorded using field-notes.
- A range of participants were interviewed at different stages in the development of their groups. For example in the research on teacher collaboration illustrated in Vignette 1 interviews were conducted with a number of policy makers, teachers and university based participants. All of the interviews were transcribed for analysis.

The iterative model of data analysis evolved draws on aspects of grounded theory (Glaser & Struass, 1967) approaches to data collection but is primarily an approach that employs a hermeneutical circle or spiral approach to understanding, in which a knowledge of the overall context is essential to understanding individual events and actions.

Vignette 1: Engaging Practitioners, Policymakers and Researchers in Collaborative Enquiry

Working in collaboration with a local council, the LLTN developed a virtual research environment (VRE) for primary and secondary school teachers with responsibility for progressing a curriculum development initiative within their own schools. The education department of the council was at-tracted to the 'community of enquiry' concept and engaged with the LLTN in exploring ways in which this could be developed. The council contacted approximately 90 teachers to inform them about the virtual environment and, if a teacher emailed a positive indication of interest, he/she was provided with username and password to access it. The primary aim of the site, determined by the education department, was to facilitate teachers in sharing their practice in formative assessment and personal learning planning with others. Teachers were encouraged to present examples of formative assessment and personal learning planning strategies used in their classrooms, to read about practices in other schools and to make comments in a discussion forum. The VRE was seen as a potentially useful resource in connecting teachers who would, under normal circumstances, find communication problematic. The potential for communication was enhanced by the variety of Sakai tools (such as discussion and chat areas as well as a list of helpful websites, notices of conferences, seminars and professional development events) that were available on the site. The local council allocated funding towards the project in terms of offering five teachers one day's salary per month, each taking responsibility for one of the five key discussion areas. In addition the LLTN encouraged a small number of academics to join the virtual environment and make contributions to the work of the group as was considered appropriate. In its early stages of development the site attracted a significant number of teachers who registered their interest by email, received usernames and passwords and were informed of how to find and access the site. Initial activity on the site however was limited to a small number of contributions from 11 participants.

A number of key issues were identified from the early stages of the project's development. Firstly, schools, on receiving the invitation to contribute to the virtual environment, recognized the request as a directive from the local education department. This meant that the school response was frequently delegated to a member of school management team with the result that some of those expected to coordinate participation had to balance this demand with other important school priorities. In addition it is likely that less experienced teachers were not then offered the opportunity to participate. Secondly, some teachers expressed concern that they needed training in how to access and use the virtual environment effectively. While the general expectation was that the site demanded low levels of IT skills, the LLTN and the local education department responded to this concern by agreeing to provide and fund training of the five teachers who had been appointed to lead the different discussion areas. However, others had to rely on the use of the software manual, existing skills, and their own intuition. Thirdly, early conversations with potential participants indicated that while they were interested in the potential of such virtual collaboration, their engagement in it remained very much peripheral to their everyday practice:

I think one of the big issues for us as well is just time to sit and do these things, you know. If I'm at my desk and think of doing anything on the computer then it will just not happen, because there are so many interruptions and the phone rings and people come in. And these are all the sort of day-to-day fire fighting things that go on all the time. So I don't really have space in school. I can't do it in school anyway.

Access to a computer was also difficult, particularly when not teaching:

The, the big thing was the computers at Easter, got wiped out basically. I mean we couldn't even get on to our email to email each other and the internet wasn't on, it was all haywire you know. So I suppose that didn't help either. There's been a lot of problems. In fact my smart board in my classroom's still not working, it's so frustrating you know because there's all this great stuff out

there and then you can't use it.

A small group of participants expressed concern that they felt vulnerable being invited to present their practice for discussion to a group of peers and academics (in excess of 90) whom they did not know. This group requested that the site be more differentiated with a smaller membership including perhaps a small cluster of local schools. For these teachers, the attraction of the virtual environment was for more intimate exchange with colleagues known to them. Some even saw the potential of the virtual environment to address difficulties of communication within their school in which there was no longer a staff room. At the time of writing the local education department was keen to differentiate the virtual environment in response to this demand.

There were other difficulties in establishing an effective virtual environment. Staff within HE who initially registered interest in the virtual environment and the opportunity to communicate with teachers, were slow to devote time to engage with the virtual environment. Researchers within the LLTN devoted considerable time to the setting up of the virtual environment and managing its membership. These were tasks which, though essential, were not recognized or funded as part of a researcher's role. Establishing the virtual environment as a 'normal' means of communication, of learning and of collaborative working remains very much an aspiration.

Vignette 2: Virtual Environments and Pupil Engagement in Learning

As the work of the LLTN progressed there was increased contact and exchange between schools and individual teachers. The ease with which researchers were able to construct virtual environments and make them accessible to schools allowed for a small number of interested teachers to explore using virtual environments in their everyday practice. One large secondary school

Figure 1. Example of AERS virtual environment (© 2009, Applied Educational Research Scheme. Used with permission)

expressed an interest in developing a virtual environment for upper secondary school pupils (aged 15-17 years). This was seen primarily as a potentially useful resource for pupils but also as an opportunity for teachers to explore new technologies and their potential for developing learning and teaching within the school. In addition, changes to school funding had resulted in the closure of the school staff room and the creation of smaller subject based staff meeting rooms. The creation of the virtual environment was seen by some teachers as a vehicle for increased communication and sharing of ideas across different subject areas.

A virtual environment was quickly developed as a means of supporting a secondary school year 5 modern studies class. The virtual environment developed with the school (as described in Figure 1 above) contained a number of practical tools and also facilitated individual and group communication. However effective communication between the research team and teachers in the school was difficult and many teachers, in the absence of detailed information and support were unable to access any support in terms of developing their ideas for virtual working. Consequently

the initial virtual space was used enthusiastically by just one teacher.

This teacher was interested in archiving lessons and resources that would then be accessible to pupils and useful to both their ongoing class work and later revision. The teacher argued that the virtual environment was also useful in encouraging pupils to take more responsibility for their work at home:

And it's nice to be able to say, well look, everything that you need, that we all covered in class, is available for you online and you can go and get it there. You don't have to come to me and say 'I wasn't in yesterday can you give the stuff' and I've got to fish it out of a folder and I've found that's really helped in terms of training my students to stop asking me '...what did we do yesterday?'

In addition, the teacher arranged to be available at set times to respond to pupil queries online. This enabled pupils to make contact with their teacher when they had specific questions or encountered difficulties outside of lesson time and normal school hours. As the potential usefulness of the virtual environment to assist teachers and engage pupils slowly became recognised by other teachers within the school. It was decided that it should be expanded to include all those pupils in years 4-6 (secondary school) studying for their 'Higher' certificate examinations. A meeting was organised by the researchers leading the development with the principal subject teachers to introduce them to the virtual environment and provide some initial training on its use. This attempt to move from a small developmental project to incorporating the virtual environment into everyday practice was partly due to the perceived benefits of enabling pupils' easy access to their coursework and assignments. Further, some of the teachers were interested in developing pupils' use of the site so that when the pupils logged on they would recognise and communicate with others also using the site and, thus, pupils would be able to interact and help each other in their learning. However in developing the virtual environments with the principal teachers in the school researchers had limited access to other teachers, many of whom were already working innovative ways with their own web-based resources. Expansion of the use of the virtual environment to a larger number of teachers and other subject areas has therefore been variable.

Some teachers have found the virtual environment a valuable addition to their teaching and an extremely useful way of managing resources and interacting with pupils. Others, less familiar with such technology and with no access to support and learning, have had difficulty in seeing ways in which the environment could be useful to them. Teachers had no access to higher education research literature (no subscription to journals) and had little knowledge of where to look for examples of innovative practice. For example, researchers drew teacher attention to the 'British Educational Communications and Technology Agency' - BECTA website (http://www.becta. org.uk) as a possible source of subject specific information. Some teachers found understanding the virtual environment, logging in and using its

various tools challenging. The small amount of practical support and training available for them, and the restrictions on their time, frustrated their attempts to get to grips with the technology. This meant that some initial barriers such as unfamiliar login procedures, or knowing how to add files have halted their (and their pupils') use of the environment. Where teachers did engage pupils in the virtual environment difficulties arose as in many classes only the teacher had access to a networked computer, pupils then had little opportunity to access their personal work and other resources during class time. Teachers echoed this difficulty:

I'm using it [virtual environment] for something that they can do at home. I can't really see a use for it as a classroom resource. By the time you get it up and the time you get logged onto a laptop your period's over. As a classroom resource, we're a long way, you know, away from that. I think as a school we need to address our lack of ICT provision for our pupils. Unless we start giving pupils a laptop, which... if we're expecting the kids to do things like this, and we're expecting them to work hard and do 5 Highers, then I think they should look at some way of providing this for them.

At the time of printing the use of this virtual environment has progressed into second year at the school and the LLTN continue to research its progress. A key development has been the employment of a teacher one day per week to help make teachers aware of the virtual environments and facilitate their development with those interested. This has resulted in a differentiation of the initial virtual environments into a number of additional subject specific environments and expedited practicalities such as enabling pupils to be registered and logged in to the system. The school environment though remains restrictive. The modern languages department of the school, for example, was keen to record narrative extracts in different languages and make these available in the virtual environment along with transcriptions and translations. A good quality digital recorder was required for this process but there was no funding for this until possibly in the second term and the plans were delayed. Of key interest in future research will be the ways in which teachers are able to make use of the technology, to support pupils in its development, and the extent to which pupils apply their experience of social networking software to an educational context.

Vignette 3. An Action Research Project in Adult Literacies

An action research project was funded for two years to develop and explore the potential for enhancing literacies learning for adults with learning difficulties by engaging with their systems of care and/or support. In the early stages of the project a virtual research environment (VRE) was constructed to facilitate the work of the project. This VRE was accessible via the web to the research team, a representative of the funding body and all tutors participating in the project. It contained a variety of tools such as chat/discussion areas, a file store, an announcement function and a group email address. Tutors were encouraged to use the VRE as a means of contacting and discussing ideas with the research team. In addition it provided a means for tutors to record, share and discuss their experiences with each other. As an administrated tool the VRE proved invaluable to the whole research group. The group email address allowed all researchers and other project participants to keep up to date with communications which could be sent to all or selected members of the VRE. Emails were also collated in the VRE for reference allowing participants to keep up to date with communications. Different forms of data generated by the project (interview recordings, film, research notes) were immediately stored in the VRE giving the research team immediate access. Transcripts were later collated in the VRE file store meaning that all data generated by the

project was collated and easily accessible via the web. In addition the location of the VRE within the wider AERS virtual environment, protected by login and password procedures, ensured that the data was secure. Such access to emerging data both in the form of dialogue on the site and stored in various formats in the file store, enabled distributed members of the research team to engage with or comment on the ongoing analysis. The following extract from a tutor's virtual diary illustrates the way in which the VRE collated information and provided a new source of data which was essential to the project development:

I [tutor] had a brief meeting with [carer] afterwards and went through what each of the learners was working on. She said that she had met one of Paul's support workers and asked her if she could start getting Paul to calculate his own money. She emphasized that he still may need support but even if he tried. She also said that when [learner] goes to the gym she tells him (and the other clients) to get their money ready to pay. Paul normally waits with his wallet expecting her to sort it out for him but she's been telling him to try himself. So far she has found that Paul can work it out on his own but just expects other people to do it for him.

There was variation in tutors' interest and available time to make use of the VRE and some corresponded with the researchers using phone calls and email. Where the VRE was used tutors felt it helpful both in enabling communication with the researchers and as a means of learning about other tutors' practice. For example several tutors kept online diaries of their experiences of the project with daily and weekly accounts of project progress and developments. This greatly facilitated the action research dimension to the project as in addition to facilitating reflexive practice it enabled researchers to clarify issues and respond to emerging difficulties. As these forms of communication and dialogue increased the VRE became a vital hub for the research activities. Access to emerging findings in terms of tutor experience of the project allowed an iterative process of enquiry and clarification to develop between researchers and tutors. Likewise a key part of the collaborative dimension of the project was to assist tutors in working with parents/carers and care providers to develop opportunities for literacy development in people's everyday lives. Tutors made use of the VRE to identify opportunities for this to occur and some of the carers involved in the project used the VRE to correspond and clarify emerging issues with tutors, an essential activity for the project. Equally all members of the research team had immediate access to data and were able to observe the project developing. In particular those leading the research were in constant touch with its development rather, as in other projects not supported by a VRE, having to rely on researchers gathering data and reporting at specific project meetings.

In summary the VRE soon became crucial to the development of the project by continually generating data which all members of the research team could analyse, reflect on and use to shape future steps in the project development. Furthermore the collation of tutor material and experience on the VRE was of interest to the funders of the research who wanted to explore producing training materials from the data to help other tutors develop their practice. Use of the VRE enabled the funders to see the project develop, to collaborate with the research team and to address emerging difficulties faced by practitioners. The use of the VRE by this project was not unproblematic and was facilitated by intensive researcher support. However it provided an innovative and extremely valuable platform for collaborative working.

DISCUSSION

The virtual environment described in Vignette 1 had aspirations of encouraging communication and dialogue between teachers and academic staff within HE. However, while there was initial teacher interest and the local council-appointed coordinators tried to seed discussion, little collaborative activity consequently emerged. The local education department had speculated that this form of collaborative working may prove useful but the key factors identified above as crucial considerations for communities of enquiry were largely not addressed. Some teachers expressed concern that practical constraints such as their differing levels of IT skills and effective access to the internet within schools were prohibiting their participation. Others expressed concern that engaging with a virtual environment requires dedicated time which they did not have opportunity or authority to devote in this way. In contrast the local authority had anticipated that the virtual environment would assist teachers in sharing practice, a task they were already required to be undertaking. This expectation from the local authority resulted in a top down implementation of the initiative which required teacher and school compliance. Schools responded to this by allocating responsibility of 'compliance' to senior teachers in the school management team. As a result those teachers with relatively little actual teaching responsibilities and considerable experience became those charged with leading the school's engagement with the virtual environment. Less experienced teachers with an interest in developing their practice were restricted in their access to the virtual environment.

Crucially, teachers expressed hesitancy at presenting their ideas and examples of their practice in such a public environment. Some explicitly expressed concern that they were fearful of embarrassing their school by exposing how far they were behind in terms of developing their ideas and contributing to the initiative. Consequently there was a demand from some teachers for more differentiated, intimate use of virtual environments involving local clusters of two to three schools rather than one large local council-based virtual environment. The local council and researchers were clearly unaware of the context in which these teachers were working, one in which the influence of performance and managerialism played a key role in shaping teacher behaviour.

While the teachers forming the potential participants in the virtual environment have been given a clear purpose with regard to sharing their practice it is clear that transferring some of this to the virtual environment offered more substantial challenge than first perceived. In such situations it is clear that the use of a virtual environment implies not just the use of an extra tool for communities of enquiry to use but a substantially new way of engaging with their work, one that is currently neither explicitly recognized by teachers or the local council. A clear example of this was the absence of access to effective technical support within schools. Where teachers in Vignette 1 met with barriers, in particular technical difficulties, there was little immediate access to support and this frustrated, even prevented, their further participation. As the site developed it offered policy-makers the opportunity to have ongoing and direct contact with practitioners. The lack of apparent interest by practitioners needed to be responded to and provided insight for policy-makers into teachers' circumstances and working conditions that were inhibitive to their required tasks.

Vignette 2 provides insight into the development of virtual environments to support class teaching and the learning challenge this poses to schools and teachers. Clearly there are similar issues to be addressed as those illustrated in Vignette 1, in particular teacher time to become familiar with the technology, develop their ideas and incorporate its use in their teaching, was extremely limited, often relying on work in their own time at home. However the senior management team within the school was supportive of the process in terms of realizing some staff time for the development of the virtual environment(s) and administrative support for logging in pupils. Teachers were generally supportive of the initiative as, along with pupils, they recognized the immediate potential of the virtual environment to support pupil learning. In addition they were interested in the more long term potential of the environments to engage pupils in active virtual discussion. What teachers were able to realize however was almost entirely determined by their personal interest in and ability to engage with the virtual environments. Crucially there was no opportunity at school level for teachers to develop a thoughtful strategic approach to incorporating the use of virtual environments into their teaching. Opportunity was not afforded to learn how virtual environments had been developed by other teachers in their subject area. A clear example of this was the fact that the school and participating teachers took time to realise the flexibility of the virtual environments to be used in different teaching situations and by different groups of teachers. While researchers were confident they had explained that virtual environments could be established for groups of one or two collaborating teachers or pupils the majority of teachers still referred to 'the school virtual environment' and conceptualized it as a single environment. It was over a year before individual teachers, having learned more about the technology and its availability to the school, approached researchers requesting environments for the purposes of collaborative work with colleagues or to complement individual class teaching. Progressing the innovation in the school has consequently been slow though nevertheless useful.

The adult literacies project (Vignette 3) faced similar difficulties in terms of tutors being restricted by the time they had available to use the site as well as difficulties with access to PCs and the internet. However in contrast to Vignettes 1 & 2 practitioner engagement in the virtual environment enabled a very effective form of collaboration to emerge. Tutors in this project, had been able to meet together on several occasions to discuss the project and use of the virtual environment, prior to developing the use of the VRE. Consequently they were familiar with each other and clearly less hesitant to share aspects of their practice. The project described in Vignette 3 was challenging to tutors as it required them to evolve a new approach to their practice and engage with learners and their wider communities on a personal level. However the purpose and aims of the project were a carefully defined and the researcher input afforded tutors the opportunity to engage in dialogue with both the research team and the funders of the project whenever further clarity was required. A more crucial difference though was that the adult literacies project benefited from having at its disposal a full-time university based researcher. The researcher facilitated tutor engagement at a number of levels including being available to facilitate tutors access to the virtual environment, troubleshoot technical problems and provide ongoing training and support in the use of the software. In contrast where teachers in Vignette 1 met with barriers, in particular technical difficulties, there was little immediate access to support and this frustrated their further participation.

FUTURE TRENDS

As referred to above the initial theoretical work within LLTN on 'community of enquiry' provided a useful conceptual framework for the development of the use of virtual environments by different groups. It also provided a useful lens through which to begin analysing the different initiatives (see Christie *et al* 2007). However while exploring factors such as climate, relationships, perspective and assumptions proved illuminative in the developing communities and their use of virtual environments more fundamental issues were unresolved. The structure and context of the different initiatives had a significant bearing on their development and in turn were crucial in determining emergent forms of dialogue and participation. As illustrated in the vignettes teachers struggled to realise time to engage with the projects. Their interest and enthusiasm for participation were suffocated

by their everyday teaching timetables, by more pressing and measureable tasks for which they were accountable. It is revealing that teachers in Vignette 1 were fearful of exposure, of revealing deficits in their practice and their school's progress. Vignette 3, while exploring a very different context nevertheless illustrates some of the benefits to the research and practitioner communities when genuine, virtual collaborative work is carefully nurtured. It would appear that Scottish Education is currently a difficult environment in which to foster the innovative forms of collaboration that virtual environments can support.

The Vignettes provide an indication then both of the possible contribution of virtual environments to teacher professional learning but also, crucially, illuminate the extent to which the landscape of teaching in Scotland needs to change to foster innovation. In this sense innovation is a challenge to all in the educational community. Researchers in this project to an extent pioneered the use of virtual environments both in terms of practically nurturing their development but also by trying to understand and theorise emergent, new ways of working. In this sense the development of virtual environments in teaching and learning in Scotland requires further, significant collaborative working between the practitioner, policy and research communities.

CONCLUSION

The new Scottish schools intranet, GLOW, will no doubt offer a platform for Scottish teachers to start and build ICT further into teaching and learning. The experience of LLTN and related research however emphasises the need for teachers to be involved closely with the development of the technology. Simply presenting teachers with a variety of tools, (as is illustrated above) may confine new ICT to a supportive role in existing pedagogy rather than one that may facilitate new approaches and furthermore matches young peoples' experience of ICT. Similarly to accept that learning involves active participation of learners implies that virtual environments for pupils need to be constructed in ways which encourage and nurture their active participation rather than passive observation. The experience of this LLTN research indicates that teachers will need time and support to discover the ways in which virtual environments may effectively support their teaching. This will also apply to efforts to encourage collaborative learning between schools and the role of virtual environments in teacher professional development. It is crucial that teacher use of virtual environments is recognized as a legitimate, alternative, and effective way of collaborative working and teaching. The experience from LLTN echoes the findings of the OECD in 2002 which indicated that 'sufficient professional development opportunities and support, compensated time off for training, and an adequate ICT infrastructure present the optimal conditions for advancing the adoption of ICT by a school staff' OECD/CERI (2002, p.24). Teachers in Scotland will need time to learn about virtual ways of working, to develop and realize their ideas. All of this points towards developing a careful, incremental development of new technology in collaboration with what teachers and schools need and value. In the current context of professional learning in Scotland, arguably governed by 'managerial professionalism' and 'performativity' discourses, such professional learning opportunity for teachers is limited. GLOW will offer teachers immediate access to new technology which many may be unprepared for and hence unable to make effective use of.

REFERENCES

Ball, S. (2006). *Educational Policy and Social Class*. London UK: Routledge.

Baron, S. (2004). The Applied Educational Research Scheme: A real opportunity for Scottish educational research. *Education Next, 12*, 41–44.

Bernstein, B. (1975). *Class, Codes and Control, 3*. London: Routledge.

Bray, J., Lee, J., Smith, L., & Yorks, L. (2000) *Collaborative inquiry in practice*. London, Sage Publications.

Carr, N., & Chambers, D. (2006). Teacher professional learning in an online community: the experiences of the National Quality Schooling Framework Pilot Project. *Technology, Pedagogy and Education, 15*(2), 143–157. doi:10.1080/14759390600769094

Carusi, A. (2006). Power and Agency in Online Text-based Collaborations . *E–Learning, 3*(1), 4–15. doi:10.2304/elea.2006.3.1.4

Cassidy, C., Christie, D., Coutts, N., Dunn, J., Sinclair, C., Skinner, D., & Wilson, A. (2008). Building communities of educational enquiry. *Oxford Review of Education, 34*(2), 217–235. doi:10.1080/03054980701614945

Christie, D., Cassidy, C., Skinner, D., Coutts, N., Sinclair, C., Rimpilainen, S., & Wilson, A. (2007). Building collaborative communities of enquiry in educational research. *Educational Research and Evaluation, 13*(3), 263–278. doi:10.1080/13803610701632091

Coffield, F. (2000). *The Necessity of Informal Learning*. Bristol: The Policy Press.

Dawson, V. (2008). Use of Information Communication Technology by Early Career Science Teachers in Western Australia, *International Journal of Science Education, 30*(2), 203-219. http://www.informaworld.com/smpp/title~cont ent=t713737283~db=all~tab=issueslist~branch es=30 - v30.

Day, C., Flores, M. A., & Viana, I. (2007). Effects of national policies on teachers' sense of professionalism: findings from an empirical study in Portugal and in England. *European Journal of Teacher Education, 30*(3), 249–265. doi:10.1080/02619760701486092

Day, C. & Sachs, J. (2005). Professionalism, performativity and empowerment: discourses in the politics and purposes of continuing professional development. In C. Day & J. Sachs (Eds) *International handbook on the continuing professional development of teachers*. Maidenhead, UK: Open University Press.

Fraser, C., Kennedy, A., Reid, L., & McKinney, S. (2007). Teachers' continuing professional development (CPD): contested concepts, understandings and models. *Journal of In-service Education, 33*(2), 153–169. doi:10.1080/13674580701292913

Friedman, A., & Philips, M. (2004). CPD programmes of UK professional associations: developing a vision. *Journal of Education and Work, 17*(3). doi:10.1080/1363908042000267432

Furlong, J., & Oancea, A. (2005). *Assessing Quality in Applied and Practice-based Educational Research.* A framework for discussion. University of Oxford. Retrieved 13th February, 2009 from http://www.aare.edu.au/05papc/fu05018y.pdf

Glaser, B., & Strauss, A. (1967). *The Discovery of Grounded Theory: Strategies for Qualitative Research.* Chicago; Aldine.

GTC Scotland (2008). Continuing Professional Development. Retrieved 13th February, 2009 from http://www.gtcs.org.uk/ProfessionalDevelopment/ProfessionalDevelopment.asp

Hakkarainen, K., Palonen, T., Paavola, S., & Lehtinen, E. (2004) *Communities of networked expertise. Professional and educational perspectives.* Oxford, European Association for Research on Learning and Instruction; Elsevier.

Hardy, I., & Lingard, B. (2008). Teacher professional development as an effect of policy and practice: a Bourdieuian analysis. *Journal of Education Policy, 23*(1), 63–80. doi:10.1080/02680930701754096

Hargreaves, A. (2000). Four ages of professionalism and professional learning. *Teachers and Teaching, 6*(2), 151–182. doi:10.1080/713698714

Kennedy, A., Christie, D., Fraser, C., Reid, L., McKinney, S., Welsh, M., Wilson, A., & Griffiths, M. (2008). Key informants' perspectives on teacher learning in Scotland. *British Journal of Educational Studies, 56*(4), 400-419.

Laterza, V., Carmichael, P., & Procter, R. (2007). The doubtful guest? A Virtual Research Environment for education. *Technology, Pedagogy and Education, 16*(3), 249–267. doi:10.1080/14759390701614363

Lave, J., & Wenger, E. (1991) *Situated learning: Legitimate Peripheral Participation.* Cambridge, Cambridge University Press.

Lipman, M. (1988). *Philosophy goes to school.* Philadelphia: Temple University Press.

Lipman, M. (1991). *Thinking in Education.* Cambridge: Cambridge University Press.

Liu, Y., & Huang, C. (2005). Concerns of teachers about technology integration in the USA. *European Journal of Teacher Education, 28*(1), 35–47. doi:10.1080/02619760500039928

McLaughlin, C., & Black-Hawkins, K. (2004). A schools–university research partnership: understandings, models and complexities. *Journal of In-service Education, 30*(2), 265–284. doi:10.1080/13674580400200319

Murphy, E., & Rodríguez-Manzanares, M. (2008). Instant messaging in a context of virtual schooling: Balancing the affordances and challenges. *Educational Media International, 45*(1), 47–58. doi:10.1080/09523980701847180

OECD/CERI. (2002). *Quo Vademus? The Transformation of Schooling in a Networked World OECD/CERI Version 8c.* Retrieved 13th February, 2009 from http://www.oecd.org/dataoecd/48/20/2073054.pdf

ONS. (2007). *First Release: Internet Access 2007 Households and Individuals.* Retrieved 13th February, 2009 from http://www.statistics.gov.uk/pdfdir/inta0807.pdf.

Ottesen, E. (2006). Learning to teach with technology: authoring practised identities. *Technology, Pedagogy and Education, 15*(3), 275–290. doi:10.1080/14759390600923568

Pachler, N., & Daly, C. (2006). Power and Agency in Online Text-based Collaborations. *E–Learning, 3*(1).

Pardales, M., & Girod, M. (2006). Community of inquiry: its past and present future. *Educational Philosophy and Theory, 38*(3), 299–309. doi:10.1111/j.1469-5812.2006.00196.x

Richards, C. (2006). Towards an integrated framework for designing effective ICT-supported learning environments: the challenge to better link technology and pedagogy. *Technology, Pedagogy and Education, 15*(2), 239–255. doi:10.1080/14759390600769771

Rimpilainen, S., & Carmichael, P. (2006). *Sakai: An Environment for Virtual Research, Ennen ja Nyt 2006.* Retrieved 13th February, 2009 from http://www.ennenjanyt.net/2006_2/rimpilainen.pdf.

Schlager, S., & Fusco, J. (2003). Teacher Professional Development, Technology, and Communities of Practice: Are We Putting the Cart Before the Horse? *The Information Society, 19*(3), 203–220. doi:10.1080/01972240309464

Smedley, L. (2001). Impediments to Partnership: a literature review of school-university links. *Teacher and Teaching: theory and practice, 7*(2), 189-209.

Somekh, B. (2004). Taking the sociological imagination to school: an analysis of the (lack of) impact of information and communication technologies on education systems. *Technology, Pedagogy and Education, 13*(2), 163–179. doi:10.1080/14759390400200178

Turner, C. (2006). Informal learning and its relevance to the early professional development of teachers in secondary schools in England and Wales. *Journal of In-service Education, 32*(3), 301–319. doi:10.1080/13674580600841885

Wilson, A., Rimpilainen, S., Skinner, D., Cassidy, C., Christie, D., Coutts, N., & Sinclair, C. (2007). Using a Virtual Research Environment to support new models of collaborative and participative research in Scottish education. *Technology, Pedagogy and Education, 16*(3), 289–304. doi:10.1080/14759390701614413

Chapter 7
Challenges of Online Teacher Professional Development Communities
A Statewide Case Study in the United States

Vassiliki I. Zygouris-Coe
University of Central Florida, USA

Bonnie Swan
University of Central Florida, USA

ABSTRACT

With so many educators needing either initial preparation or ongoing professional development to build and sustain expertise in their discipline, online professional development arises as a viable, effective, and timely vehicle for teacher training. Online learning technologies have the potential to transform the professional development of teachers; penetrate cultural, discipline, and other barriers; bring educators together to learn, share successes and challenges; and co-construct and transfer learning. This chapter presents examples of success and challenges associated with a large-scale U.S. statewide online teacher professional development community. It also makes the case for implementing a systematic approach to investigating the effectiveness of online teacher professional development communities through ongoing assessment and responsive evaluation.

INTRODUCTION

The purpose of this chapter is to "tell the tale" (i.e., mission, scope, successes, and challenges) of Florida Online Reading Professional Development (FOR-PD), a large-scale U.S. statewide online professional development project, and its impact on preK-12 teachers' knowledge about reading research and effective instruction. The authors are the project's principal investigator, an associate professor of reading education at the University of Central Florida (UCF), and the project's lead evaluator, an evaluation specialist with extensive experience in learning assessment and planning and implementing evaluations in various educational agencies at

DOI: 10.4018/978-1-60566-780-5.ch007

a variety of levels. This chapter examines the following: (a) the role of professional development on teacher quality; (b) the role of professional learning communities for supporting teacher capacity and expertise through professional development; (c) online professional development as a means of creating and sustaining teacher professional learning communities; (d) successes and challenges associated with a situated large-scale online teacher professional development community; and (e) trends and directions for the future.

BACKGROUND: TEACHER QUALITY AND PROFESSIONAL DEVELOPMENT

Teacher quality has been the focus of much policy analysis as a result of research on the role of teachers on student learning. The No Child Left Behind U.S. Public Act (NCLB) requires a highly qualified teacher in every classroom (Darling-Hammond & Sykes, 2003). The NCLB principles for high-quality professional development are comprehensive, multi-faceted, complex, and require extensive participation from administrators and teachers. In addition, the U.S. Department of Education (USDOE) indicates that effective teacher professional development is more than just coursework designed to fulfill a state or district requirement. It is a set of activities grounded in scientifically based research and producing a measurable effect on student academic achievement.

Professional development is most effective when it is part of a system-wide plan to improve and integrate teacher quality at all stages: preparation, induction, support, and ongoing development (USDOE, 2002). According to a congressional report by the National Commission on Teaching and America's Future (1997):

What teachers know and understand about content and students shapes how judiciously they select from texts and other materials and how effectively

they present material in class. Their skill in assessing their students' progress also depends upon how deeply they understand learning, and how well they can interpret students' discussions and written work. No other intervention can make the difference that a knowledgeable, skillful teacher can make in the learning process. (p. 8)

Professional development refers to those intentional, systematic, and ongoing processes and activities designed to enhance the professional knowledge, skills, and attitudes of educators so that they might improve the learning of students (Guskey, 2000). Professional development is an essential part of building teacher expertise in schools.

DuFour and Eaker (1998) recommend that the content of professional development programs should "be based on research," and used to "expand the repertoire of teachers to meet the needs of students who learn in diverse ways" (p. 276). They also recommend that the process of professional development should provide ongoing coaching that is critical to the mastery of new skills, attend to the tenets of good teaching, promote reflection and dialogue, be sustainable over time, and be evaluated at multiple levels with evidence of improved performance.

The NCLB principles for effective professional development require practices grounded in research, collaborative and strategic work, alignment with state standards, ongoing assessment, and developing a system for intervention and support to teachers and students. Although educational reform is warranted, and even mandated, change in educators' belief systems about pedagogy and learning does not occur quickly. Ongoing professional development is necessary for improving teachers' growth and instructional practice. Traditional face-to-face professional development has not resolved major educational challenges in the U.S. Many researchers (e.g., Dede, Breit, Ketelhut, McCloskey, & Whitehouse, 2005) propose that online teacher professional development has the potential to develop and support teachers' professional growth and effectiveness in their classrooms. They also acknowledge that online teacher professional development raises many challenging questions regarding access to technology, quality of materials, equity, costs, and other issues (e.g., Dede, Ketlehut, Whitehouse, Breit, & McCloskey, 2006).

PROFESSIONAL LEARNING COMMUNITIES

In education, the term *professional learning community* describes a collegial group of school administrators and faculty who are unified in their commitment to student learning. They share a common vision, work and learn collaboratively, study student data, visit other classrooms, and practice participatory decision-making (Hord, 1997). The benefits to the school and students include a reduced isolation of teachers, shared accountability, better informed and committed administrators and teachers, and academic gains for students. Professional learning communities are centered on learning, on creating a collaborative culture, on shared commitment to continuous improvement that focuses on results, and on providing timely and relevant information to teachers on students' needs and growth (Eaker, DuFour & DuFour, 2002; DuFour, 2004). The word *community* implies shared interests.

Educators working and learning collaboratively to improve both instructional practices and student achievement is an attainable goal through professional learning communities. Darling-Hammond (1993) recommends that:

Teachers should have opportunities to engage in peer coaching, team planning, and teaching, and collaborative research that enables them to construct new means for inquiring into their practice. Participation in professional communities through

school and teacher networks also deepens teachers' understanding (p. 758).

Educators who are part of a professional learning community create structures to promote a collaborative culture. This model of learning helps eliminate teacher isolation, one of the factors associated with attrition. Teaching in isolation has become the norm in many schools, especially at the secondary level. Collaboration in professional learning communities is strategic, ongoing, and systematic in that teachers work together to analyze, reflect upon, and improve their classroom practice. Teacher teamwork, collective inquiry, learning by seeking answers to questions, and collaborative learning can lead to higher levels of student achievement. A professional learning community will not only develop the professional development skills of the participating teachers but it can also strengthen social networks. According to Dufour, Eaker, and DuFour (2005), this type of professional learning contributes to increased professional morale in any setting.

ONLINE TEACHER PROFESSIONAL DEVELOPMENT

In an era marked by massive federal emphases on educational accountability in U.S. schools, the education and professional development of teachers has been receiving unprecedented attention and has been viewed as the catalyst for student achievement and educational improvement. Research shows that collaboration between teachers can be a powerful tool for professional development and a key contributor to school improvement by providing "opportunities for adults across a school system to learn and think together about how to improve their practice in ways that lead to improved student achievement" (Annenberg Institute for School Reform, 2004, p. 2).

Online learning technologies have the potential to transform professional development of teachers and the development of supportive collaborative professional learning communities, bringing teachers from across schools, states, and even nations together to learn, share successes and challenges, and co-construct and transfer learning. Information technologies can provide teachers with the professional development they need, when they need it, and where they need it.

Quality programs, flexibility, and accessibility of learning are key issues for teacher professional development. Online professional development can transcend geographical, cultural, and social barriers to accessing quality learning. Online programs can be used to assist in the development of teacher content knowledge expertise and school-level capacity. Online professional development programs can also help develop common content language in various disciplines (e.g., literacy, mathematics, science, social studies, technology, or foreign languages). They have the capability of creating and sustaining successful professional learning communities; something that is often difficult to create and sustain in traditional forms of professional development. More traditional teacher professional development includes a one-stop approach, for example where an expert visits a school for a few hours or even a few days at a time in which time she or he *sprinkles* knowledge to teachers. After the expert leaves, there is often little follow up and continuation of dialogue. On the other hand, when well crafted, online teacher professional development can bring quality learning to the teacher's fingertips and can help sustain a professional learning community for long periods.

Much professional development based on electronic technologies refers to web-based, interactive experiences that combine text, video, and sound. It can be entirely asynchronous or fully interactive. Online professional development can help teachers learn about using new technologies to grow professionally and teach students how to learn with these technologies. Not just a flexible and convenient medium for the delivery

and development of content, online professional development is instead a transformative medium for academic dialogue, academic exploration, independent, and collaborative learning. When done well it has the capability of transforming teachers' learning, instructional practices, and student achievement.

Inherent challenges with online professional development include teachers' perceptions of how learning happens, of technology and professional development, and of how and where learning can take place. In addition, teachers' knowledge of online technologies, access to technologies, and support also present obstacles to online professional development. Online teacher professional development provides a different paradigm for learning individually and collaboratively. Both traditional and online teacher professional development lack evidence and research on their effectiveness on teacher, student, and school success. As states are investing substantial funds to meet the need of keeping teachers' knowledge current in new and expanding ways, the need increases to research and effectively evaluate these methods in ways that can contribute to their success and improvement. Furthermore little is currently known about best practices for online professional development design and implementation (Dede, 2006; Whitehouse, Breit, McCloskey, Ketelhut, & Dede, 2006).

BUILD IT AND THEY WILL COME: THE CASE OF A U.S. LARGE-SCALE STATEWIDE ONLINE TEACHER PROFESSIONAL DEVELOPMENT PROJECT

One way to support the training of teachers on a large scale is by providing access to high-quality professional development using an online medium. Courses provided online are the quickest growing form of teacher training (Seal, 2003). Now, more than ever, online professional development can meet the professional needs of educators due to its flexibility, accessibility, and affordability. The flexibility of online teacher professional development can enable schools, districts, and states to tailor material to meet their individual needs.

In the area of literacy, in the U.S., there is national need for developing and supporting educators' knowledge, research, and instruction. Part of the answer to the problem of meeting the needs of a growing number of struggling readers lies in focusing more effectively on developing primary through secondary teachers' expertise about teaching reading effectively. (Snow, 2002). Research shows that historically few teachers have received adequate knowledge and preparation in teaching reading comprehension, especially at the middle and high school levels. As a result, it is evident that high-quality ongoing professional development efforts are crucial to the success of systemic and standards-based reform initiatives (Snow, Griffin, & Burns, 2005). The change needed to systematically alter the way we go about reading and teacher professional development raises many important questions.

How can thousands of teachers develop their knowledge of reading research and instruction and change their instructional practices to help students succeed and learn in reading? How can they have access to quality materials and experiences? How can they learn with and from other educators? Lastly, how can they do all of this anytime, anywhere? Florida Online Reading Professional Development (FOR-PD), Florida's *first* large-scale statewide online professional development project, has served as one avenue to meet the reading professional development needs of Florida educators. It functions as a delivery mechanism for improving teaching methods in preK-12 reading instruction.

Funded by the Florida Department of Education, FOR-PD is one of the leading projects of its kind (Kleiman, 2004). The free 14-week online course was designed to enable preK-12 teachers to keep abreast with emerging standards, current

scientifically based research, best instructional practices, and the ever-changing literacy needs of an increasingly diverse group of preK-12 students. Specifically, it was developed as a vehicle for Florida's teachers to meet teaching certification requirements. During the 2006-2007 academic year, 3,898 participants completed the FOR-PD course bringing the number up to 16,655 since the course was first implemented in 2003.

This highly collaborative project is housed, and was developed, at the University of Central Florida. It provides services to Florida's educators through all 67 Florida school districts, 7 state universities, and 6 community colleges. The mission of the FOR-PD project is to: (a) support the Florida Department of Education (FLDOE) in its statewide implementation of a reading professional development system using online delivery; (b) serve as a model for reading professional development online delivery; (c) translate scientifically based research into action, provide support, empower teachers to use innovative, creative, and effective strategies to help all children learn proficiently; (d) increase teachers' knowledge about reading; (e) improve curriculum, reading instruction, and student learning.

Successes of a Statewide Large-Scale Online Teacher Professional Development Community

For the purpose of this chapter, we will present core successes associated with the development, monitoring, and sustainability of large-scale online teacher professional development communities. Successes reflected in this large-scale online community lie in the following areas: (a) quality online professional development communities; (b) an increase in teaching and learning online; (c) professional collaborations; (d) professional knowledge and skills; (e) a model for ongoing improvement; and (f) impact on educators' knowledge and skills for teaching.

Quality Online Professional Development Communities

One way to meet the professional needs of teachers on a large scale is by providing access to high-quality professional development using a distance-online medium (Seal, 2003). Online courses are not only convenient and socially rewarding; they are also valuable in that they expose teachers to the many resources available through technology. They can also provide an opportunity for teachers to learn skills in how to use technology to enhance learning themselves. FOR-PD participants develop experiences with technology and learning online as a result of participating in a sustained 14-week long professional development. FOR-PD facilitators develop even greater knowledge of technology and using a distance online medium as they facilitate online professional development and learning over time.

In an online professional learning community, a group of individuals communicate online and share common interests, goals, knowledge, and ideas. These communications contribute to the improvement of the knowledge of each participant in the community. In the FOR-PD teacher learning community, educators learn more about scientifically based reading research and instruction as they work together for 14 weeks. The FOR-PD online medium allows educators free access to quality content about reading research and instruction and acts as a vehicle for ongoing teacher professional growth.

FOR-PD is funded on an annual basis by the FLDOE to provide quality online professional development services to preK-12 educators. It provides them with an opportunity to complete certification and re-certification requirements at a low cost to the state and at no financial cost to the educator. As a result, FOR-PD has a state-wide systemic impact on teachers' success at a low cost. In addition, FOR-PD has the ability to monitor and assess teacher progress. Participants, facilitators, school districts, universities, and other collaborators comment on the positive impact of this online teacher professional development on teacher and student success in reading.

Building and sustaining such a large-scale, research-based content-specific (in this case, reading research and instruction) online teacher learning community is no small feat. It requires vision, skill, resources, knowledge of discipline and technology, a multi-faceted infrastructure, and a model of continuous improvement. Effective recruitment, training, and ongoing professional development of online facilitators are other factors that have contributed to the success of FOR-PD.

A successful online teacher professional community requires quality facilitation and support. FOR-PD provides a multi-layered system of support to facilitators and participants. Facilitators undergo a specific application process and are selected on the basis of professional qualifications in literacy. Upon selection, FOR-PD has developed a seven-week online training course to best prepare them to facilitate online. During the course, facilitators learn alongside experienced online mentors and are given theoretical and practical training in facilitating online learning. FOR-PD sustains the community of facilitators via asynchronous and synchronous ongoing discussions, through peer mentoring, ongoing professional development online courses, frequent online chats, a monthly e-newsletter, reports on participant progress, and by providing facilitators with expert technology and literacy support.

FOR-PD participants are also supported by facilitators, the Help Desk (day, evening, and weekend telephone and online support services), online chats, a monthly e-newsletter, reports on participant progress, weekly reminders about course content and ways to collaborate with other educators in the course, several layers of course-related support on assignments and tasks, and by literacy expert support. Developing and supporting a successful online teacher professional learning community requires planning, resources, monitoring, and time.

Developing Teachers' Digital Age Skills

The experience of learning to learn online not only can improve the content knowledge and pedagogy of teachers but it also provides a significant opportunity to help teachers relate better to the needs of a new age of digitally native students--a new age of students whose learning needs are rapidly changing and are much different from what teachers have otherwise experienced as learners themselves.

The U.S. National Education Technology Plan included a recommendation that school districts and individual schools work to "Ensure that every teacher has the opportunity to take online learning courses" (USDOE, Office of Postsecondary Education, 2005, p. 15). FOR-PD has served as one such avenue to meet the reading professional development needs of Florida educators on a large scale. The web-based course meets the needs of a large and diverse group of K-12 teachers by using a digital medium to keep them abreast of timely and relevant research-based knowledge, strategies and skills.

Experiencing a well-crafted distance online literacy course, like FOR-PD, can help teachers relate better to the needs of a new age of digitally-native students. Younger people of today are highly connected, and most have had a lifetime of exposure to using the World-Wide Web and other communications and technologies, including instant messaging, text messaging, CDs, iPods, video gaming, and cellular phones. More and more online courses are being introduced, and even required, in K-12 schools.

To understand the importance of giving teachers an opportunity to participate in online learning and collaboration one only needs a glance at the growth of in the demand for online courses and computer use in K-12 schools. For example, the Sloan Consortium's first ever nation-wide survey of online learning in elementary and secondary education, K-12 online learning: A Survey of U.S. School District Administrators (Allen & Seeman, 2007), found that two in three school districts had one or more students enrolled in either a fully online or a blended course conducted during the 2005-2006 school year. The new study also estimated that 1,300,000 U.S. K-12 students were engaged in online courses in 2007-2008, which had doubled in just two years.

Due to this prevalence of technology in our everyday lives, few would argue that it is of profound importance that our teachers become tech-savvy and more knowledgeable about literacy, how to interact socially online, how to use digital research tools, and how to teach online. The trend of having the Internet and digital media available in more classrooms and homes will very likely continue. One estimate is that in 2019 about half of all high school courses in the U.S. will be delivered online (Christensen & Horn, 2008).

Professional Collaborations

Members of online learning communities share common interests and benefit from peer-to-peer communication in which they share knowledge and information. Educators in particular are in need of community building as teaching often tends to be an isolating profession. Many teachers in traditional professional development efforts (district- or school-based) do not have time to develop bonds and networks with other educators. Online professional learning communities have the capability to elicit and sustain professional collaborations over time.

FOR-PD serves a wide demographic of teachers at all levels of experience, content areas, and grade-levels. For example, in the spring of 2007, more than a third (37%) of the participants served at the high school level, 28% middle school, 20% were elementary, and 15% other. For content area teachers, 31% of the participants were identified as either language arts or reading teachers, 14% were elementary teachers, and 10% were Exceptional Student Education (ESE) teachers. About 13% classified themselves as other, which consisted

Table 1. School District Participant Primary Teaching Position and Experience, Spring 2007

Subject Area	Percent	Experience	Percent
Administration	2.7%	First Year	11.1%
Business	1.5%	1-2 years	29.7%
Elementary Teacher	13.7%	3-5 years	18.5%
ESE	10.1%	6-10 years	16.4%
ESOL	2.5%	11 years and up	24.3%
Fine Arts or Music	1.0%		
Foreign Language	1.3%		
Gifted	0.2%		
Language Arts or Reading	31.0%		
Mathematics	5.1%		
Reading Specialist/Coach	2.2%		
Science	7.2%		
Social Studies	7.5%		
Technology	0.9%		
Other	13.1%		
Total	100.0%	Total	100.0%
Note. Data were obtained from a FOR-PD participant database (n = 1,431).			

of Advanced Placement teachers, curriculum development staff, library or media specialists, and administrators, including principals and even district superintendents of schools. About 41% of the participants had more than six years of teaching experience. About 11% were first-year teachers, 30% were teaching for one to two years, and 18% were teaching for three to five years (cf. Table 1).

Because the FOR-PD course has been adopted and is offered as part of several graduate programs in seven state universities, it also allows for professional collaborations to take place among educators who are pursuing advanced graduate degrees. Currently, FOR-PD also meets program requirements in the following advanced graduate education programs: (a) at the Master's and Specialist level: early childhood education, elementary education, exceptional education, reading education, media education, school psychology, counselor education, speech and language pathology; (b) at the Doctorate level:

elementary education, curriculum and instruction, reading education, speech and language pathology, educational leadership, and exceptional education. The diversity of FOR-PD participants allows for cross-disciplinary collaborations.

As part of the FOR-PD online learning community, diverse educators work together toward a common goal: to learn more about reading, reading research, and effective reading instruction that will help all students become successful readers. This large-scale online learning community has been instrumental in breaking disciplinary boundaries (i.e., a math educator working and learning alongside a science educator, a reading teacher, an elementary teacher, or a teacher of students with varied exceptionalities) and building bridges among educators in the state of Florida. For 14 weeks they exchange ideas, lesson plans, and resources on research and instruction; visit class members and classrooms; and create chat groups and book clubs. Many continue to communicate with each other even after completing the professional development. FOR-PD does follow up and continues to provide resources and support long after they complete the course.

In addition, as a result of the FOR-PD online teacher professional learning community, diverse educators develop a common foundation or language of literacy and understanding of scientifically based reading research and instruction. This common language of literacy (e.g., what we mean when we talk about phonemic awareness, structural analysis, morphemic analysis, or explicit instruction) allows for informed dialogue and helps educators to examine reading development and instruction from the perspective of an elementary or secondary educator, a reading teacher, a literacy coach, or a principal. FOR-PD teacher professional development communities help to generate shared beliefs about what quality instruction looks like, facilitate interactions between teachers and administrators, and help develop excellence across schools and school districts. Teachers can learn from other excellent teachers. Online exchanges help to make instruction less ambiguous, provide opportunities for exchanges among teachers, and thereby create a stronger professional community.

Developing Professional Knowledge and Skills for Teaching

FOR-PD was designed to provide Florida preK-12 educators with the foundations of research-based practices. As a result, online professional learning community educators learn about the principles of scientifically based reading research as the foundation of comprehensive instruction that synthesizes and scaffolds each of the major components of the reading process toward student mastery. This large-scale online teacher professional development community provides educators with quality content, up-to-date research, cutting edge instructional practices and resources, modeling, and instructional tools to provide quality reading instruction for all students. The online medium

allows for an ongoing (and immediate) delivery of quality content, resources, activities, timely feedback from literacy experts and other educators, working with researchers and colleagues, and learning about different models of research-based instruction (via multimedia).

Other benefits of this online community support include an increase in educators' cross-curricular knowledge and skills, providing educators with opportunities to implement knowledge to make immediate instructional practices, and an opportunity to publicly reflect and converse about their instructional needs, plans and decisions.

A Model for Ongoing Improvement

Continuous improvement is based on a cyclical process: plan, implement, assess, and reflect. This model has had a major impact on the success of the FOR-PD online teacher professional development communities. Research- and data-based decisions and filtering those decisions through sample audiences (i.e., facilitators, participants, advisory boards, project staff, researchers) have contributed to the effective development, updates, and sustainability of FOR-PD online learning communities. Developing and implementing a model of ongoing improvement is a must for the success of any online teacher professional development learning community.

Collecting and acting on performance data on a large-scale. The FOR-PD evaluation process is outcome-oriented and features a mixed-method design with a client-centered/responsive approach (Stake, 1975; also see Stufflebeam 2001), which plays a key role in understanding and building on the strengths and weaknesses and establishing a coherent framework. The project evaluator obtains input from the principal investigator and other major stakeholders to update evaluation instruments and methods on an ongoing basis. The Program Evaluation Standards (Joint Committee on Standards for Educational Evaluation, 1994) of *utility, feasibility, propriety,* and *accuracy* are followed.

The electronic facet of online learning provides a wealth of opportunity to collect performance data on a on a large scale. Many of the FOR-PD evaluative efforts are automated and are well embedded in the many aspects of the project's infrastructure. Frequent analysis and reporting have been designed in a way to allow the project to operate in a continuous loop of improvement and assure that accountability requirements are met in a successful manner. Because of this, a myriad of changes in both delivery and methods based on recommendations provided to the project staff in formative reports can be implemented quickly, often before the course is offered again the following semester.

Data related to the evaluation are gathered from multiple sources using several techniques and are analyzed in multiple ways. Data sources included online surveys, interviews, quality assurance checks, focus groups, project databases that are maintained by the project staff, course content, and participants' work samples from the course including literacy logs of how they are implementing what they have learned.

The quality assurance checks and survey sources for evaluation data are described more below. Other data analyzed are in the form of document review, including, for example, correspondence between the project staff and other stakeholders and the course components. All data are collected after seeking and obtaining approval from the University of Central Florida's (UCF) Institutional Review Board and participation in surveys, focus groups, and interviews is voluntary and confidential.

Monitoring of facilitator and participant progress through quality assurance checks (QAC). Quality assurance in distance learning can be defined "as the means by which the institutions or providers set their program goals and measure results against those goals" (Council of Higher Education Accreditation, 1998, p. vi). For FOR-PD, they began as a way to incorporate both confirmatory and corrective feedback to facilitators and

to inform the project staff about the effectiveness of the course along several dimensions.

QAC are both *evaluated as a process* and used *as a process to evaluate* the effectiveness of FOR-PD. In an effort to improve completion rates and assure the project offers a high-quality online professional development courses consistently, FOR-PD implements a series of QAC for both facilitators and participants. Taking a snapshot of what has occurred at critical times enables the staff to track progress while the courses are in session and allows for customized assistance for both participants and facilitators in order to maximize their experience with the FOR-PD. This data is later used with other data to help select the best quality facilitators to manage sections in the following term.

QAC are performed two times during the 14-week course to monitor facilitator performance. In the first check—during weeks two or three of the course—four requirements are checked: (a) whether or not the facilitator has posted a welcome message containing contact information about grading, important dates, feedback procedure, and specific facilitator expectations (e.g., grammar and conventions); (b) whether or not they were actively participating in discussions; (c) a *Meet Me Here* message should be posted in lesson one for an introduction and example for participants that shows them how to post on the discussion board; and (d) that facilitators are posting grades on a regular basis (about one lesson per week). On the second check, during week eight of the course, two requirements are checked: (a) maintaining active participation in the discussion along with well-defined postings, and (b) grading.

QAC are also performed twice for participant performance. In the first check, participants are classified as either non-starters (those who never logged in and started the course), lagging (those who are behind two or more lessons), dropped, or up to date. Non-starters are contacted and soon after they are dropped if they do not catch up. In the second check, the progress of participants is classified and logged again.

Monitoring project success through Web-based surveys. Several Web-based surveys are conducted on a range of topics to monitor and enable ongoing improvement. They are described briefly below. Most items on these surveys are either multiple-choice, yes/no or Likert-type, and a few allow for open-ended responses. While some survey questions remained constant so that comparisons could be made across semesters, others changed based on the project need. For some items, teacher participants are grouped by content area, grade level, experience, and whether participants are pre- or in-service teachers. Analysis of this type helps assure that all demographic groups are being well served. Quantitative responses are analyzed using statistical software, and open-ended responses are sorted and analyzed according to themes.

FOR-PD participants complete a participant end-of-course survey. This survey focuses on several topics including rates of completion, the instructional alignment of the course, the usability of the course features and effectiveness of the design, perceived effect FOR-PD had on their professional development, facilitator effectiveness, and the effectiveness of course features in building a learning community.

Not all individuals who are registered for FOR-PD start the course and some others do not finish the course. A non-completer/non-starter survey is used to ascertain why. Survey items focus on reasons for not completing the course, the likeliness that non-completers plan to attempt the course later, and what preferences they have for delivery (online vs. other).

All facilitators are asked to complete a facilitator end-of-course survey at the close of each semester. This survey focuses on several topics including their background and levels of experience; their perceptions regarding the expectations placed upon them, the usefulness of the course components; their perceptions about the effect of FOR-PD on their professional development;

and their perceptions about the impact on their students' reading achievement.

Those who contact the FOR-PD help desk are asked to complete a Help Desk survey. This short, four-item survey contains items related to the efficiency, effectiveness, and friendliness of the help desk staff. The survey is sent via e-mail with a link to complete the survey after each call, e-mail, or instant message comes into the help desk.

Fall participants who complete FOR-PD are surveyed again using a classroom implementation survey about three months after completing the course. The purpose is to discern the impact FOR-PD may have had on their classroom instruction, whether they were using the strategies they learned, and whether they thought any changes they may have made to their course content and instruction might have helped their students learn.

Impact on Educators' Knowledge and Skills for Teaching

Overall, evaluative analysis indicates that the FOR-PD participants perceived their experiences with the online learning experience to have had a positive impact on their classroom instruction and improved their knowledge of reading. Results from evaluation reports from the fifth year of operations, in the 2006-2007 academic year (Swan, Huh, Chen, & Smith, 2008), showed that 97% of teachers who completed FOR-PD reported that their involvement resulted in positive changes made to their classroom instruction; a large majority (94%) felt FOR-PD course content was appropriate for helping them integrate literacy into their content area instruction, and the same number (94%) were comfortable, to a large or moderate extent, in using the teaching strategies taught in the course. For example, one explained "Learning for me is a complex process (as with everyone) but I have always needed to understand theory before being able to implement practical instruction. As I learn more about literacy and reading, I know I am becoming a better teacher. I am better able to instruct and implement literacy techniques and ideas in my classroom."

Almost all (96%) agreed the course content increased their knowledge of scientifically based reading research. There is a concern that only 78% of the science teachers agreed the course increased their knowledge compared to teachers in other content areas: 96% reading, 92% language arts, 94% mathematics, 94% social studies, and 91% agreed for exceptional education. Content area teachers leave the course with new understanding and appreciation for reading. "I am a chemistry teacher, but I have learned through this course that 75% or more of what I do rests on the ability of my students to read and comprehend that text. I do not think I ever really made the connection before which is kind of sad. But I sure see that connection now." Data also show that FOR-PD met the needs of teachers with regard to improving their knowledge of reading no matter what the level of experience from pre-service (93%) through 11 years or more (96%). Other results— according to results from the pre- and post-tests in the course—show significant and substantial gains in reading knowledge for teachers. Further statistical analysis that compared teachers' test scores according to middle and secondary content area (for language arts, mathematics, and science) or grade level (elementary, middle, and high school) also showed significant gains. In addition, these groups showed no significant differences in post-test results.

Completion rates for online professional development programs, whether *free* or paid, are an important factor in evaluating overall effectiveness. Unfortunately, the literature reveals little information about what an acceptable rate might be for a free (comprehensive and 14-week sustained) statewide online course like FOR-PD. There are simply too many intervening factors to make a clear assessment. Although difficult to compare, in the corporate sector, according to Meister (2002), as much as 70% of learners do not complete scheduled online learning programs.

An investigation of the FOR-PD sections database revealed average completion rates at 77% for the 5,038 who started the course during the 2006-2007 school year.

Challenges of a Statewide Large-Scale Online Professional Development Community

Several barriers exist related to the design, implementation, and sustainability of online teacher professional development communities. One is the fast pace of technological change. Another is the technological knowledge of the participants of the community and their experiences with online learning. Several challenges are associated with the development, monitoring, and sustainability of large-scale online teacher professional development communities. Challenges reflected in the FOR-PD community lie in the following areas: (a) designing, implementing, and maintaining a large-scale online teacher professional learning community; (b) participants' knowledge of (and experiences with) technology; (c) communicating and learning in an online medium; and (d) assessing the effectiveness of an online learning community.

Designing and Implementing a Large-Scale Online Teacher Professional Learning Community

Although online learning is a reflection of a technological revolution it still remains experimental and emerging (Levine & Sun, 2002), many barriers to learning at a distance are caused by a lack of resources and people (Barge, 1998). Core concerns about online professional development deal with the quality of the content, with technical issues, such as necessary equipment and knowledge of technology, and with quality standards (e.g., Dede, et al., 2006). What are key guidelines of online professional development? Treacy, Kleiman, and Peterson (2002) identified the following elements of successful online professional development (OPD). They include the following:

- Assess local professional development needs and develop an OPD plan based on these needs.
- Connect OPD with other ongoing, face-to-face professional development activities.
- Carefully select and train OPD specialist team members.
- Build a strong local team.
- Develop incentives.
- Publicize the OPD program and involve local stakeholders.
- Provide readily available and reliable access to technology and support.
- Foster a rich, interactive online learning community.
- Integrate online workshops with face-to-face meetings. (p. 44)

These nine elements are fundamental to the development and sustainability of a large-scale online teacher professional development community. In addition, costs associated with hardware, Internet access, software, maintenance, ongoing content updates, training of key staff, training and ongoing support of online facilitators, communications with key stakeholders, ongoing evaluation of the project, ongoing support of participants (even beyond program completion), and dissemination of results, are important design and implementation components of this online learning community.

FOR-PD incorporates the aforementioned elements of effective online professional development and maintains a cycle of continuous improvement in all areas of the project. Because the effect of online professional development on teachers has not been well researched (e.g., Whitehouse et al., 2006), FOR-PD strives to assess its impact on its key audiences (teachers and their students, facilitators, all participants), knowledge about reading research and instruction,

participants' attitudes and beliefs toward technology, and satisfaction of participants and all levels of collaborators (i.e., preK-12 educators, school districts, state universities, and community colleges). A sustained record of success in teacher learning has been providing state funding for FOR-PD since 2003 in Florida. This funding has made it possible (the program is offered free to all certified Florida educators) for school districts and educators to receive quality research-based training and ongoing support that will help them to make instructional decisions to improve the reading of all students in their classrooms.

The project was developed collaboratively with literacy and technology experts. The conceptual infrastructure, design, implementation, and assessment processes are not static; they are evaluated on an ongoing basis and are filtered through the key members of this large-scale online teacher professional development community. In addition, FOR-PD maintains an active community of collaborators and representatives from all strata of education. Classroom teachers (preK-12), administrators, literacy coaches, school district staff, FLDOE representatives, technology experts, instructional designers, faculty, and researchers comprise sample members of the advisory board learning community that provides feedback, direction, and ensures that the program meets state and national standards related to literacy, technology, online learning, and teacher professional development. To effectively design and maintain a large-scale online teacher professional development community requires financial support, expert support, in-house support, quality content, technology, resources, time, a mechanism for ongoing content and technology updates, and multiple voices that will help develop a common message. FOR-PD's participatory, data driven, and teacher-centered decision-making model has contributed to its ability to effectively meet the professional development needs of thousands of Florida teachers.

Participants' Limited Knowledge of (and Experiences with) Technology

Many educators taking online courses have limited experiences in online learning, online instruction, and online communities. Even today, some educators do not use online communication tools as an integral part of their professional practices. Learners need to understand and develop experiences with the capabilities of current technologies for online teaching and learning. Lack of effective technical support and troubleshooting when experiencing difficulty with technology adds to the frustration of the participating teachers.

FOR-PD assesses participants' technology knowledge and skills and provides tools, mechanisms, and support to advance their knowledge, eliminate frustrations, and support them with tools and resources they need to learn and succeed in an online learning environment. The FOR-PD design incorporates pedagogically sound and highly relevant and engaging online content, learning activities, and learner assessments. FOR-PD selects tools, resources, features and course design elements that facilitate learner interaction and learning in this large-scale online community. One of FOR-PD's goals has been to help educators change their beliefs about how effective online professional development can be for their professional growth and learning. FOR-PD data shows that educators report an increase not only in their knowledge and implementation of technology to communicate and learn with others online but also an improvement in their attitudes toward online learning and online communities after taking the FOR-PD course. Furthermore, over the last decade, a higher proportion of teachers are starting the course have already experienced taking an online course--currently about half of FOR-PD participants are new to online learning and taking their first online course, compared to 89% when FOR-PD was first being implemented.

Flexibility

Flexibility is another key factor to learning online. Because technological problems can happen, it is important to remain flexible in terms of how information and communication is shared in an online teacher professional development community. FOR-PD provides several means of access to information as well as multiple ways to share information within the online learning community. Multiple access points allow the participants to share and receive information in different ways and they can help to minimize stress for participants and help to eliminate undue burden on facilitators when technology fails. Problems might become evident in an end of course survey, or from ongoing analysis of data collected through the help desk. When recurring problems occur, they are considered as opportunities for improvement, and a process of corrective action might lead to designing and implementing a new tutorial or a change in procedure or additional correspondence.

Selecting the Right Resources

To succeed learners require the resources that will empower them to succeed. Because some technology challenges are beyond a facilitator's or a participant's control, removing the technology challenges from the learning process allows the learners' interaction in the online learning community to be positive and not filled with major technological challenges. FOR-PD provides training to online facilitators via the training course, technology-related chats, technology-related Frequently Asked Questions (FAQs) available through the course and the project website, substantial help desk support, and technology-related tutorials, facilitators, and participants. All of these tools and resources are designed to help the online community participants to work through a technology challenge when it arises. They help make the online professional development learning experience enjoyable and they enable and motivate the learner to continue participating and contributing to the community.

Communicating and Learning in an Online Medium

In the case of an online community, communication (with the facilitator and with each other) and participation (social and academic) are integral. Because the experiences of the members with communicating and learning in a virtual medium will vary, providing quality support (technological, facilitator) and models of how learners can effectively communicate and learn from one another is crucial. Without active communication (facilitator-learner and vice versa and learner-learner) and participation in discussions and other community activities, the learner cannot be a part of the community.

FOR-PD facilitators provide ongoing communication with participants and stimulate communication among participants. Because of the diversity of participants in the FOR-PD community, sub-communities are often formed based on grade level, content area, or other professional or personal interests. Participants communicate about the professional development content, experiences, and assignments, but also about their own classroom instruction, resources, ideas, or challenges they or their students may be experiencing in reading.

The shift from traditional classroom (face-to-face) education to computer-mediated distance learning presents serious challenges to facilitators and participants. Isolation has been seen as a major contributor to participant attrition (Morgan & Tam, 1999). One way FOR-PD has helped to ensure online learners feel connected, is by encouraging community building and support among participants. To scaffold learning FOR-PD focuses on encouraging learners to interact with the content, the facilitator and to reflect on their own learning and beliefs with themselves and with each other.

A review of FOR-PD discussion boards and chat sessions reveal that facilitators and participants communicate on both an academic and personal level. The project incorporates intentional activities and assignments that encourage participants to talk about their personal lives (i.e., hobbies, books they are reading, families, activities) and their successes and challenges with being a member of an online learning community (i.e., research perspectives on content, research, policy, technical problems and solutions, or time management tips) and to seek advice from each other on their professional development plans or classroom instruction.

In a large-scale online professional development, community there is opportunity for successful and less successful communities. FOR-PD places much focus on the ongoing professional development of its facilitators and on the program assignments and requirements. Facilitators play a key role in encouraging and supporting open lines of communication with themselves and learners and also among learners. We have found, through observing the interactions of participants on discussion boards, that more experienced online community members often help novice members with suggestions about technology and content. FOR-PD monitors facilitator performance and participant communication, participation, and learning to help ensure that the members of the community are having a positive learning experience.

FOR-PD participants freely share disagreements with state policy about their professional development, mandates, and future plans in public forum; facilitators help create a safe online community—a space and a place where educators can academic and non-academic topics. Thoughtful and reflective postings within the community to group-think contributions are encouraged. Participants receive basic instruction on netiquette and are encouraged to continually address group norms to maintain professional communication and to build consensus as both group and individual identities within an online learning community are significant factors.

Technology can also contribute to communication and learning challenges. In some cases, technology can exclude or discourage people from communicating as some tools can be complicated or unfamiliar to some, unavailable for a certain platform, and at times slow and cumbersome. As a result, they can all cause the communication and learning processes to be less than ideal, and members who do not actively participate may drop out of the community. The FOR-PD quality assurance checks implemented at critical semester times help prevent participant attrition and contribute to improvements in communication and learning in the online community.

In online learning communities establishing the infrastructure for communications and learning to take place in a positive, encouraging, supportive, and rewarding manner is foundational. Equally important is the monitoring, assessment, providing formative feedback and ongoing improvement to the content, to support the quality of learning that takes place in the online community.

Assessing the Effectiveness of an Online Learning Community

Building and sustaining an effective online learning community involves assessment as the cornerstone. How do we know what kinds of experiences participants are having in the online community? In the case of FOR-PD, what are they learning about literacy, learning online, and technology? Because of the size and the accountability level of this large-scale online teacher professional development community, assessment is a must; it involves a multi-faceted, ongoing and responsive process. FOR-PD assesses its impact through surveys with core audiences, pre/post assessments of teacher knowledge, classroom observations a semester after the completion of the program, focus groups, and research that examines the impact of teacher knowledge gained

at FOR-PD on instructional practice and student achievement.

Challenges with assessment include resources, training researcher assistants, closely following participants, the timing of assessments (before and during the program and a semester after completion of the program), and implementing changes in the program as a result of assessment and research. We need to continue to develop measures that will provide an accurate understanding of what teachers learn while engaged in online professional development and how and whether they use their knowledge to transform their practice and student learning. Improving practice and community building are not easy to develop. The development of quality professional communities can be a critical element in changing the practices of teachers.

FUTURE TRENDS

Online learning communities have been emerging as alternatives to traditional classroom-based, face-to-face, professional development. They are based on the desire of participants in the community to learn with and from each other. The online learning community is the main vehicle to learning online. Future trends include emerging models of technological advancements, development and access to high-quality online professional development models (Dede, et al., 2006), efforts to make teachers, administrators, and policy-makers aware of the benefits of online professional development, and involving teachers involved in all stages of online professional development (i.e., design, development, implementation, assessment, and ongoing evaluation), and teacher empowerment. Tomorrow's teachers will demand a greater degree of personalization and practicality in online learning and more networking software that will allow them to interact with others globally (Barab, Kling, & Gray, 2004; National Research Council, 2007).

The advent of online learning has provided opportunities for teachers to play a direct role in the planning and organization of professional development (Dede, et al., 2006). Online professional development excites teachers and provides them with models on how to utilize information technologies to improve their instructional practices. Online programs should be part of a continuum of learning opportunities in schools for teachers and students and schools and states should provide adequate resources of time, personnel and support systems for online teacher professional development (National Research Council, 2007).

In addition, educators and researchers should continue to raise important questions about the nature of online learning for teacher professional development, the types of learning that can be promoted by online teacher professional development communities, challenges inherent in online learning communities, and the ways in which online learning communities can be improved to promote further teacher professional development and learning.

Understanding online learning communities in the context of teachers' professional lives is a necessary element. More research needs to take place on the impact of online professional development communities on teacher knowledge, teacher networks and collaborations, teacher professional growth, and teacher instructional practice (Dede, 2006). We need to learn from successes and challenges of existing online teacher professional development communities, their design features, and ways of sustaining them and improving them. Lastly, we need to develop a body of knowledge on online teacher professional learning communities that will help facilitate the promotion of distance learning as a core vehicle for teacher professional development (Whitehouse, et al., 2006).

CONCLUSION

Teacher quality is the top contributing factor to student achievement (e.g., National Commission on Teaching & America's Future, 1997). Quality ongoing professional development contributes to teacher growth and success. The need for professional development that can meet today's educators' demanding schedules, that uses quality content and resources that are available to teachers from any place and any time, and that can deliver relevant, accessible, and ongoing support has stimulated the development of online teacher professional development programs. Online teacher professional development programs make it possible for educators to communicate, share knowledge and resources, and reflect via asynchronous interactions.

While setting up the software for developing and maintaining an online community is relatively easy, the challenging task is sustaining it over time. Online professional development providers need to be aware of the purposes of the online community, guidelines for effective sustainability of the online community, the characteristics and needs of the various participants who join an online learning community, and the kinds of activities that will meaningfully engage and facilitate learning among the members of that community.

Developing and sustaining an effective online learning community can be challenging even in the midst of an era of much technological advancement. Developing and sustaining an effective large-scale online community is even more challenging. As online teacher professional development is an emerging trend it is still a "new frontier." Educators around the world experience many demands on their knowledge, time, and professional development. Current U.S. policy and research has placed the concept of teacher quality in the spotlight due to its impact on student achievement (e.g., Hanushek, Kain, O'Brien, & Rivkin, 2005; National Commission on Teaching & America's Future, 1997; Rivkin, Hanushek, &

Kain, 2005). Some states' professional development efforts are so large that the more traditional face-to-face format may no longer be the best option for teacher training. Because of its flexibility, interest continues to grow in the use of the Internet to provide training. The need for more evidence of effectiveness is especially great in the field of online professional development where little is currently known about best practices for design and implementation (Whitehouse, et al., 2006).

Currently, in the U.S., school districts spend approximately a few hundred dollars per teacher on professional development (Killeen, Monk, & Plecki, 2002). While we need to support teachers' professional development, we need to ensure that finances, time, and effort are expended on quality programs that equip teachers to teach effectively. Policy makers and school administrators need to involve teachers in professional development programs that engage teachers in self-reflection, sharing with other educators, and learning about how to transform instructional practice (Bodzin & Park, 2000; Herringlton, Herringston, Oliver, & Omari, 2000). Online teacher professional development communities have the potential to meaningfully engage teachers in reflective knowledge making and knowledge sharing and support their growth over time.

Our goal with this large-scale online teacher professional development community is to help remove policy, attitudinal, administrative, and other barriers to online teacher learning. FOR-PD is a comprehensive, research-based, quality online professional development project that provides ongoing support to teachers beyond the program as they implement new curricula and transform instructional practice. Failure to identify, address, and prevent barriers will interfere with the effectiveness of the online learning community. Build it and they will come. But will they stay and invite others to join the community? Will they continue to come back to that community for support, resources, and further learning? We may build it and they may come, but we need to be ready to help them succeed, provide them with quality content, support technology usage, listen to educators' voices and meet their professional needs, monitor the community's progress, and be serious about ongoing assessment and evaluation of the effectiveness of the online learning community.

REFERENCES

Allen, I. E., & Seeman, J. (2007, October). *Online nation: Five years of growth in online learning.* Retrieved September 26, 2008, from http://www. sloan-c.org/

Annenberg Institute for School Reform. (2004). *Professional learning communities: Professional development strategies that improve instruction.* Retrieved June 13, 2008, from http://www.an-nenberginstitute.org/pdf/ProfLearning.pdf

Barab, S., Kling, R., & Gray, J. 2004. Introduction: Designing for virtual communities in the service of learning. In: S. Barab, R. Kling, & J. Gray (Eds.), *Designing for Virtual Communities in the Service of Learning.* Cambridge, UK: Cambridge University Press.

Bodzin, A. M., & Park, J. C. (2000). Dialogue patterns of preservice science teachers using asynchronous computer mediated communications on the World Wide Web. *Journal of Computers in Mathematics and Science Teaching, 19*(2), 161–194.

Christensen, C. M., & Horn, M. B. (Summer, 2008). How do we transform our schools? *Education Next, 8*(3). Retrieved September 29, 2008, from http://www.hoover.org/publications/ednext/18575969.html

Council for Higher Education Accreditation. (1998, April). *Assuring quality in distance learning.* Washington, DC: Institute for Higher Education Policy. Retrieved October 16, 2008, from: http://www.chea.org

Darling-Hammond, L. (1993). Reframing the school reform agenda. *Phi Delta Kappan, 74*(10), 752–761.

Darling-Hammond, L., & Sykes, G. (2003). Wanted: A national teacher supply policy for education: The right way to meet the "Highly Qualified Teacher" challenge. *Education Policy Analysis Archives, 11*(33). Retrieved October 16, 2008, from http://epaa.asu.edu/epaa/v11n33/

Dede, C. (Ed.). (2006). *Online professional development for teachers: Emerging models and methods.* Cambridge, MA: Harvard Education Press.

Dede, C., Breit, L., Ketelhut, D. J., McCloskey, E., & Whitehouse, P. (2005). *An overview of current findings from empirical research on online teacher professional development.* Cambridge, MA: Harvard Graduate School of Education.

Dede, C., Ketelhut, D., & Whitehouse, J. P., Breit, L., & McCloskey, E. (2006). *Research agenda for online teacher professional development.* Cambridge, MA: Harvard Graduate School of Education.

DuFour, R. (2004). What is a "professional learning community?". *Educational Leadership, 61*(8), 6–11.

DuFour, R., & Eaker, R. (1998). *Professional learning communities at work: Best practices for enhancing student achievement.* Alexandria, VA: National Educational Service.

DuFour, R., Eaker, R., & DuFour, R. (Eds.). (2005). *On common ground: The power of professional learning communities.* Bloomington, IN: Solution Tree.

Eaker, R., DuFour, R., & DuFour, R. (2002). *Getting started: Reculturing schools to become professional learning communities.* Bloomington, IN: National Educational Service.

Guskey, T. R. (2000). *Evaluating professional development.* Thousand Oaks, CA: Corwin Press.

Hanushek, E. A., Kain, J. F., O'Brien, D. M., & Rivkin, S. G. (2005, February). *The market for teacher quality.* National Bureau of Economic Research Working Paper 11154.

Herrington, A., Herrington, J., Oliver, R., & Omari, A. (2000). A web-based resource providing reflective online support for preservice mathematics teachers on school practice [Electronic Version]. *Contemporary Issues in Technology and Teacher Education, 1*(2), 17-140. Retrieved September 29, 2008, from http://www.citejournal.org/vol1/iss2/currentissues/general/article1.htm

Hord, S. M. (1997). Professional learning communities: What are they and why are they important? *Issues About Change, 6*(1). Retrieved September 29, 2008, from http://www.sedl.org

Joint Committee on Standards for Educational Evaluation. (1994). *The program evaluation standards.* Thousand Oaks, CA: Sage.

Killeen, K., Monk, D., & Plecki, M. (2002). School district spending on professional development: Insights available from national data. *Journal of Education Finance, 28*(1), 25–49.

Kleiman, G. L. (2004, July). *Meeting the need for high quality teachers: E-Learning solutions.* White paper written for the U.S. Department of Education Secretary's No Child Left Behind Leadership Summit Whitepaper: Increasing Options through E-Learning. Retrieved March 6, 2006, from http://www.ed.gov/about/offices/list/os/technology/plan/2004/site/documents/Kleiman-MeetingtheNeed.pdf

Levine, A., & Sun, J. (2002). *Barriers in distance education.* Washington, DC: American Council on Education.

Meister, J. (2002). *Pillars of e-learning success.* New York: Corporate University Exchange.

National Commission on Teaching and America's Future. (1997). *Doing what matters most: Investing in quality teaching.* New York: National Commission on Teaching and America's Future.

National Research Council. (2007). *Enhancing professional development for teachers: Potential uses of information technology, report of a workshop.* Washington, DC: The National Academies Press.

Reinking, D., McKenna, M., Labbo, L., & Kieffer, R. (Eds.). (1998). *Handbook of literacy and technology: Transformations in a post-typographic world.* Mahwah, NJ: Erlbaum.

Rivkin, S. G., Hanushek, E. A., & Kain, J. F. (2005). Teachers, schools, and academic achievement. *Econometrica, 73*(2), 417–458. doi:10.1111/j.1468-0262.2005.00584.x

Schofield, J. W. (2003). Bringing the Internet to schools effectively. *Global issues. The evolving Internet, 8*(8). An Electronic Journal of the U.S. Department of State. Retrieved January 29, 2009, from http://www.scribd.com/doc/3210562/the-evolving-internet

Seal, K. (2003). Transforming teaching & learning through technology. *Carnegie Reporter, 2*(2), 25–33.

Snow, C. (2002). *Reading for understanding: Toward an R & D program in reading comprehension.* Santa Monica, CA: RAND.

Snow, C., Griffin, P., & Burns, M. S. (2005). *Knowledge to support the teaching of reading: Preparing teachers for a changing world.* San Francisco, CA: Jossey-Bass.

Stake, R. (1975). *Evaluating the arts in education: A responsive approach.* Columbus, OH: Merill.

Stufflebeam, D. L. (2001). *Evaluation models.* San Francisco: Jossey-Bass.

Swan, B., Huh, J., Chen, Y.-C., & Smith, S. (2008). *Florida Online Reading Professional Development (FOR-PD) Phase V annual evaluation report fall 2006 to summer 2007.* Orlando: University of Central Florida, College of Education.

Treacy, B., Kleiman, G., & Peterson, K. (2002). Successful online professional development. *Learning and Leading with Technology, 30*(1), 42–47.

U.S. Department of Education, National Center for Education Statistics. (2006). *Internet access in U.S. public schools and classrooms: 1994–2005, 2007.* Available at http://nces.ed.gov/

U.S. Department of Education, Office of Postsecondary Education. (2005). *The Secretary's Fourth Annual Report of Teacher Quality: A highly qualified teacher in every classroom.* Washington, DC (ERIC Document Reproduction Service No. ED485858).

U.S. Department of Education (USDOE). (2002). *The Secretary's Report on Teacher Quality.* Washington, DC: U.S. Department of Education.

Whitehouse, P., Breit, L., McCloskey, E., Ketelhut, D. J., & Dede, C. (2006). An overview of current findings from empirical research on online teacher professional development. In C. Dede (Ed.), *Online professional development for teachers: Emerging models and methods* (pp. 13-30). Cambridge, MA: Harvard Education Press.

Chapter 8
Teacher Professional Development through Knowledge Management in Educational Organisations

J. Gairín-Sallán
Universitat Autònoma de Barcelona, Spain

D. Rodríguez-Gómez
Universitat Autònoma de Barcelona, Spain

ABSTRACT

Professional development has mainly centered around training processes that involve updating knowledge, yet it has made little headway as a construct that includes both the professional and personal characteristics and working conditions. It has also focused more on developing training programmes than on analysing the tools for continuous training. This chapter analyses the relationships between professional development, organisational development and the creation and management of collective knowledge. These three concepts can be interrelated and contribute to change when we place ourselves within the framework of autonomous organisations with collective projects focused on lifelong learning. It also outlines the Accelera experience of knowledge creation and management in communities, describing the model and process used. This article examines some of the findings and future prospects of the methodology presented.

INTRODUCTION

The knowledge society, and we would add the learning society, is taking shape as a new scenario with its own characteristics and requirements that differentiate it from the preceding models of society. Developing the knowledge society in education requires new curricular, didactic and/ or organisational strategies, as well as an optimal development of educational professionals (teaching staff, directors, social educators, pedagogues and educational psychologists, social integrators, etc.) if we want to contribute to increasing the competitiveness and quality demanded by the educational systems.

DOI: 10.4018/978-1-60566-780-5.ch008

In this setting, what is needed is changes in the organisation of educational efforts and in the role of the agents, which in turn requires a revision of teaching competencies within the framework of the most autonomous school, characterised by carrying out institutional projects and teamwork. In the words of David Hargreaves:

To improve schools, one must be prepared to invest in professional development; to improve teachers, their professional development must be set within the context of institutional development. (Hargreaves, 1994, p. 436)

Compared to traditional, widespread prescriptions for hiring, training and uniform working conditions, we are witnessing ever more contextualised processes and the use of new professional development strategies.

In view of these changes, this chapter presents a strategy for the continuous training and development of education professionals based on a model of knowledge creation and management.

After a brief description of today's society and an analysis of the aptness of the continuous training applied in its organisations, we interrelate knowledge management, organisational development and professional development, describing the framework in which educational organisations can be seen as learning communities. After that, we present the Accelera proposal for professional development by means of knowledge creation and management processes (henceforth KCM) which combines the creation of online learning communities (henceforth OLC) and the philosophy and technology of what is known as social software – "tools for content creation and sharing and for developing networks" (Graham, 2007, p. 6)-, along with several examples and some findings.

BACKGROUND

Constant societal changes, globalisation, increased competitiveness and technological development, as principal factors, require us to reconsider our systems and policies of training and professional development. Organisations, and not just educational ones, are required to be more innovative, creative and efficient, which entails many changes, including changing in training processes (Rubio, 2007). A changing society requires organisations that adapt and revise their coherency and ways of acting according to the needs of the environment. Innovation, which was a trait of only creative, cutting-edge organisations, has become a widespread need and a problem that is constantly being examined at different levels (a more adapted society, more adapted organisations, more adapted individuals) and with different strategies. Innovation is a change that takes place because society is changing, organisations are changing and people, their relationships and their actions and results must change.

Some necessities to be taken into account are in line with the analysis of the new training trends in 21st century organisations (Figure 1) conducted recently by the consultancy firm Overlap.

The aforementioned characteristics of the knowledge society clearly reveal the fast obsolescence of knowledge and the need for constant updating, in turn justifying the development of policies of compulsory continuous training and professional development in organisations. They contribute directly to increasing the intellectual capital of organisations, making possible educational improvements related to higher student performance and a response that more closely fits their educational and training requirements and needs.

Professional development in organisations must therefore shed its adaptive and retroactive nature and instead push for proactive actions that are one step ahead of the social and workplace changes and the advent of new technologies.

Figure 1. Types of training needs (Overlap, 2007)

Level of need	Organisational	Improved performance is focused on increasing organisational effectiveness and efficiency through training and development programmes	The goal is to align and integrate the training strategy with the other business strategies in order to generate and reinforce competitive improvements that are sustainable over time.
	Individual	The solutions focus on developing the needs detected in employees with regard to the competencies needed in the job they perform.	The strategic component is crucial and consists of improving performance by designing and implementing individual programmes to retain talent.
		Tactical	Strategic
		Focus for implementation	

In this way, in the specific case of educational organisations, the functions of teacher professional development can be reduced to just three (Day & Sachs, 2004): 1) aligning the teaching practices with educational policies; 2) improving students' results by improving the teaching activity; and 3) improving the status and profile of the teaching profession.

Continuous training, planned and developed within the framework of organisations, thus attempts to respond to both lifelong training and learning and the changing demands of society and educational services.

In this framework, knowledge creation and management (KCM) becomes a fundamental strategy as it combines personal/professional development and organisational development, in addition to doing this while respecting the conditions of the context and reinforcing collaborative work and reflection on the problems and challenges posed by the educational practice.

After careful analysis of the definitions and inherent characteristics of knowledge creation and management, we can affirm that it consists of "a series of systematic processes (the identification and gathering of knowledge; the processing, development and sharing of knowledge; and the use of knowledge) aimed at organisational and/or personal development and, consequently

at generating a competitive advantage for the organisation and/or individual". (Rodríguez, 2006, p. 32)

KCM processes make possible a true development of continuous training in organisations as opposed to the simple sum of occasional training actions, as they are characterised by the following features:

- Activities created in the day-to-day job;
- The 'learner' is responsible for acquiring the theoretical and practical knowledge, but the presence of a knowledge manager and moderator is also necessary to take responsibility for planning and developing the process;
- The learning that takes place during the KCM is generated collaboratively by the people around us;
- There may be some type of explicit "programming" that guides the KCM process and will be conducted by and agreed to by the organisation itself;
- The goals of the KCM can be diverse, yet they can include resolving problems in the immediate setting and introducing organisational changes;
- The motivation may be oriented at both achievement and emulation among

learners; and

- The knowledge and competencies will be validated via everyday practice.

KCM also dovetails with the new approaches to continuous training in organisations that take advantage of the characteristics of the workplace organisation as one of the reference points for diversifying training initiatives. As against standard, mass and homogenising training programmes, individual and contextualised approaches are thereby generated, which meet both workplace and group needs and recognise the varied nature and diversity of workplace situations.

In any event, the implementation of KCM processes entails a prioritisation, in organisations, of the acquisition and/or development of technologies, methodologies and strategies for measuring, creating and spreading individual and collective knowledge. To achieve this, internationally renowned organisations such as the OECD (2003) seriously recommend studying the processes, tools and results of knowledge creation and management.

Among the various categories of knowledge-related investments (education, training, software, R&D, etc.) KM is one of the less known, both from a quantitative and qualitative point of view as in terms of cost and economic returns. Thus, there is certainly a need to know more about these new knowledge-based activities; about the current state of KM as an organisational process within various kinds of companies and sectors; about the variety of methods and tools that are developed; and about the effects of KM practices that are currently observed. (OECD, 2003, p. 3)

KNOWLEDGE MANAGEMENT, PROFESSIONAL DEVELOPMENT AND ORGANISATIONAL DEVELOPMENT

Having discussed training, we shall use it as a springboard for relating the different stereotypes that often arise in organisations.

Training in organisations has the clear purpose of affecting people in order to modify their field of knowledge, change their attitudes or develop their skills. Providing knowledge about the workplace, empowering workers to solve problems in their profession or job, driving knowledge of new technologies, promoting teamwork skills and the like are specific manifestations of this training that might be linked to specific organisations.

However important, training that is thus oriented towards improving professional and personal performance can be considered a restrictive vision of training. First, we must understand that training is increasingly a collective responsibility if we take into account the fact that professional work is performed in organised setting whose mission is to gain the involvement and commitment of all its members. Secondly, its link to organisational development makes training the cornerstone of any transformation that the organisation would like to undertake.

Precisely the quest for new forms of training that enable organisations to place themselves in the best possible conditions for fulfilling their goals is what has fostered a change in the orientation of training. Whilst initially it focused on improving internal processes (detecting problems related to the stated mission, more efficiently executing jobs, better understanding of how groups work, etc.), the outbreak of crazy times (Peters, 1994), in reference to the turbulence of today, technology crises, impartiality and somehow also chaos have fostered an orientation towards external processes.

Under these circumstances, training is focused on restructuring, culture (the strength of an or-

Figure 2. Continuous training in relation to organisations (Pont, 1997)

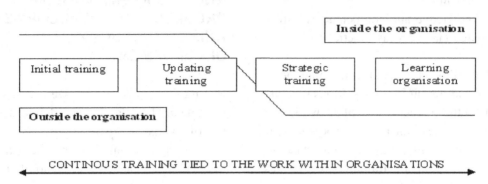

ganisation lies in the values and links it forges), learning (the ability to "read" and personally interpret a mutable, difficult to universalise reality), teams (building autonomous, self-led units with the ability to change), quality (the transversal vector of processes and products within the organisation) and vision (global thinking, shared wisdom) (Pont, 1997). Training can therefore be regarded as the prerequisite for making it possible for the organisation to achieve its purposes, as an inherent part of the organisation which acts as a tool that serves the organisation's needs, as part of the strategy that makes it possible to develop advantageous positions when faced with change, or as the essence that makes it possible for the organisation to learn. Figure 2 identifies the types of training that can be considered under this perspective.

If we view the learning organisation as one that facilitates the learning of all its members and is constantly transforming itself, we are stressing the value of learning as a cornerstone of the organisation. The organisation's development is based on the development of its people and on their ability to take on new ways of doing things inside the institution in which they work.

Organisations that are more capable of handling the future believe in themselves not because of what they are but because of their ability to cease being what they are; that is, they do not feel strong

because of the structures they have but because of their ability to build themselves other more appropriate structures when needed.

This conceptual framework in which self-learning takes place is unquestionably the benchmark that enables the organisation to head confidently into the future. People are trained and developed not just to meet the organisation's needs, which are predefined and prescribed, rather to expand their function. This new approach might even come to question certain issues related to leadership, decision-making and the established control mechanisms. It also requires new learning strategies to be explored and training systems to be modified.

Many of these training and professional development activities have often been targeted by governments to promote educational changes and reforms (Boyle, Lamprianou & Boyle, 2005, Day & Sachs, 2004). Therefore, they have set up mass encounters, workshops, classroom and distance courses that meet the informative needs of the educational administration more than meeting teachers' needs. This sole via of continuous intervention has been the main vehicle for teacher professional development, despite the existence of hosts of studies that reveal their insufficiency and inappropriateness.

Fortunately, other methodologies for training and professional development are starting to gain

Figure 3. Kinds of professional development for teaching staff

	Inside Educational Organisations	Outside Educational Organisations
Direct learning	Consulting, Mentoring	Conferences, workshops, seminars, courses
Indirect learning	Mentoring, peer coaching, active research, teamwork, school-based study circles.	Research networks, communities of practice, school-university partnerships

ground (Boyle, Lamprianou & Boyle, 2005): sharing experiences among the teachers at the same school, sharing knowledge and competencies with the teaching staff from other schools, hiring consultants to develop training programmes at the school, drawing up and developing innovation projects that include training programmes, and so forth.

Here we are addressing the right side of Figure 1, where training is linked to the institutional mission and even that might be included within the process of ongoing revision and improvement of the organisation in advanced situations. In these cases, the learning is indirect and linked to professional development, personal development and the development of the organisation (Figure 3).

Ongoing, internal training as part of the organisational strategy thus links directly up with processes of organisational learning, knowledge creation and management and, therefore, with high levels of organisational development. In short, KCM finds its chance be spearheaded as a strategy for professional development inside organisations (Rodríguez, 2006).

The goal is to take advantage of the experience and competency that the professionals who participate in organisations have amassed over years. Their knowledge in the broad sense can be related to teacher training and development, acknowledging them as the basis of KCM processes, which have been identified by Day & Sachs (2004), based on Cochrane-Smith and Lytle, as:

- Knowledge-for-practice: formal knowledge generated by researchers outside the

schools;
- Knowledge-of-practice: generated by the teaching staff based on a critical evaluation of their own classroom or school in terms of social justice, equality and student performance.
- Knowledge-in-practice: the teaching staff's practical knowledge generated by systematic inquiries related to and stimulated by the efficacy in their own classroom.
- Knowledge-of-self: generated by the teaching staff by reflecting on their own values, goals, emotions and relationships.

Actions aimed at taking advantage of and sharing professionals' intellectual capital by means of KCM serve both the organisation and the individuals involved, closing the triangle of relationships among professional development, organisational development and knowledge management.

The professional development of the members of any organisation is fundamental for the development of the organisation itself. Thus, for example, the majority of characteristics attributed to effective schools have a direct implication on the teaching staff (Bolam & McMahon, 2004; Teddie & Reynolds, 2000): they have to work collegially and cooperate to achieve common goals, have high expectations for their students, provide positive feedback, monitor students' work, etc.

Finally, Bolam & McMahon (2004), citing Fullan, mention that the learning teacher is the key to organisational learning, and that one of the means of promoting it is by investing in professional development for the teaching staff.

Learning Communities as the Framework for Teacher Professional Development

Internal cooperation among the teaching staff in schools is already usually assumed (although it is not always present in practice) based on the commitments entailed in developing curricular autonomy: setting methodological criteria for the subjects; defining basic and additional goals for the subjects being learnt; setting and coordinating criteria on student evaluation and retesting; coordinating the functions of guiding and tutoring students; proposing the organisation of the student groups; and promoting educational and extracurricular activities.

However, these are processes that are usually limited and circumscribed to the teachers, with little or no participation by parents and students. As a result, the goal is to drive communitarian projects; promote cooperative classrooms that include shared knowledge and authority among the teaching staff, students and some participation by the parents; and setting up multidisciplinary teams of teachers and students for secondary and university education or other alternatives.

The similar holds true of external cooperation processes. There are real possibilities for institutions to cooperate with each other. If there were not, we could not call to mind experiences such as: the association of schools under a single organisational umbrella; school clusters in rural areas; associations of adult learning centres; networks of schools; and cooperative actions promoted within broader settings such as the "Proyecto Educativo de Ciudad" (City Education Project). However, we can state that these cooperative experiences are few and far between, mediated by specific needs and in many cases related to deficient situations.

Preventing the isolation that certain practices have prompted can only be overcome by fostering cooperative processes, which not only serve as a framework for a powerful professional exchange but can also provide mutual support at times when difficulties arise in the teaching-learning processes.

Taking on institutional commitments to professionalisation, fostering structures for cooperative work (teaching departments and educational teams) and generating processes of internal dynamisation are personal and institutional challenges, yet they will not be possible without modifying the current macro- and micro-structural conditions that are not always present in which the professors operate. Knowledge creation and management can contribute to the development of these communities and the fulfilment of their objectives.

In any case, we are talking about collective work, shared culture and a connection between educational and organisational processes in which the teaching staff is at the core. This is the foundation upon which the new philosophy stands, as long as we have professionals capable of teamwork and accepting collective action as conditions that are inherently linked to educational quality.

Today's society requires individuals, diverse collectives, companies, organisations and institutions to know how to work and learn in networks and communities in which new knowledge is generated and processes of innovation are promoted through active dialogue. As Poley (2002) points out, working in the knowledge age requires the ability to recognise models, maintain a broad set of relationships, share ideas with communities of interest and enrich oneself with these relationships.

Learning communities are an outstanding tool for promoting improvements in educational systems. These communities can be set up among professionals from the same school, between schools and education and social services within the same town, between schools and professionals from different towns and communities, and even among professionals from different countries. Some of these types of communities have been developed as part of the Accelera project, which we shall describe below.

Valuable knowledge is not always available in

organisations, rather it must be created within the framework of the existing social systems, either intra-organisational or inter-organisational. This creation combines a social and a personal dimension. Knowledge, once validated socially, must be transformed and assimilated by each individual in particular. Therefore, we must view knowledge as a personal appropriation that does not exclude a social use and intense organisation.

Many different studies and publications confirm that the creation of networks and communities fosters the creation of knowledge and the processes of professional development (Aubuson et al., 2007; Leinonen & Järvelä, 2006; Snow-Gerono, 2005).

Aubuson et al. (2007) compile some of the essential features of these professional development communities: knowledge is shared, a progressive discourse is developed that involves identifying a meaningful phenomenon and engaging in a discussion aimed at getting a better grasp of it; mutual respect; developing a collective skill that goes beyond individual skills; true reflection and examination; and a determination to improve the communities in which they participate.

We are talking about communities, referring to the classroom, the school, a region or a online environment, viewed as a community of individuals that organise themselves in order to build and become involved in their own educational and cultural project, and that learn via cooperative, shared efforts.

Regardless of the specific guise they take, what is undeniable is that these communities all participate in a series of minimal conditions, namely:

- Institutional changes that facilitate their development.
- The pursuit of effective models for them to operate.
- To make headway in the technical innovations needed and provide tools that foster modern, flexible environments.

- Open participation and horizontal operating structures.
- Cooperative group work.
- Situating the individuals in the school.
- If these conditions obtain, the benefits can be manifold, because:
- By using dialogue as the cornerstone of the process, we achieve greater interaction and participation.
- Shared responsibility ensures that all the members of the community participate in the learning process.
- Knowledge is viewed as dynamic, and the process of building knowledge as an active, cooperative process.

The interaction among the members of the community must make it possible for each and every member to advance while strengthening a common culture and the possibility that the learning and organisational improvement becomes real.

Hislop (2005) highlights the potential of communities in relation to processes of knowledge: 1) they underlie organisational innovation by supporting and promoting the creation, development and use of knowledge; 2) they facilitate and promote individual and group learning, as well as knowledge sharing.

In this sense, we adopted the concept of community of practice proposed by Wenger (1999) to develop our KCM model. This community is based on the following indicators: mutually sustained relationships; shared methods for getting things done together; a quick flow of information; the absence of introductory preambles in conversations; and knowledge of what the others know and can do. They are extremely dynamic, with constant changes among members and the type knowledge and practices that characterise them, and learning and developing knowledge are inherent in their dynamics (Hislop, 2005).

Currently, the majority of these communities are developed and take place in online environments (Allan & Lewis, 2006; Graham, 2007;

Rosmalen et al., 2006; Wei & Chen, 2006). Indeed, technology facilitates synchronous and asynchronous communication according to users' needs. Network-based organising, virtual working, dispersed working and collaborative work, among others, are concepts and proposals that are widely known and used to refer to contemporary forms of organisation with an intensive use of ICTs.

Some of the characteristics of these online communities are:

- They are only feasible in cyberspace, inasmuch as their members communicate with each other in a space created using electronic resources.
- Their organisational model is horizontal with no vertical structures, given the fact that information and knowledge are constructed based on joint reflection.
- They share a space to build, as the participants, with their varied and variable interests, goals and jobs, are the ones to give meaning to the community.
- Their members share a goal, interest, need or activity that is the underlying reason for setting up the community. They also agree on a context, a language and conventions and protocols.
- Their members take an active stance for participation and even share emotional ties and intense common activities.
- Their members have access to shared resources and policies that govern access to these resources.
- There is reciprocity of information, support and services among their members.

In the specific case of KCM, the best-known and most successful projects have involved the use of intranets, data warehouses, decision support tools and groupware, among others. Nevertheless, we should be cautious in how we use these ICTs

if we want to avoid perverting the usefulness and meaning of KCM processes in view of the lack of proven models and valid working procedures.

The Accelera Experience

The Accelera 1.0 project was developed from 2003 to 2006 with the purpose of "delimiting and experimenting with a model that would allow knowledge to be created and shared among different members of the educational community" (teachers, education specialists, researchers, managers in the public administration and other stakeholders involved in the educational process) in an effort to make headway in creating a space in the knowledge society that had been theretofore underdeveloped in the field of education.

The creation of knowledge requires a social dimension in which processes of combination and socialisation of this knowledge can take place. This social dimension is where work, interaction and networked learning, either in person or virtually, gain meaning. (Gairín & Rodríguez, 2007, p. 10)

During the second stage of the project, Accelera 2.0, which is lasting between 2006 and 2009, the activities focus on analysing the roles of the stakeholders and processes that intervene and take part, respectively, in knowledge creation and management in online settings. There is a twofold goal:

1. To describe and analyse the characteristics of the different stakeholders that take part in KCM communities (participants, moderators and knowledge managers) as well as the strategies they use during the KCM process.
2. To analyse some of the fundamental processes and factors for the proper development of KCM model: participation, motivation,

group dynamics (cohesion, productivity, etc.), ethics, communication processes and content analysis, among others.

In line with the studies conducted by Anderson and Jones (2000) as part of the American Educational Research Association (AERA), we understand that creating KCM communities fosters the processes of personal, professional and organisational change, as unlike other proposals in which experts generate the knowledge, they allow knowledge to be created and used in the same practical setting. We therefore believe that when professionals discuss their practical problems they can be viewed as knowledge generators and may be more willing to seek and use research conducted by "outsiders".

The proposition we developed for Accelera started from three basic premises:

Figure 4. Knowledge Creation and Management Communities in the Accelera Project

	Community	Participants	Contents to be developed
Accelera 1.0	ATENEA (40 people)	Heads of primary and secondary schools (headmasters and heads of study), although education inspectors, initial training teachers, lifelong training teachers and doctoral students also took part.	Organisation and management of educational institutions. During the first two cycles of KCM the following issues were addressed: bullying and teacher motivation.
	GALATEA (25 people)	University faculty involved in the initial training of education professionals, lifelong learning teachers and primary school teachers.	Teaching the social sciences: dealing with immigration at school.
	THEMIS (34 people)	This community was primarily made up of primary, secondary and university teachers, doctoral students and experts in coeducation and gender violence from all over Spain and from a variety of organisations (the Barcelona Town Hall's Municipal Education Institute, SOS Racism, Platform Against Gender Violence, etc.).	Coeducation and gender violence.
	MOMO (10 people)	This community is made up of knowledge moderators and managers from the different KCM communities, the system administrator and other members of the research group, all of them experts in the different areas being studied in the processes and systems of knowledge management (such as: organisational culture, organisational learning, group dynamics and learning communities).	Characteristics, possibilities and limitations of Knowledge Creation and Management model.
Accelera 2.0	BABEL (15 people)	Teachers and heads of the network of Jesuit schools related to the Joan XXIII Foundation.	Proposal for developing a multilingual school.
	DEWEY (32 people)	Students, alumni, external experts and professors in the Faculty of Education at the Universitat Autònoma de Barcelona (UAB).	Drawing up a document on the new curricula in educational degrees.
	ARGOS (13 people)	Professors and heads of the La Salle network of university centres.	Defining the basic jobs to be performed in the modernisation of KCM networks among the La Salle university centres.
	IDES (–)	Professors involved in the "Teaching Innovation Unit in Higher Education" at the UAB.	Defining the characteristics and implications of the "end-of-studies project" that all degree programmes must have.
	COYHAIQUE (23 people)	Heads of schools in the town of Coyhaique, in southern Chile.	Efforts to develop the managerial functions in the region.
	REDAGE (22 people)	Staff from institutions and programmes related to educational administration and management.	Improving the administration and management of educational institutions in South America.

a. As a strategy for continuous training and professional development in organisations, KCM is linked to processes of internal. This means that it is a type of training "in" the organisation, a type of internal training that shares characteristics of both implicit / informal training and of explicit / formal training.

b. The learning must be meaningful for the person learning, and dialogue, action and intergenerational and inter-subject solidarity can contribute to this if we consider that everyone is potentially both student and teacher.

c. It assumes professionals' ability to generate new knowledge by sharing the knowledge that emerges from reflection on and structuring their own practice.

During the first stage of the Accelera project, the online space was organised into three OLC which fed a fourth OLC – MOMO – which worked as a base of knowledge for reflection on the processes and dynamics generated in the other three OLC. The composition of each is shown in Figure 4.

During the second stage of the project, the online space was made up of six intelligent OLC (Figure 5), and the seventh OLC, MOMO, was kept in place serving the same purpose it served in the previous stage of research.

The core of the KCM model (Figure 6) consists of debate as a strategy through which we attempt to generate processes of combination, socialisation, externalisation and internalisation of knowledge (Nonaka & Takeuchi, 1995), and the 'minutes' or diachronic record of what has been debated as formal documents that reflect everything that has taken place or been dealt with in this debate.

The debate takes place via a series of tools including forums, chats and wikis, and it is fed by documents, bibliographic references, examples, experiences and ideas, which both fuel it and systematise it.

One important aspect that must be taken into account is that these external contributions do not only come from experts and knowledge moderators or managers, rather the participants in the debate themselves can and should make contributions as well. For example, any document, book, article or website that is used during the debate to support any of the arguments put forth should be properly referenced in its corresponding section.

All the knowledge generated in the OLC is organised and structured by the community moderator, generating, after proposing debates or not, final contributions in the guise of articles, experiences, instruments, references and the like

Figure 5. Sequence for developing an initial KCM in a newly-created community

REFERENCE QUESTIONS	PURPOSE OF THE ANALYSIS	TOOLS	TIMING
What do we mean by ...?	Concept and characteristics	FORUM	Initial contact 1st to 12th of April 13th to 30th of April
How do we identify ...?	Examples	FORUM / CHAT	2nd to 11th of May
How can we diagnose ...?	Aspects of application	WIKI / FORUM	11th of 21st of May
Construction or drawing up of an instrument / proposal	Aspects of application	WIKI / CHAT	22nd of May to 14th of June
Intervention guidelines	Intervention guidelines	WIKI / FORUM / CHAT	15th of June to 14th of July

Figure 6. KCM Model

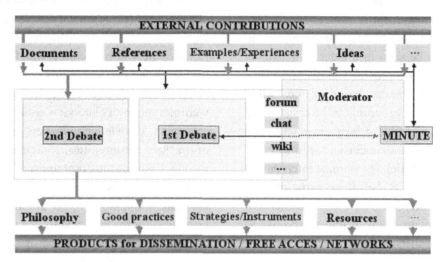

that can be used to disseminate this knowledge, or as initial contributions for other OLC or KCM cycles.

We thus shift from professionals' tacit, personal knowledge to an explicit, collective knowledge that is only vaguely organised (minutes), and then to classified knowledge that is qualified and can and should be disseminated. This, then, includes the main stages that generically speaking any knowledge management process should contain: identify, capture, share, create, disseminate and use knowledge.

Finally, from a technological standpoint, the delimited and experienced KCM model has given rise to the Accelera platform, which is based on developing and adapting a CMS (Course Management System) using open-source software such as Moodle (http://moodle.org), a type of FOSS (free, open sourced software) created originally to develop OLC and founded on educational principles about the social construction of knowledge.

For example, Figure 5 contains one of the standard sequences suggested during the early cycles of KCM for a newly-created community. It is a highly direct yet effective platform for starting the KCM process that allows the com-

munity to move forwards towards self-managed models of KCM.

The first question posed to the group (What do we mean by…?) enables us to examine the implicit assumptions that the different participants in the OLC have, as well as to negotiate meanings and explicitly outline and describe the concept, issue or problem being addressed and analysed. The forum is the instrument that facilitates interaction among the participants.

Likewise, the second reference question (How do we identify …?) serves to compile a set of contributions that enable us to identify, contextualise and clearly and unequivocally delimit the issue being addressed. The tools in this case are the forum, which is a user-friendly venue for submitting proposals and comments, and the chat, which makes simultaneous interaction on given aspects of the contributions possible.

The contributions to each of the questions are summarised periodically and presented once again to the group for its approval. Therefore, for every 15-day period, the knowledge manager, or moderator in some cases, makes two summaries (one per week) and gives two or three days for the participants to add elements that were omitted. The approved summaries then remain as references and tend not to be revised.

In this way, a concept is successively delimited and characterised, real situations are shared in which it can be seen in a clear or debatable way, instruments are provided to diagnose situations (which are created based on the "wiki" tool, which enables proposals to be constructed cooperatively), evidence of the use in practice and results are gathered, and conclusions are drawn that act as indicative guidelines to guide intervention processes. The process also allows participants to evaluate the impact, gather new forms of intervention or state new problems, if they would like to keep examining the subject.

Some Findings from Accelera

The methodology used in the Accelera Project 1.0 was the multiple-case study, an empirical inquiry that investigated contemporary phenomena in their real-life context, and specifically when the boundaries between phenomena and context are not clearly evident (Yin, 2003), with increased robustness sought in the study and its conclusions by arranging sources of information, instruments and information providers.

We consider three cases from Accelera 1.0 (see Figure 4) characterised by: a) undertaking a KCM process in a socio-educational/training context; b) organising KCM based on online learning communities and c) being based on the Accelera KCM model (Figure 6). The cases selected were: the ATENEA community (consisting of heads of primary and secondary schools), the GALATEA community (consisting of primary and secondary education teaching staff specialising in social sciences) and the THEMIS community (consisting of technicians and experts in gender-based violence working in the public administration). The number of participants in each community was 40, 25 and 34, respectively.

The data mentioned in this chapter were collected during the 2003-2004 academic year and specifically refer to one of the main functions of our initiative (professional development through KCM communities), to the key element in our KCM model (the moderator) and, finally, to some problems and barriers in this kind of OLC.

The methods used for gathering information were an exploratory interview with the institutional managers, knowledge managers and moderators of the three communities, content analysis of the forums, based on the Community of Inquiry model (Garrison, Anderson & Archer, 2001), analysis of the general operation of the communities, questionnaires for the participants and two discussion groups with the participation of some members of the communities, institutional managers and experts in various fields of KCM.

The selected results and comments presented below are organised based on three analysis categories: professional development, the moderator's tasks and functions and barriers in OLC.

As regards the link between the KCM processes and the professional development of the participants, in the absence of a thorough assessment of the impact of KCM on professional development and consequently on institutional improvement, those interviewed to date (managers, moderators and participants) all agree on the usefulness of KCM as a strategy for the training and professional development of those involved.

This undoubtedly gives you training. In other words, anyone who joins a community like this one ends up learning. [...] I've learned things, and that wasn't the objective. (participant)

[...] we sought people out and took advantage of the knowledge they already had to share it [in the OLC]. We said "we already have the subject and you're the experts"... If we manage to make the exchange take place, they're bound to learn more, because they already have solutions, they don't need an expert to come and chat to them. [...] Organisations should use these formulas

[KCM and OLC], either on a face-to-face basis or online, to complete people's full development and training. (moderator)

KCM processes are clearly based on the principles of social learning theories (Elkjaer, 2003) and this is what justifies their implementation based on OLC. In that regard, one of the participants said the following:

I think that if you participate in a community where what is being discussed is close to your knowledge area, it facilitates your professional development and the proper functioning of the community. [...] I think that knowledge is generated when other people's opinions are very different to yours, and that makes you think, and perhaps makes you move forward in terms of your knowledge. (participant)

Finally, as regards this first category of analysis, it is important to point out that although not all communities have the training and professional development of their participants as their main and explicit objective, all the KCM systems contribute in one way or another to professional development:

I can see two types of KCM communities and processes: (1) communities consisting of professionals who consider their concerns and seek alternatives to the problems they have [...] they are people whose main objective is not training, but who indirectly receive training. [...] (2) another type of community are those that are part of the formal processes that take place in universities,

in which facts and theories are researched and discussed, and which contribute to professional development. (moderator)

In communities like those which arose in the Accelera project, in which the moderator is very important, he/she has many tasks and functions, but they can only be organised in three categories (see Figure 7).

The organisational function entails preparing the subject matter, arranging it and planning the questions for discussion and the material, including focusing the discussion on critical points, asking questions and responding to the contributions made by students. One of the moderators tells us:

It is necessary to have a protocol with the moderator's tasks and the participants' tasks. There must be a clear distribution of roles. The ideal moderator is one who goes even further, adds some energy, excitement and finds a thousand ways to look at the group and keep it alive. (moderator)

The social function requires the creation of a pleasant and friendly climate which encourages participants to become involved (creating an atmosphere of co-operation which enables a community of learning to be generated). To achieve this, it is sometimes necessary to use media outside the KCM process. Some interviewees said:

For people to join the community, it is necessary to encourage participation, and provide positive feedback. To do that I send instructions by e-mail.

Figure 7. Functions of the moderator in online environments (Anderson et al, 2001, p. 4)

Anderson et al (2001)	Berge (1995)	Paulsen (1995)	Mason (1991)
Design and Organisation of the teaching plan	Management	Organisation	Organisation
Facilitating discourse	Social Function	Social Function	Social Function
Direct Teaching	Pedagogical Function	Intellectual Function	Intellectual Function

[...]. The moderator must provide leadership, and be a reference point. That way the participants' productivity can be enhanced. (manager)

The intellectual function involves summarising and compiling the main points and producing a synthesis of the points dealt with, and highlighting the emerging themes. The key task of the moderator of a KCM community is to act as a guiding intermediary for the space and to encourage the exchanges that take place in the community. He/she must thereby guarantee the relevance and quality of the contributions made based on criteria for action that can change according to the characteristics and objectives of each project.

The moderator must not touch up, filter or modify messages. He/she must respect the contributions made. He/she must make sure that the criteria for participation are met and when this is not the case, he/she must contact the participant to suggest the necessary changes and set out the reasons for which the message has not been approved, and agree on the changes necessary to adapt it to the regulations of the community in which work is being done. (moderator)

Finally, as regards the barriers and difficulties in the development of OLCs, during the implementation of the Accelera 1.0 and 2.0 projects, we found one of the main problems for the implementation of OLCs is the lack of technological skills among a significant proportion of the teaching staff involved. One of the interviewees made the following comment in this respect:

We are dealing with a population in which the age of the participants is advanced, at around 45 or 50 years old [...] Their technological skills are not very highly developed, we don't have them, I include myself in this group [...] To avoid this problem, the initial process [of registration in the community] should certainly be much simpler. (moderator)

Curiously, the person in charge of other OLCs studied said that the fact that these communities make intensive use of technology indirectly facilitates the development of technological skills among the participants:

It is a benefit that is not perhaps very tangible [...] We now have a lot of people who know how to produce blogs, add comments, make a YouTube channel, link videos... these are normal skills for any citizen, as well as English, to operate in the twenty-first century. We are achieving this way and we are becoming major awareness raisers in this field [digital literacy]. (moderator)

The introduction of any change or innovation in the organisational context always requires the support or involvement of that organisation's managers, (Gairín, 2006; Stoll & Flink, 1999). Without the support of managers, the change or innovation is doomed to failure. This can be seen in our experiences:

For me, the key was institutional support, and it is one of the things that the manuals always mention. There must be direct involvement by the managers. If the managers don't make more effort than the professionals themselves (we can win them over later) but if managers don't show willing, we can't open the door to change. (moderator)

Finally, it is important to point out that written communication is a barrier to participation for some people. Participants must be persuaded of the virtues of written communication: it is more reflective, words and ideas are measured to a greater extent; furthermore, simple economy of effort means that only what is most important is said, with no time-wasting on preliminaries.

One of the participants made the following comment:

Having to write is a barrier in itself, because we all find speaking easier than writing. If you interviewed me now in writing, I wouldn't say so much as if it was oral. [...] So written communication is a barrier, but at the same time I think it is a virtue. [...] Because you want to consider your words carefully and economise your efforts to say what is really important, when you end up giving your opinion you do so with more quality. (participant)

FUTURE TRENDS

The Accelera experience has shown the usefulness of KCM procedures based on OLCs for encouraging collaborative work among teaching staff for the improvement of educational quality, the development of the organisation and professional development.

After analysis of the operation of the various communities created, it has also shown some limitations, which are listed below:

a.   The restrictions imposed by using written language, especially for individuals with weaker language skills.

b.   The use of synchronic tools is limited, as not all the participants can access them at the same time, sometimes because of availability issues and at other times because they are working in different time brackets.

c.   The over-saturation of information and the complications involved in managing it can trigger problems if there are not enough appropriate criteria for culling and managing this information.

d.   Lack of training on the use of the platform, for both moderators and the other participants.

e.   The difficulties that schools have in getting connections and the teaching staff's excessive workload makes it difficult to attain an optimal development of the proposed model, as seen in the results of the THEMIS and

GALATEA communities.

f.   The development of OLC requires not just minimal resources (time, space, computers) but also constant guidance and support for the community which spurs it on and showcases the headway it has made.

g.   The functionality of the proposal might be limited if there is not a highly co-operative culture and close co-operation from the heads of the institution.

Taking advantage of the opportunities and diminishing the problems might be a plausible proposition as long as they are considered to overcome the challenges and uncertainties that practice has exposed. Overcoming the dogmatic nature of some training communities, avoiding the exclusion of those who do not handle ICTs fluently, constant encouragement of the participation and cohesion of users and establishing effective controls over the process and its results are issues that are worth bearing in mind.

For future KCM communities, some of the proposals for improvement that could be put forth based on our experience include (1) developing new and improved strategies for organisational development based on collective knowledge creation and management; (2) further specification and study of the determining factors of the processes of organisational knowledge creation and management; (3) examination of the idiosyncrasy inherent in KCM models that use technology intensively; and (4) definition of the profiles and functions of some of the basic figures that must take part in the "KCM Team".

These challenges are the basis for research in Accelera 2.0, and we hope that they can provide us with more alternatives in the near future. It is clear that further examination of knowledge management as a continuous training strategy is needed in order to determine whether it truly contributes to an improvement in continuous training and professional development in the different educational stakeholders and whether it leads to improvements in students' learning.

Likewise, KCM studies and practices must be targeted towards a much more comprehensive definition of the phenomenon that would enable all the existing theories on learning processes to be harnessed in a better way. As Vera & Crossan (2003) propose, a multi-paradigmatic approach to KCM is crucial.

CONCLUSION

The professional development of teaching staff is increasingly closely linked to the development of organisations and to the use of tools that enable the needs of the organisation and those of its members to be satisfied.

The Accelera experience has been the basis for the training and development of OLCs based on a collective KCM methodology, and for the identification of the problems and resistance to the development of knowledge creation processes.

Some of the main potentialities of the Accelera KCM model are that it strengthens a corporate culture based on collaboration and co-operation between schools from different environments and stages in education, and promotes synergies that stave off institutional and professional stagnation, contributing to developing a workplace learning culture in the case of communities developed at the same school (i.e. BABEL).

Development of professional communities via an intensive use of technology and the use of asynchronic tools also facilitates co-operative processes without threatening individual autonomy, fosters the participation of people who might be somewhat reluctant to speak up in real meetings, and promotes a greater use of ICTs by the teachers participating.

The Accelera KCM model fosters the creation of products that can be disseminated and used by third persons and organisations, thereby contributing to their professional and organisational development.

Contextualised professional development requires the existence of a climate and culture that are favourable to the exchange of knowledge in a community context in which the need for change is shared, as well as a professional commitment to improvement, the importance of dealing with specific problems and the idea that a professional exchange is a fundamentalism means of personal and organisational enrichment.

The focus of attention is the problems generated by professional work, with the classroom and teams of teachers (departments and educational teams) being the contexts for reference. The classroom is the space for detection of teaching problems and the teams of teachers are the place where alternatives can and must be debated.

In any event, collaborative work comes up against two essential questions. First, the collective working system is usually inefficient due to poor management of group work; second, it is not always possible to share professional concerns within a single organisation, whether this is prevented by operational issues (not enough time for meetings, too few teachers, lack of space, etc.) or relational issues (a poor climate in the workplace).

The creation and development of OLCs (not limited to specific spaces or times) is in this regard a real possibility, which enables the opportunities for exchange between professionals to multiply. This is shown in the various communities created in Accelera.

However, what seemed most important to us was the validation of a working system using questions and administrators (moderators) who produce summaries of the progress made in the community. Their work enabled progress to be to put in objective terms and satisfaction of participants to be improved.

It can therefore be said that the Accelera model for KCM provides some new features for processes of educational change. It improves and complete the teaching staff's reflection processes, by encouraging their systematisation, registration and dissemination, as well as reinforcing the creation of OLCs by using cultural strategies in group work.

Finally, as we have shown throughout this chapter, educational policies must foster and strengthen communities of education professionals, taking advantage of the possibilities afforded us by ICTs and thus contributing to the professional development of teachers, to organisational development, and presumably to an improvement in the quality and performance of our educational systems.

ACKNOWLEDGMENT

Contributions from the research "Agentes y procesos en la gestión del conocimiento en red" (Agents and process in networked knowledge management). Ministry of Education and Culture, National R&D Plan (ref. SEJ2007-67093/EDUC), supervised by Joaquín Gairín.

REFERENCES

Allan, B., & Lewis, D. (2006). The impact of membership of a virtual learning community on individual learning careers and professional identity. *British Journal of Educational Technology*, *37*(6), 841–852. doi:10.1111/j.1467-8535.2006.00661.x

Anderson, G. L., & Jones, F. (2000). Knowledge generation in Educational Administration from the inside out: The promise and perils of site-based, administrator research. *Educational Administration Quarterly*, *36*(3), 428–464. doi:10.1177/00131610021969056

Anderson, T., Rourke, L., Garrison, D. R., & Archer, W. (2001). Assessing Teaching Presence in a Computer Conferecing Context. *Journal of Asynchronous Learning Networks, 5*(2). Retrieved May 9, 2008, from http://communitiesofinquiry.com/files/Teaching%20Presence.pdf

Aubusson, P. (2007). Action learning in teacher learning community formation: informative or transformative? *Teacher Development*, *11*(2), 133–148. doi:10.1080/13664530701414746

Bolam, R., & McMahon, A. (2004). Literature, definitions and models: Towards a conceptual map. In C. Day & J. Sachs (Ed.), *International Handbook on the Continuing Professional Development of Teachers* (pp. 33-63). Berkshire: Open University Press, McGraw-Hill Education.

Boyle, B., Lamprianou, I., & Boyle, T. (2005). A longitudinal study of teacher change: what makes professional development effective? Report of the second year of the study. *School Effectiveness and School Improvement*, *16*(1), 1–27. doi:10.1080/09243450500114819

Day, C. (1999). *Developing Teachers: The Challenges of Lifelong Learning*. London: Routledge.

Day, C., & Sachs, J. (2004). Professionalism, performativity and empowerment: discourses in the politics, policies and purposes of continuing professional development. In C. Day & J. Sachs (Ed.), *International Handbook on the Continuing Professional Development of Teachers* (pp. 3-32). Berkshire: Open University Press, McGraw-Hill Education.

Elkjaer, B. (2003). Social learning theory: learning as participation in social processes. In M. Easterby-Smith & M.A. Lyles (Ed.), *Handbook of organizational learning and knowledge management* (pp. 38-53). Oxford: Blackwell Publishing.

Gairín, J. (2006). *Procesos de cambio en los centros a partir de evaluaciones externas*. Madrid: CIDE, Ministerio de Educación.

Gairín, J., & Rodríguez, D. (2007, March). *La Creación y Gestión del Conocimiento a través de la red. Notas y comentarios desde la experiencia*. Paper presented at Expolearning/VirtualCampus, Barcelona.

Garrison, D. R., Anderson, T., & Archer, W. (2001). Critical thinking, cognitive presence, and computer conferencing in distance education. *American Journal of Distance Education, 15*(1), 7–23.

Graham, A. (2007). Web 2.0 and the changing ways we are using computers for learning: What are the implications for pedagogy and curriculum? *Elearningeuropa.info*. Retrieved May 9, 2008, from http://www.elearningeuropa.info/files/media/media13018.pdf

Hargreaves, D. (1994). The new professionalism: The synthesis of professional and institutional development. *Teaching and Teacher Education, 10*(4), 423–438. doi:10.1016/0742-051X(94)90023-X

Hislop, D. (2005). *Knowledge Management in Organizations. A critical introduction*. Oxford: Oxford University Press.

Leinonen, P., & Järvelä, S. (2006). Facilitating interpersonal evaluation of knowledge in a context of distributed team collaboration. *British Journal of Educational Technology, 37*(6), 897–916. doi:10.1111/j.1467-8535.2006.00658.x

Nonaka, I., & Takeuchi, H. (1995). *The Knowledge-Creating Company*. Cambridge: Oxford University Press.

OECD. (2003). *Measuring knowledge management in the business sector: first steps*. Paris: OECD Publications.

Overlap (2007). *Tendencias de la formación 2007*. Retrieved July 1, 2007, from http://www.web.overlap.net/archivos/novedad/InformeTendencias_reducido_con_notas.pdf

Peters, T. (1994). *The Seminar*. New York: Random House.

Poley, J. (2002). La dirección de instituciones universitarias en la era del conocimiento. In D.E. Hanna (Ed.), *La enseñanza universitaria en la era digital* (pp. 173-191). Barcelona: Octaedro-EUB.

Pont, E. (1997). La formación de los recursos humanos en las organizaciones. In J. Gairín & A. Ferrández (Ed.), *Planificación y gestión de instituciones de formación* (pp. 317-341). Praxis, Barcelona.

Rodríguez, D. (2006). Modelos para la creación y gestión del conocimiento: aproximación teórica. *Educar, 37*, 25–39.

Rosmalen, P. (2006). Knowledge matchmaking in Learning Networks: Alleviating the tutor load by mutually connecting learning network users. *British Journal of Educational Technology, 37*(6), 881–895. doi:10.1111/j.1467-8535.2006.00673.x

Rubio, A. (2007). Las nuevas tendencias en la formación. *Capital Humano, 209*, 120–126.

Snow-Gerono, J. L. (2005). Professional development in a culture of inquiry: PDS teachers identify the benefits of professional learning communities. *Teaching and Teacher Education, 21*, 241–256. doi:10.1016/j.tate.2004.06.008

Stoll, L., & Fink, D. (1999). *Para cambiar nuestras escuelas. Reunir la eficacia y la mejora*. Barcelona: Octaedro.

Teddie, C., & Reynolds, D. (2000). *International Handbook of School Effectiveness Research*. London: Falmer Press.

Vera, D., & Crossan, M. (2003). Organizational Learning and Knowledge Management: Toward an Integrative Framework. In M. Easterby-Smith & M. A. Lyles (Ed.), *Handbook of Organizational learning and knowledge management* (pp. 122-141). Oxford: Blackwell Publishing.

Wei, F., & Chen, G. (2006). Collaborative mentor support in a learning context using a ubiquitous discussion forum to facilitate knowledge sharing for lifelong learning. *British Journal of Educational Technology*, *37*(6), 917–935. doi:10.1111/j.1467-8535.2006.00674.x

Wenger, E. (1999). *Communities of Practice. Learning, meaning and identity*. Cambridge: Cambridge University Press.

Chapter 9
Thinking Things Through
Collaborative Online
Professional Development

John P. Cuthell
MirandaNet Academy, UK

ABSTRACT

One of the most powerful ways of changing our thinking about how we teach and learn is to experience for ourselves the power of collaborative project-based experiential learning. Few teachers have had the opportunity to learn in this way, and this creates barriers for those who want to change their pedagogy. The Oracle Education Foundation's Project Learning Institute provides teachers with the experience of collaborative project-based learning, using ThinkQuest® to create their own curriculum project. By collaborating with their peers, tutors and mentors, teachers are able to model the projects, environment and experiences they want for their classes through a blended learning experience. This chapter describes the model of continuing professional development and its impact on schools, pedagogies and professional philosophies.

INTRODUCTION: IS TODAY'S EDUCATION FIT FOR PURPOSE?

For more than ten years groups of concerned stakeholders have focused on the apparent mis-match between the learning that school systems promote, and the needs of a changing world and its societies (Cuthell, 1998; Dockstader, 1999; Edens, 2000; Cuthell, 2003). Whilst much of the concern has been functionalist and a reaction against globalization, other voices have

identified a disjunction between the world of schools, and that of the young people in them.

"Preparing today's youth to succeed in the digital economy requires a new kind of teaching and learning. Skills such as global literacy, computer literacy, problem solving, critical thinking, creativity, and innovation have become critical in today's increasingly interconnected workforce and society – and technology is the catalyst for bringing these changes into the classroom." http://www.eschoolnews.com/resources/creating-the-21st-century-classroom/

DOI: 10.4018/978-1-60566-780-5.ch009

The utilitarian functionalist perspective has been matched by a concern that there is an increasing disjunction between the educational offerings presented to students and their real needs, interests and concerns (Preston, 2004; Trilling, 2005). The agenda that sees the embedding of creativity, critical thinking, problem-solving, working with others and other key skills in ICT-rich learning environments often seems to conflict with official prescriptions to specify, increase and test subject content in a desire to raise standards.

BACKGROUND

The MirandaNet Fellowship has worked with teachers since 1995 in a bid to effect curriculum change through professional development models based on practice-based (action) research, supported through an online community of practice (Cuthell, 2005; 2006; Cuthell & Preston, 2005; Preston, 2004; Preston et al, 2000). The MirandaNet Fellowship, founded in 1992, is an e-community of practice for international ICT policy makers, teachers, teacher educators, researchers and commercial developers who are passionate about digital technology in teaching and learning and about using technologies to promote cultural understanding and democratic participation. Currently there are over 850 members in 43 countries worldwide. The website, online forums, seminars, workshops and projects run by members are funded by international partner companies and government agencies. (http://www.mirandanet.ac.uk)

An early MirandaNet project (1999 – 2002) was with the Oracle Education Foundation, an independent, charitable, organization funded by Oracle Corporation©, which has provided ThinkQuest©, (previously known as Think.com) a free collaborative online tool for schools to use, for almost ten years. This provides a secure and protected environment for projects that can cover single classrooms, whole schools – or international collaboration. Recent work has promoted teacher and curriculum development through the integration of Project Learning, embedded ICT and the use of ThinkQuest as an online learning platform. ThinkQuest is an online community that facilitates project learning and the use of technology to help students develop vital skills for life and work in the 21st century. This initiative has been run through the Project Learning Institute©, which uses blended learning (online personal learning, mentoring and teamwork; face-to-face workshops) to promote pedagogical change and student-centred learning.

ThinkQuest is a protected, teacher-mediated environment that allows members to collaborate on learning projects within their own class – or with other schools globally, create web pages with text, pictures, multimedia components, and downloadable files, interact in online message boards, brainstorms, and debates, send messages within the protected community, participate in the ThinkQuest competition, an international project learning competition and browse an extensive library of educational resources created by students for students. This collaborative learning environment can be accessed from school and from home.

It has already been mentioned that what are termed 21st Century Skills are often presented from a utilitarian functionalist perspective. It is very easy for schools and teachers to assume that all that is necessary is for these to be taught and practiced. However, creative thinking, innovation, and the confident use of new technology, together with critical thinking, need to be practiced and deployed by learners as part of their work process. By collaborating on learning projects within an online environment, students are provided with constant opportunities to develop and hone each of these important skills.

Critical thinking develops the ability of learners to use multiple perspectives to analyse an issue or problem, create an intervention plan, and evaluate the results of the intervention. This is also combined with creativity, in demonstrating the process of generating new ideas or concepts. The use of teamwork tests the ability of learners to work cooperatively with others to achieve a shared goal and evaluate their own contributions and skills. The international dimension and opportunities for projects in ThinkQuest foster cross-cultural understanding and the ability to recognize and correctly react to people or situations that are open to misunderstanding due to cultural differences. A constant throughout the work is multimodal communication, through the demonstration of the process of exchanging information and ideas. Underpinning all of this is the use of a range of technologies to create, store, analyze, and transmit information. The whole process encourages self-direction – the ability to demonstrate work behavior that could be characterised as self-starting, self-motivated and proactive.

Many technology companies have charitable arms that support education projects across the world – Apple©, Cisco©, HP©, Intel©, Microsoft© and Oracle©, for example – and the focus on 21st Century Skills has drawn in a range of other stakeholders. Whilst some have a narrow national focus, and see the issue of 21st Century skills simply in terms of domestic competitiveness, others have a more global view, and see their role as one of empowering learners across the world.

The ThinkQuest programme supported by the OEF provides a global web-based platform that can be accessed by learners everywhere, and is available in eleven languages: Brazilian Portuguese; Chinese; Dutch; English; French; German; Hindi; Italian; Spanish; Thai and Turkish. More languages are added periodically.

The Oracle Education Foundation sponsors a teacher professional development programme called the Project Learning Institute, partnering with over 80 organisations that share its goals. To support this work the Foundation awards grants to support partners, fund projects, and increase low-income students' participation in its programmes. The project described here is part of this work.

PROJECT LEARNING

Project based learning involves the use of class-room projects with the intention of bringing about 'deep' learning (as opposed to 'surface' learning), where students use technology and inquiry to engage with issues and questions that are relevant to their lives. These classroom projects can be used to assess student's subject matter competence, rather than using more traditional testing methods.

One can define project learning as a pedagogical approach that focuses on the learning process, combining technology, curriculum content and enquiry techniques to classroom projects (Barron, 1998; Boss & Krauss, 2007). Learners create research-based investigations that focus on collaborative strategies involving design, problem solving, decision-making, and investigative activities. Learners work in groups or by themselves, with the teacher facilitating them to develop ideas, solutions and presentations.

Project learning, then, is a collaborative approach emphasising long-term, interdisciplinary and student-centered learning activities. Within the project framework learners are expected to organise their own work and manage their own time. They collaborate, working together to make sense of what is going on. The emphasis is on the creation of artefacts to demonstrate knowledge and understanding.

HOW DOES ONE CHANGE TEACHER PRAXIS? DEVELOPING A PROJECT LEARNING PEDAGOGY

Teachers who want to further develop the integration of ICT with their classroom activities can participate in the O.E.F. Project Learning Institute. By the time they have completed the Institute course, teachers have experienced for themselves what 21st Century Project learning is, and have been prepared to:

- integrate 21st century skills and technology into their curricula;
- design and implement online, standards-based learning projects that develop students' 21st century skills;
- apply best practices to their learning projects, using the OEF online project learning environment ThinkQuest Projects.

Integrating 21st Century Skills Instruction into the Curriculum

The emphasis with this approach is that, in addition to curriculum content, teachers embed the 21st Century skills into the work and learning process. The skills required for 21st Century learning are: critical thinking, creativity, teamwork, cross-cultural understanding, communication, technology and self-direction. In other words, the project structure should provide learners with as many opportunities as possible to work in these ways. This is not to say that every activity has to contain every one of these. However, the activities to support learning should promote learner autonomy as a way of achieving the curriculum outcomes.

Design and Implement Online, Standards-Based Learning Projects that Develop Students' 21st Century Skills

The move from a classroom-based, teacher-centric pedagogical mode to on online environment in which standards and outcomes are embedded with 21st century skills and processes requires teachers to think about the ways in which the activities and learning can be undertaken. What information sources should be provided for learners, and which can one expect learners to find for themselves? What skills need to be taught in advance, and which can be taught on-demand? How explicit should the outcomes and assessment criteria be for the learners – and at what stage in the process?

What should be the balance between being taught, practicing and applying?

Apply Best Practices to their Learning Projects Using the OEF Online Project Learning Environment ThinkQuest Projects

The face-to-face element of the Project Learning Institute enables the teachers to discuss their projects, engage in peer-to-peer learning and access other ThinkQuest Projects to observe other models and build their own best practice. This provides teachers with the opportunity to discuss with peers their concerns and aspirations; exchange information, skills and techniques; collaborate on skill development and curriculum approaches and experience the benefits of collaborative work. Indeed, for many teachers this is the first real opportunity to do this, since the isolated nature of the classroom and the role of the teacher naturally reinforces a didactic approach to teaching and learning. In this was there is a real understanding of the transformational nature of collaborative learning, and provides an insight into the ways in which this can be brought to their own classrooms and learners.

Such an approach – one that combines an understanding of new ways of working, the embedding of curriculum standards and outcomes and the availability of models of best practice and peer support – means that there is more likely to be a convergence between teachers' values, their pedagogical approaches and their ICT skills, competence and concepts (Holmes, et. al., 2007) than one that sees the development of ICT skills and the use of tools as separate from their curriculum implementation. The development of new pedagogical approaches must be holistic, and seen as integral to a shift in the relationship and dynamics of traditional classroom praxis. We can no longer assume that, because a teacher is ICT-literate, this will impact on their professional practice. The £230 million UK programme of training teachers to become 'confident and competent' with ICT was subject to a degree of criticism on the grounds that much of the training was divorced from curriculum applications and the school context. Indeed, Chris Yapp commented that many of the ICT professional development approaches seemed predicated on the assumption thatNew teacher = Old teacher + ICT (Selinger & Yapp, 2001, p. 20)

INVOLVING TEACHERS IN PEDAGOGICAL CHANGE

The Project Learning Institute uses of blend of three learning components: Virtual training, In-class training and Implementation and mentoring.

Virtual Training: This is a six-week online training period that provides a baseline understanding of 21st century skills and project learning and, more importantly provides direct experience for the participants of working online in the project learning institute, working online in ThinkQuest, using all the interactive tools that their pupils will use, and developing a curriculum project that they will implement. It can be seen as a form of experiential learning.

The ThinkQuest home page for the project provides all of the resources that participants will need as they work through the Project Learning Institute and ThinkQuest materials. The activities they will undertake in the Project Learning section of Oracle iLearning will be completed in ThinkQuest, and their coaches (and others in their team) provide feedback throughout the process.

Note: During the time that the materials for this chapter were created the learning environment was known as Think.com. The name ThinkQuest was used for an international project competition. From September 2008, however, the whole platform was renamed ThinkQuest and ThinkQuest projects and the competition contained within it. The screenshots, therefore, are still badged as Think.com

Throughout the process participants can post their own questions and answers to others. This routine is one that many teachers incorporate for their own learners as a way of sharing expertise, and as a way of showing their class that they may well have answers for others. The coaches will post answers on the Message Board if they feel that they are applicable to others in the group: if they are specific to an individual then they will use the email function in ThinkQuest to send a personal message.

In-Class Training

For four days, participants meet face-to-face and refine and develop their 21st century learning project to facilitate for students upon returning to school. During this phase the practical issues of implementing their project in the classroom are considered, and the communal constructivist approach to learning (Holmes et al., 2001) becomes an extremely powerful model (see Figure 2).

Implementation/Mentoring

Back at school, participants facilitate their 21st century learning project with students. ThinkQuest provides the community platform for peer support and feedback during the implementation phase of their projects, and the teachers can view one another's projects to offer additional support and collaboration.

The fact that, throughout the Institute, participants use ThinkQuest Projects to design and implement their own classroom learning projects means that their grasp of the issues for their own learners who are involved in the online aspect of learning is firmly grounded in their own experiences (see Figure 3).

This identifies the types of page that can be created, and the activities that the teachers – and learners – can incorporate into their projects. Learners can upload a range of resources for others in the class or project, and generate a number of

Figure 1. Project Learning Institute South Africa Project. (Adapted from Oracle Education Foundation ThinkQuest).

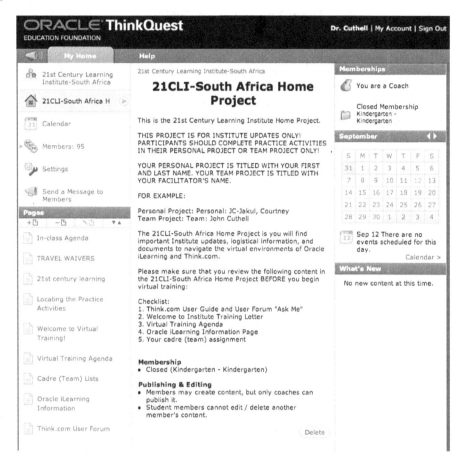

collaborative activities: Voting; Message Boards; Debates; Asking Questions and Brainstorming ideas.

Teachers also have access to a User Forum, where their questions are answered by one of the project team and where discussion about the work and its outcomes can take place.

PARTICIPANT PRE-REQUISITES AND TARGET AUDIENCE

So, who can participate in this professional development experience? To attend the Institute, participants must be fluent in English: although ThinkQuest is currently offered in eleven different languages, the Project Learning Institute materials are currently only in English. In addition, participants must be educators – primary or secondary teachers, or district technology coordinators working with school, learners and teachers. It goes without saying that hey should also be computer literate and have an understanding of using online technologies. The teachers should also be registered in ThinkQuest Projects, and committed to completing all training components.

The target audience, therefore, is K-12 teachers who want to integrate the development of 21st century skills into their curricula and design and implement learning projects with their students.

Figure 2. Project Learning Institute South Africa Project. In-class Training. (Adapted from Oracle Education Foundation ThinkQuest).

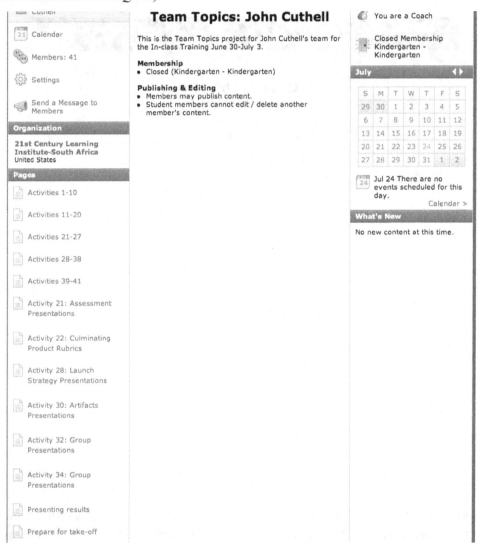

The expectation is that these teachers will be well-motivated self-starters who will act as catalysts within their own professional communities and provide models for successful learning – for colleagues as well as their own learners.

WHAT IS PROJECT LEARNING?

The Project Learning Institute teaches a variation of Project Based Learning (PBL) and refers to it as

Project Learning (PL). As previously mentioned, project learning is a dynamic approach to teaching that engages students in self-directed learning. Students acquire skills and knowledge by collaborating on projects that investigate and propose solutions to real world challenges. There are a number of key concepts that underpin the approach. Self-directed learning implies that the learners set their own objectives within the framework of the project, and scaffold their acquisition of skills and knowledge. Collaboration with peers reinforces the

Figure 3. Project Learning Institute South Africa Project. Designing Pages. (Adapted from Oracle Education Foundation ThinkQuest).

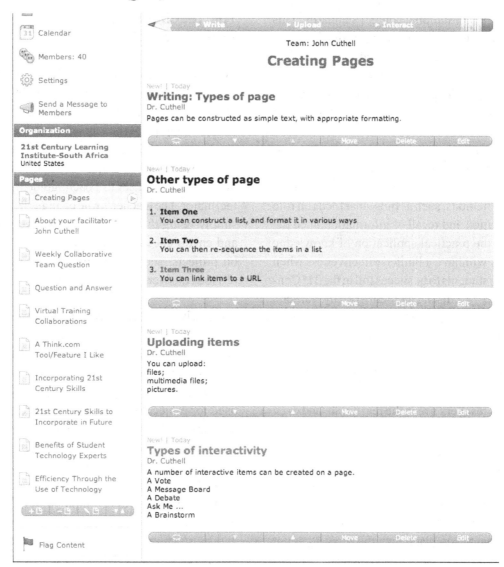

learning through communal constructivism, and the application of skills and learning to real-world challenges enables learners to transfer their skills and knowledge to other domains, embedding and further reinforcing the learning.

At its core, then, project learning fosters a complex learning environment in which students can not only develop key 21st century skills but also gain a deeper understanding of relevant curricular concepts. Knowledge retention is improved. More importantly, the learners become highly motivated and engaged in the learning process. This virtuous cycle supports and encourages further learning for teachers as well as their learners.

Pedagogical Implications of Project Learning

Project learning should be a practical teaching method incorporating collaboration, critical thinking, multimodal, written and oral communication, and the values of the work ethic, while meeting state or national content standards. This structured approach to learning bridges the gap between learning core knowledge and applied skills. In other words, it enhances the requirements that teachers have to meet, and ensures a more integrated approach to the teaching and learning process.

If teachers simply focus on meeting state or national curriculum or test requirements, using what are sometimes seen as 'tried and tested' traditional teaching methods, such as those that focus on rote memorization and recall of information, then the focus on the practical application of knowledge and skills will have a limited effectiveness when preparing students to be successful in the 21st Century. Indeed, the disengagement of many learners, who see schooling as an increasing self-reflexive irrelevance, is likely to increase.

Linking to Curriculum and Standards

However, teachers live in the real world, and even the most radical curriculum reformers know the truth of the old adage about not throwing the baby out with the dishwater. Project learning must be designed with a focus on curriculum standards, and the assessment of student learning is an important element in this. Indeed, if one cannot assess what learning has taken place then the project cannot be said to be successful. When the teachers start to plan their projects it is vital to review the applicable standards that apply to the teaching and learning for the class. Those standards that can be met through project learning should be identified. Any that cannot be met through project learning should be covered outside the project.

The project performance standards, goals, and plan assessments should be identified and set while the project learning experiences are being designed. It is also important that teachers determine where their learners should be at the completion of the project, and identify measurable indicators

that demonstrate student performance.

The Teacher's Role in Project Learning

The key to project learning is that it should be a shared, participatory experience for all members of the project, which means that many teachers have to relinquish their position at the front of the classroom and move into the main part of the room, where they are more central to the learning activities and act as coach, guide, mentor or facilitator. The teacher's role changes from that of simply being the instructor to one who supports and encourages students' thinking as they work on projects, and challenges them to go beyond obvious answers and responses.

Selecting a Learning Platform

One question that is often asked is why – given the increasing number and range of learning platforms on the market – ThinkQuest should be used for project learning. Many teachers have an awareness of a number of online environments that could be used for projects, and often display a proprietorial interest in those on which they can stamp their own individuality. There are a number of important features of ThinkQuest that are not necessarily found in other environments. First, and most important for many school managers and parents, is that ThinkQuest is a protected, online learning platform. It is only available for schools and those who work in them, which acts as a guarantor of safety and integrity as an educational environment. It is also a platform that specifically enables teachers to integrate learning projects into their classroom curriculum and students to develop 21st century skills. Think-Quest is global in its reach, infinitely scaleable, completely free to use and, most importantly, contains no advertising. ThinkQuest Projects offers an easy way for students to publish and share their work with a global audience, earn and apply

21st century skills and collaborate on teacher-led learning projects.

Supporting Child Safety

In order to support child safety, ThinkQuest Projects provides a robust, password-protected environment that is available only to schools that have been verified by the Oracle Education Foundation. The environment allows students in ThinkQuest Projects to be identified by first name and last initial only and, importantly, prohibits students from sharing personal information, such as addresses and phone numbers. It attributes all content created in ThinkQuest Projects to its author (which means that there is no anonymous content). Teachers are provided with tools to review student content, and ThinkQuest has inbuilt functionality that allows users to control privacy settings within projects: they can be viewed only by members of the project, by other classes and schools invited into the project – or by the global ThinkQuest community.

Using ThinkQuest Projects in the Classroom

The flexibility of ThinkQuest Projects enables it to be applied in many ways in the classroom. It can be used in any curricular area to support and enhance a wide range of learning activities, including projects, student collaboration, writing assignments, creative expression, peer reviews, homework assignments or cross-cultural exchanges.

The content creation tools in ThinkQuest Projects enable students to publish and store a rich variety of products, including text, images, documents, spreadsheets, presentations, and other files; message boards; votes, and debates; music and video files. Most importantly, students aren't limited to using ThinkQuest Projects in the classroom. They can continue their work from any internet-connected computer.

Conducting Online Collaborative Projects

Using ThinkQuest Projects, teachers and students can design and implement inter-school or international collaborative learning projects. Collaborative projects engage students in working together in ways that teach them important skills for work and life in the 21st century.

Once such project – Outside My Window – developed from a Project Learning Institute held in Singapore, involved three schools (Grades 4 & 5), two in the United States and one in Australia, looking outside their windows and sharing images and information. All of the schools were comparing and contrasting their immediate environments through exploring the related essential questions:

How and why would I create a plant that will make a difference to the world?
How would I survive in my backyard if I were one inch tall?
What new things can I learn about the world by looking in someone's backyard?

The project was a closed one: the project and contributions could be seen by the participant schools and their 125 members, but by no-one else.

Each of the project members had to undertake five tasks: Getting to know each other; Sharing our backyards; Bug Report; Scientific and character drawing and Narrative storyboard plan.

Each of the learners in each school had to either create a personal page or update their existing one in ThinkQuest. This was visible to all of the project members. Then the learners visited their team members in each school, read their personal pages and left them a message. This activity corresponds to Step One, Socialisation, in the Five Step Theory (Salmon, 2002). The learners use the Message Board function in ThinkQuest to communicate until they are able to use their Team pages. The final ask was for the learners to use Google Earth to locate their buddies' schools and explore the location, so that they would have a better understanding of the environment outside the school windows in each location. This project was a specific outcome of the workshop in Singapore, and consolidated the understanding of the teachers in project learning.

Mind Body and Soul

Another project set up by teachers following the Singapore workshop was an open one: people from any ThinkQuest school could participate. Over 100 members explored issues connected with Health. The essential question was contained in the title of the project: Mind, Body & Soul: Do We Really Care?

The learners were encouraged to explore the issues related to Health within their communities through a variety of sources: personal research, interviews, data collection and discussions and examining the ways in which they could make an impact on their own lives. In other words, although the project was a mechanism for delivering the curriculum, it was grounded in the learners' understanding of the topic, and its application to their own lives.

The project page contained a number of information sources for the learners to use to help structure their work, whilst at the other side of the page could be seen a number of messages, responses to questions and other contributions from the learners.

Causes of Diseases

On this page the learners were responding to two questions that the teacher had posed: Do all diseases spread to people coming into contact with a sick person? What are the diseases that are not spreading? There were a number of responses from the learners. One answer was a closed, limited one compared with the others, which were much more

expansive. All of the responses were available for everyone to view, and since they were anonymous they constituted a resource from which all could learn, both in terms of the content and the form of the answer. In other words, there was a range of models from which learners could select and apply to their own work.

These projects were outcomes of the Project Learning Institute workshops, and therefore formed a pedagogical resource for teachers new to project learning, enabling them to see the ways in which work can be structured and learners supported through different activities.

FUTURE TRENDS

These workshops demonstrated the powerful way in which existing pedagogies could be changed for the participants and concepts of teaching and learning transformed. The elements that made such a transformation possible – participating in an active learning process, embedding ICT in the whole of the learning cycle, experiencing collaborative learning and being a member of a supportive and sustaining community of practice – need to become part of the entitlement for professional development for all teachers.

For too long educational needs have been determined by those outside and beyond the profession, to the extent that many regard the role of teachers as nothing more than implementing content devised by others in ways that others have determined. Despite this, most teachers have a keen understanding of the needs of their learners, and a desire that they should be empowered and their lives transformed. The blended learning experience offered by the Project Learning Institute provides an environment in which professionalism can be nurtured and developed.

At a time when globalization and its associated technologies provides access to a world of materials and expertise the Fordist model of education and its expectations is increasingly obsolete and irrelevant. It is imperative that teachers are provided with conduits for their own development, communities of practice to which they can belong and access to ideas and examples to transform their classrooms and extend learning beyond the walls and limitations of their institutions.

The Project Learning Institute provides a model that could be said to be too utopian to be applied to all. Bringing teachers together for four days could be considered impossibly expensive and disruptive for all to experience. Despite this there are developing models of liminal spaces that can be used in similar ways: FlashMeetings; unConferences; Wikis – as well as such applications as Skype. Indeed, MirandaNet is currently trialing and evaluating such technologies in an attempt to put control of professional development firmly in the hands of the practitioners. Further evaluation and research will determine their effectiveness for the whole profession, and whether we will have an holistic model of education that addresses the needs of all learners – rather than needs perceived by agencies and those in authority.

CONCLUSION

The initial promise of ICT as a tool for transforming the teaching and learning process – identified by Cuthell (1998; 2002b); Preston et al, (2000); Holmes et al, (2007) – has never quite been realized in the classroom. Some teachers have embraced new technologies and embedded them in their praxis and their expectations for their learners (Cuthell, 2002a). Many others have simply seen the application of ICT either as a way of improving pupil productivity, or as vocational preparation, whilst a dogged rearguard refuse to accept that ICT has any place in their professional life. Indeed, in some cases teachers' ICT competence and use in their personal life is at stark variance with their use of the technology in their classroom (Cuthell, 2003).

What is true of teachers in general, however, is

a desire for all of their learners to be as successful as possible. When they can see – and experience – how their own praxis can be changed for the benefit of their learners they will embrace the change and accept ownership of it. Professional development will be owned, rather than being something that is 'done' to them. The blended approach of the Project Learning Institute situates the e-learning experience in a curriculum context that is familiar to the teachers. Snyder (1998) questioned whether e-learning could invoke new experiences, and suggested that for many it may simply be an extension of familiar behaviour and perceptions, a concern that is still true ten years later. Certainly, if e-learning is simply seen as replicating a conventional course, with set texts and expected responses, that could well be the case. The learning experience for teachers described in this paper, however, brings together new skills, new behaviour and new perceptions of how to structure learning experiences for their classes. It is experiential learning in its fullest sense.

Teachers undertake courses with a priori knowledge and expectations of what constitutes the teaching and learning process, based on prior experience, cultural background, educational expectations, and so on. These frame and shape the outcomes, and their expectations of what will be passed on to their classes and learners. The very different experiences of the Project Learning Institute are designed to create a deep understanding of what is involved in implementing it in their classrooms, and what it means to be a learner in those circumstances. As such, their praxis is more likely to be recontextualised in the light of these experiences.

The progression from disorientation to reorientation through praxis – that is, through culturally reflective action that generates personal, practical knowledge about learning, is recognized as part of the process domain of becoming a constructivist learner (Levy, 2006 p 227). Indeed, it is part of the process domain of learning through e-pedagogies.

What this project shows is that the act of participation and active learning, together with the sense of being part of a knowledge community, works for all of those who participate in the Project Learning Institute. The investment of time and effort that they make during the project provides the motivation for them to implement their insights, skills and techniques in their classrooms and change their professional practice. The knowledge that the rest of their community of learners can see all of the projects further motivates them to develop their practice (Cuthell, 2005).

And, in the process, their learners are empowered.

REFERENCES

Barron, B. (1998). Doing with understanding: Lessons from research on problem- and project-based learning. *Journal of the Learning Sciences*, 7(3), 271–311. doi:10.1207/s15327809jls0703&4_2

Boss, S., & Krauss, J. (2007). *Reinventing project-based learning: Your field guide to real-world projects in the digital age.* Eugene, OR: International Society for Technology in Education.

Cuthell, J. P. (2006). Ms. Chips and her Battle Against the Cyborgs. Embedding ICT in Educational Practice. In D. O Murchu & Sorensen, E. (Eds.), *Enhancing Learning Through Technology.* (pp. 253–268) Hershey, Idea Group

Cuthell, J. P. (2006). Online forums as learning resources: some case studies from MirandaNet. *Proceedings of IADIS International Conference: Web Based Communities, 2006*, 371–375.

Cuthell, J. P. (2006). Steering the Supertanker: Changing Teaching and Learning. In Maddux, C. (Ed.) *Computers in the Schools: Technology Applications in Education (2006) 23 1/2* Binghamton, N.Y. The Howarth Press.

Cuthell, J. P. (2008). Online forums as a resource for teacher professional development: lessons from a web-based community of practice and influence. *International Journal of Web Based Communities*, 4(3), 359–365. doi:10.1504/IJWBC.2008.019195

Cuthell, J. P., & Preston, C. (2007). *Perspectives on ICT CPD: Past, Present and Future. The experiential learning of advisers responsible for school teachers' ICT CPD programmes.* Retrieved June 6 2008 from Institute of Education, London WLE Centre Web site: http://www.wlecentre.ac.uk/cms/files/occasionalpapers/wle_op3.pdf

Dockstader, J. (1999). Teachers of the 21st Century Know the What, Why and How of Technology Integration. [Technological Horizons In Education]. *T.H.E. Journal*, 26.

Edens, K. M. (2000). Preparing Problem Solvers for the 21st Century through Problem-based Learning. *College Teaching*, 48(2), 55–60.

Holmes, B., Gardner, J., & Galanouli, D. (2007). Striking the right chord and sustaining successful professional development in information and communication technologies. *Journal of In-service Education*, 33(4), 389–404. doi:10.1080/13674580701687799

Holmes, B., Tangney, B., FitzGibbon, A., Savage, T., & Meehan, S. (2001). Communal Constructivism: Students constructing learning for as well as with others. [Norfolk, VA: Association for the Advancement of Computing in Education]. *Proceedings of SITE, 2001*, 3114–3119.

Levy, P. (2006). 'Living' theory: a pedagogical framework for process support in networked learning. *ALT-J, Research in Learning technology, 14*(3), 225-240

Maximizing the Impact. *The pivotal role of technology in a 21st century education system. ISTE, 2007.* Retrieved June 3 2008, from Partnership for 21st Century Skills Web site: http://www.setda.org/web/guest/maximizingimpactreport

McLoughlin, C., & Lee, M. J. W. (2008). *Future Learning Landscapes: Transforming Pedagogy through Social Software.* Retrieved June 3 2008, from: http://www.innovateonline.info/index.php?view=article&id=539

Preston, C. (2004). *Learning to use ICT in Classrooms: Teachers' and Trainers' perspectives.* London, MirandaNet/TTA. Retrieved June 6 2008 from MirandaNet Web site: www.mirandanet.ac.uk/tta

Preston, C., Cox, M., & Cox, K. (2000). *Teachers as Innovators: What motivates teachers to use ICT A study of expert teachers.* Retrieved June 6 2008, from MirandaNet Web site: http://www.mirandanet.ac.uk/pubs/tes_art.htm

Preston, C., & Danby, M. (2004). *Building professional capacity in new media skills - An evaluation of the European Computer Driving Licence (ECDL) for Educators.* Retrieved June 6 2008 from MirandaNet Web site: http://www.mirandanet.ac.uk/industry/astonswann.htm

Salmon, G. (2002). *E-tivities: The Key to Active Online Learning.* London: Kogan Page.

Selinger, M., & Yapp, C. (2001). *ICT Teachers.* London. Institute for Public Policy Research.

Snyder, I. (1998). *Page to Screen.* London: Routledge.

Trilling, B. (2005). *Toward Learning Societies and the Global Challenges for Learning-With-ICT.* Retrieved June 3 2008, from Tech & Learning Web site: http://news.techlearning.com/techlearning/pdf/events/techforum/ny05/Toward_Learning_Societies.pdf

Section 3
Innovations in the Use of Technology and TPD

Chapter 10

Innovations in the Use of Technology and Teacher Professional Development

Donald E. Scott
University of Calgary, Canada

Shelleyann Scott
University of Calgary, Canada

ABSTRACT

This chapter explores the innovative uses of technology for teachers' professional development as well as its impact in the classroom on learning and teaching. Two international case studies are included. The first outlines technological innovations in graduate programme delivery within the university context in Canada. The second case presents a multi-dimensional professional development initiative in Australia which has influenced teachers' and students' learning. Two models are described: the macro-oriented "Webs of Enhanced Practice" that addresses the professional development of educators and experts; and the micro-oriented "Webs of Enhanced Learning" focusing on the learning occurring at the classroom level. These two models represent innovations in the use of technology as they conceptualise the eclectic use of multi-modal, varied technologies to advance the professional development of communities of learners.

INTRODUCTION

Technology has radically altered human civilisation. Few nations have not been affected in some way by the technological advances of the 20th and 21st centuries. Evidence from the 21st century indicates that technological change and adoption is not slowing, rather it is increasing at an almost exponential pace. Education, both in the schools and institutions of higher education, has similarly been affected by increasing accessibility to technology. As Levine and Sun indicate new technologies, in particular the Internet, have greatly influenced the opportunities to access education, interact with others, and to "disseminate knowledge to an exponentially large number of people than ever before" (2002, p. 1). This also applies to opportunities for accessing ongoing teacher professional development. This chapter outlines two main perspectives in relation to innovations in the use of technology and teacher

DOI: 10.4018/978-1-60566-780-5.ch010

Copyright © 2010, IGI Global. Copying or distributing in print or electronic forms without written permission of IGI Global is prohibited.

professional development. The first perspective is that new technologies offer increased opportunities to facilitate personal reflection on practice, collegial collaboration, problem-solving, and the production and sharing of teaching resources through the creation of online professional development communities. The second perspective is that teachers need professional development to become comfortable and innovative in their use of these technologies in order to relate to technologically-adept students in schools and to integrate information communication technology (ICT) into their classroom activities.

BACKGROUND

Understanding Teacher Professional Development

Literature about effective professional development is certainly abundant with many scholars dedicating their professional research lives to investigating what works and what is largely ineffective. Research started as early as the late 1970s with significant numbers of studies emerging throughout the 1980s and 1990s. Joyce and Showers (1970-1990s) identified flaws in the prevailing view that professional development initiatives failed due to teachers' lack of motivation and engagement (Joyce & Showers, 1980, 1982; Showers & Joyce, 1996). They found that professional development must contain certain components in order for teachers to be able to transfer their learning from workshop settings into their regular repertoire of strategies. The key to success was ongoing, in-context support structures, such as peer coaching, which made significant difference in teachers' capacity to transfer these innovations into regular classroom practice (Joyce & Showers, 1995; Showers, 1984). They linked effective professional development practices with school improvement and recommended teachers along with leaders, take

ownership in shaping the school vision and approaches to improving student learning (Joyce & Showers, 1995; Showers, 1995). Lieberman and Miller identified the need to ensure teachers have constructivist learning opportunities (Lieberman, 1995; Lieberman & Miller, 2000). Lieberman and Miller along with Sparks and Hirsh (1997) emphasised the importance of teacher engagement in collegial dialogues which focused on classroom activities and improving student learning. Even with this knowledge about what constitutes effective teacher professional development, there still exists challenges in establishing and sustaining these valuable approaches.

Guskey stated professional development should be perceived as a "process, not an event … that the process is intentional … and is a systematic effort to bring about … positive change or improvement" to teachers knowledge, beliefs and/or skills (cited in Todnem & Warner, 1994, p. 63). Quick fixes and one-shot sessions, while politically desirable, are rarely effective as they lack systematic approaches or in-context support structures to aid transfer of learning into regular pedagogical practice (Scott, 2003). Frequently, professional development is introduced to ensure reforms of educational environments; however, the magnitude and pace of the requisite changes also influences the effectiveness of the staff development. Guskey reflected "asking teachers or administrators to change too many things too rapidly also may result in maintenance of the status quo … [because they] find it necessary to adopt a coping strategy that seriously distorts the change" (1994, p. 35). Therefore, leaders must understand that effective professional development processes take time and they must support the integration of these into their schools. Entrepreneurial leadership is demonstrated through creative timetabling and decision-making that facilitates collaborative teacher-teams; and building strong and positive cultures which nurture whole-staff engagement in activities that support teacher and student learning (Darling-Hammond, 1998; Darling-

Hammond & McLaughlin, 1995; Leithwood, 2007; Leithwood, Seashore Louis, Anderson, & Wahlstrom, 2004).

All of the described approaches are based on the foundation of face-to-face professional development initiatives. However, with the advances in technologies, teacher professional development must be reconceptualised to encompass online modes. Teaching is an isolating profession. Teachers may go through an entire school day and spend just a few minutes in conversation with a colleague. Coupled with this isolation within the school, many teachers are situated in rural or even remote communities. This means they have even fewer colleagues to work with, and limited choices in neighbouring schools to access support and interaction. ICT offers a solution to these challenges. Teachers no longer need experience the isolation that results from geographical distances, financial constraints, or negative school cultures. Professional development opportunities can be mediated via the Internet. A significant advantage of undertaking professional development through a technological medium is that teachers are not only learning about their discipline content, assessments, and practices, but are also potentially learning about how the technology can facilitate students' use of technologies for their own educational activities.

Technology and Professional Development

In many cases, traditional professional development focuses on 'directive' information dissemination with little prioritisation for interaction or collaboration. Chalmers and Keown state, however, professional development should "include the personal and social dimensions" (2006, p. 144). Similarly, Putnam and Borko iterate that what is learned is a "product of the interactions of groups of people over time", reinforcing the importance of collegial interactions (2000, p. 5). The advent of 1st (asynchronous) and 2nd

(synchronous) generation technologies has the capacity to radically reinvent professional growth activities. For example, early technology adopters availed themselves of online communication, such as email and the Internet, for keeping in touch with colleagues and resource development and sharing. As technology became more sophisticated, teachers found that the isolation inherent in teaching can be ameliorated through forums, bulletin boards, wikis, blogs, and now with Voice-over-Internet-Protocol (VoIP) software (e.g., Skype® and Elluminate-Live!®). These media allow communication with colleagues regardless of the distances involved and offer innovations to professional development practices.

1st Generation Technologies

Online bulletin boards and forums are repositories wherein postings about certain topics can be lodged for others to read and comment on if desired. Posts are linear and asynchronous, whereby interactions are not necessarily made in 'real time'. Participants can respond to whatever conversation thread interests them or simply read for information. Forums, unlike bulletin boards may be synchronous if two individuals are posting online in the same timeframe. Blogs and wikis are a natural progression from bulletin boards. Blogs, or bulletin board logs, are online journals whereby users can share their activities, thoughts, documents, and photographs with others who are then able to respond. Wikis are alterable web pages designed to evolve as content is added from different sources. These become ever-changing sources of information similar to encyclopaedia except the veracity of information is reliant on the contributors' knowledge. For teachers who crave social networking and access to greater pools of knowledge, forums, blogs, and wikis can offer much in their professional development. The asynchronous nature of these forums provides the freedom to participate if, and when, teachers have the time and interest to do so. Forums can also be richer sources of information and insights. This is because the asynchronous process tends to foster higher-order thinking when teachers have time to reflect on their readings prior to formulating a response. Asynchronous forums enable shy individuals to 'have their say' without fear of ridicule or intimidation by quicker or more domineering personalities (Simonson, Smaldino, Albright, & Zvacek, 2006). Riding (2001) cautions, however, that not all online forums are successful in maintaining teacher professional development involvement. He identifies a number of factors which influence the success of forum servers. Success was found when email messages were sent directly to teachers rather than having them check in on websites. Messages that focus on the topics of interest mean teachers do not have to filter out extraneous interactions. Engagement is increased when there are moderators who stimulate conversation threads with additional comments and questions. Including experts as members on forums increases teachers' interest and motivation to maintain involvement. When forums are well advertised and draw membership from a wider constituency they facilitate "more rounded 'community experience[s]'" (Riding, 2001, p. 294).

2nd Generation Technologies

Asynchronous communication, while having certain advantages lacks the spontaneity and synergy that comes with synchronous interactions. Hence, there has been a move to synchronous modes of online communication. Even though this technology has been available for many years the sophistication has increased over time. For example, initially texting was simple one-to-one text communication via computers; now individuals can join 'chat rooms' with multiple users engaged in conversations about a given topic. Some examples of this technology include MSN messenger, AOL Instant Messenger, and Yahoo! Messenger. Emotions can be captured, albeit in

a limited form, through the use of emoticons and short-hand text (e.g., ROFL – roll on floor laughing). This has the advantage of reducing the misconceptions and bluntness that can arise from the lack of non-verbal gestural cues that exist in face-to-face conversations. Chat rooms can be used by teachers to engage with multiple colleagues with similar interests where they can synchronously discuss teaching problems and strategies, and share ideas.

As synchronous technologies continue to be developed and enhanced, real time verbal communication is now possible and financially viable through the Internet. One of the first and more successful programs which utilises VoIP technology is Skype®. Skype is essentially another version of a telephone call except it is facilitated across the Internet. Even though one-to-one communication is useful, one-to-many is more synergistic and offers greater opportunities to participate in 'collective' conversations. Examples of this type of 2nd generation technology include Elluminate Live!®, Horizon Wimba®, and Centra® which are web-based audio conferencing software. They enable groups of individuals to have real-time virtual lectures, discussions, and meetings supported with PowerPoint slides, web sites, whiteboard mark-up capability and shared applications (Peters & Bell, 2006). For the first time, technology has the capacity to mirror face-to-face approaches in professional development. Teachers are able to meet colleagues and experts online to engage in live discourse, view materials together, work collaboratively on documents, watch streamed videos, and observe and participate in lectures all from the comfort of their own home. This now means that professional learning communities can be reconceptualised into virtual space.

DuFour and Eaker's (2004) "professional learning communities" and Wenger's (2003) "communities of practice" have been hailed as the 'latest and greatest' positive trend in the professional development of adults. Wenger and Snyder described communities of practice having the capacity to "drive strategy, generate new lines of business, solve problems, promote the spread of best practices, [and] develop people's professional skills" (2000, p. 140). McLaughlin and Talbert identified professional communities as facilitating the development of "new teacher materials and strategies and ... the risk taking and struggle entailed in transforming practice" (1993, p. 15). Criticism of the "professional learning communities" and "communities of practice" concepts revolve around the administrative construction and teaming of teachers for professional development purposes. Synergies experienced within effective professional development are difficult to predict, control, or structure for, as they tend to be influenced by personalities, coincidence of contexts and experiences, and personal and professional interests. Therefore, the most effective, sustained and satisfying professional development is that which encompasses the personal and the professional and is established by like-minded individuals and supported by their organisations.

"Social networking" has emerged to describe relatively unique online forms of interaction and is facilitated by software such as MySpace. com, FaceBook, and Flickr (Carter, Foulger, & Ewbank, 2008). These environments frequently represent the merging of 'personal' and 'professional' interactions within many organisations. For example, teachers who are friends can share personal experiences, anecdotes and funny situations while also collecting ideas, resource swapping, and reflecting on their professional practice. These teacher-friend networks are highly elastic as they can expand to include others or contract when friends and colleagues drop out. These social networking tools have the capacity to support the evolution of naturally forming "professional learning communities" and "communities of practice" and extend beyond artificially contrived professional development constructs.

Even though technology offers much in potentially extending professional and personal development opportunities, there are constraints

which must be recognised and overcome. Many teachers are resistant to innovations in technology and reluctant to explore virtual interactions, preferring face-to-face meetings. Some perceive time to be a barrier, as online communication requires consistent attention in nurturing communities of practice. Insufficient or inadequate technological infrastructure is as a barrier particularly in remote locations where technology may not be accessible or stable. When the technology fails or is interrupted, so too are the operations of the communities of practice. Lack of technological skill can also hold some back from participating in online professional learning (Havelock, 2004).

Exposure to these new technologies and experiencing how learning can be facilitated through the innovative use of these media can be powerful experiences for teachers (Hartnell-Young, 2006; Motteram, 2006). Like any new teaching situation, online professional learning communities take time to establish, and to develop the requisite technological expertise and user-comfort in the relatively new environment. Once comfort is achieved teachers are more likely to transfer these innovative practices utilising the familiar tools and media into their repertoire of teaching strategies. The advantage of this extension of technological expertise is that teachers can also become more creative in how they use these media to provide innovative learning experiences for their technologically-adept students. If teachers do not take up the challenges of extending their toolbox of teaching strategies into the 21st century technological context, they run the risk of losing students' and society's respect for educators.

Technology for Teaching and Learning

Technology has had a revolutionary impact on modern society. Western governments perceive technology as a means to remain competitive within an increasingly globalised society, as illustrated by Dolence and Norris' comments that "[t]hose [nations] who realign their practices most effectively to Information Age standards will reap substantial benefits. Those who do not will be replaced or diminished by more nimble competitors" (1995, p. 2). As a result of society's rapid adoption of new technologies, educators are expected to ensure students have the necessary knowledge and skills to keep abreast and be au fait with these technological trends. Walker considers the whole concept of being "educated" when he states that soon educated people would be expected to be able to "use several symbol systems … apply knowledge in life … think strategically … manage information … learn, think, and create as part of a team" through the use of technology (1999, p. 20). Walker's discussion of the possible shift in the definition of being educated is in relation to graduates of the education system and yet the same rationale equally applies to the graduates' teachers.

The changing expectations of society in relation to technology present issues for schools and universities. This includes concerns with the cost of implementation and in providing appropriate professional development for staff so that they are able and willing to use these technologies in innovative ways for teaching and learning purposes. Compounded with these issues is that many students are entering schools and universities with superior technological expertise in comparison to that of teachers (Scott & Scott, 2003). Within schools this phenomena has the potential to create discord between staff and students. This is evident when teachers perceive technologically-facilitated learning environments as reducing their levels of control; and results in frustration for students when expectations for technologically-orientated learning experiences are not met, or worse actively impeded by unconfident or uninformed teachers (Scott & Scott, 2003). The Internet offers increased opportunities for students of all ages to engage in online collaboration through the burgeoning availability of social networking technologies (Chalmers & Keown, 2006). Technology, such as WebCT®, Blackboard®, web-based bulletin boards and forums, enable students to research, share ideas and materials, and work collaboratively on projects across classrooms, schools, districts and even globally. Barbara Means (2000) states even with these advances many teachers are not using technology innovatively for pedagogical purposes. Currently many teachers are simply using technology as a "performance tool", for example, a calculator or a word processor "which enhances or changes how a task is accomplished" (Putnam & Borko, 2000, p. 10). There is therefore, an obvious need for teaching staff to engage in professional development focused on increasing, not only their "performance" skill levels with technology, but their understandings of how to utilise technology in pedagogically innovative ways.

INNOVATIONS IN THE USE OF TECHNOLOGY IN INTERNATIONAL SETTINGS

Two case studies are presented which explore teacher professional development but from differing angles. The first, a Canadian case, explores innovative uses of technology in graduate programmes designed as professional development for teachers. The second, an Australian case, presents the situation of a multi-faceted long-term professional development strategy situated within a school district context. While the first case explores the delivery of professional development within a university situation the school-based example also investigated the impact on students as a result of the professional development strategy. Both cases discuss the use of a range of technologies to support ongoing, contextualised professional development.

Using Voice-over-Internet-Protocol (VoIP) for Professional Development: A Canadian Case Study

Many educators consider postgraduate programmes as excellent professional development. Postgraduate programmes offer teachers exposure to advances in knowledge and practice emerging from scholarly research. They also facilitate teachers' networking with their peers who are also engaging in continued learning and with experts from a range of disciplines. Traditional programmes require students to attend classes at a particular university or college campus, however, they tend to exclude teachers who are situated in isolated areas or who have limited time to allocate to studies. As Webber and Scott state "[c]learly, institutions of higher learning face significant challenges as they strive to become more innovative, networked, communication savvy, cosmopolitan, and technologically literate" (2008, p. 5). They continue their discussion of the changes in higher education indicating that expectations are different and universities "look very different from how they appeared even a decade ago. Student numbers have increased dramatically and technology has reshaped how teaching and learning occurs" (Webber & Scott, 2008, p. 1).

This case study outlines an entrepreneurial approach to establishing Faculty of Education postgraduate programmes at a large university in Alberta, Canada. Social justice is a key rationale for establishing these programmes as they aim to provide equity and access for all teachers regardless of their mode of study or their geographical location. For example, some students wish to undertake their studies in a part-time mode but some programmes do not allow this. Similarly, many students are situated not only in remote regions of Alberta but also in isolated locales around the world and technology facilitates their continuing learning. Networking facilitated through these programmes include insights from colleagues and experts situated as far afield as Africa, Australia, China, Egypt, Japan, New Zealand, Qatar, United Kingdom, and the USA to name a few.

Webber and Scott (2008) defined entrepreneurship in educational organisations as encompassing six key dimensions:

1. innovative behaviour – the generation of knowledge and skills;
2. networking – information acquisition and successful adaptation to changing conditions;
3. time-space communication framework – synchronous and asynchronous communication, local and distributed communication, and learning across space and through time;
4. local-global perspective – local-national-global cultural literacy, and principled, reflective, engaged citizens;
5. educational organizations as knowledge centres – sources of knowledge creation for students, faculty members, and support staff and sites of essential learning and attention to access, resources, and community needs; and
6. integrated face-to-face and Internet-based learning – international, competitive environment, and strategic alliances (Webber & Scott, 2008).

In the six dimensions, innovation in the use of technology is a significant component of entrepreneurial activities. In this case study, Internet-based technologies provide the foundation for learning and reflective practice, interaction, engagement and networking across space and time, and the crossing of global boundaries.

Even though the programmes are focused on the Education discipline not all students are teachers, drawing from other fields such as health, higher education, the military, business, and industry. Students who enrol in the distance mode undertake the majority of their coursework through an online medium. Upon entry into the programme doctoral students are advised to attend summer courses and other holiday initiatives such as student conferences. At these events they are able to socialise with peers, faculty supervisors and other scholars, and participate in classes. These activities enable networking and the forging of relationships so essential for successful further studies. This early contact establishes positive social dynamics that tend to translate into the online environments. This blended approach overcomes many of the criticisms of fully online courses whereby social networking can be impeded due to isolation and the lack of interpersonal and social relationship linkages.

The online environment is a coalescent approach incorporating synchronous classroom environments mediated through the VoIP Elluminate Live!® software and asynchronous modes such as Blackboard® and email. Instructors are encouraged to employ a wide range of teaching strategies and learning experiences which involve many of the features these software packages enable. Some instructors use the range of Elluminate Live!® features. For example, they plan for maximum student involvement through collaborative activities. These include group presentations conducted live in synchronous classrooms, asynchronous and synchronous verbal and text interactions mediated in 'break-out rooms' in small groups, and Blackboard® forums. Instructors also encourage student reflection on learning and content materials by students posting their syntheses of theories, reactions, and ideas on discussion boards for critical review. Access to staff is also mediated through phone calls, email and live verbal interaction using Elluminate Live!®. The library and university bookstore also participate in this entrepreneurial approach by providing excellence in service, sending out texts and materials directly to students anywhere in the world, and through ready access to e-libraries.

The professional development offered within these programmes is not only related to educational theory and research but also extends to developing students' technological capabilities. Students

and staff are encouraged to access the extensive knowledge and expertise residing in the technical support services team who provide professional development on the range of Elluminate Live!® functions. Students and staff have access outside of class time to the Elluminate Live!® for group meetings, practice with this online medium, and research meetings.

Many students enter the programme with a profound lack of technical expertise and fear of technology. Course evaluation data indicates though, that learning activities, professional development on the use of the technologies, and the supportive classroom environment result in high levels of student technological comfort and efficacy within the timeframe of one course. Additionally, students report their resultant increase in 'technological efficacy' has translated to extensive and more innovative technological practice in their school classrooms and private lives. The introduction of students to innovative uses of technology has opened up pathways of communication which they may not have encountered before. With the increase of comfort with technology, some have extended their practice to socialising and networking with colleagues using Skype®.

Due to the coursework activities that put students in contact with colleagues around the world, many report the advantages of the networking opportunities that support career advancement as well as professional growth. With students situated in widely varying contexts the capacity for innovation in problem-solving is significant. Course discussion boards and forums abound with stories, ideas, and solutions to specific problems that have been developed in students' organisations. This results in creative synergies that enhance the professional development experience. Anecdotal evidence indicates that some relationships forged from course-based interactions carry over into private social networking after courses are completed.

The positives inherent in this case study may indicate that this blended approach is the panacea for professional development; however, a cautionary note must be sounded at this juncture. There are a number of issues emerging from these programmes. Although many academics enjoy teaching within the online and blended learning environments, some, like their students, are not technologically comfortable and shy away from taking up teaching opportunities within this innovative mode. Others do teach within the online environment; however, the extent of their teaching strategies is conducting lectures and occasional question and answer sessions. Even though technology-focused and teaching and learning-focused professional development are readily available, some choose not to avail themselves of it.

This case study presents an entrepreneurial approach to the provision of systematic professional development. Teachers who engage in these distance programmes have greater opportunities to develop their understandings of innovative uses of technology than their counterparts who opt for face-to-face programmes. Success is measured in the attainment of qualifications, students' self-reported technological efficacy, national and international collegial networks, and increased knowledge.

Teacher Professional Development that Supports ICT Integration in the Classroom: An Australian Case Study

As Dolence and Norris reflect "[s]ociety is undergoing a fundamental transformation from the Industrial Age to the Information Age ... all people, organizations, societies, and nations are affected" (1995, p. 2). Schools at all levels – elementary, secondary, and tertiary are increasingly under pressure from government, business and industry to produce graduates who are technologically literate. Over the past decade these societal demands have resulted in a focus on establishing infrastructure within schools in order for students to have op-

portunities to learn using technology. Teachers are expected to engage with the technology agenda for both their managerial duties and pedagogical approaches. Barbara Means highlighted the focus on the integration of technology in schools during the 1970s-1980s as being predominately "to teach about computers rather than to teach with them" and were rarely for teaching of core academic subjects (Means, 2000, p. 187). In the 1980-1990s education shifted towards greater alignment with the real workplace through use of word processing packages to support student writing for example. This influenced the core curriculum areas where technology was incorporated in terms of the applications that supported student activities. The integration of technology into curriculum received a dramatic boost with the advent of the World Wide Web in 1990 and the related search engines that enabled increased access to information from wider sources.

Increasing the collaborative and social nature of learning utilising the interactive capabilities of computer networks has emerged as an advantage of technology. This impacted on the patterns of use, with some schools becoming involved in challenging research collaborations with researchers and industry across the globe. While examples of innovative uses of technology bode well for students' learning, Means stated "although such examples of technology-enhanced, constructivist-orientated learning activities are prominent in the education literature, they do not represent mainstream educational practice" (2000, p. 194).

The Western Australian school context has been greatly influenced over the past decade by radical curriculum changes reflecting a more constructivist paradigm (Curriculum Council of Western Australia, 1998). As a result of these curriculum changes Information Technology (IT) was replaced as a stand-alone discipline to being "integrated" into all learning areas. The rationale for this significant change was to "increase the relevance and authenticity of the learning tasks, to ensure students are able to transfer their ICT skills into real research tasks, and to ensure an increased coverage of technologies" (Scott & Scott, 2003, p. 4). This has resulted in the need to prioritise technology related professional development for all discipline teachers.

This Western Australian case study is about teachers' professional development experiences with technology. It outlines the learning journey of teachers in a low socio-economic district who were the first recipients of a government initiative to provide them with subsidised laptops. Even though this was an innovation in 'teacher access to technology' no professional development was routinely provided within this initiative; hence, teachers were interested in ICT but remained at their fundamental level of technology expertise. Recognising the massive impact of this technology policy on his staff, one entrepreneurial principal within this district took a multi-dimensional approach to supporting his teachers' and students' technology-facilitated learning.

Research in this school district identified a massive disparity between student and teacher familiarity, comfort and expertise with, and regularity of use of technology (Scott & Scott, 2003). Students were advanced in all of these areas and yet their teachers were working at fundamental levels. This had the potential to create disharmony in the classroom with students strongly advocating for ICT-oriented learning activities, while their unconfident teachers shied away from experimentation. Teacher reluctance was due to fears about their lack of expertise with ICT, losing control of the class, and/or losing face. The schools in this district had large populations of indigenous, refugee, and immigrant students. The research revealed that technology-mediated learning experiences were highly valued by all of these students and acted as motivational factors to attend school and increase engagement.

Cognisant of the student motivational element afforded by technology, the principal of the secondary school collaborated with the network administrator and district office to institute a multi-dimensional long-term strategy to enhance technology-facilitated learning experiences. This strategy evolved over an eight-year period from conception to the conclusion of the evaluative research. The ultimate aim was to increase student outcomes. It facilitated increased opportunities for pedagogical professional development of teachers. Additionally, it provided teachers and students increased access to technology infrastructure and technical support. The principal's entrepreneurial approach encompassed the following:

- Funding for a full-time teacher-leader as network administrator to design, install, and maintain a cutting edge switched fibre-optic network in the school with access available to the cluster elementary schools in the district;
- Providing a system which enabled full email and Internet access for both staff and students, a school website and intranet, repositories for student and staff work, and the potential for parent access to student work from home;
- Sourcing sufficient numbers of computers to ensure a one-to-one student-to-computer ratio in the secondary school;
- Employing a full-time technician to provide the support necessary to keep the system operating within optimal parameters;
- Employing a teacher-leader to work alongside the network administrator in providing pedagogical professional development focused on innovative uses of ICT;
- Funding for the teacher-leaders to team-teach and work collaboratively with teachers and students in- and out-of-class time;
- Providing funding for district-wide professional development where elementary and secondary teachers could collaborate.

Professional Development

Professional development was established as after-school face-to-face workshops for all teachers from the secondary and elementary schools cluster. Workshops were run each week over the course of six months facilitated by the network administrator. Experts and outside teacher-leaders were invited to work with teachers introducing them to new technologies and pedagogies. Teachers were exposed to the fundamentals of computer and intranet use, email, designing web pages, Internet browsing, and MS Office applications for the development of resources. "Peer Coaching Study Teams" (Showers, 1995; Showers & Joyce, 1996) were established to facilitate in-context collegial support in their own schools. Online collaboration involved the sharing of teaching resources, strategies and problem-solving activities facilitated via email and shared intranet web pages. Teacher-leaders facilitated in-situ pedagogical and technological professional development support to all members of the cluster – in-class, during class preparation times, and outside school hours over a two-year period. School-based operational communication largely shifted from traditional paper-based to online modes: for example, daily newsletters to teachers and students; minutes of staff and committee meetings were uploaded to the intranet; and student absenteeism was recorded online by teachers.

Impact of Professional Development on Learning and Teaching

The amount of ICT-facilitated learning experiences increased during this period, as did the level of sophistication of teachers' design of these activities. As staff expertise increased specialised discipline applicable software such as Computer-Aided Design (CAD) were explored. Additionally, older technologies made way for newer, more sophisticated technologies. For example, science related videos were converted to streamed video and placed on the intranet for ready student access anywhere in the school. Interviews with students, and researchers' observation in class, revealed increased student satisfaction, engagement, and productivity within these activities. Student retention and attendance also was positively influenced.

Over the course of the eight years, significant improvements occurred in teachers' technological efficacy and their levels of comfort with integrating these into their teaching and learning repertoire. Many teachers maintained and extended their networks with colleagues, teacher-leaders and experts during and after this initiative's establishment. A key factor for success was excellence in service provided by the technical support and the professional development team.

Sustainability of this strategy was deleteriously affected by the systematic dismantling of the school's technology infrastructure, and the withdrawing of funding for professional developers and technicians by the central education authority. This was due to a new Education Ministry initiative designed to equalise the technological capacity of all schools within the state to ensure parity. Unfortunately, this negatively affected innovative schools whose administrators and teachers had prioritised ICT-facilitated learning as these schools' infrastructure and professional development processes were reduced to a 'centralised common standard'. This process effectively interrupted the consistent progress teachers had made towards innovative technology-integrated teaching practice.

This case study demonstrates how pedagogically-driven ICT-oriented professional development is effective in enhancing teachers' practice, and student motivation and outcomes. Teachers' engagement with technology for teaching promotes the critical reflection on their current teaching beliefs and practices. This frequently motivates them to move to more innovative teaching approaches regardless of the technology aspects. Success factors directly relate to:

- entrepreneurial and supportive leadership;
- considerable goodwill and participation of teachers;
- greater access for staff, students and parents to a range of technologies;
- excellence in service by technical personnel; and
- effective professional development and credible professional developers and experts.

At the forefront of this entire initiative was innovation in pedagogical practice to ensure optimal student learning outcomes. Therefore, the technology did not drive the pedagogy but it promoted the refinement of pedagogical practice.

The two case studies presented, although from differing international contexts, outline two varied forms of professional development for teachers and yet when compared yield significant similarities. The alignment between these cases is highlighted in the entrepreneurial leadership evident in both settings. Social justice was a key aim in enabling increased access to professional development not only of teachers but also for students mediated through the innovative use of technology. Technology was perceived as a means of meeting the needs of a new generation of individuals who have different expectations from learning the environment to those of their predecessors. The professional development predominantly focused on facilitating, expanding and enhancing teachers' discipline knowledge as well as their exposure to, and comfort with new technology. Additionally, important aspects for effective professional development were included. For example, collaboration and the social learning were overtly included and encompassed interaction across disciplines, within disciplines, and across contexts. An unexpected aspect to emerge was the social networking which these new technologies facilitated. Analysis of these two successful professional development initiatives leads us to explore the future trends that using innovative technologies present.

FUTURE TRENDS

Technologies that facilitate learning, collaboration and social networking abound, are becoming increasingly sophisticated, and are relatively easy to use once familiarity has been established. Even though many are using these for social purposes, there is potential for these technologies to be valuable in providing teacher professional development opportunities and to increase the learning of students in the school context. At this juncture a cautionary note must be made regarding the rationale for adopting innovative technologies and how they are used. Sound pedagogy and social justice goals must be the driving force behind the integration of technology into the professional development arena. Simply implementing professional development programmes via a technological medium or using it in the classroom just because it is available and now possible is not a valid rationale. A sound pedagogical approach to professional development and instructional design is essential, particularly when learning is mediated through technology (Price & Kirkwood, 2008). Ascough espouses placing "pedagogy before technology" to ensure high quality educational experiences regardless of the delivery mode (2002, p. 17).

Professional developers must understand how to teach effectively using innovative technologies. Their own understandings of the technology and constructivist pedagogies should be sufficiently in-depth to ensure that learning experiences are structured and facilitated in educationally optimal ways for maximum effectiveness – incorporating the principles of adult learning (Knowles, Holton III, & Swanson, 2005; Merriam, 2001). In fact, professional developers should embrace the challenges of critically reviewing their own teaching practice, thereby "advancing pedagogical strategies" with the goal of moving from a transmissive to a constructivist paradigm within the technological medium (Suen, 2005, p. 143). For example, online learning experiences must involve engagement with peers and experts, both synchronously and asynchronously, so that synergies can be developed, insightful sharing can occur, and exposure to innovations in teaching and learning is facilitated. Knowles and his associates (2005) emphasise the importance of participants' need to be self-directing and autonomous, where they are able to have input into their programme topics so that content is pragmatic and relevant. Professional development experiences are most useful if they contain problem-solving dimensions, have intrinsic interest-value, and a sound rationale for learning. Social dimensions are also important in professional development, as humans desire interaction with others, enjoy a laugh with like-minded individuals, and to share the camaraderie of common life and work experiences. These dimensions are the glue that binds professional development communities.

As previously outlined from the literature, sound professional development of teachers ensures opportunities for communicating, collaborating and problem-solving together and with experts. There are many examples in the literature of models which advocate these elements such as, "professional learning communities" (DuFour, 2004; DuFour & Eaker, 2004), "communities of practice" (Wenger, 2003), and "peer coaching study teams" (Joyce & Showers, 1995; Showers, 1995) and yet most of these are founded on the premise of face-to-face interaction. So how should professional development be reconceptualised to ensure its effectiveness and to integrate the advantages provided by the innovative use of technologies?

Webs of Enhanced Practice

This chapter presents a new model of professional development (see Figure 1), namely "Webs of Enhanced Practice" which are facilitated through blended approaches (Scott, 2009). Webs of Enhanced Practice (WoEP) represent innovation in the use of technology for teacher professional

development. This model includes four main dimensions: technology, delivery, interaction, and networking.

The technological dimension – The web-like nature of this professional development model is due to the eclectic use of many different forms of technology to meet the needs of the participants. Both 1st and 2nd generation technologies find a place in these webs as each present its own set of advantages to participants. For example, online bulletin boards, forums, email, blogs, and wikis can offer busy teachers opportunities to keep up-to-date with the knowledge-base and each other. Second generation technologies, such as text chat and VoIP, offer participants the possibilities of synergy creation and immediacy in their interactions. This model is unusual in that it advocates for utilising whatever technology is optimal and timely for the purposes defined by the participants. Therefore a range of technology which suits different purposes is encompassed in the model as it is the pedagogy and social networking, not the technology, which is crucial. The technology is simply a vehicle for delivery of services.

The multi-modal delivery dimension – Innovation is represented by the multi-modal approach facilitated through synchronous and asynchronous technologies, potentially interwoven with face-to-face activities. This blended approach provides the greatest flexibility for teachers in their frantically busy, and frequently chaotic work and personal lives. Asynchronous technologies provide opportunities for engagement at the convenience of the participants as they can access and review these when they have time.

Synchronous technologies offer less convenience as participants must be online simultaneously; however, the advantages are immediacy and increased clarity of discussion intent gleaned from the verbal cues. Many professional development participants still desire face-to-face interactions because of the human social dynamics that are possible through this mode. Face-to-face meetings represent the whole sensory package – voice, aural, touch, and gestural expressions. Face-to-face, however, is not always viable, convenient, or affordable. No one mode meets all needs and no one innovation is pre-eminently superior to another. Therefore, this model advocates for multi-modal delivery opportunities to increase the advantages and reduce the disadvantages through a coalescent approach.

The multi-faceted interaction dimension – Webs of Enhanced Practice (WoEP) teachers are in contact, not only with their peers but also with colleagues at different levels of the organisation (e.g., principals, heads of department, and teacher-leaders). WoEPs can and should snowball to incorporate discipline, technology,

Figure 1. Webs of Enhanced Practice (modified from Scott, 2009)

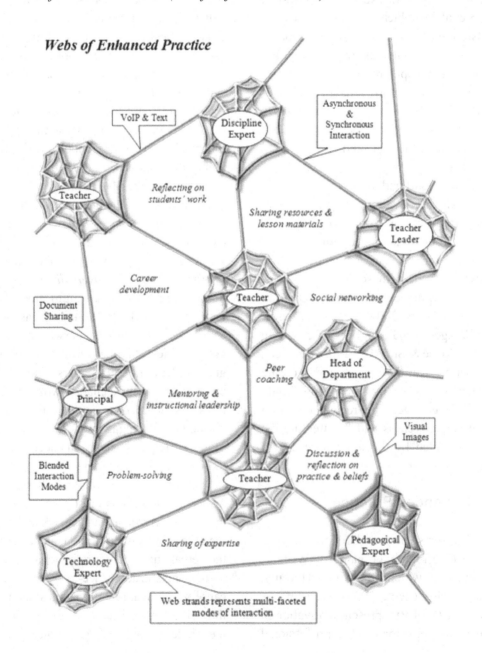

and pedagogical experts, thereby expanding the knowledge and skills 'caught within the webs'. Reciprocal learning is a significant component in the WoEPs. Experts can learn from the members and from the diversity in contexts, and may have increased access to research opportunities. Experts can also share their expertise with other experts providing professional development for these highly knowledgeable individuals. Participants can engage in discussions, reflect on personal teaching effectiveness, problem-solve, and share expertise, resources and lesson materials. The more senior members of the WoEP can support the career aspirations and development of participants by facilitating mentoring and providing instructional leadership.

Social and professional networking dimension – The WoEPs combines 'professional' and 'personal' elements, so desirable to teachers, and more accurately capture the complexity and potential existing in the technology-rich 21st century work-lifestyle. The 'professional' is encompassed in the focus on increasing the quality of teaching and the level of professionalism. The 'personal' revolves around the social networking components. It includes the socialising potential, development of friendships and mentoring relationships, nurturing of interpersonal and intrapersonal skills, and development of teacher- and self-efficacy.

The WoEP is a model set at a macro level. It involves educators at all levels of the organisation potentially within a school, across a district, province or state, or indeed across the world. Entrepreneurial technology-facilitated professional development enables the crossing of "traditional boundaries of culture, politics, time, and space" and enriches the global community (Scott & Webber, 2008, p. 764). WoEPs are not static, being in a constant state of flux with current and new members moving in and out according to their needs and preferences. Individuals may be involved in multiple webs at the same time; however, the extent of their involvement may vary from full commitment to incidental.

Webs of Enhanced Learning

While the WoEPs are predominantly focused on professional development, the implications for enhancing teaching and learning practice are explored in the magnification of the WoEP (see Figure 2). The second model "Webs of Enhanced Learning" (WoEL) (Scott, 2009) zooms in on the impact of professional development-oriented WoEPs on teachers' practices in the classroom. The WoEL focuses in on students' learning that results from teachers' architectural expertise in designing innovative experiences for students. Similar to the WoEP, the WoEL has four main dimensions – the technology, delivery, interaction, and social and professional networking.

Technological dimension – Teachers with technological efficacy from their professional development activities are more likely to be willing and able to integrate these into their students' classroom activities. Using a range of technologies to meet different learning outcomes enables students to develop both their content knowledge and technical expertise. Twenty-first century students are frequently *au fait* with a range of technologies and are regular consumers of them for largely social and recreational purposes. However, students may be exposed to technologies different to those they regularly use or have some familiarity with, because these are particularly suited to the learning outcomes. Integrating these has the potential to increase students' motivation and engagement and also to positively influence their attitudes towards school and teachers.

Multi-modal delivery dimension – Blended approaches incorporating asynchronous and synchronous technologies provide opportunities for students to work with their peers regardless of geographical location or time zones. This multi-modal delivery has the capacity to open up authentic learning tasks, that is, to have students working on projects which are of value to the wider community – business, industry or charitable organisations. Students engaged in

Figure 2. ICT-facilitated Learning and Teaching for Enhanced Practice in the 21st Century (modified from Scott, 2009)

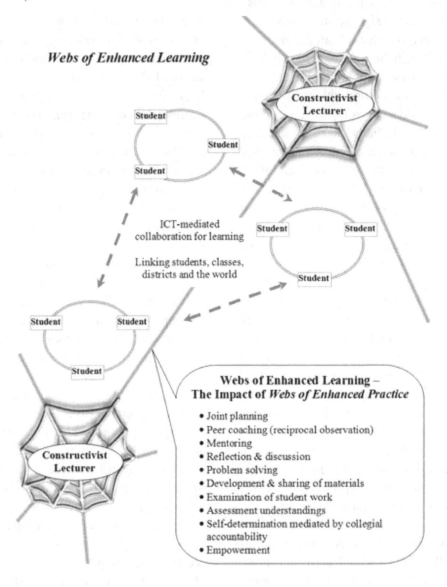

authentic learning tend to work harder and more persistently, are more conscious of producing a quality product, and respond more positively to community feedback and critique.

Social learning dimension – Social learning is a key element of any students' education. Individuals learn best when they have opportunities to engage with knowledge, construct their schema through interactions with resources and others,

and question their understandings by comparing them with those of their peers. Imagine how much richer the learning opportunities can be when students interact with global peers who have completely differing frames of reference influenced by variations in cultures, climates, political societies, and social systems. Additionally, experts from outside the classroom can be drawn from linkages available through the Webs of Enhanced Practice. Student learning is no longer restricted to what can be experienced in a traditional contained classroom, as collaboration with other cohorts around the world makes any classroom 'virtually' accessible.

Many students come to the classroom with high levels of technological expertise but lack the understandings of social etiquette related to using certain technologies. An aspect of social networking is to learn what is socially appropriate and constructive. Unfortunately, the teaching of social skills, manners, and morals frequently falls within society's expectation of school curricula. Therefore, teachers can use these WoEL to facilitate students' learning of new social networking mores and etiquette required by 21st century technological societies.

Professional and social networking dimension – Even though the other dimensions are focused on students' learning, this final dimension in the WoEL is about teachers and their context. Acknowledging the teaching isolation inherent in most schools, this WoEL model offers an amelioration of this condition. As identified in Figure 2 teachers who are teamed to facilitate their students' collaborations are also in a position to collaborate for teaching purposes. Collaborative relationships emerging from the more macro WoEP enable teachers to experience:

- *Joint planning of lessons to implement innovative teaching strategies* – This process is about reducing teacher workload and enhancing practice. It reduces feelings of isolation and has the potential of nurturing personal friendships.
- *Peer coaching (reciprocal observation)* – Implementing new complex strategies requires commitment, effort, and perseverance for transfer to occur from workshop settings into regular teaching repertoire. Observing classes and learning from how others have implemented various strategies is invaluable in embedding the innovations into practice.

- *Collegial cultures* – The teaching profession around the world is rife with early attrition of novice teachers. Mentoring relationships between experienced staff and these novices can result in increases in their satisfaction, comfort and quality of practice.
- *Reflection and discussion* – Reflection is a powerful motivator and guide to improving practice (Bandura, 2001). However, most teachers do not get enough time to engage in this. If teachers' workloads are reduced as a result of collaborative efforts there is the potential to buy out time for reflection.
- *Problem-solving* – 'A problem shared is a problem solved' is an age-old adage which resonates as a truism in the case of most teachers. Few problems exist in teaching that cannot be resolved with assistance from colleagues, superordinates and/or experts. Drawing upon the expertise and experience of participants 'caught in the webs' can assist the most isolated of teachers.
- *The development and sharing of materials* – Sharing of resources entails scrutiny and potential critique by respected colleagues. Therefore, teachers who have opportunities to share and receive lessons and materials are likely to spend more time developing better quality resources.
- *The examination of student work* – Much can be learned about the effectiveness of the teaching and learning experiences through the examination of students' work. Using samples of student work encourages teachers to critically reflect upon their own understandings of the curriculum and assessment processes. High quality samples from students are valuable in providing exemplars for others to clarify curricula outcomes.
- *Increases in understanding of sound assessment* – Assessment is always a contentious

185

area in teaching as it places the educator under the scrutiny of administrators and parents. It is desirable for collaboration to occur for the purposes of ensuring parity and moderation of marking across classrooms, schools and districts. Collaboration also enables the sharing of tests and assignment protocols, and the extension of teacher understandings about sound assessment processes and practices.

- *Self-determination moderated by collegial accountability* – A key priority for teachers is to be self-determining in relation to their professional development (Scott, 2003). However, collegial reciprocity tends to also incorporate peer-accountability. This situation can be a positive element as it acts as a motivator in implementing changes to classroom teaching behaviours. For example, teachers who have made arrangements to observe each other's lessons and to share their joint planning will be more likely to follow through due a sense of obligation to support their colleague (Joyce & Showers, 1995).

- *Empowerment* – All of these aspects within the professional and social networking dimension are about positively influencing teachers. When teachers are highly efficacious they tend to feel empowered. Empowered teachers work more effectively to produce enhanced student outcomes (Bandura, 1986; 1993).

The Webs of Enhanced Practice and Webs of Enhanced Learning models are dependent upon support from educational leaders, experts, teachers, and technical providers. Support is needed in the form of funding for technology infrastructure to support the professional development processes. Technical support and expertise is essential in establishing and maintaining the 'webs'. Support personnel must be available to train participants in best practice in the use of the technologies and

to assist in the establishing web linkages. Additionally, organisations must recognise and reward participation in these innovative forms of professional development, particularly when they affect improving student outcomes. Rewards inherent in the 'webs' are not simply intrinsic. Webs of Enhanced Practice may provide a valuable 'pool of future leaders'. Those who are prioritising ongoing, systematic professional development should be those groomed for leadership roles and career advancement, particularly if they have transferred their knowledge and skills into making a difference to student learning outcomes. Leadership should be distributed throughout the 'webs' so leaders move to another web or drop out altogether, their loss does not irreparably disrupt the linkages for other participants. Disruptions are minimised because other leaders in the 'webs' would take over the role. This integrates the evolutionary and adaptability qualities that promote ongoing sustainability.

CONCLUSION

Technology offers considerable potential in reconceptualising both professional development and teaching and learning. Innovation in the use of technology is conceptualised as the eclectic utilisation of a multi-modal range of technologies that advances the professional development of a community of learners. Constructivist professional development environments are frequently denied teachers (Lieberman & Miller, 2000) and yet these are also the most effective in bringing about positive changes in teacher behaviours and beliefs (Joyce & Showers, 1995). Collaboration between various stakeholders, such as teachers, leaders, experts, and professional developers is a key element in successful adult learning and yet it is constrained by limitations in time, finances, distance, relationships and trust. The Webs of Enhanced Practice are less constrained by these limitations as they encompass an individual's professional and *social* needs and facilitate these beyond the boundaries of space and time (Scott & Webber, 2008). They are an entrepreneurial approach to promoting the learning of educators and students. Factors essential to the success of WoEP include participants' levels of comfort and familiarity with a range of technologies; participants' willingness to engage with the webs; leadership that supports and recognises the participants' engagement and outcomes; and financial and technical support for web-like communities.

"Webs of Enhanced Learning" explore the impact in the classroom of the professional development and relationships forged in the WoEP (Scott, 2009). Teachers who have attained technological efficacy are better able to facilitate the learning of their students using innovative technologies. Students who learn within technology-rich and social learning environments have greater potential to emerge with increased academic outcomes in addition to increased social and technical skills. In fact these two 'webs' are mutually responsive and continually evolving. As stated in Joyce and Showers …

The development of a pervasive staff development system is, in itself, a major cultural change; and that change will spawn others by changing the relation of professional to professional and between all professionals and the knowledge base in the process of inquiry (1995, p. xiv).

REFERENCES

Ascough, R. S. (2002). Designing for online distance education: Putting pedagogy before technology. *Teaching Theology and Religion, 5*(1), 17–29. doi:10.1111/1467-9647.00114

Bandura, A. (1986). *Social foundations of thought and action: A Social Cognitive Theory.* Englewood Cliffs, NJ: Prentice-Hall.

Bandura, A. (1993). Perceived self-efficacy in cognitive development and functioning. *Educational Psychologist, 28*(2), 117–148. doi:10.1207/s15326985ep2802_3

Bandura, A. (2001). Social Cognitive Theory: An agentic perspective. *Annual Review of Psychology, 52,* 1–26. doi:10.1146/annurev.psych.52.1.1

Carter, H. L., Foulger, T. S., & Ewbank, A. D. (2008). Have you googled your teacher lately? Teachers' use of social networking sites. *Phi Delta Kappan, 89*(9), 681–685.

Chalmers, L., & Keown, P. (2006). Communities of practice and professional development. *International Journal of Lifelong Learning, 25*(2).

Curriculum Council of Western Australia. (1998). The curriculum framework for kindergarten to year 12 education in Western Australia [Curriculum Document]. (pp. 1-325). Perth WA: The Curriculum Council.

Darling-Hammond, L. (1998, February). Teacher learning that supports student learning. *Educational Leadership,* 6–11.

Darling-Hammond, L., & McLaughlin, M. (1995). Policies that support professional development in an era of change. *Phi Delta Kappan, 76*(8), 597–604.

Dolence, M. G., & Norris, D. M. (1995). *Transforming higher education: A vision for learning in the 21st Century.* Society for College and University Planning (SCUP): Ann Arbor, MI, USA.

DuFour, R. (2004). What is a "Professional Learning Community?". *Educational Leadership, 61*(8), 6–11.

DuFour, R., & Eaker, R. (2004). *Professional Learning Communities at work: Best practices for enhancing student achievement.* Bloomington, IN: National Educational Service.

Guskey, T. R. (1994). Results-oriented professional development: In search of an optimal mix of effective practices. *Journal of Staff Development, 15*(4), 42–50.

Hartnell-Young, E. (2006). Teachers' roles and professional learning in communities of practice supported by technology in schools. *Journal of Technology and Teacher Education, 14*(3), 461–480.

Havelock, B. (2004). Online community and professional learning in education: Research-based keys to sustainability. *Association for the Advancement of Computing in Education, 12*(1), 56–84.

Joyce, B., & Showers, B. (1980). Improving inservice training: The messages of research. *Educational Leadership, 37*(5), 379–385.

Joyce, B., & Showers, B. (1982). The coaching of teaching. *Educational Leadership, 40*(1), 416.

Joyce, B., & Showers, B. (1995). *Student achievement through staff development*. New York: Longman.

Knowles, M. S., Holton, E. F., III, & Swanson, R. A. (2005). *The adult learner: The definitive classic in adult education and human resource development* (6th ed.). Amsterdam: Elsevier.

Leithwood, K. (2007). What we know about educational leadership. In C. F. Webber, J. Burger, & P. Klinck (Eds.), *Intelligent leadership: Constructs for thinking education leaders* (pp. 41-66). Dordrecht, The Netherlands: Springer.

Leithwood, K., Seashore Louis, K., Anderson, S., & Wahlstrom, K. (2004). *How leadership influences student learning*. New York: Wallace Foundation.

Levine, A., & Sun, J. C. (2002). *Barriers to distance education*. Washington, DC: American Council on Education.

Lieberman, A. (1995). Practices that support professional development: Transforming conceptions of professional learning. *Phi Delta Kappan, 76*(8), 591–596.

Lieberman, A., & Miller, L. (2000). Teaching and teacher development: A new synthesis for a new century. In R. S. Brandt (Ed.), *Education in a new era* (pp. 47-66). VA: Association for Supervision and Curriculum Development.

McLaughlin, M., & Talbot, J. E. (1993). *Contexts that matter for teaching and learning: Strategic opportunities for meeting the nation's educational goals*. Stanford, CA: Centre for Research on the Context of Secondary School Teaching.

Means, B. (2000). Technology in America's schools: Before and after Y2K. In R. S. Brandt (Ed.), *Education in a new era*. Alexandria, VA: Association for Supervision and Curriculum Development.

Merriam, S. B. (2001). Andragogy and self-directed learning: Pillars of adult learning theory. In S. B. Merriam (Ed.), *The new update on adult learning theory, 89*, (pp. 3-13). San Francisco: Jossey-Bass.

Motteram, G. (2006). Blended education and the transformation of teachers: a long-term case study in postgraduate UK higher education. *British Journal of Educational Technology, 37*(1), 17–30. doi:10.1111/j.1467-8535.2005.00511.x

Peters, T., & Bell, L. (2006). Is web conferencing software ready for the big time? *Computers in Libraries, 26*(2), 32–36.

Price, L., & Kirkwood, A. (2008). Learning and teaching and technology. In S. Scott & K. Dixon (Eds.), *The globalised university: Trends and development in teaching and learning* (pp. 83-113). Perth: Black Swan Press.

Putnam, R. T., & Borko, H. (2000). What do new views of knowledge and thinking have to say about research on teacher learning? *Educational Researcher, 29*(1), 4–15.

Riding, P. (2001). Online teacher communities and continuing professional development. *Teacher Development, 5*(3), 283–295. doi:10.1080/13664530100200156

Scott, D. E. (2009). *Effective Voice-over-Internet-Protocol (VoIP) learning experiences: The relationship between adult learning motivation, multiple intelligences, and learning styles.* Doctoral Thesis. Curtin University of Technology.

Scott, S. (2003). Professional development: A study of secondary teachers' experiences and perspectives. *The International Journal of Learning, 10.*

Scott, S., & Scott, D. E. (2003). The integration of technology into the curriculum: The perspectives of teachers and students within a Western Australian secondary school. *The International Journal of Learning, 10.*

Scott, S., & Webber, C. F. (2008). Evidence-based leadership development: The 4L framework. *Journal of Educational Administration, 46*(6), 762–776. doi:10.1108/09578230810908343

Showers, B. (1984). *Peer coaching: A strategy for facilitating transfer of training.* Eugene, OR: Center for Educational Policy and Management.

Showers, B. (1995, April). *Designing site-based school improvement programs.* Paper presented at the Primary Principals, Education Department of Western Australia, Nedlands, Western Australia.

Showers, B., & Joyce, B. (1996). The evolution of peer coaching. *Educational Leadership, 53*(6), 12–16.

Simonson, M., Smaldino, S., Albright, M., & Zvacek, S. (2006). *Teaching and learning at a distance: Foundations of distance education.* (3rd ed.). Upper Saddle River, NJ: Pearson Merrill Prentice Hall.

Sparks, D., & Hirsh, S. (1997). *A new vision for staff development*: Association for Supervision and Curriculum Development.

Suen, L. (2005). Teaching epidemiology using WebCT: Application of the seven principles of good practice. *The Journal of Nursing Education, 44*(3), 143–146.

Todnem, G., & Warner, M. P. (1994). Demonstrating the benefits of staff development: An interview with Thomas R. Guskey. *Journal of Staff Development, 15*(3), 63–65.

Walker, D. (1999, October). Technology and literacy: Raising the bar. *Educational Leadership, 57*(2), 18–32.

Webber, C. F., & Scott, S. (2008). Entrepreneurship and educational leadership development: A Canadian and Australian perspective. *International Electronic Journal in Leadership Learning, 12*(11).

Wenger, E. (2003). Communities of practice and social learning systems. In R. Gardner, D. Nicolini, S. Gherardi & D. Yanow (Eds.), *Knowing in organizations: A practice-based approach.* Armonk, NY: M.E. Sharpe.

Wenger, E. C., & Snyder, W. M. (2000). Communities of practice: The organizational frontier. *Harvard Business Review, 78*(1), 139–146.

Chapter 11

Game Informed Virtual Patients
Catalysts for Online Learning Communities and Professional Development of Medical Teachers

Michael Begg
University of Edinburgh, UK

David Dewhurst
University of Edinburgh, UK

Michael Ross
University of Edinburgh, UK

ABSTRACT

Modern medical education necessitates a complex interleaving of issues relating to practice, professional and personal development, teaching and learning. This complexity has led, in part, to medical education being persistently located in the vanguard of eLearning development. Here, the authors describe our approach to the development of virtual patient resources and in particular how this iterative dialogue arising from the allied processes of practice, reflection and pedagogy required to create new learning tools and resources has contributed to professional development of those engaged in teaching medical students and in building online learning communities at the University of Edinburgh.

INTRODUCTION

Communication and network technologies have played an increasingly visible role in global culture since the early 1990s when the Microsoft Windows operating system and the expansion of the Internet into what we now recognise as the World Wide Web brought affordable hardware and similarly cost effective innovations in data searching, content creation and communication. The education sector has, over time, increasingly turned to information and communication technology (ICT), largely with a view to increasing capacity and reducing costs across administrative and business operations, as well as to increasing the quantity of educational resources available to teachers and students.

ICT continues to impact upon the processes of teaching and learning, and is now broadly regarded to be an integral component of the learning landscape

DOI: 10.4018/978-1-60566-780-5.ch011

(Laurillard, 1993) typified by the increasingly widespread use of Virtual Learning and Teaching Environments (VLEs), digital learning and library resources, e-assessment tools and software packages and Web 2.0 applications. The range of tools and applications available to teachers continues to grow, while eLearning literature commonly reports an increased degree of learner satisfaction, potential for rich engagement, a high degree of interactivity, and increased student adoption of self-directed learning habits. Equally compelling factors influencing the integration of digital technology into teaching and learning are contemporary cultural drivers towards mass Higher Education, widening access and lifelong learning. Numerous countries have declared ambitions to significantly increase the number of students entering into Higher Education and it is advances in ICT in general and eLearning in particular which make such ambitions possible (Littlejohn, 2003).

However, eLearning is still a relatively young area of development and can perhaps still be considered to be in a period of transition (Laurillard, 2007). It also has very broad application across different disciplines and different levels of education. In an attempt to narrow the focus, in this chapter, we have focussed on a particular community of practice – medical education – and how its various processes related to teaching, learning, reflection, professional development and activity recording are attempting to engage with the affordances the new digital technologies in the most meaningful and appropriate way.

Although the term "eLearning" is often used in very general terms about ICT in educational contexts, it is perhaps more appropriately used when considering the range of pedagogic and related activities associated with personal learning and professional development. We believe that successful eLearning offers user-centred, flexible opportunities for self-directed, reflective learning practices. It offers the potential for contextualised learning opportunities and acts as an effective agent for developing learning communities through a broad range of direct user communication options such as email, Voice-Over Internet Protocol (e.g. Skype), discussion boards and online conferencing.

More recently, the eLearning landscape has seen the introduction of a plethora of so-called Web2.0 applications, typified by social networking sites such as MySpace, Facebook and Bebo, and benefitted from the associated opportunities for content creation, syndication and management, cross platform delivery and overall user control. Blogs, wikis, podcasts and vodcasts, social bookmarking and content-tagging are all becoming increasingly commonplace within our educational institutions. Whatever threats these advancements may pose to the traditional organisational and political structures of our institutions they are unquestionably having a direct impact upon our learning communities. Learners, at every level, can now easily locate, author, share, discuss and aggregate information, establish collaborative networking relationships and project partnerships with peers and, effectively, steer their own personal and professional development.

eLEARNING

eLearning is not merely a phenomenon that impacts upon learners. The implementation of eLearning tools and applications impacts upon all other stakeholders within the learning environment – particularly teachers (Ellaway, Begg, Dewhurst, & Macleod, 2005). It would seem clear that in developing the skills required to create new learning materials in unfamiliar media, and adopting new, equally unfamiliar approaches to creating learning content and educational activities presents considerable challenges for teaching staff.

Virtual Learning Environments (VLEs) are becoming ubiquitous in European and North American Higher Education institutions and an increasing number of these institutions have integrated these "virtual" versions of their course identities so deeply as to now offer online distance learning degree programmes, often at a Masters level, whereby students undertake a full course of study without ever physically entering the fabric of the institution. The University of Edinburgh has developed a number of such online courses (http://postgraduateprogrammesonline.ed.ac. uk/) and prominent amongst those is the MSc in Clinical Education aimed at healthcare professional educators.

The needs of medical education are both singular and particular. While HE institutions may commonly acquire a license for one of a number of generic off-the-shelf VLE solutions, it is often the case in the UK and elsewhere, that medical programmes – due both to the singular structure and activity patterns of medical education and the fact that such courses are in the vanguard of new developments – will, where resources allow, opt for bespoke VLE solutions, even if this solution is viewed to sit at odds with the dominant institutional system (Cook, 2001). This inclination again towards adopting tailored solutions for the singular challenges posed by the constraints of medical education is another factor contributing towards a position of commitment towards developing, implementing and evaluating the highest possible quality of eLearning tools and activities.

Whilst, like VLEs, these highly flexible tools may sit somewhat awkwardly within the socio-political makeup of other institutional technologies (McGee & Begg, 2008), they also offer responsive opportunities for collaboration, collection, recording and community building activities within peer groups. This has seen educators effectively work "under the wire" beyond the reach of institutional systems in order to progress their teaching or professional development (Begg, Ellaway, Dewhurst, & Macleod, 2007a)

To understand why eLearning has developed such a particularly close relationship of innovation and integration with healthcare education it may be of some value to look at the evolving nature of medical education itself and how the adoption of new technologies into practice has prompted a symbiotic development of both educative and developmental domains, as clearly evinced by the emergence of virtual patients

MEDICAL EDUCATION

We use the term 'medical education' here to mean undergraduate and postgraduate training and continuing professional development of medical doctors. Evidence of medical education can be traced back at least 5,000 years (Calman, 2007), although historically very little attention has been paid to the appropriate training and support of medical teachers themselves. As with many other disciplines, there was an assumption that a good doctor would also be a good teacher - exemplified by the traditional medical adage "See one, do one, teach one". Over the past few decades, interest and research in medical education has progressed dramatically. Teaching techniques have become more complex and specialised with increasing focus on simulation, learning technologies and informatics. There has been a shift away from teaching traditional discipline-based subjects such as anatomy and physiology separately, towards more integrated systems-based approaches, where for example the anatomy, physiology, pathology, clinical presentations and treatments for diseases such as angina are learned together. Clinical case-based learning, early contact with patients and increasing emphasis on the importance of learning communication skills, ethics and practical procedures have also been given greater emphasis (Schmidt & Rickers 2007).

In almost all countries training and accreditation for those engaging in medical practice has long been carefully regulated (Parliament 1858; EU 1981; DOH 2007) - principally for reasons of patient safety. There has been no similar regulation and training for those involved in medical teaching. The relatively recent demand for more public accountability, quality assurance and transparency from the medical profession, together with the more pedagogical issues highlighted above, has had a very positive impact on medical education as a discipline. There has been a move towards all doctors being required to teach (GMC 2006a) and to include continuing professional development as a teacher in their annual appraisal (GMC, 2004). Some medical students are learning to teach as undergraduates (GMC, 2003), there is an expectation that those taking on more responsibilities in education will undertake further training or a higher degree (GMC 1999, 2006a; NES 2007; NMC 2007), and national and international organisations are working to define standards and appropriate training for medical teacher professional development (Association of American Medical Colleges 1998; GMC 2003; WFME 2003; Frank 2005; PMETB 2005; GMC 2007; Cumming & Ross 2008). Medical teaching as a discipline could therefore be said to be currently undergoing a process of 'professionalisation' (Academy of Medical Educators 2007; Calman, 2007)

Aspects of medical education that particularly stand-out from other disciplines in higher education include the teaching and learning and assessment of communication skills, clinical diagnostic skills, 'professionalism' and practical clinical procedures. Miller (1990) presents a helpful model of the stages of skill acquisition in which the learner first knows about the skill, then knows how to do it, then can show how to do it in a simulated environment, and then does it in practice. Whilst adequate exposure to real patients is essential to medical training at all levels, simulation enables core learning objectives to be contextualised without any risk to patients and is an important part of the preparation of medical students to treat real patients. Simulations include clinical problems, virtual patients, low-fidelity part-task mannequins (e.g. synthetic airways for intubation and skin for minor surgery), high-fidelity whole body simulators (used to simulate complex illnesses and emergency situations such

as cardiac arrest) and standardised ('simulated') patients or actors briefed on how to give a realistic performance of a patient.

THE NATURE OF MEDICAL PRACTICE

It is not appropriate to consider teaching, teacher development and technologies in isolation when attempting to establish a model for supporting these multiple objectives within a single integrated development environment. It may be appropriate – and more digestible – to focus on one key area of modern healthcare education that has instigated significant changes to formal curricula, approaches to teaching and learning and has explicit ramifications for professional development - namely the emergence, growth and use of virtual patients.

Members of the public generally go to a medical doctor for an opinion. They expect, amongst other things, that the doctor will diagnose what the problem is and formulate an appropriate plan to address it. Virtual patients enable students to practise these and other skills and can, therefore, help students develop some of the core skills required for effective practice as a doctor. Diagnosis and patient management are some of the most complex and challenging skills that students have to master however, consequently there must be considerable flexibility and potential for complexity in virtual patients created for this task.

Figure 1 shows a simplified medical consultation in which the doctor will first seek to establish a relationship and gather information about the patient and the reason for their attendance by listening, questioning, clinical examination and from other sources. From this information, which is often imprecise and incomplete, together with their scientific knowledge and clinical experience, they will exercise 'clinical judgement' in formulating a provisional or definitive 'diagnosis'. The doctor will then explain the problem(s) to the patient, discuss and advise on any relevant treat-

Figure 1. A simplified medical consultation

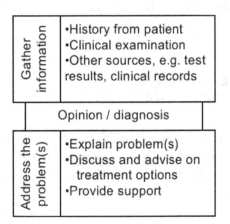

Gather information	•History from patient •Clinical examination •Other sources, e.g. test results, clinical records
	Opinion / diagnosis
Address the problem(s)	•Explain problem(s) •Discuss and advise on treatment options •Provide support

ment / management options, and provide support as required (Byrne & Long 1976).

This orderly approach in which the doctor gathers as much relevant information as possible and then formulates a diagnosis is generally referred-to as the '**Inductive**' method of diagnosis. In a study of over 2000 audio-taped consultations, it was found that most medical consultations seem to follow such a sequence (Byrne & Long, 1976). What they did not detect from the recordings, however, were the doctors' thought processes – which subsequent research has shown do not generally follow such a logical analytical sequence (Elstein, Shulman, & Sprafka, 1978; Norman, Young, & Brooks, 2007). As doctors gain experience in clinical practice and interact with many individual patients, there is evidence that they collect in memory an increasingly large number of typical patterns of illness presentation and progression, sometimes called 'illness scripts' (Schmidt & Rickers, 2007). It seems that when an expert doctor is confronted with a familiar presentation of an ill patient they will formulate a provisional diagnosis very early in the consultation, sometimes within seconds, and will then strategically seek information to prove or disprove their hypothesis. If their hypothesis is disproved, or further information is gathered which suggests

an alternative illness, a new provisional diagnosis will be made and tested. This has been referred-to as the '**Hypothetico-deductive**' method of diagnosis (Elstein, A. S., Shulman, L. S., & Sprafka, S. A., 1978; Norman, G., Young, M., & Brooks, L., 2007). It is likely that both novice and expert doctors actually use the hypothetico-deductive method in practice, although will revert to a more inductive method when confronted with an unfamiliar presentation of illness. Teaching students to use both approaches has been shown to result in improved diagnostic accuracy compared to using either alone (Kulatanga-Moruzi, Brooks, & Norman, 2001), and so this is the approach we have tried to adopt when developing virtual patients.

As an illustration of both diagnostic methods, imagine a previously healthy lady in her mid-thirties presenting to her general practitioner (GP) feeling 'tired all the time'. This is a common presentation in the UK, and statistically the most common cause by far is stress. There are numerous other potential causes of tiredness however, including depression, anaemia, thyroid problems, diabetes, chronic infections such as TB, heart or kidney failure, substance misuse, early rheumatoid arthritis, MS and various types of cancer and leukaemia (Hopcroft & Forte, 2003). An inductive approach to diagnosis in this case would involve taking a full history with questions relating to all possible causes, performing a full examination of all systems, and organising a battery of blood tests, x-rays and other investigations. The inductive doctor would then wait until they had all the information before making a diagnosis. Clearly this would take significantly longer than a typical 10-minute GP appointment. In practice, assuming the patient looks well and reports no worrying features (sometimes called 'red flags') the GP will often hypothesise early in the consultation that the cause of the tiredness might be stress, and will thus focus their questioning, examination and further management on proving or disproving this hypothesis. The hypothetico-deductive doctor will therefore focus on possible stressors, work and home situation, mood, sleep and the physical manifestations of stress. Critically, however, the doctor will also 'screen' for more serious potential causes of tiredness, with questions about weight loss, breathlessness and depression; inspection of the patient's records for previous serious illnesses; physical examination of the chest, abdomen, eyes and lymph glands; and possibly taking a blood test to check for anaemia, diabetes, thyroid problems, kidney failure and inflammation. The hypothetico-deductive doctor does not expect to find anything during this screen although remains vigilant, and does not check for all possible causes of tiredness, but seeks evidence which might refute their original hypothesis. If, for example, the patient reveals that they have lost weight without changing their calorie intake or exercise levels, or have enlarged lymph glands on examination, then more serious disease may be present and stress is less likely, so the doctor will make a new hypothesis to test.

Medical teachers are tasked with helping undergraduate students and postgraduate trainees develop and refine their expertise in clinical judgement and diagnosis. There are a number of problems inherent in trying to achieve this however, such as then high turnover and variability of patients presenting, and the lack of sufficiently detailed and immediate feedback typically available in clinical practice. These problems are being compounded by increasing student numbers, reduced numbers of hospital beds and enforced reductions on working hours for junior doctors. Becoming an expert in any field, whether sport, music or the medical diagnosis, requires a significant amount of deliberate practice. Some have even tried to quantify this in terms of the number of hours of practice required, with findings typically in the region of ten years or 10,000 hours (Ericsson, 2004; Ericsson, Krampe, & Tesch-Romer, 1993). The evidence suggests that deliberate practice is also required to maintain that expertise, and that when even highly experienced professionals are appropriately motivated they are

able to gradually improve their objective performance in representative tasks from their domain of expertise (Ericsson, Krampe, & Tesch-Romer, 1993). To do this, they need to identify an area of their performance that they want to improve, and find a way to perform the same or similar tasks repeatedly with detailed and immediate feedback on their performance (Ericsson, 2004). Unlike in music or sport however, doctors are typically introduced to their field in their late teens or early twenties rather than in early childhood, and there are often no 'gold standard' expert performances to emulate (Ericsson, 2004). Many expert doctors find it difficult to reflect-upon and articulate to a novice the thought processes that they went through to arrive at a particular clinical judgement or diagnosis. Because their diagnoses are often heavily influenced by pattern-recognition with a previous patient or 'illness script' and hypothetico-deductive diagnostic methods, they may find it difficult to tease-apart and reason the different elements of their clinical judgement to help learners understand the processes involved (Schmidt & Rickers 2007). Experts also typically find it difficult to identify where students went wrong when they make errors in their diagnoses, and how best to help them improve their skills. In considering what factors contribute to good teaching in such circumstances, the concept of scholarship in teaching (Fincher R-ME, Simpson DE, Mennin SP, Rosenfeld GC, & Rothman A., 2000; Glassic, 2000) can be a helpful guide. Integral to the concept of scholarship is the notion that the teacher is also a learner – continually trying to improve their own understanding and practice whilst teaching others to improve theirs. Part of the success of eLearning in medical education may be due to the way in which it forces expert clinicians to learn new skills and to critically reflect on their prior approaches to clinical and teaching practice.

eLEARNING IN MEDICAL EDUCATION

In the UK in the 1990s there were a number of national initiatives and a significant funding available to stimulate the use of ICT in higher education across a broad range of disciplines. Medical and biomedical education was prominent in many of these initiatives and the result was a plethora of interactive computer programs - commonly known as Computer-Assisted Learning (CAL) - and videos designed to support student learning of factual knowledge, principles and skills. Multimedia CDROMs, which incorporated a range of features to support learning (high-quality graphics; animation sequences to demonstrate dynamic principles; video (essential, for example, in illustrating abnormal gait patterns in some neurological conditions); audio; interactive self-assessments/quizzes; patient cases; simulated laboratory environments (virtual labs) in which students could collect data from simulated experiments) were the mainstay of e-learning during this period. Although this approach perhaps never achieved the cost-savings and efficiency gains predicted by those who funded such initiatives at that time, a number of studies in the biomedical sciences attempted to evaluate the educational effectiveness of these CAL programs. In general they demonstrated that students could manage their own learning very effectively, and that many of the learning objectives of the traditional teaching methods (lectures, practical classes) could be achieved (Coleman, Dewhurst, Meehan, & Williams, 1994; Dewhurst, Macleod, & Norris, 2000; Hughes, 2001; Rest, 1997; Tait, 1997)

The emergence of the Internet as a tool for supporting teaching and learning was the next major development and Virtual Learning Environments were becoming increasingly common by the end of the 20th Century.

'Virtual Learning Environments (VLEs) are a compelling and powerful way to support and manage modern medical education processes. A purposively aligned and built VLE, despite time and resource implications for development, can help to integrate and normalise procedures and provide a central access point and reference mechanism for all of a course's geographically and culturally diverse communities' (Ellaway, Dewhurst, & Cumming, 2003)

Medical education, especially the training of doctors, has always tended to be at the forefront of adoption of and innovation in eLearning. There are many possible reasons for this, including political factors and relatively good funding and support from the profession and Government, but one of the most significant factors is that of patient safety. Patient welfare is a defining principal of medical practice and training novices to make diagnoses, carry-out practical procedures and prescribe medication and other treatments is inherently fraught with potential dangers. Any method that presents a suitable opportunity to acquire the broad range of skills associated with professional practice without compromising patient safety is therefore of great interest. Case-based discussion and simulation training, using part-task mannequins, high-fidelity simulators, standardised patients and actors are examples of activities in which the core learning objectives can be contextualised and achieved without risk to patients. Another reason for early adoption of innovations in eLearning in medical education is to ensure learners are exposed to an adequate breadth of clinical experience. With increasing numbers of medical students passing through medical schools, drivers to reduce the number of patients in hospital their duration of stay, increasingly stringent directives governing doctors' working hours, and directives from governing bodies such as the UK General Medical Council declaring that "opportunistic learning" is no longer sufficient in healthcare education, it is difficult to ensure students have sufficient clinical exposure. All of these factors have stimulated the development of learning environments and resources where the virtual is increasingly expected to emulate, wherever it can, the real.

Another possible reason directly leading from this necessity for *reality*, and one which we will expand upon further, is the "practicum" nature of healthcare education. Schön (1987) defined the practicum as "a setting designed for the task of learning a practice. In a context that approximates a practice world, students learn. . . by undertaking projects that simulate and simplify practice; or they take on real-world projects under close supervision". Essentially, the suggestion is that the process of teaching should reflect as closely as possible the nature and context of the skills being taught and so the context of the teaching should, as closely as possible, reflect the reality of the practice. This sets the ground for the notion that the teacher and the pupil should, ideally, be sharing the same environment, the same resources, and, generally, accept that they are involved in a cyclical professional process of acquiring understanding, reflecting on that understanding, delivering insight, reflecting further upon feedback received, thereby returning to the point of acquiring understanding. Computer mediated activities, whether gaming, participating in an online social network such as Facebook or MySpace, or file-sharing, to name a few of the multiform activities undertaken online, are highly adaptable at connecting communities of individuals each of whom are empowered within the relevant environment. eLearning should be seen as no different in this. There can and should be appropriate representation and affordance for the full range of users in a single environment. It could, therefore, be suggested that a suitably constructed eLearning platform is a suitably aligned extension of the principles of the practicum.

CASE-BASED LEARNING AND VIRTUAL PATIENTS

Descriptions of individual patients and their medical problems, typically referred-to as 'Case Studies', have been used in medical education for centuries (Calman, 2007; Charlton & Walston, 1998). Typically they have been used to either exemplify a particular condition or clinical presentation and encourage students to generalise from the example, or alternatively to challenge generalisations and assumptions by offering exceptions to the rule and unusual or unexpected outcomes. In medicine there is also an increasing trend towards 'Narrative-based medicine' (Greenhalgh & Hurwitz, 1998), with increased awareness of the importance of patient's stories and the shortcomings of traditional positivist 'Evidence-Based Medicine' (Greenhalgh, 2006; Sackett, Straus, Richardson, Rosenberg, & Haynes, 2000). The development and use of virtual patients is an area of particularly rapid growth with several initiatives throughout Europe and the United States providing content, authoring tools and delivery platforms (Begg, 2008; Begg, Ellaway, Dewhurst, & Macleod, 2006). Meta frameworks, such as the Medbiquitous virtual patient standard have also emerged in order to maximise the potential for sharing of these virtual cases. Virtual patients are scenario-based learning activities, and are used in medical and veterinary education in numerous institutions worldwide. At the University of Edinburgh they are used in a variety of ways including: developing clinical diagnostic and decision-making skills; teaching and formatively assessing knowledge of basic and clinical sciences such as physiology and pharmacology; and enabling experiential learning ('learning through doing'). In some courses students particularly in the later years of their courses are engaged in developing their own virtual patients and this has proved to be a very effective and popular activity. The nature of the virtual patient also varies: some present a strongly didactic, linear and strictly codified exploration of key clinical data in information-gathering, diagnosis and treatment; others attempt to contextualise the learning experience by presenting believable narratives in realistic settings that invite the learner to *perform* in the role of a practitioner.

At Edinburgh the scalable creation of online resources has been facilitated by the in-house development of a range of easy to use authoring and delivery tools, suitable for academic and clinical teachers with little technical know-how. EROS (the Edinburgh Re-usable Object Sequencer), a web-based authoring tool, supports the creation of interactive, tutorial-style resources. It comprises a series of templates based on a range of common question types (MCQ, short text, extended matching, etc) which are most-often used for the development of formative self-assessment quizzes. Exemplars include a comprehensive pathology course (120+ individual modules), a number of clinical skills support resources and a wide range of case-based learning modules. These provide students with opportunities to test their understanding of the curriculum knowledge base, often within a contextualised and recognisable case narrative framework. EROS has had considerable impact in enabling content creation by academic staff with little intervention from learning technologists and to date in excess of 700 learning resources have been created in this way.

Another tool, Labyrinth, provides for the authoring of more complex "branching path" case narratives that take a game informed approach to the development of virtual patients (Begg, Dewhurst, & Macleod, 2005; Begg et al., 2006; Begg, Ellaway, Dewhurst, & Macleod, 2007b). Typically authors encourage learner engagement through a highly contextualised requirement for learners to adopt a meaningful role in the clinical scenario (e.g. junior doctor, patient, nurse), make critical clinical decisions (define the physical examination process they will follow, decide which tests to request, interpret the test data, come up with a differential diagnosis, and decide on a suitable treatment). Decisions have consequence and allowing the learner to work through even 'inappropriate' choices promotes learning. Learners apply critical, reflective reasoning whilst performing "in character" within a plausible real-life clinical scenario.

Labyrinth, like EROS, is designed to be usable by teachers with little technical knowledge, and the signs are that uptake by staff will be high. Locally, Labyrinth cases have already been embedded into the undergraduate MBChB programme in modules relating to clinical emergency training, general practice and surgery. The contextualised and character-rich cases are also playing a significant role in postgraduate training via the online distance MSc programme in Surgical Sciences, and further afield Labyrinth is being used in the development of new healthcare curricula in Malawi (Dewhurst & Chimalizeni, 2008)

The concept of game informed learning (Begg, 2008) is similar to the more familiar idea of games based learning (Prensky, 2000). Game informed learning proposes that through the concepts of play and narrative commonly attributed to successful games – contextual character roles for users, a responsive environment, a reasonable degree of empowerment for users within the game world, frequent feedback, etc – a richly compelling and immersive learning experience may be produced. Game informed learning differs from game based learning principally in that it argues that the resulting application need not be, explicitly, a game. Rather, it may be a learning activity, such as an interactive virtual patient case scenario, that applies the principals of games and narrative to enhance the impact of that activity.

Considering, once again, the level of experience and the variance of approaches that clinical practice implies we can draw parallels between diagnostic approaches and the particular style of virtual patient development accommodated by the two tools, EROS and Labyrinth. The inductive approach with its emphasis on methodical gathering of ordered evidence may be appropriately delivered via the strong linear framework of EROS, while the hypothetico-deductive approach may be best served by Labyrinth's ability to host multiple highly individualised pathways taken through a single case – allowing learners to explore multiple 'what if?' questions at each stage of their progress through a virtual case.

Figure 2. a) Example of a computer assisted learning (CAL) sequence, featuring a pair matching question concerned with Reproductive Health; b) The editing interface within the Edinburgh Reusable Object Sequencer (EROS) for the CAL self assessment page shown in figure 2a

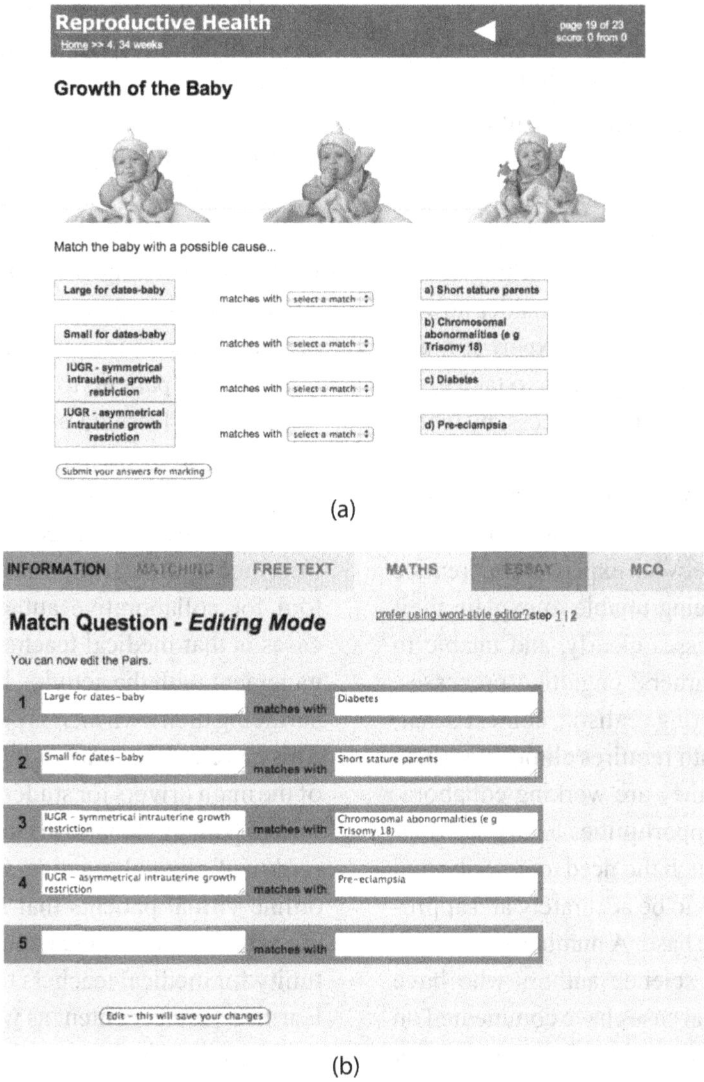

(a)

(b)

VIRTUAL PATIENT CREATION AND PROFESSIONAL DEVELOPMENT

The task of creating virtual patients requires medical teachers to reflect on their practice in a very focussed way that seems to be quite different to their reflection in normal clinical practice. This would suggest that such enhanced reflection should improve their clinical practice and encourage them to be more reflective about other aspects of their practice (Schön, 1983; Schön, 1987). Active participation might also encourage them to take a more scholarly approach to their clinical teaching and practice, and make greater use-of, and contribute more to, the literature and to academic networks of like-minded practitioners (Boyer, 1990; Glassic, 2000). In our experience, active collaboration even on this small scale has also led to the establishment of small online communities of practice, which have been previously shown to be inherently beneficial to learning (Ellaway, 2005).

We have observed, through running virtual patient authoring workshops in Edinburgh, London and Malawi with a range of healthcare professional educators, how the process of applying the principles of game informed learning to the creation of virtual patients has led, somewhat inadvertently, to game informed teaching. As an illustration of this phenomenon consider how as healthcare professionals develop expertise much of their cognitive processing seems to take place at the subconscious level. This process, by which knowledge effectively becomes tacit (Baumard, 1999) or hidden, has also been called "thin-slicing" (Gladwell, 2005). This can lead to a problem with knowledge transfer between expert and apprentice due to the experts being unable to explain their own cognitive processes clearly, and unable to identify errors in learners' cognitive processes. The process of authoring realistic, context sensitive cases in Labyrinth requires clinical teachers – particularly when they are working collaboratively with peers – opportunities to *surface* their tacit knowledge through the need to describe and capture the processes to be accurately and appropriately set out in the case. A number of clinical, academic and basic science authors who have worked on such virtual cases have commented on the difficulty and complexity of such work, but also the considerable personal and academic gains and satisfaction associated with it. This has led an increasing number of clinical teachers to submit the work they do in authoring virtual patients as part of their professional CPD commitments. It is here that we can observe an illustration of the direct and explicit linking of practice, learning and professional development. Virtual patients reflecting real life and practice, are written by practitioners who, surface tacit knowledge through the process of authoring thereby increasing personal awareness and reflectivity, and at the same time

they explicitly document these to develop and enhance the quality of a teaching resource. The issue then becomes how to frame the activities of multiple practitioners with a similar degree of flexibility and responsiveness.

PROFESSIONAL DEVELOPMENT OF MEDICAL TEACHERS

In seeking to offer undergraduate medical students a balanced education drawing on the strengths of evidence-based and narrative approaches, we have found virtual patients to offer many advantages to "traditional" learning and teaching methods.

Observation of the process of development of virtual patient case scenarios has shown that one of the positive consequences of using a game informed approach and making use of an online tool for collaborative authoring virtual patient cases is that medical teachers have, through engagement with the activity, been steered towards surfacing their own *tacit* professional knowledge. This has clear advantages if one assumes that one of the main drivers for students to undertake these virtual patient scenarios is to gain insight into the *reality* of clinical practice. Cleverly constructed online virtual patients that incorporate many of the principles of online games offer a real opportunity for medical teachers to support students in learning factual content as well as more complex skills such as the hypothetico-deductive method of diagnosis. The process of developing virtual patients also affords many direct opportunities for professional development of the teachers, including:

- Enhanced content knowledge and potentially enhanced clinical skills – whilst creating a virtual patient teachers will question, structure and identify gaps in their knowledge and are likely to go and read more about it.
- Development as educators – through

Figure 3. a) A navigation chart of a game informed virtual patient scenario authored in the Labyrinth application. The figure illustrates the degree of branching complexity that can be introduced using this kind of technology;b) A screen grab from the complex branching case virtual patient scenario mapped out in figure 3a.

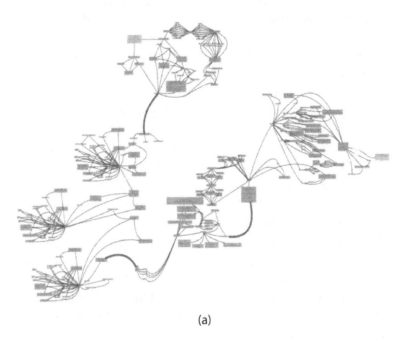

(a)

(b)

reflection on current teaching practice, learning new skills and techniques and engagement with new, often unfamiliar, educational processes and methods in creating online learning resources for students.

- Community-building – in many instances VP development is a collaborative activity with development teams often comprising a small number of practicing clinicians and other professional (e.g. in one patient case there may be a psychiatrist, a GP, a learning technologist and physiologist developing a virtual patient together in an online environment). They will share and discuss knowledge and experience in an effort to develop a highly interactive and challenging learning resource. Often there is a challenge to develop a VP where the learner can adopt different roles – that of a junior/novice doctor, that of another healthcare professional (e.g. nurse) or that of the patient. Such peer learning is a particularly valuable staff development activity for all concerned.
- Reflective practice – by reflecting in and on action, as well as enhancing professional knowledge and skills, medical teachers may also develop their abilities and attitudes towards reflective practice itself (Schön, 1987).
- Enhanced integration of clinical and teaching roles – clinicians who have been involved in the development of virtual patients become more attuned to gathering material and examples from their everyday work which might be suitable for teaching. They are likely to think about and record this in a structure and format which is suitable for educational use.
- Increased awareness of the need for professional development – clinical teachers have a responsibility to support and assess student professional development (GMC, 2003, 2006b; NMC, 2007). Virtual patients can be used as a means to achieve this in

a realistic yet safe environment. By creating realistic patient scenarios and ethical dilemmas to train and assess student professional development, educators are also forced to reflect and evaluate themselves.

Such processes of personal professional development, teaching skill and professional excellence cannot, in the present culture, be considered in isolation. There are complex interactions between all of these factors. There are also constraints on such interactions – not least of time, distance and funding. The requirements of practice, and the affordances of available technology, increasingly compel us towards a strategy that allows for integrated online environments in which such interactions and developments might take-place.

ONLINE COMMUNITIES OF MEDICAL TEACHERS

The potential benefits of interactive and supportive communities of practice are well described in the literature (Wenger, 1998). As we move into what some have described as the 'post-modern' era of education, there is increased recognition of the need to share knowledge, experience and insight between academic disciplines and professions – to break-down traditional barriers separating academic and professional groups and their exclusive 'silo' of knowledge, and to increase the value of such knowledge to society through a process of 'knowledge transfer' (Jacob, 2003; Ozga, 2007). Academics and practitioners can benefit immensely and immediately from increased interaction with similarly motivated groups, and have much to learn from each other. Traditionally there have been multiple cultural, social, financial, spatial and temporal constraints to such interaction. With the growth of transnational organisations, increasing economic integration and the rapid development of information technologies and telecommunications, sometimes collectively referred-to as 'globalisation', has come many new opportunities (Giddens, 1990). As Hudson and Lowe write:

"We may have to rethink our understanding of the nature of 'society' with its relatively fixed social structures and geographical boundaries... Globalisation is essentially about the networking of the planet – through the Internet, satellite telecommunications and rapid transport – by new forms of local, regional and transnational social connections, economic markets and political structures" (Hudson & Lowe, 2004).

Collaborative online virtual patient creation and development represents a fruitful exploration of such new opportunities, with potential benefits to those teachers and technologists involved in the creation process, students and trainees in medicine, veterinary medicine and allied health professions, and to the educational and healthcare institutions with which they are associated.

As experience of developing and using eLearning resources in medical education matures there are signs that a community lifecycle is emerging. An innovation (in this instance, virtual patients) leads to reflection on existing practice. Collaborative development of resources and adopting a novel approach (game-informed learning) to the development of resources leads to further innovation. The process of authoring itself engages further reflection and personal development (the "surfacing" of professional *tacit* knowledge) as well as indicating potential impact upon the evolution of the broader curriculum. Reflective commentary, observation, evaluation and other evidence gathering activities are gathered within the medical education community, as is data about how students engage with the innovative materials and whether they are fulfilling the learning objectives for which they were designed. The community dialogue leads (ideally) not only to further enhancement of authoring skills which might directly enhance and improve existing

virtual patients, but also to the kind of informed, reflective community dialogue that leads both to the ongoing professional development of those involved and completes the "cycle" through the generation of new innovations.

FUTURE TRENDS

The University of Edinburgh is embarking on a process of deliberately expanding the role of the *traditional* VLE to accommodate the processes, practices and reflections of the growing community of healthcare educators. It is hoped that by increasing teachers' awareness and opportunities for interaction, by aggregating previously compartmentalised activities and related knowledge and skills such as case-authoring, CPD recording, portfolio development, reflection on student feedback and evaluation, by utilising the syndication and aggregation principals of Web 2.0, and by engaging in the emerging communities of practice that are growing around innovative applications such as Labyrinth; it should be possible to enhance healthcare education delivery and professional development in a number of ways:

- Improved alignment between activity creation and delivery
- Built in mechanisms for quality assurance (QA) through opportunities for peer review
- Increased levels of "buy-in" from healthcare educators due to broader base of activities relating to personal professional development, teaching and networking
- Improved quality of teaching and learning resources accorded by the *lifecycle* support in which students become competent educators within a single supported community framework

Exemplar models for nurturing online communities of practice through these kinds of approaches are emerging. In Malawi there is a great deal of activity addressing the identified need for curricular reform in the country's quest to generate greater numbers of healthcare professionals and self directed learners. An online collaborative working environment (CWE) proved to be a powerful way of enabling geographically disparate healthcare workers (doctors, clinical officers and nurses) across Malawi to collectively discuss case development, curricular prioritisation and resource collection, whilst authoring learning activities using Labyrinth and seeking peer feedback on case authoring activities. The Malawi Healthcare CWE is forming the heart of the emergent VLE for healthcare education and, critically, the teachers have not only bought-in to the online environment, they have, in a very real sense, created it.

Similarly, in a recent project with Chest, Heart and Stroke Scotland (CHSS) and National Health Service Education Scotland (NES) a CWE platform was developed which allowed groups of nurses, clinicians and teachers to gather and describe resources and requirements for a learning resource concerning the core competencies required by those working with those affected by strokes. Learning activities were collaboratively authored addressing each of the core competencies in turn and, as the project development reached completion the same environment formed the base for users to enter and undertake the activities. A self-assessment process underpinned with formal certification was also incorporated thereby presenting another complete model of a single environment supporting learning, reflection, content and activity development, delivery and recording of achievement.

In another initiative that more explicitly taps into the potential of virtual patient authoring to impact upon personal professional reflective practice The Royal College of Surgeons in Edinburgh, who are responsible for CPD of surgeons from all around the world, have recently put forward proposals to explore the usefulness of creating and engaging with interactive, scenario-based learning pathways or mazes (initially devised by small teams of 'expert' surgeons) as a means of acquiring and demonstrating their ability to apply specialist and up-to-date knowledge as part of the recertification process essential for continued practice.

It is arguably also the case that as long as eLearning activities attract funding streams largely out-with core institutional teaching and learning budgets, issues of related staff development – including teacher professional development – may also be forced out-with traditional institutional frameworks. Clinical teachers at the University of Edinburgh, as elsewhere, currently acquire information and knowledge from disparate sources such as subject specific special interest groups, practitioner mailing lists such as the UK's jiscmail service, as well as through the more traditional professional discourse afforded by institutional training, conferences, journals, networking, etc. Potentially such an outward search for support and information could isolate teachers from their own local context and community. In Edinburgh, we are actively seeking to capitalise on such external online resources, communities and activities by pooling them into 'ClinED' - an online collaborative learning environment for clinical educators, encouraging a shared collective engagement with external agencies (Ross, Blaney, Cameron, Begg, & Cumming, 2008). This online educator community environment is closely aligned to the Virtual Learning Environments for undergraduate medical teaching and the MSc in Clinical Education programme (www.clinicaleducation.mvm. ed.ac.uk). The anticipation is that, over time, the divide between different groups of clinical teachers undertaking professional development activities will become increasingly narrowed.

CONCLUSION

This chapter has focused on professional development of medical educators and in particular how their involvement in designing and creating innovative, scenario-based learning resources (virtual patients) has contributed to that activity. The formation of online communities of practice in medical education has also been explored and ways in which the technologies at their disposal in an online environment can support multi-specialty and multi-professional development have been described. It is clear that eLearning and ICT more generally can provide a vehicle for enhancing professional engagement with the education of students and for self-development in numerous ways.

Game informed virtual patients have proved to be extremely useful in helping students learn complex skills such as medical diagnosis. As a very welcome by-product of virtual patient construction, we have witnessed members of clinical and academic staff become more cohesive as a community, develop their understanding and skills in teaching and practice, and become more aware of themselves as learners and reflective practitioners. Whilst the training of medical teachers, the development of online learning communities and the creation of virtual patients themselves are all still at a relatively early stage, already there seems to be considerable potential gains for all involved.

Medical education is often in the vanguard of innovation and it is possible that what we are describing and observing in medical education practice now will extend into teacher professional development in other disciplines and at all levels in the future.

REFERENCES

Academy of Medical Educators. (2007). 14th December 2007, from http://www.medicaleducators.org/

Association of American Medical Colleges. (1998). *Learning objectives for medical student education.* Retrieved 15th April 2007, from www.aamc.org/meded/msop

Baumard, P. (1999). *Tacit knowledge in organizations.* London, UK: Sage.

Begg, M. (2008). Leveraging Game Informed Learning in Higher Education. *Medical Teacher, 30*(2), 155–158. doi:10.1080/01421590701874041

Begg, M., Dewhurst, D., & Macleod, H. (2005). Game Informed Learning: Applying computer game processes to Higher Education. *Innovate, 1*(6).

Begg, M., Ellaway, R., Dewhurst, D., & Macleod, H. (2006). Virtual Patients: considerations of narrative and gameplay. In M. Burmester, D. Gerhard, & F. Thissen (Eds.), *Digital Game Based Learning: 4th International Symposium for Information Design* (pp. 101 - 113). Stuttgart Media University: Universitatsverlag Karlsruhe.

Begg, M., Ellaway, R., Dewhurst, D., & Macleod, H. (2007a). *Logos and Mythos: the political dilemmas of Web 2.0 in an accreditation-driven educational environment.* Paper presented at the Ice 2007 - Ideas in Cyberspace Education, Loch Lomond, UK.

Begg, M., Ellaway, R., Dewhurst, D., & Macleod, H. (2007b). Transforming Professional Healthcare Narratives Into Structured Game Informed Learning Activities. *Innovate, 3*(6).

Boyer, E. L. (1990). *Scholarship reconsidered: priorities of the professoriate.* Princeton, New Jersey: Carnegie Foundation for the Advancement of Teaching.

Byrne, P., & Long, B. E. L. (1976). *Doctors talking to Patients.* London: HMSO.

Calman, K. C. (2007). *Medical education: past, present and future.* Edinburgh: Elsevier.

Charlton, B. G., & Walston, F. (1998). Individual case studies in clinical research. *Journal of Evaluation in Clinical Practice, 4*(2), 147–155. doi:10.1046/j.1365-2753.1998.00011.x

Coleman, I., Dewhurst, D., Meehan, A. S., & Williams, A. D. (1994). A computer simulation for learning about the physiological response to exercise. *The American Journal of Physiology, 11*, s2–s9.

Cook, J. (2001). *JTAP 623 - The Role of Virtual Learning Environments in UK Medical Education* (No. JTAP 623). UK: Institute for Learning and Research Technologyo. Document Number)

Cumming, A. D., & Ross, M. T. (2008). *The Tuning Project (medicine) – learning outcomes / competences for undergraduate medical education in Europe*. Edinburgh: The University of Edinburgh. Available online: www.tuning-medicine. com. Document Number)

Dewhurst, D., & Chimalizeni, Y. (2008). *Collaborative development of online virtual patients for medical and healthcare professional education in Malawi*. Paper presented at the eLearning Africa.

Dewhurst, D., Hardastle, J., Hardcastle, P. T., & Stuart, E. (1994). Comparison of a computer simulation program with a traditional laboratory practical class for teaching the principles of intestinal absorption. *The American Journal of Physiology, 12*(1), s95–s103.

Dewhurst, D., Macleod, H., & Norris, T. (2000). Independent Student Learning Aided by Computers: An Acceptable Alternative to Lectures? *Computers & Education, 35*, 223–241. doi:10.1016/S0360-1315(00)00033-6

DOH. (2007). *Trust, assurance and safety - the regulation of health professionals for the 21st Century*. London: Department of Health, HMSOo. Document Number)

Ellaway, R., Begg, M., Dewhurst, D., & Macleod, H. (2005). In A Glass Darkly: identity, agency and the role of the learning technologist in shaping the learning environment. *E-Learning, 3*(1), 75-87.

Ellaway, R., Dewhurst, D., & Cumming, A. (2003). Managing and supporting medical education with a virtual learning environment: the Edinburgh Electronic Medical Curriculum. *Medical Teacher, 25*(4), 372–380. doi:10.1080/0142159031000136789

Ellaway, R. H. (2005). *Evaluating a Virtual Learning Environment in Medical Education.* Unpublished PhD, University of Edinburgh, Edinburgh.

Elstein, A. S., Shulman, L. S., & Sprafka, S. A. (1978). *Medical problem solving: an analysis of clinical reasoning*. Cambridge, MA: Harvard University Press.

Ericsson, K. A. (2004). Deliberate practice and the acquisition and maintenance of expert performance in medicine and related domains. *Academic Medicine, 79*(10Supplement), S70–S81. doi:10.1097/00001888-200410001-00022

Ericsson, K. A., Krampe, R. T., & Tesch-Romer, C. (1993). The role of deliberate practice in the acquisition of expert performance. *Psychological Review, 100*(3), 363–406. doi:10.1037/0033-295X.100.3.363

EU. (1981). Council Directive 81/1057/EEC of 14 December 1981 concerning the mutual recognition of diplomas, certificates and other evidence of the formal qualifications of doctors, nurses responsible for general care, dental practitioners and veterinary surgeons respectively, with regard to acquired rights.

Fincher, R.-M. E., Simpson, D. E., Mennin, S. P., Rosenfeld, G. C., Rothman, A., & McGrew, M. C. (2000). Scholarship in teaching: an imperative for the 21st Century. *Academic Medicine, 75*(9), 887–894. doi:10.1097/00001888-200009000-00009

Frank, J. R. (2005). *The CanMEDS 2005 physician competency framework. Better standards. Better physicians. Better care.* Ottowa: The Royal College of Physicians and Surgeons of Canadao. Document Number)

Giddens, A. (1990). *The Consequences of Modernity.* Cambridge: Polity Press.

Gladwell, M. (2005). *Blink: the power of thinking without thinking.* New York: Little Brown & Co.

Glassic, C. E. (2000). Boyer's expanded definition of scholarship, the standards for assessing scholarship, and the elusiveness of the scholarship of teaching. *Academic Medicine, 75*(9), 877–880.

GMC. (1999). *The doctor as teacher.* London: General Medical Council.

GMC. (2003). *Tomorrow's doctors: recommendations on undergraduate medical education.* London: General Medical Council.

GMC. (2004). *Continuing professional development.* London: General Medical Council.

GMC. (2006a). *Good medical practice.* London: General Medical Council.

GMC. (2006b). *Strategic proposals for student fitness to practice: call for informal feedback.* London: General Medical Councilo. Document Number)

GMC. (2007). *The new doctor.* London: General Medical Council.

Greenhalgh, T. (2006). *How to read a paper: the basics of evidence-based medicine.* Oxford: Blackwell Publishing Ltd.

Greenhalgh, T., & Hurwitz, B. (1998). *Narrative based medicine.* London: BMJ Books.

Hopcroft, K., & Forte, V. (2003). *Symptom sorter* (2nd ed.). Abingdon: Radcliffe Medical Press Ltd.

Hudson, J., & Lowe, S. (2004). *Understanding the Policy Process: analysing welfare policy and practice.* Bristol: The Policy Press.

Hughes, I. E. (2001). Do computer simulations of laboratory practicals meet learning needs? *Trends in Pharmacological Sciences, 22,* 71–74. doi:10.1016/S0165-6147(00)01605-9

Jacob, M. (2003). Rethinking Science and Commodifying Knowledge. *Policy Futures in Education, 1*(1), 125–142. doi:10.2304/pfie.2003.1.1.3

Kulatanga-Moruzi, C., Brooks, L. R., & Norman, G. R. (2001). Co-ordination of analytical and similarity-based processing strategies and expertise in dermatological diagnosis. *Learning and Teaching Medicine, 13,* 110–116. doi:10.1207/S15328015TLM1302_6

Laurillard, D. (1993). *Rethinking University Teaching - A framework for the effective use of educational technology.* UK: Routledge

Laurillard, D. (2007). In H. Beetham & R. Sharpe (Eds.), *Rethinking Pedagogy for a Digital Age.* Oxford: Routledge.

Leathard, H. L., & Dewhurst, D. (1995). Comparison of the cost-effectiveness of a computer assisted learning program with a tutored demonstration to teach intestinal motility to medical students. *Assoc for Learning Technology Journal, 3*(1), 118–125.

Littlejohn, A. (2003). Issues in reusing online resources. In A. Littlejohn (Ed.), *Reusing Online Resources: a sustainable approach to eLearning* (pp. 1-6). London: Kogan Page.

McGee, J. B., & Begg, M. (2008). What medical educators need to know about "Web 2.0". *Medical Teacher, 30*(2), 164–169. doi:10.1080/01421590701881673

Miller, G. E. (1990). The Assessment of CLinical Skills / Competence / Performance. *Academic Medicine, 65*(9), 63–67. doi:10.1097/00001888-199009000-00045

NES. (2007). *NES survey of Scottish consultant workforce*. Edinburgh: NHS Education for Scotlando. Document Number)

NMC. (2007). *Standards to support learning and assessment in practice: NMC standards for mentors, practice teachers and teachers*. Available online: http://www.nmc-uk.org/: Nursing and Midwifery Council.

Norman, G., Young, M., & Brooks, L. (2007). Non-analytical models of clinical reasoning: the role of experience. *Medical Education, 41*, 1140–1145.

Ozga, J. (2007). Knowledge and Policy: Research and Knowledge Transfer. *Critical Studies in Education, 48*(1), 63–78. doi:10.1080/17508480601120988

PMETB. G. a. (2005). *Principles of good medical education and training*. London: General Medical Council and Postgraduate Medical Education and Training Board.

Prensky, M. (2000). *Digital Game Based Learning*: McGraw-Hill.

Rest, T. (1997). Using video for teaching chemistry: A phoenix? *TLTP Newsletter*.

Ross, M. T., Blaney, D., Cameron, H. S., Begg, M., & Cumming, A. D. (2008). *ClinEd: developing a web-based collaborative learning environment for clinical educators at the University of Edinburgh*. Paper presented at the All Together Better Health IV.

Sackett, D. L., Straus, S. E., Richardson, W. S., Rosenberg, W., & Haynes, R. B. (2000). *Evidence-based medicine: how to practice and teach EBM*. London: Churchill Livinstone.

Schmidt, H. G., & Rickers, R. M. J. P. (2007). How expertise develops in medicine: knowledge encapsulation and illness script formation. *Medical Education, 41*, 1133–1139.

Schön, D. A. (1983). *The reflective practitioner: how professionals think in action*. London: Temple Smith.

Schön, D. A. (1987). *Educating the reflective practitioner: toward a new design for teaching and learning in the professions*. San Fransisco: Jossey-Bass.

Tait, B. (1997). Constructive Internet Learning. *Active Learning, (7)*, 3-8.

The Medical Act (1858). UK Government.

Wenger, E. (1998). *Communities of Practice: Learning, Meaning and Identity*. New York: Cambridge University Press.

WFME. (2003). *Basic medical education: WFME global standards for quality improvement*. Copenhagen: World Federation for Medical Education.

Chapter 12
VideoPaper as a Bridging Tool in Teacher Professional Development

Trond Eiliv Hauge
University of Oslo, Norway

Svein Olav Norenes
University of Oslo, Norway

ABSTRACT

This study demonstrates the possibilities of new media and affordable technological tools that support teacher professional development in a workplace setting. A team of 5 mathematics teachers in a secondary school is followed over a period of six months as they work jointly to improve their teaching and team practice using a multimedia Web developer system (VideoPaper). VideoPaper is an easy-to-use tool for developing and sharing of Web documents that integrates video resources, images, and texts reflecting local practices. The framework of Developmental Work Research methods aligned to historical-cultural activity theory (Engeström, 2001, 2008) was adapted to the local needs and workplace conditions. The findings point to changes in teachers' conceptual approaches to learning and teaching, and to the significance of technology-enhanced support for professional development. The study contributes to an understanding of the complexities in bridging practices between social and technological design for teacher development and the development of learning communities.

INTRODUCTION

In modern knowledge organizations, practices for facilitating collaboration, creation, advancement, and sharing of knowledge are considered some of the most important challenges for professional and institutional development (Gherardi, 2006; Hakarainen, Palonen, Paavola, & Lehtinen, 2004; Nonaka

& Takeuchi, 1995). However, the school development and teacher professional learning literature does not reveal a straightforward solution to the complexity of these challenges (Darling-Hammond & Bransford, 2005; Fullan, Hill, & Crévola, 2006; Hubbard, Mehan, & Stein 2006; Leithwood & Louis, 1998; MacBeath & Mortimore, 2001).

A growing body of studies concerns the use of new technologies in schools to facilitate collaborative learning, knowledge building and knowledge

DOI: 10.4018/978-1-60566-780-5.ch012

advancement among students (Scardamalia & Bereiter, 1994, 2006; Stahl, 2006; Wasson, Ludvigsen, & Hoppe, 2003). However, there is a lack of knowledge related to how technology may support advanced workplace learning and professional development among teachers (Paavola & Hakarainnen, 2005). A promising field of research that moves beyond some of these limits is the development of online and inquiry-based learning environments where teachers create and share lessons plans, learning resources, and descriptions of classroom practices through case stories and videos. The Inquiry Learning Forum (IFL) (Barab, MaKinster, & Scheckler, 2003), the LeMill learning toolbox (Calibrate, 2005), and the multimedia authoring tool VideoPaper (Beardsley, Cogan-Dew, & Olivero, 2007) are examples of inquiry-oriented technologies that focus on the community aspect of teachers' learning. However, there is a need for further research on the integration of such technologies in real workplace settings that support teacher professional development, for example, in nested improvement design of classroom practices. Research on online design reveals the complexities of bridging practices between net-based and social levels for teacher professional development (cf., Barab, Kling, & Gray, 2004; Kling & Courtright, 2003).

In this chapter, we present and examine a small-scale intervention study in a workplace setting for mathematics teachers in an upper secondary school that explores the systematic development of classroom practices supported by a multimedia web-developer system (*VideoPaper*), i.e., an easy-to-use tool for the joint development and sharing of web-documents that integrate video resources, images, and texts reflecting local practices. The tool was accessible online through a restricted domain open to the participants. The VideoPaper technology was originally designed to support student teachers/teachers in reflecting upon their practices (Beardsley, Cogan-Drew, & Olivero, 2007; Olivero, Sutherland, & John, 2004); however, the actual study extends this

user scenario by including experienced teachers in a workplace and communal setting for professional development. The study focuses on how the teachers become aware of the salient features of their instruction when participating in different spaces for design, assessment, and reflection. We seek to understand how the actual technology may support professional practices in a real workplace setting. This integral design perspective seems to be a necessary extension of existing approaches to online learning (cf., Barnett, 2006; Schlager & Fusco, 2003).

TOOLS AND RESEARCH DESIGN

VideoPaper Technology

The Java-based VideoPaper Builder software, developed by the U.S. Concord Consortium and TERC (2000) (http://vpb.concord.org/), enables the user to insert and in various ways interlink texts, images, and video resources, and to publish the combined resources as a user-friendly multimedia web document. The possibility of publishing text and video side-by-side makes *VideoPaper* a powerful tool to annotate digital video, cf. Figure 1.

Figure 1 depicts a screenshot of VideoPaper divided into three sectors: A, B, and C. Sector A is where the video and slides are imported and displayed, sector B is where the navigation buttons and menus are generated, and sector C is where textual annotation and descriptions are described and presented by the writers of the VideoPaper. Content is added with easy-to-use text formatting tools and is connected to multimedia content by simple control buttons. Control buttons are easily inserted in the text as triggers for 1) video playback, 2) overlays adjustable to the video, and 3) slides or pictures to appear below the video playback window. The activity of interconnecting video, images, and text with the help of the VideoPaper builder allows the production of the textual sto-

Figure 1. VideoPaper screenshot

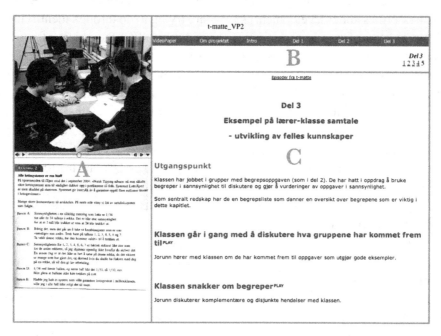

ries to be narrowed by resources brought into the VideoPaper by the user.

A core idea behind the VideoPaper technology has been to support teachers in combining educational research and theory with factual classroom practice. Although the use of some sort of theory or practice is essential to any process concerning teachers' learning, innovative and structured use of a combination of the two is less frequent. Studies of knowledge representations among teachers reveal that they largely describe their profession through communicative and instructional activities and attributes belonging to the classroom, whereas academic researchers belong to a different discourse tradition, with explicit structures, terms, expressions, and values (Bartels, 2003). The idea of supporting a reflective practice is the second essential aspect behind the VideoPaper technology. Pre-service and in-service teacher building of VideoPapers has been proved to support reflective practice by engaging teachers in demonstrating and sharing ideas and theory behind successful teaching among colleagues (Beardsley, Cogan-Drew, & Olivero,

2007). In these projects, teachers use technology to merge a theory or an academic discourse with examples from the practitioner's own classroom activity. While these studies emphasize the value of VideoPaper as a tool for bridging the gap between educational research and a professional teacher's discourse, these VideoPaper projects do not specifically address collective discourse practices and institutional dimensions related to how a bridging discourse may support teacher professional development. The actual study examines how a designed linkage between online and workplace learning can illuminate these questions.

Theoretical Framework

In conceptualizing the research intervention and technology use, we draw on theoretical perspectives from Cultural-Historical Activity Theory (CHAT) (Engeström, 1987, 1999a; Leont'ev, 1978, 1981; Vygotsky, 1978). As activity theory is deeply contextual and historically oriented toward practices, their objects, mediating artifacts, and social organization (Cole & Engeström, 1993), this theory fits well into the study at hand, which explore the teachers' professional development as part of the collective history of the school. Activity theory is also based on a dialectical conception of knowledge and thinking focusing on the creative potential in human cognition; in addition, the theory seeks to explain and influence changes in human practices over time (Engeström, 1999b). We find this framework useful in understanding the design of technology-enhanced practices.

According to Engeström (1987, 1999a), an activity system is made up of individuals or groups (subjects) acting to accomplish the end of an activity, an outcome, which may be characterized as the object of activity. This system thinking recognizes a special status of culturally developed artifacts as fundamental mediators of actions, relating subjects and the object of activity in a dynamic three-way interaction. However, in an extended version of the activity system, Engeström takes into consideration a set of interrelated collective and regulative forces represented by the community involved, work distribution, and rules at work. This extended activity model has to be understood as a collective phenomenon, which moves beyond mere individual activities. It is developmental in nature, object-oriented, and collective and based on culturally mediated activities (Engeström, 1999b).

Research Design and Methods

The research study began as a school-based development project in mathematics for the school year 2006-07, initiated by the leadership of the school but collaboratively organized by 5 teachers at the first grade level. This development design was gradually changed when the principal invited the research group to join the school project. The final research design is based on the Developmental Work Research (DWR) framework (Engeström, 2001, 2007), which are also known as Change Laboratory methods. DWR is a form of research that aims to enable participants to move from everyday to scientific understandings of what they are trying to do through identifying, working on, and expanding the object of activity with tools offered in activity theory. A modified version of DWR was applied in our study (cf., approaches by Edwards & Fox, 2005; Ellis & Edwards, 2007), which means that the researchers are not only consultants but also directly involved in the change processes together with the participants in trying to understand in greater depth the object of activity and the practices at stake. The research design was created through joint planning and discussions with the teachers, the principal, and the deputy head for school development. A sequence of classroom observations, teacher team discussions, video recording of jointly designed lessons, and a set of workshops over a period of 6 months followed. The activities were designed to support the teachers in describing, analyzing, and improving their teaching practices according to the aims of classroom development. Research data in the present study belong to different phases of this development work.

We draw on a rich set of data from various phases of the development work research as data emerged in interviews, design and implementation of lesson plans, observation and videos of classroom practices, technology use, and workshop discussions. Table 1 gives an overview of the different episodes, time periods, documentation forms, and actors involved in the project.

Analytical Framework

Figure 2 depicts a dual picture of the emerging activity systems (cf. Engeström, 1987, 1999b) observed when the researchers collaborated with the teachers during the developmental work research period. The left-hand picture reflects teacher activities in the pre-study period, while the right-hand picture describes activities during the intervention period that used lessons plans and VideoPaper technology. The teachers worked independently in their everyday practice but came

Table 1. Overview of project activities

Actions	Date/time period	Documentation	Actors
Phase I: Pre-studies	Sept. – Dec. 2006		
Project initiation	Sept. 2006	Development plan for Math 1. Grade Email Meeting notes Contract/agreement	Heads of the school Math teacher team Research group
Field observations	Nov. 2006	Field notes from classroom activities Field notes from teacher team meetings	Four Math classes Math teacher team Research group
Project plan development	Dec. 2006	Description of action plan Meeting notes	Heads of the school and research group
Phase II: VideoPaper activities	**Jan. – May 2007**		
VP Activity 1 Teacher team meetings	Jan. 2007	Field notes	Math teacher team and researcher group
VP Activity 2 Planning of instructional designs in two classes	Feb. 2007	Planning documents Schedules for instruction Schedules for recording Email	Two teachers in the Math teacher team Research group
VP Activity 3 Performing and recording in two classes	Feb. 2007	Videotapes Field notes	Two Math classes (teachers and students) Research group
VP Activity 4 VideoPaper building 1	Feb. 2007	VideoPaper work files and final web documents	Research group
VP Activity 5 VideoPaper workshop 1	March 2007	Videotapes Field notes	Math teacher team Research group
VP Activity 6 VideoPaper building 2	March 2007	VideoPaper work files and final web documents	Research group
VP Activity 7 VideoPaper workshop 2	March 2007	Videotapes Field notes	Math teacher team Deputy head for school development Research group
VP Activity 8 VideoPaper demonstration and discussion	April 2007	Audio recording	Heads of the school Research group
VP Activity 9 Post-interview	May 2007	Audio recordings Field notes	Two teachers in the Math teacher team Research group

Figure 2. Analytical framework for the study of teaching practice and tool use

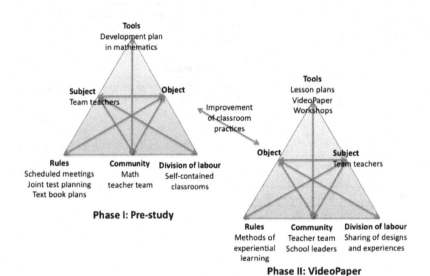

together weekly to coordinate their time schedules, textbook progression, and student assessment plans. The activity system is weak in its collective structure, activities are fragmented, and the team framework is primarily used for coordination of formal grade-level activities. When the team moved into the intervention phase, the collective activities of the team were strengthened by regular meetings, shared design work and lesson planning, and tools used for observation and discussion of classroom practices. The objects of activity in both phases focused on the overall goal of improvement of classroom practices. Against this background, the activity systems in Figure 2 will be used as an analytical framework for the exploration of the activities and tools used in the study.

In the following section, activities in phase I of the study are described by looking at the motives for change as part of a wider school development strategy. Next, we use observations in the pre-study phase to learn how the teachers work in their everyday practice. Descriptions of the ac-

tivities in phase I are based on the data generated through shared planning and discussions with the teachers. Descriptions of the activities in phase II draw on data from the joint lesson planning with the teachers and interactions with the teachers in the workshops that used VideoPaper as the driving force for work analyses. This means that we include information from the collaborative design work with the teachers as well the technology supported discussions in the workshops as sources for descriptions of the activities and assessment of practice transformation.

Two conceptual designs of workplace learning will then be explored in this development work research study: 1) the multimedia authoring tool VideoPaper designed to support teachers in observing and analyzing their instructional practices and 2) the teacher team as a workplace unit for collaborative planning and teaching and the nurturing of classroom development work. Phase II of the study integrated these aims. A mix of the designs explore what Schlager and Fusco (2003) mention as a major weakness of online technologies that support teacher professional development: the problems of how online activities connect to real workplace settings, local communities, and participants' predominant practices.

DRIVING MOTIVES OF CHANGE

The project can be traced back to the developmental needs and challenges brought up by annual school surveys of students' satisfaction and the rating of numerous aspects of teaching and learning in the school. In June 2006, a survey of first-year mathematics students showed a lower general score in mathematics than in other topics. In addition to this finding, for some time, the leadership of the school had wanted to support the Math teachers to improve their instruction, as part of the overall strategy for school development. When the research group was invited, the goals and teacher team structure had already been chosen. The teacher team consisted of the 5 teachers at the first grade level and the deputy head for school development, who also was a member of the school leadership group. In the kick-off meeting of the local project in June 2006, the following goal was stated for the school year 2006-07:

The goal for this project is that in June 2007 we have pupils [in mathematics] who have an average score of 2.5 on variation in instruction, use of learning resources, and assessment practice. The pupils feel that they learn what is expected of them (Math-project description, June 2006).

The goal visualizes key features of the evaluation system used in the school, in which a broad set of national survey instruments is used annually for a continuous assessment of practices involving students, teachers, and parents. Follow-up discussions with individual teachers, teacher teams, and the staff as a whole are institutionalized practices. Over time, this evaluation history

has given the leadership of the school valuable insights into the teaching cultures in various departments and subject fields. In the post-project discussions with the principal and the deputy head for school development, which took place after the VideoPaper try-out, it appears that they were very much concerned about the culture of teaching and teamwork among the mathematics teachers in the school. The principal commented:

I believe that the Math department and the teacher team have a history that is quite important. Because they have been working as they have for such a long time . . . Seen from the outside, the Math group has been looked upon as a group that works tightly and well together . . . However, they are not able to utilize their internal resources as a group, because what they are doing is . . . eh . . . copying in a way what the others are doing. We do it this way, they are saying. That's it, you know . . .].

Math teachers move into a culture. Many of them are novices and pretty new in our school, but they move into a tradition, where Math teachers are among the ones who collaborate the most in making plans, constructing the same tests, and keeping up with the same pace. However, if we look at new constellations in subjects like Social Sciences, then we see a different way of working, where people are sharing things, but by also making it into their own. It means in a way that you lift what others have done into your own [work] and you do yours better. You know what I mean? Thus, it becomes more productive than this, which is merely a bit instrumental and mechanical . . . way of working.

These statements communicate an understanding of the Math team teachers as not being able to renew and change patterns of instrumentality and individuality into joint efforts and collaboration by using and exploring the span between collective team practice and their own teaching practices. However, if we listen to the voices of the teachers and their understanding of development goals and motives of the project, we find that they are not as certain as the school leaders about why they need to be engaged in the project. During a post-interview session, one of the team members explained:

Janet: It was the leadership of the school who wanted to do something with the Math instruction, because of the results of the student surveys. [. . .] I believe it was because of the low score on variation in working methods and assessment practices in mathematics and the higher scores in other subjects taught by the same teachers. If you have one class in natural science and one in Math, then the students have different opinions about variation in working method variation. So therefore, I believe the principal asked the Math teachers to come . . . and explain how to go further. We have asked ourselves a bit about the same, ok . . . the students are saying there is little variation, but we don't know if they want more variation, and to what extent. So we thought the goal should be . . . a little more variation . . . that would be for the good . . . And so we agreed upon a goal together with the leadership . . . [. . .] we thought, okay, if we could have as a goal to move up to two point five on variation on the math issues there, then we felt this would be good enough (quiet laughter).

As can be discerned from the excerpts, the goals and motives behind the development project differ between the actors. However, the teachers and the school leaders agreed to take steps to improve instructional practices to a higher satisfactory score on important parameters. In many ways, the data reveal that the Math development project was quite open-ended in the beginning but regulated by a common goal of improving the working methods in Math. As researchers, we observed tensions and discrepancies between

the actors with regard to the *what, how,* and *why* of the project, which created a set of challenges for the developmental work research, e.g., defining the object of improvement, motivating the exchange of classroom experiences, and redesigning instructional practices. However, according to our analytical framework, at this development phase of the study we observed different opinions between the school leadership and the teachers concerning the goals, description of teaching practices, and need to change. The next phase of the research project involved challenging the perspectives on how the goals and need for improvement could be clarified and transformed into realistic change tasks for the teachers in their everyday practice and remodeled into input for the VideoPaper building.

TRANSFORMATIVE DESIGN ACTIVITIES

Transformative Activity I

Two sets of activities were initiated in November 2006 to clarify the object of activity and the design of the VideoPaper. We visited all the teachers in their classes and observed them to get an overview of the ongoing practices. We also observed activities in four weekly 1-hour team meetings. As a result of these observations, we decided to follow 1 teacher and her implementation of a project work in mathematics over a period of 6 hours. This decision was made as part of a continuous discussion with the teacher team and the deputy head for school development regarding the need to have a clear focus in the joint development work research.

During the observation and talks with the teachers, one overall basic curricular skill surfaced from time to time as a shared issue or activity, namely, the students' ability to participate in mathematical discourses. This basic skill is written as a goal statement in the national curriculum and copied into the students' textbook in mathematics (Sandvold et. al., 2006, p. 338):

To express oneself in mathematics involves making assumptions, asking questions, arguing, and explaining a way of thinking with the help of mathematics. Further, it entails participating in conversations, communicating ideas, and debating problems and solution strategies with others.

The project work that was implemented in one of the classes can be looked upon as an effort to explore and highlight this curriculum goal in a more specific way than is normally practiced. According to the teachers, this work addressed the need for variation in instructional practices. Therefore, the team openly supported the individual teacher in bringing experiences from her project work into the group for further discussions. However, as observers, we noticed a gap between the inquiry- and collaboratively oriented goal description in the curriculum and the actual project practice. The instructional script was, to a large extent, oriented toward single teacher-student interactions. In communications with teachers, we emphasized this situation and the possibility of including a broader set of activities that support students' "talking-to-learn."

During the observations, an object of shared development work for the teachers gradually emerged. As researchers, we witnessed how a joint need materialized in the collective discussions, and developed robustness to shape and energize further activities. As a result, the goals and activities for the development work research were revised and helped design the VideoPaper and teacher workshops.

Transformative Activity II

The idea of supporting teacher development by writing a reflective VideoPaper incorporates capturing video of classroom activity, selecting, editing and preparing video episodes for import into the VideoPaper, deciding on the learning theory or model, and reflecting upon learning by linking the prepared resources (Nemirovsky, Galvis, Kaplan, Gogan-Drew, & DiMattia, 2005). As the first step in constructing the VideoPaper, we discussed the need for authentic video material with the teachers. This resulted in a close collaborative work design with 2 of the teachers who planned one double lesson each that addressed how students transform mathematics into spoken words through dialogue, which could be videotaped. The teachers developed a joint lesson plan that focused on group work and inquiry-oriented learning on the topic of probability. The planning resulted in the lesson and video observation plan shown in Table 2.

Table 2 illustrates how student and teacher activities run through a common set of assignments given in the students' textbooks. The lesson plan shifted between teacher-led instruction, small group discussions by the students, teacher-group interactions, and group presentations to the whole class.

Transformative Activity III

The construction of the actual VideoPaper and its content was guided by three principles. First of all, all 5 teachers were invited into the technological environment, and the activities were directed to illuminate the classroom improvement project, the lesson design, and students' learning in the actual classes. The selection of video-films and discussion categories had to support these aims. Secondly, while the VideoPaper in general is designed to support reflection on practice and theory as part of an education course model, we wanted to create a solution that could focus on methods of professional learning in a workplace setting.

Thus, we emphasized methods of experiential learning (cf. Engeström, 1987, 2001; Kolb & Fry, 1975) and collegial learning and supervision (Lauvaas & Handal, 2000). This means a careful

Table 2. Lesson activity plan – Math classes

Acti-vity se-quence	Sche-duled time	Activity in class	Who in focus	Recording plan
0	5-10 min	Recap from Thursday 1.2 Students explicate list of terms taken from the probability chapter	Students	No recording
1	10 min	Discussion about the Lotto-example 6.2, example nr 2, in groups of four Each student in the group takes one role each (A-D) and argues for this person's solution. After, they discuss together and take notes on important aspects	Groups of stu-dents	• Camera A on group 1 • Camera B on group 2
2	5 min	Groups sum up in front of the class. Teacher guides the conversation, and the groups present	Groups of stu-dents	• Camera A focus on teacher • Camera B focus on students talking
3	5 min	Each group illustrates and discusses occurrences of probability in everyday life	Groups of stu-dents	(Camera on same groups as in sequence 1)
4	5 min	Teacher takes notes on the board while students present their everyday occurrences	Teacher and groups of students	• Camera A on teacher • Camera B on whole class
5	10 min	Whole class discussion about assignment 6.2 to il-luminate core probability facets. Uses list of terms and asks for examples from the students	Teacher and whole class	• Camera A on teacher • Camera B on whole class
6	1-2 min	Information about shift in orientation and tasks	Teacher	No recording
7	20-30 min	Students work together in groups looking through chapter 6.1-6.18 for terms and assignments that illustrates key concepts	Groups of stu-dents	Cameras follow new groups of students

orchestration of questions at different levels of exploration, starting with neutral descriptions of video-film episodes and ending up with how people would like to assess their practices. Thirdly, our application differs from other use studies of VideoPaper in the sense that we as researchers are doing the actual building of the VideoPaper document. Early negotiations during the pre-study period (see Table 1 for an overview) made it clear that the teachers could not be involved in the technical building of the VideoPaper-document because of the teachers' restricted time resources allocated to the project and the estimated workload the building of the paper would require. Reports from other VideoPaper projects also revealed that the building of VideoPaper web documents is a time- and resource-consuming process. For example, Rider and Hunting (2006) reported that the critical success factors for teachers and stu-dents completing the building of their own web

documents were the availability of technology, realistic understanding of the time involved, a vision for the finished product, and technological proficiency.

Two VideoPapers were created; they included a combination of video, pictures, and textual information into the following: 1) "exploratory enquiries" simply to get the teachers to express how they interpreted and recognized episodes from the two classes and 2) theoretically "fixated enquiries" that directed the teachers' focus to essential com-ponents of student group work and how students acted when they discussed mathematical problems or were engaged in "learning-in-and-by-talk" (cf. Dysthe, 2000; Mercer & Wegerif, 1998). Thus, theoretical ideas concerning productive interac-tion by use of talk in classroom mathematics were coupled with the goals in the national curriculum. While the first VideoPaper focused on productive talk in student groups and student-teacher interac-

Figure 3. Video episode of productive talk

tions, the second one focused on productive talk in relation to the pedagogical design features of the group work, content, and procedures at work for the students.

Information from episodes of classroom practices, some focusing on 20 seconds of talk, others on 5 to 10 minutes of activity, together with the conceptual and methodological ideas described above, transformed the VideoPapers into interactive and responsive displays that supported discussions among the teachers (cf. the example in Figure 3).

Transformative Activity IV

The two VideoPapers were presented to the teachers in two successive workshops, in February and March 2007. The content resources and working structures in the VideoPaper design regulated the discussions. As the researchers, we operated a mixed online and social collaborative system with the teachers following the adapted DWR methods and principles of experiential learning.

ANALYSES OF WORKSHOP INTERACTIONS

The outcomes of the workshops based on discussions among the teachers are presented under three headings: Teachers zoom in on students' learning, implications for design of teaching, and rethinking the object of classroom practice improvement.

Teachers Zoom in on Students' Learning

The following dialogue from VideoPaper 1 and the first workshop is representative of how the team teachers interpreted students' discussion in the classroom. The quotation gives insight into how the teachers perceived the object of improvement of classroom practices supported by the work procedures in the workshop. The discussion occurred after the teachers watched a video of 3 students discussing complementary events, outcome, sample space, and other probability terms related to the assignment they were currently solving. In the video episode, 1 of the students explains for the others in the group the differences between outcome and sample space.

Table 3.

1	Linn:	I'm not sure whether that sank in.
2	All	[Laughter]
3	Janet:	No.
4	Oscar:	No, that depends.
5	All	[Laughter]
6	Linn:	Would have enjoyed having that sequence as a cartoon [Laughs]
7	Researcher:	What can be said about this conversation?
8	Kari:	Well, it is at least apparent that Fanny has understood what complementary events means.
9	Janet:	Yeah, that previous one yes, "clever girl" [imitating the student on the tape]
10	All	[Laughing]
11	Janet:	But we have one teacher and two e::h- and one listener and one e::h-
12	Oscar:	One student yeah-
13 14 15 16	Janet:	And one, should we say a watcher, in this group. She, because the last one here, she was kind of busy with something completely different and was doing her own [small math tasks, but then she was caught by this sample space lecture (1.0) and then it began, yes so-
17	Several others	Yes- [[inaudible]
18 19 20 21 22	Janet:	So we kind of see some very distinct e::h roles that they take here (2.0) and then we witness something that we sure know e::h, s::h: o::: i::, as teachers, that the clever pupils (0.5) when they take that role as she does there (0.5) so that they have to explain (1.3) then they get even more clever (2.0). So, it is that thing to come- to get the weaker to begin to explain which is the challenge, because (1.5) yes (1.0) actually
23 24 25	Researcher:	Before we enter into the didactical discussion, or the desire to think new and differently, let's just take a short round. What is that you take notice of, Jonas, of what you have seen of this group here? What is it that you first notice?
26 27 28	Jonas:	No, e::h noting special, I guess it is a little as the previous episode, that there is somebody who doesn't exactly know (...) what (...), what this is, and then you have another who tries her best to::to explain (...) explain what it is, a::nd does it I guess eventually two times pretty similar.
29	Researcher:	Yeah (5.0). Yes, take a little [Gives sign with his hand symbolizing another circle around the table]
30 31 32 33 34 35 36 37	Oscar:	Well, I'm sitting thinking whether e::h (1,5) e::h (0.8) the outcome is much greater for the one who gets to tell and explain (0.5) that for the other two. That she e:h (0.8) the e::h teacher, the one who takes the role as the teacher, she gets very certain and secure on e::h (1.0) gets to show what she can (1.0) but e::h (2.0) I don't know (1.0) I don't think that the others learn it properly until they get further situations where they make use of it, and that they themselves are allowed to express it and are explain how they understand it. So I'm a little there (0.3) am sitting a little with that kind of thought (1.0) what is the gain for the ones who are explained to?
38	Researcher:	What do you think, Linn?
39 40 41 42	Linn:	I was thinking that the first explanation we got there, the one with the sixth quarter (0.5) there, I think one could almost distinguish how things ting came together in the head of the one who sat there and explained. (1.5) She started a little floundering, and suddenly she had her whole little midst-complex example avail-able in her head.
43	Several others	[Mm
44	Linn:	[Interesting
45 46	Janet:	Yes, she became more and more certain now as well, became more and more explicit on OR and AND e::h [1[e::h if you ask me.
47	Oscar:	[1[Yes
48	Oscar:	[2[I haven't though- [inaudible]

Table 3. continued

49 50	Janet:	[2][And, but you know, there is something about that-, and you know from when you are talking yourself (0.5) suddenly things fit together
51	Oscar:	Mm
52	Janet:	And then you are completely sure
53	Oscar:	Yes

Transcript notation

[] Brackets indicating comments and interpretations

[[/ [¹[¹ Left-hand brackets indicate overlapping utterances

(2.0) Indicating seconds of pause in speech

::: Indicting prolongation of a sound

- Hyphen indicates abrupt halt or interruption in utterance

When the sequence ended, the following discussion (see Table 3) took place between the teachers and the researcher as a moderator.

The student class and the practice unfolding in the video episode are Kari's, who is one of the teachers. Janet also knew the students very well from other settings. In addition, all the teachers worked on the same textbook chapter and had recent experience in teaching the topic of probability. In the transcript, which starts as the video playback finished, lines 1-6, Linn and the other teachers indicated that they are uncertain whether the two students actually learned what the third one explained to them. The teachers laughed a little. This occurred also as they watched the individual student explaining and emphasizing her understanding of the differences between the concept's outcome and the sample space. Further, in line 7, the researcher asked the teachers what can be said about the conversation. The teachers started commenting on the students taking different roles (8-18), whom the teachers felt understood or not, and subsequently the teachers discussed how they interpreted who was actually learning. In lines 18-25, Janet followed up this part of the discussion and turned the discussion into how important it is to get "weak" students into positions where they have to explain. After the researchers' discussion about focusing on what the others made of this episode (23-25) Jonas explained that he didn't notice anything particular. Afterwards (30-37),

Oscar mentioned that he wondered whether the outcome of the discussion was greater for the one who was talking and the others. Linn then (39-42) emphasized how bits and pieces came together for the student as she was explaining to the others. In lines 43-53, more of the teachers agreed with this interpretation.

Janet, Oscar, and Linn were the most active of the teachers. However, all the teachers joined the conversations, one way or another. This was a descriptive discussion based on observations of the episode, but we also see how the teachers linked their explanations to concrete mechanisms for learning. The discourse developed successively into a deeper elaboration of the learning taking place. We observed how the teachers gradually unpacked the students' activity by linking it to *different roles* and *types of talk* in learning.

In this video episode, the teachers were confronted with their teaching in a new way. From being in charge of lesson planning and implementation involving a varied set of learning activities in their individual classes, the teachers now took on the role of an observer, commented on each other's practices and the students' learning, and offered explanations for what happened when the students were forced to explain their mathematical understanding. Compared to how the teachers were arguing and talking about "learning-in-and-by-talk" in the planning phase, the actual concept of learning is discussed far more and linked to actual practices. The VideoPaper resources and the workshop procedures seem to have given the teachers a new arena for focused exploration of the students' learning.

Implications for Design of Teaching

The second VideoPaper session/workshop included 2 more teachers from the Math department in addition to the deputy head for school development. The intention was to move a bit deeper into the object of classroom improvement by looking at the instructional activities and content matter of the lessons framing "learning-in-and-by-talk" and to talk about possible implications of the VideoPaper experiences concerning the teaching design. The data excerpts presented below reflect general opinions expressed by the discussion group. Actually, the teachers were excited to see how the students were using mathematical concepts and talking about the problems at hand.

It was great to see how well the pupils were able to argue within the group, even if I was a totally different place in the classroom, they are still sitting talking mathematics, trying to find out things together and learning from each other. I observed some of mine who sat there explaining to the others some of the terms. And it was great fun to see how they may help each other like that. I think, as such, that they learned a lot of talking together the way they did.

In the above quotation, the teacher giving the lesson explained that she enjoyed witnessing how well her students were arguing and supporting each other when discussing in the group, although she was working in another area of the classroom. Learning took place, she believed, through their discussion. One of the other teachers commented on the video episode by looking at the students' mathematical language, and how they were searching for words and expressions suited for the task (transcript below). In her opinion, the students

were uncertain about how to express their understanding, something the teachers should consider to support better in future teaching.

What I think was apparent in the group was that they actually experience that to talk in mathematics is a language that they . . . they don't know the language, so they experience that they are lacking, they are lacking a vocabulary. So that would . . . it must eh could probably be smart to get them to work further with. Because you notice that they are searching, how they are searching for . . . So that there is something to follow up here is nothing to even consider.

Another teacher (transcript below) appreciated what he has been part of during the project. The designed group work should be followed up by further development. However, he emphasized that students also need to practise and explain what they already know, not only explore new things. As teachers, they should enhance such learning in ordinary class settings when students are presenting their work.

This work is so absolutely a good initiative, what we have done here and what we have seen here today. It shows one good way of doing things. I think maybe in the future, to develop it even further, but it is also important for students to explain things they already know. Not only to explore something new. But to work through things they know, by for example having a presentation like we had last fall, with poster about geometry, where they in a sense are allowed to go the whole way in beforehand and are allowed to explain the road from start to finish. Not just floundering ahead like they do in the groups here, so that there is something that is followed-up, something that it must contain.

Several teachers in the group agreed with what was explained in the excerpts above. They all seemed to think that the students needed help to express their mathematical thoughts through the discussion sessions, and the mathematical language used in classroom discourses should be enforced by instructional support structures. We may conclude from these quotations that the object of classroom improvement work has gained value and importance for the teachers through the various activities that took place. Their classroom practices seem to have become more open for discussion and shared reconfiguration than before.

Rethinking the Object of Classroom Practice Improvement

The descriptions above point to important aspects of the object of classroom practice improvement and features of instructional designs among the teachers. The development work seems to have opened a new area for rethinking classroom practices. In the second workshop, we explored how far the teachers wanted to go in this new direction by using a wider set of resources in the VideoPaper, e.g., curriculum guidelines and goals of the school development project. The 2 teachers involved in the actual lessons were challenged to respond.

At least I am sure that I have extended my consciousness about . . . that to get real group going requires that one has to plan carefully both the instruction and the tasks. Tasks they are working on and the follow-up work, my mind about these things have been extended. If it will become any better, I don't know, but the mind has at least expanded. So that one can take it more seriously . . . maybe . . .

The teacher's awareness of the project, as shown above, has certainly come to a higher level of consciousness with regard to the curriculum design, instruction, construction of Math assignments, and students' follow-up work. She really hoped to utilize her insight more. Another teacher emphasized that the project has contributed to the teachers rethinking their collaboration and planning work in the teacher team. In particular, the observation method and highlighting of selected instructional activities were useful. However, as the discussion continued, the group was reluctant to define concrete actions to take to redesign their practices.

The deputy head for school development (when participating in workshop 2), in her assessment of the project, especially focused on the importance of the video clips being presented as a unique way of reflecting on teaching practices. The tools used for discussing practices and object development contributed to new insight.

But, just to have the video clips makes the discussion—first of all, you are seeing the same thing—I mean you don't, everyone has their own filters, but to tell the story of what happened in my class, then first of all you get only my version and I'm only able to catch a little here and a little there, and there is so much slipping away. So to sit and look at these very exact things and discuss it, I find that extremely . . . I am very thankful for having . . ., now we have watched yours, but I am very thankful for being allowed to take part in it, because I think that this is a very unique opportunity. Just from my own experience, from my own teacher team, that is, what do we actually talk about when it comes to things we have experienced? [. . .] Because I think that when you are watching these clips, then you get to see things that is otherwise not very easy to catch when you stand there (when teaching).

In this workshop, the teachers' planning and teaching design was put under pressure by structures in the VideoPaper. We observed that the teachers contributed quite eagerly in the analysis and discussions of teaching as an individual practice. However, when it came to the collective level of team practices, the teachers were far more reluctant and vague when trying to describe future solutions.

DISCUSSION

This chapter has presented the features and possibilities of VideoPaper technology utilized in a school-based development project supported by a research intervention. With the help of the Cultural-Historical Activity Theory framework, we have analyzed teachers' use of resources in the VideoPaper by focusing on emerging collective representations of a shared object of development work, the improvement of classroom practices in mathematics. In the intervention study we used the VideoPaper to expand the focus of analyses beyond the professional development of individual teachers, and designed for a collective-oriented perspective on development work. The approach relies on a mix of technology and social structures of workplace learning, and is highly contextual in its object formation and development. The core elements are formed by the VideoPaper technology (Nemirovsky, Galvis, Kaplan, Gogan-Drew, & DiMattia, 2005) and the Developmental Work Research methodology (Engeström, 2001, 2007). This means that the VideoPaper was used as a tool for mirroring and analyzing classroom practices in a step-wise strategy for deliberate and object-oriented practice transformation.

During the developmental work research, we carefully planned potential "third spaces" (Gutierrez, Basquedano-Lopez, Alvarez, & Chio, 1999) that may function as cultural "neutral spaces" for discussions. The third spaces in our case were placed outside the everyday, work-based discourses and practices of the teachers. These spaces are represented by the VideoPaper and workshop sessions, where the participants demonstrated the ability to work on new conceptual meanings and instruction models. The study seems to confirm that the VideoPaper technology played a major role in creating content and communal activities in these workshops. Being involved in the spaces means a deliberate process of "objectification" (Engeström, 2007) of activities that stimulate the teachers to redesign their instructional practices.

The study shows the potential of these "neutral" spaces for sharing experiences and creating new perspectives on teaching and learning.

The study has examined institutional practices and activity systems, the creation of new spaces for discussion and change, and followed objects and tools in transformative activities. We have looked at how the collective features of the activity system for the mathematics teachers evolved during the development work, and how the tools significantly mediated changes in the teachers' practice. This contextual approach has shown how the teachers productively were identifying and elaborating the shared object pursued by the school leadership. We notice how the object of classroom practice improvement has gained meaning and developed as an integrated activity of the VideoPaper and the follow-up workshops. The findings seem to indicate that the actual object of activity developed as a tool for future actions and reflections. Studies by Edwards (2005), Miettinen and Virkunnen (2005), Foot (2002), and Lund and Hauge (in press) in other settings confirm that such activity transformation is possible. However, the teachers´ design considerations in our study are mostly oriented toward to the individual teachers' classroom practices. Collective teamwork and curriculum practices are not addressed to the same degree.

The importance of the conceptual tools introduced and elaborated through the developmental work research is directly related to the role of the researchers. Indeed, the researchers were simultaneously and successively designers, participants, and analysts of the interventions. As pointed out by Engeström, Engestöm, and Kerosuo (2003), the challenge was to make these roles and their implications visible and analyzable for the participants. We carefully framed the interventions, design implications, and follow-up actions of the study by not intruding on institutional priorities; however, we did not hide the mission and interests of the various partners (principal, teachers, and researchers).

TECHNOLOGY DESIGN CONSIDERATIONS: FUTURE TRENDS

Two conceptual designs of workplace learning have been explored by integrating VideoPaper technology and teacher team activities in the present study. Barab et al. (2001) strongly argue for the need to relate online activities to goals and conditions in the workplace setting for the enhancement of participants' learning. Their study emphasizes what Orlikowski (1992) calls "the duality of technology," i.e., how technology influences organizational behavior and reverse, which means that the interaction between technology and the organization (in our case, the workplace situation for the teachers) must be understood dialectically. As a consequence, a mix of technology and institutional constraints was explored in our case. The VideoPaper has been optimized to cultivate and support professional activities, comprising a wide range of resources for learning through reflection on practice. Thus, the VideoPaper resembles other online tools that support individuals as well communities of teachers, see, e.g., the Inquiry Learning Forum (Kling & Courtright, 2003), Tapped In (Schlager & Fusco, 2003), and LeMill (Calibrate, 2005). However, at the same time the actual resources work as an integral part of the real workplace setting for the teachers. In this context, we may look at the VideoPaper as a bridging tool between two different representations of the instructional worlds played out in the videos of classroom practices and real classroom lessons. This dual perspective seems to be a necessary means for optimizing use value of web-based or online support structures for professional learning, so far as our study reveals.

CONCLUSION

The VideoPaper model used in the study, visualizes how institutional goals and an emerging object of instructional improvement are interlinked and become energizers and tools for classroom development work. Thus, these "real institutional objects" also have become driving forces for structuring and applying technology. The findings point to changes in teachers' conceptual approaches to learning and teaching and consequences for technology-enhanced support for professional development. The richness of the actual developmental work research, incorporating both design and practices, contributes to the understanding of the complexities in bridging practices between social and technological design for teacher development. We urge that the design of web-based or online learning systems that foster teachers' professional development must seek to explore and find innovative ways to support transformative actions, where participants are able to create, discuss, and connect representations of collective objects of activity to their workplace setting.

ACKNOWLEDGMENT

This research was supported by the University of Oslo through the research initiative Competence and Media Convergence (CMC), 2003-2008, and the EU project: Knowledge Practices Laboratory (KP-Lab), IST -27490 (IP). We would like to give special thanks to the mathematics teachers and the principal of the case study school who so willingly participated in the research project. We will also like to thank the reviewers for valuable comments in revising the manuscript.

REFERENCES

Barab, S., MaKinster, J. G., Moore, J., Cunningham, D., & ILF Design Team. (2001). Designing and building an online community: The struggle to support sociability in the Inquiry Learning Forum. *Educational Technology Research and Development, 49*(4), 71–96. doi:10.1007/BF02504948

Barab, S. A., MaKinster, J., & Scheckler, R. (2003). Designing system dualities: Characterizing a web-supported teacher professional development community. *The Information Society, 19*(3), 237–256. doi:10.1080/01972240309466

Barab, S. A., Kling, R., & Gray, J. S. (Eds.). (2004). *Designing for virtual communities in the service of learning.* Cambridge: Cambridge University Press.

Barnett, M. (2006). Using web-based professional development system to support preservice teachers in examining authentic classroom practice. *Journal of Technology and Teacher Education, 14*(4), 701–729.

Bartels, N. (2003). How teachers and researchers read academic articles. *Teaching and Teacher Education, 19*, 737–753. doi:10.1016/j.tate.2003.06.001

Beardsley, L., Cogan-Drew, D., & Olivero, F. (2007). VideoPaper: Bridging research and practice for pre-service and experienced teachers. In B. Barron, S. Derry, R. Goldman, & R. Pea (Eds.), *Video research in the learning sciences* (pp. 479-493). Mahwah, NJ: Erlbaum.

Calibrate – Learning resources for schools. (2005). Retrieved September 15, 2008, from http://calibrate.eun.org/ww/en/pub/calibrate_project/home_page.htm

Cole, M., & Engeström, Y. (1993). A cultural–historical approach to distributed cognition. In G. Salomon (Ed.), *Distributed cognitions: Psychological and educational considerations* (pp. 1–46). New York: Cambridge University Press.

Darling-Hammond, L., & Bransford, J. (Eds.). (2005). *Preparing teachers for a changing world. What teachers should learn and be able to do.* San Francisco: Jossey-Bass.

Dysthe, O. (Ed.). (2001). *Dialog, interaction and learning.* Oslo: Abstrakt forlag

Edwards, A. (2005). Relational agency: Learning to be a resourceful practitioner. *International Journal of Educational Research, 43*(3), 168–182. doi:10.1016/j.ijer.2006.06.010

Edwards, A., & Fox, C. (2005). Using activity theory to evaluate a complex response to social exclusion. *Educational and Child Psychology, 22*(1), 50–60.

Ellis, V., & Edwards, A. (2007, August). *Reconfiguring pre-service teacher education: Developmental work research as a methodology for teacher educators' expansive learning.* Paper presented at the Conference of EARLI, Budapest, Hungary.

Engeström, Y. (1987). *Learning by expanding: An activity-theoretical approach to developmental research.* Helsinki: Orienta-Konsultit Oy.

Engeström, Y. (1999a). Activity theory and individual and social transformation. In Y. Engeström, R. Miettinen, & R. L. Punamäki (Eds.), *Perspectives on activity theory* (pp. 19–39). Cambridge: Cambridge University Press.

Engeström, Y. (1999b). Innovative learning in work teams: Analyzing cycles of knowledge creation practices. In Y. Engeström, R. Miettinen, & R. L. Punamäki (Eds.), *Perspectives on activity theory* (pp. 377–404). Cambridge: Cambridge University Press.

Engeström, Y. (2001). Expansive learning at work: Towards an activity theoretical reconceptualization. *Education and Work, 14*(1), 133–156. doi:10.1080/13639080123238

Engeström, Y. (2007). Putting Vygotsky to work. The change laboratory as an application of double stimulation. In H. Daniels, M. Cole, & J. V. Wertsch (Eds.), *Cambridge companion to Vygotsky* (pp. 363-383). Cambridge: Cambridge University Press.

Engeström, Y. (2008). *From teams to knot. Activity-theoretical studies of collaboration and learning at work*. Cambridge: Cambridge University Press.

Engeström, Y., Engeström, R., & Kerosuo, H. (2003). The discursive construction of collaborative care. *Applied Linguistics, 24*(3), 286–315. doi:10.1093/applin/24.3.286

Foot, K. A. (2002). Pursuing an evolving object: A case study in object formation and identification. *Mind, Culture, and Activity, 9*(2), 132–149. doi:10.1207/S15327884MCA0902_04

Fullan, M., Hill, P., & Crévola, C. (2006). *Breakthrough*. New York: Corwin Press.

Gherardi, S. (2006). *Organizational knowledge: The texture of workplace learning*. Malden, MA: Blackwell.

Gutierrez, K., Basquedano-Lopez, P., Alvarez, H. H., & Chio, M. M. (1999). Building a culture of collaboration through hybrid language practices. *Theory into Practice, 32*(2), 87–93.

Hakarainnen, K., Palonen, T., Paavola, S., & Lehtinen, E. (2004). *Communities of networked expertise. Professional and educational perspectives*. Amsterdam: Elsevier.

Hubbard, L., Mehan, H., & Stein, M. K. (2006). *Reform as learning. School reform. Organizational culture, and community practrices in San Diego*. New York: Routledge.

Kling, R., & Courtright, C. (2003). Group behavior and learning in electronic forums: A socio-technical approach. *The Information Society, 19*(3), 221–236. doi:10.1080/01972240309465

Kolb, D. A., & Fry, R. (1975). Towards an applied theory of experiential learning. In C. L. Cooper (Ed.), *Theories of group processes* (pp. 33–58). London: Wiley.

Lauvaas, P., & Handal, G. (2000). *Supervision and theory of practice*. Oslo: Cappelen Akademisk Forlag.

Leithwood, K., & Louis, K. S. (1998). *Organizational learning in schools*. Lisse, the Netherlands: Swets & Zeitlinger.

Leont'ev, A. N. (1978). *Activity, consciousness, and personality*. Englewood Cliffs, NJ: Prentice-Hall.

Leont'ev, A. N. (1981). *Problems of the development of the mind*. Moscow: Progress.

Lund, A., & Hauge, T. E. (in press). Changing objects in knowledge creation practices. In S. Ludvigsen, A. Lund, I. Rasmussen, & S. Säljö (Eds.), *Learning across sites: New tools, infrastructures and practices*. London: Pergamon.

MacBeath, J., & Mortimore, P. (Eds.). (2001). *Improving school effectiveness*. Buckingham, England: Open University Press.

Mercer, N., & Wegerif, R. (1998). Is 'exploratory talk' productive talk? In K. Littleton & P. Light (Eds.), *Learning with computers: analyzing productive interactions* (pp. 79-102). London: Routledge

Miettinen, R., & Virkkunen, J. (2005). Epistemic objects, artefacts and organizational change. *Organization, 12*(3), 437–456. doi:10.1177/1350508405051279

Nemirovsky, R., Galvis, A., Kaplan, J., Cogan-Drew, D., & DiMattia, C. (2005). *VideoPaper Builder* (Version 3.0). Concord, MA: Concord Consortium.

Nonaka, I., & Takeuchi, H. (1995). *The knowledge creating company*. Oxford: Oxford University Press.

Olivero, F., Sutherland, R., & John, P. (2004). Seeing is believing: Using videopapers to transform teachers' professional knowledge and practice. *Cambridge Journal of Education, 34*(2), 179–191. doi:10.1080/0305764041 0001700552

Orlikowski, W. J. (1992). The duality of technology: Rethinking the concept of technology in organizations. *Organization Science, 3*(3), 398–427. doi:10.1287/orsc.3.3.398

Paavola, S., & Hakkarainen, K. (2005). The knowledge creation metaphor – An emergent epistemological approach to learning. *Science & Education, 14*, 535–557. doi:10.1007/s11191-004-5157-0

Sandvold, K. E., Øgrim, S., Flakstad, H., Bakken, T., Skrindo, K., & Pettersen, B. (2006). *Sigma, Mathematics.* Oslo: Gyldendal Norsk Forlag AS.

Scardamalia, M., & Bereiter, C. (1994). Computer support for knowledge building communities. *Journal of the Learning Sciences, 3*, 265–283. doi:10.1207/s15327809jls0303_3

Scardamalia, M., & Bereiter, C. (2006). Knowledge-building: Theory, pedagogy and technology. In K. Sawyer (Ed.), *The Cambridge handbook of the learning sciences,* (pp. 97–115). Cambridge, MA: Cambridge University Press.

Schlager, M. S., & Fusco, J. (2003). Teacher professional development, technology, and communities of practice: Are we putting the cart before the horse? *The Information Society, 19*, 203–220. doi:10.1080/01972240309464

Stahl, G. (2006). *Group cognition. Computer support for building collaborative knowledge.* Cambridge, MA: MIT Press.

Vygotsky, L. S. (1978). *Mind in society: The development of higher psychological processes.* Cambridge, MA: Harvard University Press.

Wasson, B., Ludvigsen, S., & Hoppe, U. (2003). *Designing for change in networked learning environments.* Dordrecht, the Netherlands: Kluwer.

Section 4
Pedagogies Afforded by Technology in TPD

Chapter 13
TPD as Online Collaborative Learning for Innovation in Teaching

Diana Laurillard
Institute of Education, UK

Elizabeth Masterman
University of Oxford, UK

ABSTRACT

This chapter focuses on supporting university teachers in the UK in the more innovative use of digital technologies. Although the use of these technologies is now widespread and increasing, it is not always optimised for effective learning. It is important that teachers' use of technology should be directed towards innovation and improvement in teaching and learning, and should not merely replicate their current practice in a digital medium. The authors therefore make the case for an online collaborative environment to scaffold teachers' engagement with technology-enhanced learning. The chapter outlines the findings of our recent research into a blended approach to TPD, and use these to identify the requirements for an online collaborative environment: tools for learning design, guidance, and access to relevant resources to support teachers in their discovery of new forms of technology-enhanced teaching and learning. Such an environment, they argue, would provide a framework for a "community of innovation" in which teachers participate both as learners and researchers.

INTRODUCTION

The social and political context within which most higher education (HE) systems operate is making increasing demands on improvements in both the quality and the scale of teaching and learning. The Lisbon strategy on lifelong learning, agreed in 2000, aimed to make the EU the world's most competitive and dynamic knowledge-based economy by 2010, and called on member states

...to create the necessary conditions to enable universities to improve their performance, to modernise themselves and to become more competitive – in short, to become leaders in their own renaissance and to play their part in the creation of the knowledge-based society envisaged under the Lisbon strategy. (CEC, 2006)

DOI: 10.4018/978-1-60566-780-5.ch013

The current thinking at national level in the EU is exemplified in a recent education strategy document from the UK (DfES, 2005, p. 94). This set an agenda for further and higher education that includes the provision of high quality university courses with excellent teaching; access to university for those with the potential to benefit; and greater, and more flexible, opportunities to study. The emphasis on both higher quality and broader reach is thus a direct response to the Lisbon strategy. One major source of these increased requirements is the incursion of digital technologies into every aspect of employment, which means that the education system must both adapt in response to the changing technology environment and equip its graduates to do likewise.

However, these ambitious aims for the education system are not matched by commensurate increases in funding. Furthermore, at the post-compulsory level (i.e. education beyond the age of 16) the burden of cost is increasingly being transferred to the students. Schemes under which graduates contribute retrospectively to the cost of their learning have been implemented or are under consideration in many EU countries. However, the widening participation agenda, which aims to open up HE to those in lower socio-economic groups, calls the affordability of these ambitions into question unless universities can also find ways of improving the productivity of learning and teaching. If we are to improve both quality and reach, as governments demand, improving productivity will be essential.

Technology-enhanced learning (TEL) is one possible option for remedying this state of affairs. Digital technologies can be harnessed to serve every aspect of teaching and learning because they now provide the electronic equivalent of every educational technology invented so far. Paper, books, libraries, chalkboards, notebooks, pens, broadcasting: all are mirrored in different kinds of digital technologies, often bearing the same names, such as e-*book*, digital *library*, interactive white*board*, *notebook*, light-*pen*, pod*casting*, web*casting*.

Because of this capacity to support diverse kinds of teaching-learning interactions, TEL has the potential to help in meeting the demands of governments. It can improve both quality (e.g. by adapting to individual learners' needs) and reach (e.g. by offering greater flexibility in the mode and location of learning), and because it can also support economies of scale, could improve productivity as well, making expansion affordable without commensurate increases in funding.

Although the potential of TEL is very exciting, however, it is challenging to realize. It presupposes radical innovation, both in the way learners are supported and in teachers' approaches to pedagogy. Responsibility for such innovation is therefore a key issue, and one that cannot be entrusted solely to the educational publishers and software houses that control the market in online educational resources. It is our contention that the academic community itself must take responsibility for re-thinking the nature of teaching and learning in the light of the new opportunities afforded by digital technologies. However, if academics are to be innovative in teaching and learning, they will need considerable support. In this chapter we introduce the idea of an online "community of innovation," in which the individual professional teacher can embrace the role of innovator through participating in a supportive online environment as learner and researcher alongside their peers.

THE FEASIBILITY OF TEACHER-LED INNOVATION

In this section we review the situation that currently pertains vis-à-vis support for university teachers in the UK as they engage with TEL. We identify the emergent practices on which our vision of teacher-led innovation through a professional support network is founded.

The majority of educational institutions are adapting to the pressure for more students by injecting high levels of investment into ICT infrastructure, so that staff and students have good access to personal computing and to the internet. However, the mere provision of access is not sufficient. It is clear that, for many teachers, introducing TEL has ramifications for the whole of their practice and may require them to redesign courses they have perhaps taught for years (Masterman, 2008a). Unfortunately, a relatively small proportion of ICT investment has been directed at changing practice. Teachers in post-compulsory education have no compulsory professional training, as schoolteachers typically do, yet they are expected to embrace significant changes in the way they carry out their professional duties, and build considerable knowledge of how to use TEL (Armstrong et al., 2005; Dutton, Cheong, & Park, 2004; Kennewell & Morgan, 2003) with little time and with minimal training or resources (JISC, 2004; Britain, 2004). Where there are institutional initiatives in TPD for TEL, they tend to focus mainly on the local "virtual learning environment" (VLE).

The disparity between levels of investment in infrastructure and professional development was recognised in the review of HE in the UK in 1997, known as the Dearing Report. Its recommendation that "all institutions should, over the medium term, review the changing role of staff as a result of Communications and Information Technology" (NCIHE, 1997, p. 43) led to targeted funding for teaching quality enhancement, a national teaching fellowship scheme, and a specialist institute

to accredit programmes of training for higher education teachers; to commission research and development in learning and teaching practices; and to stimulate innovation. (ibid., p. 126)

These developments in the UK were important because they legitimised and motivated innovation and research on teaching and learning. Further support is available to university teachers through the provision of regular workshops run by national organisations such as JISC (http://www.jisc.ac.uk)

and ALT (http://www.alt.ac.uk/); a learning and teaching support network of discipline-oriented advice centres run by universities (LTSN); digital libraries of resources (e.g. the British Library); and through national and international repositories of TEL resources and learning objects such as JORUM (http://www.jorum.ac.uk).

Even so, the shift of direction in the culture towards a greater focus on learning and teaching has not yet led to the significant investment that would be needed to make radical changes. Other, equally profound, changes are required if HE is to exploit technology fully in the service of its ambitions. One of the most significant lies in teachers' perspective on their own practice: they need to think of themselves also as *learners* and to think of teaching as, in part, a *learning profession*.

Although a number of institutions have active professional development programmes for TEL (e.g. Sharpe, Benfield, & Francis, 2006; Salmon, Jones & Armellini, 2008), these are only able to reach small numbers of academics, rather than the thousands that constitute their teaching populations. True, individual teachers have been prepared to experiment with TEL, and this action research approach has generated the bulk of the successful practice now documented, for example, in recent case studies (Comber et al., 2002; JISC, 2004; JISC, 2007), as well as in the learning technology journals. However, individual efforts cannot suffice. Moreover, while teachers are often prepared to share and reuse their own ideas (Day, Stobart, Sammons, & Kington, 2006), the exchange of professional practice within and across institutions and sectors is hampered by factors that include: the variation in learning cultures and approaches (Hodkinson & James, 2003); differences among subject disciplines (Knight, Tait, & Yorke, 2006); the context-dependent nature of many teaching materials; and the privileging of research over teaching (Masterman & Lee, 2005).

All these difficulties mean that, although many teachers are using TEL in some form by now, they are primarily replicating their current practice in a digital environment, rather than exploring ways in which they can use that environment for genuine innovation. Much of their use of technology is limited to PowerPoint presentations, online reading materials, and discussion forums in the VLE. There are relatively few who can find the time to explore the genuine benefits of TEL, such as new forms of interaction with their students, productive online collaborative learning, and learning through interaction with adaptive models of the subject domain.

Does this relative conservatism in teachers' use of TEL matter? Yes, because if education is to achieve the improvements in quality and reach identified in the previous section, then teachers must be able to innovate using digital technologies. To achieve this, they need encouragement and practical guidance in understanding how best to design TEL activities for their learners, whether they work in "conventional" educational institutions (Beetham & Sharpe, 2007; Webb & Cox, 2004), or in part-time, distance, or workplace settings (Eraut, 2004; Weller, Pegler, & Mason, 2005).

Our own recent research suggests that, where teachers are prepared to seek inspiration and new ideas, they tend to do so informally, enacting professional development as part of everyday practice through consultations with colleagues and Web searches, rather than within formal TPD programmes. This is a promising beginning; however, given the level of innovation that is both needed and expected of education, teachers will have to become learners in a more formal sense: a profession that continually renews itself, adapting to the changing cultural and economic conditions, and learning from their own and others' experience. Since no government has provided sufficient incentives, time or support for the major renewal process that this implies, we argue that this change can only happen, over time, by becoming part of the way teachers do their job.

We therefore propose to capitalise on the informal community-based learning that already

prevails among teachers, and raise it to the level of a professional process that makes it possible for academic teachers both to build their own professional support network, and to take responsibility for the necessary innovation themselves.

In the remainder of this chapter we address the feasibility of this question from two perspectives: the pedagogic and the social. From the pedagogic perspective, we propose an online "learning design" environment comprising a set of digital tools and resources; from the social perspective, we outline a vision of the kind of community in which these tools and resources might function, through mediating a long overdue dialogue between teachers and educational researchers.

SUPPORTING PEDAGOGIC INNOVATION

Outline of Previous Work

Our case for supporting pedagogic innovation through a set of online tools and resources is founded on two complementary projects to research and develop proof-of-concept prototype "pedagogy planning" tools at the Universities of London and Oxford: "The London Pedagogy Planner" (LPP) (San Diego et al., 2008) and "Phoebe" (Masterman, 2008b). These tools belong to an emergent genre intended to support teachers and lecturers in making appropriate and effective use of digital technologies in their teaching. The conceptual framework underpinning the tools was "learning design," an approach which is concerned – significantly for this chapter – with modelling and sharing practice in the creative use of technology (Agostinho, 2008) and emphasises the aspects of a learning experience that can be planned, or "designed for," in advance (cf. JISC, 2006). Learning design operates at multiple levels of granularity, from whole programmes of study down to individual learning "sessions" (e.g. seminars, tutorials, or lab classes).

The development of the two planning tools was preceded by a research phase, in which each project worked closely with teachers to elicit their normal practice in planning for learning at all levels of granularity and, hence, to determine the design requirements for the tool in question.

For example, the Phoebe project found the most frequent learning design activity to be at the level of the creation and revision of individual learning sessions. It uncovered a relative consistency in the core components of the task, but a wide variation in the actual approaches adopted. This suggested that a pedagogy planning tool should be capable of supporting a variety of routes through the design, as well as supporting teachers' underlying pedagogic approach, whether derived from a formal theory of learning (e.g., constructivist, situated, behaviorist) or from personal experience.

Both projects also found that many teachers produce formal structured plans, often to meet institutional requirements and using institution-specific terminology. This indicated that the planning tool would need a degree of customizability in the output representations (finished plans). Moreover, in order arrive at the finished plan, individual teachers sometimes produce a number of intermediate representations, some on paper and others created in digital tools. Therefore, a planning tool needs to be capable of re-representing the same information in multiple formats.

Extending the scope of the activity to collaboration, data from the Phoebe project showed that, more often than not, teachers plan together. Therefore, communication mechanisms, and the means both to create and to store the shared representations, are central to effective working.

The Prototype Tools

The LPP was based on a model of the critical relationships among the components of learning design and aimed to support lecturers from the initial curriculum requirements, learner needs and resource constraints, through to the TEL activities

in which their students would engage (San Diego et al., 2008). It took the user through a series of design decisions, displaying their consequences in multiple dynamic numerical and graphical representations of their learning design. Figure 1 shows a sample screen where the user is allocating the total credit hours available to a selection of teaching methods (lectures, tutorials, etc.). The LPP then gives feedback in terms of the likely amount of time for which each method will elicit the different kinds of cognitive activity on the part of the learner (attention, inquiry, etc.).

By attempting to give feedback on the users' actions, the LPP faced the challenge of supporting the teacher's underlying pedagogic approach, while at the same time making clear its own conceptual model (i.e. the model underpinning the guidance that it offered). To achieve this balance, the LPP used Laurillard's Conversational Framework (Laurillard, 2002) to distil theories and principles of learning into successive design decisions and parameters that were neither overly simplistic nor overly complex. These were intended to stimulate ways of thinking about learning design, but not to force the user's hand in any way. For example, on the screen shown in Figure 1, the Conversational Framework is used to interpret the design in terms of the nature of the learning experience it offers. As the teacher assigns a number of hours to a teaching method, the tool calculates the proportion of time likely to be spent on the five distinct forms of learning: attention, inquiry, discussion, practice, and production. However, the user can edit these figures to suit the specific circumstances of the learning experience they are designing.

In contrast with the LPP, Phoebe was a predominantly text-based online planning tool with an extensive resource bank of conceptual and practical guidance, as shown in Figure 2. It provided a simple authoring environment that allowed the creation of learning designs from pre-defined templates. This enabled users to bring together the key components of a learning design, and record ideas and requirements as they

Figure 1. The London Pedagogy Planner enabled teachers to plan the distribution of learners' time across different teaching methods, and see the result in terms of the different kinds of cognitive activity (attention, inquiry, etc.) elicited.

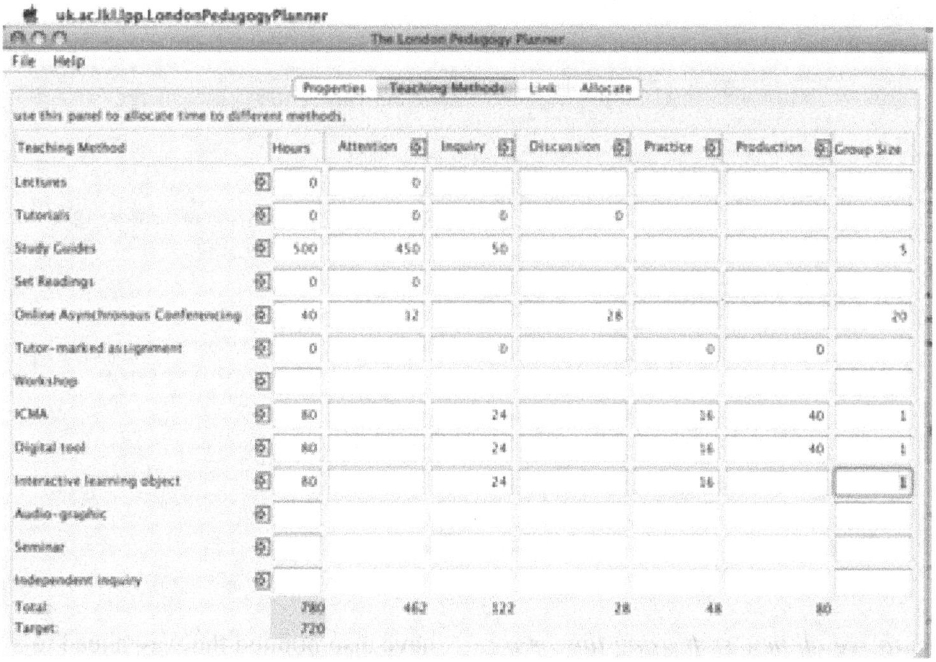

designed the activities that make up a learning experience. As the user worked through a design they had access to context-specific help, as well as to resources intended to encourage exploration, adaptation and improvement in their use of TEL and in their pedagogy.

In keeping with the principles of learning design, Phoebe promoted the sharing of users' work by a) including illustrative designs in the support system and b) allowing users to make designs created within Phoebe available to other users of the tool. This is complementary to the approach taken by the LPP, which could link to the resources and designs generated in Phoebe, and then analyse them with respect to pedagogic theory and the course-planning requirements of users' own institutions.

Key Findings from the Evaluation

The LPP and Phoebe projects each evaluated its own prototype pedagogy planning tool independently through a series of practical workshops involving both experienced and trainee teachers, who worked with the relevant tool to design a learning session of their own. Data were collected through observation and online surveys.

Although the tools were "proof-of-concept" prototypes only, and as such did not fully implement the requirements elicited in the research phase, it was clear that teachers value this kind of online support. Quantitative data collected by the LPP Project showed that 85% of the 59 participants in the evaluation viewed such tools as a worthwhile development, and this was reinforced by enthusiastic comments from evaluators of Phoebe, e.g.:

Figure 2. The Phoebe pedagogy planning tool, showing the context-specific help available to teachers as they edit a learning design. The relative sizes of the "design area" and "guidance area" can be adjusted according to requirements.

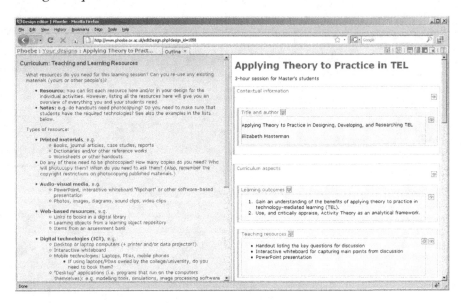

I would like to see all new staff using this as a way of: a) developing a real appreciation of the learning process; b) gaining confidence in their delivery because of a comprehensive planning process which they will then be able to use again; c) develop relatively high-level ICT skills.

I would like experienced lecturers to use Phoebe to: a) develop a better appreciation of how technology can be used to enhance traditional learning approaches; b) develop the courage to move out of their comfort zone and 'have a go' [...] c) use it to work more collaboratively with their subject colleagues. (Lecturer quoted in Masterman, 2008b, pp. 27–8)

Overall, the LPP and Phoebe projects confirmed, from the teachers' point of view, the potential value of an online "learning design environment" of tools and resources to guide them in using digital technologies to improve the quality and flexibility (reach) of their students' learning. The research and evaluation phases have also pointed the way ahead to a more full-featured prototype that can build on the outcomes of both projects.

However, as we have made clear, teachers cannot act alone to innovate in a successful and sustainable manner: rather, novel ideas and approaches need to be propagated through and across communities. Significantly for our purposes, the evaluation of the LPP and Phoebe also shed light on teachers' perceptions of the social (community) context in which an online learning design environment might function. First, the role of the community is pivotal since, left to their own devices, teachers may not voluntarily engage with such tools: "It is about people and events which encourage practitioners to engage with such tools" (university lecturer quoted in Masterman, 2008b, p. 54). Second, although that community may be located within an institution, it must be one in which individuals participate voluntarily and are motivated by intrinsic factors: that is, teachers must sense the potential benefits of such tools *to themselves*:

it depends on whether [the tools] are able to engender a sense of 'ownership' of a genuinely creative process which puts the learner at its heart, rather than create the impression of a mechanistic process. (University lecturer quoted in Masterman, 2008b, p. 55)

Teacher-led innovation within a framework of institutional support: this is the message from practitioners that we take forward into the next section of this chapter.

SUPPORTING AN ONLINE COMMUNITY IN COLLABORATIVE INNOVATION

What does it take to support an online community that learns through collaboration? The TEL research community has developed a strong interest in using digital technologies to support online collaborative learning communities of students; in this section we discuss how the same technologies might be adapted to support a collaborative learning community of *teachers*.

The Value of Tools as a Catalyst for Change

The LPP and Phoebe projects showed, even in a small way, how supportive design tools have the potential to help change teachers' practice. Indeed, the use of tools is one of the most powerful ways in which humans do change their behaviour:

…it was technology—the ability to physically interact with the environment—that made life easier. Just consider things as simple as the basket and the wheel. The adaptive evolutionary advantage in making tools was enormous. (Wolpert, 2003, p. 1741)

Nowadays, the environment in which learners interact with resources and with their peers in formal education is often virtual (i.e. online) rather than physical, requiring the tools and technologies of communication and design, rather than those to which Wolpert refers. Nevertheless, the essential point of technology has always been that it "[makes] life easier" or better, in some way. Therefore, once a tool has demonstrated its benefits to its early adopters, it is rapidly disseminated through the community by and for which it has been created. Our premise is that an online tool (or set of tools) that is usable, useful and genuinely relevant to teachers' needs, will provide the mechanism by which the teaching community disseminates its own ideas and thereby adapts more rapidly to its changing political and social environment. In this section, therefore, we present a model for an online collaborative environment that capitalises on the experience and wisdom of the teaching community, and enables teachers to progress their knowledge by building on each others' work.

Modelling the Design Process as a Social Practice

The picture of learning design that emerged from our previous work has resonances with Martin Oliver's characterisation of curriculum design as "a social practice that involves orientation to historical precedents, accessible resources [and] local values" (Oliver, 2002, pp. 13–14), rather than one that is governed by a "rationalistic and linear" model (Oliver, 2003). This has substantial ramifications for the design of an online environment to support practice, especially for building a computational model of the learning design process.

Oliver's picture is further complicated because, although practitioners may be designing primarily at the session level, they are governed by the decisions made at the module or course level, including the allocation of resources, teaching methods, and timing. Conversely, their decisions at the session level may have an impact on the higher level. Moreover, the process at each level may involve a succession of phases or, even, an iterative cycle. For example, Beetham (2008) has identified four core activities in the construction of a learning session: i) creating a design (plan) for the session; ii) "instantiating," or setting up the learning environment (e.g. preparing a laboratory for a practical class, or uploading resources and activities to a VLE); iii) realising, or running, the design with students in that environment; and iv) reviewing (reflecting on, evaluating) the design and the learning session that was realised from it.

Given that design is a social practice, with teachers belonging to a professional community even when they are working in physical isolation (Masterman, 2008a), the individual activities at all levels must be embedded into their social context. Moreover, where that professional community is also a *learning* community, the plans, resources and reflections associated with one learning session need to be captured so that other members of the community may learn from it. In relation to the four core activities listed in the previous paragraph, this means that:

i.   Design is not simply an individual creative activity, but one that builds on the work of other teachers, using existing designs as stimuli for new ones, or as the basis for re-design, or as part of a broader design. It therefore presupposes access to a repository of existing ideas and resources generated by the community.

ii.   Instantiating a design must take account of the learning environment – physical or virtual – already inhabited by the students, as well as by other teachers. It must therefore be compatible with what the rest of that teaching community is doing.

iii. When a design is realised with students, data must also be gathered both on its usage and on students' performance, to enable the teaching community to understand, and learn from, that design.

iv.   Reviewing the design, in terms of the way it was used and students' feedback, enables the individual teacher to report what he or she has learned from the experience to the rest of the community, or to improve on the design as a contribution to the resources of the community.

As the individual teacher embeds their own design process in this context of a professional learning community, they become more like a researcher, discovering how to improve the effectiveness of their teaching (Laurillard, 2008). However, for this to be possible, an online collaborative design environment must, at the minimum, enable teachers to record their decisions and, most important, capture data from the "realisation" phase that can help others judge whether the design is adaptable to their own needs. Ideally, it will support all of the above capabilities, as well as others at higher levels of granularity (i.e. module, course, or programme).

Scaffolding Teachers' Engagement with the Work of Others

A key function of an online collaborative design environment lies, of course, in teachers' professional development: providing tools and context-specific guidance for planning and design. In the early stages of their engagement with TEL, we must enable teachers to benefit from work already done by others. This can be done by providing links from the various tools within the design environment to relevant online materials, such as learning objects and resources, learning patterns, case studies, and summaries that take the findings of research into pedagogy and TEL and distil them into recommendations for effective practice. Teachers who wish to explore the use of TEL will have access to what their peers have already done, some ideas to build on, and guidance from the fruits of other teachers' experience. Of course, such resources are currently limited, as the teaching profession has barely begun to build these kinds of practices, still less to record their outcomes for the benefit of others.

Although it is, in principle, relatively straightforward to link to existing online resources, the lack of good metadata often makes them difficult for search engines to discover. Moreover, many research reports and papers are too lengthy for this purpose, since teachers need only short, easily digestible, summaries. Digital libraries and learning object repositories do exist, but we have not yet built the teaching community into the kind of online professional learning community that is able to improve these libraries, nor improve their own teaching by using them. An online collaborative design environment that scaffolds their introduction into this kind of practice would help to accelerate the developing of such an online learning community.

This will be important, because our own research, as well as others', has underscored the importance of a community approach both to teachers' initial engagement with TEL and to the promotion of good practice and sharing of learning designs: "Human support remains an essential feature of learning design implementations" (Beetham, 2008). Although such support may well begin with intensive one-to-one support from experts, it usually moves on to "collaborative support networks" based around a particular discipline, pedagogic focus or, even, institution: "This is how academic staff naturally seek evidence and principles to support their practice." (Beetham, 2008). Where teachers are co-located, such networks may be blended: collaborating face to face, but sharing their work online. Where they are dispersed geographically, fully online communities may develop.

Bearing in mind that the majority of teachers already engage in some form of collective design activity, we conclude that an online learning design environment needs the functionality for collaboration a) within communities in the form of support for multiple authoring, customisation of terms and outputs, and links to resources in "local" institutional repositories, and b) across communities – enabling, for example, users to interrogate resource banks in other institutions and consult the contents of these for inspiration and/or repurposing for use with their own learners.

The Role of the Practitioner Community in Developing and Sustaining an Online Design Environment

If the community for which a tool is intended is truly to "own" it, then that community must participate in its design, development and maintenance. Recognising the importance of starting from teachers' personal planning context and needs, we advocate an approach successfully adopted in the Phoebe project: working with a small group of informant-practitioners, whose role is to inform the (iterative) functional design and contribute to the development of the guidance and support *from the very beginning of the project*. This will be a permanent feature of such a tool because the demands of the community will keep developing, becoming gradually more sophisticated.

The role of the informant-practitioner is derived from the framework of "informant design" put forward by Scaife and Rogers (1999). In our conceptualisation, informant design involves the input of various representatives of the TEL community at the specific stages of the project where their contribution will be of the most value. For example, in the Phoebe project the diverse group of informant-practitioners had very different dispositions towards TEL depending on their situation, at the individual, departmental or institutional level. In the LPP project, each version of the prototype became a catalyst for further demands as practitioners saw what was possible, and using it triggered ideas for new types of functionality they could not have imagined before. Also – and this is a key aspect of the informant design approach – experienced practitioners are in a position to articulate the perspectives and needs of those teachers who have travelled less far along the TEL road.

An online learning design environment to support the professional development of teachers also needs to be adaptable for local use so that through the experience of planning learning, analysing design decisions, and sharing resources and pedagogic design, each institutional community can build a collective understanding of learning design that is relevant to it. Conversely, it needs to be able to feed the best of its local knowledge and expertise back to the educational community at large. Resources of this kind need continuous development if users are to continually return to them for help and inspiration.

FUTURE TRENDS

In this section, we take our empirical findings regarding the role of online learning communities in the development, uptake and sustainability of a collaborative learning design environment forward to propose a new kind of community: a community in which teachers go beyond the mere sharing of resources and receiving of wisdom dispensed by researchers to actually working with researchers, and eventually developing a research-like approach to innovation in their practice within a voluntary or "self-identified" (Beetham, 2008) community.

Advancing the Understanding and Use of TEL through Dialogue between Researchers and Practitioners

The idea of online communities of practice for teachers' professional development is important for two reasons. Firstly, as Lucas and her colleagues have concluded from their research among academics in higher education, staff who work collaboratively – whether formally or informally – are more likely to be involved in innovative teaching and learning (Lucas, 2008). Secondly – and more relevant to the theoretical position we propose in this chapter – such communities could help to create more permeable boundaries between teachers and educational researchers.

Educational researchers themselves are now beginning to argue for the importance of online communities enabling teachers to engage more directly with them, because such communities "transform research findings into practical action which has an immediate impact on classroom practice and pedagogy" (Armstrong & Curran, 2006, p. 337). When teachers and researchers collaborate closely on how best to introduce digital technologies into normal teaching, their greater sense of control and ownership leads to a shift in the teachers' aspirations, as they go beyond their craft knowledge, "eager to find more formal, external warrants for their thinking and practice" (Triggs & John, 2004, p. 431). As teachers begin to think more like researchers, so they begin to lose their sense of isolation, to exchange and transform their knowledge, and to analyse how to improve their practice (Laurillard, 2008).

However, what these researchers have not argued so far is that the influence can usefully operate in the reverse direction as well, enabling research to be more responsive to teachers' needs, and to feed its output more directly into practice. We see this as being an important contribution of this online collaborative environment approach to teachers' professional development: i.e. that it attempts to embody research findings in the way it offers support. We envisage three ways in which this might be achieved: i) transferring the findings of research directly to practitioners, ii) translating theories and research findings into supportive frameworks for practice, and iii) disseminating effective practice that is the outcome of teachers' own action research.

The transfer of research findings to practice is, in effect, a one-way process that makes available to teachers the outcomes of research into teaching and learning, case study accounts of successful implementations, and outlines of theoretical principles. However, just as a busy practising teacher would be unlikely to receive kindly an educational researcher who handed them a full-length academic paper to "read, absorb and inwardly digest," so the users of an online support system cannot be expected to read such material verbatim. As we have already noted, easily comprehensible summaries and digests are needed for the first method to work.

However, the mere transfer of findings from researcher to teacher does not necessarily mean that they will be turned into practice. What is also needed is their translation into a supportive framework in which the teacher can make informed decisions about a particular learning design: something that can be provided by an online environment designed with a strong awareness of learning theories. Moreover, in underpinning the teacher's decision-making these theories are put to a very direct test by the learning session that is realised from the design. In that sense, the process allows not just transfer of theory into practice, but also feedback from practice to validate (or, conversely, challenge) the theory.

The third way in which research findings can inform practice is through the adoption and dissemination of effective practice. If a teacher designs an effective learning session or module, then other teachers can inspect it, analyse why it works, and decide how to adapt it for their own use. If they succeed in improving it, then their improved version can be inspected and adapted by yet other teachers. This iterative, collaborative process is a form of action research by the teaching practitioners, who are creating and disseminating their own research findings in a tight iterative loop of practice, research, dissemination, and further practice. The expectations of an online learning design environment in this respect are twofold:

i. It should optimise the likelihood that the initial design will be successful (i.e. through the theory-informed supportive framework embedded in the technology);

ii. Through storing teachers' completed learning designs in a communal online environment, it would make them available on a far wider scale than hitherto (cf. our earlier discussion on the barriers to the sharing and reuse of designs).

Of course, there is no certainty that refined effective practice will be distilled back into explicit formal theory, as the reinterpretation of practice at the level of theory has not hitherto been a concern of teachers. This is where the researcher steps in, to reflect on the implications of the progressive refinements of practice embodied in the learning designs for the theory underpinning them, and then feeding those reflections back into online support.

The Characteristics of a Community of Innovation

By developing an online tool to support teachers' professional development, we are conceptualising this online learning community as a computer-supported collaborative learning (CSCL) community (Stahl, Koschmann, & Suthers, 2006). That is, we propose to emulate for teachers the collaborative learning process currently advocated for students. There is extensive support in the literature for the idea of collaborative learning, which is closely linked to the social constructivist view of learning. Digital tools to support CSCL have been developed and researched for some time, so it is important that a CSCL environment for teachers should learn from the findings of previous research into how to promote the exchange of ideas and the sharing of feedback (Scardamalia & Bereiter, 2006), how to develop a tool-mediated design (Hmelo-Silver, 2003), and how to construct a shared representation (Jermann & Dillenbourg, 2003; Kobbe et al., 2007).

However, the context for teachers is very different from that for students. Research on CSCL has shown that learners' motivation to collaborate has to be carefully nurtured by the teacher. In contrast, when the collaborating partners are teachers, and learning takes place outside (or beyond) formal TPD programmes, there is no-one to orchestrate the process. Moreover, the motivation to share their designs is probably outweighed by the requirement to teach, and by the lack of reward for sharing teaching as opposed to sharing research. There are other differences from students' collaborative learning, too: peers with whom one might share similar interests and challenges may reside in different institutions, and there may be competition (i.e. to attract students to one's own programme) as well as collaboration.

The online collaborative environments that we provide for teachers' professional development must therefore be careful to recognise and adapt to the realities of teachers' mainstream work. Working contexts vary greatly, but teachers who develop their own "micro-communities" of practice to explore the use of ICT become "enabled professionals" (Triggs & John, 2004). These communities might be centred on a particular subject area, but they can embrace professionals with different perspectives. The micro-communities could then combine to form meso-communities: i.e. across different institutional contexts, but with a similar core focus on improving practice. In Triggs and John's empirical work in this area, the significance of professional learning in this context meant that, for the teachers:

new forms of engagement equipped them to deal confidently with and actively pursue pedagogic challenge and development. In each case, it was not knowledge transacting that held the key but the process of knowledge transformation within their practice. And in each case it was the activity within the "micro-" and "meso-" communities of practice that enabled this transformation to occur.

(Triggs & John, 2004, p. 434)

The premise is that the mere exchange or transfer of knowledge, such as the advice and guidance offered in an online environment, is insufficient for professional learning. Rather, knowledge must be "encountered and transformed in and through action", as in Wenger's concept of communities of practice (Triggs & John, 2004, p. 428; Wenger, 1999). The forms of interaction between teachers that we build into our online learning communities must therefore respect the same requirements. We need to facilitate the continual iteration between sharing, discussing, challenging, adopting, testing, adapting, and disseminating: in other words, all the activities of computer-supported collaborative learning.

The Supportive Institutional Context

As we have already noted, teachers must be motivated to develop the potential of TEL themselves, and the benefit of using online learning design tools, and of engaging in professional development, must be visible *to them* through the improved quality and productivity of their work. However, the benefit must also be recognised by their institution. This means that the work must be seen in the context of institutional strategies to support teachers in the long process of innovation and improvement to meet their strategic aims:

Technology makes its best contribution when it is implemented in the service of high-level strategic ambitions, less so when we use it 'because it's there.' (Laurillard et al., 2009, p. 299)

Otherwise put, universities and colleges must become "learning organisations" in the fullest sense. The teaching community orients itself towards what it perceives to be the principal incentives and drivers, and these rarely focus on the quality of teaching innovation or on extending the same quality to a larger number of students.

This means that institutions themselves must take responsibility for enabling and motivating their academic communities to take on the task of professional development in order to innovate, and improve practice, but, as we noted from the Phoebe evaluation data, to do this in a non-coercive manner.

CONCLUSION

Within the context of increasing demand for improvements in the quality and scale of lifelong learning consequent on the Lisbon strategy, this chapter is based on the assumption that technology-enhanced learning (TEL) will be needed because of its potential to improve the quality of students' learning and broaden access to HE without commensurate increases in funding. However, progress is currently hampered, in part by a lack of comprehensive TPD for TEL at the institutional level that both reaches the numbers of teaching staff required and stimulates the kinds of radical change to their teaching approach (pedagogy) and real innovation in the use of TEL that are needed to effect meaningful change.

We have argued that innovation in teaching and learning must be led by the teaching profession. Many teachers are undertaking TEL initiatives either individually or in small groups, but this will not achieve the best results for learners, and will certainly not achieve improved productivity without a collective effort that builds knowledge of how to do this well. In this chapter we set ourselves the challenge to capitalise on this grassroots activity by providing teachers and lecturers with an online collaborative environment for TPD and the model of a community of innovation that might be nurtured by this environment. We conceptualise an online learning community for TPD as online collaborative learning by teachers who are embarking on the discovery of how best to use technology to enhance learning.

Building a digital environment to support TPD

will formalise the process and product of learning design because it will result in a system that explicitly embodies the stages of the process, the design decisions made, the theories in use, the existing materials available for access and adaptation, and the process of collaboration across the community (see the Learning Design Support Environment project http://www.ldse.org.uk). The online environment will no doubt always be imperfect, and incomplete, but by articulating TPD as a process of collaborative learning design TPD itself will be more clearly inspectable and testable, more easily subjected to critique and change, than is possible now. Professional development knowledge is articulated in many texts, events and practices, but by capturing at least some of these in a digital tool, we have a way of developing both theory and practice in an iterative and explicit way.

This task will be far from straightforward. Our own previous research into pedagogy planning tools has demonstrated the complex, ill-structured nature of designing, instantiating, realising and reviewing learning experiences, and the challenges to modelling educational intent and theories of learning computationally. We will also need to accommodate, *inter alia*, teachers' needs and preferences regarding the formats in which intermediate designs and final products are represented. But fundamental to our approach is the sense that the teaching profession must be given the tools to enable them to take the lead in the pedagogic innovations needed throughout our education systems.

In the long term, we envisage that an online learning design environment for teachers will be owned and maintained by the teaching community itself, working across all sectors of education and training, identifying and responding to its own needs, and sharing its creative ideas as a "community of innovation". In reality, of course, this will be an agglomeration of layered communities: individual organisations with their own discourses and forms of representation, and communities that cross institutional boundaries, knitting together these diverse forms in a common understanding and purpose.

The ambitions for higher education in particular, and education in general, demand a more effective and more professional approach to the use of learning technologies. By supporting teachers in the innovative use of digital technologies, enabling teaching to become the collaborative online learning community of innovative professional practice it needs to be, we will be better placed to succeed in those ambitions.

ACKNOWLEDGMENT

Funding for the Phoebe and LPP projects was made available by the Joint Information Systems Committee (JISC) in the UK, and the Centre for Distance Education, University of London.

REFERENCES

Agostinho, S. (2008). Learning Design Representations to Document, Model, and Share Teaching Practice. In L. Lockyer, S. Bennett, S. Agostinho, & B. Harper (Eds.), *Handbook of Research on Learning Design and Learning Objects: Issues, Applications and Technologies* (pp. 1–19). Hershey, PA: IGI Global.

Armstrong, V., Barnes, S., Sutherland, R., Curran, S., Miller, S., & Thompson, I. (2005). Collaborative research methodology for investigating teaching and learning: the use of interactive whiteboard technology. *Educational Review, 57*(4), 457–469. doi:10.1080/00131910500279551

Armstrong, V., & Curran, S. (2006). Developing a collaborative model of research using digital video. *Computers & Education, 46*(3), 336–347. doi:10.1016/j.compedu.2005.11.015

Beetham, H. (2008). *Review: Design for Learning programme phase 2*. Unpublished report. Bristol: JISC.

Britain, S. (2004). *A Review of Learning design: Concept, Specifications and Tools. A report for the JISC E-learning Pedagogy Programme*. Retrieved February 4, 2009, from http://www.jisc.ac.uk/media/documents/programmes/elearningpedagogy/learningdesigntoolsfinalreport.pdf

CEC. (2006). *Delivering on the modernisation agenda for universities: Education, research and innovation*. Brussels: Commission of the European Communities.

Comber, C., Watling, R., Lawson, T., Cavendish, S., McEune, R., & Paterson, F. (2002). *Impact2: Learning at home and school: Case studies*. Coventry, UK: Becta.

Day, C., Stobart, G., Sammons, P., & Kington, A. (2006). Variations in the work and lives of teachers: relative and relational effectiveness. *Teachers and Teaching: theory and practice, 12*(2), 169–192.

DfES. (2005). *Five Year Strategy for Children and Learners*. Retrieved February 4, 2009, from http://www.dfes.gov.uk/publications/5yearstrategy/

Dutton, W., Cheong, P. H., & Park, A. (2004). An Ecology of Constraints on e-Learning in Higher Education: The Case of a Virtual Learning Environment. *Prometheus, 22*(2), 131–149. doi:10.1080/0810902042000218337

Eraut, M. (2004). Informal learning in the workplace. *Studies in Continuing Education, 26*(2), 247–273. doi:10.1080/158037042000225245

Hmelo-Silver, C. E. (2003). Analyzing collaborative knowledge construction: multiple methods for integrated understanding. *Computers & Education, 41*(4), 397–420. doi:10.1016/j.compedu.2003.07.001

Hodkinson, P., & James, D. (2003). Transforming Learning Cultures in Further Education. *Journal of Vocational Education and Training, 55*(4), 389–406. doi:10.1080/13636820300200236

Jermann, P., & Dillenbourg, P. (2003). Elaborating new arguments through a CSCL script. In J. Andriessen, M. Baker, & D. Suthers (Eds.), *Arguing to learn: Confronting cognitions in computer-supported collaborative learning environments* (pp. 205–226). Dordrecht, The Netherlands: Kluwer.

JISC. (2004). *Effective Practice with e-Learning*. Higher Education Funding Council for England.

JISC. (2006). *Background to the JISC Circular 1/06: Design for Learning Programme* (briefing document). Bristol: JISC. Retrieved January 20, 2009, from http://www.jisc.ac.uk/fundingopportunities/funding_calls/2006/02/funding_01_06.aspx

JISC. (2007). *Effective Practice with e-Assessment*. Higher Education Funding Council for England.

Kennewell, S., & Morgan, A. (2003). *Student teachers' experiences and attitudes towards using interactive whiteboards in the teaching and learning of young children*. Paper presented at the ACM International Conference Proceeding Series, Sydney, Australia.

Knight, P., Tait, J., & Yorke, M. (2006). The professional learning of teachers in higher education. *Studies in Higher Education, 31*(3), 319–339. doi:10.1080/03075070600680786

Kobbe, L., Weinberger, A., Dillenbourg, P., & Harrer, A., Hämäläinen, R., Häkkinen, P., & Fischer, F. (2007). Specifying computer-supported collaboration scripts. *International Journal of Computer-Supported Collaborative Learning, 2*(2-3), 211–224. doi:10.1007/s11412-007-9014-4

Laurillard, D. (2002). *Rethinking university teaching: a Conversational Framework for the effective use of learning technologies* (2nd ed.). London: RoutledgeFalmer.

Laurillard, D. (2008). The teacher as action researcher: Using technology to capture pedagogic form. *Studies in Higher Education, 33*(2), 139–154. doi:10.1080/03075070801915908

Laurillard, D., Oliver, M., Wasson, B., & Hoppe, U. (2009). Implementing technology enhanced learning. In N. Balacheff, S. Ludvigsen, T. de Jong, A. Lazonder, & S. Barnes (Eds.), *Technology Enhanced Learning: Principles and Products* (pp. 285–302). Dordrecht, The Netherlands: Springer.

Lucas, L. (2008). *Towards a Socio-cultural understanding of academics' experiences of linking research and teaching*. Seminar given at the Oxford Learning Institute, University of Oxford, UK, May 29, 2008.

Masterman, E. (2008a). Activity Theory and the Design of Pedagogic Planning tools. In L. Lockyer, S. Bennett, S. Agostinho, & B. Harper (Eds.), *Handbook of Research on Learning design and Learning Objects: Issues, Applications and Technologies* (pp. 209-227). Hershey, PA: IGI Global.

Masterman, L. (2008b). *Phoebe Pedagogy Planner Project: Evaluation Report*. Oxford, UK: University of Oxford, Technology-Assisted Lifelong Learning Unit and Oxford University Computing Services. Retrieved February 4, 2009, from http://www.jisc.ac.uk/media/documents/programmes/elearningpedagogy/Phoebeevaluationreportsept08.pdf

Masterman, L., & Lee, S. (2005). *Reusing learning materials in English Literature and Language: Perspectives from three universities*. Egham, UK: Higher Education Academy English Subject Centre. Retrieved February 4, 2009, from http://www.english.heacademy.ac.uk/explore/projects/archive/technology/tech10.php

NCIHE. (1997). *Higher Education in the Learning Society. Summary Report* (Document No. NCIHE/97/849). London: HMSO.

Oliver, M. (2002). *Creativity and the curriculum design process: a case study*. York, UK: Higher Education Academy. Retrieved February 4, 2009, from http://www.heacademy.ac.uk/resources/detail/id153_Creativity_and_the_curriculum_design_process_a_case_study

Oliver, M. (2003). *Curriculum Design as acquired social practice: a case study*. Paper presented at the 84th Annual Meeting of the American Educational Research Association, Chicago, IL.

Salmon, G., Jones, S., & Armellini, A. (2008). Building institutional capability in e-learning design. *ALT-J, 16*(2), 95–109. doi:10.1080/09687760802315978

San Diego, J., Laurillard, D., Boyle, T., Bradley, C., Ljubojevic, D., Neumann, T., & Pearce, D. (2008). Towards a user-oriented analytical approach to learning design. *ALT-J, 16*(1), 15–29. doi:10.1080/09687760701850174

Scaife, M., & Rogers, Y. (1999). Kids As Informants: Telling Us What We Didn't Know or Confirming What We Knew Already? In A. Druin (Ed.), *The Design of Children's Technology* (pp. 27–50). San Francisco, CA: Morgan Kaufmann.

Scardamalia, M., & Bereiter, C. (2006). Knowledge Building: Theory, Pedagogy and Technology. In K. Sawyer (Ed.), *Cambridge Handbook of the Learning Sciences* (pp. 97–118). Cambridge, UK: Cambridge University Press.

Sharpe, R., Benfield, G., & Francis, R. (2006). Implementing a university e-learning strategy: Levers for change within academic schools. *ALT-J, 14*(2), 135–151. doi:10.1080/09687760600668503

Sharpe, R., & Oliver, M. (2007). Designing courses for e-learning. In H. Beetham & R. Sharpe (Eds.), *Rethinking Pedagogy for a Digital Age: Designing and delivering e-learning* (pp. 41–51). London: Routledge.

Stahl, G., Koschmann, T., & Suthers, D. (2006). Computer-supported collaborative learning: An historical perspective. In R. K. Sawyer (Ed.), *Cambridge handbook of the learning sciences* (pp. 409–426). Cambridge, UK: Cambridge University Press.

Triggs, P., & John, P. (2004). From transaction to transformation: information and communication technology, professional development and the formation of communities of practice. *Journal of Computer Assisted Learning, 20*(6), 426–439. doi:10.1111/j.1365-2729.2004.00101.x

Webb, M., & Cox, M. (2004). A review of pedagogy related to information and communications technology. *Technology, Pedagogy and Education, 13*(3), 235–286. doi:10.1080/14759390400200183

Weller, M., Pegler, C., & Mason, R. (2005). Use of innovative technologies on an e-learning course. *The Internet and Higher Education, 8*(1), 61–71. doi:10.1016/j.iheduc.2004.10.001

Wenger, E. (1999). *Communities of Practice: Learning, Meaning, and Identity*. Cambridge, UK: Cambridge University Press.

Wolpert, L. (2003). Causal belief and the origins of technology. *Philosophical Transactions of the Royal Society of London, Series A, 361*(1809), 1709–1719.

Chapter 14

Online Pedagogy Design and Development
New Models for 21ˢᵗ Century Online Teacher Professional Development

Pamela Whitehouse
West Virginia University, USA

Erin McCloskey
Harvard Graduate School of Education, USA

Diane Jass Ketelhut
Temple University, USA

ABSTRACT

The purpose of this chapter is to examine the shifting priorities of online teacher professional development design, particularly through the lens of online pedagogies. Whether one's purpose is to design an online teacher learning community or formal professional development program, decisions about technology use will mediate how the learning communities or training programs function. Designers, when choosing communication tools or digital media for inclusion in their program, ideally draw from their technological pedagogical content knowledge, or TCPK – that is, their understanding of which technologies will support pedagogy appropriate for the content and learners being targeted. The model we offer for online teacher professional development program design makes visible the interaction between the technology, the content, the pedagogy and the learner.

INTRODUCTION

The purpose of this chapter is to examine the shifting priorities of online teacher professional development design, particularly through the lens of online pedagogies. The teaching profession is changing as a

response to multiple outside pressures and the rising importance of digital media and digital literacies in teaching and learning. United States federal policy mandates, such as the No Child Left Behind Act (United States Department of Education, 2002), now require evidence of teacher quality, thereby pushing the profession to become more data-driven in terms of providing empirical evidence of the efficacy

DOI: 10.4018/978-1-60566-780-5.ch014

of teacher professional development programs. Additionally, there are new standards, such as the second edition of the *National Educational Technology Standards for Teachers (*NETS-T*)* published by the International Society for Technology in Education (International Society for Technology in Education, 2009), that state, among other things, that teachers should be able to teach and model the effective uses of digital media such as blogs, wikis, and other social networking tools. At the same time, the global workplace and the Information Age economy are demanding new skills of graduates (Dede, 2000b), which require the shifting of priorities within K12 curricula and challenge teachers to teach new content in new ways to help students develop those skills. For example, we have seen a shift in the role that the Internet occupies in education. At first, the Internet (now known as Web 1.0) was exalted for its copious amounts of information that provided new worlds of knowledge and content created for our consumption. The Internet has evolved, however, from a simple information source to a communicative and creative platform. Now we find ourselves immersed in a world of Web 2.0, where we create our own digital media, build and maintain a participatory culture through social networking, and communicate instantly in real-time through chat and instant messaging (Jenkins, 2006; Solomon & Schrum, 2007).

As a result, NETS-T (International Society for Technology in Education, 2009) also states that 21st century teachers must be lifelong learners and reflective practitioners who are able to adjust to rapidly changing expectations. Where teachers from previous generations strove to develop a core set of relatively static skills that would serve them well in their professional lives, today's teachers need to keep learning and developing new skills to adjust for these changing needs and expectations (Darling-Hammond & Bransford, 2005). Emerging research on how children learn impacts our understanding of how teachers learn, as well as what it means to think, write, and teach as a professional educator (Bransford, Darling-Hammond, & LePage, 2005). Changing patterns in Internet usage, new understandings about how teachers and students learn, and shifting priorities about what is important to teach raise a crucial question: What might 21st century teacher professional development (TPD) look like if it is to respond to these trends and concerns? TPD programs that are delivered online assume new importance in this changing landscape, offering the potential to expand beyond the traditional 'sit and get' model of professional development to embrace a model that utilizes and targets 21st century tools, skills and learning styles in order to reach 21st century students and learning goals. Offering TPD online and nothing more, however, does not guarantee relevance to those goals, alignment with how people learn, or an updated approach. Development of online TPD programs has proliferated extensively as designers, providers and funders have seen its potential to address a variety of priorities for teachers' and students' learning. Research in the field of online TPD is also expanding rapidly, with early findings pointing the way to empirical research models that guide the design of online teacher professional development programs. This chapter explores the question of 21st century teacher professional development from the perspective of online pedagogy, exploring the unique territory that emerges when technology and pedagogy intersect and offering a model for online pedagogy to consider when designing teacher professional development in the digital age.

BACKGROUND

Until recently, as with many online learning environments, online TPD was characterized by the simple transfer of face-to-face pedagogy and text-based materials to a web-based container, frequently with an asynchronous discussion tool and archival databases (Stevens-Long & Crowell, 2002). Today, however, more sophisticated digital media such as video and audio support the content, while new pedagogical models for online learning are being developed (Bruckman, 2004). However, despite the promise of reaching large numbers of teachers through an online environment and providing quality TPD while cutting costs, online TPD programs have experienced varying degrees of success. For example, many online TPD programs fail to achieve their goals, and many teachers drop out or exhibit little 'presence' in the online environment, through a lack of participation or insufficient media literacy (Brown & Green, 2003; Perkins, 2000).

Some members of the education research community suggest online teacher *learning communities* are more successful because they offer teachers opportunities that go beyond what formal online TPD can provide. For example, Vavasseur and MacGregor (2008) argue that while online TPD offers the affordances of distance learning classes, a more effective option features online communities of practice, or teacher learning communities, where teachers can work together on problems of their choosing that relate directly to their practice. Embedded in their argument is the idea that online TPD, with its traditional content, predetermined curriculum, and formal learning structures, is about training rather than developing one's practice through collaborative online learning experiences. This issue has often been the problem for both traditional and online TPD programs, which Borko (2004) has characterized as frequently "fragmented, intellectually superficial" (p. 3) learning experiences.

Whether one's purpose is to design a teacher learning community, or a more formal online TPD course or program, decisions about technology use will mediate how the learning communities or training programs function. Designers, when choosing communication tools or digital media for inclusion in their program, ideally draw from their *technological pedagogical content knowledge*, or TPCK – that is, their understanding of which *technologies* (T) will support a *pedagogy*

(P) that is appropriate for the *content* (C) and *learners* being targeted (Koehler & Mishra, 2008). Although this is not a traditional approach to thinking about pedagogical content knowledge (PCK), we argue that TPCK *must* also take into account the *learners* in relation to the technology, as well as the learners' relation to the content and pedagogy. These design decisions are based on the designers' expert knowledge of the learners, the content that teachers will likely discuss in the online learning community, the ways that they will want to manipulate that content, and the forms of collaboration that will best support teachers' needs. In short, TPCK informs design whether the intention is to provide training via more traditional direct instructional methods or to enact theories of social construction through teacher learning communities. The remainder of this chapter explores the affordances and constraints that mediate the alignment of pedagogy, technology and teachers-as-learners in online learning environments. We do this by reviewing the research on online TPD, with a focus on pedagogy, examining some exemplary programs and offering a continuum that makes visible the alignment (or lack of) between pedagogy, learners and technology.

ISSUES, CONTROVERSIES AND PROBLEMS

Online TPD innovations are shifting traditional TPD from "teaching by telling" (Dede, 2000b) or "sit and get" (in front of a computer) workshops (Bowskill, Foster, Lally, & McConnell, 2000) to "learning by doing" (Dede, 2000a) or constructivist pedagogies (Jonassen, Peck, & Wilson, 1999) that merge communities of practice theory (Barab, Kling, & Gray, 2004; Wenger, 1998) with constructivist design principles (Barab, MaKinster, & Scheckler, 2004; Cradler, Freeman, Cradler, & McNabb, 2002; Dede, 2000b; Riel & Polin, 2004). These changes in thinking about how to design online TPD for better teacher learning have led to the formation of online "learning communities" or "communities of practice," which are intended to provide teachers with effective collaborative learning experiences meant to improve their teaching and student outcomes (Barab, Kling et al., 2004; Bean & Stevens, 2002; Bintrim, 2002; Brown & Green, 2003; Epanchin & Colucci, 2002; Fawcett & Juliana, 2002; Mehlinger & Powers, 2002; Mouza, 2002). The central tenet of a *community of practice* is that learning is a social process of mutual engagement, joint enterprise, and shared language that evolves through mutual histories of learning (Wenger, 1998) and, in this case, takes place online. *Learning communities* are similar but may have more explicit learning goals and include guidance toward particular outcomes not found in communities of practice (Riel & Polin, 2004). Overall, many innovative design models provide important affordances for teacher learning online.

In support of the change toward online collaborative learning models for teacher professional development, Schlager and Fusco (2004) suggest that researchers, practitioners and policymakers are evolving toward a shared vision of TPD that includes online communities of practice or professional learning communities. They argue that "the large scale and distributed nature of many reform projects, along with an imperative to sustain and upscale change" have encouraged researchers to consider online learning communities as a powerful lever in TPD (p.127). This shared vision across the arenas of research, policy and practice represents a significant change in thinking about teacher learning, and it challenges designers of online TPD to develop new research models that make visible the interplay of online pedagogy, the technological tools through which pedagogy is enacted, and the unique needs of teacher-learners. Such an undertaking represents a particular challenge to online pedagogy because, as noted in the introduction, assumptions about pedagogy (and about learning, by extension) are embedded in the design of online TPD, whether they are implicitly

acknowledged or not. In the next sections, we discuss current and emerging models of online pedagogy, and how these new ideas advance online TPD from 20th century Web 1.0 knowledge containers and purveyors to Web 2.0 knowledge creation and social networking tools.

Issues in Online Pedagogy

Both formal online teacher professional development programs and less prescriptive teacher learning communities are often innovative in design, but their pedagogical strategies are not, in many cases. Rudestam and Schoenholtz-Read (2002) have asserted that "electronic teaching developed from advances in communications technology, not from innovative changes in pedagogy" (p 15). It follows, then, that pedagogy in online learning, much like reading materials that have been digitized to function within the electronic medium, has simply been transferred into, but not transformed by, the new environment: same stuff, different container. This transfer approach to pedagogy often results in a lack of alignment with the needs of the learners and with the technical tools chosen to support online learning.

The issue of alignment has recently gained prominence in writings about online pedagogy. For example, Kuan-Chou and Keh-Wen's generic e-Learning system model identifies teaching and learning as a continuum that is intersected by pedagogy and technology (Kuan-Chou & Keh-Wen, 2008). They argued that pedagogy and technology must align with how students learn, or less learning will occur. Figure 1 represents their rendering of the model.

These researchers envisioned technology as a divider between the teacher and the student because they believe the non-verbal signals necessary to bolster student understanding are not visible. This general perspective –that technologies would divide rather than unite program participants – mediated the pedagogy and learning activities of many online learning designs, as evidenced

Figure 1. Generic e-Learning Model by Kuan-Chou and Keh-Wen (©2008, Waset.org).

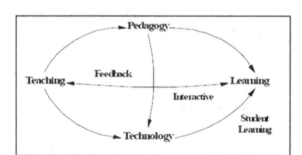

by web-based course shells or containers that are primarily text-based and designed from the standpoint that the pedagogical strategies would include direct instruction and discussion, and that most teacher/student interactions would be asynchronous and text-based.

Technological Pedagogical Content Knowledge

Despite designs that divorce technology from pedagogy, Bruckman and colleagues (2004) have argued that technological design and pedagogy have the potential to co-evolve to new models of teaching and learning within online learning environments. In fact, technology design and pedagogy have evolved over the last few years, and there are new theories and models of technological pedagogical content knowledge (TPCK) that extend the innovations that have informed the design of online TPD and teacher learning communities. In a recent study, Mishra and Koehler discussed technological pedagogical content knowledge as a dynamic framework defined by pedagogy, content, and technology (AACTE Committee on Innovation and Technology, 2008; Koehler & Mishra, 2008; Mishra & Koehler, 2006). They posit that this model extends the work of Shulman, who argued that teaching focused on either pedagogy or content falls short in developing good teaching practice and that, rather, one must consider the dynamic interplay between them (Shulman,

1987). Mishra and Koehler built upon Shulman's work by developing a new model of pedagogy, content and technology that takes into account the dynamics created at the intersections in a more complex fashion.

The framework they developed for TPCK emphasizes the need to think about developing good teaching at the overlapping areas of Pedagogical Content Knowledge (which teaching strategies best match a particular content area), Technological Content Knowledge (which technological tools best represent and illuminate that content), and Technological Pedagogical Knowledge (how technologies can transform teaching and which tools support different pedagogies). The importance of this work is clear. As Mishra and Koehler (2006) write, it moves the field beyond the idea that learning how to use hardware and software, or acquiring basic computing skills, is sufficient for teachers to effectively use new technologies in their classrooms. An ability to make fluid decisions of what pedagogical strategy is best while in the moment is needed, which goes beyond knowing the technology; TPCK requires knowing *which* learning goals the technology can meet, and *how*. Despite the importance of TPCK in the design of online learning and online TPD programs in particular, research on online TPD has rarely investigated these areas.

Issues: Online Pedagogy

In order to bring these issues of pedagogy and technology into clearer focus, we draw from the larger study that preceded the issues discussed in this chapter. The larger study included a scan of over 400 hundred of research articles on online TPD, with the goal of identifying online TPD research that was empirical, rather than anecdotal, theoretical, conceptual or polemical, in order to define the current research landscape in online TPD (Whitehouse, Breit, McCloskey, Ketelhut, & Dede, 2006). It was not limited to any particular theoretical approach or method. Rather, studies were selected because they had clear research questions, rigorous data collection, and thorough analysis.

Overall, the pedagogies represented in the research studies we examined were informed by a social constructivist or communities of practice approach (Wenger, 1998), although the definitions of these terms, as well as their enactments, varied widely across studies. Most of the studies we examined had overlapping pedagogical approaches, and research activities focused on interactions among individuals and groups, as well as the contexts that supported those interactions. Making pedagogy visible through theory and research-based models illuminates the assumptions the designers make about how teachers learn, and as discussed in the previous paragraphs, highlights the need for thinking about the interplay between pedagogy, learners and technology. However, truly visible pedagogy was rarely achieved in the studies we examined, remaining outside the discussion and research focus. Nevertheless, though often invisible, TPCK was still a major force in the design decisions made by the researchers and designers, particularly given the shift towards social constructivist approaches to online TPD design.

RESEARCH FINDINGS: MODELS OF ONLINE PEDAGOGY

Our analysis of these online TPD studies revealed three pedagogical models of online TPD (writ large) that form the foundational pedagogical strategies for many online TPD programs. The analysis drew from the pedagogical descriptions given in the research articles reviewed where such description existed. In some cases, where there were no explicit descriptions of the pedagogical approach, the analysis drew from the description of the program design. The models are:

- *neo-traditional*
  - instructor is the primary source of knowledge;
  - learning is focused on acquisition of knowledge, but the relationship between teacher-learners and instructors must be negotiated across distance
  - learners are often conceived of as receivers of knowledge, but this may be mediated by activities that lead them to reconstruct the knowledge in ways useful to their learning purposes
- *social constructivist* (communities of practice are included in this category)
  - learners make meaning of the content, both individually and within the group
  - co-construction of knowledge may not be located only in course content
- *tele-mentoring*
  - online mentoring falls into three main categories:
    - ask an expert,
    - pair mentoring and
    - group mentoring in both synchronous and asynchronous environments
  - learners generally follow the apprenticeship model of learning from the master, although some programs

Figure 2. Pedagogical Continuum (© 2009, Pamela L. Whitehouse. Used with permission).

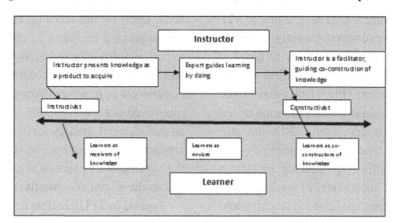

support a co-mentoring model in which learners share their expertise

In order to better understand these models, we devised a pedagogical design continuum, represented in Figure 2.

Conceptions of instructor and of the learner were used to help surface the pedagogical assumptions in each model. Articulating the roles of instructor and learner via this graphic was a useful way to think about how to make online pedagogy visible, but as will become apparent in the *Emerging Models* section of this chapter, the graphic was also limiting because it left the technical design invisible, as well as its interactions with the learner and the instructor. At this point overall, the continuum serves as a useful reference when reading the fuller descriptions of each model.

Neo-Traditional

The neo-traditional pedagogical model represents the traditional direct instruction of teaching while the "neo" indicates that teaching online requires a different sort of negotiation between teacher, technical design and learner. Within this model, key "traditional" pedagogical characteristics—a hierarchical structure where the instructor is the

'expert' and content is created and/or presented by the instructor—may remain (Perkins, 2006). Instructors often use computer-mediated communications and a website as a delivery system for course content. This model exhibits important components of traditional face-to-face TPD by assuming that the teachers are the "basic source of curriculum knowledge" and that program design is guided by an "emphasis on the acquisition of knowledge and the primary role of subject matter" (Klein, 2001, p. 4). The programs are structured to provide a set curriculum developed by the instructor or other teaching entity. As noted in the neo-traditional bullet above, this model accommodates different conceptions of the learner; it might frame learners as passive recipients of knowledge or encourage learners to make use of received knowledge in substantial and personally relevant ways (Perkins, 2006). Formal instruction ends with the course completion date, although participants might retain ongoing access to course materials, online discussion forums, or other resources.

The EdTech Leaders Online (ETLO) is a good example of the neo-traditional model. Working with organizations across the United States such as school districts, departments of education and universities, ETLO's primary approach is "enabling clients to develop their own organizational capacity to provide effective online professional development" (Kleiman & Treacy, 2006, p. 31). As such, ETLO offers client organizations a standardized sequence of online courses to develop this capacity. Beginning with an online course about facilitating online TPD, clients experience online learning as learners, become familiarized with crucial issues in developing TPD, and gain knowledge about emerging technologies and online learning. Follow-up courses include a teaching practicum and a series of workshop options addressing important issues in teaching and learning, which clients choose depending on their professional development needs. The learner in these standardized courses receives and absorbs a lot of information, suggesting a more passive conception of the learner. However, by collaborating with colleagues in devising a locally relevant plan to develop and implement online TPD on site, the learners take their acquired knowledge and shape it to meet their purposes, which demand a more active stance of the learner. Facilitated asynchronous discussions about the content of online workshops also offer learners the opportunity to engage with others in meaning co-construction.

Social Constructivist Model

The social constructivist pedagogical model emerges from theories of social context and constructivism. This model posits that knowledge creation is not the absorption and assimilation of information by a learner, but rather an active process in which learners make meaning of content, both in individual construction and in co-construction with other learners in that particular context (Alexander, 1999; Jonassen et al., 1999; Maddux, 2001). Social context theory arises from both situated learning theory [learning is an integral and inseparable aspect of social practice (Lave & Wenger, 1991)] and from theories of context [social, physical and political factors form a context that shapes learning experiences (Tessmer & Richey, 1997)]. These theories per-

ceive the learner as both acting upon and being acted upon by the learning environment; rather than a passive recipient or observer, the learner exercises autonomy and agency within a dynamic and iterative process of constructing meaning. A *community of practice* (Wenger, 1998) model is often cited as a common form of social constructivist pedagogical strategy for online TPD, but there are many interpretations of what this means, so the variations of enactment paint broad swathes across the social constructivist landscape.

Tapped In 2 (TI2) offers a useful example of a social constructivist pedagogical model because it was designed to provide a community of practice for K16 educators from United States school districts, museums, foundations, and research and development organizations, as they "learn the ropes of their profession, implement new practices, and apply content knowledge" (M. S. Schlager, Fusco, & Schank, 2002, p. 2). Its design also took into account certain limitations and priorities of TPD. TI2 was intended to provide a test bed for research on teacher professional development, and offered a model that could scale up to support thousands of teachers' professional activities. Another important goal of the project is to provide a professional community of practice based on analysis of research findings from the (largely traditional) professional development programs that were most successful in supporting school reform (M. S. Schlager et al., 2002). The role of the learner in TI2 is highly constructivist because the program offers no set curriculum or required courses, but instead provides teachers with the tools they need to develop their own learning experiences based on their own priorities and needs and with groups of their choosing. For example, educators using the TI2 environment could choose to be involved in online mentoring, or not, and have complete autonomy to determine their learning goals. In a recent study of TI2, the researchers found three design elements that are key to sustainability to support a teacher learning community: investing in bonding social capital (the relationships developed in a homogeneous community), providing multiple online gathering places, and reinforcing leadership roles that emerge from the work of individual members (Farooq, Schank, Harris, Fusco, & Schlager, 2007). The findings indicate new levels of TPCK, in that the researchers have found that there are particular design aspects that promote sustainable learning.

Tele-Mentoring Model

In contrast, the third pedagogical model, tele-mentoring (mentoring), prescribes a relationship between the mentor and mentee that is based on computer-mediated communication, such as the telephone, email, listservs, or discussion forums (Wighton, 1993). It does not necessarily draw directly upon social constructivist or neo-traditional strategies, and it features an apprenticeship in which learning-by-doing guided by an expert in a pre-specified field is the chief learning goal. Riel identified three main types of mentoring: ask an expert, pair mentoring, and group mentoring (Riel, 1999). Designs of tele-mentoring programs emerge from various interpretations of Vygostkian theory (e.g., zones of proximal development, situated learning) that invoke notions of apprenticeship and development in similar fashion to traditional modes of face-to-face mentoring (Lave & Wenger, 1991).

Mentoring has often been described as a pairing of a novice with an expert in a hierarchical relationship, although more recently mentoring has also been considered a reciprocal relationship between peers (Danielson, 2002). Tele-mentoring programs for educators are generally meant to help overcome geographical or social/cultural isolation of teachers and to provide them with new outlets for professional development. Some online mentoring programs are particularly designed to foster reflective dialogue among teachers and to make the action of teaching visible through sharing experiences and knowledge (Spitzer, Wedding, & DiMauro, 1994). Learners in tele-mentoring

models are usually perceived as novices, and program design is focused on creating access to experts, whether in a paired or group setting, with differing notions about the role and importance of reciprocity in the relationship. Depending on the relationship to the expert, the learner might enact a more neo-traditional role, by receiving and then applying knowledge in an apprenticeship, or a more social constructivist role, by reflecting on the learning-by-doing under the guidance of the expert or in relationships with peers.

An example of a large scale group mentoring program is the Electronic Emissary, a research project originally coordinated from the University of Texas at Austin and funded by the Texas Center for Educational Technology and by J.C. Penney. Dr. Judi Harris, principal investigator, believes this is the longest running online tele-mentoring project in existence (Harris, 2003). The program uses email and the telephone as communication sources; the purpose of the project is to form teams by matching teachers and students from around the globe with experts for the dual purposes of professional development and enrichment of student learning experiences. Each team is composed of a K12 educator, a group of students, a content expert (mentor), and a facilitator from the Electronic Emissary. The team format derives from the idea that the teacher and students are novices who work with a subject matter expert toward completing a specific project, with the help of an online facilitator from the Electronic Emissary to support communications. In this case, the conception of the learner falls toward the more neo-traditional pedagogical model because teachers are in a structured relationship with an expert, who gives instruction and advice. Discussions about teaching and learning generally take place with the Electronic Emissary assistants.

Model Synthesis

The three models share important commonalities that are mediated by the online learning environment. The online environment poses a "construc-

Table 1. Revised Pedagogical Model (© 2009, Pamela Whitehouse. Used with permission).

Pedagogical Models	Pedagogical Approach/ Instruction	Technical Design	Conception of Learner Ranges	Exemplars
Neo-traditional	Traditional curriculum theory[i], research-based pedagogies, direct instruction and training; instructor provides knowledge	Mainly Web 1.0 tools: access to course content; acquiring course content; online resources	Receiver of knowledge; acquirer of knowledge[ii] to learner as constructor of knowledge	EdTech Leaders Online Learning to Teach with Technologies Studio
Social Constructivist (Community of practice)	Constructivist practice, social context for knowledge creation; little direct instruction; instructor guides learners' meaning-making	Focused on Web 2.0 tools: access to and creation of collaborative learning groups, knowledge management tools	Constructor and/or co-constructor of knowledge	Tapped In 2 Inquiry Learning Forum
Mentoring (Tele-mentoring)	Vygostkian zones of proximal development, situated learning; instructor (expert) guides learning-by-doing	Overall focus on Web 1.0 tools: access to an expert; searchable databases	Apprentice to master/ peer/group, role can vary from receiver to co-constructor	Electronic Emissary eMSS Project

tivist challenge to the authority of a particular, grounded matrix of knowledge," and the traditional tools of the trade (lectures, books) "no longer carry prescriptive meaning; they just open up possible alternative interpretations that students differentially select" (Rudestam & Schoenholtz-Read, 2002a, p. 16). As a result, programs that fall within each model often contain – intentionally or not – constructivist characteristics, although these characteristics can vary widely, and any model might incorporate any singular constructivist element. In this sense these aren't three pedagogical models that 'stand alone' without ever overlapping each other. Rather, each carries a primary pedagogical perspective that becomes visible through the technologies and course structures that are chosen. This argument is similar to the TPCK design proposed by Mishra and Koehler (2006), but it takes a different tack by making the learner visible instead of the content. Table 1 extends the scope of our original pedagogical continuum by introducing the component of technical design and how it interacts with pedagogy and the learner.

The overlap between models, particularly in their conception of the learner, indicates some interesting contradictions. The pedagogy, content and technology do not align in ways one might expect, especially in light of the strong emphasis on aligning pedagogical strategies with clear learning objectives, activities and assessment in school curriculum and lesson planning. For example, some online TPD programs provide collaboration tools but utilize direct instruction as the central pedagogical strategy and skills practice as the main learner activity, leaving those (potentially constructivist) collaboration tools either unused or used for non-collaborative tasks such as logistical communications. Interestingly, the constructivist characteristics most clearly manifest themselves in the technical design of each model. For example, some online TPD programs use collaboration tools such as Google Docs that foster a high degree of learner autonomy and co-creation of knowledge, or discussion forums designed to extend thinking about a topic.

Figure 3. Revised Pedagogical Continuum. (© 2009, Pamela Whitehouse. Used with permission).

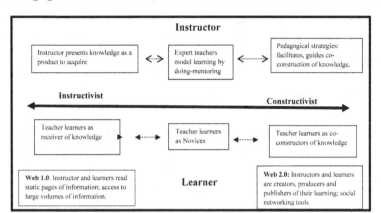

SOLUTIONS: EMERGING MODELS OF ONLINE PEDAGOGY

Mishra and Koehler (2006) envisioned TPCK as a series of overlapping circles (content, pedagogy, and technology) that highlight the need to view content, pedagogy and technology as dynamic variables that require a more complex approach for design and implementation of online TPD. This model provides an integrated perspective of important design factors in online TPD, as well as for other learning purposes. The model makes visible the interplay of pedagogy, content and technology; however, the learner becomes invisible.

Further analysis of the literature revealed that it is possible to conceive of a continuum from Instructivist to Constructivist that embraces the learner, the pedagogy (instructor) and the technology. The pedagogical continuum we offer illustrates how the online pedagogical approach informs the instructor's role, the conception of the learner, and technical design. In this Revised Pedagogical Continuum depiction (Figure 3), the dynamic interplay is between the intersections of pedagogy, content, technology, and the learner.

The left end of the continuum represents the neo-traditional idea of teaching, in which teaching is a highly structured activity, teacher learners are conceptualized as acquirers of knowledge,

and course content is pre-determined. Technical design aligned with this category would likely be focused on delivering content and guiding structured discussion and use Web 1.0 technologies that allow learners to gather information, discuss the information and create their own products individually.

The middle, mentoring area imagines the teacher learner as an apprentice, who learns-by-doing under the guidance of an expert. Technical design aligned with this area on the continuum would most likely be focused on providing learning-by-doing activities, which could be technically-mediated, and might use digital media or simulations in addition to providing content and written advice. Tele-mentoring would most likely blend Web 1.0 and Web 2.0 tools, depending on the nature of the content, goals, expert-novice relationship, and mentoring structure (group or peer, for example).

At the right (constructivist) end of the continuum, learners co-create knowledge within a social constructivist context, blurring the lines between learner and instructor, as participants may move freely between both roles. Technical design aligned with this area on the continuum would likely be Web 2.0 media such as blogs, wikis, and other tools that support social networking, collaboration, and production and creation of learning objects and artifacts. Teachers as learners decide what content and skills they want to develop, and find others to work with them. For example, the Globaloria program of West Virginia provides public school teachers and students with blogs and wikis to share and collaborate together and in separate peer groups as they create educational games using Adobe Flash and other high-end gaming software. The key idea is to support all learners as they explore, develop and create their games (Caperton, 2009).

FUTURE TRENDS

The West Virginia Globaloria program mentioned in the previous section is an advanced example of innovative online TPD that is ongoing, embedded in the school, project-based and teacher-led. The educator wiki is provided and supported by the Globaloria staff to support co-creation of new TPCK strategies in a collaborative space, and it includes on-demand technical support from experts who enter the classroom via desktop video conferencing and a rich archive of teacher- and student-created tutorials. The networked environment not only blurs rather than blends face-to-face learning environments with online learning spaces; it makes teaching and learning visible in ways that have not been possible before the advent of the Internet (Whitehouse, Reynolds, & Caperton, 2009). For example, researchers and teachers alike may trace the ongoing digital conversations that reveal knowledge-building and creativity, as well as gaps in learning. Video of students and teachers in specific learning contexts can provide examples of exemplary teaching; as well provide the base for online conversations that allow all participants to stretch their imaginations and their reflection on practice.

As outlined in this chapter, a 21st century model of online TPD and TPD must take into account the changing needs of teachers as professional educators, and model as well as teach the effective use of digital media. As we have indicated, one way to support and develop this type of online TPD is to further examine the importance of aligning the pedagogy, content, the needs of the learners and the technical design. A tight alignment may not be mandatory, but even flexible arrangements should be carefully considered and deliberately enacted. It is necessary to consciously align the pedagogical strategies, content and technological design with the needs of the learners—whether the learning context is for training or for learning communities. In the case of online TPD, teaching and modeling this alignment seems important, especially as classroom teaching itself (as well as student learning) becomes more technologically-mediated as learning contexts blur the virtual and the face-to-face. Teachers as learners are not well understood, however we do know what does not work. We believe that further exploration on the interplay between pedagogy, technical design and needs of the learners will shed further light on how to best support 21st century teachers as learners. The model we offer has much room for further development, but we believe it is useful for thinking about the possible alignments and interplay between technology, content, pedagogy and learners.

CONCLUSION

In the near future, online TPD as well as face-to-face TPD must move away from the 19th and 20th century models that favor direct instruction and standardized content without taking into account individualized classroom contexts, that conceive of teachers as receivers of knowledge rather than as multi-faceted adaptive experts, and that provide technical tools designed for communication and logistical purposes rather than teaching and meaning-making purposes. Today's teacher must have the tools and resources at hand for leading students in project-based and inquiry-based classrooms where direct instruction becomes not the primary pedagogical strategy, but one option within a constellation of strategies at the teacher's disposal. The central focus needs to be on creating learning experiences that reach far beyond the classroom walls into a world where distance and geography are not barriers to engagement with real world problems, but are simply part of the project management shared by students and teachers. Teachers must teach and model for their students how to manage learning experiences across distance, time, geography and culture. In its turn, online TPD programs must model and teach these skills and concepts with innovative programs where technology, pedagogy, content and the learner are clearly conceived and aligned with the needs of the learners and the learning goals.

REFERENCES

AACTE Committee on Innovation and Technology (Ed.). (2008). *Handbook of Technological Pedagogical Content Knowledge (TPCK) for educators*. New York: Routledge.

Alexander, J. O. (1999). Collaborative Design, Constructivist Learning, Information Technology Immersion, & Electronic Communities: A Case Study [Electronic Version]. *Interpersonal Computing and Technology: An Electronic Journal for the 21st Century, 7*. Retrieved October 1999 from http://www.emoderators.com/ipct-j/1999/n1-2/alexander.html.

Barab, S. MaKinster, J., & Scheckler, R. (2004). Designing System Dualities: Characterizing Online Community. In S. Barab, R. Kling, & J. Gray (Eds.), *Designing for Virtual Communities in the Service of Learning*. Cambridge, MA: Cambridge University Press.

Barab, S., Kling, R., & Gray, J. H. (Eds.). (2004). *Designing for Virtual Communities in the Service of Learning*. Cambridge, United Kingdom: Press Syndicate of the University of Cambridge.

Bean, T. W., & Stevens, L. P. (2002). Scaffolding Reflection for Preservice and Inservice Teachers. *Reflective Practice, 3*(2), 205–219. doi:10.1080/14623940220142343

Bintrim, L. (2002). Redesigning Professional Development. []. Association for Supervision & Curriculum Development.]. *Educational Leadership, 59*, 96.

Borko, H. (2004). Professional Development and Teacher Learning: Mapping the Terrain. *Educational Researcher, 33*(8), 3–15. doi:10.3102/0013189X033008003

Bowskill, N., Foster, J., Lally, V., & McConnell, D. (2000). *Networked professional development: issues and strategies in currrent practice*. Retrieved April 7, 2003, 2003, from http://www.tandf.co.uk/journals

Bransford, J., Darling-Hammond, L., & LePage, P. (2005). Introduction. In L. Darling Hammond & J. Bransford (Eds.), *Preparing Teachers for a Changing World*. San Francisco: Jossey-Bass.

Brown, A., & Green, T. (2003). Showing Up to Class in Pajamas (or Less!) The Fantasies and Realities of On-Line Professional Development. *Clearing House (Menasha, Wis.), 76*(3), 148–152.

Bruckman, A. (2004). Co-Evolution of Technological Design and Pedagogy in an Online Learning Community. In S. A. Barab, R. Kling, & J. H. Gray (Eds.), *Designing for Virtual Communities in the Service of Learning* (pp. 239-255). Cambridge, UK: Cambridge University Press.

Caperton, I. (2009). *The Case for Globaloria Network in West Virginia: Empowering West Virginia youth to create and collaborate online with a 21st century game-making curriculum*. New York: World Wide Workshop.

Cradler, J., Freeman, M., Cradler, R., & McNabb, M. (2002). Research Implications for Preparing Teachers to Use Technology. *Learning & Leading with Technology, 30*(1), 50–54.

Danielson, L. (2002). Mentoring in the Professions. *Clearing House (Menasha, Wis.), 75*(4), 183.

Darling-Hammond, L., & Bransford, J. (2005). Introduction. In L. Darling Hammond & J. D. Bransford (Eds.), *Preparing Teachers for a Changing World* (pp. 1-39). San Francisco: Jossey-Bass.

Dede, C. (2000a). Emerging Influences of Information Technology on School Curriculum. *Journal of Curriculum Studies, 32*(2), 281–303. doi:10.1080/002202700182763

Dede, C. (2000b). A New Century Demands New Ways of Learning. In D. T. Gordon (Ed.), *The Digital Classroom* (pp. 171-178). Cambridge, MA: Harvard Education News Letter.

Education, U. S. D. o. (2002). *Introduction: No Child Left Behind.* Retrieved March 17, 2003, 2003, from http://www.nclb.gov/next/overview/index.html

Epanchin, B. C., & Colucci, K. (2002). The Professional Development School Without Walls. *Remedial and Special Education, 23*(6), 350–359. doi:10.1177/07419325020230060501

Farooq, U., Schank, P., Harris, A., Fusco, J., & Schlager, M. (2007). Sustaining a Community Computing Infrastructure for Online Teacher Professional Development: A Case Study of Designing Tapped In. *Computer Supported Cooperative Work: The Journal of Collaborative Computing, 16*(4-5), 397–429. doi:10.1007/s10606-007-9049-0

Fawcett, G., & Juliana, M. (2002). Teaching in the Digital Age: "Teaching as You Were Taught" Won't Work. In P. Rogers (Ed.), *Designing Instruction for Technology Enhanced Learning* (pp. 71-82). Hershey, PA: Idea Group Publishing.

Harris, J. (2003). Professor, College of William and Mary. In P. Whitehouse (Ed.) (pp. phone conversation). Fall River MA.

International Society for Technology in Education. (2009). National Education Technology Standards (NET-T) and Performance Indicators for Teachers [Electronic Version]. Retrieved Jan. 20, 2009 from http://www.iste.org/Content/NavigationMenu/NETS/ForTeachers/2008Standards/NETS_T_Standards_Final.pdf.

Jenkins, H. (2006). *Fans, bloggers, and gamers: Exploring participatory culture.* New York, NY: New York University Press.

Jonassen, D. H., Peck, K. L., & Wilson, B. G. (1999). *Learning with Technology A Constructivist Perspective.* Upper Saddle River, NJ: Merrill, an imprint of Prentice Hall.

Kleiman, G., & Treacy, B. (2006). EdTech Leaders Online. In C. Dede (Ed.), *Online professional development for teachers: Emerging models and methods* (pp. 31-47). Cambridge, MA: Harvard Education Press.

Klein, M. F. (2001). Approaches to Curriculum Theory and Practice. In J. T. Sears & J. D. Marshall (Eds.), *Teaching and Thinking about Curriculum* (pp. 3-14). Troy, NY: Educator's International Press, Inc.

Koehler, M. J., & Mishra, P. (2008). Introducing TPACK. In A. A. o. C. f. T. E. C. o. I. a. Technology (Ed.), *Handbook of Technological Pedagogical Content Knowledge (TPACK) for educators* (pp. 3-29). New York: Routledge.

Kuan-Chou, C., & Keh-Wen, C. (2008). Building an e-Learning System Model with Implications for Research and Instructional Use. *Proceedings of World Academy of Science: Engineering & Technology, 30*, 479–481.

Lave, J., & Wenger, E. (1991). *Situated Learning Legitimate Peripheral Participation*. New York: Cambridge University Press.

Maddux, C. D. (2001). *Educational Computing: Learning with Tomorrow's Technologies*. Needham Heights, MA: Allyn & Bacon.

Mehlinger, H. D., & Powers, S. M. (2002). *Technology and Teacher Education*. Boston: Houghton Mifflin.

Mishra, P., & Koehler, M. J. (2006). Technological pedagogical content knowledge: A framework for teacher knowledge [Electronic Version]. *Teachers College Record, 108*, 1017-1054. Retrieved 7/16/2008 from http://www.tcrecord.org.

Mouza, C. (2002). Learning to Teach with New Technology: Implications for Professional Development. *Journal of Research on Technology in Education, 35*(2), 272–289.

Perkins, D. (2000). "The big question is how to show up without showing up". In D. T. Gordon (Ed.), *The Digital Classroom* (pp. 87-89). Cambridge, MA: Harvard Education News Letter.

Perkins, D. (2006). *Feedback on dissertation*. In P. Whitehouse (Ed.). Cambridge, MA.

Riel, M. (1999, March 1999). *Telementoring on the Web*. Retrieved March 2, 2003, 2003, from http://www.iearn.org/circles/mentors.html

Riel, M., & Polin, L. (2004). Online Learning Communities: Common Ground and Critical Differences in Designing Technical Environments. In S. Barab, R. Kling, & J. H. Gray (Eds.), *Designing for Virtual Communities in the Service of Learning* (pp. 16-50). New York: Cambridge University Press.

Rudestam, K. E., & Schoenholtz-Read, J. (2002a). The Coming of Age of Adult Online Education. In K. E. Rudestam & J. Schoenholtz-Read (Eds.), *Handbook of Online Learning*. Thousand Oaks: Sage.

Rudestam, K. E., & Schoenholtz-Read, J. (2002b). Overview: The Coming of Age of Adult Online Education. In K. E. Rudestam & J. Schoenholtz-Read (Eds.), *Handbook of Online Learning* (pp. 3-28). Thousand Oaks, CA: Sage Publications.

Schlager, M., Fusco, J., Barab, S., Kling, R., & Gray, J. H. (2004). Teacher professional development, technology, and communities of practice: Are we putting the cart before the horse? In R. Pea, J. S. Brown & C. Heath (Eds.), *Designing for Virtual Communites in the Service of Learning* (pp. 120-153). Cambridge, MA: Cambridge University Press.

Schlager, M. S., Fusco, J., & Schank, P. (2002). Evolution of an On-line Education Community of Practice. In K. A. Renninger & W. Shumar (Eds.), *Building Virtual Communities: Learning and Change in Cyberspace* (pp. 129-158). New York: Cambridge University Press.

Shulman, L. S. (1987). Knowledge and teaching: Foundations of the new reform. *Harvard Educational Review, 57*(1), 1–22.

Solomon, G., & Schrum, L. (2007). *Web 2.0 new tools, new schools*. Eugene, OR: International Society for Technology in Education.

Spitzer, W., Wedding, K., & DiMauro, V. (1994). *Fostering Reflective Dialogues for Teacher Professional Development*. Retrieved Feb. 17, 2003, 2003, from http://www.terc.edu/papers/labnet/Guide/03-Introduction.html

Stevens-Long, J., & Crowell, C. (2002). The Design and Delivery of Iteractive Online Graduate Education. In K. E. Rudestam & J. Schoenholtz-Read (Eds.), *Handbook of Online Learning* (pp. 151-169). Thousand Oaks, CA: Sage Publications.

Tessmer, M., & Richey, R. C. (1997). The Role of Context in Learning and Instructional Design. *Educational Technology Research and Development, 45*(2), 85–115. doi:10.1007/BF02299526

Vavasseur, C. B., & MacGregor, S. K. (2008). Extending Content-Focused Professional Development through Online Communities of Practice. *Journal of Research on Technology in Education, 40*(4), 517–536.

Wenger, E. (1998). *Communities of Practice*. Cambridge, UK: Press Syndicate of the University of Cambridge.

Whitehouse, P., Breit, L., McCloskey, E., Ketelhut, D. J., & Dede, C. (2006). Overview of Current Findings from Empirical Research on Online Teacher Professional Development. In C. Dede (Ed.), *Online Teacher Professional Development: Emerging Models and Methods*. Cambridge MA: Harvard Education Publishing Group.

Whitehouse, P., Reynolds, R., & Caperton, I. (2009). *The Development of a research framework to examine teacher professional development and educator experiences in Globaloria: Pilot year 1*. Paper presented at the Society for Technology in Education (SITE).

Wighton, D. J. (1993). Telementoring: An Examination of the Potential for an Educational Network. Retrieved March 2, 2003, 2003, from http://mentor.creighton.edu/htm/telement.htm

ENDNOTES

[i]   See *Curriculum Studies The Reconceptualization*; 2000, edited by William Pinar (Troy NY: Educator's International Press, Inc.) for an in depth discussion of curriculum theory. In this case, the pedagogical model is based on a traditional curriculum theory.

[ii] See Belenky et al. for a thorough discussion of learners as receivers of knowledge (Belenky, Clinchy, Goldberger, & Tarule, 1986)

Chapter 15
Challenges for the Teacher's Role in Promoting Productive Knowledge Construction in Computer–Supported Collaborative Learning Contexts

Maarit Arvaja
University of Jyväskylä, Finland

Raija Hämäläinen
University of Jyväskylä, Finland

Helena Rasku-Puttonen
University of Jyväskylä, Finland

ABSTRACT

This chapter discusses challenges related to teachers' pedagogical activities in facilitating productive discussions among students in Computer-Supported Collaborative Learning (CSCL) contexts. In the light of two different cases from secondary-level and higher education contexts, the authors examine how teachers' pedagogical choices influenced the quality of students' activity, namely Web-based discussion. The results of our studies indicated that rich moments of collaboration were rare and distributed unequally among the students. The obvious weakness from the perspective of teachers' pedagogical activities was that in neither of the studies was the students' interaction in the discussion forum supported in any way. A future challenge is, therefore, to develop both pedagogical and technological tools to support the monitoring and enhancement of students' learning process during online learning. Furthermore, we discuss how teachers' professional development (TPD) is challenged by new technological tools in formal learning environments.

DOI: 10.4018/978-1-60566-780-5.ch015

INTRODUCTION

New technological tools challenge teachers' pedagogical activities and professional development (TPD). Recent empirical studies share the idea of teachers' learning as a lifelong and collaborative process in which learning environments are to support the growth of both individual and collective professional knowledge of teachers (Zellermayer & Munthe, 2007). This chapter explores teachers' pedagogical activities in facilitating productive knowledge construction and discussions among students in Computer-Supported Collaborative Learning (CSCL) contexts. We define collaboration as the process of shared knowledge construction in which knowledge is created and built on each other's ideas and thoughts (e.g., Baker, 2002; Barron, 2000; Dillenbourg, 1999). At their best, new technological applications offer tools for supporting collaboration within teams (e.g., Cobos & Pifarre, 2008; Fischer, Bruhn, Gräsel, & Mandl, 2002; Koschmann, 1996). However, often the web has been overrated as a tool for collaboration, and the term itself is in danger of losing its meaning, while most web facilities intended for correspondence or coordination across distances are marketed as "collaboration tools" (Lipponen, 2001; Roschelle & Pea, 1999). In addition, the new kinds of social networking technologies and content management systems, often called Web 2.0 technologies (O'Reilly, 2005), as well as more established communication technologies themselves are rarely designed with learning and teaching in mind (Laurillard, 2009). Hence, teaching with such technologies sets high demands and challenges for pedagogy and TPD. As learning is conceived as an active process of knowledge construction, the teacher should be seen as a facilitator who supports and guides students' participation and knowledge construction processes (Fischer & Dillenbourg, 2006; Rasku-Puttonen, Eteläpelto, Arvaja & Häkkinen, 2003). However, the transmission mode of instruction – the teacher showing and telling what students should know and then testing it – is well alive and present in schools even today (Weinstein, 1989; Wells & Arauz, 2006), and reflected also in students' shared activities (Arvaja, 2005). Even though this mode of instruction can be regarded as important for passing on cultural meanings, knowledge and practices valued in the culture, students also need more opportunities to explore alternative perspectives, and possibilities to develop and enrich the acquired knowledge and practices (Wells & Arauz, 2006). However, many recent studies imply that fostering student engagement in productive discussions and enhancing the dialogic mode of instruction are far from being an easy task (e.g. Alexander, 2006; Lyle, 2008). In this chapter, the key aims will be to characterize the nature of productive collaborative learning, that is, interaction that promotes learning; to illustrate teachers' instructional activities and pre-structuring in CSCL contexts with relation to students' collaborative knowledge construction; and to sum up the results in the form of concrete messages for practical applications.

THEORETICAL BACKGROUND

Collaboration and collaborative learning have become common terms occurring frequently in discussion among teachers, researchers, and politicians. In school curricula, collaboration and collaborative learning are mentioned as important means for developing learning and instruction in schools. This has been an answer to the requirements that an information society sets for its citizens. Contemporary work requires the ability to work productively with others, since a lot of work today is done in groups, teams, and larger networks. Furthermore, it has been suggested that modern work requires the ability to communicate, negotiate, and anticipate what is to be done in practice rather than just doing the job as such (Iedema & Scheeres, 2003). However, from the teachers' perspective, there are also other current values in support of collaboration and collaborative learning than just the mission to prepare future workers. Many studies have demonstrated that students do learn better in groups than individually (e.g., Fisher et al., 2002; Howe & Tolmie, 1999; Light, Littleton, Messer & Joiner, 1994). In addition, teachers have acknowledged the motivating value of doing things together. Furthermore, collaboration is seen as one way to support students' own active knowledge construction instead of knowledge transferred from teachers to students (Wells & Arauz, 2006).

What are collaboration and collaborative learning, after all? Both in everyday discussions among practitioners in the schools and among researchers in the field of learning and instruction, the term collaboration is sometimes used very loosely, and the definition of collaboration is blurred. In many notions, it has been regarded as similar to co-operation, which is a typical activity in school projects, where the students work toward a shared goal, usually a shared product, but the actual work is divided (Cohen, 1994). In addition, collaboration is sometimes referred to very generally as a shared activity of the students, interaction between students, or participation in learning communities (e.g. Lipponen, 2001). However, in those notions, the nature of activity, interaction, or participation is not specified. Here collaboration refers to a specific type of activity, where the students are engaged together in the construction of shared knowledge or understanding about the issues addressed (e.g., Baker, 2002; Barron, 2000; Dillenbourg, 1999). According to Mercer (1996), different types of talk represent different ways in which the participants in a dialogue engage in the joint construction of knowledge. Exploratory talk, which is beneficial for collaborative knowledge construction, occurs when the participants engage critically but constructively with each other's ideas. Thus, within collaborative discourse different kinds of activities can be identified such as elaboration (e.g., van Boxtel, van der Linden & Kanselaar, 2000), asking questions (King, 1999),

or argumentation that are beneficial to learning (e.g., Baker, Andriessen, Lund, van Amelsvoort, & Quignard, 2007; Weinberger & Fischer, 2006).

Research on collaborative learning and the use of information and communication technologies has been integrated in the research area called Computer-Supported Collaborative Learning (CSCL) (Koschmann, 1996). Although there is no unified theory of CSCL, the common feature of different viewpoints is to focus either on how collaboration can be supported by technology or how technology can be used collaboratively (Lipponen, 2001). Furthermore, the crucial question in CSCL is how peer interaction and work in groups in computer-mediated contexts can enhance sharing and construction of knowledge—that is, collaborative learning. (Arvaja, Häkkinen & Kankaanranta, 2008)

It is argued that the promotion of collaboration requires approaches that help support and structure collaborative learning situations since free-form collaboration does not systematically produce learning (De Laat & Lally, 2004; Dillenbourg, 2002; King, 1999; Lehtinen, 2003; Lipponen, 2000). Structures are intended to facilitate collaborative learning processes and guide learners' activities. At its best, some amount of structuring may help to manage collaborative learning situations and enable teams to achieve effective collaboration (Dillenbourg, 1999; Kollar, Fischer & Hesse, 2003). One way to structure interactions is to design collaboration *scripts* in CSCL environments (Kobbe, Weinberger, Dillenbourg, Harrer, Hämäläinen, Häkkinen, & Fischer, 2007). The main idea in scripted collaboration is to provide support and structure for groups in otherwise open learning environments. These scripts are sets of teacher's pre-defined instructions to favor the emergence of productive interactions. In practice, scripts can, for example, prescribe how students should form groups, how they should interact and collaborate, and how they should solve problems (Dillenbourg & Jermann, 2006).

TEACHERS' INSTRUCTIONAL ACTIVITIES AND THE QUALITY OF STUDENTS' LEARNING ACTIVITIES

In this section, we take a look at teachers' instructional activities and their relationship to students' learning activities during web-based learning activity. We especially focus on discussing how teachers' pedagogical choices influence the quality of students' activity, namely web-based discussion. We do this by discussing a history learning project conducted with two teachers in two different secondary schools (Arvaja, Rasku-Puttonen, Häkkinen & Eteläpelto, 2003; Rasku-Puttonen, Eteläpelto, Häkkinen & Arvaja, 2002). The participants in this learning project were two secondary school classes from two separate schools (a total of 36 students) and their teachers, who made general plans for learning activities in collaboration. The aim of the history project was to study the theme of imperialism through a role-play in collaboration with another school. The students chose different kinds of occupational or social roles (e.g., railway technician, farmer, Hindu priest) representing different perspectives. One school represented British society and the other school Indian society. The purpose was to encourage students to construct, share, and seek knowledge about the lives of Indians and the British during the age of imperialism in the 19th century from the perspective of each student's own fictional role character through using a shared web-based learning environment.

Teachers' Instructional Activities

Next, we will compare the instructional activities of the teachers in the two schools. We compare the nature of task structuring and the teachers' roles as they define themselves.

One difference between the schools in realizing the project concerned the specificity of the instructions given by the teachers about working through role characters in the face-to-face classroom context and in sending messages in the web-based environment (Table 1). For example, in school A, most of the messages were based on tasks that the teacher had assigned to the students:

Mr Pandit: You are very interested in India. You will discuss with Doctor Lister and Miss Aarti Saha about the conditions in India. You decide to write a letter to a doctor living in India and tell your thoughts about how India could be reformed.

From teacher A's instructions above, we can see that the task was assigned to a group of students. Thus, the task supported collaborative working. The task was quite open-ended, leaving a space for creativity, but at the same time, the task supported reasoning. In contrast, in school B the teacher did not give any specific instructions for students to follow while writing the messages. He told the students to plan the messages themselves from the perspective of their own roles by using their own imagination and knowledge from books. He also instructed students to make contacts with role characters that would be feasible from the perspective of that historical time, but did not specify with whom, as the teacher in school A did.

Table 1. Differences in teachers' activities in the two schools

	Degree/nature of task structuring	Role of the teacher	Support for web-based interaction
School A	High structuring	Controller	No
School B	Low structuring	Guide	No

Earlier studies have demonstrated that shared knowledge construction in web-based discussion typically occurs in situations where the task itself triggers reasoning (Arvaja, 2007; Hämäläinen, 2008). It has been suggested that complex tasks, dealing with ill-defined and open-ended problems, facilitate productive interaction, such as elaborative talk, more effectively than tasks with well-structured problems and closed questions with one right answer (Cohen, 1994; van Boxtel et al., 2000). In addition, for example, explanation-seeking tasks are more likely than fact-seeking tasks to trigger such activities as reasoning, comparing, arguing, or explaining (Cohen, 1994), thus enhancing the mechanisms important to knowledge construction. Teacher A's task assignments dealt with open-ended tasks that were aimed at triggering reasoning without a requirement of 'right answers' implied in the example above. Also, teacher B gave his students instructions to be creative, thus supporting open-endedness. However, the instructions were quite ill-structured and lacked a clear goal about what and to whom to write.

Differences in teachers' instructional activities were seemingly related to their own perceptions of their role as a teacher (Table 1). The teachers defined their roles quite differently (Rasku-Puttonen et al., 2002). In an interview school A's teacher (called the Controller-Teacher here) characterized himself as a controller who wants to hold the reins. According to his opinion, a teacher needs to know the goal and the direction of the learning processes. School B's teacher (called the Guide-Teacher) described his role as a guide and a resource for the students. He wanted to encourage the students to engage in self-regulated learning.

The Controller-Teacher used to organize whole class sessions in the beginning and in the end of each learning session because he aimed to teach the concepts of the history domain. In his opinion, small group work alone will not produce good learning outcomes. He also preferred explicitly defined tasks to ill-defined ones. He thought that clear instruction and task assignments are the best ways to prepare students to work in a self-regulated manner toward the goals of the task.

The Guide-Teacher let the students start their work as soon as they entered the classroom. He let the students work with their friends in pairs or in small groups along their own wishes. He did not organize the student groupings. The Guide-Teacher described his role as an expert in the classroom, someone to whom the students could come for information and who would give guidance based on the students' needs. He allowed space for the students' own imagination and creativity to progress towards the goal of the task. To sum up, the main difference between the two teachers' instructional activities was the level of structuring, which was related to their perception of their role as a teacher. How then was the teachers' activity related to the students' work on the history project?

The Relationship between Teachers' Instructional Activities and the Quality of Students' Web-Based Discussion

Table 2 below illustrates students' learning activities in the two schools evaluated by the knowledge level in the web-based messages.

The quality of the messages the students sent between the schools was evaluated by their knowledge level. In the first level (*activity in the role*), students described the activities of their

Table 2. Differences in the knowledge level of the web-based messages in the two schools (Level 1, the lowest) (adapted from Arvaja et al., 2003)

	School A (*n*=24)	School B (*n*=29)
Level 1	21%	52%
Level 2	37%	31%
Level 3	25%	14%
Level 4	17%	3%

own role character without sharing any relevant knowledge about the theme under study; in the second level (*surface level knowledge sharing*), students described activities of own role character by sharing surface level knowledge about one issue relevant to the theme under study; in the third level (*surface level knowledge sharing*), students shared surface level knowledge about more than one issue relevant to the theme under study, whereas, in the fourth level (*advanced level knowledge sharing*), students shared advanced level knowledge through their roles about the theme under study by explaining, reasoning, or comparing knowledge. As we can see from Table 2, in school A, 42% of the messages reached the two highest levels (Levels 3 and 4), while in school B only 17% of the messages met this standard. Thus, it seemed that the Controller-Teacher's students in school A were able to reach more high-level activity than their fellow students in school B. In addition, in school A, about 30% (7) of the messages were written collaboratively. Most of these messages (5) reached the two highest levels. In school B, it seemed that without the Guide-Teacher's clear instructions, the students operated at the two lowest levels without sharing any relevant knowledge about the theme under study (Level 1) or presenting just one surface-level issue under that theme (Level 2). Furthermore, none of the messages were written collaboratively. In the interviews, the students of school B expressed this lack of instruction: "I didn't know what to write", "I'm glad the first message came from the other school, otherwise I wouldn't have had any idea what to write" or "I didn't know whom to write and what to write". Thus, even though the Guide-Teacher stressed the importance of using students' own imagination and creativity, this did not seem to succeed without instruction about the content and purpose of the messages.

There is an extensive field of study on associations between teacher's interpersonal behavior and students' achievements that supports our findings (e.g., den Brok, Brekelmans & Wubbles, 2004;

Goh & Fraser, 1998; Henderson & Fisher, 2008; Wubbles & Brekelmans, 2005). Those studies have demonstrated that teachers' interpersonal qualities such as leadership, helping, and understanding behavior led to better student outcomes. Leadership behavior was described in terms, which reminds the activity of the Controller-Teacher, such as lead, organize, set tasks, and structure the classroom situation. However, teacher interpersonal behavior stressing students' responsibility or freedom behavior, such as the Guide-Teacher's behavior in our study, was not related to better outcomes. These results suggest that shifting responsibility from teachers to learners presupposes on the one hand sufficient structuring of the student activities and on the other hand teacher's active support for student self-regulation (Rasku-Puttonen et al., 2003).

From a collaboration point of view, the shared work in the web-based environment was not successful. First of all, 36% of the messages were never replied (Arvaja et al., 2003). Although there were 12 interaction cycles (cycle = chain of messages) in the web-based discussion, only half were collaborative according to Baker's (2002) categorization (see more Arvaja et al., 2003). Baker (2002) defines collaboration as a symmetrical and aligned form of co-operation, where the students either agree (co-construction) or disagree (co-argumentation). In four of these collaborative interaction cycles, the knowledge level of the messages was at level two or higher, meaning that the knowledge construction dealt with the subject under study. However, in only one of these interaction cycles did the knowledge construction occur at a high level (Level 4). In this interaction cycle, the students were able to construct shared knowledge by explaining and comparing. Further, in this interaction cycle, the questions the students presented to each other were exploratory in nature. In three other interaction cycles dealing with the subject, it was typical that students equally shared mainly surface-level factual knowledge with each other. In these and all other interaction cycles, the questions were either fact-seeking questions or rhetorical questions, which could be answered simply yes or no. Thus, it seemed that the 'quality' of maintaining features of the interaction (e.g., Baker, Hansen, Joiner & Traum, 1999; Mäkitalo, Häkkinen, Leinonen & Järvelä, 2002) regulated the quality of interaction as a whole and thus also the quality of collaborative activity. It has been demonstrated that in order to induce collaboration between students, it is crucial to construct tasks that compel them to work together, as most students first attempt to carry out the tasks on their own, joining forces with other learners only when they realize it is necessary to solve a problem (Hämäläinen, 2008; Hämäläinen, Oksanen & Häkkinen, 2008).

To sum up, from the teachers' activity point of view, it seemed that clear instructions were able to guarantee that at the individual message level the students reached better results. However, support for collaboration *during* the web-based interaction was minimal (Table 1). Thus, even though the students in school A had a clear educational goal to find out some historical knowledge or information according to the teacher's instructions, it was up to the students to decide how they coordinated and maintained interaction on the web - whether they, for example, asked a question or challenged others' ideas or just sent an informative letter without any obligation to reply. However, it has been suggested that students do not ask thought-provoking questions (King, 1999) or interact at a high level unless they are taught or instructed to do so (Wegerif, Mercer & Dawes, 1999).

TEACHER'S PRE-STRUCTURING ACTIVITIES AND STUDENTS' COLLABORATIVE KNOWLEDGE CONSTRUCTION

In this section, we will discuss teacher's pre-structuring activities and their relationship to students' collaboration based on our earlier studies

carried out in the higher education context (Arvaja & Hämäläinen, 2008; Hämäläinen & Arvaja, 2009). We will discuss the main findings from the perspective of how teacher's pre-structuring of the task supported student groups' collaborative knowledge construction. We will, firstly, illustrate the scripted task and elaborate how Groups A and B followed the pre-structured case script, and secondly present the main differences and similarities between the groups in students' knowledge construction activity.

Teacher's Pre-Structuring Activities

The participants in the study consisted of first-year teacher education students studying the pedagogy of pre-primary and primary education. Two small groups with 4 (Group A) and 5 (Group B) students participated in the study. The leading idea of the teacher's pre-structuring of the task was to structure the student group processes and to trigger engagement in cognitive activities by means of a script, while they were working in an asynchronous virtual learning environment. In the case script, the main idea was to solve an authentic learning problem (e.g., Brown, Collins, & Duguid, 1989; Zualkernan, 2006) with complementary knowledge construction (e.g., Perkins, 1993). The case exercise took about four weeks during which the students were supposed to proceed through five different phases. Moving from one phase to the next presupposed that the previous task has been completed. The students were not penalized in any way, however, if they failed to go through the script. Thus, the script carefully guided the students step by step through the task and also offered necessary material, but neither gave instructions for student interaction as such nor penalized students if they failed to go through the phases.

In the case script, the learners worked in small groups to prepare an individualized teaching plan for one particular learner (Matti). Matti had special needs with respect to the teaching plan. The case script comprised five phases: Firstly, the students familiarized themselves with an authentic learning problem concerning learning readiness (of two different learners, Matti and Timo). In this phase, each group read a comic where Matti and Timo are working together. Secondly, the groups read theoretical background material about Matti's case. After this, they entered a shared web discussion about constructing a shared plan for a personal curriculum for Matti. Based on this discussion, the students accomplished a shared plan for this personal curriculum as a group. And, finally, the groups commented on other groups' curriculum plans for Timo and evaluated how realistic the plan was with regard to supporting the learning readiness of the learner in question.

Both Groups A and B went through the first phase of the script, and the authentic learning problem grounded their work through the task. From the second phase (reading theoretical background material), we did not get an exact participation rate, but Group A used the case material whereas Group B did not ground their work in the readings as was expected in the script (see next subsection and Table 3). In the third phase, both groups used shared web discussion. However, as will be described in the following section, the function of discussion differed greatly between the groups. In the final phase of the script, the groups were expected to use complementary knowledge construction (e.g., De Laat & Lally, 2004) and to comment on the other groups' curriculum plans with a different case. However, within this script both groups squeaked through the phase rather than actively used complementary knowledge construction to

increase the quality of their teaching plans (see Hämäläinen & Arvaja, 2009). Next, we will take a closer look at one phase of the script, namely the web-based discussion, where the students were supposed to discuss Matti's special needs for a personal curriculum based on the case description. We will see if the script succeeded in supporting students' collaborative knowledge construction and engagement in productive discussions.

The Relationship between Teacher's Pre-Structuring Activities and the Quality of Students' Collaborative Knowledge Construction

The students' collaborative knowledge construction activity in the web-based discussion was analyzed in terms of communicative functions (Kumpulainen & Mutanen, 1999) and contextual resources (Linell, 1998). (For a more specific discussion about the methodology and its theoretical grounds, see Arvaja, 2007; Arvaja, Salovaara, Häkkinen & Järvelä, 2007.) Table 3 presents the main differences and similarities between the two groups in the use of the communicative functions and contextual resources during the web-based discussion related to the designed script.

The functional analysis of the web-based messages focused on the purposes for which language was used in the given context. Additionally, communicative functions were used to indicate the cognitive quality of the discussions. As was stated earlier, it has been proposed that communicative functions, such as elaborating, asking questions, and arguing, enhance under-

Table 3. The main functions of communication and contextual resources used by Groups A and B in the case task (adapted from Arvaja & Hämäläinen, in press)

	Communicative functions (%)		Contextual resources (%)
Group A (*n*=104)	Knowledge providing (22%) Reasoning (22%) Commenting (13%) Organizational (13%)	Group A (*n*=111)	Case material (17%) Co-text (15%) Own idea (14%) Own conception (13%)
Group B (*n*=136)	Organizational (21%) Commenting (20%) Social (15%) Interrogative (13%)	Group B (*n*=99)	Document (33%) Co-text (17%) Own idea (10%) Own conception (10%)

standing and (individual) learning (e.g., Baker et al., 2007; Weinberger & Fischer, 2006). As can be seen from Table 3 in the case task, the main function of communication regarding students in Group A was to provide knowledge (22%) and to reason (22%). Thus, the students gave suggestions, information, or concrete examples relating to the topic of discussion (knowledge providing), and they justified the knowledge or reasoned about it (reasoning). They also organized the activities in the discussion forum or generally on the task (13%) and gave comments (13%) in the form of positive/negative feedback or expressed (dis) agreement to other participants.

Linell's (1998) notion of *contextual resources* was adapted and used as an analytical tool in studying the resources students used in their knowledge construction activity. Contextual resources refer to those aspects of the potential context that the participants make relevant in the ongoing activity. Potential contexts can relate to prior discourse (co-text) that is used for "a new act of sense-making" (Linell, 1998, p. 132) to concrete resources, such as course material available (e.g., books, links) or to more abstract resources, such as students' prior knowledge, opinions, attitudes, and experiences. The notion of co-text is particularly important from the collaboration point of view, because it shows whether the students build their thoughts and discussion on other students' thoughts and discussion (Arvaja, 2007). Co-text is manifested in such communicative functions as elaborating, reasoning, or answering questions. Thus, it indicates whether the content of the previous discussion is developed further. As can be seen from the use of contextual resources and, more specifically, the figure for co-text (15%), the knowledge was co-constructed in Group A (Table 3). Thus, the students built on each other's thoughts. The knowledge was mainly constructed by discussing the case (17%) and by using one's own ideas (14%) and conceptions (13%). Students' own ideas were usually manifested in practical or concrete suggestions (e.g., action or activity

descriptions) and conceptions in interpretations of issues or knowledge (e.g., application of theoretical knowledge). From the task aim point of view, this group shared (no co-text) and constructed (co-text) knowledge by using the case description as their main resource as had been intended by the designed script.

Generally, Group A followed the phases of the script and the pedagogical core idea of the script, as the results of this one particular phase demonstrate. However, the students' activities were not symmetrical. Of four students, only two actively contributed to content-based activities (e.g., knowledge providing and reasoning), whereas the two other students mainly commented on others' ideas (see Arvaja & Hämäläinen, 2008). However, despite the unequal participation, the group had members who reached collaboration (see Hämäläinen & Arvaja, 2009).

Group B followed the phases of the script; however, the students did not proceed according to the predefined pedagogical core idea of the script. In terms of the discussion, Group B differed notably from Group A (Table 3). The main functions of Group B were organizing activities (21%), commenting on other students' thoughts (20%), and maintaining a good atmosphere (social, 15%). Thus, instead of focusing on content-based goals, the students had a strong social orientation in their work. Their main reference was clearly the document base (33%), which indicates that the discussion forum was used for commenting on the ideas to be included in the document (personal curriculum) and organizing the process of writing the document. Thus, the forum was not extensively used for developing ideas relating to the problem-solving task (case) but to coordinate activities that took place elsewhere. However, the knowledge provided, elaborated, and reasoned in the forum was co-constructed as the figure for co-text (17%) shows (Table 3). Students' own ideas or conceptions were also among the four main contextual resources (Table 3). However, the case, the main resource in terms of the aim of the task, was hardly referred to during the discussion (see Arvaja & Hämäläinen, 2008). This supports the notion that content-based activity mainly took place during the document writing and not in the discussion forum, where it was supposed to happen according to the script. Additionally, the work of Group B was not collaborative, which the group members also noticed was problematic, as shown in the following student comment (see Hämäläinen & Arvaja, 2009):

We already have an awful lot of stuff in our plan, good stuff definitely, but somehow it should be edited for the final version, shouldn't it? It seems that we don't have any sort of division of labour here now and I, for one, find this very chaotic now... we should finish the plan, right, but it doesn't help at all if everybody is doing something on their own, but we lack an explicit framework for what to do. Or am I just all lost with this myself...? For my part, I could try to find tonight some clear "headings" or themes according to which the final plan would be easier to compile? (I have to rush to work now!) What do you think? Bye for now. (Hämäläinen & Arvaja, 2009).

To sum up, whereas Group A used the discussion forum as a place for their shared problem-solving activity and the case material and each other as resources in that activity, Group B students focused mostly on organizing their activities and commenting on others' suggestions or ideas without using the resources (case material) designed in the script. The student comment above represents well the nature and function of Group B's discussion - to organize activities in the shared document. However, this is not to say that Group A succeeded and Group B failed in the given task. Both groups succeeded in completing personal curricula for different learners, which was the supposed outcome of the task. Furthermore, in the personal curriculum, Group B students also used the case material, but the curriculum was written on an individual basis as the student comment also

indicates: "everybody is doing something on their own." Generally, the main difference between the groups' activities was that Group A students proceeded through the different steps of the script as was designed, whereas Group B students partly failed to use the discussion forum for discussing the case, but still used the case material in their document writing.

Furthermore, if we take a look at the quality of the discussion (Table 3), we can see that among the four main functions there was only one function in both of the groups that can be regarded as cognitively high level (e.g., King, 1999; Mercer, 1996; Weinberger & Fischer, 2006). The Group A students reasoned the knowledge, and the Group B students asked questions (interrogative). However, in the analysis, it was not differentiated whether the questions asked were exploratory, factual, or rhetoric, which all have quite different impacts on thinking and learning (King, 1999). As the student comment demonstrates, the questions asked in Group B employed the techniques of rhetoric. In the discussions, both groups also used elaboration (Group A, 11%; Group B, 5%), even though it was not among the main functions of communication (Arvaja & Hämäläinen, 2008). However, neither group used such functions as argumentation or counter-argumentation (Arvaja & Hämäläinen, 2008). Thus, it seemed that the knowledge was more cumulatively (Mercer, 1996) shared (no co-text) and constructed (co-text) than critically evaluated (Arvaja, 2007).

FUTURE TRENDS

Our studies show that promoting students' productive (e.g., argumentative and elaborative) discussions in the online courses was a challenging task for the teachers. As regards the role of technology, the students used rather typical asynchronous communication tools in their shared discussions. An asynchronous web-based discussion tool, however, can be regarded as a challenging tool for argumentation, because it does not allow for a very rapid exchange of ideas. Instead, synchronous discussion tools, such as chat, have proved efficient in supporting argumentative discussions (e.g. Marttunen & Laurinen, 2007). On the other hand, open problem solving tasks, such as the ones used in this study, do not necessarily call for a rapid exchange of knowledge. An asynchronous discussion tool can also be regarded as a challenging tool for shared knowledge construction, because it allows for long monologues which may be difficult to 'grab' as a whole and develop further by others. However, as a 'public memory' (Lipponen, 2001) an asynchronous discussion tool allows for more careful and perhaps deeper reflection on the other students' thoughts than a synchronous tool. As is already evident, in the future the benefits of new technologies should be utilized more extensively. At the moment the rise of Web 2.0 technologies, such as blogs, wikis and tools for instant messaging, give new possibilities for collaborative activities and also boost for new ways of communication. However, the pedagogical challenge still remains. As was stated earlier, these new tools (nor the preceding Web 1.0 technologies) are not designed for learning and teaching purposes as such (Laurillard, 2009). Designing and establishing new social environments for learning are demanding processes, which call for close collaboration between different fields of expertise (e.g. technical developers, specialists with pedagogic and field-specific expertise) (Hämäläinen, Oksanen & Häkkinen, 2008). In the future, pedagogically justified technologies are needed. According to recent studies, pedagogically designed technologies can serve, at their best, as shared operational environments for shared knowledge construction (e.g. Bluemink & Järvelä, 2009; Hämäläinen, 2008; Ravenscroft, Sagar, Baur & Oriogun, 2009). However, human responsibility for learning and teaching cannot be replaced by even the most advanced technology. The problematic nature of supporting human learning still remains; it is always a matter of dealing with

complex interaction of social, cognitive, motivational and emotional aspects and the features of the learning context (Arvaja et al., 2007). In addition, it has been argued that the new technologies call for research to assume whole new methodologies and theoretical perspectives (Peters, Slotta, Forte, Bruckman et al., 2008).

The asynchronous discussion forum used in our university case can be called as an established communication tool in the sense that online courses in Finnish universities are typically constructed around such tools. However, the most popular and in many cases the only accustomed web-based activity at the secondary level of education is searching knowledge from the Internet. Such use of ICT reflects and supports the transmission mode of instruction (Wells & Arauz, 2006). Even though the secondary schools in Finland are technologically well equipped with Internet access (100%), active and varied utilization of technology in teaching is still rare, as the SITES 2006 study demonstrates (Kankaanranta & Puhakka, 2008; Law, Pelgrum & Plomp, 2008). In addition, although many students are using different social networking (e.g. Facebook, Messenger) and content management tools (e.g. blogs, wikis) on a daily basis in their free time, more 'productive' use of these tools in formal education is almost non-existent at the secondary level and even at the university level still in its infancy. It is also typical that the use of technology in schools and universities rests on the shoulders of only few active teachers. To sum up, there is a huge gap between the reality of youngsters and that of formal education when it comes to technology. Therefore, the rise of Web 2.0 technologies sets new strains on the TPD as teachers have to integrate these new technologies into more or less traditional learning methods, curricula and schools' everyday life. Thus, from the TPD point of view, teachers need support and guidance in the use of new technological tools. They need possibilities to share their thoughts, reflections and good ideas for making progress (Mouza, 2007). Promoting the use of ICT in education should include helping teachers to integrate new pedagogical innovations into their daily work. For this purpose we need collaborative projects that are tailored to teachers' everyday work.

CONCLUSION

Our results from both studies show that if the success of collaborative work is measured through cognitive quality of discussions, both endeavors were not very successful. In both cases, rich moments of collaboration were rare and distributed unequally among the students. Thus, this study indicates that the process of collaboration is not easy to support and structure. Our findings are in line with Dillenbourg and Jermann's (2006) notion that structuring collaborative interactions is a complicated challenge that can be hindered by either too much or too little guidance. If there is not enough guidance, students may not reach the goals set for interaction, or in the worst case, there is no real interaction at all.

The obvious weakness from the perspective of teachers' structuring activities was that in neither of our studies was the students' interaction in the discussion forum supported in any way. Once the instructions were given, the responsibility for coordinating the interaction in the forums was only on the learners' side. However, as the results of the studies show, some of the students were not capable of engaging in productive collaboration. They had difficulties organizing the shared activity productively (Group B in the case script) and even difficulties detecting the purpose of their activity (School B students in the history project). Thus, it seemed that when the groups had to put more effort into organizational issues, it decreased the quality of their content-based activity and collaboration. However, when the students had clear instructions (School A students) and had no need to put too much effort on organizing activities (Group A), the students reached higher-level collaboration.

However, supporting and structuring collaboration are more complicated than designing detailed instructions in technical environments. Since the central idea in collaboration is creative interaction between learners, it is not predictable. Even though detailed instruction (such as scripts) at their best support collaborative learning (e.g., Weinberger, Stegmann & Fischer, 2007), they typically also suffer from the problem of being restrained to a specific learning platform and learning context (Kobbe et al., 2007). There is also a danger of over-structuring collaboration (Dillenbourg, 2002). If there is too much guidance, it may limit the richness of natural collaboration (Dillenbourg & Tchounikine, 2007; Hämäläinen & Häkkinen, 2009), or structuring can become counter-productive (Tchounikine, 2008). Therefore, the future challenge is to find ways to engage the whole group in the collaboration process (Fredricks, Blumenfeld, & Paris, 2004), while still leaving space for participants' own ideas and creativity (Vass, Carroll & Shaffer, 2002).

In order to better understand the contextual factors involved in the construction of a web-based learning environment, we should be able to specify the factors that are relevant in the interplay between teachers' instructional and students' learning activities. In our studies, the students would have needed the teacher's support in order to achieve more equal participation, in deepening their discussions, and in guiding them to use the resources as intended –that is, in supporting collaborative knowledge construction. Then again, studies on teachers' role in supporting group work give contradictory evidence about their contribution (e.g. Gillies, 2004) and students' own problem solving (Oortwijn, Boekaerts & Vedder, 2008). Pöysä and colleagues (2007), in turn, have shown that students need and expect the teacher's support while working in web-based learning environments. Still, as they also have demonstrated, students are often left on their own to manage their own learning process. Thus, it would be necessary for teachers to continuously monitor individual students' participation and activities on web-based exercises. Careful monitoring would give feedback to the teachers and help them adjust their instructional activities and scaffolding to meet the diverse needs of their students during a long-term learning process. In the cases studied, the web-based environment did not, however, enhance teachers' monitoring, which as such was too time consuming for the teachers struggling with time limitations. Therefore, in the future, it would be necessary to develop technological tools in terms of supporting teachers' awareness of students' learning process.

Many teachers and researchers working within the field of education have been interested in producing learning environments that support active student participation and shared responsibility for learning. Computer-Supported Collaborative Learning environments have been assumed to provide such an opportunity for students to construct and progressively improve their understanding through productive discussions. The transformation of monologic classroom cultures to dialogic ones and the attendant assumptions about teacher-student relationship, however, seem to be very demanding for many teachers and students. Given this, our examples give evidence of teachers' desire and abilities to produce and implement pedagogically innovative learning environments (e.g., Rasku-Puttonen, Eteläpelto, Lehtonen, Nummela, & Häkkinen, 2004). In interviews, teachers said that they would have needed still more time for joint discussions on the learning goals and needed to give students more detailed instructions. In order to learn more from each other, they also wished to have sessions to observe each other's authentic teaching activities. We suggest that in order to get support for professional development teachers need more systematically constructed programs for their productive workplace learning. Based on our research, we perceive teacher collaboration within work communities as a powerful element

in teachers' workplace learning (see also Meirink, Meijer, & Verloop, 2007), one that will ultimately enhance student learning and achievement (Vescio, Ross, & Adams, 2008).

REFERENCES

Alexander, R. (2006). *Towards dialogic teaching* (3rd ed.) New York: Dialogos.

Arvaja, M. (2005). *Collaborative knowledge construction in authentic school contexts.* Unpublished doctoral dissertation, University of Jyväskylä, Institute for Educational Research.

Arvaja, M. (2007). Contextual perspective in analysing collaborative knowledge construction of two small groups in web-based discussion. *International Journal of Computer-Supported Collaborative Learning, 2*(2-3), 133–158. doi:10.1007/s11412-007-9013-5

Arvaja, M., Häkkinen, P., & Kankaanranta, M. (2008). Collaborative learning and computer-supported collaborative learning environments. In J. Voogt & G. Knezek (Eds.), *International handbook of information technology in primary and secondary education* (pp. 267-279). New York: Springer.

Arvaja, M., & Hämäläinen, R. (2008). Collaborative knowledge construction during structured tasks in an online course at higher education context. In G. Ollington (Ed.), *Teachers and teaching: Strategies, innovations and problem solving.* New York: Nova Science Publishers.

Arvaja, M., Rasku-Puttonen, H., Häkkinen, P., & Eteläpelto, A. (2003). Constructing knowledge through a role-play in a web-based learning environment. *Journal of Educational Computing Research, 28*(4), 319–341. doi:10.2190/4FAV-EK1T-XV4H-YNXF

Arvaja, M., Salovaara, H., Häkkinen, P., & Järvelä, S. (2007). Combining individual and group-level perspectives for studying collaborative knowledge construction in context. *Learning and Instruction, 17*(4), 448–459. doi:10.1016/j.learninstruc.2007.04.003

Baker, M., Andriessen, J., Lund, K., van Amelsvoort, M., & Quignard, M. (2007). Rainbow: A framework for analysing computer-mediated pedagogical debates. *International Journal of Computer-Supported Collaborative Learning, 2*(2-3), 315–357. doi:10.1007/s11412-007-9022-4

Baker, M., Hansen, T., Joiner, R., & Traum, D. (1999). The role of grounding in collaborative learning tasks. In P. Dillenbourg (Ed.), *Collaborative learning: Cognitive and computational approaches* (pp. 31-63). Oxford: Elsevier Science.

Baker, M. J. (2002). Forms of cooperation in dyadic problem-solving. *Revue d'Intelligence Artificielle, 16*(4-5), 587–620. doi:10.3166/ria.16.587-620

Barron, B. (2000). Achieving coordination in collaborative problem-solving groups. *Journal of the Learning Sciences, 9*(4), 403–436. doi:10.1207/S15327809JLS0904_2

Bluemink, J., & Järvelä, S. (2009). Discourse processes and shared understanding in virtual multiplayer game collaboration. (Submitted).

Brown, J. S., Collins, A., & Duguid, P. (1989). Situated cognition and the culture of learning. *Educational Researcher, 18*(1), 32–42.

Cobos, R., & Pifarre, M. (2008). Collaborative knowledge construction in the web supported by the KnowCat system. *Computers & Education, 50*(3), 962–978. doi:10.1016/j.compedu.2006.09.009

Cohen, E. (1994). Restructuring the classroom: Conditions for productive small groups. *Review of Educational Research, 64*(1), 1–35.

De Laat, M., & Lally, V. (2004). It's not so easy: Researching the complexity of emergent participant roles and awareness in asynchronous networked learning discussions. *Journal of Computer Assisted Learning, 20*(3), 165–171. doi:10.1111/j.1365-2729.2004.00085.x

den Brok, P., Brekelmans, M., & Wubbles, T. (2004). Interpersonal teacher behaviour and students outcomes. *School Effectiveness and School Improvement, 15*, 407–422. doi:10.1080/09243450512331383262

Dillenbourg, P. (1999). Introduction: What do you mean by collaborative learning? In P. Dillenbourg (Ed.), *Collaborative learning: Cognitive and computational approaches* (pp. 1-19). Oxford: Pergamon.

Dillenbourg, P. (2002). Over-scripting CSCL: The risks of blending collaborative learning with instructional design. In P. A. Kirschner (Ed.), *Three worlds of CSCL. Can we support CSCL* (pp. 61-91). Heerlen, Open Universiteit Nederland.

Dillenbourg, P., & Jermann, P. (2006). Designing integrative scripts. In F. Fischer, H. Mandl, J. Haake, & I. Kollar (Eds.), *Scripting computer-supported collaborative learning: Cognitive, computational and educational perspectives.* New York: Springer.

Dillenbourg, P., & Tchounikine, P. (2007). Flexibility in macro-scripts for computer-supported collaborative learning. *Journal of Computer Assisted Learning, 23*(1), 1–13. doi:10.1111/j.1365-2729.2007.00191.x

Fischer, F., Bruhn, C., Gräsel, C., & Mandl, H. (2002). Fostering collaborative knowledge construction with visualization tools. *Learning and Instruction, 12*(2), 213–232. doi:10.1016/S0959-4752(01)00005-6

Fischer, F., & Dillenbourg, P. (2006, April). *Challenges of orchestrating computer-supported collaborative learning*. Paper presented at the 87th Annual Meeting of the American Educational Research Association (AERA), San Francisco, US.

Fredricks, J. A., Blumenfeld, P. C., & Paris, A. H. (2004). School engagement: potential of the concept, state of the evidence. *Review of Educational Research, 74*, 59–109. doi:10.3102/00346543074001059

Gillies, R. M. (2004). The effects of cooperative learning on junior high school students during small group learning. *Learning and Instruction, 14*(2), 197–213. doi:10.1016/S0959-4752(03)00068-9

Goh, S., & Fraser, B. (1998). Teacher interpersonal behaviour, classroom environment and student outcomes in primary mathematics in Singapore. *Learning Environments Research, 1*, 199–229. doi:10.1023/A:1009910017400

Hämäläinen, R. (2008). Designing and evaluating collaboration in a virtual game environment for vocational learning. *Computers & Education, 50*(1), 98–109. doi:10.1016/j.compedu.2006.04.001

Hämäläinen, R., & Arvaja, M. (2009). Scripted collaboration and group-based variations in a higher education CSCL context. *Scandinavian Journal of Educational Research, 53*(1), 1-16.

Hämäläinen, R., & Häkkinen, P. (2009). *Group variations in scripted collaboration: The case of Grid-Script*. (Submitted).

Hämäläinen, R., Oksanen, K., & Häkkinen, P. (2008). Designing and analyzing collaboration in a scripted game for vocational education. *Computers in Human Behavior, 24*(6), 2496–2506. doi:10.1016/j.chb.2008.03.010

Henderson, D., & Fisher, D. (2008). Interpersonal behaviour and student outcomes in vocational education classes. *Learning Environments Research, 11*, 19–29. doi:10.1007/s10984-007-9034-z

Howe, C., & Tolmie, A. (1999). Productive interaction in the context of computer-supported collaborative learning in science. In K. Littleton & P. Light (Eds.), *Learning with computers* (pp. 24-45). London: Routledge.

Iedema, R., & Scheeres, H. (2003). From doing work to talking work: Renegotiating knowing, doing and identity. *Applied Linguistics, 24*(3), 316–337. doi:10.1093/applin/24.3.316

Kankaanranta, M., & Puhakka, E. (2008). *Kohti innovatiivista tietotekniikan opetuskäyttöä. Kansainvälisen SITES 2006 – tutkimuksen tuloksia*. Jyväskylä: Jyväskylän yliopistopaino.

King, A. (1999). Discourse patterns for mediating peer learning. In A. O'Donnell & A. King (Eds.), *Cognitive perspectives on peer learning* (pp. 87-115). Mahwah, NJ: Lawrence Erlbaum Associates.

Kobbe, L., Weinberger, A., Dillenbourg, P., Harrer, A., Hämäläinen, R., Häkkinen, P., & Fischer, F. (2007). Specifying Computer-Supported Collaboration Scripts. *International Journal of Computer-Supported Collaborative Learning, 2*(2-3), 211–224. doi:10.1007/s11412-007-9014-4

Kollar, I., Fischer, F., & Hesse, F. W. (2003). Cooperation scripts for computer-supported collaborative learning. In B. Wasson, R. Baggetun, U. Hoppe, & S. Ludvigsen (Eds.), *Proceedings of the International Conference on Computer Support for Collaborative Learning: CSCL 2003 Community events - Communication and interaction* (pp. 59-61). Bergen: InterMedia.

Koschmann, T. (Ed.). (1996). *CSCL: Theory and practice of an emerging paradigm*. Mahwah, NJ: Lawrence Erlbaum Associates.

Kumpulainen, K., & Mutanen, M. (1999). The situated dynamics of peer group interaction: An introduction to an analytic framework. *Learning and Instruction, 9*(5), 449–473. doi:10.1016/S0959-4752(98)00038-3

Laurillard, D. (2009). The pedagogical challenges to collaborative technologies. *International Journal of Computer-Supported Collaborative Learning, 4*(1), 5–20. doi:10.1007/s11412-008-9056-2

Law, N., Pelgrum, W., & Plomp, T. (2008). *Pedagogy and ICT use in schools around the world. Findings from the IEA SITES 2006 study*. The University of Hong Kong: Comparative Education Research Centre.

Lehtinen, E. (2003). Computer-supported collaborative learning: An approach to powerful learning environments. In E. de Corte, L. Verschaffel, N. Entwistle, & J. van Merriëboer (Eds.), *Powerful learning environments: Unraveling basic components and dimensions* (pp. 35-54). Amsterdam: Pergamon.

Light, P., Littleton, K., Messer, D., & Joiner, R. (1994). Social and communicative processes in computer-based problem solving. *European Journal of Psychology of Education, 9*(1), 93–109.

Linell, P. (1998). *Approaching dialogue. Talk, interaction and contexts in dialogical perspectives*. Amsterdam: John Benjamins.

Lipponen, L. (2000). Towards knowledge building discourse: From facts to explanations in primary students' computer-mediated discourse. *Learning Environments Research, 3*(2), 179–199. doi:10.1023/A:1026516728338

Lipponen, L. (2001). *Computer-supported collaborative learning: From promises to reality*. Unpublished doctoral dissertation, University of Turku.

Lyle, S. (2008). Dialogic teaching: Discussing theoretical contexts and reviewing evidence from classroom practice. *Language and Education, 22*(3), 222–240.

Mäkitalo, K., Häkkinen, P., Leinonen, P., & Järvelä, S. (2002). Mechanisms of common ground in case-based web-discussions in teacher education. *The Internet and Higher Education, 5*(3), 247–265. doi:10.1016/S1096-7516(02)00112-4

Marttunen, M., & Laurinen, L. (2007). Collaborative learning through chat discussions and argument diagrams in secondary school. *Journal of Research on Technology in Education, 40*(1), 109–126.

Meirink, A., Meijer, P., & Verloop, N. (2007). A closer look at teachers' individual learning in collaborative settings. *Teachers and teaching . Theory into Practice, 13*(2), 145–164.

Mercer, N. (1996). The quality of talk in children's collaborative activity in classroom. *Learning and Instruction, 6*(4), 359–377. doi:10.1016/S0959-4752(96)00021-7

Mouza, C. (2007). A socio-cultural approach to the design of a virtual practicum. In M. Zellermayer & E. Munthe (Eds.), *Teachers learning in communities* (pp. 165-187). Rotterdam: Sense Publishers.

O'Reilly, T. (2005). *What Is Web 2.0. Design Patterns and Business Models for the Next Generation of Software*. Retrieved, January 9, 2009, from http://www.oreillynet.com/pub/a/oreilly/tim/news/2005/09/30/what-is-web-20.html

Oortwijn, M., Boekaerts, M., & Vedder, P. (2008). The impact of the teacher's role and pupils' ethnicity and prior knowledge on pupils' performance and motivation to cooperate. *Instructional Science, 36*(3), 251–268. doi:10.1007/s11251-007-9032-7

Perkins, D. N. (1993). Person-plus: A distributed view of thinking and learning. In G. Salomon, (Ed.), *Distributed cognitions. Psychological and educational considerations* (pp. 88-110). New York: Cambridge University Press.

Peters, V., Slotta, J., Forte, A., Bruckman, A., Lee, J. J., Gaydos, M., et al. (2008). Learning and research in the Web 2 Era: Opportunities for research. In G. Kanselaar, V. Jonker, P. A. Kirschner & F. J. Prins (Eds.), *Proceedings of the International Conference of the Learning Sciences.* International Society of the Learning Sciences. Utrecht. Retrieved January 5, 2009, from http://www.fi.uu.nl/en/icls2008/505/paper505.pdf

Pöysä, J., Hurme, T-R., Launonen, A., Hämäläinen, T., Järvelä, S., & Häkkinen, P. (2007). *Millaista on laadukas yhteisöllinen oppiminen verkossa. Osallistujalähtöinen näkökulma yhteisöllisen oppimisen ja toiminnan käytänteisiin Suomen virtuaaliyliopiston tieteenalaverkostojen verkkokursseilla.* Suomen virtuaaliyliopiston julkaisuja 3.

Rasku-Puttonen, H., Eteläpelto, A., Arvaja, M., & Häkkinen, P. (2003). Is successful scaffolding an illusion? - Shifting patterns of responsibility and control in teacher-student interaction during a long term learning project. *Instructional Science, 31*(6), 377–393. doi:10.1023/A:1025700810376

Rasku-Puttonen, H., Eteläpelto, A., Häkkinen, P., & Arvaja, M. (2002). Teacher's instructional scaffolding in an innovative ICT-based history-learning environment. *Teacher Development, 6*(2), 269–287. doi:10.1080/13664530200200180

Rasku-Puttonen, H., Eteläpelto, A., Lehtonen, O., Nummila, L., & Häkkinen, P. (2004). Developing teachers' professional expertise through collaboration in an innovative ICT-based learning environment. *European Journal of Teacher Education, 27*(1), 47–60. doi:10.1080/0261976042000211829

Ravenscroft, A., Sagar, M., Baur, E., & Oriogun, P. (in press). Ambient pedagogies, meaningful learning and social software. In S. Hatzipanagos & S. Warburton (Eds.), *Social software & developing community ontologies.* IGI Global Publishing.

Roschelle, J., & Pea, R. (1999). Trajectories from today's WWW to a powerful educational infrastructure. *Educational Researcher, 28*(5), 22–25.

Tchounikine, P. (2008). Operationalizing macro-scripts in CSCL technological settings. *International Journal of Computer-Supported Collaborative Learning, 3*(2), 193–233. doi:10.1007/s11412-008-9039-3

van Boxtel, C., van der Linden, J., & Kanselaar, G. (2000). Collaborative learning tasks and the elaboration of conceptual knowledge. *Learning and Instruction, 10*(4), 311–330. doi:10.1016/S0959-4752(00)00002-5

Vass, M., Carroll, J., & Shaffer, C. (2002). Supporting creativity in problem solving environments. *Proceedings of the 4th Conference on Creativity & Cognition* (pp. 31-37). Loughborough, UK.

Vescio, V., Ross, D., & Adams, A. (2008). A review of research on the impact of professional learning communities on teaching practice and student learning. *Teaching and Teacher Education, 24,* 80–91. doi:10.1016/j.tate.2007.01.004

Wegerif, R., Mercer, N., & Dawes, L. (1999). From social interaction to individual reasoning: An empirical investigation of a possible sociocultural model of cognitive development. *Learning and Instruction, 9*(6), 493–526. doi:10.1016/S0959-4752(99)00013-4

Weinberger, A., & Fischer, F. (2006). A framework to analyze argumentative knowledge construction in computer-supported collaborative learning. *Computers & Education, 46,* 71–95. doi:10.1016/j.compedu.2005.04.003

Weinberger, A., Stegmann, K., & Fischer, F. (2007). Knowledge convergence in collaborative learning: Concepts and assessment. *Learning and Instruction, 17*(4), 416–426. doi:10.1016/j.learninstruc.2007.03.007

Weinstein, C. S. (1989). Teacher education students' preconceptions of teaching. *Journal of Teacher Education, 40*(2), 53–60. doi:10.1177/002248718904000210

Wells, G., & Arauz, R. M. (2006). Dialogue in the classroom. *Journal of the Learning Sciences, 15*(3), 379–428. doi:10.1207/s15327809jls1503_3

Wubbles, T., & Brekelmans, M. (2005). Two decades of research on teacher-student relationships in class. *International Journal of Educational Research, 43*, 6–24. doi:10.1016/j.ijer.2006.03.003

Zellermayer, M., & Munthe, E. (2007). Teachers learning in communities. In M. Zellermayer & E. Munthe (Eds.), *Teachers learning in communities* (pp. 1-6). Rotterdam: Sense Publishers.

Zualkernan, I. A. (2006). A framework and a methodology for developing authentic constructivist e-Learning environments. *Educational Technology & Society, 9*(2), 198–212.

Compilation of References

AACTE Committee on Innovation and Technology (Ed.). (2008). *Handbook of Technological Pedagogical Content Knowledge (TPCK) for educators*. New York: Routledge.

Academy of Medical Educators. (2007). 14th December 2007, from http://www.medicaleducators.org/

Achinstein, B. (2006). New teacher and mentor political literacy: reading, navigating and transforming induction contexts. *Teachers and Teaching: theory and practice, 12*(2), 123-138.

ACOT. (1996/2006). *Changing the conversation about teaching, learning and technology: A report on 10 years of ACOT research*. Retrieved September 7, 2008, from http://www.images.apple.com/education/k12/leadership/acot/pdf/10yr.pdf

AERA. American Educational Research Panel. Retrieved 27th of December from: http://www.aera.net/newsmedia/?id=763

Agostinho, S. (2008). Learning design Representations to Document, Model, and Share Teaching Practice. In L. Lockyer, S. Bennett, S. Agostinho, & B. Harper (Eds.), *Handbook of Research on Learning design and Learning Objects: Issues, Applications and Technologies* (pp. 1–19). Hershey, PA: Information Science Reference.

Alberta Education. (2008). *Facts about the Alberta Initiative for School Improvement (AISI)*, from http://education.alberta.ca/admin/aisi/about/whatisaisi.aspx

Albion, P., & Ertmer, P. A. (2002). Beyond the foundations: The role of vision and belief in teachers' preparation for integration of technology. *TechTrends, 46*(5), 34–38. doi:10.1007/BF02818306

Alexander, J. O. (1999). Collaborative Design, Constructivist Learning, Information Technology Immersion, & Electronic Communities: A Case Study [Electronic Version]. *Interpersonal Computing and Technology: An Electronic Journal for the 21st Century, 7*. Retrieved October 1999 from http://www.emoderators.com/ipct-j/1999/n1-2/alexander.html.

Alexander, R. (2006). *Towards dialogic teaching* (3rd ed.) New York: Dialogos.

Allan, B., & Lewis, D. (2006). The impact of membership of a virtual learning community on individual learning careers and professional identity. *British Journal of Educational Technology, 37*(6), 841–852. doi:10.1111/j.1467-8535.2006.00661.x

Allen, I. E., & Seeman, J. (2007, October). *Online nation: Five years of growth in online learning*. Retrieved September 26, 2008, from http://www.sloan-c.org/

American Association for the Advancement of Science. (1993). *Benchmarks for Science Literacy*. New York: Oxford University Press.

Anderson, G. L., & Jones, F. (2000). Knowledge generation in Educational Administration from the inside out: The promise and perils of site-based, administrator research. *Educational Administration Quarterly, 36*(3), 428–464. doi:10.1177/00131610021969056

Anderson, R., & Demeulle, L. (1998). Portfolio use in twenty-four teacher education programs. *Teacher Education Quarterly, 25*(1), 23–32.

Anderson, T., Rourke, L., Garrison, D. R., & Archer, W. (2001). Assessing Teaching Presence in a Computer

Conferecing Context. *Journal of Asynchronous Learning Networks, 5*(2). Retrieved May 9, 2008, from http://communitiesofinquiry.com/files/Teaching%20Presence.pdf

Annenberg Institute for School Reform. (2004). *Professional learning communities: Professional development strategies that improve instruction.* Retrieved June 13, 2008, from http://www.annenberginstitute.org/pdf/ProfLearning.pdf

Arfwedson, G. (1984). Why schools are different (In Norwegian). Oslo: Tanum.

Armstrong, V., & Curran, S. (2006). Developing a collaborative model of research using digital video. *Computers & Education, 46*(3), 336–347. doi:10.1016/j.compedu.2005.11.015

Armstrong, V., Barnes, S., Sutherland, R., Curran, S., Miller, S., & Thompson, I. (2005). Collaborative research methodology for investigating teaching and learning: the use of interactive whiteboard technology. *Educational Review, 57*(4), 457–469. doi:10.1080/00131910500279551

Arvaja, M. (2005). *Collaborative knowledge construction in authentic school contexts.* Unpublished doctoral dissertation, University of Jyväskylä, Institute for Educational Research.

Arvaja, M. (2007). Contextual perspective in analysing collaborative knowledge construction of two small groups in web-based discussion. *International Journal of Computer-Supported Collaborative Learning, 2*(2-3), 133–158. doi:10.1007/s11412-007-9013-5

Arvaja, M., & Hämäläinen, R. (in press). Collaborative knowledge construction during structured tasks in an online course at higher education context. In G. Ollington (Ed.), *Teachers and teaching: Strategies, innovations and problem solving.* New York: Nova Science Publishers.

Arvaja, M., Häkkinen, P., & Kankaanranta, M. (2008). Collaborative learning and computer-supported collaborative learning environments. In J. Voogt & G. Knezek (Eds.), *International handbook of information technology in primary and secondary education* (pp. 267-279). New York: Springer.

Arvaja, M., Rasku-Puttonen, H., Häkkinen, P., & Eteläpelto, A. (2003). Constructing knowledge through a role-play in a web-based learning environment. *Journal of Educational Computing Research, 28*(4), 319–341. doi:10.2190/4FAV-EK1T-XV4H-YNXF

Arvaja, M., Salovaara, H., Häkkinen, P., & Järvelä, S. (2007). Combining individual and group-level perspectives for studying collaborative knowledge construction in context. *Learning and Instruction, 17*(4), 448–459. doi:10.1016/j.learninstruc.2007.04.003

Ascough, R. S. (2002). Designing for online distance education: Putting pedagogy before technology. *Teaching Theology and Religion, 5*(1), 17–29. doi:10.1111/1467-9647.00114

Association of American Medical Colleges. (1998). *Learning objectives for medical student education.* Retrieved 15th April 2007, from www.aamc.org/meded/msop

Aubusson, P. (2007). Action learning in teacher learning community formation: informative or transformative? *Teacher Development, 11*(2), 133–148. doi:10.1080/13664530701414746

Baker, M. J. (2002). Forms of cooperation in dyadic problem-solving. *Revue d'Intelligence Artificielle, 16*(4-5), 587–620. doi:10.3166/ria.16.587-620

Baker, M., Andriessen, J., Lund, K., van Amelsvoort, M., & Quignard, M. (2007). Rainbow: A framework for analysing computer-mediated pedagogical debates. *International Journal of Computer-Supported Collaborative Learning, 2*(2-3), 315–357. doi:10.1007/s11412-007-9022-4

Baker, M., Hansen, T., Joiner, R., & Traum, D. (1999). The role of grounding in collaborative learning tasks. In P. Dillenbourg (Ed.), *Collaborative learning: Cognitive and computational approaches* (pp. 31-63). Oxford: Elsevier Science.

Ball, S. (2006). *Educational Policy and Social Class.* London UK: Routledge.

Bandura, A. (1986). *Social foundations of thought and action: A Social Cognitive Theory*. Englewood Cliffs, NJ: Prentice-Hall.

Bandura, A. (1993). Perceived self-efficacy in cognitive development and functioning. *Educational Psychologist, 28*(2), 117–148. doi:10.1207/s15326985ep2802_3

Bandura, A. (1997). *Self-efficacy: The exercise of control*. New York: Freeman.

Bandura, A. (2001). Social Cognitive Theory: An agentic perspective. *Annual Review of Psychology, 52*(1), 1–26. doi:10.1146/annurev.psych.52.1.1

Bandura, A. (2001). Social Cognitive Theory: An agentic perspective. *Annual Review of Psychology, 52*, 1–26. doi:10.1146/annurev.psych.52.1.1

Barab, S. A., Kling, R., & Gray, J. S. (Eds.). (2004). *Designing for virtual communities in the service of learning*. Cambridge: Cambridge University Press.

Barab, S. A., MaKinster, J., & Scheckler, R. (2003). Designing system dualities: Characterizing a web-supported teacher professional development community. *The Information Society, 19*(3), 237–256. doi:10.1080/01972240309466

Barab, S. MaKinster, J., & Scheckler, R. (2004). Designing System Dualities: Building Online Community. In S. Barab, R. Kling & J. Gray (Eds.), *Designing virtual communities in the service of learning*. Cambridge, UK: Cambridge University Press.

Barab, S. MaKinster, J., & Scheckler, R. (2004). Designing System Dualities: Characterizing Online Community. In S. Barab, R. Kling, & J. Gray (Eds.), *Designing for Virtual Communities in the Service of Learning*. Cambridge, MA: Cambridge University Press.

Barab, S., Kling, R., & Gray, J. 2004. Introduction: Designing for virtual communities in the service of learning. In: S. Barab, R. Kling, & J. Gray (Eds.), *Designing for Virtual Communities in the Service of Learning*. Cambridge, UK: Cambridge University Press.

Barab, S., Kling, R., & Gray, J. H. (Eds.). (2004). *Designing for Virtual Communities in the Service of Learning*.

Cambridge, United Kingdom: Press Syndicate of the University of Cambridge.

Barab, S., MaKinster, J. G., Moore, J., Cunningham, D., & ILF Design Team. (2001). Designing and building an online community: The struggle to support sociability in the Inquiry Learning Forum. *Educational Technology Research and Development, 49*(4), 71–96. doi:10.1007/BF02504948

Barnett, M. (2006). Using web-based professional development system to support preservice teachers in examining authentic classroom practice. *Journal of Technology and Teacher Education, 14*(4), 701–729.

Baron, S. (2004). The Applied Educational Research Scheme: A real opportunity for Scottish educational research. *Education Next, 12*, 41–44.

Barron, B. (1998). Doing with understanding: Lessons from research on problem- and project-based learning. *Journal of the Learning Sciences, 7*(3), 271–311. doi:10.1207/s15327809jls0703&4_2

Barron, B. (2000). Achieving coordination in collaborative problem-solving groups. *Journal of the Learning Sciences, 9*(4), 403–436. doi:10.1207/S15327809JLS0904_2

Bartels, N. (2003). How teachers and researchers read academic articles. *Teaching and Teacher Education, 19*, 737–753. doi:10.1016/j.tate.2003.06.001

Baumard, P. (1999). *Tacit knowledge in organizations*. London, UK: Sage.

Bean, T. W., & Stevens, L. P. (2002). Scaffolding Reflection for Preservice and Inservice Teachers. *Reflective Practice, 3*(2), 205–219. doi:10.1080/14623940220142343

Beardsley, L., Cogan-Drew, D., & Olivero, F. (2007). VideoPaper: Bridging research and practice for pre-service and experienced teachers. In B. Barron, S. Derry, R. Goldman, & R. Pea (Eds.), *Video research in the learning sciences* (pp. 479–493). Mahwah, NJ: Erlbaum.

Becta (2007). *Harnessing Technology Review 2007: progress and impact of technology in education*. Coventry: Becta.

Beetham, H. (2008). *Review: Design for Learning programme phase 2*. Unpublished report. Bristol: JISC.

Begg, M. (2008). Leveraging Game Informed Learning in Higher Education. *Medical Teacher, 30*(2), 155–158. doi:10.1080/01421590701874041

Begg, M., Dewhurst, D., & Macleod, H. (2005). Game Informed Learning: Applying computer game processes to Higher Education. *Innovate, 1*(6).

Begg, M., Ellaway, R., Dewhurst, D., & Macleod, H. (2006). Virtual Patients: considerations of narrative and gameplay. In M. Burmester, D. Gerhard, & F. Thissen (Eds.), *Digital Game Based Learning: 4th International Symposium for Information Design* (pp. 101 - 113). Stuttgart Media University: Universitatsverlag Karlsruhe.

Begg, M., Ellaway, R., Dewhurst, D., & Macleod, H. (2007a). *Logos and Mythos: the political dilemmas of Web 2.0 in an accreditation-driven educational environment.* Paper presented at the Ice 2007 - Ideas in Cyberspace Education, Loch Lomond, UK.

Begg, M., Ellaway, R., Dewhurst, D., & Macleod, H. (2007b). Transforming Professional Healthcare Narratives Into Structured Game Informed Learning Activities. *Innovate, 3*(6).

Beijaard, D., Korthagen, F., & Verloop, N. (2007). Understanding how teachers learn as a pre-requisite for promoting teacher learning. *Teachers and Teaching, 13*(2), 105–108. doi:10.1080/13540600601152298

Bell, B., & Gilbert, J. (1994). Teacher development as professional, personal, and social development. *Teaching and Teacher Education, 10*(5), 483–497. doi:10.1016/0742-051X(94)90002-7

Bernstein, B. (1975). *Class, Codes and Control, 3*. London: Routledge.

Biesta, G. (2007). Why "what works" won't work: Evidence-based practice and the democratic deficit in educational research. *Educational Theory, 57*(1), 1–22. doi:10.1111/j.1741-5446.2006.00241.x

Bintrim, L. (2002). Redesigning Professional Development. []. Association for Supervision & Curriculum Development.]. *Educational Leadership, 59*, 96.

Bluemink, J., & Järvelä, S. (2009). Discourse processes and shared understanding in virtual multiplayer game collaboration. (Submitted).

Bodzin, A. M., & Park, J. C. (2000). Dialogue patterns of preservice science teachers using asynchronous computer mediated communications on the World Wide Web. *Journal of Computers in Mathematics and Science Teaching, 19*(2), 161–194.

Bolam, R., & McMahon, A. (2004). Literature, definitions and models: Towards a conceptual map. In C. Day & J. Sachs (Ed.), *International Handbook on the Continuing Professional Development of Teachers* (pp. 33-63). Berkshire: Open University Press, McGraw-Hill Education.

Bolam, R., McMahon, A., Stoll, L., Thomas, S., & Wallace, M. (2005). *Creating and Sustaining Effective Professional Learning Communities.* London: Department for Education and Skills.

Bond, P. (2004). Communities of practice and complexity: Conversation and culture. *Organisations and People, 11*(4), 1–7.

Borko, H. (2004). Professional Development and Teacher Learning: Mapping the Terrain. *Educational Researcher, 33*(8), 3–15. doi:10.3102/0013189X033008003

Borko, H., & Putnam, R. T. (1995). Expanding a teacher's knowledge base: A cognitive psychological perspective on professional development. In T. R. Guskey & M. Huberman (Eds.), *Professional development in education: New paradigms and practices* (pp. 35-65). New York: Teachers College Press.

Boss, S., & Krauss, J. (2007). *Reinventing project-based learning: Your field guide to real-world projects in the digital age.* Eugene, OR: International Society for Technology in Education.

Bowskill, N., Foster, J., Lally, V., & McConnell, D. (2000). *Networked professional development: issues and strategies in currrent practice.* Retrieved April 7, 2003, 2003, from http://www.tandf.co.uk/journals

Boyer, E. L. (1990). *Scholarship reconsidered: priorities of the professoriate*. Princeton, New Jersey: Carnegie Foundation for the Advancement of Teaching.

Boyle, B., Lamprianou, I., & Boyle, T. (2005). A longitudinal study of teacher change: what makes professional development effective? Report of the second year of the study. *School Effectiveness and School Improvement, 16*(1), 1–27. doi:10.1080/09243450500114819

Boyle, B., While, D., & Boyle, T. (2004). A longitudinal study of teacher change: What makes professional development effective? *Curriculum Journal, 15*(1), 45–68. doi:10.1080/1026716032000189471

Brandt, R. (1994). Reflections on 25 years of staff development. *Journal of Staff Development, 15*(4), 2–25.

Bransford, J., Darling-Hammond, L., & LePage, P. (2005). Introduction. In L. Darling Hammond & J. Bransford (Eds.), *Preparing Teachers for a Changing World*. San Francisco: Jossey-Bass.

Bray, J., Lee, J., Smith, L., & Yorks, L. (2000) *Collaborative inquiry in practice*. London, Sage Publications.

Britain, S. (2004). *A Review of Learning design: Concept, Specifications and Tools. A report for the JISC E-learning Pedagogy Programme*. Retrieved February 4, 2009, from http://www.jisc.ac.uk/media/documents/programmes/elearningpedagogy/learningdesigntoolsfinalreport.pdf

Brown, A. (1994). The Advancement of Learning. *Educational Researcher, 23*(8), 4–12.

Brown, A., & Campione, J. (1994). Guided discovery in a community of learners. In K. McGilly (Ed.), *Classroom lessons: integrating cognitive theory and classroom practice* (pp. 229-270). Cambridge, MA: Bradford Books.

Brown, A., & Green, T. (2003). Showing Up to Class in Pajamas (or Less!) The Fantasies and Realities of On-Line Professional Development. *Clearing House (Menasha, Wis.), 76*(3), 148–152.

Brown, J. S., Collins, A., & Duguid, P. (1989). Situated cognition and the culture of learning. *Educational Researcher, 18*(1), 32–42.

Bruckman, A. (2004). Co-Evolution of Technological Design and Pedagogy in an Online Learning Community. In S. A. Barab, R. Kling, & J. H. Gray (Eds.), *Designing for Virtual Communities in the Service of Learning* (pp. 239-255). Cambridge, UK: Cambridge University Press.

Byrne, P., & Long, B. E. L. (1976). *Doctors talking to Patients*. London: HMSO.

Calderhead, J. (1989). Reflective teaching and teacher education. *Teaching and Teacher Education, 5*(1), 43–51. doi:10.1016/0742-051X(89)90018-8

Calderhead, J., & Robson, M. (1991). Images of teaching: Student teachers' early conceptions of classroom practice. *Teaching and Teacher Education, 7*(1), 1–8. doi:10.1016/0742-051X(91)90053-R

Calibrate – Learning resources for schools. (2005). Retrieved September 15, 2008, from http://calibrate.eun.org/ww/en/pub/calibrate_project/home_page.htm

Calman, K. C. (2007). *Medical education: past, present and future*. Edinburgh: Elsevier.

Caperton, I. (2009). *The Case for Globaloria Network in West Virginia: Empowering West Virginia youth to create and collaborate online with a 21st century game-making curriculum*. New York: World Wide Workshop.

Carr, N., & Chambers, D. (2006). Teacher professional learning in an online community: the experiences of the National Quality Schooling Framework Pilot Project. *Technology, Pedagogy and Education, 15*(2), 143–157. doi:10.1080/14759390600769094

Carr, W., & Kemmis, S. (1986). *Becoming Critical: Education, Knowledge and Action Research*. Basingstoke: Falmer Press.

Carter, H. L., Foulger, T. S., & Ewbank, A. D. (2008). Have you googled your teacher lately? Teachers' use of social networking sites. *Phi Delta Kappan, 89*(9), 681–685.

Carusi, A. (2006). Power and Agency in Online Text-based Collaborations . *E–Learning, 3*(1), 4–15. doi:10.2304/elea.2006.3.1.4

Cassidy, C., Chrisite, D., Coutts, D., Dunn, J., Sinclair, C., Skinner, D., & Wilson, A. (2008). Building communities of educational inquiry. *Oxford Review of Education, 34*(2), 217–235. doi:10.1080/03054980701614945

Cassidy, C., Christie, D., Coutts, N., Dunn, J., Sinclair, C., Skinner, D., & Wilson, A. (2008). Building communities of educational enquiry. *Oxford Review of Education, 34*(2), 217–235. doi:10.1080/03054980701614945

CEC. (2006). *Delivering on the modernisation agenda for universities: Education, research and innovation.* Brussels: Commission of the European Communities.

Chalmers, L., & Keown, P. (2006). Communities of practice and professional development. *International Journal of Lifelong Learning, 25*(2).

Charlton, B. G., & Walston, F. (1998). Individual case studies in clinical research. *Journal of Evaluation in Clinical Practice, 4*(2), 147–155. doi:10.1046/j.1365-2753.1998.00011.x

Chen, T.-L., & Chen, T.-J. (2002). *A strategic analysis of the online learning community for continuing professional development of university faculty in Taiwan: A SWOT analysis.* Paper presented at the International Conference on Computers in Education (ICCE'02).

Christensen, C. M., & Horn, M. B. (Summer, 2008). How do we transform our schools? *Education Next, 8*(3). Retrieved September 29, 2008, from http://www.hoover.org/publications/ednext/18575969.html

Christie, D., Cassidy, C., Skinner, D., Coutts, N., Sinclair, C., Rimpilainen, S., & Wilson, A. (2007). Building collaborative communities of enquiry in educational research. *Educational Research and Evaluation, 13*(3), 263–278. doi:10.1080/13803610701632091

Clardy, A. (2005). *Andragogy: Adult learning and education at its best?* Towson, Maryland.

Clarke, D., & Hollingsworth, H. (1994). *Reconceptualising teacher change.* Paper presented at the 17th Annual Conference of the Mathematical Education Research Group of Australasia, Southern Cross University, Lismore, Australia.

Cobos, R., & Pifarre, M. (2008). Collaborative knowledge construction in the web supported by the Know-Cat system. *Computers & Education, 50*(3), 962–978. doi:10.1016/j.compedu.2006.09.009

Cochran-Smith, M., & Lytle, S. (1999). The teacher research movement: a decade later. *Educational Researcher, 28*(7), 15–25.

Cochran-Smith, M., & Zeichner, K. M. (Eds.). (2005). *Studying teacher education: the report of the AERA panel on research and teacher education.* Mahwah, NJ: Lawrence Erlbaum.

Coffield, F. (2000). *The Necessity of Informal Learning.* Bristol: The Policy Press.

Cohen, E. (1994). Restructuring the classroom: Conditions for productive small groups. *Review of Educational Research, 64*(1), 1–35.

Cole, M., & Engeström, Y. (1993). A cultural–historical approach to distributed cognition. In G. Salomon (Ed.), *Distributed cognitions: Psychological and educational considerations* (pp. 1–46). New York: Cambridge University Press.

Coleman, I., Dewhurst, D., Meehan, A. S., & Williams, A. D. (1994). A computer simulation for learning about the physiological response to exercise. *The American Journal of Physiology, 11*, s2–s9.

Comber, C., Watling, R., Lawson, T., Cavendish, S., McEune, R., & Paterson, F. (2002). *Impact2: Learning at home and school: Case studies.* Coventry, UK: Becta.

Cook, J. (2001). *JTAP 623 - The Role of Virtual Learning Environments in UK Medical Education* (No. JTAP 623). UK: Institute for Learning and Research Technologyo. Document Number)

Cordingley, P., Bell, M., Evans, D., & Firth, A. (2005). The impact of collaborative continuing professional development (CPD) on classroom teaching and learning. Review: How do collaborative and sustained CPD and sustained but not collaborative CPD affect teaching and learning? In *Research Evidence in Education Library.* London: EPPI-Centre, Social Science Research Unit, Institute of Education, University of London.

Cordingley, P., Bell, M., Isham, C., Evans, D., & Firth, A. (2007). What do specialists do in CPD programmes for which there is evidence of positive outcomes for pupils and teachers? In *Research Evidence in Education Library*. London, EPPI-Centre, Social.

Cornu, B. (2004). Networking and collecting intelligence for teachers and learners. In A. Brown & N. Davis (Eds.), *Digital Technology, communities and education* (pp. 40-45). London: Routledge Falmer.

Council for Higher Education Accreditation. (1998, April). *Assuring quality in distance learning*. Washington, DC: Institute for Higher Education Policy. Retrieved October 16, 2008, from: http://www.chea.org

Couros, A. (2006). *Examining the open movement: possibilities and implications for education*. Unpublished doctoral dissertation, University of Regina, Saskatchewan.

Cox, M., Webb, M., Abbott, C., Blakeley, B., Beauchamp, T., & Rhodes, V. (2003). *ICT and pedagogy. A review of the research literature*. London: Becta for the Department for Education and Skills.

Cradler, J., Freeman, M., Cradler, R., & McNabb, M. (2002). Research Implications for Preparing Teachers to Use Technology. *Learning & Leading with Technology, 30*(1), 50–54.

Crystal, J. (2001). Building from within: Two professional development models that work. *Technology & Learning, 22*(2), 62–66.

Cumming, A. D., & Ross, M. T. (2008). *The Tuning Project (medicine) – learning outcomes/competences for undergraduate medical education in Europe*. Edinburgh: The University of Edinburgh. Available online: www.tuning-medicine.com. Document Number)

Curriculum Council of Western Australia. (1998). The curriculum framework for kindergarten to year 12 education in Western Australia [Curriculum Document]. (pp. 1-325). Perth WA: The Curriculum Council.

Cuthell, J. P. (2006). Ms. Chips and her Battle Against the Cyborgs. Embedding ICT in Educational Practice.

In D. O Murchu & Sorensen, E. (Eds.), *Enhancing Learning Through Technology*. (pp. 253–268) Hershey, Idea Group

Cuthell, J. P. (2006). Online forums as learning resources: some case studies from MirandaNet. *Proceedings of IADIS International Conference: Web Based Communities, 2006*, 371–375.

Cuthell, J. P. (2006). Steering the Supertanker: Changing Teaching and Learning. In Maddux, C. (Ed.) *Computers in the Schools: Technology Applications in Education (2006) 23 1/2* Binghamton, N.Y. The Howarth Press.

Cuthell, J. P. (2008). Online forums as a resource for teacher professional development: lessons from a web-based community of practice and influence. *International Journal of Web Based Communities, 4*(3), 359–365. doi:10.1504/IJWBC.2008.019195

Cuthell, J. P., & Preston, C. (2007). *Perspectives on ICT CPD: Past, Present and Future. The experiential learning of advisers responsible for school teachers' ICT CPD programmes*. Retrieved June 6 2008 from Institute of Education, London WLE Centre Web site: http://www.wlecentre.ac.uk/cms/files/occasionalpapers/wle_op3.pdf

Danielson, L. (2002). Mentoring in the Professions. *Clearing House (Menasha, Wis.), 75*(4), 183.

Darling-Hammond, L. (1993). Reframing the school reform agenda. *Phi Delta Kappan, 74*(10), 752–761.

Darling-Hammond, L. (1994). *Professional Development Schools: schools for developing a profession*. New York: Teachers' College Press.

Darling-Hammond, L. (1998). Teacher learning that supports student learning. *Educational Leadership, 55*(5), 6–11.

Darling-Hammond, L., & Bransford, J. (2005). Introduction. In L. Darling Hammond & J. D. Bransford (Eds.), *Preparing Teachers for a Changing World* (pp. 1-39). San Francisco: Jossey-Bass.

Darling-Hammond, L., & Bransford, J. (Eds.). (2005). *Preparing teachers for a changing world. What teach-*

ers should learn and be able to do. San Francisco: Jossey-Bass.

Darling-Hammond, L., & McLaughlin, M. (1995). Policies that support professional development in an era of change. *Phi Delta Kappan, 76*(8), 597–604.

Darling-Hammond, L., & Snyder, J. (2000). Authentic assessment of teaching| in context. *Teaching and Teacher Education, 16*(5-6), 523–545. doi:10.1016/S0742-051X(00)00015-9

Darling-Hammond, L., & Sykes, G. (2003). Wanted: A national teacher supply policy for education: The right way to meet the "Highly Qualified Teacher" challenge. *Education Policy Analysis Archives, 11*(33). Retrieved October 16, 2008, from http://epaa.asu.edu/epaa/v11n33/

Darling-Hammond, L., Chung, R., & Frelow, F. (2002). Variation in teacher preparation. How well do different pathways prepare teachers to teach? *Journal of Teacher Education, 53*(4), 286–302. doi:10.1177/0022487102053004002

Dawson, V. (2008). Use of Information Communication Technology by Early Career Science Teachers in Western Australia, *International Journal of Science Education, 30*(2), 203-219. http://www.informaworld.com/smpp/title~content=t713737283~db=all~tab=issueslist~branches=30 - v30.

Day, C. & Sachs, J. (2005). Professionalism, performativity and empowerment: discourses in the politics and purposes of continuing professional development. In C. Day & J. Sachs (Eds) *International handbook on the continuing professional development of teachers.* Maidenhead, UK: Open University Press.

Day, C. (1999). *Developing Teachers: The Challenges of Lifelong Learning.* London: Routledge.

Day, C., & Gu, Q. (2007). Variations in the conditions for teachers' professional learning and Development: sustaining commitment and effectiveness over a career. *Oxford Review of Education, 33*(4), 423–443. doi:10.1080/03054980701450746

Day, C., & Sachs, J. (2004). Professionalism, performativity and empowerment: discourses in the politics, policies and purposes of continuing professional development. In C. Day & J. Sachs (Ed.), *International Handbook on the Continuing Professional Development of Teachers* (pp. 3-32). Berkshire: Open University Press, McGraw-Hill Education.

Day, C., Flores, M. A., & Viana, I. (2007). Effects of national policies on teachers' sense of professionalism: findings from an empirical study in Portugal and in England. *European Journal of Teacher Education, 30*(3), 249–265. doi:10.1080/02619760701486092

Day, C., Stobart, G., Sammons, P., & Kington, A. (2006). Variations in the work and lives of teachers: relative and relational effectiveness. *Teachers and Teaching: theory and practice, 12*(2), 169–192.

De Laat, M., & Lally, V. (2004). It's not so easy: Researching the complexity of emergent participant roles and awareness in asynchronous networked learning discussions. *Journal of Computer Assisted Learning, 20*(3), 165–171. doi:10.1111/j.1365-2729.2004.00085.x

Dede, C. (2000). Emerging Influences of Information Technology on School Curriculum. *Journal of Curriculum Studies, 32*(2), 281–303. doi:10.1080/002202700182763

Dede, C. (2000). A New Century Demands New Ways of Learning. In D. T. Gordon (Ed.), *The Digital Classroom* (pp. 171-178). Cambridge, MA: Harvard Education News Letter.

Dede, C. (2006). *Online Professional Development for Teachers.* Cambridge, MA: Harvard Education Press.

Dede, C. (Ed.). (2006). *Online professional development for teachers: Emerging models and methods.* Cambridge, MA: Harvard Education Press.

Dede, C., Breit, L., Ketelhut, D. J., McCloskey, E., & Whitehouse, P. (2005). *An overview of current findings from empirical research on online teacher professional development.* Cambridge, MA: Harvard Graduate School of Education.

Dede, C., Ketelhut, D., & Whitehouse, J. P., Breit, L., & McCloskey, E. (2006). *Research agenda for online teacher professional development.* Cambridge, MA: Harvard Graduate School of Education.

den Brok, P., Brekelmans, M., & Wubbles, T. (2004). Interpersonal teacher behaviour and students outcomes. *School Effectiveness and School Improvement, 15,* 407–422. doi:10.1080/09243450512331383262

Department for Children. Schools and Families (2008). *Harnessing Technology: Next Generation Learning 2008-14.* Coventry: Becta.

Department of Education Science and Training [DEST]. (2004). *Australian Government Quality Teacher Programme Updated Client Guidelines, 2004 - 05.* Canberra.

Department of Education Science and Training [DEST]. (2005). *An Evaluation of the Australian Government Quality Teacher Programme 1999 to 2004.* Canberra: Atelier Learning Solutions Pty Ltd.

Department of Education. Science and Technology (DEST) (2004). *PD 2000 Australia - National mapping of school teacher professional development.* Retrieved September 5, 2004, from http://www.qualityteaching. dest.gov.au/Content/SubSection_PD2000.htm

Devereux, C. (2009). *Beyond the curriculum: The positive effects of Continual Professional Development for a group of post-16 science teachers.* Occasional Paper, London: WLE Centre, Institute of Education.

Dewey, J. (1910). *How we think.* Boston: DC Heath & Co.

Dewey, J. (1938). *Experience and education.* New York: Collier Books.

Dewey, J. (1938/1986). *Logic: The theory of inquiry. John Dewey: The later works 1925-1953, 12,* 1-506 J. A. Boydston. Carbondale, Southern Illinois University Press.

Dewhurst, D., & Chimalizeni, Y. (2008). *Collaborative development of online virtual patients for medical and healthcare professional education in Malawi.* Paper presented at the eLearning Africa.

Dewhurst, D., Hardastle, J., Hardcastle, P. T., & Stuart, E. (1994). Comparison of a computer simulation program with a traditional laboratory practical class for teaching the principles of intestinal absorption. *The American Journal of Physiology, 12*(1), s95–s103.

Dewhurst, D., Macleod, H., & Norris, T. (2000). Independent Student Learning Aided by Computers: An Acceptable Alternative to Lectures? *Computers & Education, 35,* 223–241. doi:10.1016/S0360-1315(00)00033-6

DfES. (2005). *Five Year Strategy for Children and Learners.* Retrieved February 4, 2009, from http://www.dfes. gov.uk/publications/5yearstrategy/

Dillenbourg, P. (1999). Introduction: What do you mean by collaborative learning? In P. Dillenbourg (Ed.), *Collaborative learning: Cognitive and computational approaches* (pp. 1-19). Oxford: Pergamon.

Dillenbourg, P. (2002). Over-scripting CSCL: The risks of blending collaborative learning with instructional design. In P. A. Kirschner (Ed.), *Three worlds of CSCL. Can we support CSCL* (pp. 61-91). Heerlen, Open Universiteit Nederland.

Dillenbourg, P., & Jermann, P. (2006). Designing integrative scripts. In F. Fischer, H. Mandl, J. Haake, & I. Kollar (Eds.), *Scripting computer-supported collaborative learning: Cognitive, computational and educational perspectives.* New York: Springer.

Dillenbourg, P., & Tchounikine, P. (2007). Flexibility in macro-scripts for computer-supported collaborative learning. *Journal of Computer Assisted Learning, 23*(1), 1–13. doi:10.1111/j.1365-2729.2007.00191.x

Dochy, F., Segers, M., & Sluijsmans, D. (1999). The use of self, and peer, and co-assessment in higher education: A review. *Studies in Higher Education, 24*(3), 331–350. doi:10.1080/03075079912331379935

Dockstader, J. (1999). Teachers of the 21st Century Know the What, Why and How of Technology Integration. [Technological Horizons In Education]. *T.H.E. Journal, 26.*

DOH. (2007). *Trust, assurance and safety - the regulation of health professionals for the 21st Century.* London: Department of Health, HMSOo. Document Number)

Dolence, M. G., & Norris, D. M. (1995). *Transforming higher education: A vision for learning in the 21ˢᵗ Century.* Society for College and University Planning (SCUP): Ann Arbor, MI, USA.

Dreyfus, H. L., & Dreyfus, S. E. (1986). *Mind over machine: the power of human intuition and expertise in the era of the computer.* New York: The Free Press.

DuFour, R. (2004). What is a "professional learning community?" . *Educational Leadership, 61*(8), 6–11.

DuFour, R. (2004). What is a "Professional Learning Community"? *Educational Leadership, 1*(8), 6–11.

DuFour, R., & Eaker, R. (1998). *Professional learning communities at work: Best practices for enhancing student achievement.* Alexandria, VA: National Educational Service.

DuFour, R., & Eaker, R. (2004). *Professional Learning Communities at work: Best practices for enhancing student achievement.* Bloomington, IN: National Educational Service.

DuFour, R., & Eaker, R. (2004). *Professional Learning Communities at work: Best practices for enhancing student achievement.* Bloomington, IN: National Educational Service.

DuFour, R., Eaker, R., & DuFour, R. (Eds.). (2005). *On common ground: The power of professional learning communities.* Bloomington, IN: Solution Tree.

Duncan-Howell, J. (2007). *Online Communities of Practice and their role in the professional development of teachers.* Unpublished doctoral thesis, Queensland University of Technology, Brisbane, Australia.

Dutton, W., Cheong, P. H., & Park, A. (2004). An Ecology of Constraints on e-Learning in Higher Education: The Case of a Virtual Learning Environment. *Prometheus, 22*(2), 131–149. doi:10.1080/0810902042000218337

Dwyer, D. C., Ringstaff, C., & Sandholtz, J. H. (1990). *Teacher beliefs and practices (Part 1): Patterns of change. The evolution of teachers' instructional beliefs and practices in high-access-to technology classrooms* (ACOT Report #8). Cupertino, CA: Apple Computer.

Dysthe, O. (Ed.). (2001). *Dialog, interaction and learning.* Oslo: Abstrakt forlag

Eaker, R., DuFour, R., & DuFour, R. (2002). *Getting started: Reculturing schools to become professional learning communities.* Bloomington, IN: National Educational Service.

Edens, K. M. (2000). Preparing Problem Solvers for the 21st Century through Problem-based Learning. *College Teaching, 48*(2), 55–60.

Education Department of Western Australia (2000b). *Technology 2000 Expanding Learning Horizons: Draft Strategic Plan Overview 1999-2001*: Education Department of Western Australia. Retrieved 29th Dec. 2000

Education Department of Western Australia. (2000a). *Learning Technologies Project: 1999 School Computer and Connectivity Census Report.* Perth, AU: Education Department of Western Australia.

Education, U. S. D. o. (2002). *Introduction: No Child Left Behind.* Retrieved March 17, 2003, 2003, from http://www.nclb.gov/next/overview/index.html

Edwards, A. (2005). Relational agency: Learning to be a resourceful practitioner. *International Journal of Educational Research, 43*(3), 168–182. doi:10.1016/j.ijer.2006.06.010

Edwards, A., & Fox, C. (2005). Using activity theory to evaluate a complex response to social exclusion. *Educational and Child Psychology, 22*(1), 50–60.

Elkjaer, B. (2003). Social learning theory: learning as participation in social processes. In M. Easterby-Smith & M.A. Lyles (Ed.), *Handbook of organizational learning and knowledge management* (pp. 38-53). Oxford: Blackwell Publishing.

Ellaway, R. H. (2005). *Evaluating a Virtual Learning Environment in Medical Education.* Unpublished PhD, University of Edinburgh, Edinburgh.

Ellaway, R., Begg, M., Dewhurst, D., & Macleod, H. (2005). In A Glass Darkly: identity, agency and the role of the learning technologist in shaping the learning environment. *E-Learning, 3*(1), 75-87.

Ellaway, R., Dewhurst, D., & Cumming, A. (2003). Managing and supporting medical education with a virtual learning environment: the Edinburgh Electronic Medical Curriculum. *Medical Teacher, 25*(4), 372–380. doi:10.1080/0142159031000136789

Elliot, J. (1991). *Action research for educational change.* Milton: Open University Press.

Ellis, V., & Edwards, A. (2007, August). *Re-configuring pre-service teacher education: Developmental work research as a methodology for teacher educators' expansive learning.* Paper presented at the Conference of EARLI, Budapest, Hungary.

Ellminn, R., & Elminn, B. (2005). Working with portfolio. (In Norwegian). Oslo: Interface Media A/S.

Elstein, A. S., Shulman, L. S., & Sprafka, S. A. (1978). *Medical problem solving: an analysis of clinical reasoning.* Cambridge, MA: Harvard University Press.

Engeström, J. (2005). *Why some social network services work and others don't – Or: the case for object-centred sociality.* Retrieved June 10th, 2007, from: http://www.typepad.com/t/trackback/242863/2243067

Engeström, Y. (1987). *Learning by expanding: An activity-theoretical approach to developmental research.* Helsinki: Orienta-Konsultit Oy.

Engeström, Y. (1999). Activity theory and individual and social transformation. In Y. Engeström, R. Miettinen, & R. L. Punamäki (Eds.), *Perspectives on activity theory* (pp. 19–39). Cambridge: Cambridge University Press.

Engeström, Y. (1999). Innovative learning in work teams: Analyzing cycles of knowledge creation practices. In Y. Engeström, R. Miettinen, & R. L. Punamäki (Eds.), *Perspectives on activity theory* (pp. 377–404). Cambridge: Cambridge University Press.

Engeström, Y. (2001). Expansive learning at work: Towards an activity theoretical reconceptualization. *Education and Work, 14*(1), 133–156. doi:10.1080/13639080123238

Engeström, Y. (2007). Putting Vygotsky to work. The change laboratory as an application of double stimulation. In H. Daniels, M. Cole, & J. V. Wertsch (Eds.), *Cambridge companion to Vygotsky* (pp. 363-383). Cambridge: Cambridge University Press.

Engeström, Y. (2008). *From teams to knot. Activity-theoretical studies of collaboration and learning at work.* Cambridge: Cambridge University Press.

Engeström, Y., Engeström, R., & Kerosuo, H. (2003). The discursive construction of collaborative care. *Applied Linguistics, 24*(3), 286–315. doi:10.1093/applin/24.3.286

Epanchin, B. C., & Colucci, K. (2002). The Professional Development School Without Walls. *Remedial and Special Education, 23*(6), 350–359. doi:10.1177/07419325020230060501

Eraut, M. (2004). Informal learning in the workplace. *Studies in Continuing Education, 26*(2), 247–273. doi:10.1080/158037042000225245

Ericsson, K. A. (2004). Deliberate practice and the acquisition and maintenance of expert performance in medicine and related domains. *Academic Medicine, 79*(10Supplement), S70–S81. doi:10.1097/00001888-200410001-00022

Ericsson, K. A., Krampe, R. T., & Tesch-Romer, C. (1993). The role of deliberate practice in the acquisition of expert performance. *Psychological Review, 100*(3), 363–406. doi:10.1037/0033-295X.100.3.363

EU. (1981). Council Directive 81/1057/EEC of 14 December 1981 concerning the mutual recognition of diplomas, certificates and other evidence of the formal qualifications of doctors, nurses responsible for general care, dental practitioners and veterinary surgeons respectively, with regard to acquired rights.

Evans, L. (2002). What constitutes teacher development? *Oxford Review of Education, 28*(1), 123–137. doi:10.1080/03054980120113670

Farooq, U., Schank, P., Harris, A., Fusco, J., & Schlager, M. (2007). Sustaining a Community Computing Infrastructure for Online Teacher Professional Development: A

Case Study of Designing Tapped In. *Computer Supported Cooperative Work: The Journal of Collaborative Computing, 16*(4-5), 397–429. doi:10.1007/s10606-007-9049-0

Fawcett, G., & Juliana, M. (2002). Teaching in the Digital Age: "Teaching as You Were Taught" Won't Work. In P. Rogers (Ed.), *Designing Instruction for Technology Enhanced Learning* (pp. 71-82). Hershey, PA: Idea Group Publishing.

Fielding, M., Bragg, S., Craig, J., Cunningham, I., Eraut, M., Gillinson, S., et al. (2005). *Factors Influencing the Transfer of Good Practice.* London: Department for Education and Skills.

Fincher, R.-M. E., Simpson, D. E., Mennin, S. P., Rosenfeld, G. C., Rothman, A., & McGrew, M. C. (2000). Scholarship in teaching: an imperative for the 21st Century. *Academic Medicine, 75*(9), 887–894. doi:10.1097/00001888-200009000-00009

Firestone, A. W. (1996). Images of Teaching and Proposals for Reform: A Comparison of Ideas from Cognitive and Organizational research. *Educational Administration Quarterly, 32*(2), 209–235. doi:10.1177/0013161X96032002003

Fischer, F., & Dillenbourg, P. (2006, April). *Challenges of orchestrating computer-supported collaborative learning.* Paper presented at the 87th Annual Meeting of the American Educational Research Association (AERA), San Francisco, US.

Fischer, F., Bruhn, C., Gräsel, C., & Mandl, H. (2002). Fostering collaborative knowledge construction with visualization tools. *Learning and Instruction, 12*(2), 213–232. doi:10.1016/S0959-4752(01)00005-6

Fisher, T., Higgins, C., & Loveless, A. (2006). *Teachers Learning with Digital Technologies: a review of research and projects.* Futurelab series, No 14. Retrieved December 20th 2006, from: http://www.futurelab.org.uk/research/lit_reviews.htm#lr14 20.12.06).

Flores, M. A., & Day, C. (2006). Contexts which shape and reshape new teachers' identities: A multy-perspective study. *Teaching and Teacher Education, 22,* 219–232. doi:10.1016/j.tate.2005.09.002

Foot, K. A. (2002). Pursuing an evolving object: A case study in object formation and identification. *Mind, Culture, and Activity, 9*(2), 132–149. doi:10.1207/S15327884MCA0902_04

Frank, J. R. (2005). *The CanMEDS 2005 physician competency framework. Better standards. Better physicians. Better care.* Ottawa: The Royal College of Physicians and Surgeons of Canadao. Document Number)

Fraser, C., Kennedy, A., Reid, L., & McKinney, S. (2007). Teachers' continuing professional development (CPD): contested concepts, understandings and models . *Journal of In-service Education, 33*(2), 153–169. doi:10.1080/13674580701292913

Fredricks, J. A., Blumenfeld, P. C., & Paris, A. H. (2004). School engagement: potential of the concept, state of the evidence. *Review of Educational Research, 74,* 59–109. doi:10.3102/00346543074001059

Freire, P. (1972). *Pedagogy of the oppressed.* Harmondsworth: Penguin.

Friedman, A., & Philips, M. (2004). CPD programmes of UK professional associations: developing a vision. *Journal of Education and Work, 17*(3). doi:10.1080/1363908042000267432

Fullan, M. (1998). Leadership for the 21st Century breaking the bonds of dependency. *Educational Leadership, 55*(7).

Fullan, M. (2007). *The new meaning of educational change* (3rd ed.). New York, NY: Routledge.

Fullan, M. G., & Hargreaves, A. (1991). Interactive professionalism and guidelines for action. In *Working Together for Your School* (pp. 63-111). Hawthorn, Vic: ACEA.

Fullan, M., Hill, P., & Crévola, C. (2006). *Breakthrough.* New York: Corwin Press.

Fuller, F. F., & Bown, O. H. (1975). Becoming a teacher. In K. Ryan (Ed.), *Teacher Education The 74th Yearbook of the National Society for the Study of Education, Part 11.* Chicago: University of Chicago Press.

Furlong, J., & Oancea, A. (2005). *Assessing Quality in*

Applied and Practice-based Educational Research. A framework for discussion. University of Oxford. Retrieved 13th February, 2009 from http://www.aare.edu.au/05papc/fu05018y.pdf

Gairín, J. (2006). *Procesos de cambio en los centros a partir de evaluaciones externas.* Madrid: CIDE, Ministerio de Educación.

Gairín, J., & Rodríguez, D. (2007, March). *La Creación y Gestión del Conocimiento a través de la red. Notas y comentarios desde la experiencia.* Paper presented at Expolearning/VirtualCampus, Barcelona.

Gal, S. (1993). Teachers and teaching. *Journal of Research in Rural Education, 9*(1), 38–42.

Gall, M. D., Renchler, R. S., Haisley, F. B., Baker, R. G., & Perez, M. (1985). *Effective staff development for teachers: A research-based model:* College of Education, University of Oregon.

Galland, P. (2002). Techie teachers — Web-based staff development at your leisure. *TechTrends, 46*(3), 11–16. doi:10.1007/BF02784836

Garet, M. S., Porter, A. C., Desimone, L., Birman, B. F., & Yoon, K. S. (2001). What makes professional development effective? Results from a national sample of teachers. *American Educational Research Journal, 38*(4), 915–945. doi:10.3102/00028312038004915

Garmston, R. (1991). Staff developers as social architects. *Educational Leadership, 49*(3), 64–65.

Garrison, D. R., Anderson, T., & Archer, W. (2001). Critical thinking, cognitive presence, and computer conferencing in distance education. *American Journal of Distance Education, 15*(1), 7–23.

Gherardi, S. (2006). *Organizational knowledge: The texture of workplace learning.* Malden, MA: Blackwell.

Giddens, A. (1990). *The Consequences of Modernity.* Cambridge: Polity Press.

Gillies, R. M. (2004). The effects of cooperative learning on junior high school students during small group learning. *Learning and Instruction, 14*(2), 197–213. doi:10.1016/S0959-4752(03)00068-9

Ginns, I., Heirdsfield, A., Atweh, B., & Watters, J. (2001). Beginning teachers becoming professionals through action research. *Educational Action Research, 9*(1), 111–133. doi:10.1080/09650790100200140

Gitlin, A., Barlow, L., Burbank, M. D., Kauchak, D., & Stevens, T. (1999). Pre-service teachers thinking on research: implications for inquiry oriented teacher education. *Teaching and Teacher Education, 15*(7), 753–769. doi:10.1016/S0742-051X(99)00015-3

Gladwell, M. (2005). *Blink: the power of thinking without thinking.* New York: Little Brown & Co.

Glaser, B., & Strauss, A. (1967). *The Discovery of Grounded Theory: Strategies for Qualitative Research.* Chicago; Aldine.

Glassic, C. E. (2000). Boyer's expanded definition of scholarship, the standards for assessing scholarship, and the elusiveness of the scholarship of teaching. *Academic Medicine, 75*(9), 877–880.

GMC. (1999). *The doctor as teacher.* London: General Medical Council.

GMC. (2003). *Tomorrow's doctors: recommendations on undergraduate medical education.* London: General Medical Council.

GMC. (2004). *Continuing professional development.* London: General Medical Council.

GMC. (2006). *Good medical practice.* London: General Medical Council.

GMC. (2006). *Strategic proposals for student fitness to practice: call for informal feedback.* London: General Medical Councilo. Document Number)

GMC. (2007). *The new doctor.* London: General Medical Council.

Goh, S., & Fraser, B. (1998). Teacher interpersonal behaviour, classroom environment and student outcomes in primary mathematics in Singapore. *Learning Environments Research, 1,* 199–229. doi:10.1023/A:1009910017400

Goldenberg, C., & Gallimore, R. (1991). Changing teaching takes more than a one-shot workshop. *Educational Leadership, 49*(3), 69–72.

Goodlad, J. (1994, April). The national network for educational renewal. *Phi Delta Kappan*, 632–638.

Graham, A. (2007). Web 2.0 and the changing ways we are using computers for learning: What are the implications for pedagogy and curriculum? *Elearningeuropa. info*. Retrieved May 9, 2008, from http://www.elearningeuropa.info/files/media/media13018.pdf

Green, H., & Hannon, C. (2007). *Their Space. Education for a digital generation*. London: Demos (available at www.demos.co.uk).

Greenhalgh, T. (2006). *How to read a paper: the basics of evidence-based medicine*. Oxford: Blackwell Publishing Ltd.

Greenhalgh, T., & Hurwitz, B. (1998). *Narrative based medicine*. London: BMJ Books.

GTC Scotland (2008). Continuing Professional Development. Retrieved 13th February, 2009 from http://www.gtcs.org.uk/ProfessionalDevelopment/ProfessionalDevelopment.asp

Guskey, T. R. (1985). Staff development and teacher change. *Educational Leadership*, *42*(7), 56–60.

Guskey, T. R. (1986). Staff development and the process of teacher change. *Educational Researcher*, *15*(5), 5–20.

Guskey, T. R. (1994). Results-oriented professional development: In search of an optimal mix of effective practices. *Journal of Staff Development*, *15*(4), 42–50.

Guskey, T. R. (2000). *Evaluating professional development*. Thousand Oaks, CA: Corwin Press.

Guskey, T. R. (2002). Professional development and teacher change. *Teachers and Teaching*, *8*(3), 381–391. doi:10.1080/135406002100000512

Guskey, T. R. (2005). Taking a second look at accountability. *Journal of Staff Development*, *26*(1), 10–18.

Guskey, T. R., & Sparks, D. (1991). What to consider when evaluating staff development. *Educational Leadership*, *49*(3), 73–74.

Guskey, T. R., & Sparks, D. (2002). Linking professional development to improvements in student learning. In *American Educational Research Association*. New Orleans, LA.

Gutierrez, K., Basquedano-Lopez, P., Alvarez, H. H., & Chio, M. M. (1999). Building a culture of collaboration through hybrid language practices. *Theory into Practice*, *32*(2), 87–93.

Haberman, M. (1991). The pedagogy of poverty versus good teaching. *Phi Delta Kappan*, *73*(4), 290–294.

Hakarainnen, K., Palonen, T., Paavola, S., & Lehtinen, E. (2004). *Communities of networked expertise. Professional and educational perspectives*. Amsterdam: Elsevier.

Hakkarainen, K., Palonen, T., Paavola, S., & Lehtinen, E. (2004) *Communities of networked expertise. Professional and educational perspectives*. Oxford, European Association for Research on Learning and Instruction; Elsevier.

Hall, G., & Hord, S. (1987) *Change in schools: Facilitating the process*. New York: State University of New York Press.

Hämäläinen, R. (2008). Designing and evaluating collaboration in a virtual game environment for vocational learning. *Computers & Education*, *50*(1), 98–109. doi:10.1016/j.compedu.2006.04.001

Hämäläinen, R., & Arvaja, M. (in press). Scripted collaboration and group-based variations in a higher education CSCL context. *Scandinavian Journal of Educational Research*.

Hämäläinen, R., & Häkkinen, P. (2009). *Group variations in scripted collaboration: The case of Grid-Script*. (Submitted).

Hämäläinen, R., Oksanen, K., & Häkkinen, P. (2008). Designing and analyzing collaboration in a scripted game for vocational education. *Computers in Human Behavior*, *24*(6), 2496–2506. doi:10.1016/j.chb.2008.03.010

Hammersley, M., & Atkinson, P. (1983). Ethnography: Principles in practice (second ed.). London: Routledge.

Handal, G., & Lauvås, P. (1987). *Promoting reflective teaching: supervision in practice.* Milton Keynes, UK: SRHE/Open University Enterprises.

Hanushek, E. A., Kain, J. F., O'Brien, D. M., & Rivkin, S. G. (2005, February). *The market for teacher quality.* National Bureau of Economic Research Working Paper 11154.

Hardy, I., & Lingard, B. (2008). Teacher professional development as an effect of policy and practice: a Bourdieuian analysis. *Journal of Education Policy, 23*(1), 63–80. doi:10.1080/02680930701754096

Hargreaves, A. (1992). Cultures of teaching: A focus for change. In A. Hargreaves & F. Michael (Eds.), *Understanding teacher development* (pp. 216 - 241). New York: Teachers College Press, Columbia University.

Hargreaves, A. (1994). *Changing teachers, changing times: Teachers' work and culture in the postmodern age.* Great Britain: Redwood Books.

Hargreaves, A. (2000). Four ages of Professionalism and Professional Learning. *Teachers and Teaching: History and Practice, 6*(2), 151–182.

Hargreaves, A. (2000). Four ages of professionalism and professional learning. *Teachers and Teaching, 6*(2), 151–182. doi:10.1080/713698714

Hargreaves, A., & Fullan, M. G. (1992). Introduction. In A. Hargreaves & F. Michael (Eds.), *Understanding teacher development* (pp. 1-8). New York: Teachers College Press, Columbia University.

Hargreaves, D. (1994). The new professionalism: The synthesis of professional and institutional development. *Teaching and Teacher Education, 10*(4), 423–438. doi:10.1016/0742-051X(94)90023-X

Harris, J. (2003). Professor, College of William and Mary. In P. Whitehouse (Ed.) (pp. phone conversation). Fall River MA.

Hartnell-Young, E. (2006). Teachers' roles and professional learning in communities of practice supported by technology in schools. *Journal of Technology and Teacher Education, 14*(3), 461–480.

Havelock, B. (2004). Online community and professional learning in education: Research-based keys to sustainability. *Association for the Advancement of Computing in Education, 12*(1), 56–84.

Hawkes, M. (1999). Exploring network-based communication in teacher professional development. *Educational Technology, 39*(4), 45–52.

Haythornthwaite, C. (2002). Building social networks via computer networks: Creating and sustaining distributed learning communities. In K. A. Renninger & W. Shumar (Eds.), *Building virtual communities: Learning and change in cyberspace* (pp. 159-190). Cambridge: Cambridge University Press.

Helleve, I. (2007). In an ICT-based teacher- education context: Why was our group "The magic group"? *European Journal of Teacher Education, 30*(3), 267–284. doi:10.1080/02619760701486118

Henderson, D., & Fisher, D. (2008). Interpersonal behaviour and student outcomes in vocational education classes. *Learning Environments Research, 11*, 19–29. doi:10.1007/s10984-007-9034-z

Herring, S., Martinson, A., & Scheckler, R. (2002). Designing for community: The effects of gender representation in videos on a web site. *Proceedings of the Thirty-Fifth Hawaii International Conference on System Sciences.* Los Alamitos: IEEE Computer Society Press.

Herrington, A., Herrington, J., Oliver, R., & Omari, A. (2000). A web-based resource providing reflective online support for preservice mathematics teachers on school practice [Electronic Version]. *Contemporary Issues in Technology and Teacher Education, 1*(2), 17-140. Retrieved September 29, 2008, from http://www.citejournal.org/vol1/iss2/currentissues/general/article1.htm

Hirsh, S. (2004). Putting comprehensive staff development on target. *Journal of Staff Development, 25*(1), 12–15.

Hislop, D. (2005). *Knowledge Management in Organizations. A critical introduction.* Oxford: Oxford University Press.

Hmelo-Silver, C. E. (2003). Analyzing collaborative knowledge construction: multiple methods for integrated understanding. *Computers & Education, 41*(4), 397–420. doi:10.1016/j.compedu.2003.07.001

Hodkinson, P., & James, D. (2003). Transforming Learning Cultures in Further Education. *Journal of Vocational Education and Training, 55*(4), 389–406. doi:10.1080/13636820300200236

Hoffman-Kipp, P., Artiles, A., & Lopez-Torres, L. (2003). Beyond reflection: Teacher learning as praxis. *Theory into Practice, 42*(3), 248–254.

Holmes, B., Gardner, J., & Galanouli, D. (2007). Striking the right chord and sustaining successful professional development in information and communication technologies. *Journal of In-service Education, 33*(4), 389–404. doi:10.1080/13674580701687799

Holmes, B., Tangney, B., FitzGibbon, A., Savage, T., & Meehan, S. (2001). Communal Constructivism: Students constructing learning for as well as with others. [Norfolk, VA: Association for the Advancement of Computing in Education]. *Proceedings of SITE, 2001*, 3114–3119.

Hopcroft, K., & Forte, V. (2003). *Symptom sorter* (2nd ed.). Abingdon: Radcliffe Medical Press Ltd.

Hord, S. M. (1997). Professional learning communities: What are they and why are they important? *Issues About Change, 6*(1). Retrieved September 29, 2008, from http://www.sedl.org

Howe, C., & Tolmie, A. (1999). Productive interaction in the context of computer-supported collaborative learning in science. In K. Littleton & P. Light (Eds.), *Learning with computers* (pp. 24-45). London: Routledge.

Hoyle, E. (1974). Professionality, professionalism, and control in teaching. *London Educational Review, 3*, 13–19.

Hubbard, L., Mehan, H., & Stein, M. K. (2006). *Reform as learning. School reform. Organizational culture, and community practrices in San Diego.* New York: Routledge.

Huberman, M. (2001). Networks that alter teaching: Conceptualisations, exchanges and experiments. In J. Soler, A. Craft & H. Burgess (Eds.), *Teacher development: Exploring our own practice.* (pp. 141-159). London: Paul Chapman.

Hudson, J., & Lowe, S. (2004). *Understanding the Policy Process: analysing welfare policy and practice.* Bristol: The Policy Press.

Hughes, I. E. (2001). Do computer simulations of laboratory practicals meet learning needs? *Trends in Pharmacological Sciences, 22*, 71–74. doi:10.1016/S0165-6147(00)01605-9

Hunter, B. (2002). Learning in the virtual community depends upon changes in local communities. In K. A. Renninger & W. Shumar (Eds.), *Building virtual communities* (pp. 96-126). Cambridge: Cambridge University Press.

Iedema, R., & Scheeres, H. (2003). From doing work to talking work: Renegotiating knowing, doing and identity. *Applied Linguistics, 24*(3), 316–337. doi:10.1093/applin/24.3.316

International Society for Technology in Education. (2009). National Education Technology Standards (NET-T) and Performance Indicators for Teachers [Electronic Version]. Retrieved Jan. 20, 2009 from http://www.iste.org/Content/NavigationMenu/NETS/ForTeachers/2008Standards/NETS_T_Standards_Final.pdf.

Jacob, M. (2003). Rethinking Science and Commodifying Knowledge. *Policy Futures in Education, 1*(1), 125–142. doi:10.2304/pfie.2003.1.1.3

Jenkins, H. (2006). *Fans, bloggers, and gamers: Exploring participatory culture.* New York, NY: New York University Press.

Jermann, P., & Dillenbourg, P. (2003). Elaborating new arguments through a CSCL script. In J. Andriessen, M. Baker, & D. Suthers (Eds.), *Arguing to learn: Confronting cognitions in computer-supported collaborative learning environments* (pp. 205–226). Dordrecht, The Netherlands: Kluwer.

JISC. (2004). *Effective Practice with e-Learning.* Higher Education Funding Council for England.

JISC. (2006). *Background to the JISC Circular 1/06: Design for Learning Programme* (briefing document). Bristol: JISC. Retrieved January 20, 2009, from http://www.jisc.ac.uk/fundingopportunities/funding_calls/2006/02/funding_01_06.aspx

JISC. (2007). *Effective Practice with e-Assessment.* Higher Education Funding Council for England.

Joint Committee on Standards for Educational Evaluation. (1994). *The program evaluation standards.* Thousand Oaks, CA: Sage.

Jonassen, D. H., Peck, K. L., & Wilson, B. G. (1999). *Learning with Technology A Constructivist Perspective.* Upper Saddle River, NJ: Merrill, an imprint of Prentice Hall.

Joyce, B., & Showers, B. (1980). Improving inservice training: The messages of research. *Educational Leadership, 37*(5), 379–385.

Joyce, B., & Showers, B. (1980). Improving inservice training: The messages of research. *Educational Leadership, 37*(5), 379–385.

Joyce, B., & Showers, B. (1982). The coaching of teaching. *Educational Leadership, 40*(1), 416.

Joyce, B., & Showers, B. (1995). *Student achievement through staff development.* New York: Longman.

Joyce, B., & Weil, M. (1986). *Models of teaching* (3rd ed.). New York: Prentice Hall.

Joyce, B., Weil, M., & Calhoun, E. (2004). *Models of teaching* (7th ed.). New York: Allyn & Bacon.

Joyce, B., Weil, M., & Showers, B. (1992). *Models of teaching* (4th ed.). New York: Allyn & Bacon.

Kankaanranta, M., & Puhakka, E. (2008). *Kohti innovatiivista tietotekniikan opetuskäyttöä. Kansainvälisen SITES 2006 tutkimuksen tuloksia.* Jyväskylä: Jyväskylän yliopistopaino.

Kelly, P. (2006). What is teacher learning? A sociocultural perspective. *Oxford Review of Education, 32*(4), 505–519. doi:10.1080/03054980600884227

Kennedy, A., Christie, D., Fraser, C., Reid, L., McKinney, S., Welsh, M., Wilson, A., & Griffiths, M. (2008). Key informants' perspectives on teacher learning in Scotland. *British Journal of Educational Studies, 56(4), 400-419.*

Kennewell, S., & Morgan, A. (2003). *Student teachers' experiences and attitudes towards using interactive whiteboards in the teaching and learning of young children.* Paper presented at the ACM International Conference Proceeding Series, Sydney, Australia.

Killeen, K., Monk, D., & Plecki, M. (2002). School district spending on professional development: Insights available from national data. *Journal of Education Finance, 28*(1), 25–49.

King, A. (1999). Discourse patterns for mediating peer learning. In A. O'Donnell & A. King (Eds.), *Cognitive perspectives on peer learning* (pp. 87-115). Mahwah, NJ: Lawrence Erlbaum Associates.

King, K. (2002). *A journey of transformation: A model of educators' learning experiences in educational technology.* Paper presented at the Adult Education Research Conference, Raleigh NC, May. ED 472069.

Kleiman, G. L. (2004, July). *Meeting the need for high quality teachers: E-Learning solutions.* White paper written for the U.S. Department of Education Secretary's No Child Left Behind Leadership Summit Whitepaper: Increasing Options through E-Learning. Retrieved March 6, 2006, from http://www.ed.gov/about/offices/list/os/technology/plan/2004/site/documents/Kleiman-MeetingtheNeed.pdf

Kleiman, G., & Treacy, B. (2006). EdTech Leaders Online. In C. Dede (Ed.), *Online professional development for teachers: Emerging models and methods* (pp. 31-47). Cambridge, MA: Harvard Education Press.

Klein, M. F. (2001). Approaches to Curriculum Theory and Practice. In J. T. Sears & J. D. Marshall (Eds.), *Teaching and Thinking about Curriculum* (pp. 3-14). Troy, NY: Educator's International Press, Inc.

Klenowski, V. (2002). *Developing Portfolios for Learning and Assessment*. London: Routledge Falmer.

Kling, R., & Courtright, C. (2003). Group behavior and learning in electronic forums: A socio-technical approach. *The Information Society, 19*(3), 221–236. doi:10.1080/01972240309465

Knight, P., Tait, J., & Yorke, M. (2006). The professional learning of teachers in higher education. *Studies in Higher Education, 31*(3), 319–339. doi:10.1080/03075070600680786

Knowles, M. S., Holton, E. F., III, & Swanson, R. A. (2005). *The adult learner: The definitive classic in adult education and human resource development* (6th ed.). Amsterdam: Elsevier.

Knowles, M. S., Holton, E. F., III, & Swanson, R. A. (2005). *The adult learner: The definitive classic in adult education and human resource development* (6th ed.). Amsterdam: Elsevier.

Kobbe, L., Weinberger, A., Dillenbourg, P., & Harrer, A., Hämäläinen, R., Häkkinen, P., & Fischer, F. (2007). Specifying computer-supported collaboration scripts. *International Journal of Computer-Supported Collaborative Learning, 2*(2-3), 211–224. doi:10.1007/s11412-007-9014-4

Kobbe, L., Weinberger, A., Dillenbourg, P., Harrer, A., Hämäläinen, R., Häkkinen, P., & Fischer, F. (2007). Specifying Computer-Supported Collaboration Scripts. *International Journal of Computer-Supported Collaborative Learning, 2*(2-3), 211–224. doi:10.1007/s11412-007-9014-4

Koehler, M. J., & Mishra, P. (2008). Introducing TPACK. In A. A. o. C. f. T. E. C. o. I. a. Technology (Ed.), *Handbook of Technological Pedagogical Content Knowledge (TPACK) for educators* (pp. 3-29). New York: Routledge.

Kolb, D. A. (1984). *Experiential Learning: Experience as the Source of Learning and Development*. Englewood Cliffs, New Jersey: Prentice Hall.

Kolb, D. A., & Fry, R. (1975). Towards an applied theory of experiential learning. In C. L. Cooper (Ed.), *Theories of group processes* (pp. 33–58). London: Wiley.

Kollar, I., Fischer, F., & Hesse, F. W. (2003). Cooperation scripts for computer-supported collaborative learning. In B. Wasson, R. Baggetun, U. Hoppe, & S. Ludvigsen (Eds.), *Proceedings of the International Conference on Computer Support for Collaborative Learning: CSCL 2003 Community events - Communication and interaction* (pp. 59-61). Bergen: InterMedia.

Korthagen, F. (2001). Teacher education a problematic enterprise. In F.A.J. Korthagen, J.P. Kessels, B. Koster; B. Lagerwerf, & T. Wubbels (Eds.), *Linking practice and theory. The pedagogy of realistic teacher education* (pp. 1- 19). Mahwah, N.J.: Lawrence Erlbaum Associates.

Korthagen, F., & Kessels, J. P. (1999). Linking theory and practice: Changing the pedagogy of teacher education. *Educational Researcher, 28*(4), 4–17.

Korthagen, F., & Vasalos, A. (2005). Levels in reflection: core reflection as a means to enhance professional growth. *Teachers and Teaching, 11*(1), 47–71. doi:10.1080/1354060042000337093

Korthagen, F., & Wubbels, T. (2001). Learning from practice. In F.A.J. Korthagen, J.P. Kessels, B. Koster; B. Lagerwerf, & T. Wubbels (Eds.), *Linking practice and theory. The pedagogy of realistic teacher education* (pp. pp. 32-50). Mahwah, N.J.: Lawrence Erlbaum Associates.

Korthagen, F., Keesels, J., Koster, B., Lagerwerf, B., & Wubbels, T. (Eds.). (2001). *Linking practice and theory. The pedagogy of realistic teacher education*. Mahwah, NJ: Lawrence Erlbaum Associates.

Korthagen, F., Klaassen, C., & Russel, T. Simons, R. J., van der Linden, J., & Duffy, T. (Eds.). (2000). *New learning in teaching training. New learning*. Dordrecht, The Netherlands: Kluwer Academic.

Koschmann, T. (Ed.). (1996). *CSCL: Theory and practice of an emerging paradigm*. Mahwah, NJ: Lawrence Erlbaum Associates.

Koster, B., Brekemans, M., Korthagen, F., & Wubbels, T. (2005). Quality requirements for teacher educators. *Teaching and Teacher Education, 21*, 157–176. doi:10.1016/j.tate.2004.12.004

Kress, G., & Pachler, N. (2007). Thinking about the 'm' in m-learning. In N. Pachler (Ed.), *Mobile learning: towards a research agenda* (pp. 7-32). London: WLE Centre, Institute of Education. Available at: http://www.wlecentre.ac.uk/cms/files/occasionalpapers/mobilelearning_pachler_2007.pdf

Kuan-Chou, C., & Keh-Wen, C. (2008). Building an e-Learning System Model with Implications for Research and Instructional Use. *Proceedings of World Academy of Science: Engineering & Technology, 30*, 479–481.

Kulatanga-Moruzi, C., Brooks, L. R., & Norman, G. R. (2001). Co-ordination of analytical and similarity-based processing strategies and expertise in dermatological diagnosis. *Learning and Teaching Medicine, 13*, 110–116. doi:10.1207/S15328015TLM1302_6

Kumpulainen, K., & Mutanen, M. (1999). The situated dynamics of peer group interaction: An introduction to an analytic framework. *Learning and Instruction, 9*(5), 449–473. doi:10.1016/S0959-4752(98)00038-3

LaBosky, V. K. (1994). *Development of reflective practice: A study of preservice teachers.* New York: Teachers College Press.

Laterza, V., Carmichael, P., & Procter, R. (2007). The doubtful guest? A Virtual Research Environment for education. *Technology, Pedagogy and Education, 16*(3), 249–267. doi:10.1080/14759390701614363

Latour, B. (1987). *Science in action.* Cambridge, MA: Harvard University Press.

Laurillard, D. (1993). *Rethinking University Teaching - A framework for the effective use of educational technology.* UK: Routledge

Laurillard, D. (2002). *Rethinking university teaching: a Conversational Framework for the effective use of learning technologies* (2nd ed.). London: RoutledgeFalmer.

Laurillard, D. (2007). In H. Beetham & R. Sharpe (Eds.), *Rethinking Pedagogy for a Digital Age*. Oxford: Routledge.

Laurillard, D. (2008). The teacher as action researcher: Using technology to capture pedagogic form. *Studies in Higher Education, 33*(2), 139–154. doi:10.1080/03075070801915908

Laurillard, D. (2009). The pedagogical challenges to collaborative technologies. *International Journal of Computer-Supported Collaborative Learning, 4*(1), 5–20. doi:10.1007/s11412-008-9056-2

Laurillard, D., Oliver, M., Wasson, B., & Hoppe, U. (2009). Implementing technology enhanced learning. In N. Balacheff, S. Ludvigsen, T. de Jong, A. Lazonder, & S. Barnes (Eds.), *Technology Enhanced Learning: Principles and Products* (pp. 285–302). Dordrecht, The Netherlands: Springer.

Lauvaas, P., & Handal, G. (2000). *Supervision and theory of practice*. Oslo: Cappelen Akademisk Forlag.

Lave, J., & Wenger, E. (1991). *Situated learning: Legitimate peripheral participation*. Cambridge: Cambridge University Press.

Law, N., Pelgrum, W., & Plomp, T. (2008). *Pedagogy and ICT use in schools around the world. Findings from the IEA SITES 2006 study*. The University of Hong Kong: Comparative Education Research Centre.

Learning Cultures Consulting Inc. (2006). *One-to-one mobile computing – Literature review*. Report for Alberta Education.

Leathard, H. L., & Dewhurst, D. (1995). Comparison of the cost-effectiveness of a computer assisted learning program with a tutored demonstration to teach intestinal motility to medical students. *Assoc for Learning Technology Journal, 3*(1), 118–125.

Lechner, S. (1998). Teachers of the N-Gen need reflective online communities. *Journal of Online Learning, 9*(3), 20–24.

Lederman, N. G., & Niess, M. L. (1997). Action research: our actions may speak louder than our words. *School Science and Mathematics, 97*(8), 397–399.

Lehtinen, E. (2003). Computer-supported collaborative learning: An approach to powerful learning environments. In E. de Corte, L. Verschaffel, N. Entwistle, & J. van Merriëboer (Eds.), *Powerful learning environments: Unraveling basic components and dimensions* (pp. 35-54). Amsterdam: Pergamon.

Leinonen, P., & Järvelä, S. (2006). Facilitating interpersonal evaluation of knowledge in a context of distributed team collaboration. *British Journal of Educational Technology, 37*(6), 897–916. doi:10.1111/j.1467-8535.2006.00658.x

Leithwood, K. (2007). What we know about educational leadership. In C. F. Webber, J. Burger, & P. Klinck (Eds.), *Intelligent leadership: Constructs for thinking education leaders* (pp. 41-66). Dordrecht, The Netherlands: Springer.

Leithwood, K., & Louis, K. S. (1998). *Organizational learning in schools*. Lisse, the Netherlands: Swets & Zeitlinger.

Leithwood, K., Seashore Louis, K., Anderson, S., & Wahlstrom, K. (2004). *How leadership influences student learning*. New York: Wallace Foundation.

Leithwood, K., Seashore, L. K., Anderson, S., & Wahlstrom, K. (2004). *How leadership influences student learning*. New York: Wallace Foundation.

Leont'ev, A. N. (1978). *Activity, consciousness, and personality*. Englewood Cliffs, NJ: Prentice-Hall.

Leont'ev, A. N. (1981). *Problems of the development of the mind*. Moscow: Progress.

Levin, B. B., & Rock, T. C. (2003). The effects of collaborative action research on preservice and experienced teacher partners in professional development schools. *Journal of Teacher Education, 54*(2), 135–149. doi:10.1177/0022487102250287

Levine, A., & Sun, J. (2002). *Barriers in distance education*. Washington, DC: American Council on Education.

Levine, A., & Sun, J. C. (2002). *Barriers to distance education*. Washington, DC: American Council on Education.

Levy, P. (2006). 'Living' theory: a pedagogical framework for process support in networked learning. *ALT-J, Research in Learning technology, 14*(3), 225-240

Lieberman, A. (1995). Practices that support professional development: Transforming conceptions of professional learning. *Phi Delta Kappan, 76*(8), 591–596.

Lieberman, A., & Miller, L. (2000). Teaching and teacher development: A new synthesis for a new century. In R. S. Brandt (Ed.), *Education in a new era* (pp. 47-66). Virginia: Association for Supervision and Curriculum Development.

Lieberman, A., & Miller, L. (2000). Teaching and teacher development: A new synthesis for a new century. In R. S. Brandt (Ed.), *Education in a new era* (pp. 47-66). VA: Association for Supervision and Curriculum Development.

Lieberman, A., & Pointer Mace, D. H. (2008). Teacher learning: The key to educational reform. *Journal of Teacher Education, 59*(3), 226–234. doi:10.1177/0022487108317020

Light, P., Littleton, K., Messer, D., & Joiner, R. (1994). Social and communicative processes in computer-based problem solving. *European Journal of Psychology of Education, 9*(1), 93–109.

Linell, P. (1998). *Approaching dialogue. Talk, interaction and contexts in dialogical perspectives*. Amsterdam: John Benjamins.

Lipman, M. (1988). *Philosophy goes to school*. Philadelphia: Temple University Press.

Lipman, M. (1991). *Thinking in Education*. Cambridge: Cambridge University Press.

Lipponen, L. (2000). Towards knowledge building discourse: From facts to explanations in primary students' computer-mediated discourse. *Learning Environments Research, 3*(2), 179–199. doi:10.1023/A:1026516728338

Lipponen, L. (2001). *Computer-supported collaborative learning: From promises to reality.* Unpublished doctoral dissertation, University of Turku.

Little, J. W. (1990). The mentor phenomenon and the social organization of teaching. *Review of Research in Education, 16,* 297–351.

Littlejohn, A. (2003). Issues in reusing online resources. In A. Littlejohn (Ed.), *Reusing Online Resources: a sustainable approach to eLearning* (pp. 1-6). London: Kogan Page.

Liu, Y., & Huang, C. (2005). Concerns of teachers about technology integration in the USA. *European Journal of Teacher Education, 28*(1), 35–47. doi:10.1080/02619760500039928

Lloyd, M., & Cochrane, J. (2006). Celtic knots: Interweaving the elements of effective teacher professional development in ICT. *Australian Educational Computing, 21*(2), 16–19.

Lloyd, M., Cochrane, J., & Beames, S. (2005). *Towards a model of effective professional development in ICT for teachers.* Commissioned report for Queensland Society for Information Technology in Education (QSITE). Retrieved September 13, 2008, from http://www.qsite.edu. au/publications/position/PD

Long, H. B. (2004). Understanding adult learners. In M. W. Galbraith (Ed.), *Adult Learning Methods: A Guide for Effective Instruction* (3rd ed.). Florida, USA: Krieger Publishing.

Loughran, J. (2006). *Developing a Pedagogy for Teacher Education.* London: Routledge.

Lucas, L. (2008). *Towards a Socio-cultural understanding of academics' experiences of linking research and teaching.* Seminar given at the Oxford Learning Institute, University of Oxford, UK, May 29, 2008.

Lund, A., & Hauge, T. E. (in press). Changing objects in knowledge creation practices. In S. Ludvigsen, A. Lund, I. Rasmussen, & S. Säljö (Eds.), *Learning across sites: New tools, infrastructures and practices.* London: Pergamon.

Lunenberg, M., Korthagen, F., & Swennen, A. (2007). The teacher educator as a role model. *Teaching and Teacher Education, 23*(5), 586–601. doi:10.1016/j. tate.2006.11.001

Lyle, S. (2008). Dialogic teaching: Discussing theoretical contexts and reviewing evidence from classroom practice. *Language and Education, 22*(3), 222–240.

MacBeath, J., & Mortimore, P. (Eds.). (2001). *Improving school effectiveness.* Buckingham, England: Open University Press.

Maddux, C. D. (2001). *Educational Computing: Learning with Tomorrow's Technologies.* Needham Heights, MA: Allyn & Bacon.

Mäkitalo, K., Häkkinen, P., Leinonen, P., & Järvelä, S. (2002). Mechanisms of common ground in case-based web-discussions in teacher education. *The Internet and Higher Education, 5*(3), 247–265. doi:10.1016/S1096-7516(02)00112-4

Marttunen, M., & Laurinen, L. (2007). Collaborative learning through chat discussions and argument diagrams in secondary school. *Journal of Research on Technology in Education, 40*(1), 109–126.

Masterman, E. (2008). Activity Theory and the Design of Pedagogic Planning tools. In L. Lockyer, S. Bennett, S. Agostinho, & B. Harper (Eds.), *Handbook of Research on Learning design and Learning Objects: Issues, Applications and Technologies* (pp. 209-227). Hershey, PA: IGI Global.

Masterman, L. (2008). *Phoebe Pedagogy Planner Project: Evaluation Report.* Oxford, UK: University of Oxford, Technology-Assisted Lifelong Learning Unit and Oxford University Computing Services. Retrieved February 4, 2009, from http://www.jisc.ac.uk/media/ documents/programmes/elearningpedagogy/Phoebe-evaluationreportsept08.pdf

Masterman, L., & Lee, S. (2005). *Reusing learning materials in English Literature and Language: Perspectives from three universities.* Egham, UK: Higher Education Academy English Subject Centre. Retrieved February 4,

2009, from http://www.english.heacademy.ac.uk/explore/projects/archive/technology/tech10.php

Matei, S. A. (2005). *From counterculture to cyberculture: Virtual community discourse and the dilemma of modernity.* Retrieved August 10, 2008, from http://jcmc.indiana.edu/vol10/issue3/matei.html

Matusov, E. (1998). When Solo Activity Is Not Privileged: Participation and Internalization Models of Development. *Human Development, 41,* 326–249. doi:10.1159/000022595

Maximizing the Impact. *The pivotal role of technology in a 21st century education system. ISTE, 2007.* Retrieved June 3 2008, from Partnership for 21st Century Skills Web site: http://www.setda.org/web/guest/maximizingimpactreport

McEwan, N. (2006). *Improving Schools Investing in Our Future.* Edmonton: Alberta Education.

McGee, J. B., & Begg, M. (2008). What medical educators need to know about "Web 2.0". *Medical Teacher, 30*(2), 164–169. doi:10.1080/01421590701881673

McKenzie, J. (1998). Creating learning cultures with just-in-time support. *Adult Technology Learning.* Retrieved July 27, 2000, from http://www.staffdevelop.org/adult.html

McLaughlin, C., & Black-Hawkins, K. (2004). A schools–university research partnership: understandings, models and complexities. *Journal of In-service Education, 30*(2), 265–284. doi:10.1080/13674580400200319

McLaughlin, M., & Talbot, J. E. (1993). *Contexts that matter for teaching and learning: Strategic opportunities for meeting the nation's educational goals.* Stanford, CA: Centre for Research on the Context of Secondary School Teaching.

McLoughlin, C., & Lee, M. J. W. (2008). *Future Learning Landscapes: Transforming Pedagogy through Social Software.* Retrieved June 3 2008, from: http://www.innovateonline.info/index.php?view=article&id=539

McNiff, J. (2002). *Action Research. Principles and Practice.* London: Routledge Falmer.

Means, B. (2000). Technology in America's schools: Before and after Y2K. In R. S. Brandt (Ed.), *Education in a new era.* Alexandria, VA: Association for Supervision and Curriculum Development.

Mehlinger, H. D., & Powers, S. M. (2002). *Technology and Teacher Education.* Boston: Houghton Mifflin.

Meirink, A., Meijer, P., & Verloop, N. (2007). A closer look at teachers' individual learning in collaborative settings. *Teachers and teaching . Theory into Practice, 13*(2), 145–164.

Meister, J. (2002). *Pillars of e-learning success.* New York: Corporate University Exchange.

Mercer, N. (1996). The quality of talk in children's collaborative activity in classroom. *Learning and Instruction, 6*(4), 359–377. doi:10.1016/S0959-4752(96)00021-7

Mercer, N., & Wegerif, R. (1998). Is 'exploratory talk' productive talk? In K. Littleton & P. Light (Eds.), *Learning with computers: analyzing productive interactions* (pp. 79-102). London: Routledge

Merriam, S. B. (2001). Andragogy and self-directed learning: Pillars of adult learning theory. In S. B. Merriam (Ed.), *The new update on adult learning theory* (Vol. 89, pp. 3-13). San Francisco: Jossey-Bass.

Merriam, S. B. (2001). Andragogy and self-directed learning: Pillars of adult learning theory. In S. B. Merriam (Ed.), *The new update on adult learning theory, 89,* (pp. 3-13). San Francisco: Jossey-Bass.

Mevarech, Z. (1997). The U-Curve process that trainee teachers experience in integrating computers into the curriculum. In D. Passey & B. Samways (Eds.), *Information technology: Supporting change through teacher education.* London: Chapman & Hall.

Meyer, T. (2002). Novice teacher learning communities: An alternative to one-on-one mentoring. *American Secondary Education, 31*(1), 1–27.

Miettinen, R., & Virkkunen, J. (2005). Epistemic objects, artefacts and organizational change. *Organization, 12*(3), 437–456. doi:10.1177/1350508405051279

Miller, G. E. (1990). The Assessment of CLinical Skills / Competence / Performance. *Academic Medicine, 65*(9), 63–67. doi:10.1097/00001888-199009000-00045

Mishra, P., & Koehler, M. J. (2006). Technological pedagogical content knowledge: A framework for teacher knowledge [Electronic Version]. *Teachers College Record, 108*, 1017-1054. Retrieved 7/16/2008 from http://www.tcrecord.org.

Moreno, J. M. (2007). Do the initial and continous teachers' professional development sufficiently prepare teachers to understand and cope with the complexities of today and tomorrow's education? *Journal of Educational Change, 8*(2), 169–172. doi:10.1007/s10833-007-9027-9

Moss, G., Jewitt, C., Levacic, R., Armstrong, V., Cardini, A., & Castle, F. (2007). *The interactive whiteboards, pedagogy and pupil performance evaluation: an evaluation of the Schools Whiteboard Expansion (SWE) project: London Challenge.* Nottingham: DfES.

Motteram, G. (2006). Blended education and the transformation of teachers: a long-term case study in postgraduate UK higher education. *British Journal of Educational Technology, 37*(1), 17–30. doi:10.1111/j.1467-8535.2005.00511.x

Mouza, C. (2002). Learning to Teach with New Technology: Implications for Professional Development. *Journal of Research on Technology in Education, 35*(2), 272–289.

Mouza, C. (2007). A socio-cultural approach to the design of a virtual practicum. In M. Zellermayer & E. Munthe (Eds.), *Teachers learning in communities* (pp. 165-187). Rotterdam: Sense Publishers.

Mulford, B. (2008). *The leadership challenge: Improving learning in schools.* Camberwell, Victoria: Australian Council for Educational Research.

Murphy, E., & Rodríguez-Manzanares, M. (2008). Instant messaging in a context of virtual schooling: Balancing the affordances and challenges. *Educational Media International, 45*(1), 47–58. doi:10.1080/09523980701847180

Murray, J., & Male, T. (2005). Becoming a teacher educator: evidence from the field. *Teaching and Teacher Education, 21*, 125–142. doi:10.1016/j.tate.2004.12.006

National Commission on Teaching and America's Future. (1997). *Doing what matters most: Investing in quality teaching.* New York: National Commission on Teaching and America's Future.

National Research Council. (2007). *Enhancing professional development for teachers: Potential uses of information technology, report of a workshop.* Washington, DC: The National Academies Press.

NCIHE. (1997). *Higher Education in the Learning Society. Summary Report* (Document No. NCIHE/97/849). London: HMSO.

Nemirovsky, R., Galvis, A., Kaplan, J., Cogan-Drew, D., & DiMattia, C. (2005). *VideoPaper Builder* (Version 3.0). Concord, MA: Concord Consortium.

NES. (2007). *NES survey of Scottish consultant workforce.* Edinburgh: NHS Education for Scotlando. Document Number)

Nespor, J. (1987). The role of beliefs in the practice of teaching. *Journal of Curriculum Studies, 19*(4), 317–328. doi:10.1080/0022027870190403

Nespor, J. (1997). *Tangled up in school: Politics, space, bodies, and signs in the educational process.* Mahwah, NJ: Lawrence Erlbaum Associates.

Nielsen, K., & Kvale, S. (1999). Apprenticeship. (In Norweigian). Oslo: AdNotam.

Niemi, H. (2002). Active learning- a cultural change needed in teacher education and schools . *Teaching and Teacher Education, 18*(7), 763–780. doi:10.1016/S0742-051X(02)00042-2

NMC. (2007). *Standards to support learning and assessment in practice: NMC standards for mentors, practice teachers and teachers.* Available online: http://www.nmc-uk.org/: Nursing and Midwifery Council.

Noddings, N. (1992). *The challenge to care in schools.* New York: Teachers' College Press.

Nonaka, I., & Takeuchi, H. (1995). *The knowledge creating company.* Oxford: Oxford University Press.

Nonaka, I., & Takeuchi, H. (1995). *The Knowledge-Creating Company.* Cambridge: Oxford University Press.

Norman, G., Young, M., & Brooks, L. (2007). Non-analytical models of clinical reasoning: the role of experience. *Medical Education, 41,* 1140–1145.

O'Reilly, T. (2005). *What Is Web 2.0. Design Patterns and Business Models for the Next Generation of Software.* Retrieved, January 9, 2009, from http://www.oreillynet.com/pub/a/oreilly/tim/news/2005/09/30/what-is-web-20.html

OECD. (2003). *Measuring knowledge management in the business sector: first steps.* Paris: OECD Publications.

OECD/CERI. (2002). *Quo Vademus? The Transformation of Schooling in a Networked World OECD/CERI Version 8c.* Retrieved 13th February, 2009 from http://www.oecd.org/dataoecd/48/20/2073054.pdf

Oliver, M. (2002). *Creativity and the curriculum design process: a case study.* York, UK: Higher Education Academy. Retrieved February 4, 2009, from http://www.heacademy.ac.uk/resources/detail/id153_Creativity_and_the_curriculum_design_process_a_case_study

Oliver, M. (2003). *Curriculum Design as acquired social practice: a case study.* Paper presented at the 84th Annual Meeting of the American Educational Research Association, Chicago, IL.

Olivero, F., Sutherland, R., & John, P. (2004). Seeing is believing: Using videopapers to transform teachers' professional knowledge and practice. *Cambridge Journal of Education, 34*(2), 179–191. doi:10.1080/03057640410001700552

ONS. (2007). *First Release: Internet Access 2007 Households and Individuals.* Retrieved 13th February, 2009 from http://www.statistics.gov.uk/pdfdir/inta0807.pdf.

Oortwijn, M., Boekaerts, M., & Vedder, P. (2008). The impact of the teacher's role and pupils' ethnicity and prior knowledge on pupils' performance and motivation to cooperate. *Instructional Science, 36*(3), 251–268. doi:10.1007/s11251-007-9032-7

Orlikowski, W. J. (1992). The duality of technology: Rethinking the concept of technology in organizations. *Organization Science, 3*(3), 398–427. doi:10.1287/orsc.3.3.398

Ottesen, E. (2006). Learning to teach with technology: authoring practised identities. *Technology, Pedagogy and Education, 15*(3), 275–290. doi:10.1080/14759390600923568

Overlap (2007). *Tendencias de la formación 2007.* Retrieved July 1, 2007, from http://www.web.overlap.net/archivos/novedad/InformeTendencias_reducido_con_notas.pdf

Ozga, J. (2007). Knowledge and Policy: Research and Knowledge Transfer. *Critical Studies in Education, 48*(1), 63–78. doi:10.1080/17508480601120988

Paavola, S., & Hakkarainen, K. (2005). The knowledge creation metaphor – An emergent epistemological approach to learning. *Science & Education, 14,* 535–557. doi:10.1007/s11191-004-5157-0

Pachler, N., & Daly, C. (2006). Power and Agency in Online Text-based Collaborations. *E–Learning, 3*(1).

Pachler, N., & Daly, C. (2008). Narrative and social networking technologies. In Y. Gächter, H. Ortner, C. Schwarz, & A. Wiesinger, (Eds.), *Storytelling – Reflexionen im Zeitalter der Digitalisierung / Storytelling – Reflections in the Age of Digitalization* (pp. 196-201). Innsbruck: iup.

Pachler, N., & Daly, N. (2006). Online communities and professional teacher learning: affordances and challenges. In E. Sorensen & D. Murchú, (Eds,), *Enhancing learning through technology* (pp. 1-28). Hershey, PA: Idea Group.

Pachler, N., Barnes, A., & Field, K. (2008). *Learning to teach modern foreign languages in the secondary school.* (3rd ed.). London: Routledge.

Palmer, P. J. (1998). *The Courage to Teach. Exploring the Inner Landscape of a Teacher's Life.* San Fransisco: Jossey-Bass.

Pardales, M., & Girod, M. (2006). Community of inquiry: its past and present future. *Educational Philosophy and Theory, 38*(3), 299–309. doi:10.1111/j.1469-5812.2006.00196.x

Perkins, D. (2000). "The big question is how to show up without showing up". In D. T. Gordon (Ed.), *The Digital Classroom* (pp. 87-89). Cambridge, MA: Harvard Education News Letter.

Perkins, D. (2006). *Feedback on dissertation.* In P. Whitehouse (Ed.). Cambridge, MA.

Perkins, D. N. (1993). Person-plus: A distributed view of thinking and learning. In G. Salomon, (Ed.), *Distributed cognitions. Psychological and educational considerations* (pp. 88-110). New York: Cambridge University Press.

Peters, T. (1994). *The Seminar.* New York: Random House.

Peters, T., & Bell, L. (2006). Is web conferencing software ready for the big time? *Computers in Libraries, 26*(2), 32–36.

Peters, V., Slotta, J., Forte, A., Bruckman, A., Lee, J. J., Gaydos, M., et al. (2008). Learning and research in the Web 2 Era: Opportunities for research. In G. Kanselaar, V. Jonker, P. A. Kirschner & F. J. Prins (Eds.), *Proceedings of the International Conference of the Learning Sciences.* International Society of the Learning Sciences. Utrecht. Retrieved January 5, 2009, from http://www.fi.uu.nl/en/icls2008/505/paper505.pdf

Pickering, J., Pachler, N., & Daly, C. (Eds.). (2007). *New designs for teachers' professional learning.* Bedford Way Papers. London: Institute of Education, UoL

PMETB. G. a. (2005). *Principles of good medical education and training.* London: General Medical Council and Postgraduate Medical Education and Training Board.

Poley, J. (2002). La dirección de instituciones universitarias en la era del conocimiento. In D.E. Hanna (Ed.), *La enseñanza universitaria en la era digital* (pp. 173-191). Barcelona: Octaedro-EUB.

Pont, E. (1997). La formación de los recursos humanos en las organizaciones. In J. Gairín & A. Ferrández (Ed.), *Planificación y gestión de instituciones de formación* (pp. 317-341). Praxis, Barcelona.

Pöysä, J., Hurme, T-R., Launonen, A., Hämäläinen, T., Järvelä, S., & Häkkinen, P. (2007). *Millaista on laadukas yhteisöllinen oppiminen verkossa. Osallistujalähtöinen näkökulma yhteisöllisen oppimisen ja toiminnan käytänteisiin Suomen virtuaaliyliopiston tieteenalaverkostojen verkkokursseilla.* Suomen virtuaaliyliopiston julkaisuja 3.

Preece, J., & Maloney-Krichmar, D. (2005). Online communities: Design, theory, and practice. *Journal of Computer-Mediated Communication, 10*(4).

Prensky, M. (2000). *Digital Game Based Learning*: McGraw-Hill.

Preston, C. (2004). *Learning to use ICT in classrooms: teachers' and trainees' perspectives. An evaluation of the English NOF ICT teacher training programme 1999 – 2003* London: Mirandanet and the Teacher Training Agency

Preston, C. (2004). *Learning to use ICT in Classrooms: Teachers' and Trainers' perspectives.* London, MirandaNet/TTA. Retrieved June 6 2008 from MirandaNet Web site: www.mirandanet.ac.uk/tta

Preston, C., & Cuthell, J. (2007). *Perspectives on ICT CPD: The experiential learning of advisers responsible for school teachers' ICT CPD programmes.* London: WLE Centre Occasional Papers in Work-based Learning 3.

Preston, C., & Danby, M. (2004). *Building professional capacity in new media skills - An evaluation of the European Computer Driving Licence (ECDL) for Educators.* Retrieved June 6 2008 from MirandaNet Web site: http://www.mirandanet.ac.uk/industry/astonswann.htm

Preston, C., Cox, M., & Cox, K. (2000). *Teachers as Innovators: What motivates teachers to use ICT A study of expert teachers.* Retrieved June 6 2008, from

MirandaNet Web site: http://www.mirandanet.ac.uk/pubs/tes_art.htm

Price, L., & Kirkwood, A. (2008). Learning and teaching and technology. In S. Scott & K. Dixon (Eds.), *The globalised university: Trends and development in teaching and learning* (pp. 83-113). Perth: Black Swan Press.

Putnam, R. T., & Borko, H. (2000). What do new views of knowledge and thinking have to say about research on teacher learning? *Educational Researcher, 29*(1), 4–15.

Rasku-Puttonen, H., Eteläpelto, A., Arvaja, M., & Häkkinen, P. (2003). Is successful scaffolding an illusion? - Shifting patterns of responsibility and control in teacher-student interaction during a long term learning project. *Instructional Science, 31*(6), 377–393. doi:10.1023/A:1025700810376

Rasku-Puttonen, H., Eteläpelto, A., Häkkinen, P., & Arvaja, M. (2002). Teacher's instructional scaffolding in an innovative ICT-based history-learning environment. *Teacher Development, 6*(2), 269–287. doi:10.1080/13664530200200180

Rasku-Puttonen, H., Eteläpelto, A., Lehtonen, O., Nummila, L., & Häkkinen, P. (2004). Developing teachers' professional expertise through collaboration in an innovative ICT-based learning environment. *European Journal of Teacher Education, 27*(1), 47–60. doi:10.1080/0261976042000211829

Ravenscroft, A., Sagar, M., Baur, E., & Oriogun, P. (in press). Ambient pedagogies, meaningful learning and social software. In S. Hatzipanagos & S. Warburton (Eds.), *Social software & developing community ontologies*. IGI Global Publishing.

Reinking, D., McKenna, M., Labbo, L., & Kieffer, R. (Eds.). (1998). *Handbook of literacy and technology: Transformations in a post-typographic world*. Mahwah, NJ: Erlbaum.

Rest, T. (1997). Using video for teaching chemistry: A phoenix? *TLTP Newsletter*.

Richards, C. (2006). Towards an integrated framework for designing effective ICT-supported learning environments: the challenge to better link technology and pedagogy. *Technology, Pedagogy and Education, 15*(2), 239–255. doi:10.1080/14759390600769771

Richardson, V. (1990). Significant and worthwhile change in teaching practice. *Educational Researcher, 19*(7), 10–18.

Richardson, V. (1992). The agenda-setting dilemma in a constructivist staff development process. *Journal of Teaching and Teacher Education, 8*(3), 287–300. doi:10.1016/0742-051X(92)90027-Z

Richardson, V., & Placier, P. (2001). Teacher change. In V. Richardson (Ed.), *Handbook of research on teaching.* (4th ed., pp. 905-947). Washington, DC: American Educational Research Association.

Riding, P. (2001). Online teacher communities and continuing professional development. *Teacher Development, 5*(3), 283–295. doi:10.1080/13664530100200156

Riel, M. (1987). The intercultural learning network. *The Computing Teacher, 14*, 27–30.

Riel, M. (1990). Cooperative learning across rooms. *Instructional Science, 19*, 445–466. doi:10.1007/BF00119390

Riel, M. (1999, March 1999). *Telementoring on the Web*. Retrieved March 2, 2003, 2003, from http://www.iearn.org/circles/mentors.html

Riel, M., & Polin, L. (2004). Online Learning Communities: Common Ground and Critical Differences in Designing Technical Environments. In S. Barab, R. Kling, & J. H. Gray (Eds.), *Designing for Virtual Communities in the Service of Learning* (pp. 16-50). New York: Cambridge University Press.

Rimpilainen, S., & Carmichael, P. (2006). *Sakai: An Environment for Virtual Research, Ennen ja Nyt 2006*. Retrieved 13th February, 2009 from http://www.ennenjanyt.net/2006_2/rimpilainen.pdf.

Ritter, J. K. (2007). Forging a pedagogy of teacher education: The challenges of moving from classroom teacher to teacher educator. *Studying Teacher Education, 3*(1), 5–22. doi:10.1080/17425960701279776

Rivkin, S. G., Hanushek, E. A., & Kain, J. F. (2005). Teachers, schools, and academic achievement. *Econometrica*, *73*(2), 417–458. doi:10.1111/j.1468-0262.2005.00584.x

Rodríguez, D. (2006). Modelos para la creación y gestión del conocimiento: aproximación teórica. *Educar*, *37*, 25–39.

Rogoff, B. (1994). Developing Understanding of the Idea of Communities of Learners. *Mind, Culture, and Activity*, *1*(4), 209–299.

Rogoff, B., Matusov, E., & White, C. (1996). Models of teaching and learning: Participation in a community of learners. In D. R. Olsen & N. Torrance (Eds.). *Handbook of education and human development* (pp. 388-415). Cambridge: Blackwell Publishers.

Roschelle, J., & Pea, R. (1999). Trajectories from today's WWW to a powerful educational infrastructure. *Educational Researcher*, *28*(5), 22–25.

Rosmalen, P. (2006). Knowledge matchmaking in Learning Networks: Alleviating the tutor load by mutually connecting learning network users. *British Journal of Educational Technology*, *37*(6), 881–895. doi:10.1111/j.1467-8535.2006.00673.x

Ross, M. T., Blaney, D., Cameron, H. S., Begg, M., & Cumming, A. D. (2008). *ClinEd: developing a web-based collaborative learning environment for clinical educators at the University of Edinburgh*. Paper presented at the All Together Better Health IV.

Rots, I., Aelterman, A., Vlerick, P., & Vermeulen, K. (2007). Teacher education graduates. Teaching commitment and entrance into the teaching profession. *Teaching and Teacher Education*, *23*, 543–556. doi:10.1016/j.tate.2007.01.012

Rubio, A. (2007). Las nuevas tendencias en la formación. *Capital Humano*, *209*, 120–126.

Rudestam, K. E., & Schoenholtz-Read, J. (2002a). The Coming of Age of Adult Online Education. In K. E. Rudestam & J. Schoenholtz-Read (Eds.), *Handbook of Online Learning*. Thousand Oaks: Sage.

Rudestam, K. E., & Schoenholtz-Read, J. (2002b). Overview: The Coming of Age of Adult Online Education. In K. E. Rudestam & J. Schoenholtz-Read (Eds.), *Handbook of Online Learning* (pp. 3-28). Thousand Oaks, CA: Sage Publications.

Russell, A. (1995). Stages in learning new technology: Naïve adult email users. *Computers & Education*, *25*(4), 173–178. doi:10.1016/0360-1315(95)00073-9

Sachs, J. (2003). *The Activist Teaching Profession*. Buckingham: Open University Press.

Sackett, D. L., Straus, S. E., Richardson, W. S., Rosenberg, W., & Haynes, R. B. (2000). *Evidence-based medicine: how to practice and teach EBM*. London: Churchill Livinstone.

Salmon, G. (2002). *E-tivities: The Key to Active Online Learning*. London: Kogan Page.

Salmon, G., Jones, S., & Armellini, A. (2008). Building institutional capability in e-learning design. *ALT-J*, *16*(2), 95–109. doi:10.1080/09687760802315978

San Diego, J., Laurillard, D., Boyle, T., Bradley, C., Ljubojevic, D., Neumann, T., & Pearce, D. (2008). Towards a user-oriented analytical approach to learning design. *ALT-J*, *16*(1), 15–29. doi:10.1080/09687760701850174

Sandvold, K. E., Øgrim, S., Flakstad, H., Bakken, T., Skrindo, K., & Pettersen, B. (2006). *Sigma, Mathematics*. Oslo: Gyldendal Norsk Forlag AS.

Scaife, M., & Rogers, Y. (1999). Kids As Informants: Telling Us What We Didn't Know or Confirming What We Knew Already? In A. Druin (Ed.), *The Design of Children's Technology* (pp. 27–50). San Francisco, CA: Morgan Kaufmann.

Scardamalia, M. (2002). Collective cognitive responsibility for the advancement of knowledge. In B. Smith (Ed.), *Liberal education in a knowledge society* (pp. 67-98). Chicago, IL: Open Court.

Scardamalia, M., & Bereiter, C. (1994). Computer support for knowledge building communities. *Journal of the Learning Sciences*, *3*, 265–283. doi:10.1207/s15327809jls0303_3

Scardamalia, M., & Bereiter, C. (2006). Knowledge Building: Theory, Pedagogy and Technology. In K. Sawyer (Ed.), *Cambridge Handbook of the Learning Sciences* (pp. 97–118). Cambridge, UK: Cambridge University Press.

Scardamalia, M., & Bereiter, C. (2006). Knowledge-building: Theory, pedagogy and technology. In K. Sawyer (Ed.), *The Cambridge handbook of the learning sciences,* (pp. 97–115). Cambridge, MA: Cambridge University Press.

Scheckler, R. K., & Barab, S. (in press). Designing for inquiry as a social practice. In J. K. Falk & B. Drayton (Eds.), *Creating and Sustaining Online Professional Learning Communities*. New York: Teachers College Press.

Schifter, C. (2008). *Infusing Technology into the Classroom: Continuous Practice Improvement.* IGI Global.

Schlager, M. S., & Fusco, J. (2003). Teacher professional development, technology, and communities of practice: Are we putting the cart before the horse? *The Information Society, 19*, 203–220. doi:10.1080/01972240309464

Schlager, M. S., Fusco, J., & Schank, P. (2002). Evolution of an On-line Education Community of Practice. In K. A. Renninger & W. Shumar (Eds.), *Building Virtual Communities: Learning and Change in Cyberspace* (pp. 129-158). New York: Cambridge University Press.

Schlager, M., Fusco, J., & Schank, P. (2002). Evolution of an on-line education community of practice. In K.A. Renninger, & W. Shumar, (Eds.), *Building virtual communities: Learning and change in cyberspace* (pp. 129-158). New York: Cambridge University Press.

Schlager, M., Fusco, J., Barab, S., Kling, R., & Gray, J. H. (2004). Teacher professional development, technology, and communities of practice: Are we putting the cart before the horse? In R. Pea, J. S. Brown & C. Heath (Eds.), *Designing for Virtual Communites in the Service of Learning* (pp. 120-153). Cambridge, MA: Cambridge University Press.

Schlager, S., & Fusco, J. (2003). Teacher Professional Development, Technology, and Communities of Practice: Are

We Putting the Cart Before the Horse? *The Information Society, 19*(3), 203–220. doi:10.1080/01972240309464

Schmidt, H. G., & Rickers, R. M. J. P. (2007). How expertise develops in medicine: knowledge encapsulation and illness script formation. *Medical Education, 41*, 1133–1139.

Schofield, J. W. (2003). Bringing the Internet to schools effectively. *Global issues. The evolving Internet, 8*(8). An Electronic Journal of the U.S. Department of State. Retrieved January 29, 2009, from http://www.scribd.com/doc/3210562/the-evolving-internet

Schön, D. (1983). *The reflective practitioner: How professionals think in action.* New York: Basic.

Schön, D. (1987) *Educating the reflective practitioner.* San Francisco. Jossey-Bass.

Schön, D. A. (1987). *Educating the reflective practitioner: toward a new design for teaching and learning in the professions.* San Fransisco: Jossey-Bass.

Scott, D. E. (2009). *Effective Voice-over-Internet-Protocol (VoIP) learning experiences: The relationship between adult learning motivation, multiple intelligences, and learning styles.* Doctoral Thesis. Curtin University of Technology.

Scott, D. E. (2009). *Effective Voice-over-Internet-Protocol (VoIP) learning experiences: The relationship between adult learning motivation, multiple intelligences, and learning styles.* Doctoral Thesis. Curtin University of Technology.

Scott, S. (2002). *Professional development: A study of secondary teachers' experiences and perspectives.* Doctoral Thesis. Curtin University of Technology. http://adt.curtin.edu.au/theses/available/adt-WCU20030312.145827/.

Scott, S. (2003). Professional development: A study of secondary teachers' experiences and perspectives. *The International Journal of Learning, 10*.

Scott, S. (2003). Professional development: A study of secondary teachers' experiences and perspectives. *The International Journal of Learning, 10*.

Scott, S., & Scott, D. E. (2003). The integration of technology into the curriculum: The perspectives of teachers and students within a Western Australian secondary school. *The International Journal of Learning, 10.*

Scott, S., & Webber, C. F. (2008). Evidence-based leadership development: The 4L framework. *Journal of Educational Administration, 46*(6), 762–776. doi:10.1108/09578230810908343

Scottish Executive (2002). *Standard for Charted Teachers, Continuing Professional Development.* GTC Scotland: Scottish Executive.

Seal, K. (2003). Transforming teaching & learning through technology. *Carnegie Reporter, 2*(2), 25–33.

Selinger, M., & Yapp, C. (2001). *ICT Teachers.* London. Institute for Public Policy Research.

Sergiovanni, T. J. (1993, April 13). *Organisations or communities? Changing the metaphor changes the theory.* Paper presented at the annual meeting of the American Educational Research Association, Atlanta, Georgia.

Sharpe, R., & Oliver, M. (2007). Designing courses for e-learning. In H. Beetham & R. Sharpe (Eds.), *Rethinking Pedagogy for a Digital Age: Designing and delivering e-learning* (pp. 41–51). London: Routledge.

Sharpe, R., Benfield, G., & Francis, R. (2006). Implementing a university e-learning strategy: Levers for change within academic schools. *ALT-J, 14*(2), 135–151. doi:10.1080/09687760600668503

Showers, B. (1984). *Peer coaching: A strategy for facilitating transfer of training.* Eugene, OR: Center for Educational Policy and Management.

Showers, B. (1995, April). *Designing site-based school improvement programs.* Paper presented at the Primary Principals, Education Department of Western Australia, Nedlands, Western Australia.

Showers, B., & Joyce, B. (1996). The evolution of peer coaching. *Educational Leadership, 53*(6), 12–16.

Showers, B., & Joyce, B. (1996). The evolution of peer coaching. *Educational Leadership, 53*(6), 12–16.

Shulman, L. S. (1987). Knowledge and teaching: Foundations of the new reform. *Harvard Educational Review, 57*(1), 1–22.

Shulman, L., & Shulman, J. (2004). How and what teachers learn: a shifting perspective. *Journal of Curriculum Studies, 36*(2), 257–271. doi:10.1080/0022027032000148298

Simonson, M., Smaldino, S., Albright, M., & Zvacek, S. (2006). *Teaching and learning at a distance: Foundations of distance education.* (3rd ed.). Upper Saddle River, NJ: Pearson Merrill Prentice Hall.

Skovholt, T. (2001). *The Recilient Practitioner.* Boston: Allyn & Bacon.

Smedley, L. (2001). Impediments to Partnership: a literature review of school-university links. *Teacher and Teaching: theory and practice, 7*(2), 189-209.

Smith, K., & Sela, O. (2005). Action research as a bridge between pre-service teacher education and in-service professional development for students and teacher educators. *European Journal of Teacher Education, 28*(3), 293–310. doi:10.1080/02619760500269418

Smith, K., & Tillema, H. (1998). Evaluating portfolio use as a learning tool for professionals. *Scandinavian Journal of Educational Research, 42*(2), 193–205. doi:10.1080/0031383980420206

Smith, K., & Tillema, H. (2001). Long-term Influences of Portfolios on Professional development. *Scandinavian Journal of Educational Research, 45*(2), 183–203. doi:10.1080/00313830120052750

Snow, C. (2002). *Reading for understanding: Toward an R & D program in reading comprehension.* Santa Monica, CA: RAND.

Snow, C., Griffin, P., & Burns, M. S. (2005). *Knowledge to support the teaching of reading: Preparing teachers for a changing world.* San Francisco, CA: Jossey-Bass.

Snow-Gerono, J. L. (2005). Professional development in a culture of inquiry: PDS teachers identify the benefits of professional learning communities. *Teaching and Teacher Education, 21*, 241–256. doi:10.1016/j.tate.2004.06.008

Snyder, I. (1998). *Page to Screen.* London: Routledge.

Solomon, G., & Schrum, L. (2007). *Web 2.0 new tools, new schools.* Eugene, OR: International Society for Technology in Education.

Somekh, B. (2004). Taking the sociological imagination to school: an analysis of the (lack of) impact of information and communication technologies on education systems. *Technology, Pedagogy and Education, 13*(2), 163–179. doi:10.1080/14759390400200178

Songer, N. B., Lee, H.-S., & Kam, R. (2002). Technology-rich inquiry science in urban classrooms: What are the barriers to inquiry pedagogy? *Journal of Research in Science Teaching, 39*(2), 128–150. doi:10.1002/tea.10013

Sorge, D. H., & Russell, J. D. (2000). A strategy for effective change in instructional behavior: Staff development that works. *Educational Technology, 40*(6), 46–49.

Sparks, D., & Hirsh, S. (1997). *A new vision for staff development*: Association for Supervision and Curriculum Development.

Sparks, D., & Hirsh, S. (1997). *A new vision for staff development*: Association for Supervision and Curriculum Development.

Sparks, D., & Hirsh, S. (2000). *A National Plan for Improving Professional Development.* Oxford, OH: National Staff Development Council.

Spilkova, V. (2001). Professional development of teachers and student teachers through reflection on practice. *European Journal of Teacher Education, 18*(7), 815–830.

Spitzer, W., Wedding, K., & DiMauro, V. (1994). *Fostering Reflective Dialogues for Teacher Professional Development.* Retrieved Feb. 17, 2003, 2003, from http://www.terc.edu/papers/labnet/Guide/03-Introduction.html

Stahl, G. (2006). *Group cognition. Computer support for building collaborative knowledge.* Cambridge, MA: MIT Press.

Stahl, G., Koschmann, T., & Suthers, D. (2006). Computer-supported collaborative learning: An historical perspective. In R. K. Sawyer (Ed.), *Cambridge handbook of the learning sciences* (pp. 409–426). Cambridge, UK: Cambridge University Press.

Stake, R. (1975). *Evaluating the arts in education: A responsive approach.* Columbus, OH: Merill.

Stake, R. E. (2000) Case studies. In N. K. Denzin (Ed.), *Handbook of qualitative research* (2nd ed.). London: Sage Publications.

Steffy, B. E., Wolfe, M. P., Pasch, S. H., & Enz, B. J. (Eds.). (2000). *Life cycle of the career teacher.* Thousand Oaks: Kappa Delta Pi and Corwin Press, Inc.

Stenhouse, L. (1975). *An introduction to curriculum research and development.* London: Heinemann.

Stevens-Long, J., & Crowell, C. (2002). The Design and Delivery of Iteractive Online Graduate Education. In K. E. Rudestam & J. Schoenholtz-Read (Eds.), *Handbook of Online Learning* (pp. 151-169). Thousand Oaks, CA: Sage Publications.

Stoll, L., & Fink, D. (1999). *Para cambiar nuestras escuelas. Reunir la eficacia y la mejora.* Barcelona: Octaedro.

Strauss, A., & Corbin, J. (1990). *Basics of qualitative research: Grounded theory procedures and techniques.* London: Sage Publications.

Strehle, E. L., Whatley, A., Kurz, K. A., & Hausfather, S. J. (2001). Narratives of collaboration: Inquiring into technology integration in teacher education. *Journal of Technology and Teacher Education, 10*(1), 27–47.

Stufflebeam, D. L. (2001). *Evaluation models.* San Francisco: Jossey-Bass.

Suen, L. (2005). Teaching epidemiology using WebCT: Application of the seven principles of good practice. *The Journal of Nursing Education, 44*(3), 143–146.

Surowiecki, J. (2005). *The wisdom of crowds.* New York: Random House.

Swan, B., Huh, J., Chen, Y.-C., & Smith, S. (2008). *Florida Online Reading Professional Development (FOR-PD) Phase V annual evaluation report fall 2006 to summer 2007.* Orlando: University of Central Florida, College of Education.

Tait, B. (1997). Constructive Internet Learning. *Active Learning,* (7), 3-8.

Tchounikine, P. (2008). Operationalizing macro-scripts in CSCL technological settings. *International Journal of Computer-Supported Collaborative Learning, 3*(2), 193–233. doi:10.1007/s11412-008-9039-3

Teachers Matter. (2005). *Attracting, developing and retaining effective teachers, OECD rapport.* Retrieved Oct.ober 9, 2007, from: http://www.oecd.org/document/5 2/0,3343,en_2649_201185_34991988_1_1_1_1,00.html

Teddie, C., & Reynolds, D. (2000). *International Handbook of School Effectiveness Research.* London: Falmer Press.

Tessmer, M., & Richey, R. C. (1997). The Role of Context in Learning and Instructional Design. *Educational Technology Research and Development, 45*(2), 85–115. doi:10.1007/BF02299526

The Medical Act (1858).

Todnem, G., & Warner, M. P. (1994). Demonstrating the benefits of staff development: An interview with Thomas R. Guskey. *Journal of Staff Development, 15*(3), 63–65.

Treacy, B., Kleiman, G., & Peterson, K. (2002). Successful online professional development. *Learning and Leading with Technology, 30*(1), 42–47.

Triggs, P., & John, P. (2004). From transaction to transformation: information and communication technology, professional development and the formation of communities of practice. *Journal of Computer Assisted Learning, 20*(6), 426–439. doi:10.1111/j.1365-2729.2004.00101.x

Trilling, B. (2005). *Toward Learning Societies and the Global Challenges for Learning-With-ICT.* Retrieved June 3 2008, from Tech & Learning Web site: http://news. techlearning.com/techlearning/pdf/events/techforum/ ny05/Toward_Learning_Societies.pdf

Trinidad, S., Newhouse, C. P., & Clarkson, B. (2004). A framework for implementation of ICT in schools. Paper presented at the Australian Computers in Education Conference. July 2004, Adelaide, Australia.

Turner, C. (2006). Informal learning and its relevance to the early professional development of teachers in secondary schools in England and Wales. *Journal of In-service Education, 32*(3), 301–319. doi:10.1080/13674580600841885

U.S. Department of Education (USDOE). (2002). *The Secretary's Report on Teacher Quality.* Washington, DC: U.S. Department of Education.

U.S. Department of Education, National Center for Education Statistics. (2006). *Internet access in U.S. public schools and classrooms: 1994–2005, 2007.* Available at http://nces.ed.gov/

U.S. Department of Education, Office of Postsecondary Education. (2005). *The Secretary's Fourth Annual Report of Teacher Quality: A highly qualified teacher in every classroom.* Washington, DC (ERIC Document Reproduction Service No. ED485858).

U.S. Department of Education. (1999). *TIMSS 1999 Results.* Retrieved 2/14/2009, from http://nces.ed.gov/ timss/

Valli, L. (2000). Connecting teacher development and school improvement: ironic consequences of a preservice action research course. *Teaching and Teacher Education, 16*(7), 715–730. doi:10.1016/S0742-051X(00)00021-4

van Boxtel, C., van der Linden, J., & Kanselaar, G. (2000). Collaborative learning tasks and the elaboration of conceptual knowledge. *Learning and Instruction, 10*(4), 311–330. doi:10.1016/S0959-4752(00)00002-5

Vass, M., Carroll, J., & Shaffer, C. (2002). Supporting creativity in problem solving environments. *Proceedings of the 4th Conference on Creativity & Cognition* (pp. 31-37). Loughborough, UK.

Vavasseur, C. B., & MacGregor, S. K. (2008). Extending Content-Focused Professional Development through Online Communities of Practice. *Journal of Research on Technology in Education, 40*(4), 517–536.

Vera, D., & Crossan, M. (2003). Organizational Learning and Knowledge Management: Toward an Integrative Framework. In M. Easterby-Smith & M. A. Lyles (Ed.), *Handbook of Organizational learning and knowledge management* (pp. 122-141). Oxford: Blackwell Publishing.

Vescio, V., Ross, D., & Adams, A. (2008). A review of research on the impact of professional learning communities on teaching practice and student learning. *Teaching and Teacher Education*, *24*, 80–91. doi:10.1016/j.tate.2007.01.004

Vygotsky, L. S. (1978). *Mind in society: The development of higher psychological processes.* Cambridge, MA: Harvard University Press.

Waks, L. J. (1999). The Means-Ends Continuum and the Reconciliation of Science and Art in the Later Works of John Dewey. *Transactions of the Charles S. Peirce Society*, *XXXV*(3), 595–611.

Walker, D. (1999, October). Technology and literacy: Raising the bar. *Educational Leadership*, *57*(2), 18–32.

Wasson, B., Ludvigsen, S., & Hoppe, U. (2003). *Designing for change in networked learning environments.* Dordrecht, the Netherlands: Kluwer.

Watzke, J. L. (2007). Longitudinal research on beginning teacher development: Complexity as a challenge to concerns-based stage theory. *Teaching and Teacher Education*, *23*, 106–122. doi:10.1016/j.tate.2006.04.001

Webb, M., & Cox, M. (2004). A review of pedagogy related to information and communications technology. *Technology, Pedagogy and Education*, *13*(3), 235–286. doi:10.1080/14759390400200183

Webber, C. F., & Scott, S. (2008). Entrepreneurship and educational leadership development: A Canadian and Australian perspective. *International Electronic Journal in Leadership Learning, 12*(11).

Webber, C. F., Aitken, N., Runté, R., Lupart, J., & Scott, S. (2008, 30th May-4th June). *Alberta student assessment study: Stage one findings.* Paper presented at the Annual Meeting of the Canadian Society for the Study of Education, Vancouver.

Wegerif, R. (2007). *Dialogic Education and Technology.* New York: Springer.

Wegerif, R., Mercer, N., & Dawes, L. (1999). From social interaction to individual reasoning: An empirical investigation of a possible sociocultural model of cognitive development. *Learning and Instruction*, *9*(6), 493–526. doi:10.1016/S0959-4752(99)00013-4

Wei, F., & Chen, G. (2006). Collaborative mentor support in a learning context using a ubiquitous discussion forum to facilitate knowledge sharing for lifelong learning. *British Journal of Educational Technology*, *37*(6), 917–935. doi:10.1111/j.1467-8535.2006.00674.x

Weinberger, A., & Fischer, F. (2006). A framework to analyze argumentative knowledge construction in computer-supported collaborative learning. *Computers & Education*, *46*, 71–95. doi:10.1016/j.compedu.2005.04.003

Weinberger, A., Stegmann, K., & Fischer, F. (2007). Knowledge convergence in collaborative learning: Concepts and assessment. *Learning and Instruction*, *17*(4), 416–426. doi:10.1016/j.learninstruc.2007.03.007

Weinstein, C. S. (1989). Teacher education students' preconceptions of teaching. *Journal of Teacher Education*, *40*(2), 53–60. doi:10.1177/002248718904000210

Weller, M., Pegler, C., & Mason, R. (2005). Use of innovative technologies on an e-learning course. *The Internet and Higher Education*, *8*(1), 61–71. doi:10.1016/j.iheduc.2004.10.001

Wells, G., & Arauz, R. M. (2006). Dialogue in the classroom. *Journal of the Learning Sciences*, *15*(3), 379–428. doi:10.1207/s15327809jls1503_3

Wenger, E. (1998). *Communities of Practice.* Cambridge, UK: Press Syndicate of the University of Cambridge.

Wenger, E. (1998). *Communities of Practice: Learning, Meaning and Identity.* New York: Cambridge University Press.

Wenger, E. (2003). Communities of practice and social learning systems. In R. Gardner, D. Nicolini, S. Gherardi, & D. Yanow (Eds.), *Knowing in organizations: A practice-based approach.* Armonk, NY: M.E. Sharpe.

Wenger, E. (2003). Communities of practice and social learning systems. In R. Gardner, D. Nicolini, S. Gherardi & D. Yanow (Eds.), *Knowing in organizations: A practice-based approach*. Armonk, NY: M.E. Sharpe.

Wenger, E. (n.d). *Communities of practice*. Retrieved 2/14/2009, from http://www.ewenger.com/theory/

Wenger, E. C., & Snyder, W. M. (2000). Communities of practice: The organizational frontier. *Harvard Business Review, 78*(1), 139–146.

Wenger, E., McDermott, R., & Snyder, W. M. (2002). *Cultivating communities of practice: a guide to managing knowledge*. Boston: Harvard Business School Press.

WFME. (2003). *Basic medical education: WFME global standards for quality improvement*. Copenhagen: World Federation for Medical Education.

Whitehouse, P., Breit, L., McCloskey, E., Ketelhut, D. J., & Dede, C. (2006). An overview of current findings from empirical research on online teacher professional development. In C. Dede (Ed.), *Online professional development for teachers: Emerging models and methods* (pp. 13-30). Cambridge, MA: Harvard Education Press.

Whitehouse, P., Breit, L., McCloskey, E., Ketelhut, D. J., & Dede, C. (2006). Overview of Current Findings from Empirical Research on Online Teacher Professional Development. In C. Dede (Ed.), *Online Teacher Professional Development: Emerging Models and Methods*. Cambridge MA: Harvard Education Publishing Group.

Whitehouse, P., Reynolds, R., & Caperton, I. (2009). *The Development of a research framework to examine teacher professional development and educator experiences in Globaloria: Pilot year 1*. Paper presented at the Society for Technology in Education (SITE).

Wideen, M., Mayer-Smith, J., & Moon, B. (1998). A critical analysis of research on learning to teach: Making the case for an ecological perspective on inquiry. *Review of Educational Research, 68*(2), 130–178.

Wighton, D. J. (1993). Telementoring: An Examination of the Potential for an Educational Network. Retrieved March 2, 2003, 2003, from http://mentor.creighton.edu/htm/telement.htm

Wilson, A., Rimpilainen, S., Skinner, D., Cassidy, C., Christie, D., Coutts, N., & Sinclair, C. (2007). Using a Virtual Research Environment to support new models of collaborative and participative research in Scottish education. *Technology, Pedagogy and Education, 16*(3), 289–304. doi:10.1080/14759390701614413

Wilson, E. K. (2006). The impact of an alternative model of student teacher supervision: Views of the participants. *Teaching and Teacher Education, 22*, 22–31. doi:10.1016/j.tate.2005.07.007

Windschitl, M. (2002). Framing constructivism in practice as the negotiation of dilemmas: An analysis of the conceptual, pedagogical, cultural, and political challenges facing teachers. *Review of Educational Research, 72*, 131–175. doi:10.3102/00346543072002131

Wlodkowski, R. J. (2004). Strategies to enhance adult motivation to learn. In M. W. Galbraith (Ed.), *Adult Learning Methods: A Guide for Effective Instruction* (3rd ed., pp. 91-112). Florida. USA: Krieger Publishing.

Wolpert, L. (2003). Causal belief and the origins of technology. *Philosophical Transactions of the Royal Society of London, Series A, 361*(1809), 1709–1719.

Wubbels, T. (2007). Do we know a community of practice when we see one? *Technology, Pedagogy and Education, 16*(2), 225–233. doi:10.1080/14759390701406851

Wubbels, T., & Korthagen, F. (1990). The effects of a pre-service teacher training program for the preparation of reflective teachers. *Journal of Education for Teaching, 16*(1), 29–43. doi:10.1080/0260747900160102

Wubbles, T., & Brekelmans, M. (2005). Two decades of research on teacher-student relationships in class. *International Journal of Educational Research, 43*, 6–24. doi:10.1016/j.ijer.2006.03.003

Zeichner, K. (2005). Becoming a teacher educator: A personal perspective. *Teaching and Teacher Education, 22*, 32–41.

Zeichner, K. (2007). Accumulation knowledge across self-studies in teacher education. *Journal of Teacher Education, 58*(1), 36–46. doi:10.1177/0022487106296219

Zeichner, K., & Bekisizwe, N. (2008). Contradictions and tensions in the place of teachers in educational reform: Reflections on teacher preparation in the USA and Namibia. *Teachers and Teaching: Theory and Practice, 14*(4), 331–343.

Zeichner, K., & Liston, D. (1998). *Reflective teaching.* NJ: Lawrence Erlbaum.

Zellermayer, M., & Munthe, E. (2007). Teachers learning in communities. In M. Zellermayer & E. Munthe (Eds.), *Teachers learning in communities* (pp. 1-6). Rotterdam: Sense Publishers.

Zualkernan, I. A. (2006). A framework and a methodology for developing authentic constructivist e-Learning environments. *Educational Technology & Society, 9*(2), 198–212.

About the Contributors

J. Ola Lindberg earned his PhD in Education at Umeå University, Sweden. Dr. Lindberg is a senior lecturer and his main research interest lies in TPD and distance education supported by ICT. His research conducted departs from a philosophical hermeneutical approach with an overall aim at understanding social and ethical processes of teaching and fostering. In TPD and distance education his focus is on how the participants negotiate meaning in OLCs. He has contributed with book-chapters, conference-papers and journal articles on this specific topic. He is member of the international network 'The Research Network on Online Learning Communities'. A list of publications may be found at http://spica.utv.miun.se/medarbetare/detail.lasso?ID=P10019

Anders D. Olofsson, PhD, is a senior lecturer in learning & ICT at the Department of Education, Umeå University, Sweden. From a philosophical hermeneutical approach his research is aimed at understanding the meaning of social processes of teaching, fostering- and professional development, establishing the meaning of for example ethics, democracy, learning and teaching, in OLCs. Dr. Olofsson is the scientific leader for a research group titled LICT (Learning & ICT) and is in addition involved in several development- and research projects within the field of medical education. He has contributed with book-chapters, journal articles and papers to conference proceedings on this specific topic. Dr. Olofsson is member of the international network 'The Research Network on Online Learning Communities'. A list of publications may be found at http://www.pedag.umu.se/personal/olofsson_a/index.html

* * *

Maarit Arvaja, PhD, in Educational sciences, is currently working as a senior researcher at the Finnish Institute for Educational Research, University of Jyväskylä, Finland. Her research interests comprise collaborative learning and computer-supported collaborative learning. She is particularly interested in studying the process of collaborative knowledge construction, and the ways in which different cultural tools mediate that process. Her methodological areas of interests comprise qualitative research methodologies.

Michael Begg, MSc, is the eLearning Manager for the University of Edinburgh's Learning Technology Section within the College of Medicine and Veterinary Medicine. He is co-Theme Leader for Medical Informatics for the undergraduate medical programme. He also chairs the Scottish Deans Medical Education Group's subgroup for educational informatics, and is a Specialist Subject Advisor for gaming and simulation to the Higher Education Academy's MEDEV subject centre (Medicine, Dentistry and

Veterinary Medicine). His research into narrative, game based and game informed learning provided the theoretical underpinning on which the Labyrinth system was - and continues to be - developed.

Donald Christie, professor, was appointed to the Chair in Childhood and Primary Studies in the Faculty of Education at the University of Strathclyde in Glasgow in 2005 and has been Convenor of the Learners, Learning and Teaching Network, part of the Applied Educational Research Scheme in Scotland (www.aers.org), since 2004. A Chartered Psychologist and former primary teacher, he has 25 years of experience in teacher education. He researches children's social development and the process of collaboration in different contexts, including classroom learning and teachers' professional learning. He was closely involved in the creation of the framework of professional standards for teachers in Scotland, which include a significant element of practitioner research and enquiry and he is an advocate of collaborative approaches to educational research modelled on the concept of "community of enquiry".

John Cuthell, PhD, is a Research and Implementation director at the MirandaNet Academy. He has developed practice-based research accreditation for teachers; worked on a range of e-learning and change management projects involving work with varied web-based communities, and co-ordinated MirandaNet action research projects with teachers in England, Mexico, China and South Africa. From 2004 – 2005 John worked with a team of MirandaNet Fellows to support the introduction of computers into schools in Free State Province, South Africa. He has also developed and run a number of e-learning and e-facilitation courses. Current projects include the implementation of Visual Learning and the role of professional development (particularly with web-based communities of practice). Dr. Cuthell is Visiting Research Fellow at the School of Education and Professional Development, University of Huddersfield and is a Consultant at the Centre for Educational Innovation & Technology, Bath Spa University.

Caroline Daly is a senior lecturer at the Institute Of Education, University of London. She is assistant director of the Centre for Excellence in Work-based Learning for Education Professionals, which involves the initiation and co-ordination of research projects investigating work-based learning and learning with technologies. She has developed e-learning courses in national and international contexts and is currently a module leader on a mixed-mode professional masters programme for teachers. Her research background is in teacher education and professional learning in e-learning contexts and her PhD research was on the impact on professional learning of online discussion communities. She has led projects investigating e-learners' experiences and has a background in staff development to embed technologies within institution-based programme development, based on research-informed training. She has published widely for both research and practitioner audiences.

David Dewhurst, BSc, PhD, is professor of e-learning at the University of Edinburgh, UK. As an assistant principal of e-learning and e-health, he has a university-wide role in supporting these areas. He is also the director of the Learning Technology Section (LTS) within the College of Medicine and Veterinary Medicine, which provides academic support in e-learning, information technology, and medical illustration. He has over 25 years experience in teaching physiology and pharmacology to students in the biosciences, health professions, and medicine, and he has been using technology to enhance this teaching for many years.

Jennifer Duncan-Howell, PhD, is a lecturer in Information and Communication Technologies (ICT) and teacher education in the School of Mathematics, Science and Technology Education, Faculty of Education at Queensland University of Technology. Her research focuses on online communities, continuing teacher professional development, elearning, mlearning, Web 2.0 technologies, building teacher capacity, STEM (Science, Technology, Engineering and Mathematics) Education and electronic research methodology. During her 15 year career as an educator she has worked in Australia, the United Kingdom, Hong Kong, the Philippines and India. She has developed several online initiatives, *The eMerge Community,* for pre-service teachers and *The Teachers' Capacity Network (TCN),* a beginning teachers professional development initiative. Address for correspondence: Jennifer Duncan-Howell, MSTE, Faculty of Education, Queensland University of Technology,Victoria Park Road, Kelvin Grove, QLD 4059 Australia. Email: j.duncanhowell@qut.edu.au

Joaquín Gairin-Sallán is a professor of Teaching and Educational Administration, Director of the Organisational Development Research Group (EDO) and international advisor. He is member of the Faculty of Education at the Universitat Autònoma de Barcelona and former director of Educational Sciences Institute, former Director of Applied Pedagogy Department and former Dean of the Faculty of Education at the Universitat Autònoma de Barcelona. His research interest includes knowledge management, organisational learning, organisational development and professional development. The most recent research activities supervised by Joaquin Gairin are: (1) Agents and process in networked knowledge management (Ministry of Education and Culture, Spanish R&D Plan); (2) Drop-out at Catalan Universities (Catalan University Quality Assurance Agency); (3) Evaluation of Social Sciences Competences (Catalan University Quality Assurance Agency); (4) TVET Standards in Metal (Leonardo Project) and (5) TT-TVET Standards (Asia-link project).

Trond Eiliv Hauge is professor of Education at InterMedia, University of Oslo. InterMedia is a multidisciplinary research center working in the intersections between design, communication and learning in digital environments. His recent publications include the co-edited books *Undervisning i endring. ICT, aktivitet, design* (Teaching in Transformation. ICT, Activity, Design), *The Life and Work of Teachers. International Perspectives,* co-authored chapters in *World Class Schools. International Perspectives on School Effectiveness* and *Learning across sites: New Tools, Infrastructures and Practices.*

Ingrid Helleve is a lecturer in Pedagogy in the Department of Teacher Education at the University of Bergen in Norway. She teaches various courses for student teachers and also for mentors in upper secondary schools. She has worked as a teacher and a principal in primary and lower secondary schools. The doctoral research is on collaborative learning in ICT-supported learning communities. Her research interests include computer-supported collaborative learning for pupils and students. She is also engaged in research on novice teachers' situation as well as professional development for teachers and teacher educators and how educational technology can support collaborative activities across communities.

Raija Hämäläinen, PhD, is a researcher at the Finnish Institute for Educational Research, University of Jyväskylä, Finland. Her main research interest deal with collaborative learning processes in technology-based and virtual learning environments, design of the 3D-game environments for collaborative learning and scripted computer-supported collaborative learning. Her recent publications include articles in Computers & Education, Scandinavian Journal of Educational Research and Computers in Human Behavior.

Diane Jass Ketelhut is an assistant professor of Science Education at Temple University. Her research interests center on scientific inquiry, specifically looking at the effects of inquiry on science self-efficacy; using emerging technologies to deliver scientific inquiry curricula on student learning and engagement; professional development in scientific inquiry on helping teachers integrate scientific inquiry into their curricula; and different methods of assessing science and scientific inquiry. Her current federally-funded projects include "SAVE Science," an innovative game-based system for evaluating learning in science for middle school years, "Science in the City," a standards-based scientific inquiry after-school curriculum project for elementary and middle-school students, and e=mc², an alternative mid-career math and science middle school teacher education program. In her teaching, she provides students with scientific inquiry experiences, both technological and hands-on, meant to engage them and challenge them to confront their own preconceptions. She holds certification in secondary school science and was a science curriculum specialist and teacher (science and math) for grades 5-12 for 12 years. Diane received a Sc.B. in Bio-Medical Sciences from Brown University, an M.Ed. in Curriculum and Instruction from the University of Virginia and her Ed.D. in Learning and Teaching from Harvard University

Diana Laurillard, professor, PhD, holds the chair of Learning with Digital Technoligies at the London Knowledge Lab, Institute of Education. She is leading research projects on a learning design support environment, and on software interventions for dyscalulia and low numeracy. Her research is the substance of her widely-cited book *Rethinking University Teaching: A conversational framework for the effective use of learning technology* (2002). Most recent appointments were as Head of the e-Learning Strategy Unit, Department for Education and Skills, and Pro-Vice-Chancellor for learning technologies and teaching at The Open University. Currently she is on the Boards of the Observatory for Borderless HE, the UNESCO Institute for IT in Education, the Centre for Applied Research in Educational Technologies (Cambridge), and the FernUniversität (Hagen).

Margaret Lloyd, PhD, is a senior lecturer in the School of Maths, Science and Technology Education, Queensland University of Technology with a specialisation in ICT education. Since leaving classroom teaching, she has successfully taught and coordinated both under- and post- graduate ICT courses, led offshore programs, supervised higher degree research students, managed online professional communities, undertaken consultancies and taken a leading role in curriculum change. She has published widely (including a co-authored ICT textbook for junior secondary students) and received awards and international acknowledgment for her innovative online curriculum projects. Dr Lloyd's current research interests include the dynamics of online communication, the measurement of integration of ICT in the classroom, and the definition of effective professional development for teachers. She is currently involved in a research project concerned with ICT in the classroom funded by the Norwegian Research Council. Address for correspondence: Margaret Lloyd, MSTE, Faculty of Education, Queensland University of Technology, Victoria Park Road, Kelvin Grove, QLD 4059 Australia. Email: mm.lloyd@qut.edu.au

Elizabeth Masterman, PhD, has 12 years' experience researching and evaluating learning technologies at all educational levels, having previously worked for 15 years in the commercial IT sector. She obtained her PhD in Educational Technology from the University of Birmingham, UK, and is currently Senior Researcher with the Learning Technologies Group, University of Oxford. Since 2004 Elizabeth has worked on a number of projects investigating the tools and processes involved in learning design, and also has a longstanding interest in the integration of cognitive and socio-cultural approaches in the design and evaluation of technology-mediated learning. She is currently collaborating on a multi-institutional project to develop a Learning Design Support Environment, led by prof. Diana Laurillard.

Erin M. McCloskey is a doctoral candidate at the Harvard Graduate School of Education, where she does research on online teacher professional development, focusing on the relationship between technologically-mediated learning and intercultural learning. Her dissertation is a qualitative investigation of how a culturally diverse group of foreign languages teachers, in the context of an online professional development course, develop their intercultural competence and build capacity to foster similar skills in their classrooms. Prior to doctoral studies, Erin was a high school Spanish teacher, an English as a Foreign Language teacher, and a language curriculum developer. Erin received her A.B. in Comparative Literature from Brown University and her M.Ed. in Technology, Innovation and Education from Harvard University.

Svein Olav Norenes is a PhD candidate at InterMedia, University of Oslo. InterMedia is a multi-disciplinary research center working in the intersections between design, communication and learning in digital environments. His main research interest is learning and organizational development from a socio-cultural perceptive and how to utilize computer supported practices in school and workplace contexts. In his PhD project he focuses on ICT-mediated learning within the domain of Mathematics and Science Education.

Norbert Pachler is reader in Education and Co-Director of the Centre for Excellence in Work-based Learning for Education Professionals at the Institute of Education, University of London. Apart from the application of new technologies in teaching and learning, his research interests include teacher education and development and all aspects of foreign language teaching and learning. He has published widely and supervises in these fields. Since 2007 he is the convenor of the London Mobile Learning Group (http://www.londonmobilelearning.net) which brings together an international, interdisciplinary group of researchers from the fields of cultural studies, sociology, semiotics, pedagogy and educational technology.

Helena Rasku-Puttonen is professor of Psychology in Education at the Department of Teacher Education, University of Jyväskylä, Finland. Currently she is acting as the Head of Research Activities at the Department of Teacher Education. Her areas of interest include learning communities, collaboration and social interaction in school and working life contexts.

David Rodriguez-Gomez is an assistant professor in Teaching and Educational Administration, collaborator of the Organisational Development Research Group (EDO) and member of the Faculty of Education at the Universitat Autònoma de Barcelona. He holds a Pedagogy degree and a Master from Autonomous University of Barcelona. He is also PhD student in Quality and Innovation Process in Education. His research interest includes knowledge management, professional development, organisational learning, organisational development, learning technologies and university drop-out. David Rodriguez's most recent research activities are: (1) Agents and process in networked knowledge management (Ministry of Education and Culture, National R&D Plan); (2) Drop-out at Catalan Universities (Catalan University Quality Assurance Agency); (3) Evaluation of Social Sciences Competences (Catalan University Quality Assurance Agency).

Michael Ross, BSc (Hons) MBChB MRCGP, PhD, is joint director of the online MSc in Clinical Education and coordinator of staff development for the undergraduate medical programme at the University of Edinburgh. He also has responsibilities for peer assisted learning and undergraduate medical students learning to teach. He was a clinical lecturer in general practice for four years and continues to work part time as a general practitioner in Fife. He has a particular interest in the training, support and continuing professional development of medical teachers.

Rebecca Scheckler, PhD, is an educational technologist in the College of Health and Human Services at Radford University, Box 6970, Radford, VA, 24142, 540-831-7663, rscheckler@radford.edu, where she advises faculty on implementing educational technologies, formulates and implements policy for college wide educational technologies, and teaches research methods to masters students. She was previously an associate professor in the Department of Education and Knowledge Technologies at the University of Cincinnati where she taught and advised doctoral students in educational technology. She has taught Computer Science, and Biology to college students and is on the editorial board of "The Journal of Research in Science Teaching". Her research interests include the social effects of digital technologies, feminist pedagogies in online instruction, feminist pedagogies for science teaching, and the philosophy and theory of teaching digital technologies.

Donald Scott is an instructor in the Graduate Division of Educational Research, Faculty of Education, University of Calgary. Mr. Scott recently completed doctoral studies in the field of technology-facilitated learning environments. He is an experienced educator and professional developer with 30 years classroom experience. He has held the roles of teacher, network administrator, senior administrator, and university professor. He has provided information technology consultancy advice to business and government organisations. Mr. Scott's research interests encompass exploring the role of technology to support learning for both teachers and students; exploring students' and teachers' technological efficacy; and investigating the viability of technological solutions to increasing communication between agencies and schools to provide better support of at-risk youth.

Shelleyann Scott, PhD, is an associate professor at the Faculty of Education at the University of Calgary. Dr. Scott teaches in the postgraduate leadership programs and supervises doctoral and masters students. She is an experienced tertiary and secondary educator with expertise in professional development, simple and complex instructional strategies, curriculum design and evaluation, and information communication technology as it applies to learning environments. Dr. Scott's research interests include establishing and evaluating professional development within educational, business, and government contexts; the creation and maintenance of learning communities; the use of technology to support educational experiences for students and teachers; and developing and supporting quality improvement cycles. Dr. Scott has an established publishing record within national and international journals and conferences. She is an experienced professional developer and has designed and facilitated programmes in Australia, Canada, Hong Kong, Indonesia, Malaysia, Philippines, Singapore, and Sri Lanka.

Bonnie Swan is an evaluation specialist and with extensive experience in learning assessment and planning and implementing evaluations in various educational agencies at a variety of levels. She has recently been an outside evaluator in the U.S. for projects sponsored by the Florida Department of Education, the National Aeronautics and Space Administration (NASA), the National Science Foundation (NSF), and the Environmental Protection Agency (EPA). She received her Ph.D. in Education and M.Ed. in Mathematics Education from UCF and her undergraduate work focused on Economics. She has taught at the secondary and post-secondary level. Dr. Swan is an active writer and frequently presents on topics related to evaluation, online learning, professional development and student achievement.

Anne Turvey is a lecturer in Education at the Institute of Education in London. She is chair of the London Association for the Teaching of English (LATE) and a member of the National Association for the Teaching of English (NATE) Initial Teacher Education committee. She has been a tutor on the PGCE course since 1989 after teaching for many years in a London secondary school. She has published on the development of English subject knowledge in the early years of teaching and on the processes involved in becoming an English teacher. She has a long-standing research interest in teachers' professional development, and teaches on a mixed-mode masters degree which accredits practice-based learning.

Pamela Whitehouse is an assistant professor of Instructional Design and Technology at West Virginia University. Her current research projects include Globaloria, a project focused on developing educational programs to create opportunities for students and educators to engage in social and collaborative game design using digital media; From Watching to Learning, a research project designed to provide an interactive collaborative mentoring environment for pre- and in-service teachers using video cases they create themselves, and a research project to improve in-service teacher math and writing skills, using an array of digital media. She also developed and teaches online courses in Instructional Design and Technology, and a 21st Century Learning and Teaching summer certificate program for in-service teachers. She received a B.A. in Humanities and Social Sciences from University of Massachusetts Dartmouth, a Masters degree in Political Science from the University of Rhode Island, and a M.Ed. and Ed.D. in Learning and Teaching from Harvard University.

Alastair Wilson is currently senior research fellow, in the Applied Educational Research Centre, Department of Educational Studies, University of Strathclyde. Formerly he was Research Co-ordinator of the Learners, Learning & Teaching Network, which formed part of the Applied Educational Research Scheme, a consortium of Edinburgh, Stirling and Strathclyde universities engaged in a 5 year programme to increase educational research capability in Scottish HE institutions. During this period Alastair was the lead researcher in the programme's development of a virtual research environment. This work has had three key strands of activity, examining the value of virtual research environments as a means of supporting collaborative research, engaging practitioners in research and exploring the use of a VRE as a means to engage with research participants and generate new forms of data.

Vassiliki Zygouris-Coe is associate professor of reading education at the University of Central Florida, College of Education. She is also the principal investigator of the Florida Online Reading Professional Development (FOR-PD) project, Florida's first large-scale online professional development project (http://forpd.ucf.edu). Dr. Zygouris-Coe's research interests lie in literacy and teacher education, online professional development, teacher knowledge, and the role of reading in the content areas. She is an active writer and frequently presents at national and international conferences on topics related to literacy, online learning, and professional development.

Index

Symbols

1st generation technologies 171
2nd generation technologies 172
21st Century skills 155, 156, 157, 167

A

Accelera experience 142
Accelera project 140, 144, 147
action research 1, 2, 3, 7, 8, 11, 12, 14,
    16, 17, 19
AERS 96, 97, 98, 102, 105, 107
AERS virtual environment 102
AISI 30, 31, 32, 38
Alberta Initiative for School Improvement
    (AISI) Project 30
Applied Educational Research Scheme (AERS)
    96

C

CHAT 211
CLC 77, 78, 83, 84, 86, 91, 92
collaborative enquiry 97, 102
collaborative knowledge construction 264,
    265, 269, 270, 274, 275, 276
collaborative learning 155, 157, 163, 164,
    230, 233, 237, 240, 241, 242, 243,
    245, 246
collaborative online professional development
    154–167
collaborative working 96, 97, 98, 101, 102,
    104, 108, 110, 111
collaborative working environment (CWE) 204
community of enquiry 97, 98, 103, 110
community of enquiry, concept 98

community of learners 12, 13, 14, 15, 18
community of practice (COP) 12, 13, 19, 42
computer-assisted learning (CAL) 196
computer-supported collaborative learning
    (CSCL) 264
constructivist 158, 165
constructivist learning 37, 170
continuing professional development (CPD) 78
continuous training 134, 135, 136, 137,
    143, 144, 149
conversational framework 234, 245
COP 42, 44, 46, 47, 56
CPD 78, 79, 80, 81, 82, 83, 84, 85, 86,
    87, 91, 92, 93, 94, 95, 99, 112
CSCL 263, 264, 265, 276, 277, 279
Cultural-Historical Activity Theory (CHAT)
    211
CWE 204

D

developmental work research
    212, 216, 224, 225
digitally native students 120

E

eLearning 190, 191, 192, 195, 196, 197,
    203, 204, 205, 206, 207
eLearning in medical education 196
entrepreneurial leadership 170
EROS 198, 199
EROS (the Edinburgh Re-usable Object Se-
    quencer) 198
evaluation of professional development 26

Q

S

T

V

W